FUTURE
English for Results

4

TEACHER'S EDITION
AND LESSON PLANNER

Lida Baker

Series Consultants

Beatriz B. Díaz

Ronna Magy

Federico Salas-Isnardi

PEARSON
Longman

Future 4
English for Results
Teacher's Edition and Lesson Planner

Pearson Education, 10 Bank Street, White Plains, NY 10606

Staff credits: The people who made up the **Future 4** team, representing editorial,
production, design, and manufacturing, are Rhea Banker, Eleanor Barnes,
Maretta Callahan, Elizabeth Carlson, Aerin Csigay, Dave Dickey, Nancy Flaggman,
Irene Frankel, Mike Kemper, Katie Keyes, Jessica Miller-Smith, Linda Moser,
Liza Pleva, Sherry Preiss, Stella Reilly, Loretta Steeves, Marian Wassner, and Martin Yu.

Cover design: Rhea Banker
Cover photo: Kathy Lamm/Getty Images
Text design: Lisa Delgado
Text composition: ElectraGraphics, Inc.
Text font: Minion Pro

ISBN-13: 978-0-13199157-6
ISBN-10: 0-13-199157-4

Printed in the United States of America

1 2 3 4 5 6 7 8 9 10—CJK—14 13 12 11 10 09

Contents

Methodology of the *Future* Program

The instructional design of *Future* has been carefully crafted and draws on tried-and-true methods. In *Future*, current research findings are put into practice. Each of the skill sections reflects sound pedagogy and offers a logical progression from unit to unit within a level as well as from one level to the next throughout the series. The instructional design is tailored to meet the interests and needs of students at their language level and at the same time to fulfill curriculum mandates.

Future has been designed to help students persist in their English studies. The program motivates students to keep coming to class through its situational contexts that reflect students' real lives, its touches of humor, and its community–building group work and team projects. If outside factors cause students to miss classes, the strategies and study skills presented in the Student Book, along with the Practice Plus CD-ROM, help students continue their studies until they are able to return to class.

Future also helps students make a successful transition into academic programs. The levels of *Future* progressively introduce academic skills so that students feel empowered to continue their education. By continuing on into academic programs, students improve their chances of entering the job market with all the skills and tools they need to be successful.

Future is truly an integrated-skills course: listening, speaking, reading, and writing are woven together throughout the lessons, just as they are naturally woven together outside the classroom. For example, students practice their speaking skills not just on the Listening and Speaking page but also in the Life Skills lesson and in other lessons throughout the unit.

Following are some of the key pedagogical features of the skill sections of *Future 4*.

Vocabulary

- **Multiple encounters with target vocabulary.** Vocabulary is recycled throughout the unit so students have numerous exposures to the same words. Current research shows that the more encounters learners have with a target word, the more likely they are to retain that word.[1]
- **Vocabulary in context exercises.** Exercises that follow the reading selections direct students to use context clues to get the meaning of boldfaced words, giving students practice with this skill.
- **Learning strategies and supplemental vocabulary practice in the Workbook.** Each unit of the Future 4 Workbook culminates with a vocabulary lesson that reviews and expands on the vocabulary presented in the student book. This vocabulary lesson includes a learning strategy tip, such as using visuals to help remember new words. In addition, some units contain dictionary skills lessons that provide instruction and practice to help students get the most out of their dictionaries.

Listening

- **Multiple genres.** Throughout *Future*, students are exposed to a variety of listening types such as conversations, interviews, and radio talk shows.
- **Natural language.** The listening selections in *Future* use natural discourse so that students hear authentic language models. The listening selections are recorded at natural speed, reflecting what students will hear outside of class.
- **Pre-listening activities.** Before students listen to each selection, they complete pre-listening activities, which help activate students' background knowledge. Students also make predictions about what they will hear. This helps develop students' critical thinking skills[2] and is an important strategy for successful listening in a second language.[3]
- **True listening practice.** Students listen to the audio without seeing the audio script on the page. This serves two purposes: 1) It ensures that the listening exercise is truly checking students' listening skills, rather than their reading skills; and 2) It helps students prepare for standardized tests in which they are asked to listen to audio selections and answer questions without seeing the script. Students who need extra support can read the audio script printed in the back of the Student Book.
- **Multiple exposures to the same listening selection.** Students listen to the same listening material several times, but for different reasons: to check predictions, to get the main idea, and to get specific information. By hearing the same text more than once, students become more comfortable with the content and increase their comprehension.

Speaking

- **Model conversations provide support and build confidence.** Students first read and listen to model conversations and then practice the conversation in pairs. Limiting what they are at first expected to produce helps students become more confident speakers.
- **Progression from controlled to open-ended activities.** Each listening/speaking lesson concludes with a Make It Personal or Role Play activity. These activities are scaffolded to ensure that students have time to think about what they are going to say, but are open-ended, giving students an opportunity to build fluency.
- **Negotiation of meaning.** Many of the exercises in each unit require students to work together to negotiate meaning. Giving students the opportunity to interact and negotiate meaning supports development of their language skills.[4]
- **Problem-solving tasks.** In each unit, students have the opportunity to discuss solutions to a particular problem related to the unit theme. These tasks engage students' critical thinking skills and allow them to focus on fluency.

[2] Bloom, B.S. (1956). *Taxonomy of Educational Objectives, Handbook I: The Cognitive Domain,* New York: David McKay Co Inc.

[3] Rost, M. (2002). *Teaching and Researching Listening.* Harlow, England: Pearson Education.

[4] Mackey, A. (1999). Input, interaction, and second language development: An empirical study of question formation in ESL. *Studies in Second Language Acquisition, 21,* 557–587.

[1] Folse, K. (2006). The Effect of Type of Written Exercise on L2 Vocabulary Retention. *TESOL Quarterly,* Vol. 40, No. 2, 273–93.

Pronunciation

- **Systematic pronunciation syllabus.** The pronunciation syllabus was developed to support the listening/speaking lessons in the book. The specific pronunciation point is modeled in the listening text and subsequently practiced in the model conversation.
- **Focus on stress and intonation.** The pronunciation syllabus focuses primarily on the natural stress, intonation, and rhythm of English. Information about the pronunciation point is provided in the Pronunciation Watch note.

Grammar

- **Grammar input in the listening text.** Grammar in *Future* is first presented receptively through the text in the Listening/Speaking lesson so students first encounter the target language in a meaningful way, in context.
- **Grammar charts display the target.** Grammar charts at the beginning of the grammar lesson explicitly show the target structures. Grammar Watch notes provide explanations, as needed, and the Grammar Reference in the back of the book expands on the grammar when appropriate.
- **Practice with both meaning and form.** Presentations focus on meaning as well as form, enabling learners to incorporate more new structures into their language use.[5]
- **Discovery, then controlled, then productive practice.** Exercises progress from receptive to productive and from controlled to communicative, providing students with ample written and spoken practice in the target structure.
- **Contextualized, content-based activities.** Exercises are contextualized, recycling themes and vocabulary from the unit. In many cases, the grammar exercise also presents new, related content so that students are gaining additional information as well as grammar practice.
- **Numerous pair and group activities.** Pair and small group work allow students to work with new language structures in a safe, motivating environment, as well as offering further opportunities for students to negotiate meaning.
- **Opportunities for students to show what they know.** *Show what you know!* activities at the end of every grammar lesson allow students to put together the vocabulary, structures, and competencies they have learned.

Reading

- **High-interest, informative articles.** The reading articles in *Future* present interesting, useful information related to the unit theme. The structures and vocabulary in the texts are controlled so students can be successful readers.
- **Pre-reading activities.** As in the Listening lessons, the Reading lessons have pre-reading activities to help build students' cultural schema, an important factor in successfully completing a reading task.[6]

- **Recorded reading selections.** The readings in *Future* are recorded so that students can listen as they read along. Research has shown that listening while reading can have a positive effect on reading fluency.[7]
- **Opportunity to apply the information.** A *Show what you know!* activity at the end of the reading lesson allows students to synthesize and apply the information they have just learned through a speaking or writing task.
- **Building of reading skills.** Skills such as finding the main idea, identifying the topic, and scanning for information are explicitly presented and then practiced.
- **Inclusion of document and environmental literacy.** *Future* also gives students practice reading and completing forms and other documents that they are likely to encounter in their everyday lives.

Writing

- **Balanced writing syllabus.** The writing syllabus focuses on writing paragraphs, letters, and e-mails, providing a balanced approach to academic and practical writing.
- **Writing Tips.** Writing Tips provide helpful information about the structure of the writing students are about to do.
- **Exercises guide students through the writing process.** Pre-writing activities activate students' background knowledge and build schema. Writing skills are then presented and modeled. Before writing their own essay, students plan and organize their writing through graphic organizers. After writing, students review and check that they have successfully completed the assignment and incorporated the writing skill. Teachers can then ask students to write additional drafts.

Review and Assessment

- **Checkpoints to track progress.** Every unit begins with a list of competencies to be covered. As students complete each lesson, they check off the goal they have completed. At the end of the unit, students are directed to review the goals list to see their progress. Keeping track of goals completed motivates students and reinforces their sense of success.
- **Opportunities for ongoing assessment.** Teachers can use the *Show what you know!* activities at the end of most lessons and at the end of every unit to assess their students' progress. For teachers who want to do a more formal assessment, the *Tests and Test Prep* with **Exam**View® *Assessment Suite* book provides reproducible unit tests as well as a midterm and a final test. Additionally, the **Exam**View *Assessment Suite* gives teachers the option to create their own customized tests.

---

[5] Ellis, R., Basturkmen, H., & Loewen, S. (2001). Learner uptake in communicative ESL lessons. *Language Learning, 51*, 281–318.

[6] Burt, M., Peyton, J. K., & Adams, R. (2003). *Reading and adult English language learners: A review of the research.* Washington, DC: Center for Applied Linguistics.

[7] Kruidenier, J. (2002). *Research-based principles for adult basic education reading instruction.* Washington, D.C.: National Institute for Literacy, Partnership for Reading.

Each unit begins with **a list of course components** that can be used in class or assigned for homework.

3

Community Life

Classroom Materials/Extra Practice

| CD 1 Tracks 27–37 | Interactive Practice Unit 3 | Workbook Unit 3 |

Unit Overview

Goals
- See the list of goals on the facing page.

Grammar
- Participial adjectives
- *Wish* in the present and future
- Verb + object + infinitive

Pronunciation
- Pronunciation of unreleased final stop consonants
- Weak and blended pronunciation of *to*

Reading
- Read an article about community gardens
- *Reading Skill:* Making inferences

Writing
- Write a paragraph about your neighborhood

Life Skills
- Give and follow directions

Preview
- Say the unit title. Ask: *What do you think this unit will be about?*
- Hold up your book or have students look at their books. Set the context by asking the preview questions. You can also ask: *What do you see in the photo? What are the people doing? What kind of neighborhood is this? Does your neighborhood look like this?*

Unit Goals
- Point to the Unit Goals. Have students read them silently.
- Tell students they will be studying these goals in Unit 3.
- Say each goal and explain unfamiliar vocabulary as needed, for example, *festival: a large celebration; issues: problems or topics that people care about.*
- Tell students to circle one or more goals that are very important to them. Call on several volunteers to say the goals they circled.
- Write a checkmark (✓) on the board. Say: *We will come back to this page again. You will write a checkmark next to the goals you learned in this unit.*

A comprehensive **list of competencies and skills** provides an overview of the unit.

Teaching ideas for the unit opener picture help teachers establish the context of the unit and get students ready for the unit theme.

Teaching notes are organized in **a lesson plan**: Getting Started, Presentation, Controlled Practice, Communicative Practice. **Suggested times** for each part of the lesson plan are based on a 60-minute class. This time may vary depending on class size.

Culture Connections provide the teacher with information about cross-cultural issues, as well as activities that stimulate classroom discussions about culture.

Lesson 1   Talk about cultural festivals and traditions

Getting Started   5 minutes

1 BEFORE YOU LISTEN

CLASS. **Look at the picture. What kind...**

• Hold up your book and point to the photo or have students look at their books. Read the questions and have volunteers answer.

Presentation   10 minutes

2 LISTEN

A 🎧 **Mali Prem and Eric Torres...**

• Have students look at the photo. Ask: *Who are the speakers? Where are they from? How old are they? Where are they? What is their relationship?*
• Remind students to listen specifically for the answer to the question. It is not necessary to understand every word.
• Play CD 1, Track 27.
• Have students compare answers with a classmate.
• Call on a volunteer to answer the question.

Answer: Mali and Eric are going to the festival.

Controlled Practice   10 minutes

B 🎧 **Read the questions. Then listen...**

• Have students read the questions and predict the answers.
• Play Track 27 again.
• Call on students to read the questions and answers. Write the letters of the answers on the board.
• If students have difficulty answering a question, play the corresponding part of the recording again.

Culture Connection

The Thai New Year festival is called *songkram*. It is usually celebrated for three days, beginning on April 13. Thai people celebrate by eating traditional foods, thoroughly cleaning their homes, and visiting their temples and bringing food to the monks, as well as by participating in a variety of customs involving water—especially throwing water on one another! These same customs are followed by many immigrants living in Thai neighborhoods in the U.S.

Communicative Practice   10 minutes

C GROUPS. **What things are common...**

• Give an example from a U.S. perspective. For example, many immigrants and visitors to the U.S. are surprised that Americans eat turkey and pumpkin pie on Thanksgiving. Ask the class: *Which American customs surprised you when you first arrived?*
• If possible, group students from different countries.
• Give a time limit for discussion.
• While students are talking, walk around and provide help as needed.
• To wrap up, select a number of students and ask: *What was the most surprising thing you learned in your group's discussion?*

■■■ Expansion: Speaking Practice for 2C

• Have students prepare short oral reports about New Year customs and celebrations in their cultures.
• On the board, write topics associated with New Year celebrations, for example, *date and season, food, clothing, gifts, greetings, home customs, religious customs,* and *other customs.*
• Have students from the same culture work together. Have them divide up the topics so that each student reports on one aspect of the holiday. Pre-level students can report on simpler aspects of the New Year holiday, such as the date and season, food, or gifts. Above-level students should report on the more complex aspects of the holiday, such as home and religious customs.
• Give a time limit for preparation. While students are working, walk around and provide help as needed.
• Bring the class together. Have each group do a report to the class.

UNIT 3   **T-46**

Expansions provide more practice with specific skills.

Ideas for multilevel instruction help teachers meet the needs of all learners in a classroom.

Lesson 2 Describe feelings about a neighborhood

2 PRACTICE

A Read the sentences about...

- Read item 1. Ask: *Why is* disappointed *correct?* (It describes the way Maria feels.)
- Have students work alone or in pairs.
- Write the numbers *2* through *5* on the board. Call up students to write the answers. Point to each item and ask: *Is this correct?* If there is an error, elicit the correction and write it on the board.

Expansion: Speaking Practice for 2A

- Discuss the cultural aspects of items 2 and 3. Read item 2 and ask: *Why doesn't the neighbor wait for an answer? When people say* How are you? *in the U.S., are they really asking about your health?*
- Read item 3. Ask: *In the U.S., is it polite to ask someone about his or her age? Is it polite in your culture?*
- Ask: *What other topics should you not ask about in the U.S.?* (how much money people make and how much they paid for things such as their house, etc.)
- Have volunteers share their ideas with the class.

B Complete the sentences with...

- Read the first sentence and point out that although the story is in the past, the *-ed* and *-ing* forms do not change.
- Have students complete the exercise alone or in pairs. Walk around and provide help as needed.
- Have students compare answers with a partner.
- Call on students to read the sentences with the answers they filled in. Write them on the board. Point to each item and ask the class: *Is this correct?* Elicit corrections as needed.

Communicative Practice 20 minutes

Show what you know!

STEP 1. **Check (✓) three adjectives to describe...**

- As an example, say how you feel about your own neighborhood, for example, *I'm encouraged by the friendliness of my neighbors.* Write the sentence on the board.

MULTILEVEL INSTRUCTION for STEP 1

Pre-level Have students write just one or two sentences.

Above-level Have students write more than three sentences.

STEP 2. GROUPS. **Discuss.**

- Form cross-ability groups. Have each group select a timekeeper, a note taker, and a reporter.
- For item 1, tell students to share their sentences from Step 1. For item 2, the note taker should write down each student's answer.
- Give a time limit.
- Walk around as students are talking and provide help as needed.
- To wrap up, reporters should say how many people in their group were happy and unhappy and describe their classmates' reasons.
- Create a chart on the board with the headings *Happy* and *Unhappy*. As reporters are speaking, write their reasons in the proper column.

Expansion: Speaking Practice for STEP 2

- Tell students to remain in groups.
- Have them look at the reasons in the *Unhappy* column on the board.
- Have them discuss solutions to the problems and say what advice they would give to a person with this problem.
- Have a representative from each group choose one problem and share the group's solution.

Progress Check

Can you . . . describe feelings about . . .

Say: *We have practiced describing feelings about a neighborhood. Now, look at the question at the bottom of the page. Can you describe feelings about a neighborhood? Write a checkmark in the box.*

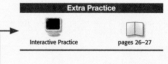

Extra Practice

Interactive Practice | pages 26–27

T-49 UNIT 3

Cross-references to relevant pages in course components at the end of each lesson allow the teacher to plan additional in-class or at-home activities.

Progress Checks allow students to reflect on their ability to use the competencies presented in the lesson.

Step-by-step teaching notes help teachers give **clear grammar presentations**. Teachers can also refer students to the **Grammar Reference section** starting on page 278 in the back of the student book.

Lesson 8 Identify community problems

Getting Started 5 minutes

- Write on the board: *I want to find a job.* Ask the class: *What is the verb? (want) What is the infinitive? (to find)*
- Using a different color, insert *my brother* between *want* and *to* in the sentence above. Ask the class: *What's the difference between the sentences? (The second sentence has an object. It changes the meaning. In the first sentence, the speaker wants to find a job. In the second sentence, the speaker wants a different person—his or her brother—to find a job.)*
- Say: *In this lesson, we're going to practice sentences that have the structure verb + object + infinitive.*

Presentation 10 minutes

▶ **Verb + object + infinitive**

- Copy the grammar chart onto the board. Read the sentences. Circle the verbs, draw a line under the objects, and draw two lines under the infinitives.
- Explain *urge*. Say: *To urge means to suggest something very strongly. For example, if you have a high fever, I urge you to see a doctor.*
- Read the first Grammar Watch note. Point to the infinitives in the examples.
- Read the second note. Point to *us* in the second example. Point to *the city* in the first example and explain that the object can also be a noun.

Language Note
Other verbs that can be followed by an object and an infinitive include *ask, advise, tell, teach, remind, encourage, expect,* and *warn.*

▨ **Expansion: Grammar Practice**

- Write several scrambled sentences on the board, for example: *expects / on time / The teacher / us / our homework / to complete,* and *Parents / the truth / their children / encourage / always / to tell,* and *to speak / I / the teacher / more slowly / asked.*
- Pair students and have them unscramble the sentences. Have them raise their hands when they are ready.
- Call on different students to say the unscrambled sentences.

Controlled Practice 25 minutes

1 PRACTICE

🅐 **Read the conversation from a...**

- Read the first two sentences and copy the example on the board.
- Have students complete the exercise alone or in pairs. Walk around and provide help as needed.
- Ask the class: *How many verbs did you circle? What's the first one?* Elicit each verb + object + infinitive. Circle and underline the appropriate words.

▨ **Expansion: Speaking Practice for 1A**

- Pair students and have them read the conversation.
- Remind students to use the relaxed pronunciation of *to.*
- Call on pairs to perform the conversation for the class.

🅑 **Cross out the noun object in each...**

- Read item 1. Ask: *Why is them correct?* (It replaces *the sanitation workers*—third person plural)
- Have students complete the exercise alone or in pairs. Walk around and provide help as needed.
- Write the numbers *2* through *6* on the board. Have students come up and write the crossed-out noun and the pronoun that replaces it, as in the example.
- Call on students to read the sentences with the pronouns out loud.

▨ **Expansion: Grammar Practice for 1B**

- Have students circle the verbs in Exercise 1B.
- Tell them to make a list of verbs that can be followed by verb + object + infinitive, beginning with the verbs they circled in Exercises 1A and 1B.
- Ask the class if they know other verbs that belong on the list. Elicit an example sentence with each correct verb. Have students add each verb to their list.

UNIT 3   **T-60**

Language Notes offer insightful and helpful information about English. The notes also offer ideas for **Community Building** in the classroom to help students get to know their classmates.

Teaching Tips give helpful teaching techniques and strategies.

Persistence Activities give teachers more ideas for community building, as well as focusing on goal setting and study skills. **Team Projects** help teachers focus on community building and recycling content in every unit.

Review & Expand — Show what you know!

1 REVIEW

Turn to page 247 for the Grammar Review.

2 ACT IT OUT

STEP 1. CLASS. Review the conversation...

- Play CD 1, Track 37. Have students listen as they read the script on page 59.

STEP 2. ROLE PLAY. PAIRS. Role-play this situation.

> **Teaching Tip**
>
> While pairs are performing role plays, use the scoring rubric for speaking on page T-xiii to evaluate each student's vocabulary, grammar, fluency, and how well he or she completes the task. You may want to review the completed rubric with the students.

- Have students look at the illustration. Ask: *Where are the people? What are they doing?*
- Read the role descriptions.
- Model the role play with an above-level student. Play the role of Student B. Student A can begin like this: *I'm organizing a spring cleanup in the park next Saturday.*
- Tell students to practice out loud at least twice.
- Have volunteers role-play for the class.

▇▇ MULTILEVEL INSTRUCTION FOR 2

Pre-level Have students write their dialogue. Tell Student A to give just one reason why the cleanup is a good idea. Tell Student B to give one reason why he or she cannot participate.

Above-level Have students practice without notes. Tell Student A to give three reasons why the cleanup is important or why Student B will benefit from participating. Have Student B give three reasons why he or she cannot participate.

3 READ AND REACT

STEP 1. GROUPS. Read about Lydia's problem.

- Read the paragraph while students follow along silently.

STEP 2. GROUPS. What is Lydia's problem?...

- Form groups of three or four. Have each group choose a timekeeper, a note taker, and a reporter.
- Give a time limit for discussion.
- Walk around and provide help as needed.
- Have the reporter from each group share the group's ideas. Write all the ideas on the board.
- Have the class vote on the best solution.

▇▇ Expansion: Speaking Practice for STEP 2

- Ask students if they have had a similar experience and how they dealt (or are dealing) with it.
- If students don't have a similar experience, have students share their opinions about whether this would be a problem for them. If so, how would they deal with it?

4 CONNECT

Turn to page 258 for the Community-Building Activity and page 265 for the Team Project. See page T-xi for general notes about teaching these activities.

▶ Progress Check

Which goals can you check off? Go back to page 45.
Ask students to turn to page 45 and check off any remaining goals they have reached. Call on students to say which goals they will practice outside of class.

▇ Go to the CD-ROM for more practice.

If your students need more practice with the vocabulary, grammar, and competencies in Unit 3, encourage them to review the activities on the CD-ROM.

Students check their progress at the end of each unit by reviewing the vocabulary, grammar, and competencies and then checking off the unit goals.

The **Practice Plus CD-ROM** in the back of the student book offers more practice with the unit material. It also provides an opportunity for students to make up the lesson if they missed a class.

Persistence Activities and Team Projects

A **Persistence Activity** and a **Team Project** for each unit of *Future 4* are in the back of the book. Cross-references at the end of the unit indicate at what point each activity should be completed. Following are some general notes that apply to all of the activities within each section.

Persistence Activities: Community Building, Planning for Learning, and Self-Evaluation

The Persistence Activities are classroom-tested activities that support students in continuing their studies. Recent research has shown us that students are more likely to persist when they feel they are part of a learning community, when they organize and plan for their learning, when they monitor their learning, and when they are able to set educational goals they believe they can achieve. Each Persistence Activity in *Future* fits one of these categories: community building, planning for learning, and self-evaluation.

Step 1: Introduce the activity
- Say the name of the activity. Then explain the objective of the activity. For example, for Unit 2, say: *We're going to talk about the characteristics of a good learner. This will help you organize and plan for your learning.*
- Put students in pairs or groups, if necessary, for the activity.

Step 2: Get ready
- Read the directions for the first part of the activity and make sure students understand what they need to do.
- Review any language students need for the activity. If students will need to write sentences, write an example sentence on the board.
- Model the activity. If the activity has students working in groups of three, call two on- or above-level students to the front of the room. Model the activity with them, taking one part yourself. If the activity requires students to work independently, write the exercise on the board and call on a few students to give sample responses. Write their responses on the board.

Step 3: Start the activity
- Have students start working in pairs, groups, or independently, as appropriate for the activity. Walk around the room while students are working, checking to make sure they are on task and providing help as needed.
- If the activity has a second part, check to make sure all students have had sufficient time to complete the first part before moving on. When students are ready, repeat Steps 2 and 3 for the second part of the activity.

Step 4: Wrap up
- After students have completed all parts of the activity, call on a few students to share their work with the class.

Team Projects

The Team Projects give students an opportunity to use the language they have learned throughout the unit to produce a product such as a booklet, poster, or chart. Students work in teams. Each team member is assigned a specific role: Captain, Co-captain, Assistant, or Spokesperson. The teacher can assign roles that match each student's strength. For example, since the tasks performed by the Co-captain are not language-intensive, the teacher may want to assign this role to a pre-level student.

Step 1: Introduce the objective
- Explain the objective of the activity. For example, for Unit 2, say: *We're learning about job-search resources in your community.*

Step 2: Form teams
- Form groups of four students. Assign students the roles of Captain, Co-captain, Assistant, or Spokesperson.
- If necessary, students can share one role. For example, a pre-level student and an above-level student can perform the role of the Assistant together. Also, one student can have two roles if necessary.

Step 3: Get ready
- Gather the materials in the note and have them ready.
- Read the directions for all team members. Go over any examples provided.
- Tell the co-captain to watch the clock to track the time and to tell the team when they have one minute left.
- Monitor as students complete the task.

Step 4: Create
- Have Co-captains retrieve needed materials.
- Read the directions for the Co-captains and team. Each team can decide who will do what to create the product.
- Have the Co-captain watch the clock and tell the team when they have one minute left.
- Walk around and check that all students have a role and are on task.

Step 5: Report
- Call on each Spokesperson to tell the class about the group's project. The goal of the presentation is to make sure the audience (the other students) understands all the information presented.
- Have the other students in the class write down a question for the team that is presenting. Call on students to ask follow-up questions that the spokesperson can answer. For example, for Unit 2, a student may ask, *Have you or any of your team members ever used these resources?*

Step 6: Collect
- Some projects require the captains to collect the project materials and put them together, for example, for Unit 2, to make a booklet.

Speaking and Writing Activities

Future provides students with multiple opportunities to build their speaking and writing skills. Speaking tasks are integrated throughout the course, and each unit culminates with a role play and a problem-solving activity. Each unit also contains a writing lesson that teaches students a practical approach to the writing process and culminates in a writing assignment. If you wish to formally assess students' speaking or writing, you may use the rubrics provided on pages T-xiii and T-xiv.

Speaking Activities

The final page of every unit of *Future* contains an Act It Out activity and a problem-solving activity. These activities offer students an opportunity to demonstrate their ability to use the vocabulary, grammar, and competencies from the unit and the course in less structured speaking activities.

After students have practiced the activity in pairs or small groups, allow some students to perform the activity in front of the whole class. If you wish to use this activity for evaluation purposes, use the Speaking Rubric on page T-xiii to make notes about each student's performance. For each category listed in the rubric (Vocabulary, Grammar, Fluency, and Task Completion), include comments about both *strong points* and *weak points*. You can then use those comments to give each student a rating of 1, 2, or 3 for each category.

The purpose of this kind of evaluation is to give fair and clear feedback to students and to give them specific points to work on so they can improve their fluency. It is important to use language that a student can understand and to give examples of what the student did or didn't say when possible. For example, you might say, *You used a lot of vocabulary related to the unit theme* or *You need to work on phrasal verbs. Review the grammar charts in the unit.* Feedback should be given to students in a timely manner in order to be most effective and helpful.

Writing Activities

Each unit of *Future* includes a two-page writing lesson that guides students in the process of composing a clear and coherent paragraph or piece of correspondence. The writing task gives students an opportunity to implement the tip they learned about writing structure. The task also gives them a chance to apply their knowledge of the grammar and vocabulary they have learned in the unit and throughout the course while also allowing them to build their writing skills and develop their writing fluency.

If you wish to evaluate students' writing formally, use the Writing Rubric on page T-xiv to make notes. For each category listed in the rubric (Vocabulary, Grammar, Mechanics and Format, and Task Completion), include comments about both *strong points* and *weak points*. You can then use those comments to give each student a rating of 1, 2, or 3 for each category.

The purpose of this kind of evaluation is to give fair and clear feedback to students and to give them specific points to work on so they can improve their writing skills. It is important to use language that a student can understand and to give examples of what the student did or did not do when possible. For example, you might say: *You used the present perfect correctly* or *You need to work on sentence structure. Remember to capitalize names.* Feedback should be given to students in a timely manner in order to be most effective and helpful.

Speaking Rubric

Name: _____

Class: _____   Date: _____

Activity: _____   Unit: _____   Page: _____

Vocabulary	Score	Comments
Uses a variety of vocabulary words and expressions related to the unit theme	3	
Uses some vocabulary words and expressions related to the unit theme	2	
Uses few vocabulary words or expressions related to the unit theme	1	
Grammar	**Score**	**Comments**
Uses grammar with control and accuracy	3	
Uses grammar with less control and accuracy	2	
Uses grammar with little control or accuracy	1	
Fluency	**Score**	**Comments**
Speech is authentic and fluent; there is authentic communication with partner	3	
Speech is overly rehearsed at points; is not true communication	2	
Speech is not authentic; student is not really listening to and communicating with partner	1	
Task completion	**Score**	**Comments**
Student completed the task successfully	3	
Student mostly completed the task; student went off topic at various points	2	
Student was not able to successfully complete the task: see comments	1	

Writing Rubric

Name: _____

Class: _____ Date: _____

Activity: _____ Unit: _____ Page: _____

Vocabulary	Score	Comments
Uses a variety of vocabulary words and expressions appropriate for the task and/or related to the unit theme	3	
Uses some vocabulary words and expressions appropriately, but sometimes misuses a word or fails to vary wording	2	
Uses many vocabulary words or expressions inappropriately	1	
Grammar	**Score**	**Comments**
Uses grammar with control and accuracy	3	
Makes some grammatical errors; uses grammar with less control and accuracy	2	
Uses grammar with little or no control or accuracy	1	
Mechanics (Spelling, Punctuation, Capitalization) and Format	**Score**	**Comments**
Very few or no mechanical errors; follows format and structure of model	3	
Some mechanical errors that do not affect comprehensibility; follows format of model with some errors	2	
Many mechanical errors that reduce comprehensibility; does not follow format of model	1	
Task completion	**Score**	**Comments**
Student completed the task successfully; the writing is focused, well-organized, and complete	3	
Student mostly completed the task; the writing is complete, but is sometimes off topic and disorganized	2	
Student was not able to successfully complete the task: the writing is incomplete and lacks focus and organization	1	

FUTURE
English for Results
4

TEACHER'S EDITION
AND LESSON PLANNER

Acknowledgments

The author and publisher would like to extend special thanks to our Series Consultants whose insights, experience, and expertise shaped the course and guided us throughout its development.

Beatriz B. Díaz Miami-Dade County Public Schools, Miami, FL
Ronna Magy Los Angeles Unified School District, Los Angeles, CA
Federico Salas-Isnardi Texas LEARNS, Houston, TX

We would also like to express our gratitude to the following individuals. Their kind assistance was indispensable to the creation of this program.

Consultants

Wendy J. Allison Seminole Community College, Sanford, FL
Claudia Carco Westchester Community College, Valhalla, NY
Maria J. Cesnik Ysleta Community Learning Center, El Paso, TX
Edwidge Crevecoeur-Bryant University of Florida, Gainesville, FL
Ann Marie Holzknecht Damrau San Diego Community College, San Diego, CA
Peggy Datz Berkeley Adult School, Berkeley, CA
MaryAnn Florez D.C. Learns, Washington, D.C.
Portia LaFerla Torrance Adult School, Torrance, CA
Eileen McKee Westchester Community College, Valhalla, NY
Julie Meuret Downey Adult School, Downey, CA
Sue Pace Santa Ana College School of Continuing Education, Santa Ana, CA
Howard Pomann Union County College, Elizabeth, NJ
Mary Ray Fairfax County Public Schools, Falls Church, VA
Gema Santos Miami-Dade County Public Schools, Miami, FL
Edith Uber Santa Clara Adult Education, Santa Clara, CA
Theresa Warren East Side Adult Education, San Jose, CA

Piloters

MariCarmen Acosta American High School, Adult ESOL, Hialeah, FL
Resurrección Ángeles Metropolitan Skills Center, Los Angeles, CA
Linda Bolognesi Fairfax County Public Schools, Adult and Community Education, Falls Church, VA
Patricia Boquiren Metropolitan Skills Center, Los Angeles, CA
Paul Buczko Pacoima Skills Center, Pacoima, CA
Matthew Horowitz Metropolitan Skills Center, Los Angeles, CA
Gabriel de la Hoz The English Center, Miami, FL
Cam-Tu Huynh Los Angeles Unified School District, Los Angeles, CA
Jorge Islas Whitewater Unified School District, Adult Education, Whitewater, WI
Lisa Johnson City College of San Francisco, San Francisco, CA
Loreto Kaplan Collier County Public Schools Adult ESOL Program, Naples, FL
Teressa Kitchen Collier County Public Schools Adult ESOL Program, Naples, FL
Anjie Martin Whitewater Unified School District, Adult Education, Whitewater, WI
Elida Matthews College of the Mainland, Texas City, TX
Penny Negron College of the Mainland, Texas City, TX
Manuel Pando Coral Park High School, Miami, FL
Susan Ritter Evans Community Adult School, Los Angeles, CA
Susan Ross Torrance Adult School, Torrance, CA
Beatrice Shields Fairfax County Public Schools, Adult and Community Education, Falls Church, VA
Oscar Solís Coral Park High School, Miami, FL
Wanda W. Weaver Literacy Council of Prince George's County, Hyattsville, MD

Reviewers

Lisa Agao Fresno Adult School, Fresno, CA
Carol Antuñano The English Center, Miami, FL
Euphronia Awakuni Evans Community Adult School, Los Angeles, CA
Jack Bailey Santa Barbara Adult Education, Santa Barbara, CA
Robert Breitbard District School Board of Collier County, Naples, FL
Diane Burke Evans Community Adult School, Los Angeles, CA
José A. Carmona Embry-Riddle Aeronautical University, Daytona Beach, FL
Donna Case Bell Community Adult School, Huntington Park, CA
Veronique Colas Los Angeles Technology Center, Los Angles, CA
Carolyn Corrie Metropolitan Skills Center, Los Angeles, CA
Marti Estrin Santa Rosa Junior College, Sebastopol, CA
Sheila Friedman Metropolitan Skills Center, Los Angeles, CA
José Gonzalez Spanish Education Development Center, Washington, D.C.
Allene G. Grognet Vice President (Emeritus), Center for Applied Linguistics
J. Quinn Harmon-Kelley Venice Community Adult School, Los Angeles, CA
Edwina Hoffman Miami-Dade County Public Schools, Coral Gables, FL
Eduardo Honold Far West Project GREAT, El Paso, TX
Leigh Jacoby Los Angeles Community Adult School, Los Angeles, CA
Fayne Johnson Broward County Public Schools, Ft. Lauderdale, FL
Loreto Kaplan, Collier County Public Schools Adult ESOL Program, Naples, FL
Synthia LaFontaine Collier County Public Schools, Naples, FL
Gretchen Lammers-Ghereben Martinez Adult Education, Martinez, CA
Susan Lanzano Editorial Consultant, Briarcliff Manor, NY
Karen Mauer ESL Express, Euless, TX
Rita McSorley North East Independent School District, San Antonio, TX
Alice-Ann Menjivar Carlos Rosario International Public Charter School, Washington, D.C.
Sue Pace Santa Ana College School of Continuing Education, Santa Ana, CA
Isabel Perez American High School, Hialeah, FL
Howard Pomann Union County College, Elizabeth, NJ
Lesly Prudent Miami-Dade County Public Schools, Miami, FL
Valentina Purtell North Orange County Community College District, Anaheim, CA
Barbara Raifsnider San Diego Community College, San Diego, CA
Mary Ray Fairfax County Adult ESOL, Falls Church, VA
Laurie Shapero Miami-Dade Community College, Miami, FL
Felissa Taylor Nause Austin, TX
Meintje Westerbeek Baltimore City Community College, Baltimore, MD

Thanks also to the following contributing authors for the Persistence Activities and Team Projects.

MaryAnn Florez D.C. Learns, Washington, D.C.
Lisa Johnson City College of San Francisco, San Francisco, CA

About the Series Consultants and Author

SERIES CONSULTANTS

Dr. Beatriz B. Díaz has taught ESL for more than three decades in Miami. She has a master's degree in TESOL and a doctorate in education from Nova Southeastern University. She has given trainings and numerous presentations at international, national, state, and local conferences throughout the United States, the Caribbean, and South America. Dr. Díaz is the district supervisor for the Miami-Dade County Public Schools Adult ESOL Program, one of the largest in the United States.

Ronna Magy has worked as an ESL classroom teacher and teacher-trainer for nearly three decades. Most recently, she has worked as the ESL Teacher Adviser in charge of site-based professional development for the Division of Adult and Career Education of the Los Angeles Unified School District. She has trained teachers of adult English language learners in many areas, including lesson planning, learner persistence and goal setting, and cooperative learning. A frequent presenter at local, state and national, and international conferences, Ms. Magy is the author of adult ESL publications on life skills and test preparation, U.S. citizenship, reading and writing, and workplace English. She holds a master's degree in social welfare from the University of California at Berkeley.

Federico Salas-Isnardi has worked for 20 years in the field of adult education as an ESL and GED instructor, professional development specialist, curriculum writer, and program administrator. He has trained teachers of adult English language learners for over 15 years on topics ranging from language acquisition and communicative competence to classroom management and individualized professional development planning. Mr. Salas-Isnardi has been a contributing writer or consultant for a number of ESL publications, and he has co-authored curriculum for site-based workforce ESL and Spanish classes. He holds a master's degree in applied linguistics from the University of Houston and has completed a number of certificates in educational leadership.

AUTHOR

Jane Curtis began teaching ESOL in Barcelona, Spain. She has been a classroom teacher, materials writer, and teacher trainer for nearly thirty years. Jane currently teaches in the English Language Program at Roosevelt University, where she also serves as special programs coordinator.

Scope and Sequence

UNIT	LISTENING	SPEAKING AND PRONUNCIATION	GRAMMAR
Pre-Unit **Getting Started** *page 2*	• Listen for personal information	• Give personal information	• Verb tense review
1 **Catching Up** *page 5*	• Listen to two acquaintances catching up • Listen to a conversation about goals • Listen to a radio show about entrepreneurs	• Talk about yourself and your family • Describe changes in routines • Describe a successful person • Discuss short-term and long-term goals • Talk about people's past experiences • Pronunciation of stressed words in sentences • Reduced pronunciation of *did you*	• Simple present and present continuous • Future with *will, be going to,* and present continuous • Simple past and *used to*
2 **Tell Me about Yourself** *page 25*	• Listen to a conversation between an employment specialist and a jobseeker • Listen to advice on finding a job • Listen to a job interview	• Talk about work-related goals • Discuss job-related skills and abilities • Talk about your experiences with job-hunting • Talk about job-interview questions • Respond to common interview questions • Describe previous work experience and duties • Pronunciation of silent syllables • Pronunciation of stressed syllables in words	• Infinitives and gerunds • Gerunds as objects of prepositions • Simple past and perfect present
3 **Community Life** *page 45*	• Listen to a conversation about a festival • Listen to a conversation about community problems • Listen to a conversation about ways to improve a community	• Talk about cultural festivals and traditions • Describe your feelings about your neighborhood • Describe community issues • Talk about community services • Talk about making changes in a community • Discuss ways to improve a community • Pronunciation of unreleased final stop consonants • Weak and blended pronunciation of *to*	• Participial adjectives • *Wish* in the present and future • Verb + Object + Infinitive
4 **On the Job** *page 65*	• Listen to an on-the-job training session • Listen to medical personnel discussing patients • Listen to an employee's performance review	• Talk about your experiences at a new job • Communicate with supervisors and co-workers • Check your understanding of a situation at work • Ask and answer questions about performance reviews • Give and follow work-related instructions • Stress in phrasal verbs • Pronunciation of auxiliary verbs	• Phrasal verbs • Negative *Yes/No* questions • Indirect instructions, commands, and requests

LIFE SKILLS	READING	WRITING	PROBLEM SOLVING	PERSISTENCE
	• Scanning for specific information	• Write about classmates		• Orientation to book

• Interpret and complete a school application	• Read about a successful immigrant
	• *Reading Skills:*
	  ◦ Skim for the main idea
	  ◦ Scan for specific information
		• Write sentences about your short-term goals
		• Write a biographical paragraph
		• *Writing Tip:* Put information in chronological order
			• Make suggestions to a friend for how to meet his goal of buying a house	• Community building
				• *Team Project*: Make a Venn diagram about your routines

• Interpret and write a résumé	• Read about some methods of finding a job • Read about job-interview questions • *Reading Skill:* Use details to understand important ideas	• Write sentences about your work-related goals • Write a cover letter • *Writing Tip*: Don't include unnecessary information	• Discuss ways to avoid being late for a job interview	• Planning for learning • *Team Project*: Make a brochure of job-search resources
• Listen for and give information and directions	• Read about a community garden • *Reading Skill:* Make inferences	• Write sentences describing your feelings about your neighborhood • Write a paragraph about your neighborhood • *Writing Tip*: Include details such as examples	• Discuss things a family can do to continue living in a changing community	• Community building • *Team Project*: Make a poster for a community service in your area
• Read an employee handbook	• Read about common workplace injuries • *Reading Skill*: Recognize restatements	• Write instructions for a simple procedure • Write a memo to a supervisor • *Writing Tip*: Use language that is direct and clear in a memo.	• Discuss solutions to problems caused by work schedules	• Planning for learning • *Team Project*: Make an outline for a presentation on how to be a successful team player

Text in red = Civics and American culture

UNIT	LISTENING	SPEAKING AND PRONUNCIATION	GRAMMAR
5 **Safe and Sound** *page 85*	• Listen to a fire-safety class • Listen to a radio interview with a meteorologist • Listen to a public-service announcement about making a 911 call	• Identify ways to improve fire safety in your home • Discuss what to do in case of fire • Talk about natural disasters • Talk about dangerous weather • Discuss weather reports • Communicate in a 911 emergency • Talk about emergencies • Intonation in sentences with two clauses • Pronunciation of the vowels /i/ and /ɪ/	• Present real conditionals • Adverb clauses of time • Expressing degrees of certainty
6 **Moving In** *page 105*	• Listen to a conversation about a new apartment • Listen to an expert discuss tenants' rights on a radio talk show • Listen to a conversation about bothersome neighbors	• Identify tenant responsibilities • Talk about landlord responsibilities • Discuss problems with neighbors • Intonation in tag questions • Intonation in exclamations	• Expressing expectation and permission • Tag questions with *be* • Reported speech
7 **Behind the Wheel** *page 125*	• Listen to a conversation about buying a car • Listen to a radio show host talk about ways to keep vehicles in good working order • Listen to a conversation about a car accident	• Talk about things to consider when buying a car • Describe preferences in cars • Discuss car maintenance and repairs • Describe a car accident • Stress and intonation used to highlight information. • Pronunciation of a pronoun + *'d*	• *Would rather* and *Would prefer* to express preferences • Embedded *Wh-* questions • Embedded *Yes/No* questions • Past perfect
8 **How Are You Feeling?** *page 145*	• Listen to a conversation between a patient and a doctor • Listen to two 911 calls about medical emergencies • Listen to a public service announcement about children's immunizations	• Communicate with medical personnel • Describe symptoms • Report a medical emergency • Describe ways to reduce health risks • Discuss ways to stay healthy • Beginning consonant clusters • Stress in words ending in *-cal, -ity, -tion, -ize,* and *-ate*	• Present perfect continuous • *Such . . . that* and *So . . . that* • *Should, Ought to, Had better,* and *Must*

LIFE SKILLS	READING	WRITING	PROBLEM SOLVING	PERSISTENCE
• Read an evacuation map • Understand ways to prepare for a hurricane	• **Read about preparing for natural disasters** • *Reading Skill:* Identify an author's purpose	• Write suggestions for what to do after a 911 call • Write a plan for an emergency situation • *Writing Tip:* Put the steps of a process in a logical order	• **Determine which emergency supplies should be bought first**	• **Planning for learning** • *Team Project:* Make a disaster-readiness poster
• Interpret a lease	• Read about moving trends in the U.S. • *Reading Skill:* Distinguish an author's main ideas from details	• Write a letter of complaint to a landlord • *Writing Tip:* Clearly state the problem and ask for a solution in a complaint letter	Suggest how a person might get to know his or her neighbors better.	• Self-evaluation • *Team Project:* Design a website page for newcomers about renting an apartment
• Read a car insurance renewal notice • Interpret information about buying car insurance	• Read about consumer-protection laws • *Reading Skill:* Use visuals	• **Write car-care tips** • Write about a good or bad purchase • *Writing Tip:* Use time words and phrases to signal the steps in a process	• **Discuss solutions to a problem a driver is having with her car**	• **Planning for learning** • *Team Project:* Design an Internet ad for a used car
• Interpret and complete a medical history form • Interpret and complete a health insurance form	• Read about preventive health practices • *Reading Skill:* Scan a list for details	• **Write sentences about advice, suggestions, recommendations, or requirements for good health** • Describe a personal experience with health care • *Writing Tip:* Use sensory details to help the reader see, hear, feel, smell, or taste what you are describing	• **Give advice for changes that can be made to have a healthier diet**	• **Community building** • *Team Project:* Make a booklet about ways to reduce stress

Text in red = Civics and American culture

UNIT	LISTENING	SPEAKING AND PRONUNCIATION	GRAMMAR
9 **Partners in Education** *page 165*	• Listen to a conversation between a parent and a guidance counselor • Listen to a parent talking to a secretary about enrolling a child in school • Listen to a school principal talking to a group of parents, teachers, and community leaders	• Communicate with school personnel about a student's progess • Ask about enrolling a child in school • Talk about parents' rights and responsibilities • **Talk about after-school programs** • **Talk about improving schools** • **Talk about school safety** • **Contrastive stress** • **Pronunciation of past modals**	• Adverb clauses of reason • Infinitives and adverb clauses of purpose • Adjective clauses • Past modals
10 **Safety First** *page 185*	• Listen to a conversation between a contractor and a subcontractor • Listen to two co-workers discussing safety on the job • Listen to a manager telling an employee she has been promoted	• Give a progress report • Talk about work requirements • **Discuss ways to prevent accidents at work** • Make requests, suggestions, and offers at work • **Linking a final consonant to a beginning vowel** • **Pronunciation of the letter *o***	• *Make/let/have/get* + verb • Reflexive pronouns • *Could you / I . . . ? / Why don't I . . . ? / Would you mind . . . ?*
11 **Know the Law!** *page 205*	• Listen to a conversation about a misdemeanor • Listen to a couple discussing courtroom TV shows • Listen to a talk show about traffic violations	• Identify and discuss misdemeanors • Talk about legal problems • Describe what goes on in a courtroom • Talk about DNA evidence • Discuss traffic laws • Weak pronunciation of *be* • Weak words in sentences	• Past continuous for interrupted action • Passives: present and simple past • Adverb clauses of condition and contrast
12 **Saving and Spending** *page 225*	• Listen to a conversation between a customer service officer and a bank customer • Listen to a financial expert giving a caller advice on a radio show • Listen to two friends talking about what they would do with a lot of money	• Describe bank services • Talk about opening a business • Talk about your monthly budget • Talk about your dreams for the future • Stress in compound nouns • Pronunciation of *would you*	• Indefinite and definite articles • Future real conditionals • Present unreal conditionals

LIFE SKILLS	READING	WRITING	PROBLEM SOLVING	PERSISTENCE
• Interpret a report card • Correspond with a teacher	• Read an opinion about after-school programs • *Reading Skill:* Distinguish fact from opinion	• Write a note to a teacher • Write a letter to the editor • *Writing Tip:* Put similar information together in each paragraph	• Discuss ways to improve communication between school and parents	• **Self-efficacy** • *Team Project:* Make a booklet about after-school programs
• Interpret and complete an employee accident report	• Read about workplace safety • *Reading Skill:* Look for words that show chronological order	• Write an e-mail to a supervisor suggesting a solution to a problem • *Writing Tip:* When writing about a problem, identify the problem, explain the cause, and suggest a solution	• Discuss ways for restaurant workers to prevent accidents	• **Self-evaluation** • *Team Project:* Write a work-related letter and response to an advice column
• Identify people in a courtroom	• **Read about DNA evidence** • *Reading Skill:* Understand long sentences	• Write a paragraph comparing and contrasting legal rights of accused people in your country and the U.S. • *Writing Tip:* When comparing and contrasting, use words that signal similarities and differences	• Discuss what someone should do when she thinks her car was towed away unfairly	• **Self-evaluation** • *Team Project:* Make a poster about citizens' rights and responsibilities in the U.S.
• Create a budget • Interpret an income tax form	• Read about someone whose dream of opening a restaurant came true • *Reading Skill:* Write a summary that includes the main idea and the most important information in a text to show that you understand it. • **Read about income tax in the U.S.**	• Write about a charity that you would support • *Writing Tip:* Focus a paragraph by asking a question and answering it	• Discuss ways a couple can save to buy a house	• **Self-efficacy** • *Team Project:* Make a poster about a business

Text in red = Civics and American culture

Corrletions

UNIT	CASAS Reading Basic Skill Content Standards	CASAS Listening Basic Skill Content Standards	
1	**U1:** 3.2; 3.6; **L2:** 3.3; **L4:** 3.5; 6.1; 6.4; 7.2; **L4:** 3.4; **L5:** 3.3; **L6:** 3.4; **L8:** 3.3; **L9:** 3.3; 4.3; 4.9; **SWYK Review and Expand:** 3.3	**U1:** 2.7; 4.2; **L1:** 4.6; 6.4; **L2:** 3.2; **L3:** 5.8; **L4:** 4.6; **L5:** 3.1; **L7:** 1.5; 4.6; 4.11; **L8:** 3.9; **SWYK Review and Expand:** 4.6; 4.7	
2	**U2:** 3.2; 3.6; **L2:** 3.5; **L3:** 4.7; 4.8; **L4:** 3.2; 3.4; **L5:** 3.3; **L6:** 2.12; 3.5; 6.1; 7.2; 7.2; **L7:** 2.10; 3.3; **L8:** 3.3; **L9:** 3.4; 4.1; 4.3; 4.8; **SWYK Review and Expand:** 3.3	**U2:** 2.7; 4.2; **L1:** 4.2; 4.6; 6.4; **L4:** 4.6; **L7:** 1.6; 4.6; **L8:** 3.9; 3.13; **SWYK Review and Expand:** 4.6; 4.7	
3	**U3:** 3.2; 3.6; **L3:** 3.5; 4.8; 4.9; **L6:** 6.1; 7.2; 7.9; 7.12; **L7:** 7.13; **L8:** 3.3; **L9:** 3.5; 7.12; **SWYK Review and Expand:** 3.3	**U3:** 2.7; 4.2; **L1:** 4.6; 4.7; **L3:** 4.6; 5.5; **L4:** 4.7; **L5:** 3.1; **L7:** 1.5; 4.6; 5.8; **SWYK Review and Expand:** 4.6	
4	**U4:** 3.2; 3.6; **L3:** 3.7; **L5:** 3.5; 3.6; **L6:** 3.5; 7.2; 7.3; **L8:** 3.7; **L9:** 3.4; **SWYK Review and Expand:** 3.3	**U4:** 2.7; 4.2; **L1:** 1.4; 2.8; 4.6; **L2:** 2.3; 3.13; 4.6; **L4:** 1.4; 4.6; **L5:** 3.5; 3.6; **L6:** 2.7; 5.6; 6.8; **L7:** 4.6; 5.6; **L8:** 3.13; **SWYK Review and Expand:** 4.6	
5	**U5:** 3.2; 3.6; **L1:** 3.12; **L2:** 3.4; **L3:** 3.5; 6.1; 6.5; 7.2; 7.11; **L4:** 3.4; **L5:** 3.4; 7.5; **L6:** 4.9; **L9:** 3.5; 7.5; **SWYK Review and Expand:** 3.3	**U5:** 2.7; 4.2; **L1:** 1.7; 4.6; 5.9; **L2:** 3.13; **L4:** 4.6; 4.11; **L7:** 1.1; 4.11; **SWYK Review and Expand:** 4.6; 5.5	
6	**U6:** 3.2; 3.6; **L2:** 3.6; 4.10; **L3:** 4.7; **L6:** 2.12; 3.5; 3.13; 7.2; 7.3; **L8:** 3.5; **L9:** 3.5; 4.3; **SWYK Review and Expand:** 3.3	**U6:** 2.7; 4.2; **L4:** 1.4; 3.14; 4.11; **L5:** 3.5; 3.14; **L7:** 1.7; 4.6; **L8:** 3.8; 3.13; **SWYK Review and Expand:** 4.6	
7	**U7:** 3.2; 3.6; **L2:** 3.5; **L3:** 4.7; **L4:** 3.5; **L6:** 3.5; 3.13; 4.8; 4.9; 4.10; 6.1; **L8:** 7.4; **L9:** 3.3; **SWYK Review and Expand:** 3.3	**U7:** 2.7; 4.2; **L1:** 4.6; **L3:** 4.6; 6.5; **L4:** 1.7; 4.6; 4.11; **L5:** 3.6; 3.14; **L6:** 5.9; **L7:** 2.4; 3.3; 4.6; **L8:** 3.13; **SWYK Review and Expand:** 4.6	
8	**U8:** 3.2; 3.6; **L1:** 3.3; 4.6; 5.5; **L2:** 3.3; **L3:** 4.7; **L5:** 3.4; **L6:** 3.5; 4.10; 6.3; 6.5; 6.6; **L8:** 3.3; 3.5; **L9:** 3.5; 7.1; **SWYK Review and Expand:** 3.3	**U8:** 2.7; 4.2; **L1:** 2.4; 4.6; **L2:** 3.13; 3.64; 4.6; **L4:** 4.11; **L5:** 3.7; **L6:** 5.8; **L7:** 1.6; 4.6; 4.11; **SWYK Review and Expand:** 4.6	
9	**U9:** 3.2; 3.6; **L2:** 3.4; **L3:** 4.5; 4.7; **L4:** 4.6; **L6:** 3.5; 6.1; 7.10; **L8:** 3.3; **L9:** 3.5; **SWYK Review and Expand:** 3.3	**U9:** 2.7; 4.2; **L1:** 1.4; 4.6; **L4:** 4.6; **L6:** 5.9; **L7:** 3.9; 4.6; 5.8; **L8:** 3.9; 4.6; **SWYK Review and Expand:** 4.6	
10	**U10:** 3.2; 3.6; **L2:** 3.1; 3.8; **L3:** 2.12; 3.5; 3.12; 7.5; **L5:** 3.3; **L6:** 4.7; **L8:** 3.3; **L9:** 3.5; **SWYK Review and Expand:** 3.3	**U10:** 2.7; 4.2; **L1:** 4.6; **L2:** 3.1; 3.8; **L3:** 3.11; 5.9; **L4:** 4.6; **L5:** 3.2; **L7:** 4.6; **SWYK Review and Expand:** 4.6	
11	**U11:** 3.2; 3.6; **L1:** 2.1; **L2:** 3.3; **L3:** 3.3; **L5:** 3.3; **L6:** 3.5; 3.9; **L7:** 2.1; **L9:** 3.5; **SWYK Review and Expand:** 3.3	**U11:** 2.7; 4.2; **L1:** 4.6; **L2:** 3.9; 3.13; **L4:** 1.7; 4.6; **L5:** 3.1; 3.9; **L6:** 5.8; **L7:** 1.7; 2.4; 4.6; 4.11; **SWYK Review and Expand:** 4.6	
12	**U12:** 3.2; 3.6; **L1:** 3.3; **L2:** 3.3; **L3:** 3.13; 7.7; **L4:** 4.4; 4.5; 4.8; **L5:** 4.4; **L6:** 3.3; 4.4; 4.7; **L7:** 1.5; **L8:** 3.3; **L9:** 3.4; 4.4; **SWYK Review and Expand:** 4.8	**U12:** 2.7; 4.2; **L1:** 1.4; 2.9; 4.6; **L3:** 5.8; **L4:** 4.11; **L5:** 3.13; 4.6; **L7:** 1.5; 4.6; **L8:** 3.13; **SWYK Review and Expand:** 4.6	

CASAS Competencies	LAUSD ESL High Intermediate Competencies	Florida Adult ESOL Curriculum Standards
U1: 0.1.2; 0.1.5; 0.1.7; 0.2.1; 0.2.4; **L1:** 0.1.8; 0.2.4; **L4:** 7.1.1; 7.1.2; **L5:** 7.1.1; 7.1.2; **L6:** 0.2.2; 4.1.2; **SWYK Review and Expand:** 7.1.1; 7.2.2	**A Course:** 2; 3; 5a; 5b; 7a; 7b; 7c; 7d; 8b; 11b; 42; 44 **B Course:** 1a; 3; 5; 6a; 8a; 8d; 9a; 10b; 35; 37; 40	5.03.02; 5.03.05; 5.03.13
U2: 0.1.2; 0.1.5; 0.1.7; 0.2.1; 0.2.4; **L1:** 4.1.3; 7.1.1; **L2:** 7.1.1; **L3:** 4.1.2; **L4:** 4.13; **L5:** 4.1.2; 4.1.8; **L6:** 4.1.5; **L7:** 4.1.5; 4.1.7; **L8:** 4.1.5; **L9:** 4.1.2; **SWYK Review and Expand:** 4.1.3; 4.1.5	**A Course:** 1b; 4b; 5a; 5b; 7a; 7b; 7c; 7d; 8b; 34, 36, 37, 42, 44 **B Course:** 4; 5; 6a; 6c; 8a; 8d; 29; 30; 31a; 31b; 31c; 37; 40	5.03.02; 5.03.03; 5.03.04
U3: 0.1.2; 0.1.5; 0.1.7; 0.2.1; 0.2.4; **L1:** 2.7.9; **L2:** 0.1.8; **L3:** 2.2.1; 2.2.5; 2.5.9; **L4:** 2.5.8; 2.8.9; **L5:** 2.8.9; **L6:** 2.6.1; 2.8.9; **L7:** 2.8.9; 5.1.6; 5.1.7; **L8:** 5.1.6; 5.1.7; **SWYK Review and Expand:** 2.6.3	**A Course:** 5a; 5b; 6; 7a; 7b; 7c; 7d; 8b; 8c; 16a; 42; 44; 45 **B Course:** 5; 6a; 6c; 7; 8a; 8d; 9b; 12; 37; 40; 41b	5.02.02; 5.02.03
U4: 0.1.2; 0.1.5; 0.1.7; 0.2.1; 0.2.4; **L1:** 0.1.6; 4.6.1; 4.8.1; 4.8.2; **L2:** 4.6.1; 4.8.1; 4.8.2; **L3:** 4.2.4; 4.2.5; **L4:** 4.8.1; 4.8.2; **L5:** 4.8.1; 4.8.2; **L6:** 4.3.2; **L7:** 4.4.1; 4.4.4; **L8:** 4.6.1; 4.6.5; **L9:** 4.6.2; 4.6.5; **SWYK Review and Expand:** 4.2.4; 4.6.1; 4.8.1; 4.8.2	**A Course:** 5a; 5b; 7a; 7b; 7c; 7d; 8b; 38a; 38b; 38c; 39c; 40b; 41; 42; 44 **B Course:** 4; 5; 6a; 6c; 8a; 8d; 32; 33a; 33b; 34a; 37; 40	5.03.06; 5.03.07; 5.03.11
U5: 0.1.2; 0.1.5; 0.1.7; 0.2.1; 0.2.4; **L1:** 0.1.3; 3.4.2; **L2:** 2.5.1; **L3:** 3.4.8; **L4:** 2.3.3; 3.4.8; **L5:** 2.3.3; **L6:** 3.4.8; **L7:** 2.5.1; **L8:** 2.5.1; **L9:** 3.4.8; **SWYK Review and Expand:** 2.5.1; 3.4.8	**A Course:** 5a; 5b; 7a; 7b; 7c; 7d; 8b; 12; 32; 42; 44 **B Course:** 5; 6a; 6c; 8c; 8d; 28; 37; 40	5.02.05
U6: 0.1.2; 0.1.5; 0.1.7; 0.2.1; 0.2.4; **L1:** 1.4.6; 1.4.7; **L2:** 1.4.5; **L3:** 1.4.3; **L4:** 1.4.5; **L5:** 1.4.5; **L7:** 0.1.3; 0.1.8; 7.3.1; 7.3.2; **L8:** 0.1.3; 0.1.8; 7.3.1; 7.3.2; **L9:** 1.4.7; **SWYK Review and Expand:** 1.4.7	**A Course:** 5a; 5b; 7a; 7b; 7c;7d; 23; 24; 42; 44 **B Course:** 5; 6a; 6c; 8a; 8d; 20; 37; 40; 41b	5.04.04; 5.04.05
U7: 0.1.2; 0.1.5; 0.1.7; 0.2.1; 0.2.4; **L1:** 1.9.5; **L2:** 1.9.5; **L3:** 1.9.5; 1.9.8; **L4:** 1.9.6; **L5:** 1.9.6; **L6:** 1.6.3; **L7:** 1.9.7; 1.9.9; **L8:** 1.9.7; **SWYK Review and Expand:** 0.1.8; 1.9.6; 1.9.7	**A Course:** 5a; 5b; 7a; 7b; 7c; 7d; 8b; 25b; 42; 44; 45 **B Course:** 5; 6a; 8a; 8d; 14; 15; 16; 24a; 37; 40	5.06.04
U8: 0.1.2; 0.1.5; 0.1.7; 0.2.1; 0.2.4; **L1:** 0.18; 3.1.3; 3.2.1; 3.3.1; 3.6.4; **L3:** 3.1.6; **L4:** 2.1.2; 2.5.1; **L5:** 3.5.9; **L6:** 3.5.9; **L7:** 3.1.3; 3.4.6; **L8:** 3.5.2; 3.5.9; **L9:** 2.7.9; **SWYK Review and Expand:** 3.5.2	**A Course:** 3; 5a; 5b; 7a; 7b; 7c; 7d; 28; 30a; 30b; 30c; 44; 45 **B Course:** 3;5; 6a; 6c; 8a; 8d; 26; 27; 37; 38b; 40	5.05.01; 5.05.03
U9: 0.1.2; 0.1.5; 0.1.7; 0.2.1; 0.2.4; **L1:** 2.8.6; **L2:** 2.8.9; **L3:** 0.2.3; 2.8.4; 2.8.6; 2.8.8; **L4:** 2.8.3; 2.8.6; **L5:** 2.8.8; 2.8.9; **L6:** 2.5.9; 2.8.3; **L7:** 2.8.6; **L8:** 2.8.6; **L9:** 2.8.6; 2.8.8; **SWYK Review and Expand:** 2.8.6; 2.8.8; 2.8.9	**A Course:** 5a; 5b; 7a; 7b; 7c; 7d; 8a; 8b; 10b; 11a; 44 **B Course:** 4; 5; 6a; 6b; 6c; 8a; 8d; 10a; 11; 37; 40	5.02.07; 5.02.08
U10: 0.1.2; 0.1.5; 0.1.7; 0.2.1; 0.2.4; **L1:** 4.6.1; 4.6.4; 4.6.5; **L2:** 4.4.6; 4.6.1; **L3:** 4.3.1; 4.3.2; **L4:** 4.3.3; 4.5.1; 4.5.7; **L5:** 4.3.2; 4.3.3; 4.3.4; **L6:** 4.3.4; **L7:** 4.4.2; **L8:** 0.1.3; 4.6.1; 4.6.5; **L9:** 4.6.2; **SWYK Review and Expand:** 4.3; 4.4	**A Course:** 3; 5a; 5b; 7a; 7b; 7c; 7d; 8b; 32; 33; 38a; 38b; 38c; 39a; 39b; 40c; 44 **B Course:** 3; 5; 6a; 6b; 6c; 8a; 8d; 32; 33a; 34b; 37; 40	5.03.05; 5.03.06; 5.03.07; 5.03.08; 5.03.14; 5.03.15
U11: 0.1.2; 0.1.5; 0.1.7; 0.2.1; 0.2.4; **L1:** 5.3.1; 5.3.7; **L2:** 5.3.1; 5.3.2; **L3:** 5.3.3; **L4:** 5.3.3; **L5:** 5.3.3; **L6:** 5.7.3; **L7:** 1.9.1; 1.9.2; 5.3.1; **L8:** 1.9.2; 5.3.1; 5.3.7; **L9:** 2.7.9; 5.3.2; **SWYK Review and Expand:** 5.3.1; 5.3.2; 5.3.7	**A Course:** 5a; 5b; 7a; 7b; 7c; 7d; 8b; 25b; 44 **B Course:** 5; 6a; 6b; 6c; 7; 8a; 8d; 23a; 37; 40	05.02.04; 05.07.02
U12: 0.1.2; 0.1.5; 0.1.7; 0.2.1; 0.2.4; **L1:** 1.8.1; 1.8.3; **L2:** 1.8.1; 1.8.3; 1.8.4; **L3:** 5.4.5; **L4:** 1.5.1; 1.5.2; **L5:** 1.5.1; **L6:** 5.4.1; **L8:** 7.1.2; **L9:** 5.7.6; **SWYK Review and Expand:** 1.5.1; 7.3.1	**A Course:** 5a; 5b; 7a; 8b; 7c **B Course:** 5; 6a; 6c; 8a; 8d; 9b; 19	5.04.07; 5.04.08

All units of *Future* meet most of the EFF **Content Standards**. For details, as well as for correlations to other state standards, go to www.pearsonlongman.com/future.

To the Teacher

Welcome to *Future*
English for Results

Future is a six-level, four-skills course for adults and young adults correlated to state and national standards. It incorporates research-based teaching strategies, corpus-informed language, and the best of modern technology.

KEY FEATURES

Future provides everything your students need in one integrated program.

In developing the course, we listened to what teachers asked for and we responded, providing six levels, more meaningful content, a thorough treatment of grammar, explicit skills development, abundant practice, multiple options for state-of-the-art assessment, and innovative components.

Future serves students' real-life needs.

We began constructing the instructional syllabus for *Future* by identifying what is most critical to students' success in their personal and family lives, in the workplace, as members of a community, and in their academic pursuits. *Future* provides outstanding coverage of life skills competencies, basing language teaching on actual situations that students are likely to encounter and equipping them with the skills they need to achieve their goals. The grammar and other language elements taught in each lesson grow out of these situations and are thus practiced in realistic contexts, enabling students to use language meaningfully, from the beginning.

Future grows with your students.

Future takes students from absolute beginner level through low-advanced proficiency in English, addressing students' abilities and learning priorities at each level. As the levels progress, the curricular content and unit structure change accordingly, with the upper levels incorporating more academic skills, more advanced content standards, and more content-rich texts.

Level	Description	CASAS Scale Scores
Intro	True Beginning	Below 180
1	Low Beginning	181–190
2	High Beginning	191–200
3	Low Intermediate	201–210
4	High Intermediate	211–220
5	Low Advanced	221–235

Future is fun!

Many of the conversations and other listenings texts are designed to be amusing or interesting—something to anticipate with pleasure and to then take great satisfaction in once it is understood. In addition, many activities have students interacting in pairs and groups. Not only does this make classroom time more enjoyable, it also creates an atmosphere conducive to learning in which learners are relaxed, highly motivated, and at their most receptive.

Future puts the best of 21st-century technology in the hands of students and teachers.

In addition to its expertly developed print materials and audio components, *Future* goes a step further.

- Every **Student Book comes with a Practice Plus CD-ROM** for use at home, in the lab, or wherever students have access to a computer. The Practice Plus CD-ROM can be used both by students who wish to extend their practice beyond the classroom and by those who need to "make up" what they missed in class.
- The **CD-ROM** also includes the entire class audio program as MP3 files so students can get extra listening practice at their convenience.
- The **Tests and Test Prep** book comes with the *Future* **Exam**View® *Assessment Suite*, enabling teachers to print ready-made tests, customize these tests, or create their own tests for life skills, grammar, listening, and reading.
- The **Teacher Training DVD** provides demo lessons of real teachers using *Future* with their classes. Teachers can select from the menu and watch a specific type of lesson, such as a grammar presentation, or a specific type of activity, such as a role-play activity, at their own convenience.
- The **Companion Website** provides a variety of teaching support, including a pdf of the Teacher's Edition and Lesson Planner notes for each unit in the Student Book.

Future provides all the assessment tools you need.

- The **Placement Test** evaluates students' proficiency in all skill areas, allowing teachers and program administrators to easily assign students to the right classes.
- The **Tests and Test Prep** book for each level provides:
  - **Printed unit tests** with accompanying audio CD. These unit tests use standardized testing formats, giving students practice "bubbling-in" responses as required for CASAS and other standardized tests. In addition, reproducible test prep worksheets and practice tests provide invaluable help to students unfamiliar with such test formats.

- The *Future* **Exam** *View* **Assessment Suite** is a powerful program that allows teachers to create their own unique tests or to print or customize already prepared tests.
- **Performance-based assessment:** Lessons in the Student Book end with a "practical assessment" activity such as Role Play, Make It Personal, or Show What You Know. Each unit culminates with both a role-play activity and a problem-solving activity, which require students to demonstrate their oral competence in a holistic way. The **Teacher's Edition and Lesson Planner** provides speaking rubrics to make it easy for teachers to evaluate students' oral proficiency.
- **Self-assessment:** For optimal learning to take place, students need to be involved in setting goals and in monitoring their own progress. *Future* has addressed this in numerous ways. In the Student Book, checkboxes at the end of lessons invite students to evaluate their mastery of the material. End-of-unit reviews allow students to see their progress in grammar. And after completing each unit, students go back to the goals for the unit and reflect on their achievement. In addition, the CD-ROM provides students with continuous feedback (and opportunities for self-correction) as they work through each lesson, and the Workbook contains the answer keys, so students can check their own work outside of class.

Future addresses multilevel classes and diverse learning styles.

Using research-based teaching strategies, *Future* provides teachers with creative solutions for all stages of lesson planning and implementation, allowing them to meet the needs of all their students.

- The **Teacher's Edition and Lesson Planner** offers pre-level and above-level variations for every lesson plan as well as numerous optional and extension activities designed to reach students at all levels.
- The **Practice Plus CD-ROM** included with the Student Book is an extraordinary tool for individualizing instruction. It allows students to direct their own learning, working on precisely what they need and practicing what they choose to work on as many times as they like. In addition, the CD-ROM provides all the audio files for the book, enabling students to listen as they wish to any of the material that accompanies the text.
- The **Workbook**, similarly, allows students to devote their time to the lessons and specific skill areas that they need to work on most.
- The **Tests and Test Prep** book, as noted on page xiv, includes *Future* **Exam** *View* **Assessment Suite**, which allows teachers to customize existing tests or create their own tests using the databank.

Future's persistence curriculum motivates students to continue their education.

Recent research about persistence has given us insights into how to keep students coming to class and how to keep them learning when they can't attend. Recognizing that there are many forces operating in students' lives—family, jobs, childcare, health—that may make it difficult for them to come to class, programs need to help students:
- Identify their educational goals
- Believe that they can successfully achieve them
- Develop a commitment to their own education
- Identify forces that can interfere with school attendance
- Develop strategies that will help them try to stay in school in spite of obstacles
- Find ways to continue learning even during "stopping out" periods

Future addresses all of these areas with its persistence curriculum. Activities found throughout the book and specific persistence activities in the back of the book help students build community, set goals, develop better study skills, and feel a sense of achievement. In addition, the Practice Plus CD-ROM is unique in its ability to ensure that even those students unable to attend class are able to make up what they missed and thus persist in their studies.

Future supports busy teachers by providing all the materials teachers need, plus teacher support.

The **Student Book** and **Workbook** were designed to provide teachers with everything they need in the way of ready-to-use classroom materials so they can concentrate on responding to their students' needs. The **Future Teacher Training DVD** gives teachers tips and models for conducting various activity types in their classroom.

Future provides ample practice, with flexible options to best fit the needs of each class.

The Student Book provides 60–100 hours of instruction. It can be supplemented in class by using:
- Teacher's Edition and Lesson Planner expansion ideas
- Workbook exercises
- Tests
- CD-ROM activities
- Activities on the Companion Website (longmanusa.com/Future)

TEACHING MULTILEVEL CLASSES

Teaching tips for pair and group work

Using pair and group work in an ESL classroom has many proven benefits. It creates an atmosphere of liveliness, builds community, and allows students to practice speaking in a low-risk environment. Many of the activities in *Future* are pair and small-group activities. Here are some tips for managing these activities:

- Limit small groups to three or four students per group (unless an activity specifically calls for larger groups). This maximizes student participation.
- Change partners for different activities. This gives students a chance to work with many others in the class and keeps them from feeling "stuck."
- If possible, give students a place to put their coats when they enter the classroom. This allows them to move around freely without worrying about returning to their own seats.
- Move around the classroom as students are working to make sure they are on task and to monitor their work.
- As you walk around, try to remain unobtrusive, so students continue to participate actively, without feeling they are being evaluated.
- Keep track of language points students are having difficulty with. After the activity, teach a mini-lesson to the entire class addressing those issues. This helps students who are having trouble without singling them out.

Pairs and groups in the multilevel classroom

Adult education ESL classrooms are by nature multilevel. This is true even if students have been given a placement test. Many factors—including a student's age, educational background, and literacy level—contribute to his or her ability level. Also, the same student may be at level in one skill, but pre-level or above-level in another.

When grouping students for a task, keep the following points in mind:

- *Like-ability* groups (in which students have the same ability level) help ensure that all students participate equally, without one student dominating the activity.
- *Cross-ability* groups (in which students have different ability levels) are beneficial to pre-level students who need the support of their at- or above-level classmates. The higher-level students benefit from "teaching" their lower-level classmates.

For example, when students are practicing a straightforward conversation substitution exercise, like-ability pairings are helpful. The activity can be tailored to different ability levels, and both students can participate equally. When students are completing the more complex task of creating their own conversations, cross-ability pairings are helpful. The higher-level student can support and give ideas to the lower-level student.

The *Future* Teacher's Edition and Lesson Planner provide specific suggestions for when to put students in like-ability versus cross-ability groups, and how to tailor activities to different ability levels.

Unit Opener

Each unit starts with a full-page photo that introduces the themes and vocabulary of the unit.

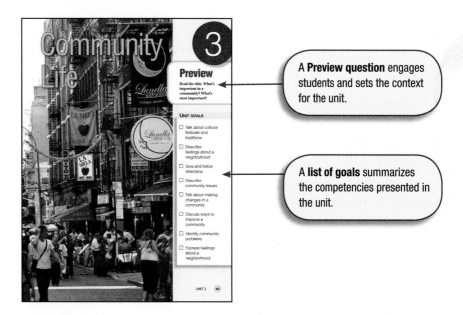

A **Preview question** engages students and sets the context for the unit.

A **list of goals** summarizes the competencies presented in the unit.

Listening and Speaking

Three listening lessons present the core competencies and language of the unit.

The **Pronunciation Watch** and pronunciation exercises focus on the sound patterns, stress, and intonation of English.

Before You Listen activities introduce new language and cultural concepts.

Listening comprehension questions focus first on topic or main idea and then on specific information.

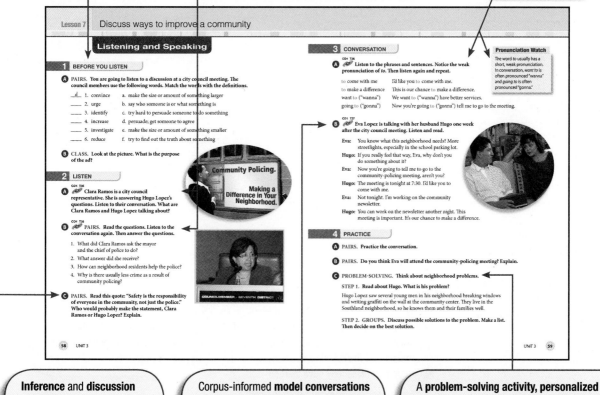

Inference and **discussion questions** often conclude the Listening sections.

Corpus-informed **model conversations** use target grammar and competencies to model spoken language.

A **problem-solving activity, personalized activity,** or **supported role play** reinforces the concepts and language learned in the lesson.

Grammar

Each unit presents three grammar points in a logical, systematic grammar syllabus.

> **Grammar charts** clearly present the target grammar.

> **Grammar Watch** notes call attention to specific aspects of the grammar point.

> Contextualized **grammar practice** progresses from controlled to open-ended exercises.

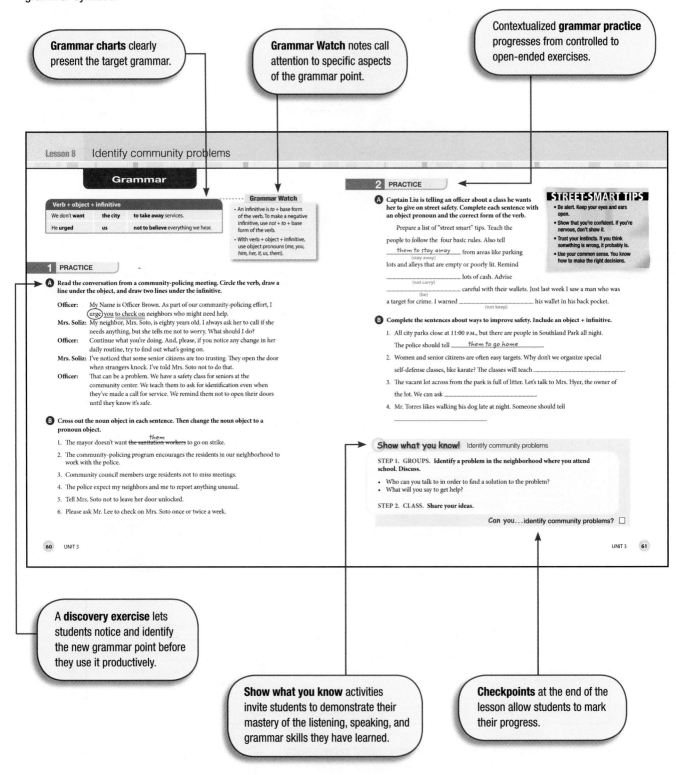

Lesson 8   Identify community problems

Grammar

Verb + object + infinitive		
We don't **want**	**the city**	**to take away** services.
He **urged**	**us**	**not to believe** everything we hear.

Grammar Watch
- An infinitive is *to* + base form of the verb. To make a negative infinitive, use *not* + *to* + base form of the verb.
- With verb + object + infinitive, use object pronouns (*me, you, him, her, it, us, them*).

1 PRACTICE

A Read the conversation from a community-policing meeting. Circle the verb, draw a line under the object, and draw two lines under the infinitive.

Officer: My Name is Officer Brown. As part of our community-policing effort, I urge you to check on neighbors who might need help.
Mrs. Soliz: My neighbor, Mrs. Soto, is eighty years old. I always ask her to call if she needs anything, but she tells me not to worry. What should I do?
Officer: Continue what you're doing. And, please, if you notice any change in her daily routine, try to find out what's going on.
Mrs. Soliz: I've noticed that some senior citizens are too trusting. They open the door when strangers knock. I've told Mrs. Soto not to do that.
Officer: That can be a problem. We have a safety class for seniors at the community center. We teach them to ask for identification even when they've made a call for service. We remind them not to open their doors until they know it's safe.

B Cross out the noun object in each sentence. Then change the noun object to a pronoun object.

1. The mayor doesn't want ~~the sanitation workers~~ to go on strike. *them*
2. The community-policing program encourages the residents in our neighborhood to work with the police.
3. Community council members urge residents not to miss meetings.
4. The police expect my neighbors and me to report anything unusual.
5. Tell Mrs. Soto not to leave her door unlocked.
6. Please ask Mr. Lee to check on Mrs. Soto once or twice a week.

2 PRACTICE

A Captain Liu is telling an officer about a class he wants her to give on street safety. Complete each sentence with an object pronoun and the correct form of the verb.

Prepare a list of "street smart" tips. Teach the people to follow the four basic rules. Also tell ___them to stay away___ from areas like parking (stay away) lots and alleys that are empty or poorly lit. Remind _____ lots of cash. Advise (not carry) _____ careful with their wallets. Just last week I saw a man who was (be) a target for crime. I warned _____ his wallet in his back pocket. (not keep)

B Complete the sentences about ways to improve safety. Include an object + infinitive.

1. All city parks close at 11:00 P.M., but there are people in Southland Park all night. The police should tell ___them to go home___
2. Women and senior citizens are often easy targets. Why don't we organize special self-defense classes, like karate? The classes will teach _____
3. The vacant lot across from the park is full of litter. Let's talk to Mrs. Hyer, the owner of the lot. We can ask _____
4. Mr. Torres likes walking his dog late at night. Someone should tell _____

STREET-SMART TIPS
- Be alert. Keep your eyes and ears open.
- Show that you're confident. If you're nervous, don't show it.
- Trust your instincts. If you think something is wrong, it probably is.
- Use your common sense. You know how to make the right decisions.

Show what you know! Identify community problems

STEP 1. GROUPS. Identify a problem in the neighborhood where you attend school. Discuss.

- Who can you talk to in order to find a solution to the problem?
- What will you say to get help?

STEP 2. CLASS. Share your ideas.

Can you... identify community problems? ☐

60   UNIT 3

UNIT 3   61

> A **discovery exercise** lets students notice and identify the new grammar point before they use it productively.

> **Show what you know** activities invite students to demonstrate their mastery of the listening, speaking, and grammar skills they have learned.

> **Checkpoints** at the end of the lesson allow students to mark their progress.

Reading

High-interest articles introduce students to cultural concepts and useful, topical information. Students read to learn while learning to read in English.

Before You Read exercises activate students' background knowledge and build other pre-reading skills.

Comprehension questions check understanding of the article and build reading skills.

Essential **reading skills**, such as making inferences, are explicitly taught and practiced.

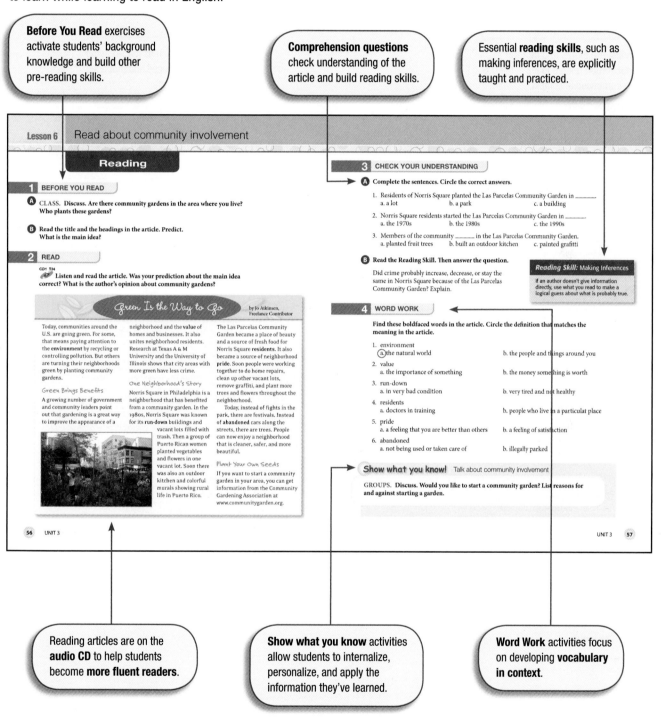

Lesson 6 — Read about community involvement

Reading

1 BEFORE YOU READ

A CLASS. Discuss. Are there community gardens in the area where you live? Who plants these gardens?

B Read the title and the headings in the article. Predict. What is the main idea?

2 READ

CD1 T34

Listen and read the article. Was your prediction about the main idea correct? What is the author's opinion about community gardens?

Green Is the Way to Go
by Jo Atkinsen, Freelance Contributor

Today, communities around the U.S. are going green. For some, that means paying attention to the **environment** by recycling or controlling pollution. But others are turning their neighborhoods green by planting community gardens.

Green Brings Benefits

A growing number of government and community leaders point out that gardening is a great way to improve the appearance of a neighborhood and the **value** of homes and businesses. It also unites neighborhood residents. Research at Texas A & M University and the University of Illinois shows that city areas with more green have less crime.

One Neighborhood's Story

Norris Square in Philadelphia is a neighborhood that has benefited from a community garden. In the 1980s, Norris Square was known for its **run-down** buildings and vacant lots filled with trash. Then a group of Puerto Rican women planted vegetables and flowers in one vacant lot. Soon there was also an outdoor kitchen and colorful murals showing rural life in Puerto Rico.

The Las Parcelas Community Garden became a place of beauty and a source of fresh food for Norris Square **residents**. It also became a source of neighborhood **pride**. Soon people were working together to do home repairs, clean up other vacant lots, remove graffiti, and plant more trees and flowers throughout the neighborhood.

Today, instead of fights in the park, there are festivals. Instead of **abandoned** cars along the streets, there are trees. People can now enjoy a neighborhood that is cleaner, safer, and more beautiful.

Plant Your Own Seeds

If you want to start a community garden in your area, you can get information from the Community Gardening Association at www.communitygarden.org.

56 UNIT 3

3 CHECK YOUR UNDERSTANDING

A Complete the sentences. Circle the correct answers.

1. Residents of Norris Square planted the Las Parcelas Community Garden in _____.
   a. a lot   b. a park   c. a building

2. Norris Square residents started the Las Parcelas Community Garden in _____.
   a. the 1970s   b. the 1980s   c. the 1990s

3. Members of the community _____ in the Las Parcelas Community Garden.
   a. planted fruit trees   b. built an outdoor kitchen   c. painted grafitti

B Read the Reading Skill. Then answer the question.

Did crime probably increase, decrease, or stay the same in Norris Square because of the Las Parcelas Community Garden? Explain.

Reading Skill: Making Inferences
if an author doesn't give information directly, use what you read to make a logical guess about what is probably true.

4 WORD WORK

Find these boldfaced words in the article. Circle the definition that matches the meaning in the article.

1. environment
   a. the natural world   b. the people and things around you

2. value
   a. the importance of something   b. the money something is worth

3. run-down
   a. in very bad condition   b. very tired and not healthy

4. residents
   a. doctors in training   b. people who live in a particulat place

5. pride
   a. a feeling that you are better than others   b. a feeling of satisfaction

6. abandoned
   a. not being used or taken care of   b. illegally parked

Show what you know! Talk about community involvement

GROUPS. Discuss. Would you like to start a community garden? List reasons for and against starting a garden.

UNIT 3   57

Reading articles are on the **audio CD** to help students become **more fluent readers**.

Show what you know activities allow students to internalize, personalize, and apply the information they've learned.

Word Work activities focus on developing **vocabulary in context**.

Life Skills

The Life Skills lesson in each unit focuses on functional language, practical skills, and authentic printed materials, such as schedules, maps, labels, and signs.

> **Civics, life skills,** and **cultural information** related to life in the U.S. are introduced in context.

> **Study skills,** such as map-reading skills, are introduced and practiced in real-life contexts.

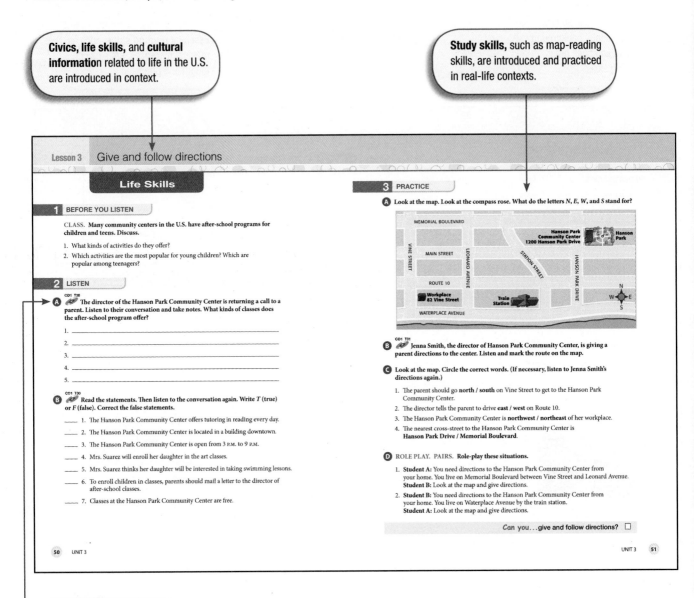

Lesson 3   Give and follow directions

Life Skills

1 BEFORE YOU LISTEN

CLASS. Many community centers in the U.S. have after-school programs for children and teens. Discuss.

1. What kinds of activities do they offer?
2. Which activities are the most popular for young children? Which are popular among teenagers?

2 LISTEN

CD1 T30
A The director of the Hanson Park Community Center is returning a call to a parent. Listen to their conversation and take notes. What kinds of classes does the after-school program offer?

1. _____
2. _____
3. _____
4. _____
5. _____

CD1 T30
B Read the statements. Then listen to the conversation again. Write *T* (true) or *F* (false). Correct the false statements.

_____ 1. The Hanson Park Community Center offers tutoring in reading every day.

_____ 2. The Hanson Park Community Center is located in a building downtown.

_____ 3. The Hanson Park Community Center is open from 3 P.M. to 9 P.M.

_____ 4. Mrs. Suarez will enroll her daughter in the art classes.

_____ 5. Mrs. Suarez thinks her daughter will be interested in taking swimming lessons.

_____ 6. To enroll children in classes, parents should mail a letter to the director of after-school classes.

_____ 7. Classes at the Hanson Park Community Center are free.

3 PRACTICE

A Look at the map. Look at the compass rose. What do the letters *N, E, W,* and *S* stand for?

CD1 T31
B Jenna Smith, the director of Hanson Park Community Center, is giving a parent directions to the center. Listen and mark the route on the map.

C Look at the map. Circle the correct words. (If necessary, listen to Jenna Smith's directions again.)

1. The parent should go **north / south** on Vine Street to get to the Hanson Park Community Center.
2. The director tells the parent to drive **east / west** on Route 10.
3. The Hanson Park Community Center is **northwest / northeast** of her workplace.
4. The nearest cross-street to the Hanson Park Community Center is **Hanson Park Drive / Memorial Boulevard**.

D ROLE PLAY. PAIRS. Role-play these situations.

1. Student A: You need directions to the Hanson Park Community Center from your home. You live on Memorial Boulevard between Vine Street and Leonard Avenue.
   Student B: Look at the map and give directions.
2. Student B: You need directions to the Hanson Park Community Center from your home. You live on Waterplace Avenue by the train station.
   Student A: Look at the map and give directions.

Can you...give and follow directions? ☐

50   UNIT 3

UNIT 3   51

> Meaningful practice mirrors **real-life tasks**.

Writing

Writing instruction is process-based, leading students to write well-organized paragraphs about familiar topics.

Before You Write activities **stimulate thinking** about the topic and provide a student **model paragraph** for the assignment.

Thinking on Paper presents pre-writing strategies and graphic organizers that students can use to plan their writing.

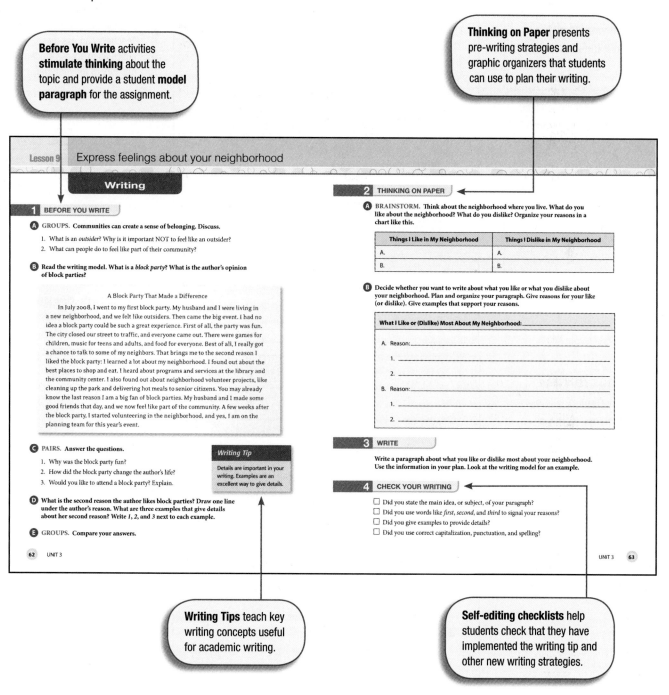

Lesson 9   Express feelings about your neighborhood

Writing

1 BEFORE YOU WRITE

A GROUPS. Communities can create a sense of belonging. Discuss.

1. What is an *outsider*? Why is it important NOT to feel like an outsider?
2. What can people do to feel like part of their community?

B Read the writing model. What is a *block party*? What is the author's opinion of block parties?

A Block Party That Made a Difference

In July 2008, I went to my first block party. My husband and I were living in a new neighborhood, and we felt like outsiders. Then came the big event. I had no idea a block party could be such a great experience. First of all, the party was fun. The city closed our street to traffic, and everyone came out. There were games for children, music for teens and adults, and food for everyone. Best of all, I really got a chance to talk to some of my neighbors. That brings me to the second reason I liked the block party: I learned a lot about my neighborhood. I found out about the best places to shop and eat. I heard about programs and services at the library and the community center. I also found out about neighborhood volunteer projects, like cleaning up the park and delivering hot meals to senior citizens. You may already know the last reason I am a big fan of block parties. My husband and I made some good friends that day, and we now feel like part of the community. A few weeks after the block party, I started volunteering in the neighborhood, and, yes, I am on the planning team for this year's event.

C PAIRS. Answer the questions.

1. Why was the block party fun?
2. How did the block party change the author's life?
3. Would you like to attend a block party? Explain.

Writing Tip

Details are important in your writing. Examples are an excellent way to give details.

D What is the second reason the author likes block parties? Draw one line under the author's reason. What are three examples that give details about her second reason? Write *1, 2,* and *3* next to each example.

E GROUPS. Compare your answers.

62   UNIT 3

2 THINKING ON PAPER

A BRAINSTORM. Think about the neighborhood where you live. What do you like about the neighborhood? What do you dislike? Organize your reasons in a chart like this.

Things I Like in My Neighborhood	Things I Dislike in My Neighborhood
A.	A.
B.	B.

B Decide whether you want to write about what you like or what you dislike about your neighborhood. Plan and organize your paragraph. Give reasons for your like (or dislike). Give examples that support your reasons.

What I Like or (Dislike) Most About My Neighborhood: _____

A. Reason: _____

   1. _____

   2. _____

B. Reason: _____

   1. _____

   2. _____

3 WRITE

Write a paragraph about what you like or dislike most about your neighborhood. Use the information in your plan. Look at the writing model for an example.

4 CHECK YOUR WRITING

☐ Did you state the main idea, or subject, of your paragraph?
☐ Did you use words like *first, second,* and *third* to signal your reasons?
☐ Did you give examples to provide details?
☐ Did you use correct capitalization, punctuation, and spelling?

UNIT 3   **63**

Writing Tips teach key writing concepts useful for academic writing.

Self-editing checklists help students check that they have implemented the writing tip and other new writing strategies.

Review & Expand

The final page of the unit allows students to review and expand on the language, themes, and competencies they have worked with throughout the unit.

Cross-references direct students to the **Grammar Review, Persistence Activity,** and **Team Project** for that unit.

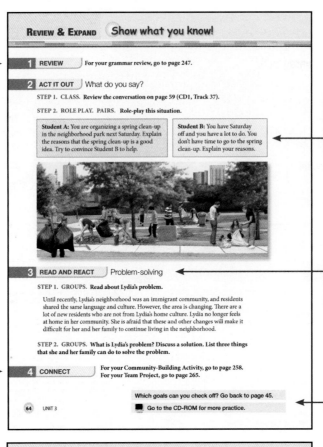

REVIEW & EXPAND Show what you know!

1 REVIEW For your grammar review, go to page 247.

2 ACT IT OUT What do you say?

STEP 1. CLASS. Review the conversation on page 59 (CD1, Track 37).

STEP 2. ROLE PLAY. PAIRS. Role-play this situation.

Student A: You are organizing a spring clean-up in the neighborhood park next Saturday. Explain the reasons that the spring clean-up is a good idea. Try to convince Student B to help.

Student B: You have Saturday off and you have a lot to do. You don't have time to go to the spring clean-up. Explain your reasons.

3 READ AND REACT Problem-solving

STEP 1. GROUPS. Read about Lydia's problem.

Until recently, Lydia's neighborhood was an immigrant community, and residents shared the same language and culture. However, the area is changing. There are a lot of new residents who are not from Lydia's home culture. Lydia no longer feels at home in her community. She is afraid that these and other changes will make it difficult for her and her family to continue living in the neighborhood.

STEP 2. GROUPS. What is Lydia's problem? Discuss a solution. List three things that she and her family can do to solve the problem.

4 CONNECT For your Community-Building Activity, go to page 258.
For your Team Project, go to page 265.

Which goals can you check off? Go back to page 45.

■ Go to the CD-ROM for more practice.

64 UNIT 3

Lively **Role-Play** activities motivate students, allowing them to feel successful. Teachers can use these activities to assess students' mastery of the material.

Problem-solving tasks encourage critical thinking and allow students to demonstrate understanding of topics.

Checkpoints allow students to see the unit goals they have accomplished.

Grammar Review

Grammar Review allows students to check their mastery of the unit grammar.

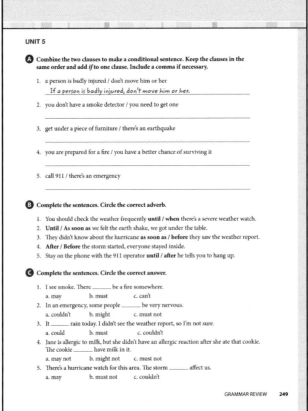

UNIT 5

A Combine the two clauses to make a conditional sentence. Keep the clauses in the same order and add *if* to one clause. Include a comma if necessary.

1. a person is badly injured / don't move him or her
   If a person is badly injured, don't move him or her.

2. you don't have a smoke detector / you need to get one

3. get under a piece of furniture / there's an earthquake

4. you are prepared for a fire / you have a better chance of surviving it

5. call 911 / there's an emergency

B Complete the sentences. Circle the correct adverb.

1. You should check the weather frequently **until / when** there's a severe weather watch.
2. **Until / As soon as** we felt the earth shake, we got under the table.
3. They didn't know about the hurricane **as soon as / before** they saw the weather report.
4. **After / Before** the storm started, everyone stayed inside.
5. Stay on the phone with the 911 operator **until / after** he tells you to hang up.

C Complete the sentences. Circle the correct answer.

1. I see smoke. There _____ be a fire somewhere.
   a. may   b. must   c. can't
2. In an emergency, some people _____ be very nervous.
   a. couldn't   b. might   c. must not
3. It _____ rain today. I didn't see the weather report, so I'm not sure.
   a. could   b. must   c. couldn't
4. Jane is allergic to milk, but she didn't have an allergic reaction after she ate that cookie. The cookie _____ have milk in it.
   a. may not   b. might not   c. must not
5. There's a hurricane watch for this area. The storm _____ affect us.
   a. may   b. must not   c. couldn't

GRAMMAR REVIEW   249

Persistence Activities

Persistence activities build community in the classroom, help students set personal and language goals, and encourage students to develop good study skills and habits.

> Controlled activities provide scaffolding for the **real-life application activities** that follow.

Unit 9   Then and Now

Ⓐ Think about how a pre-school child learns to speak a language, whether it is English or a native language. Then think of how you, as an adult, are learning English. Complete the chart below.

	Learning as a child	Learning as an adult
What strategies do children or adults use to learn a language? By imitating? By listening to an audio? By reading?		
Where do children or adults learn a language? At home? At school? In the playground?		
What do children or adults learn when learning a language? Vocabulary? Conversation? Grammar?		
From your observation, who is the faster learner, a child or an adult?		
In your opinion, what is the best way for children or adults to learn a language?		

Ⓑ PAIRS. Share your answers to Exercise A. How do you feel about learning English as an adult?

Unit 10   How Students Learn Best

Ⓐ Think of how you've been learning English. Check (✓) five types of activities you liked best.

- ☐ working alone
- ☐ working in pairs
- ☐ working in groups
- ☐ reading activities
- ☐ conversations
- ☐ grammar activities
- ☐ listening activities
- ☐ writing activities
- ☐ vocabulary activities
- ☐ using life skills materials (maps, graphs, forms, etc.)
- ☐ Other: _____

Ⓑ Look at the activities you checked. What did you like about them? How did they help you learn English?

Ⓒ PAIRS. Talk about other activities in the book. Which activities didn't you like? Why?

Ⓓ GROUPS. Compare your answers to Exercises A, B, and C. What are some similarities in the ways you prefer to learn English? Make a list of activities that help students learn effectively.

Ⓔ CLASS. Present your list to the class. Explain why these activities help students learn. Also discuss the activities that you didn't include. Why do you think those activities aren't as effective?

SELF-EFFICACY/SELF-EVALUATION   **261**

Team Projects

Each unit includes a collaborative project that integrates all of the unit themes, language, and competencies in a community-building activity.

> A **graphic organizer** helps students collect the information they need for the project.

> Students work in teams to create a **poster**, **chart**, **graph**, or **booklet** that relates to the unit theme.

Unit 7   Used Car for Sale   DESIGN AN INTERNET AD

Materials
- large paper
- markers
- magazine or Internet car advertisements (optional)

TEAMS OF 4   Captain, Co-captain, Assistant, Spokesperson

GET READY   Team: Imagine you have a used car that you want to sell.
Captain: Ask your teammates to describe the car you're selling.
Co-captain: Keep time. You have ten minutes.
Assistant: Take notes in the chart.

Make and model	
Year	
Mileage	
Options	
Other information	

CREATE   Co-captain: Get the materials. Then keep time. You have fifteen minutes.
Team: Create an Internet ad for your car. Use the information from your chart. Add art if you want.

REPORT   Spokesperson: Share your ad with the class. Describe the car you want to sell.

> Teams give **oral presentations** to share their project with the class.

TEAM PROJECTS   **269**

Getting Started

Pre-Unit

Welcome to Class

1 LEARN ABOUT YOUR BOOK

A CLASS. **Turn to page iii. Answer the questions.**

Contents
1. What information is on this page?
2. How many units are in this book? 12
3. Which unit is about health? Unit 8

4. Which unit is about money? Unit 12
5. Which unit is about work? Unit 4

B CLASS. **Where is the Practice Plus CD-ROM? What kind of practice does it provide?**

C CLASS. **Sometimes you will need to go to the back of the book to do activities. Where will you find the following? Find each section. Write the page number.**

Grammar Review _p. 245_   Persistence Activities _p. 257_   Team Projects _p. 263_

D PAIRS. **There is additional information for you at the back of the book. Find each section. Write the page number.**

Grammar Reference _p. 278_   Audio Script _p. 285_   Index _p. 295_

2 LEARN ABOUT YOURSELF

A Take the Learning Styles Survey on page 3.

B Count the number of *a*, *b*, and *c* answers. Write the numbers.

_____ a answers   _____ b answers   _____ c answers

C GROUPS. **Discuss your learning styles.**

- If you scored mostly *a*'s, you may have a visual learning style. You learn by seeing and looking.
- If you scored mostly *b*'s, you may have an auditory learning style. You learn by hearing and listening.
- If you scored mostly *c*'s, you may have a kinesthetic learning style. You learn by touching and doing.

Knowing your learning style can help you understand why some things are easier for you than other things.

1. Are you surprised by the results you got? Explain.
2. Do you think knowing your learning style will help you in your class? In what ways?

Getting Started

Presentation   5 minutes

1 LEARN ABOUT YOUR BOOK

A CLASS. **Turn to page iii. Answer the questions.**

- Have students turn to page iii. Say the word *Contents.* Ask: *What does it mean?* Elicit: Contents are what is inside something.

- Read question 1. Instruct students to look at the page and notice that the contents are divided into three parts. Briefly explain the contents of each part as follows: The first section is an introduction. Page xiv, for example, is for teachers. It tells them how to use the book. Page xvi is for students. It explains the different parts of a chapter. (Note: You may wish to do the unit tour with your students. If class time is limited, assign it for homework.)

- Have students look at the middle section of page iii. Ask: *What information do you find here?* Elicit: The units, their names, and page numbers. Ask: *What are units?* Elicit: Lessons or chapters.

- Direct students to look at the bottom section of page iii. Explain: This section contains "extra" activities and reference material.

- Instruct students to read and answer questions 2–5 on page 2. Have them compare answers with a partner.

- Call on volunteers to answer each question.

Controlled Practice   15 minutes

B CLASS. **Where is the Practice Plus CD-ROM?...**

- Read the two questions. Invite students to look for the answers.

Answers: The Practice Plus CD-ROM is at the back of the book. It has extra practice for each lesson in the book.

C CLASS. **Sometimes you will need to go to the back...**

- Tell students to look at the bottom section of page iii to find the answers, or show them how to look at the back of the book, where they can also find the answers.

- Have them fill in the page numbers. Check answers.

- Define terms as needed (for example, *persistence: the quality of continuing steadily despite problems or difficulties. Persistence activities are designed to encourage students to keep coming to class.*)

- Ask students to turn to each page and study the type of activities offered. Ask: *What activities do you find in this section?* Explain as needed.

D PAIRS. **There is additional information for you...**

- Have students look at the bottom of page iii to find the answers.

- Have them fill in the page numbers. Check answers.

- Define terms as needed (for example, *index: an alphabetical list of topics, people, or titles, and the page numbers where they are mentioned in a text*)

- Ask students to turn to each page and study the type of activities offered. Ask: *What information do you find here?*

Presentation

2 LEARN ABOUT YOURSELF

Note: This section refers to page 2.

A Take the Learning Styles survey on page 3.

- Introduce the activity by asking the class: *How do you prefer to learn? By seeing, by hearing, or by doing things?* Call on several students to answer. It may be helpful to provide a context for the question, for example, *How do you prefer to learn new words?* Or *Do you have a cell phone? How did you learn to use it?*

- If possible, make an overhead transparency of the page and project it as you proceed through the following steps. If this is not possible, hold up your book and point to items as you discuss them.

- Read the survey title and explain *learning style*. Say: *Your learning style is the way you prefer to learn new things—by seeing, by hearing, or by doing.*

- If you feel comfortable, tell the class about your own learning style. As an example, you might tell the class how you learn new vocabulary. Do you, for example, make flash cards and review them regularly? (visual style) Do you hear the word, then rehearse it in your mind or out loud over the next few days? (auditory style) Do you say the word and "feel" it in your mouth, or do you like to use plastic letters and spell out the word by manipulating the letters? (kinesthetic style)

- Read each question and the answer choices out loud. Explain vocabulary as needed. Students may select their answers as you read each item.

- Allow, but do not encourage, students to translate if needed. Watch for students who translate a great deal; they may need to be placed in a lower-level class.

- If students say that none of the answer choices are correct for them, instruct them to choose the answer that is closest to their preference.

- Leave time for students to review their answer choices.

B Count the number of a, b, and c answers....

- If you are using a transparency of the quiz, demonstrate counting the answers. Circle an answer to each item, then tally the a, b, and c answers.

- If you are not using a transparency, circle sample answers in the book (perhaps your own preferences). Walk around and show students your book. Count the a, b, and c answers and write the numbers on the board.

- On the board, write the words *visual, auditory, kinesthetic.* Ask students if they know what the words mean. Elicit: *Visual* is related to seeing; *auditory* is related to hearing; *kinesthetic* is related to touching or doing.

Communicative Practice   20 minutes

C GROUPS. Discuss your learning styles.

- Read the bulleted explanations of the scores. Ask: *How many of you scored mostly a's? b's? c's?* Some students will probably be "mixed," that is, they will have circled an equal number of a's, b's, and c's. Tell these students: *You have a mixed learning style.*

- Ask the class: *Why is it useful to know your learning style?* Select students to answer; then read the last sentence of the box.

- Read the two questions. Using your own results, if you took the survey, answer the questions. (For example, for question 2: *Knowing your own learning style can help you understand your students better.*)

- Form groups of four or five students. To form groups, use one of the following techniques or a technique that you prefer: 1. If your class has 25 students or fewer, have them number off by 4s or 5s. All students with the same number form a group. 2. Form groups consisting of students who are sitting near each other. 3. Form groups consisting of people who speak different languages.

- Provide instructions for how students should conduct themselves in a group. For example, say that "discussion" means that everyone has a chance (and a responsibility) to talk. It's polite to listen while someone else is speaking, but in a good discussion people also ask each other questions.

- Give a time limit for discussion. While students are talking, walk around, listen, and provide help as needed.

- To wrap up, call on at least one volunteer from each group to share his or her answers with the class.

What's Your Learning Style?

**Choose the first answer that you think of.
Circle *a*, *b*, or *c*.**

1 When I study, I like to _____.
   a. read notes or read diagrams and illustrations
   b. repeat information silently to myself
   c. write notes on cards or make diagrams

2 When I listen to music, I _____.
   a. picture things that go with the music
   b. sing along
   c. tap my feet

3 When I solve a problem, I _____.
   a. make a list of things to do and check them off as I do them
   b. talk about the problem with experts or friends
   c. make a diagram of the problem

4 When I read for pleasure, I prefer _____.
   a. a travel book with a lot of pictures
   b. a novel with a lot of conversation
   c. a crime story where you have to solve a mystery

5 When I'm learning to use a computer or new equipment, I prefer _____.
   a. watching a DVD about it
   b. listening to someone explain it
   c. using the equipment and figuring it out for myself

6 When I'm at a party, the next day I will remember _____.
   a. the faces of the people I met there, but not their names
   b. the names of the people there, but not their faces
   c. what I did and said there

7 When I tell a story, I'd rather _____.
   a. write it
   b. tell it out loud
   c. act it out

8 When I'm trying to concentrate, the thing I find most distracting is _____.
   a. things I see, like people moving around
   b. things I hear, like other people's conversations
   c. things I feel, like hunger, worry, or neck pain

9 When I don't know how to spell a word, I will usually _____.
   a. write it out to see if it looks right
   b. sound it out
   c. write it out to see if it feels right

10 When I'm standing in a long line, I'll usually _____.
   a. read a newspaper
   b. talk to the person in line in front of me
   c. tap my foot and move around

3 MEET YOUR CLASSMATES

A 💿 **Read and listen to the conversation.**

Ivan: Hi. My name is Ivan.

Ruth: Hi. My name is Ruth. Nice to meet you.

Ivan: Nice to meet you, too. Where are you from, Ruth?

Ruth: Colombia. What about you?

Ivan: I'm from Ukraine.

Ruth: Oh! How long have you been here?

Ivan: Three years. I came here when I finished school.

Ruth: Wow! You speak English very well.

Ivan: Thank you, but I need to study more.

Ruth: Well, I've been a student here for a year now.
It's an excellent school. You'll learn a lot here.

Ivan: Great! I think you speak well, too. Why are you studying English?

Ruth: I'm planning to go to college. I'm going to apply next year.

Ivan: That's terrific. I'm hoping to get a better job.

B **PAIRS.** Practice the conversation.

C **PAIRS.** Make similar conversations. Use your own names and information.

4 REVIEW VERB TENSES

GROUPS. Look at the conversation between Ivan and Ruth. Find one example of each of the following verb tenses and write the sentence on the line. There may be more than one correct answer.

Simple present   is, (I)'m, am, speak, need, think

Simple past   came, finished

Future   (You)'ll learn, (I)'m going to apply

Present perfect   (I)'ve been, have you been

Present continuous   are (you) studying, (I)'m planning, (I)'m hoping

Presentation 5 minutes

3 MEET YOUR CLASSMATES

Ⓐ   **Read the listen to the conversation.**

- Read the section title. Instruct students to look at the photo. Say: *The man's name is Ivan. The woman's name is Ruth.*
- Read the directions. Then play CD 1, Track 2.
- Instruct students to close their books. Play the recording again. (*Optional:* Point out that listening without reading may be easier for auditory learners; students can experiment to find out what works better for them.)
- Ask questions to check comprehension. For example: Where is Ivan from? Where is Ruth from? How long has Ivan/Ruth been here? Why is Ivan/Ruth studying English?

Controlled Practice 5 minutes

Ⓑ **PAIRS. Practice the conversation.**

- Form pairs consisting of students who are sitting near each other. Instruct them to read the conversation, then switch roles and read it again.
- Call on volunteers to read the conversation in front of the class.

Communicative Practice 10 minutes

Ⓒ **PAIRS. Make similar conversations. Use...**

- Model the activity with a student. (If possible, choose an above-level student to role play with you.) Use your own name, but make up the rest of the information.
- If you think it will be helpful, have two students role play the conversation for the class.
- Pair students and have them make similar conversations. While students are talking, walk around, listen, and provide help as needed.

- Alternately, do the activity as a mixer. Have students get up (with their books) and walk around. Ring a bell or clap your hands to signal that they should stop, pair up with a student near them, and make the conversation. Repeat the process several times.
- As a follow-up, have each student stand up, and have the class say everything they can remember about the person (i.e., the student's name and country, how long the student has been here, and why he or she is studying English.)

Controlled Practice 10 minutes

4 REVIEW VERB TENSES

GROUPS. Look at the conversation between...

- If necessary, explain *verb* and *tense*: Verbs express an action (like *walk, eat, write*) or a state (like *be, become, seem*). Tense refers to the various forms of verbs that express different times (e.g., past, present, future).
- Give an example. On the board, write *I _____ breakfast.* Say: *Let's fill in the blank with the verb* eat *in different tenses. What is the simple present form?* Elicit: *eat.* Elicit the other tenses listed in the exercise as well. To clarify meaning, add time expressions to the kernel sentence on the board, for example, *I (eat) breakfast every day, I (ate) breakfast yesterday,* etc.
- Form small groups and have students do the exercise. While students are working, walk around and provide help as needed.
- To check answers, make a five-row chart on the board, one row for each tense. Make several columns. Then, for each tense, ask students to state the verbs they wrote.

Catching Up

Classroom Materials/Extra Practice

CD 1
Tracks 3–15

Interactive Practice
Unit 1

Workbook
Unit 1

Unit Overview

Goals
- See the list of goals on the facing page.

Grammar
- Simple present and present continuous
- Future with *will*, *be going to*, and present continuous
- Simple past
- *Used to*

Pronunciation
- Pronunciation of stressed words in sentences
- Reduced pronunciation of *did you*, *did your*

Reading
- Read an article about a success story
- Read a school application
- *Reading Skill:* Skimming

Writing
- Write a paragraph about the person you admire most

Life Skills
- Complete a school application

Preview
- Say the unit title. Ask: *What does* catching up *mean?* If students need help, ask: *Do we catch up with people we see every day or people we haven't seen in a while? What do people talk about when they're catching up? Do you like to catch up by phone, by e-mail, or in person?*
- Hold up your book or have students look at their books. Set the context by asking the preview questions. You can also ask: *Where are the people? How do they look? What do you think will happen next?*

Unit Goals
- Point to the Unit Goals. Have students read the goals silently.
- Tell students they will be studying these goals in Unit 1.
- Say each goal and explain unfamiliar vocabulary as needed. For example, *routine: the usual things people do every day. When I'm working, my morning routine is the same every day; role model: a person we respect and want to imitate. My grandmother is my role model.*
- Tell students to circle one or more goals that are very important to them. Call on several volunteers to say the goals they circled.
- Write a checkmark (✓) on the board. Say: *We will come back to this page again. You will write a checkmark next to the goals you achieved in this unit.*

Catching
Up

Preview

Read the title. Who are the people? What are they saying to each other?

UNIT GOALS

☐ Talk about yourself and your family

☐ Describe routines

☐ Discuss goals

☐ Interpret and complete a school application

☐ Discuss ways to succeed

☐ Discuss people's past experiences

☐ Write about a role model

Listening and Speaking

1   BEFORE YOU LISTEN

CLASS. Look at the picture. Arturo Pérez and Brenda Kraig work at the Café Royale, a restaurant in a large hotel. What do you think they're talking about?

2   LISTEN

CD1 T3

A Listen to the first part of the conversation between Arturo and Brenda. Then complete the sentences.

1. Brenda is ordering <u>a burger, fries, and</u>
   <u>a garden salad</u>.

2. Arturo is surprised at the customer's order
   because <u>it's 10:00 in the morning</u>.

B **PAIRS.** Arturo knows Brenda's name. Predict. How do Arturo and Brenda know each other?

CD1 T4

C Read the questions. Then listen to the whole conversation. Circle the correct answers.

1. How do Arturo and Brenda know each other?
   a. Their families lived next door to each other.
   b. They dated in high school.
   c. They worked together at another restaurant.

2. When did Arturo begin working at the Café Royale?
   a. a week ago   b. a month ago   c. a year ago

3. What time of day does Arturo usually work?
   a. in the morning   b. in the afternoon   c. in the evening

4. What is Manny, the regular cook, doing today?
   a. looking for a new job   b. taking care of personal things   c. enjoying his vacation

D **PAIRS.** Discuss. What do you think Arturo and Brenda are going to talk about during their break?

Getting Started 5 minutes

BEFORE YOU LISTEN

CLASS. Look at the picture. Arturo Pérez...

- Hold up your book and point to the photo or have students look at their books. Ask: *What do you think is happening? What is Arturo's job? What is Brenda's job? How old are they?* Call on students to answer the questions.
- Ask: *What do you think they're talking about?* Write students' guesses on the board.
- Say: *We're going to listen to a conversation between Arturo and Brenda. Let's see if you guessed correctly.*

Possible answers: a customer's order; an item on the menu

Presentation 10 minutes

2 LISTEN

A **Listen to the first part...**

- Have students read the sentences silently.
- Play CD 1, Track 3. Have students listen and complete the sentences.
- Have students compare answers with a classmate.
- Have two volunteers write their sentences on the board. Review the sentences as a class.
- Have the class look back at the list of guesses from Exercise 1. Ask: *Did you guess correctly?*

Teaching Tip

If students need additional support, tell them to read the Audio Script on page 285 as they listen.

B PAIRS. Arturo knows...

- Explain that *predict* means the same as guess.
- You may want to play Track 3 again.
- Call on pairs to write their answers on the board.
- Say: *Soon we're going to hear the whole conversation. Then we'll see who predicted correctly.*

Possible answers: They worked together at another restaurant; their children attend the same school.

Community Building

On the first day of class, write every student's name on an index card. Use the cards to learn students' names, assign roles, pair or group students, and call on students to speak.

Controlled Practice 10 minutes

C **Read the questions. Then listen...**

- Play CD 1, Track 4.
- Check answers. Write the numbers *1* through *4* on the board. Call on students to read the questions and answers. Write the answers on the board.
- Play Track 4 again and stop at the spot where the answer to the question is. Ask the class to repeat the information that gives the correct answer.
- Point to students' predictions from Exercise 2B. Ask: *Which prediction was correct?*

Teaching Tip

After a student provides the answer to a question, involve the class in checking the answer by asking: *Is this correct? Do you agree with the answer?*

D PAIRS. Discuss. What do you think...

- Pair students and give them a time limit for discussion.
- Walk around and provide help as needed.
- Call on pairs to answer. Write the answers on the board.
- Say: *In the next part of the lesson, we'll see if your ideas are correct.*

Expansion: Speaking Practice for 2D

- If possible, pair students from different countries. Have students describe a routine workday in their country. Ask: *How many hours do people typically work? How long is their lunch period? How many breaks do they get?*

Presentation   10 minutes

3 CONVERSATION

Pronunciation Watch

- Introduce the concept of stressed words. Write on the board: *My husband gets up early on weekdays.*
- Read the sentence naturally, stressing the words *husband*, *gets*, *early*, and *weekdays*.
- Ask: *Which words were louder, higher in pitch, longer, or clearer?*
- Read the sentence again. Elicit the answers *husband*, *gets*, *early*, and *weekdays* and circle them.
- On the board, write *stressed words* and draw arrows to the words you circled. Then read the Pronunciation Watch note.

A 🎵 **Listen to the sentences. Notice...**

- Write the first sentence on the board. Say the sentence. Clap on the stressed words. Have the class repeat.
- Play CD 1, Track 5. Have students listen.
- Play Track 5 again. Have students listen and repeat.

Controlled Practice   10 minutes

B 🎵 **Listen to the sentences. Which...**

- Write the first sentence on the board. Say it. Have the class repeat. Put dots over *How's* and *family*.
- Read the directions. Play CD 1, Track 6.
- Have volunteers read the sentences with correct stress. Write the stressed words on the board.

C 🎵 **Arturo and Brenda are talking...**

- Play CD, 1 Track 7. Have students listen and read along silently.
- Check comprehension. Ask: *Where does Arturo live? Does he like it? How many children does he have? What does his wife do?*

4 PRACTICE

A 🎵 **PAIRS. Practice the conversation.**

- Form pairs and have students take turns reading each role in Exercise 3C.

- Have students switch partners and practice again.
- Ask volunteers to perform the conversation.

Community Building

When correcting errors in student speech, repeat the incorrect words or sentence and then ask: *Is this correct? What should it be?* Elicit the correct form and then have the class repeat.

Communicative Practice   15 minutes

Teaching Tip

While pairs are performing role plays, use the scoring rubric for speaking on page T-xiii to evaluate each student's vocabulary, grammar, fluency, and how well he or she completes the task. You may want to review the completed rubric with the students.

B **ROLE PLAY. PAIRS. Role-play a conversation...**

- Have students read the role descriptions.
- Model the conversation with an above-level student, following the model in Exercise 3C.
- Form similar-ability pairs. Tell students they may use real or imaginary information.
- Have volunteers perform their conversation for the class. Take notes on errors in sentence structure.
- Select a few key errors. Say the incorrect structure. Have a volunteer respond with the correct structure. Have the class repeat.

▬▬ MULTILEVEL INSTRUCTION for 4B

Pre-level Prepare a handout of the conversation in Exercise 3C. Delete names, addresses, family members, and types of jobs. Have students fill in the blanks with their own information and then practice reading the conversation.

Above-level Tell students to practice with their books closed. Have them perform without books.

Extra Practice

Interactive Practice

CD1 T5

A Listen to the sentences. Notice the stressed words. Then listen again and repeat.

Where are you **liv**ing?

We **have** an a**part**ment on **Fifth** Street.

It's a **lit**tle **nois**y, but we **like** it.

Pronunciation Watch

The important words in a sentence are *stressed*. They sound louder and longer than the other words. Stressed words usually have a clear meaning, such as nouns, verbs, adjectives, adverbs, and question words.

CD1 T6

B Listen to the sentences. Which words are important? Put a dot (•) over the stressed words.

1. How's your family?
2. My wife is working at a restaurant.
3. She usually works at night.
4. She's planning to go to school.
5. What does she want to study?
6. She wants to study nursing or nutrition.

CD1 T7

C Arturo and Brenda are talking during their break at the Café Royale. Listen and read their conversation.

Brenda: So how's everything going? Where are you living now?
Arturo: We have an apartment on Fifth Street. It's a little noisy, but we like it.
Brenda: We? So tell me about your family!
Arturo: We have three beautiful kids. Isabel is eight. Michelle is five. And Arturo Jr. is two.
Brenda: How wonderful! And your wife?
Arturo: Oh, yeah…my wife. My wife is great. She's working in a lawyer's office. She's a receptionist now, but she's planning to go to school to be a paralegal.

4 PRACTICE

A PAIRS. Practice the conversation.

B ROLE PLAY. PAIRS. Role-play a conversation between two acquaintances. Both of you worked at the same company five years ago, but you haven't seen each other since then. Make up the information.

Student A: You are standing in line at a supermarket near your home. You see Student B, an old work acquaintance, walk by. Tell about your life.

Student B: You're shopping at a supermarket near your job. You see Student A, an old work acquaintance, standing in the checkout line. Tell about your life.

Describe routines

Grammar

Simple present and present continuous

Simple present	Present continuous
I always **work** later in the day.	I'**m working** in the morning this week.
Manny **doesn't** usually **work** at night.	Manny **isn't working** today.
How often **do** Arturo and Brenda **work** together?	**Are** Brenda and Arturo **working** today?
Do you **work** mornings or evenings?	Where **are** you **working** these days?

Grammar Watch

- Use the simple present to talk about usual activities or general statements of fact.
- Use the present continuous to talk about things that are happening now (today, this week, this month) or things that are happening temporarily.
- Stative (non-action) verbs are commonly used in the simple present, not the present continuous: I **have** a small apartment on Fifth Street now. *(See page 278 for a list of stative verbs.)*

1 PRACTICE

A Read the conversation. Draw one line under the simple present verbs. Draw two lines under the present continuous verbs.

Brenda: Hi, Arturo. How come you're cooking breakfast again today?

Arturo: I'm helping Manny out. He needs some more time off this week.

Brenda: I don't understand. Why is Manny missing work? Is he sick?

Arturo: No, he's fine. He and his fiancée are preparing for their wedding this week. His family is visiting from Mexico, so it's a good time to discuss the plans.

B Complete the paragraph. Circle the correct words.

Arturo and Brenda **catch up /** ⟨**are catching up**⟩ during their break. They ⟨**have**⟩**/ are having** the same schedule because Manny **takes /** ⟨**is taking**⟩ some time off this week. They **talk /** ⟨**are talking**⟩ about Brenda's older brother, Edward. When Edward was young, he wanted to travel around the world, but he ⟨**doesn't care**⟩**/ isn't caring** about a life of adventure anymore. Instead, he ⟨**takes**⟩**/ is taking** a short two-week vacation every year and ⟨**works**⟩**/ is working** as a computer programmer the other fifty weeks of the year. He ⟨**thinks**⟩**/ is thinking** his life is wonderful.

Getting Started 5 minutes

- Say: *In this lesson we're going to review the simple present and present continuous.*

- Write on the board: *I go to work every weekday. Today is Sunday, so I'm not going to work.* Underline the verbs and circle the time expressions.

- Point to each sentence and ask: *Is this simple present or present continuous? What is the time? Does this activity happen regularly, all the time, or just now, today?*

- Review the verb forms. For example, for the simple present, T: *Work. I . . .* Ss: *work;* T: *You . . .* Ss: *work;* T: *He or she . . .* Ss: *works.* For the present continuous, for example, T: *I . . .* Ss: *am working;* T: *You . . .* Ss: *are working;* T: *He or she . . .* Ss: *is working.* Write the forms on the board. Circle the third-person singular *-s* in the simple present and *be* + verb-*ing* in the present continuous.

Presentation 15 minutes

Simple present and present continuous

- Copy the grammar chart onto the board. Read the sentences, underline the verbs, and ask: *What is the form?* (simple present or present continuous) Circle the time expressions and ask: *What is the time?* (*always, usually, this week,* etc.)

- Read out loud the first Grammar Watch note. Point to the simple present time expressions on the board and ask: *What are some time expressions that we use to talk about usual activities? Do you know any others?* Elicit answers and write them on the board.

- Read out loud the second note. Point to the present continuous time expressions and ask: *What are some time expressions that we use to talk about activities that are happening now or temporarily? Do you know any others?* Elicit answers and write them on the board.

- Read out loud the third note. Say: *Stative verbs are verbs like* love, believe, *and* be *that don't describe actions. Stative verbs are not usually used in the present continuous.*

Expansion: Grammar Practice

- Write the following headings on the board: *Mental States, Emotional States, Possession, Senses,* and *Other.* Write one stative verb in each category, for example, *forget, enjoy, own, see,* and *cost.* Divide the class into teams and give a time limit. Have students write as many additional stative verbs as they can. When time is up, call up a representative from each group to write the group's verbs on the board. Make corrections as needed. Finally, refer students to the list of stative verbs on page 278.

Controlled Practice 20 minutes

1 PRACTICE

Ⓐ Read the conversation. Draw...

- Have students complete the exercise. Walk around and provide help as needed.

- Check answers. Write the headings *Simple Present* and *Present Continuous* on the board. Call on students to write answers under the correct headings. Then go over each verb with the class and ask: *Is it correct?* Elicit corrections as needed.

Ⓑ Complete the paragraph. Circle...

- Copy the first sentence onto the board, including the circle. Point to the circled words and ask: *Why is the present continuous correct in this sentence?* (It's happening now.)

- Have students work alone or in pairs. Walk around and provide help as needed.

- Check answers. Have one student read each sentence with the correct verb. Write the verbs on the board. For each verb, ask: *Why is the (simple present / present continuous) correct here?* Make corrections as needed.

Community Building

One way to make sure all students have a chance to participate in whole-class activities is to use name cards. Write each student's name on an index card. At the beginning of each class, shuffle the cards. Choose a card each time you want a student to answer a question, correct an error, read a direction line, or share an idea. Then put the card at the bottom of the pile.

2 PRACTICE

A Complete the conversation. Use...

- Read the first sentence. Ask: *Why is the present continuous correct and not the simple present?* Do the second item with the whole class.

- Have students work alone or in pairs. Walk around and provide help as needed.

- Have two above-level students read the conversation out loud. Write their answers on the board. Then point to each answer and ask: *Is this correct?* Elicit corrections from students and write them on the board.

■ **Expansion: Speaking Practice for 2A**

- Pair students and have them practice reading the conversation.

B Read the conversations. Find...

- Write the first sentence, with the error, on the board. Model crossing out the word *Are* and replacing it with *Do*. Ask: *Why is Do correct?*

- Form cross-ability pairs and have them complete the exercise. Provide help as needed.

- Copy the items onto the board. Call students to the board to make corrections. Then read each corrected line and ask the class: *Is this correct?* Make corrections as needed.

Communicative Practice   20 minutes

Show what you know!

STEP 1. Think about three things...

- Give examples from your own life. For example, say: *I'm taking a Spanish class. I'm painting my kitchen. I'm volunteering at my daughter's school.* Write the sentences on the board.

- Remind students to use the present continuous.

- Walk around and provide help as needed.

■ **MULTILEVEL INSTRUCTION for STEP 1**

Pre-level Students can write just one or two sentences.

Above-level Students can write more than three sentences.

STEP 2. GROUPS. Discuss the three things...

- Model the activity using one of the sentences you wrote on the board. For example, say: *I'm taking a Spanish class this month. Usually I don't have time to take classes, but I'm not working this month, so I have more time.*

- Form cross-ability groups. Tell students to speak about the sentences they wrote in Step 1.

- Walk around and provide help as needed. Take notes on errors with the simple present and the present continuous.

- To wrap up, bring the class together and do an error-correction activity. Select sentences from your notes and write them on the board. Have a volunteer read each sentence and correct the error.

■ **Expansion: Speaking Practice for STEP 2**

- On the board, draw a picture of a page from a day planner, for example, a "Day-at-a-Glance." Write the date at the top and insert the hours from 9 A.M. to 5 P.M. Have students copy it into their notebooks.

- Tell students to imagine they are a famous person (a movie star, singer, politician, etc.). Have them fill in the schedule with the schedule of that person for one day.

- Model the activity. For example, pretend that you are a famous actor. On the board in the 9:00 A.M. space, write: *Meet with agent.* Say: *Today I am meeting with my agent at 9 A.M.*

- Form cross-ability pairs or groups and have students describe their schedules. Remind them to use the simple present for activities they do regularly and the present continuous for activities that are happening only today.

Progress Check

Can you . . . describe routines?

Say: *We have practiced describing routines. Now, look at the question at the bottom of the page. Can you describe routines? Write a checkmark in the box.*

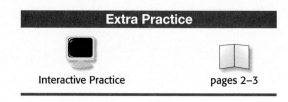

Extra Practice	
Interactive Practice	pages 2–3

A Complete the conversation. Use the simple present or the present continuous.

Arturo: I _'m trying_ to remember the name of your old friend from Juniper
              (try)
        Street. Oh, I _know_. Her name was Teresa, right?
                  (know)

Brenda: Right. You _have_ a great memory.
                (have)

Arturo: How _is_ she _doing_ these days? _Do_ you
             (do)   (see)   (do)
        see her anymore?
        (see)

Brenda: Teresa and I _are_ both really busy, so we _don't talk_
                (be)   (not talk)
        very often. But she and my sister usually _hang out_ together. They
                                       (hang out)
        are studying at the community college this semester. They both
        (study)
        want to be accountants.
        (want)

B Read the conversations. Find and correct the mistakes in each conversation.

              Do
1. **Arturo:** ~~Are~~ you always work during the day?
                  prefer
   Brenda: Yes. I ~~am preferring~~ a daytime schedule. I always feel tired when ~~I'm~~ work~~ing~~
        at night.

           do
2. **Arturo:** How ʌyou spend your evenings?
                                               go
   Brenda: I usually watch TV, but sometimes my sister and I ~~are going~~ to a movie.

          Do you have
3. **Arturo:** ~~Are you having~~ a boyfriend now?
                         is visiting
   Brenda: Yes, but at the moment, he ~~visits~~ his grandmother in Poland. ~~I'm~~ really
        miss~~ing~~ him!

Show what you know!   Describe routines

STEP 1. Think about three things you're doing this month. Make a list.

> 1. I'm taking courses at the community college.

STEP 2. GROUPS. Discuss the three things you're doing this month. Are they
different from what you usually do? Explain.

                                          Can you... describe routines? ☐

Reading

1 BEFORE YOU READ

A CLASS. What is "the American dream"?
Is it possible for this "dream" to come true?

B Read the Reading Skill. Then skim the article.
Underline the title and the section headings.
Predict. What is the main idea of the article?

> **Reading Skill:** Skimming
>
> Before you read a text for complete
> understanding, skim it, that is, read it
> quickly for a general idea. Look at the
> title, the heading of each section, and
> the illustrations or photos.

2 READ

CD1 T8

Listen and read the article. Was your prediction about the main idea correct?
Who is Devorah Hernandez? Why is she an interesting person to read about?

Ready, Set, Go!

Devorah Hernandez knows how to
set goals and do what's necessary
to achieve them.

**A Search for the
American Dream**

In 1988, Devorah and her husband
left Mexico to find a better future
for themselves and their children.
However, when they first arrived
in Salinas, California, they had
financial difficulties. In Mexico,
Devorah was a bank secretary.
In the U.S., she got a job in a
fast-food restaurant and earned
additional money babysitting.
When her family moved to
Watsonville, California, she
became a farm worker. Devorah
wanted more. She decided her
first step would be to learn
English.

The First Difficult Steps

Devorah enrolled in classes
at Watsonville/Aptos Adult
Education. It wasn't easy to
go to school, take care of her
family, and work as a part-time
housekeeper and a jewelry
salesperson. In her first year
of school, she learned basic
English, completed her GED in
Spanish, and studied office skills.
And that was just the beginning.

New Goals, New Achievement

Devorah continued to work and
study, taking computer and ESL
classes at Cabrillo College. In
addition, she fulfilled her dream
of becoming a U.S. citizen.
Eventually, she returned to
the agriculture industry when
Driscoll's, a California company

that grows and sells berries,
offered her a job as a quality-
control inspector. Devorah is now
the head of the company's food-
safety department.

Several years ago, Devorah
Hernandez received the Latin
People Succeed Award. That was
a great honor, but she is still trying
to **get ahead**. Her current goals
are to **make the most of** what life
offers, try new things, and work
hard for success.

Getting Started 10 minutes

 BEFORE YOU READ

A CLASS. **What is "the American dream"...**

- Draw a spoke-and-wheel graphic organizer on the board. Draw a circle and write the words *the American dream* in the center. Draw writing lines—spokes—from the circle outward.
- Ask: *What is the American dream?* Write each student response on a different spoke.
- Ask: *Is it possible for this dream to come true?* Call on volunteers to answer.
- Say: *You're going to read a story about an immigrant who achieved the American dream.*

Culture Connection

"The American dream" is the traditional belief that every American has an equal chance to succeed through hard work and perseverance. For many immigrants, the dream means the opportunity to achieve more success than they could in their native countries.

Presentation 15 minutes

Reading Skill: **Skimming**

- Read the Reading Skill. Explain that skimming can help students read faster and understand better. Say: *Now we're going to skim the article together.*

B **Read the Reading Skill. Then skim...**

- Have the class look at the photo. Ask: *Who is this person? What is she holding?*
- Read the directions. Explain: *The main idea is the topic of the article. It's what the article is about. You can use the title and headings to predict the main idea.*
- Read the title and the headings. Have students underline them. Then write them on the board.
- Point to the title "Ready, Set, Go!" Ask: *Why are these words used? How are they related to the topic of the American dream? What do you think the article will be about?* Write students' predictions on the board.

Answer: The main idea is that it is important to set goals and work hard in order to achieve the American dream.

- Read the first heading. Ask: *What else do you think the article is about?* Add ideas to the list on the board.
- Read the second heading. Ask: *What will this part of the reading be about?* Write students' ideas on the board.
- Read the third heading. Ask: *What do you think this part of the article is about?* Write students' ideas on the board.
- Summarize. Say: *Now that you've read the title and the headings, do you think this will be an interesting article? Do you want to read it?*

Language Note

The words *Ready, set, go!* are used at the beginning of a foot race. Runners get *ready* when they move into position. Then they get *set*—they crouch down. When they hear *go*, they spring up and begin running.

2 READ

 Listen and read the article. Was...

- Play CD 1, Track 8. Ask students to listen and read along with the article.
- Note: Do not preteach the boldfaced words. They will be taught in Exercise 4.
- When students have finished reading, point to their predictions on the board and ask: *Were your predictions correct?*
- Read the other questions in the directions and call on volunteers to answer.

Possible answer: Devorah Hernandez is an immigrant to the U.S. from Mexico. She is an interesting person to read about because she struggled and succeeded in her new life in the U.S.

Controlled Practice   15 minutes

3 CHECK YOUR UNDERSTANDING

A Look back at...

- Model the activity. Hold up your book and demonstrate reading rapidly for a word related to *babysitter* by moving your finger across each line of text.
- Have students use the same technique to search for the remaining items. Walk around and make sure they are not reading the text word for word.
- Have students compare answers with one another.
- Check answers. Say each job and have students say *check* or *no check*.

B Complete the sentences. Circle...

- Have students read rapidly to find the answers. Make sure they are not reading word for word.
- Check answers. Call on students to read the sentences and say the correct answers.

C GROUPS. Discuss. Why do you think...

- Form cross-ability groups of three or four.
- Walk around and provide help as needed.
- To wrap up, call on a student from each group to share the group's answer to the question.

Community Building

Group work will be more productive if each student has a task. For example: 1. **Timekeeper:** Keeps track of the time limit. (This task can be done by a pre-level student.) 2. **Discussion manager:** Keeps the discussion on track and makes sure that each member of the group participates. 3. **Note taker:** Takes notes as group members speak. 4. **Reporter:** Presents the group's ideas to the whole class. (This is a good task for an above-level student.)

4 WORD WORK

Find the boldfaced words...

- Tell students to find each item in the text, read the sentence in which it appears, and choose the meaning that best fits the context.

- Do item 1 with the class. Have students reread the second paragraph. Ask: *What kind of difficulties did Devorah's family have at first?* (financial) *Why did Devorah take a job as a babysitter?* (to earn more money) *What does* financial *mean?* (money)
- Have students do the other items alone or in pairs.
- Have volunteers say the answers and explain how they guessed the meaning. Correct as needed.

Communicative Practice   20 minutes

Show what you know!

GROUPS. Discuss the meaning...

- Read each word out loud as students follow along silently.
- Read each word again and have students repeat.
- Say: *These are some of the words that we usually use to describe a successful person.*
- On the board, write: *A _____ person is someone who . . .* Use the word *determined* to demonstrate. Say: *A determined person is someone who works hard to succeed and never gives up.*
- Form cross-ability groups. Tell students they can use the formula on the board to define the remaining terms.
- To wrap up, have one student from each group share the group's answers to the two questions. Write the words for describing successful people.

Possible answers: energetic, focused, lucky, organized.

Expansion: Vocabulary Practice for Show what you know!

- Have students write new words in a vocabulary notebook. Model a notebook entry. For example, an entry can include the word to be learned, a definition (in English and/or the student's first language), the part of speech, and an example sentence. Encourage students to study their words at every opportunity.

Extra Practice

Interactive Practice   pages 4–5

3 CHECK YOUR UNDERSTANDING

A **Look back at the article. Check (✓) each job that Devorah Hernandez has done.**

☑ babysitter   ☑ fast-food worker   ☑ farm worker   ☐ factory worker
☐ teacher's aide   ☑ housekeeper   ☑ quality-control inspector   ☑ jewelry salesperson

B **Complete the sentences. Circle the correct answers.**

1. Devorah Hernandez came to the U.S. _____.
   a. to work in a bank   b. to study English   **c.** to find a good life for her family

2. At Cabrillo College, Devorah Hernandez studied _____.
   a. office skills   b. for her GED   **c.** computer skills

C **GROUPS. Discuss. Why do you think Devorah Hernandez received the Latin People Succeed Award?**

4 WORD WORK

Find the boldfaced words in the article. Complete the sentences. Circle the correct answers.

1. **Financial** difficulties are problems related to _____.
   a. transportation   b. health   **c.** money

2. If we do something **eventually**, we do it _____.
   a. quickly   **b.** after a long time   c. carefully

3. One way to **get ahead** is to_____.
   a. move to a cheaper apartment   b. start your own company   **c.** take another English class

4. When you **make the most of** something, you _____.
   a. use an opportunity well   b. waste your time   c. ask a lot of questions

Show what you know!   Describe a successful person

GROUPS. Discuss the meaning of each word below. Which word best describes Devorah Hernandez? What other words describe a successful person?

> determined   disciplined   goal-oriented   hardworking   smart

Listening and Speaking

1 BEFORE YOU LISTEN

PAIRS. Arturo Pérez is an ambitious person. What does the word *ambitious* mean? Are you ambitious? Explain.

2 LISTEN

CD1 T9

A Read the list of positions at the Café Royale. Then listen to the first part of the conversation. Check (✓) the job that Arturo has now. Circle the job he wants next.

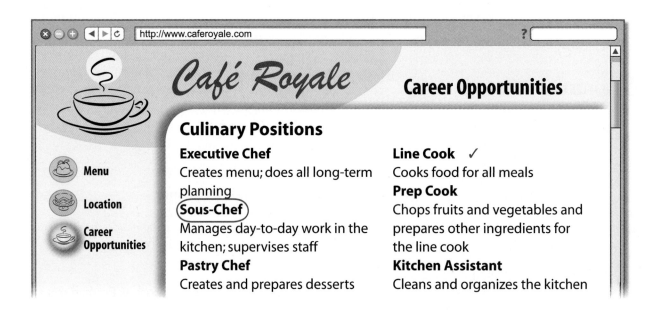

Café Royale   **Career Opportunities**

- Menu
- Location
- Career Opportunities

Culinary Positions

Executive Chef
Creates menu; does all long-term planning

(**Sous-Chef**)
Manages day-to-day work in the kitchen; supervises staff

Pastry Chef
Creates and prepares desserts

Line Cook ✓
Cooks food for all meals

Prep Cook
Chops fruits and vegetables and prepares other ingredients for the line cook

Kitchen Assistant
Cleans and organizes the kitchen

CD1 T10

B Read the questions. Listen to the whole conversation. Then answer the questions.

1. What is Arturo going to do next month?
2. What is Arturo's long-term goal? (What does he want to do ten years from now?)
3. What will Arturo do after he finishes the program?
4. What is Arturo going to do about his job at the Café Royale?

C GROUPS. Discuss. What do you think about Arturo's plans?

Lesson 4 Discuss goals

Getting Started 5 minutes

1 BEFORE YOU LISTEN

PAIRS. Arturo Pérez is an ambitious...

- Elicit the meaning of *ambitious* from the class. Ask: *Is an ambitious person someone who doesn't want to succeed?* (no) *Is an ambitious person someone who has a strong desire to succeed?* (yes) Write the definition on the board: *An ambitious person has a strong desire to succeed.* Ask students if they know of any ambitious people, for example, friends, family, or celebrities.
- Form pairs. Repeat the question: *Are you ambitious?* Give a time limit for talking.
- Call on a few students to share their answers with the class.

Presentation 10 minutes

2 LISTEN

A 💿 **Read the list of positions...**

- Hold up the book and point to the illustration. Ask: *What is this?* (a Web page showing jobs available at the Café Royale) *What are* career opportunities? (jobs available)
- Read each position and its description. If necessary, check students' understanding of vocabulary words. For example, ask: *Does a pastry chef cook food for meals?* (no) *Does a pastry chef make desserts?* (yes)
- Play CD 1, Track 9. Remind students to listen for the job Arturo has now and the job he wants to have.
- Call on students to say which job they checked and which one they circled.

Language Note

Many words related to cooking come from French, for example, *sous-chef. Sous* means *under* in French.

Teaching Tip

If students need additional support, tell them to read the Audio Script on page 285 as they listen.

Controlled Practice 10 minutes

B 💿 **Read the questions. Listen...**

- Have students read the questions and predict the answers.
- Ask: *What is the meaning of* long-term goal? (a goal someone wants to accomplish far in the future) *What is the opposite?* (a short-term goal) *What does it mean?* (a goal someone wants to accomplish soon; often short-term goals are steps along the road to a long-term goal).
- Play CD 1, Track 10.
- Call on students to answer the questions.

Answers: 1. He's going to start a cooking class. 2. He wants to have his own restaurant. 3. He will work as a sous-chef. 4. He's going to keep it.

Teaching Tip

If students are unable to answer a listening comprehension question, replay the specific part of the recording that answers the question. Stop the recording and ask them to repeat what they heard. Then have them answer the question again.

Expansion: Listening Practice for 2B

- Draw a time line on the board, like this:

Now   Short-term   Long-term

- If necessary, have students listen to Track 10 again.
- Have students write Arturo's goals on the time line.

Teaching Tip

Graphic organizers can be an excellent aid to listening comprehension. Many students benefit from converting information they hear into information they can see.

C **GROUPS. Discuss. What do you...**

- Form cross-ability groups.
- Give a time limit for discussion.
- Walk around and provide help as needed.
- To wrap up, call on a student from each group to share the group's answer to the question.

Presentation 10 minutes

3 CONVERSATION

A GROUPS. Discuss. What additional steps...

- Write on the board: *take daytime cooking classes, work in the evening*, and *become a sous-chef*. Say: *These are the steps Arturo is taking to achieve his long-term goal: to open his own restaurant in ten years.*
- Read the discussion question. Form cross-ability groups.
- Give a time limit.
- Walk around and provide help as needed.
- Call on a student from each group to share the group's ideas with the class. Write all the suggestions on the board.

Possible answers: He needs to find financing, find a location for his restaurant, employees, and perhaps find a business partner.

Expansion: Speaking Practice for 3A

- Have students vote on the step they think is most important for Arturo to take. Ask why students think it is the most important.

B Arturo and his cousin...

- Have students look at the photo. Ask: *Where are the speakers? How old is Diana?*
- Play CD 1, Track 11. Have students listen and read along silently.
- *Optional:* Have above-level students listen with their books closed.
- Check comprehension. For example, ask: *Where does Diana work?* (in a restaurant or a store) *Has she decided where she wants to study?* (not yet) *What is she going to do first, second, third?* (First, she's going to do more research. Second, she's going to visit schools. Third, she's going to send in her applications.)

Controlled Practice 10 minutes

4 PRACTICE

A PAIRS. Practice the conversation.

- Form pairs and have them switch roles and practice again.
- Have pairs perform the conversation for the class.

MULTILEVEL INSTRUCTION for 4A

Pre-level Have students practice the conversation several times with the same partner.

Above-level Have students continue the conversation for another two or three exchanges, using their own ideas.

Communicative Practice 15 minutes

B MAKE IT PERSONAL. Think about your...

STEP 1. Think of a long-term goal...

- Tell students to write down one goal and at least three activities that will help them achieve it.
- Walk around and provide help as needed.

STEP 2. GROUPS. Share your ideas.

- Form cross-ability groups of three or four students. Have them select a discussion manager and a timekeeper. The discussion manager should make sure everyone has a chance to speak.
- Give a time limit for discussion.
- Bring the class together and have groups share their ideas with the class.

Expansion: Speaking Practice for 4B

- Have the class sit in a circle. Go around and have each student say his or her long-term goal and at least one activity that will help him or her achieve it. Start by speaking about your own goals.

Extra Practice

Interactive Practice

3 CONVERSATION

(A) GROUPS. Discuss. What additional steps do you think Arturo must take to achieve his long-term goal?

(B) CD1 T11

Arturo and his cousin Diana are talking about her plans for the future. Diana's long-term goal is to be a store manager. Listen and read.

Diana: I don't want to be a cashier my whole life. Eventually, I want to be a manager. I think it's time for me to go to school.

Arturo: Have you decided where to study?

Diana: Not yet. First I need to do more research. I'm looking at different business programs online.

Arturo: Are you going to visit any schools?

Diana: Yes, a few. I'll start sending in my applications by the end of the month.

Arturo: It sounds like you have a plan.

4 PRACTICE

(A) PAIRS. Practice the conversation.

(B) MAKE IT PERSONAL. Think about your short-term goals.

STEP 1. Think of a long-term goal you have at work, school, or home. How are you going to achieve your goal? Take notes.

STEP 2. GROUPS. Share your ideas.

Grammar

Future with *will*, *be going to*, and present continuous

Will	Be going to	Present continuous
I'll take daytime classes and work in the evening.	I'm going to take cooking classes in August.	I'm starting classes there next month.

1 PRACTICE

A Read the e-mail that Brenda Kraig wrote to her sister. Underline the examples of future with *will*, *be going to*, and present continuous.

> **Grammar Watch**
>
> • Use *will*, *be going to*, or present continuous to talk about the future.
> • Use *will* to express a willingness or promise to do something: *I'll do it tomorrow*.
> • Use *be going to* or present continuous to talk about plans or things that someone intends to do.

Subject : New Plans

Hi, Kayla!

I just want to let you know that everything is fine. I'm happy, but I need to think about where I'll be five years from now.

Pawel and I aren't going to get married anytime soon—in fact, he's in Poland now and won't be back until next month. In the meantime, I'm going to make a few decisions about my life. The community college near my apartment is having an open house later this week. That will give me a chance to visit the campus and find out about classes. I'm also going to talk to a counselor at the career center to find out what's best for me.

So what will Pawel say? I'm writing to him tonight. I'll let you know how everything goes.

Brenda

B Complete the sentences with the correct future form.

1. My sister _____is getting married_____ next week.
   (*present continuous*/get married)

2. Do you have any idea where you _____'ll be (*or* will be)_____ in twenty years?
   (will/be)

3. My neighbors _____are going to have_____ a party on Friday night.
   (be going to/have)

4. We hope the party _____won't be (*or* will not be)_____ too loud.
   (will/not/be)

5. I 'm going to tell (*or* am going to tell) my neighbors that I _____'ll bring (*or* will bring)_____ a cake.
   (be going to/tell)   (will/bring)

6. I have to leave early because I _____'m starting (*or* I am starting)_____ a class at the community
   (*present continuous*/start)
   college tomorrow morning at 9 o'clock.

Getting Started
5 minutes

- Say: *In this lesson we're going to review three ways of talking about the future.*
- Write three example sentences on the board and underline each verb. For example, *Janet <u>will start</u> college in September 2010. She is <u>going to work</u> in a law office this summer. She and her parents <u>are having</u> dinner with friends tonight.*
- Read each sentence. Circle the time expressions and ask: *What's the time of the verb—past, present, or future?*
- On the board, write *I, you, he/she/it, we, they.* Quickly review the conjugation of verb + *be going to.* For example, T: *Study. I am going to study. You* . . . Ss: *are going to study.* T: *He or she* . . . Ss: *is going to study.* Write all forms on the board.

Presentation
10 minutes

Future with *will*, *be going to*, and present continuous

- Copy the grammar chart onto the board.
- Read the first Grammar Watch note. Explain: *All three forms are used to talk about the future.* Read the sentences on the board. Ask: *What's the verb? What's the time expression?* Underline the verbs and circle the time expressions.
- Say: *Some future forms have unique meanings.* Read the second Grammar Watch note. Explain: *If you are willing to do something, it means you volunteer to do it or you don't mind doing it.* Read the example sentence.
- Read the third note. Explain that *intends* is similar to *plans.*

Language Note

The present continuous is used only for future activities that are planned. In contrast, both *will* and *be going to* can be used to talk about predicted future events. For example, it is correct to say *It's going to rain tonight* or *It will rain tonight.* However, *It is raining tonight* is incorrect.

Controlled Practice
10 minutes

1 PRACTICE

A Read the e-mail...

- Read the e-mail out loud while students read silently.
- Tell the class to find the first future verb and underline it. Ask: *Which verb did you underline?* (*'ll*)
- Have students continue working alone or in pairs. Walk around and provide help as needed.
- Have students compare answers with each other.
- Check answers. Call on students to read each sentence of the e-mail and say which words they underlined.

B Complete the sentences with...

- Do item 1 with the class. Elicit the correct answer (*is getting married*) and write it on the board.
- Tell students to complete the exercise alone or in pairs. Walk around and provide help as needed.
- Have students compare answers.
- Call on students to write answers on the board. Have other students say if they are correct.

Teaching Tip

Whenever possible, try to involve students in correcting errors. Point to items written on the board or restate oral items with errors. For example, ask the class: *Is this correct? What do we need to change here? Does anyone have a different answer?*

▬▬▬ Expansion: Grammar Practice for 1B

- Write on the board several sentences with blanks and have students provide all possible future forms. For example: *1. Tomorrow is Ana's birthday, and her friends _____ (have) a party for her.* (are having / are going to have) *2. Don't worry. I promise I _____ (give) you a ride to the party.* (will give) *3. Ana _____ (meet) her parents for dinner this weekend.* (is meeting / is going to meet) *4. Lola _____ (bake) a chocolate cake tonight.* (is going to bake / is baking)

Controlled Practice   15 minutes

2 PRACTICE

Ⓐ Complete the sentences. Use...

- Do the first item with the class. Elicit the correct answer (*is going to go*) and write it on the board.
- There are three verbs in the box and six blanks. Remind students that some verbs will be used more than once.
- Tell students to complete the exercise alone or in pairs. Walk around and provide help as needed.
- Have students compare answers.
- Call on students to write answers on the board. Have other students say if they are correct.

Ⓑ Look at Marta's...

- Read Marta's goals and activities.
- Call on above-level students to model a sentence with *will* or *be going to*. For example, *Marta is going to attend a job-search workshop next month.* Write the sentence on the board.
- Have students complete the activity on notepaper alone or in pairs. Give a time limit. Walk around and provide help as needed.
- Have volunteers write their sentences on the board.
- Check answers. Have students read the sentences on the board. Point to each sentence and ask: *Is the sentence correct?* Elicit corrections from the class and write them on the board.

Possible answers: 1. She's going to register for classes. 2. She's going to ask for more scholarship money. 3. She will attend a job search workshop. 4. She's going to search for jobs online. 5. She will continue her volunteer work at the community center.

■■■ **MULTILEVEL INSTRUCTION for 2B**

Pre-level Have students write one sentence with *will* and one sentence with *be going to*.
Above-level Have students write four sentences with *will* and four with *be going to*.

Communicative Practice   20 minutes

Show what you know!

STEP 1. Write two or three short-term...

- Write *Goals for next month* on the board.
- Tell the class two or three of your goals. Write them on the board.
- Have students write their goals in their notebooks.

STEP 2. What can you do to meet...

- Model the activity. Choose one goal you wrote on the board and write two activities next to it.
- Have students write their activities in their notebooks. Remind them to use the correct forms of *will* and *be going to*.

■■■ **Expansion: Writing Practice for STEP 2**

- Have students write complete sentences about their activities. Collect the papers and correct errors involving *will* and *be going to*.

STEP 3. GROUPS. Take turns sharing your ideas...

- Point to the goal and activities you wrote on the board and tell the class about them. You can say: *One of my short-term goals is _____. To reach this goal, I'm going to _____. I'm also going to _____*
- Form cross-ability groups. Give a time limit. Walk around and provide help as needed.
- Call on volunteers to share their ideas and opinions with the whole class.

Progress Check

Can you . . . discuss goals?

Say: *We have practiced discussing goals. Now, look at the question at the bottom of the page. Can you discuss goals? Write a checkmark in the box.*

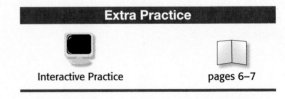

Extra Practice	
Interactive Practice	pages 6–7

A Complete the sentences. Use one of the verbs in the box with the correct future form.

go   have   start

I just saw Mike Cho in the street. Remember Mike? He's doing well, but he's thinking

about getting a better job. He ____*is going to go*____ back to school, and he
                              (be going to)

____*will start*____ in September. Canyon College ____*is having*____ an
     (will)   (present continuous)

information session next week, and Mike ____*is going to go*____ to it. The college
                                              (be going to)

____*will have*____ some counselors there to talk about the program—and
     (will)

Mike hopes they ____*will have*____ refreshments!
                     (will)

B Look at Marta's short-term goals and activities for the next month. Write three sentences with *be going to* and two sentences with *will*.

Goals for Next Month
1. Plan for next semester's classes
   - register for classes
   - ask for more scholarship money
2. Prepare for job after finishing school
   - attend job/search workshop
   - search for jobs online
   - continue volunteer work at community center

Show what you know!   Discuss goals

STEP 1. Write two or three short-term goals you would like to achieve in the coming year.

STEP 2. What can you do to meet your goals for this year? Write two activities for each of your short-term goals.

STEP 3. GROUPS.   Take turns sharing your ideas and giving your opinions.

Can you... discuss goals? ☐

Interpret and complete a school application

Life Skills

1 READ AN APPLICATION

A CLASS. What kinds of application forms have you completed? What information do most applications ask for?

B Read the application that Arturo Pérez completed for the Helman Culinary School.

2 PRACTICE

A Find these words in the form. Match the words with the definitions.

___e___ 1. credit   a. a document that shows student classes and grades

___f___ 2. fee   b. money that cannot be returned to you after you pay it

___d___ 3. maiden name   c. not required, but something you can choose to do

___b___ 4. non-refundable   d. the family name a woman had before marriage

___c___ 5. optional   e. a unit to measure college or university work

___a___ 6. transcript   f. money you pay to do something

B Read the statements about Arturo. Write *T* (true) or *F* (false). Correct the false statements.

                  Spring

___F___ 1. He wants to start classes in ~~Fall~~ 2010.   ___T___ 4. He completed his GED in August 2007.

___F___ 2. His phone number at home is   ___T___ 5. He was a prep cook before he became
          858-555-~~1492~~. 3410   a line cook.

___T___ 3. He is a U.S. citizen.   ___F___ 6. He worked as a prep cook for just
                                             under ~~a year~~. two years

C PAIRS. Answer the questions.

1. How much money did Arturo pay when he submitted his application?
2. What address did Arturo send his completed application to?
3. What languages does Arturo speak?

D Find an application for a school in your area. Use the Internet or visit a school admissions office. Bring the application to class.

E GROUPS. Complete your applications. Help one another with vocabulary.

Interpret and complete a school application

Getting Started   5 minutes

1   READ AN APPLICATION

A CLASS. What kinds of application forms...

- Survey the class. Ask: *How many of you are planning to apply to a school? Which one? What do you want to study? Have you filled out an application yet?*
- Tell students that in this lesson they will practice reading and filling out a school application.
- On the board, write the headings *Kinds of Applications* and *Information They Ask for.*
- Read the questions and have volunteers answer them. Write answers under the correct headings.
- Ask: *What information is usually found on all forms?* (name, address, phone numbers, etc.) *What information is found on certain forms but not others?* (For example, citizenship is required for school applications but not for apartment rentals or bank accounts.)

Teaching Tip

When you use charts to organize information on the board, give each column a heading, for example, *Kinds of Applications* and *Information They Ask for.*

Presentation   15 minutes

B Read the application...

- Remind the class that Arturo Pérez was one of the speakers in Lesson 1. He was a line cook at the Café Royale. His goal was to become a sous-chef and eventually to open his own restaurant.
- Give students a time limit for reading.
- Walk around and provide help as needed.

Culture Connection

In the U.S., it is illegal for organizations to require people to state their age, marital status, or ethnicity on applications. Organizations may ask for this information, but applicants are not required to provide it.

Note: The notes for Exercise 2 appear on page T-17.

Controlled Practice   25 minutes

2 PRACTICE

Ⓐ Find these words...

- Model the technique for matching words with their definitions. Have students look at the example. Read the word *credit* and the definition. Say: *How do we know that letter e is correct?* Have students find the word *credit* in the application. Tell them to read the word in context and choose the definition that fits the way the word is used.
- Have students complete the exercise alone or in pairs. Give a time limit.
- Check answers. Write the numbers *2* through *6* on the board. Say each number and call on a student to say the letter of the definition. If an answer is incorrect, have the class look at the item in context again and correct the error.

Ⓑ Read the statements...

- Write item 1 on the board. Demonstrate how to correct a false statement by crossing out the error in the sentence and writing the correction above it.
- Have students complete the exercise alone or in pairs. Give a time limit.
- Check answers. Write the numbers *2* through *6* on the board. Call on students to write the answers on the board. For false items, tell students to write the incorrect part of the sentence on the board, draw a line through it, and write the correction above the line.

Ⓒ PAIRS Answer the questions.

- Have students take turns reading the questions.
- Have them look back at the application, underline the answers to the questions, and write the question numbers in the margin.
- Check answers. Have students read the questions and say their answers.

Answers: 1. $25.00 2. 1075 First Avenue, San Diego, CA 92101 3. Spanish and English

Ⓓ Find an application...

- Print out several applications and bring them to class for students who were not able to find their own.
- *Optional:* Make a class set of one application and give one to each student.

Community Building

If your class has an Internet connection, show students how to search for an online application. If possible, search for an application to your school.

Communicative Practice   15 minutes

Ⓔ GROUPS. Complete your applications....

- Form cross-ability groups. Have above-level students help pre-level students with vocabulary.
- Give a time limit.
- Walk around and provide help as needed.

Progress Check

Can you . . . interpret and complete...

Say: *We have practiced interpreting and completing a school application. Now, look at the question at the bottom of the page. Can you interpret and complete a school application? Write a checkmark in the box.*

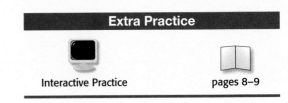

Extra Practice

Interactive Practice   pages 8–9

Helman Culinary School
www.helman.edu • 619-555-4000

Office of Admissions | 1075 First Avenue, San Diego, CA 92101

Submit the following:
1. Application
2. $25 non-refundable application fee
3. Official transcripts of high school and college
4. Personal Statement

Applying for:
- ☐ Fall 20 ____
- ☑ Spring 20 _10_
- ☐ Summer ____

Specializing in:
- ☑ Cooking
- ☐ Event Planning
- ☐ Management

Contact Information

Pérez
Last Name:

Maiden Name:

Arturo
First Name:

Antonio
Middle Name:

2492 Jefferson St.
Street Address

San Diego
City

CA
State

92110
Zip

858-555-3410
Home Phone

858-555-1492
Cell Phone

Arturo1989@gotmail.com
E-mail

Personal

Date of Birth: 06/27/75
(MM/DD/YY)

123-89-0000
Social Security Number

Gender:
- ☑ Male
- ☐ Female

Citizenship:
- ☑ United States
- ☐ Other

Native Language:
- ☐ English
- ☑ Other _bilingual in Spanish and English_

Optional: Helman Culinary School is an equal opportunity institution. This information is requested to comply with federal law and will not affect consideration of your application.

Ethnicity:
- ☐ African American, Black
- ☐ American Indian/Alaskan
- ☐ Asian or Pacific Islander
- ☐ Hispanic or Latino
- ☐ White, Non-Hispanic
- ☐ Other
- ☐ Prefer not to answer

Education

Delgado H.S., San Diego, CA
Last High School Attended

Central College, San Diego, CA
Colleges Attended

- ☐ High School Graduate: _____ (mm/yy)
- ☑ Passed GED Test: 08/07 (mm/yy)

Most Credits or Highest Degree Earned
- ☐ Associate's Degree
- ☐ Some Credits: _____
- ☐ Bachelor's Degree
- ☐ Certificate: _____

Work History (Begin with most recent employer.)

Employer: Café Royale
Job Title: Line Cook
City and State: San Diego, CA
Dates Employed: from 08/09 to present

Employer: Café Royale
Job Title: Prep Cook
City and State: San Diego, CA
Dates Employed: from 09/07 to 08/09

Employer: Mi Comida
Job Title: Kitchen Assistant
City and State: San Diego, CA
Dates Employed: from 03/06 to 09/07

Applicant signature: Arturo Pérez

Date: 12/01/10

Can you...interpret and complete a school application? ☐

Discuss ways to succeed

Listening and Speaking

1 BEFORE YOU LISTEN

GROUPS. Check (✓) the information that you believe is true about entrepreneurs. Help one another with new vocabulary. Then discuss the qualities of entrepreneurs and give examples of entrepreneurs.

> An *entrepreneur* is a person who starts a business and takes risks to make a profit.

Entrepreneurs . . .

- [ ] have creative ideas.
- [ ] are usually happy working for big companies.
- [ ] want to be self-sufficient or independent.
- [ ] usually have a lot of self-confidence.
- [ ] are not afraid to take financial risks.
- [ ] are usually young.

2 LISTEN

A CD1 T12 Holly Maxwell is the host of "Real-Life Entrepreneurs," a weekly radio show. Listen. What is the focus of her show this week?

B CD1 T12 Read the questions. Listen to Holly Maxwell again. Then answer the questions.

1. What kind of business did Nadia Gorsky start?
2. What is a three-generation household?
3. Where is Nadia's grandmother from?
4. Why did Nadia's grandmother take care of her when Nadia was a child?
5. What did Nadia help her grandmother do?
6. What degrees did Nadia get?
7. What was her career goal when she was in school?
9. What did Nadia dream of doing?

C GROUPS. Discuss. What did Nadia's parents use to tell her? How did that advice help Nadia to become successful?

Getting Started   5 minutes

1 BEFORE YOU LISTEN

GROUPS. **Check (✓) the information...**

- Write the word *entrepreneur* on the board, say it, and have the class repeat it.
- Read the definition. Give examples of famous entrepreneurs (*Bill Gates, Steven Jobs, Estée Lauder*).
- On the board, write *An entrepreneur is someone who . . .* and *Entrepreneurs are . . .* Say: *What are the qualities of entrepreneurs?* Point to the first sentence beginning and say, *For example, an entrepreneur is someone who is not afraid to take risks.* Point to the second sentence beginning and ask, *What's another quality of entrepreneurs?*
- Form cross-ability groups. Encourage the above-level students to help the pre-level students.
- Read each item in the list and have students raise their hands if they checked it. Summarize by saying: *It looks like we agree that entrepreneurs. . . .* (Read the items that most students checked.)
- Have students say their ideas about the qualities of entrepreneurs and write them under the sentences you wrote on the board previously.
- Create a new list on the board with the heading *Examples.* Have students say their examples.

▮ EXPANSION: Speaking Practice

- Write this question on the board: *Do you think you could be an entrepreneur? Why or why not?*
- Form groups. Give a time limit for discussion.
- Have groups share their answers.

Presentation   5 minutes

2 LISTEN

Ⓐ **Holly Maxwell is the host of...**

- Explain: *Focus* means the topic or main idea.
- Have the class look at the photo. Ask: *Where is the woman? What is her job?*
- Play CD 1, Track 12. Play it again if necessary.
- Call on a volunteer to answer the question.

Answer: The focus is on entrepreneurs in California.

Teaching Tip

To help students listen for the focus, remind them that they don't need to understand every word. They should listen for the main idea only.

Controlled Practice   10 minutes

Ⓑ **Read the questions. Listen to...**

- Have students read the questions before listening.
- Play Track 12 again.
- Have students compare answers with a partner.
- Stop the recording after the name of Nadia's company. Read question 1. Have the class answer.
- Call on students to read the questions and answers.

Answers: 1. a frozen soup company. 2. a household in which grandparents, parents, and children live together. 3. Russia. 4. because her parents went to work early in the morning 5. make soup. 6. a bachelor's and a master's in biology 7. to be a nutritionist. 8. opening her own business.

Teaching Tip

If students have difficulty answering listening comprehension questions, replay the recording in chunks. Read each question and play the section that contains the answer. Stop after the answer and have the class repeat it and answer the question.

Communicative Practice   10 minutes

Ⓒ GROUPS. **Discuss. What did Nadia's parents...**

- Form cross-ability groups to discuss.
- Bring the class together. Have a representative from each group share the group's answers.

Answers: They used to tell her she could be anything she wanted to be. The advice probably gave her confidence.

▮ Expansion: Speaking Practice for 2C

- Write on the board: *What advice did your parents give you? Did it help you become successful?*
- Have volunteers share their answers with the class.

Presentation   10 minutes

3   CONVERSATION

Pronunciation Watch

- Read the Pronunciation Watch note.
- On the board, write: *What did you do last night?*
- Read the sentence slowly, enunciating each word separately. Then read the sentence naturally. Be sure to pronounce *did you* as *didja.*
- Ask: *Do the sentences sound the same?* (no) *How are they different?* (There is a /j/ between *did* and *you*, and *you* is reduced to *ya.*)
- On the board, write *Did your car start this morning?* Say the sentence slowly, enunciating every word. Then say the sentence naturally. Be sure to pronounce *Did your* as *Didjer.* Again, ask: *Do the sentences sound the same?* (no) *How are they different? (Did your* changes to *didjer.)*

A   Listen to the pronunciation of...

- Tell students to listen for *didja* and *didjer.*
- Play CD 1, Track 13. Have students listen.
- Play Track 13 again. Have students repeat.
- Call on students to say each sentence. If necessary, model pronunciation and have students repeat.

Controlled Practice   10 minutes

B   Listen to the sentences. Circle...

- Write item 1 on the board. Pronounce it both ways. With *Do you*, instruct students to listen for the /u/ vowel. With *Did you*, remind students to listen for the /j/ sound and the reduced *ya.*
- Play CD 1, Track 14. Have students listen.
- Play Track 14 again. Have students repeat.
- Pair students and have them say the sentences to each other.
- Call on students to say the sentences with *did.*

C   Before the show, Holly Maxwell talked...

- Play CD 1, Track 15. Have students listen and read silently.
- Ask: *Where did Mrs. Gorsky grow up? What was her job? What was her first job in the U.S.? What did her husband do? What does her daughter do?*

4   PRACTICE

A   PAIRS. Practice the conversation.

- Form cross-ability pairs and have students take turns reading each role.
- Have students switch partners and practice again.
- Walk around and listen as students are practicing. Take notes on students' pronunciation of *did you.*
- If necessary, model the pronunciation of *did you* and have the class repeat.
- Ask volunteers to perform the conversation for the class.

▬▬ MULTILEVEL INSTRUCTION for 4A

Cross-ability Tell lower-level students to read the role of Holly Maxwell. Have above-level students read the role of Mrs. Gorsky.

Communicative Practice   10 minutes

B   MAKE IT PERSONAL. PAIRS. Talk about where...

- Model the activity with an above-level student. Interview the student, using the conversation in Exercise 3C as a model.
- Give a time limit for speaking.
- Walk around and provide help as needed.
- Have pairs role-play their interview for the class.

▬▬ MULTILEVEL INSTRUCTION for 4B

Pre-level Tell students to write down ideas before role-playing the interview.

Above-level Write additional interview questions on the board, for example: *Do you think you will be successful in the future? What are you doing to prepare for success?* Have pairs extend their interview, using the additional questions.

Extra Practice

Interactive Practice

CD1 T13

A Listen to the pronunciation of *did you* and *did your*. Then listen again and repeat.

did you ("didja")   Where did you grow up?

What did you do when you came here?

Did you work in a factory?

did your ("didjer")   Where did your daughter learn to cook?

CD1 T14

B Listen to the sentences. Circle the words you hear.

1. Where (do) / did you work?
2. **Do** / (**Did**) you ever think about starting a business?
3. What (do) / did you like to do after work?
4. How many hours **does** / (did) your daughter work?
5. **Does** / (**Did**) your daughter always like to cook?

CD1 T15

C Before the show, Holly Maxwell talked to Nadia's mother. Listen and read.

Holly Maxwell: Where did you grow up, Mrs. Gorsky?

Mrs. Gorsky: I grew up in Moscow. Things were tough.

Holly Maxwell: Did you work there?

Mrs. Gorsky: Yes. I used to work in a factory. I was a garment worker.

Holly Maxwell: And what about when you came to the U.S.? What did you do when you came here?

Mrs. Gorsky: My first job here was as a cleaning woman in an office building. My husband was a baker. We both used to work nights. We didn't have much, and we worked hard. But we were happy....We've had a good life here.

Holly Maxwell: That's terrific!

Mrs. Gorsky: And now my daughter is a successful entrepreneur!

4 PRACTICE

A PAIRS. Practice the conversation.

B MAKE IT PERSONAL. PAIRS. Talk about where you grew up and what you did before you came to this country. Mention any successes that you and your family had before or after you came to this country.

Discuss people's past experiences

Grammar

Simple past
Nadia **realized** that she **wasn't** satisfied.
She **began** to dream about owning her own business.
She **didn't forget** her grandmother's recipe.
Did you **work there**?

Grammar Watch

- Use the simple past to talk about actions, feelings, or situations in the past.
- *See page 279 for a list of verbs that are irregular in the simple past.*

1 PRACTICE

A Read the information about Ali Pashko. Find all of the verbs in the simple past. Write them in a chart like the one below. Then write the correct base form.

Ali Pashko had a hard life when he first arrived in the U.S. He got a job at a gas station and often worked more than eighty hours a week. Most days he started at 4:00 P.M., and he didn't finish until 9:00 or 10:00 the next morning. He didn't have a car, so he took the bus. He never got much sleep, and he often fell asleep as soon as he found a seat on the bus. Ali worked hard for several years and saved a lot of money. Last year he got a better job. And he finally bought a car.

Regular Verbs		Irregular Verbs	
Simple past	**Base**	**Simple past**	**Base**
arrived	arrive	had	have

B Complete the conversation between Holly Maxwell and her station manager. Use the simple past.

Manager: I ___enjoyed___ your show yesterday about California entrepreneurs.
      (enjoy)

Holly: Thank you, sir. A lot of our listeners ___called___ the station
      (call)

and ___sent___ e-mails after the show to say how much they
    (send)

___liked___ it.
  (like)

Manager: I can see why you ___decided___ to talk about Nadia Gorsky on the
      (decide)

program. She ___didn't have___ much money when she was a child, and
    (not have)

now she's a successful entrepreneur. It's a great story.

Getting Started   5 minutes

- Say: *We're going to review the simple past forms of regular and irregular verbs.*
- On the board, write example sentences with the regular and irregular past and underline the verbs. For example, *The (fall) semester <u>began</u> (one week ago). Adam <u>enrolled</u> in a computer class.*
- Point to each sentence and ask: *What's the time of the verb?* (past) *Is the action finished?* (yes) *What is the base form of the verb?* (begin, enroll)
- On the board, draw a three-column chart with the headings *Affirmative, Negative,* and *Question.* Under *Affirmative,* write: *I worked last night.*
- Ask the class: What's the negative? Elicit *I didn't work last night* and write it in the second column.
- Ask: *What's the yes/no question?* Elicit *Did you work last night?* and write it in the third column.
- Practice with four more verbs—two regular and two irregular verbs, for example, *study, go, clean,* and *buy.* Write the verbs in the chart on the board.

Language Note

The base form of a verb is the simple present form with no endings. For example, the base form of *went, goes,* and *gone* is *go.*

Presentation   10 minutes

Simple past

- Copy the chart onto the board.
- Read out loud the first Grammar Watch note. Read the chart sentences and underline the verbs.
- Read the second note. Point to *realized* in the first grammar chart sentence and say: *Some verbs have regular past forms. They end with -ed.* Point to *began.* Say: *Some verbs have irregular past forms. They don't end in -ed.*
- Ask: *What other verbs have regular past forms? What other verbs have irregular past forms?* Write a separate list. Refer students to page 279 for a list of verbs that are irregular in the simple past.

Expansion: Grammar Practice

- Play a game to review irregular past verbs. Divide the class into several teams. Have each team stand in a single-file line.

- Say a verb in the present form. Ask for the simple past form of the verb. Only the student at the front of each team may speak. The first student to say the correct form wins a point for his or her team. Students who were at the front of their team's line move to the back.

Controlled Practice   10 minutes

1 PRACTICE

Ⓐ Read the information about...

- Copy the chart onto the board, without examples.
- Read out loud the first sentence of the paragraph. Write *arrived* and *had* in the correct columns. Elicit the base form of the verbs (*arrive, have*) and write them in the correct columns.
- Read the rest of the paragraph. Have students underline the past verbs.
- Have students copy the chart into their notebooks, fill in the chart with the verbs they underlined, and write the base form for each verb.
- Call seven students to the board. Assign each student one sentence of the paragraph. Have them write the verbs from their sentence in the chart.

Answers:

Regular Verbs		Irregular Verbs	
Simple past	Base	Simple past	Base
arrived	arrive	had	have
worked	work	got	get
started	start	didn't have	have
didn't finish	finish	took	take
saved	save	fell	fall
		found	find
		bought	buy

Ⓑ Complete the conversation between...

- Read the first sentence.
- Have students work alone or in pairs to complete the conversation.
- Have two volunteers read the conversation out loud. Write the verbs on the board.

Presentation   10 minutes

Used to

- Copy the chart onto the board.
- Write the following headings on the board: *Affirmative, Negative,* and *Question.*
- Write *used to* under *Affirmative.* Say: *In the affirmative, used to is spelled with -ed, like other past forms.*
- Read the second sentence, elicit *didn't use to,* and write the phrase under *Negative.*
- Point to and read the third sentence. Write *did . . . use to* under *Question.*
- To summarize, ask: *Which form has an -ed ending?* (only the affirmative)
- Read the first Grammar Watch note. Point to the first sentence and ask: *In the past, did Nadia use to help her grandmother around the house?* (yes) *Does she help her now?* (no)
- Read the second Grammar Watch note. Say: *The word but shows the contrast between the past and the present.*
- Read the first sentence again. Add *but* and have students complete the sentence: *Nadia used to help her grandmother around the house, but . . .* (now she doesn't).

Controlled Practice   10 minutes

2 **PRACTICE**

Ⓐ Complete the sentences. Use...

- Read item 1, calling students' attention to *but.*
- Remind students to use the information in the second part of the sentence to decide if the first part should use the affirmative or negative form of *used to.*
- Have students read the sentences with the answers. Write the answers on the board.

Ⓑ Read the paragraph. Find...

- Write the first part of the sample sentence, with the error, on the board. Cross out *worked* and write *work* above. Read the second part of the sentence and ask: *Is there an error here?* Have students find the error (*dream*) and say the correction (*dreamed*). Write it on the board.

Communicative Practice   15 minutes

Show what you know!

STEP 1. GROUPS. Prepare five questions...

- Help students form questions with the simple past and *used to,* for example: *Did you have a car?* or *Did you use to have a car? Where did you work? How did you use to travel to and from work?*
- Have students write two questions with *used to.*

STEP 2. PAIRS. Choose a partner. Use...

- Model the activity with an above-level student.
- Form similar-ability pairs. Tell students to use the questions they wrote in Step 1. Give a time limit.
- Walk around and provide help as needed. Take notes on errors with the simple past and *used to.* Review errors with the class.
- To wrap up, select sentences from your notes and write them on the board. Have a volunteer read each sentence and correct the error.

STEP 3. CLASS. Take turns reporting...

- Model the activity. Say two sentences using the simple past and *used to* about the student interviewed in Step 2.

▆▆▆ MULTILEVEL INSTRUCTION for STEP 3
Pre-level Have students say one sentence using the simple past.
Above-level Have students form sentences contrasting the past and present, for example: *Matilda used to work in a factory, but now she works in a restaurant.*

Progress Check

Can you . . . discuss people's past experiences?
Say: *Look at the question at the bottom of the page. Can you discuss people's past experiences? Write a checkmark in the box.*

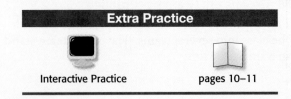

Extra Practice

Interactive Practice   pages 10–11

Used to
Nadia **used to help** her grandmother around the house.
Nadia's mother **didn't use to work** during the day.
How many hours a day **did** Nadia's mother **use to work** when she first came here?

Grammar Watch

- Use **used to** + base form for repeated past actions, feelings, or situations.
- Use **used to** for contrast between the past and the present: *I **didn't use to have** a car, but now I have one.*

2 PRACTICE

A **Complete the sentences. Use *used to* or *didn't use to* and a verb from the box.**

drive	go	listen	live	take

1. Sandra Castillo ___used to live___ in New York, but now she has a home in California.

2. She ___didn't use to drive___, but now she goes everywhere by car.

3. She ___used to take___ the bus to work, but she no longer takes public transportation.

4. She ___didn't use to listen___ music on the radio, but now her car radio is always on.

5. She ___used to go___ to concerts, but now she spends most of her time working.

B **Read the paragraph. Find and correct four more mistakes.**

    Claudio Rialto used to ~~worked~~ *work* as a cook in a big restaurant, but he always dream *ed* of having his own business. He wanted to make the delicious pasta dishes that his grandmother always use *d* to prepare when Claudio was young. He worked long hours for many years and saved a lot of money. One day he hear *d* about a man who was looking for a partner to start a restaurant. Claudio invited the man to lunch. When the man ~~try~~ *tried* Claudio's pasta, he immediately asked Claudio to be his partner.

Show what you know!   Discuss people's past experiences

STEP 1. GROUPS. Prepare five questions to find out about your classmates' lives when they first arrived in the U.S.

STEP 2. PAIRS. Choose a partner. Use your questions to interview each other.

STEP 3. CLASS. Take turns reporting what you learned about your classmates.

Can you. . . discuss people's past experiences? ☐

Write about a role model

Writing

1 BEFORE YOU WRITE

A GROUPS. Discuss. What is a *role model*? Is it important to have role models in your life? Explain.

B Read the writing model. Why does the author want to be like Mrs. Popa?

Lifelong Learning

Romina Popa is my next-door neighbor and my role model. I can learn a lot from her example. Mrs. Popa came to the U.S. from Moldova in 1995. At that time, she was married and had two young children. Her family was the most important part of her life, but she wanted to do other things, too. Her first goal was to learn English, so she took classes at the local community college. Her next goal was to get an associate's degree in nursing. She began her studies in 1998 and graduated in 2001. By then, her children were in school during the day, so she got a job as an emergency room nurse and did volunteer work. Although she was very busy taking care of her family, working, and volunteering, she went back to school for a bachelor's degree in nursing in 2003 and graduated in 2005. Mrs. Popa is now fifty years old. Her children are in college, and she is, too. She's taking classes for a master's degree. I really admire Mrs. Popa. She sets goals and works hard to reach them. I want to be a lifelong learner just like her.

C PAIRS. Answer the questions.

1. How does the author know Mrs. Popa?
2. How old is Mrs. Popa?
3. What is Mrs. Popa's current goal?

> **Writing Tip**
>
> When you write a biographical paragraph, put information about the person's life in chronological (time) order.

D Add information about Mrs. Popa to the timeline.

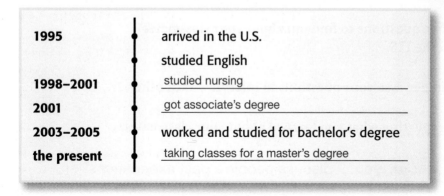

1995	•	arrived in the U.S.
	•	studied English
1998–2001	•	studied nursing
2001	•	got associate's degree
2003–2005	•	worked and studied for bachelor's degree
the present	•	taking classes for a master's degree

Getting Started — 5 minutes

1 BEFORE YOU WRITE

A GROUPS. DISCUSS. **What is a...**

- On the board, write *A role model is a person who* _____.
- Ask: *How can we finish the sentence? What's your idea?* Elicit students' answers and write them on the board.
- Ask: *Why is it important to have role models in your life? What's your idea?* Form cross-ability groups. Give a time limit.
- Walk around and provide help as needed.
- Bring the class together.
- Have a representative from each group share the group's answer.

Presentation — 10 minutes

B Read the writing model. **Why...**

- Tell the class they're going to read about a woman from Moldova. Ask: *Where is Moldova?* (in Eastern Europe, northeast of Romania)
- Read the paragraph out loud as students read along silently.

Answer: The writer wants to be like Mrs. Popa because she sets goals and works hard to reach them and because she is a lifelong learner.

Culture Connection

The U.S. has two-year colleges, called community colleges, and four-year colleges, called colleges or universities. Community colleges award a diploma called an associate's degree. Universities award a diploma called a bachelor's degree after four years of study. They award a master's degree after one or two additional years of study and a Ph.D. following another two to four years, on average.

Controlled Practice — 15 minutes

C PAIRS. **Answer the questions.**

- Form cross-ability pairs. Give a time limit.
- Walk around and provide help as needed.
- Check answers. Call on students to read the questions and say the answers.

Answers: 1. She is the writer's next-door neighbor. 2. She is fifty. 3. Her goal is to get a master's degree.

Expansion: Speaking Practice for 1C

- Write the following additional discussion questions on the board: *What was Mrs. Popa's first goal?* (to learn English) *How did she meet her goal?* (She took classes at the local community college.) *What was her second goal, and what did she do to accomplish it?* (to get an associate's degree in nursing. She went to school at night and worked during the day.) *What is Mrs. Popa doing now?* (She's studying for a master's degree.)

Writing Tip: **Using Chronological Order**

- Read the Writing Tip.
- On the board, write: *biographical* and *chronological*. Define the terms. Say: *biographical: the story of a person's life; chronological: in order of time, from earliest to latest.*
- Ask: *What is a biographical paragraph?* (a paragraph about someone's life) *How is the paragraph about Mrs. Popa organized?* (in chronological order)
- Say: *In this lesson you will write a biographical paragraph about a person you admire.*

D Add information about...

- Copy the timeline onto the board. Say: *This is called a timeline. You can see the dates in chronological order, from earliest to latest, on the left. On the right are important events in Mrs. Popa's life.*
- Have students work alone or in pairs to complete the timeline. Give a time limit.
- Check answers. Call on three students to go up to the board and fill in the missing information on the timeline.
- To wrap up, ask the class: *Are the answers correct?* Elicit corrections as needed and write them on the board.

Controlled Practice 15 minutes

2 THINKING ON PAPER

Ⓐ BRAINSTORM. Who are the people...

- Write the word *brainstorm* on the board. Say: *What do you think* brainstorm *means?* (to quickly think of a lot of ideas and write them down)

- Say: *Brainstorming is a good way to think of ideas for writing.* Hold up your book, point to the chart, and say: *When you brainstorm, it's useful to write your ideas in a chart.*

- Demonstrate brainstorming. Copy the headings *People I Admire* and *Reasons* on the board. Say: *I'm going to brainstorm a list of people I admire.* Write three to four names. Then say: *Now I'm going to choose one person and brainstorm the reasons why I admire (him or her).* Write reasons, for example, *always supports me, gives good advice, honest.* Write notes, not complete sentences.

- Pair students and have them share their charts.

Ⓑ Plan and organize your own...

- Read question 1. Point to the list of people you admire on the board and select one. Circle the name. On the board, write: *The person I admire most is _____.*

- Read question 2. Point to the list of reasons. Rewrite one or two reasons as sentences. For example, *I admire _____ because he always knows what to do when there's a problem.*

- Read question 3. Draw a timeline on the board and fill it in with three to four things the person you selected did. For example, *2000: arrived in the U.S. Got a job as a busperson* (the worker who clears tables in a restaurant). *2003: got a job as a waiter. 2005: worked and took English classes at night. 2007: decided to go to culinary school.*

- Write sentences to match the items in the timeline. For example, *_____ arrived in the U.S. in 2000 and got a job as a busperson. In 2003 he got a job as a waiter. In 2005 ...*

- Read question 4. Ask: *What does* lesson *mean here?* (a suggestion to help you live your life better) Tell the class the lesson you learned from your role model. Write a sentence on the board, for example, *I learned from _____ that I need to work hard and be patient if I want to succeed.*

- Have students write answers to the questions.

▄▄ MULTILEVEL INSTRUCTION for 2B

Pre-level Tell students to answer each question with one sentence. For example, they can choose just one thing their role model did in the past.

Above-level Tell students to write two to three sentences for questions 2, 3, and 4. Encourage them to write about all the items in their timeline.

Communicative Practice 15 minutes

3 WRITE

Write a paragraph about the person...

- Say: *Now use the sentences you wrote in Exercise 2B and write them as a paragraph. It's OK to change or add sentences while you are writing.*

- Review paragraph format. Remind students to give their paragraph a title, indent the first line, and begin each sentence with a capital letter.

- Tell students to look at the writing model in Exercise 1B and circle the time words and phrases (*at that time, first, next, by then, now*). Remind students to follow chronological order.

4 CHECK YOUR WRITING

Teaching Tip

You may want to collect student papers and provide feedback. Use the scoring rubric for writing on page T-xiv to evaluate each student's vocabulary, grammar, mechanics and how well he or she has completed the task. You may want to review the completed rubric with the students.

- Have students read their paragraphs and check off the questions in the checklist.

- Collect papers and make corrections as needed in paragraph format, verb forms, and writing checklist items.

Extra Practice

Interactive Practice   page 12

A BRAINSTORM. Who are the people that you admire? Why do you admire them? Organize your ideas in a chart like this.

People I Admire	Reasons

B Plan and organize your own paragraph. Answer the questions.

1. Who do you admire most?
2. Why do you admire this person?
3. What did this person do? What is this person doing now? (Use chronological order.)
4. What important lesson can you learn from this person?

3 WRITE

Write a paragraph about the person you admire most. Give reasons to explain why you admire the person. Use the information in your chart. Look at the writing model for an example.

4 CHECK YOUR WRITING

☐ Did you describe the person's achievements?
☐ Did you put information about the person's life in chronological order?
☐ Did you give reasons to explain why you admire the person?
☐ Did you use correct capitalization, punctuation, and spelling?

1 REVIEW   For your grammar review, go to page 245.

2 ACT IT OUT   What do you say?

STEP 1. Review the conversations on pages 6-7 (CD1 Tracks 4 and 7).

STEP 2. ROLE PLAY. PAIRS. Role-play this situation.

Student A: Yesterday you saw an old high school friend for the first time in almost ten years. You found out about your old friend's job, family, and life in general. Now you are at a party and talking to another high school friend.

Student B: You are talking to an old high school friend at a party. Yesterday, your friend saw another high school friend for the first time in almost ten years. You want to know everything about that person's job, family, and life in general.

3 READ AND REACT   Problem-solving

STEP 1. Read about the problem.

Your good friend started talking about buying a house three years ago, but he is still renting an apartment. He hasn't taken any steps toward buying a house and needs help. He wants to know how to meet his goal.

STEP 2. GROUPS. What is the problem? Discuss a solution. Make a list of two short-term goals for your friend. Write two activities for each short-term goal.

4 CONNECT   For your Community-Building Activity, go to page 257.
For your Team Project, go to page 263.

Which goals can you check off? Go back to page 5.

 Go to the CD-ROM for more practice.

1 REVIEW

Turn to page 245 for the Grammar Review.

2 ACT IT OUT

STEP 1. CLASS. **Review the conversations...**

- Play CD 1, Tracks 4 and 7. If necessary, direct students to the script for Track 4 at the top of page 285 and for Track 7 on page 7.

STEP 2. ROLE PLAY. PAIRS. **Role-play this situation.**

> **Teaching Tip**
>
> While pairs are performing role plays, use the scoring rubric for speaking on page T-xiii to evaluate each student's vocabulary, grammar, fluency, and how well he or she completes the task. You may want to review the completed rubric with the students.

- Have students look at the photo. Ask: *Where are the people? What is their relationship?*
- Read the role descriptions. If necessary, clarify the situation. Say: *Students A and B are good friends. At the party, they are talking about an old high school friend of theirs whom Student A ran into yesterday.*
- Model the role play with an above-level student. Play the role of Student A. You can begin like this: *Hey, guess who I saw yesterday?*
- Write on the board the grammar points taught in this unit: the simple present and present continuous; the future with *will, be going to*, and present continuous; the simple past and *used to*. Remind students to use the unit grammar.
- Have students write out their dialogues.
- Tell students to practice out loud at least twice.
- Have volunteers role-play for the class.

■■■ MULTILEVEL INSTRUCTION for 2

Pre-level Simplify the situation as follows: Student A and Student B went to high school together. They see each other at a party and spend time catching up on each other's jobs, friends, families, and life in general. They make plans to get together soon and catch up some more. Have students write out their dialogue and then practice it at least twice.

Above-level Do a three-way role play, including Student C, who is the old friend that Student A ran into yesterday. Imagine that you are at a real party and speak without notes.

3 READ AND REACT

STEP 1. **Read about the problem.**

- Read the directions while students follow along silently.

STEP 2. GROUPS. **What is the problem? Discuss...**

- On the board, make two lists with the headings *Goals* and *Activities*.
- Form groups of three or four. Have each group choose a timekeeper, a note taker, and a reporter.
- Have the reporter from each group share the group's ideas.

4 CONNECT

- Turn to page 257 for the Community-building Activity and page 263 for the Team Project. See page T-xi for general notes about teaching these activities.

Progress Check

Which goals can you check off? Go back to page 5.

Ask students to turn to page 5 and check off any remaining goals they have reached. Call on students to say which goals they will practice outside of class.

 Go to the CD-ROM for more practice.

If your students need more practice with the vocabulary, grammar, and competencies in Unit 1, encourage them to review the activities on the CD-ROM.

Tell Me about Yourself

Classroom Materials/Extra Practice

CD 1
Tracks 16–26

Interactive Practice
Unit 2

Workbook
Unit 2

Unit Overview

Goals

- See the list of goals on the facing page.

Grammar

- Infinitives and gerunds
- Gerunds as objects of prepositions
- Simple past and present perfect

Pronunciation

- Pronunciation of silent syllables
- Pronunciation of stressed syllables

Reading

- Read a résumé
- Read an article about job interviews
- *Reading Skill:* Using details to understand important ideas

Writing

- Write a cover letter

Life Skills

- Write a résumé

Preview

- Say the unit title. Ask: *What do you think this unit will be about?*
- Hold up your book or have students look at their books. Set the context by asking the preview questions. You can also ask: *Where are they? What is she holding? How does she look?*

Unit Goals

- Point to the Unit Goals. Have students read the goals silently.
- Tell students they will be studying these goals in Unit 2.
- Say each goal and explain unfamiliar vocabulary as needed. For example, *résumé: a written document showing a person's previous work experience, skills, and education; cover letter: a short introductory letter written by an applicant for a job.*
- Tell students to circle one or more goals that are very important to them. Call on several volunteers to say the goals they circled.
- Write a checkmark (✓) on the board. Say: *We will come back to this page again. You will write a checkmark next to the goals you learned in this unit.*

Tell Me about Yourself

2

Preview

Read the title. Who are the people? What are they saying to each other?

UNIT GOALS

☐ Talk about work-related goals

☐ Interpret and write a résumé

☐ Use job-information sources

☐ Discuss job-related skills and abilities

☐ Respond to common interview questions

☐ Describe previous work experiences and duties

☐ Write a cover letter

Listening and Speaking

1 BEFORE YOU LISTEN

A CLASS. Why do people go to career centers?
What can employment specialists do for their clients?

B GROUPS. When you are *motivated*, you really want to be successful at doing something. Discuss. What are you motivated to do?

2 LISTEN

CD1 T16

A Listen to the first part of a conversation between Catherine Tote, an employment specialist, and her client, Nedim Buric. Then answer the questions.

1. What are two reasons that clients come to Sun County Career Center?

   a. to learn English
   _____

   b. to take training classes
   _____
      to use the computer center

2. What does Nedim want to do?

   to find a job as soon as possible
   _____

B PAIRS. Predict. What is the first thing that Catherine and Nedim will discuss: his work experience, his skills, or his education? What other things do employment specialists ask clients about?

CD1 T17

C Read the statements. Then listen to the whole conversation. Write *T* (true) or *F* (false). Correct the false statements.

__F__ 1. Today is Nedim's ~~second~~ *first* meeting with Catherine Tote.

__F__ 2. Nedim ~~has~~ *doesn't have* a job but is looking for ~~a new~~ one.

__T__ 3. Nedim has good computer skills.

__T__ 4. Nedim pays attention to details.

__F__ 5. Nedim *didn't* graduated ~~from~~ from a university in Bosnia.

__F__ 6. Catherine has *not yet* ~~already~~ found a job for Nedim.

Getting Started 5 minutes

1 BEFORE YOU LISTEN

A CLASS. **Why do people go to...**

- Read the questions. Ask: *What is a career center? Have you ever been to one? What is an employment specialist?* Ask several students to share their experiences. Then have them answer the questions in the book.

Possible answers: People go to career centers to get help finding a job or job training. Employment specialists can help clients with these things.

B GROUPS. **When you are *motivated*...**

- Say the word *motivated* and have the class repeat.
- Tell the class something you are motivated to do. Write your sentence on the board, demonstrating *motivated to* + verb, for example: *I am very motivated to lose 10 pounds.*
- Form cross-ability groups. Tell students to take turns answering the question.
- Call on students to share their ideas with the class.

Presentation 10 minutes

2 LISTEN

A **Listen to the first part...**

- Have students look at the photo. Ask questions to prepare them for listening, for example: *Where are the speakers? Who is the man? Why is he there? Who is the woman?*
- Tell students to read the questions before listening.
- Play CD 1, Track 16. Have students listen and write their answers.
- Have students compare answers with a classmate.
- Have two volunteers write the answers on the board. Make corrections as needed.

Teaching Tip

Have students read listening comprehension questions before listening. Knowing the questions will help students focus their listening.

B PAIRS. **Predict. What is the first thing...**

- Read the first question and take a class vote. For example, ask: *How many people think they will talk about Nedim's work experience first?*
- Read the second question. Elicit students' answers and write them on the board.

Possible answers: Employment specialists ask clients what kind of job they are looking for, if they need help with their résumé, if they have special skills, etc.

Community Building

Whole-class votes and surveys are a way to involve all students in class activities, regardless of their proficiency level.

Controlled Practice 10 minutes

C **Read the statements. Then listen...**

- Have students read the statements silently and predict whether they are true or false.
- Play CD 1, Track 17.
- Have students complete the exercise alone or in pairs.
- Check answers. Call on students to read each statement and say whether it is true or false. If it is false, ask the student to correct it. Write the answers on the board.

Expansion: Speaking Practice for 2C

- With the class, review Nedim's experience, skills, and education. Write them on the board, for example, *two years of university, worked in a lawyer's office, organized.*
- Form cross-ability groups. Have each group select a timekeeper, a note taker, and a reporter. Tell students to think of three jobs that would be good for Nedim.
- Give a time limit.
- Have each group's reporter share his or her group's ideas and say why the jobs the group picked would be good for Nedim.

Presentation   10 minutes

3 CONVERSATION

Pronunciation Watch

- On the board, write: *chocolate, vegetable, every,* and *favorite.* Ask a number of students to read the words.
- Read the Pronunciation Watch note.
- Say the words on the board naturally, as follows: *chocolate → choclat; vegetable → vegtable; every → evry; favorite → favrit.*
- Have students show with fingers how many syllables they hear.

A Listen to the words. Notice...

- Play CD 1, Track 18. Have students listen and hold up fingers indicating the number of syllables they hear.
- Play Track 18 again. Have students listen and repeat.

Controlled Practice   10 minutes

B GROUPS. Discuss. What is an example of...

- Ask: *What is an entry-level job?* (*in a company, the job with the lowest pay and fewest responsibilities*) Elicit some examples of entry-level jobs. For example, ask: *What's an entry-level job in a restaurant?* (*busperson* or *kitchen helper*)
- Form cross-ability groups. Tell each group to choose a timekeeper, a note taker, and a reporter.
- Give a time limit. Write the headings *Entry-level job, Advantages,* and *Disadvantages* on the board.
- Have reporters share their group's answers. Take notes on the board.

Possible answers: *Examples:* mailroom clerks, cleaning staff, store clerks, grocery-store baggers. *Advantages:* joining a company, learning new skills, making contacts. *Disadvantages:* low pay, little responsibility.

- Call on students to read the notes on the board and say whether they agree.

▨ Expansion: Speaking Practice for 3B

- Have volunteers describe the entry-level jobs they have had. Have them talk about what they liked or disliked about the jobs.

C Nedim's friend Tatiana is looking...

- Play CD 1, Track 19. Have students listen and read along silently.
- Check comprehension. Ask: *What is Tatiana interested in?* (photography) *What job does Nedim suggest?* (salesperson in a camera store) *Why is this a good job for Tatiana?* (She's friendly, helpful, and motivated.)

4 PRACTICE

A PAIRS. Practice the conversation.

- Form cross-ability pairs and have students take turns reading each role.
- Have students switch partners and practice again.
- Walk around and listen. Take notes on students' pronunciation of *interested* and *camera.*
- Ask volunteers to perform the conversation.

Communicative Practice   15 minutes

B MAKE IT PERSONAL. Think about...

STEP 1. What job would you like...

- Model the activity. Copy the chart onto the board. Interview an above-level student. For example, ask: *What is your goal? What are you most interested in? What are your personal qualities?* etc. Write the student's information in the chart.
- Have students fill in the charts in their books.

STEP 2. GROUPS. Discuss.

- Form cross-ability groups.
- Model answering the questions using the model chart on the board.
- Bring the class together. Have volunteers answer the questions using their own chart.

Extra Practice

Interactive Practice

CONVERSATION

CD1 T18

A Listen to the words. Notice that one syllable is not pronounced. Then listen again and repeat.

camera (2 syllables)   interested (3 syllables)

family (2 syllables)   different (2 syllables)

B GROUPS. Discuss. What is an example of an entry-level job? What are the advantages and disadvantages of this type of job?

CD1 T19

C Nedim's friend Tatiana is looking for a job in the Help Wanted section of the newspaper. Listen and read.

Nedim: What kind of job are you looking for?

Tatiana: Well, I'm interested in photography. And I'd like to find a job with some opportunity for the future.

Nedim: Here's something at a camera store. Would you consider doing this?

Tatiana: Hmm. It's a position as a salesperson. It's a good entry-level job.

Nedim: You're certainly the right kind of person for the job. You're friendly and helpful.

Tatiana: And motivated. I'll work during the day and take classes at night.

4 **PRACTICE**

A PAIRS. Practice the conversation.

B MAKE IT PERSONAL. Think about your work-related goals.

STEP 1. What job would you like to have? Write information about yourself.

Goal: I want to work as a(n) _____.			
Interests: what I'm most interested in	**Personal Qualities:** kind of person I am	**Skills:** what I know how to do	**Steps:** ways to get the job I want

STEP 2. GROUPS. Discuss.

1. In what ways are you qualified for the job you would like to have?

2. What additional skills do you need? How will you get them?

3. How long will it take to achieve your goal?

Grammar

Infinitives and gerunds

Verb + Infinitive	Verb + Gerund
I **want** *to find* a job.	They **discussed** *finding* a job.
I **decided** *to come* to the U.S.	My uncle **recommended** *finishing* my degree in the U.S.
We can **start** *to look at* available positions.	We can **start** *looking at* available positions.

Grammar Watch

- Use an infinitive after verbs such as *agree, decide, need, wait, want,* and *would like.*
- Use a gerund after verbs such as *enjoy, discuss, finish,* and *recommend.*
- Use either an infinitive or a gerund after verbs such as *begin, continue, like quit, prefer* and *start.*
- *See page 280 for a list of verbs.*

1 PRACTICE

A Read the newspaper article. Underline the examples of verb + infinitive. Circle the examples of verb + gerund.

Sun County Career Center

Sun County Career Center (SCCC) began helping jobseekers thirty years ago. SCCC always planned to offer English and work-skills training to immigrants who needed to find employment, but in 2000, they decided not to limit their services and opened their doors to anyone who was looking for a job. The organization continues to offer ESL classes and job training. It recently started offering job placement and counseling services as well.

B Complete the conversation between Catherine Tote and Mi Young Park, her co-worker at SCCC. Circle the correct words.

Catherine: I met with an interesting client earlier today. When he came in, he wanted **to look** / **looking** at the job listings immediately. He couldn't wait **to find** / **finding** a job.

Mi Young: Did he finally agree **to discuss** / **discussing** the kind of work that might be good for him?

Catherine: Yes, after I explained why we needed **to talk** / **talking** about his personal qualities and his skills. He finally understood how important it is to look for a job that he can enjoy **to do** / **doing**.

Getting Started   5 minutes

- Say: *In this lesson we're going to learn about infinitives and gerunds.*
- Write on the board: *After class, I want to do my homework in the library. I enjoy walking early in the morning.*
- Point to the first sentence and say: *Infinitives have the form* to + verb. Underline the verb *want* and double underline the infinitive.
- Point to the second sentence and say: *Gerunds have the form verb* + -ing. Underline the verb *enjoy* and double underline the gerund.
- Read both sentences and have students repeat.
- To reinforce, ask several students: *What do you want to do after class? What do you enjoy doing in the morning?*

Presentation   10 minutes

Infinitives and gerunds

- On the board, draw a three-column chart with the following headings: *Verb + Infinitive, Verb + Gerund, Verb + Infinitive or Gerund.*
- Read the sentences in the grammar chart and have students repeat. Then ask: *Which verbs come before an infinitive? Which verbs come before a gerund? Which verbs come before an infinitive or a gerund?* Write the verbs in the appropriate columns.
- Read the Grammar Watch note.
- Point to each column on the board. Ask: *Which verbs should I write here?* Have students refer to the Grammar Watch note and repeat the verbs in each category.
- Have volunteers choose one verb from each category and make a sentence with it.

Expansion: Grammar Practice

- Have students create a three-column chart in their notebooks like the one on the board.
- Have students look at the list of verbs followed by infinitives and gerunds on page 280. Give them several minutes to study the list.
- Pair students. Give a time limit. Have them write as many verbs as they can remember in their charts.
- Have students read the verbs on their lists. Write them on the board.

Controlled Practice   15 minutes

1   PRACTICE

A Read the newspaper article. Underline...

- Write the first sentence on the board. Have a student read it. Circle *began helping.* Ask: *What's the verb?* (began) *What comes after it, an infinitive or a gerund?* (a gerund)
- Read the article out loud. Have students listen and complete the exercise.
- Check answers. Call on students to read the sentences and say which phrases they underlined or circled. Write the phrases on the board. Make corrections as needed.

B Complete the conversation between...

- Form cross-ability pairs and tell them to complete the exercise.
- Walk around and provide help as needed.
- Call on students to read the sentences with the correct forms. Make corrections as needed.
- Have a pair of students read the dialogue with the correct forms.

Expansion: Grammar Practice for 1B

- Form cross-ability pairs.
- Have students choose four verbs from each column on the board and write a sentence for each verb.
- Call on pairs to read their sentences and write them on the board. Make corrections as needed.

Controlled Practice   10 minutes

2 PRACTICE

Complete the conversation between...

- Read the first and second sentences. Point out that with the verb *continue* it's possible to use either an infinitive or a gerund.
- Have students continue working alone or in pairs. Give a time limit. Walk around and provide help as needed.
- Call on two students to read the conversation out loud. Write their answers on the board. After each answer, ask the class: *Is this correct?* Elicit corrections from students and write them on the board.

Expansion: Speaking Practice for 2

- Form cross-ability pairs and have students practice the conversation.
- Call on pairs to perform the conversation for the class.

Communicative Practice   20 minutes

Show what you know!

STEP 1. Complete the sentences about...

- To model the activity, give examples from your own life. For example, say: *I really enjoy teaching Level 4. I hope to teach Level 4 again next semester. Someday, I'm going to learn to design a Web page.*
- Have students complete the sentences with their own information.

Expansion: Grammar Practice for STEP 1

- On the board, write additional verbs that can be used to talk about goals, for example, *decide, need, want, would like, consider, finish, recommend,* and *start.*
- Have students use these verbs to write additional sentences about their goals.

STEP 2. GROUPS. Discuss. What are the...

- Form cross-ability groups of five or six people. Have each group select a timekeeper, a note taker, and a reporter.
- Tell students to read their sentences to their classmates. The note taker should write down the group members' answers.
- Give a time limit.
- Walk around and provide help as needed.
- At the end of the discussion, tell note takers to tally the group's answers and determine which ones are the most popular.
- To wrap up, have each group's reporter tell the class about their group's most popular answers.

Progress Check

Can you . . . talk about work-related goals?

Say: *We have practiced talking about work-related goals. Now, look at the question at the bottom of the page. Can you talk about work-related goals? Write a checkmark in the box.*

Extra Practice

Interactive Practice   pages 14–15

Complete the conversation between another SCCC career specialist and his client.
Use infinitives and gerunds. Where appropriate, write two answers.

Michael: Yesterday we discussed ____*setting*____ long-term and short-term goals.
(set)
Let's continue __*to talk/talking*__ about that today.
(talk)

Violette: I finished ____reading____ the information you gave me about goal-
(read)
setting, and I'd really like ____to take____ the time to think about my
(take)
goals. But I need ____to earn____ some money right now.
(earn)

Michael: OK. Then you should consider ____taking____ a job that might lead to a
(take)
better position later.

Violette: That's a good idea. I can start ____to make / making____ money while I'm planning
(make)
for the future. As I think you know, I prefer ____to work / working____ in an office.
(work)

Michael: Yes. Let's see . . . You like ____to do / doing____ research, don't you?
(do)

Violette: Definitely. That's what I liked most about my last job. The only reason I quit
____working____ there was that I moved.
(work)

Show what you know! Talk about work-related goals

STEP 1. Complete the sentences about your work-related goals.

1. I really enjoy _____.

2. My friends think I should try _____.

3. I hope _____.

4. A teacher recommended _____.

5. Someday, I am going to learn _____.

**STEP 2. GROUPS. Discuss. What are the most popular answers for
questions 1, 2, and 3?**

Can you...talk about work-related goals? ☐

Life Skills

1 INTERPRET A RÉSUMÉ

A CLASS. A *résumé* is typed information about your education, skills, and experience. Have you used a résumé to find a job? Do people usually give a résumé to an employer before or after a job interview?

B GROUPS. Skim Francis Kouadio's résumé. What kind of information is in the *Objective* section of the résumé? In the *Qualifications* section? In the *Related Experience* section?

Francis Kouadio
2038 Crabtree Court, Barrington, IL 60010
847-555-1054
frankkouadio@mymail.com

OBJECTIVE: To work as a software programmer and developer

QUALIFICATIONS
- Creative in the design of new computer software
- Skilled at analyzing and solving problems
- Proficient in computer programming languages such as C/C++, Java, and SQL
- Able to work with PC, Macintosh, and Linux platforms

RELATED EXPERIENCE

Technology Specialist
2008–present
RescueMe Computing
Barrington, IL

Started RescueMe at-home visits for computer set-up and repair. Helped clients with business and personal computer needs. Designed database software for doctors and dentists.

Sales Associate
2005–2008
Ted's Electronics
Lake Zurich, IL

Answered customer questions and assisted in purchase of computers, televisions, and other equipment. Received an award for most sales in December 2008.

Volunteer
2004–2005
District 10 Middle School

Taught an after-school program: Computer Skills for the Classroom

EDUCATION
Cutter College, Chicago, IL

B.S., Computer Science, June 2005

References available upon request.

Getting Started   5 minutes

1 INTERPRET A RÉSUMÉ

A CLASS. A *résumé* is typed information about...

- Find a model résumé on the Internet. Print it out and make copies for the class, or project the page for the class to see.
- Read the definition of *résumé* in the directions.
- Have students look at the model and point out the sections showing the person's education, skills, and experience.
- Read the first question in the directions. Have students raise their hands if they have used a résumé.
- Read the second question. Have a volunteer answer.

Answer: People usually give a résumé to an employer before a job interview.

- Say: *In this lesson, we will read a résumé and learn how to write one.*

B GROUPS. Skim Francis Kouadio's...

- Review skimming. Say: *Skimming is reading rapidly to discover what something is about. When you skim, you should not read every word.*
- Read the first question. Have the class skim the *Objective* section. Call on a volunteer to answer the question.

Answer: The *Objective* section describes the type of job the applicant is applying for.

- Group students who are sitting near one another. Have them skim the résumé for the contents of the *Qualifications* and *Related Experience* sections.
- Go over answers with the class.

Answers: The *Qualifications* section includes the skills and accomplishments that make the applicant a good candidate for the job. The *Related Experience* section includes previous jobs and volunteer experience.

Culture Connection

Certain types of information should **not** be included in a résumé, including an applicant's Social Security number; personal information (weight, height, health, marital status, number of children); reasons for leaving jobs; and salary information.

Expansion: Reading Practice for 1B

- Bring real résumés to class, one for each group.
- Divide the class into small groups.
- Have students skim each résumé for the applicant's objective, qualifications, and experience.
- Time permitting, have groups switch résumés and skim again.

Lesson 3 Interpret and write a résumé

Presentation   10 minutes

2 READ

A Read Francis Kouadio's résumé.

- Make a list of vocabulary that students ask about.
- Write new words and definitions on the board. Encourage students to enter them in their vocabulary notebooks.

Controlled Practice   10 minutes

B GROUPS. Discuss.

- Form cross-ability groups. Tell students to take turns reading the questions.
- To wrap up, read each question and have volunteers answer.

Answers: 1. This information is at the top so that the employer can easily contact him. 2. These achievements show that he has initiative and he is an excellent worker. 3. The volunteer work gave him useful experience that probably helped him get his first paid job. Volunteer work also shows that a person is interested in his or her community.

Communicative Practice   10 minutes

C CLASS. *References* are people who...

- Tell the class about a time you applied for a job and the people you used as references.
- Form cross-ability groups. Have groups choose a timekeeper and a reporter.
- Have reporters share their group's answers to question 1 and write them on the board.

Answer: 1. Former employers, teachers, athletic coaches, supervisors in volunteer positions, members of the clergy.

Controlled Practice   10 minutes

3 WRITE

A BRAINSTORM. Think about...

- Give an example of each item and write it on the board.
- Tell students they can make up information.
- As students work, walk around and provide help.

Teaching Tip

If some students have never had a job, pair them with students who have worked or tell them to make up their own information.

B Write an objective for a job...

- Read Francis Kouadio's objective on page 30. Tell students to begin the objective with an infinitive.
- Call on several students to share their objectives with the class.

Communicative Practice   15 minutes

C Write your own résumé. Use...

- Look at Francis Kouadio's résumé on page 30. Point out: In the *Qualifications* section, all items begin with adjectives; in the *Related Experience* section, all items begin with verbs; positions are listed with the most recent one first; the entire résumé is on one page; the last item on the page is *References available upon request.*
- Have students write a draft résumé in class. While students work, walk around and provide help.
- Collect the drafts and give feedback.

Progress Check

Can you . . . interpret and write a résumé?
Say: *Look at the question at the bottom of the page. Can you interpret and write a résumé? Write a checkmark in the box.*

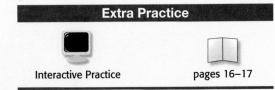

Extra Practice

Interactive Practice   pages 16–17

2 READ

A Read Francis Kouadio's résumé.

B GROUPS. Discuss.

1. Why does Francis Kouadio include his address, telephone number, and e-mail address at the top of his résumé?

2. Why does Francis include achievements such as "started RescueMe at-home visits" and "received an award for most sales in December 2008" in his work experience?

3. Why does Francis include a volunteer position along with his paid jobs?

C CLASS. *References* are people who can describe your personal qualities, skills and abilities, and experience. Discuss.

1. What kinds of people can provide references?

2. Who would you use as a reference?

3 WRITE

A BRAINSTORM. Think about your education and training, experience, and skills. Record your information in a chart like this.

Schools Attended	
Degrees or Certificates	
Places of Employment	
Titles and Responsibilities	
Achievements and Awards	
Skills and Abilities	
Personal Qualities	
Interests	

B Write an objective for a job that you would like.

C Write your own résumé. Use the information and the job objective that you wrote for Exercises A and B. Use Francis Kouadio's résumé as a model.

Can you...interpet and write a résumé? ☐

Use job-information sources

Listening and Speaking

1 BEFORE YOU LISTEN

GROUPS. Discuss the information in the Job-Search Tips. Have you ever followed any of the tips to find a job? What happened?

2 LISTEN

CD1 T20

A Lisa Wong is talking to her niece Angela at a family party. Listen to Lisa's advice on finding a job. What are some ways Lisa suggests that Angela could find a job?

CD1 T20

B Read the questions. Then listen to Lisa again. Circle the correct answers.

1. When did Lisa get her first job in the U.S.?
   a. twelve years ago
   b. twenty years ago
   c. twenty-five years ago

2. Where was Lisa's first job in the U.S.?
   a. in a newspaper office
   b. in a flower shop
   c. in a job-placement agency

3. How did Lisa find her job?
   a. by reading a newspaper ad
   b. by going into a store with a "Help Wanted" sign
   c. by networking

4. Who did Lisa talk to before she was hired?
   a. the manager
   b. the owner
   c. the secretary

C Read the Job-Search Tips again. According to Angela's aunt, what is the best way to find a job? Circle your answer.

Job-Search Tips

Are you getting tired of looking for work? Use one of these proven methods for finding a job.

- Look at want ads in the job section of your local newspaper.
- Go online. Do research on one of today's many job-related websites.
- Look for "Help Wanted" signs in your neighborhood.
- Take advantage of the services of a job-placement agency.
- Get information about possible jobs by networking (talking with people you know and trying to meet new people to help you find work).

Getting Started 5 minutes

1 BEFORE YOU LISTEN

GROUPS. Discuss the information...

- Read the job-search tips out loud while students read along silently.
- Explain vocabulary as needed, for example: *proven method: a method that is certain to work because it has been tried by many people;* and *want ads: the same as classified ads.*
- Group students. Give a time limit for discussion. While students are talking, walk around and provide help as needed.
- To wrap up, call on volunteers to share their answers with the class.

Culture Connection

Job searchers who sign up with a job placement agency do not have to pay a fee. The fee is paid by employers who use the agency to obtain lists of applicants.

Presentation 10 minutes

2 LISTEN

A **Lisa Wong is talking to...**

- Have students look at the photo. Ask: *Where are the speakers? How old are they? What's their relationship?*
- Tell students to listen specifically for Lisa's advice. Encourage them to take notes as they listen.
- Play CD 1, Track 20. If students need extra support, tell them they may read the Audio Script on page 285 as they listen.
- Call on a volunteer to answer the question. If students need a hint, ask: *How many suggestions did Lisa give?* (five) *What were they?* Write the suggestions on the board.

Answers: She could look in the newspaper, go online, go into businesses that have a "Help Wanted" sign in the window, use a job placement agency, and network with family, friends, and neighbors.

Teaching Tip

Encourage students to take notes whenever they listen. Explain that when they take notes, they shouldn't try to write every word. Instead, they should write down the key words that make up a message, such as nouns, verbs, and adjectives.

Controlled Practice 20 minutes

B **Read the questions. Then listen...**

- Have students read the questions silently and predict the answers.
- Play Track 20 again.
- Check answers. Call on students to read the questions and answers. If a student makes a mistake, ask the class: *Do you agree?* or *Is that correct?*
- If students are having difficulty with one question, replay the segment of the listening passage that answers the question. Have students repeat what they heard, then answer the question again.

C **Read the Job-Search Tips...**

- Give students time, if necessary, to reread the tips and select their answer.
- Have a volunteer answer the question.

Expansion: Speaking Practice for 2C

- Ask: *Do you agree that networking is the best way to find a job?* Have volunteers share their opinions.

Lesson 4 Use job-information sources

3 CONVERSATION

A GROUPS. Discuss.

- Form cross-ability groups. Make sure each group has a reporter.
- Have reporters share their group's answers. Write them on the board.

Possible answers: 1. the salary, hours, and responsibilities 2. newpaper ad, company website, other employees of the company, the company's personnel office, a career placement service

B Angela is talking to her neighbor...

- Play CD 1, Track 21. Have students listen and read along silently.
- *Optional:* Have above-level students listen with their books closed.
- Check comprehension. Ask: *How has Angela sent her résumé?* (online) *Has she gotten any responses?* (no) *What does Harold suggest?* (going to an employment agency and getting help at the library) *What is Angela going to do?* (She's going to go to the library to use their computers.)

4 PRACTICE

A PAIRS. Practice the conversation.

- Form cross-ability pairs and have students take turns reading each role.
- Have students switch partners and practice again.
- Walk around and listen as students are practicing. Provide help as needed.
- Ask volunteers to perform the conversation.

Communicative Practice   25 minutes

B ROLE PLAY. PAIRS. Role-play a conversation...

Teaching Tip

While pairs are performing, use the scoring rubric for speaking on page T-xiii to evaluate each student's vocabulary, grammar, fluency, and how well he or she completes the task.

- Have students reread the Job-Search Tips on page 32, if necessary.
- Model the activity with an above-level student. Play the role of Harold.
- Form cross-ability pairs. Tell them to follow the conversation in Exercise 3B, replacing Harold's suggestions with the information they choose.
- Give a time limit. Walk around and provide help as needed.
- Have volunteers role-play their conversation.

■■ MULTILEVEL INSTRUCTION for 4B

Cross-ability Ask the higher-level student to play Harold and to give at least three suggestions.

C MAKE IT PERSONAL. GROUPS. Discuss...

- Share one of your experiences with job-hunting and say whether or not you were successful.
- Form cross-ability groups and give students a time limit for talking.
- Encourage students to use infinitives and gerunds.
- Walk around while students are talking and provide help as needed.
- Take notes on errors with infinitives and gerunds.
- Call on volunteers to share their experience with the class.
- To wrap up, go over errors with infinitives and gerunds. Say the incorrect forms you heard. Have the class correct them.

Community Building

If your school has a job placement office, invite one of the counselors to come speak to your class. Have the class choose the topic of the visit (for example, how to use the Internet to search for jobs). Before the counselor's visit, have students prepare questions they would like to ask.

Extra Practice

Interactive Practice

A GROUPS. Discuss.

1. What kinds of information might you want to learn about a job before applying?
2. Where can you get information about a job before you apply?

CD1 T21

B Angela is talking to her neighbor Harold. Listen and read.

Harold: Hi, Angela. How's your job-hunt going?

Angela: It's going OK. I've been sending my résumé out online, but I haven't heard back from anyone yet.

Harold: Have you thought about going to an employment agency?

Angela: Yeah, but I don't want to pay to get a job.

Harold: But you don't pay! The employer usually pays!

Angela: Really? That's great. I'll definitely try that then!

Harold: Also, what about getting help at the library? I think they give job-search workshops. Maybe they can give you some ideas.

Angela: That would be a big help. I was planning on going to the library anyway to use their computers. I'll check it out.

4 PRACTICE

A PAIRS. Practice the conversation.

B ROLE PLAY. PAIRS. Role-play a conversation between a person looking for a job and a friend who is suggesting ideas for finding a job. Use the Job-Search Tips on page 32. Use the ideas below for places to get help.

> community career center   job fair   library   school

C MAKE IT PERSONAL. GROUPS. Discuss your experiences with job-hunting. What did you do to find a job? Were you successful?

Discuss job-related skills and abilities

Grammar

Gerunds as objects of preposition

I'm **thinking about** *applying for* a position at a hair salon.

I was **worried about** *not having* enough money to live on.

Adjective + Preposition		Verb + Preposition	
capable of	interested in	believe in	plan on
good at	excited about	choose between	think about

Grammar Watch

- Use a gerund (verb + *-ing*)—not an infinitive (*to* + base form of verb)—after a preposition.
- *See page 281 for a list of verbs + prepositions and for a list of adjectives + prepositions.*

1 PRACTICE

A Read the conversation between friends. Underline the prepositions. Circle the gerunds.

Carmen: What's the matter? You look worried. Are you concerned about (getting) a job?

Min-Ji: Yes. I didn't plan on (looking) for work for so long. I'm beginning to wonder if I'll ever find a job! And I'm getting tired of (going) on interviews.

Carmen: I know. It's not much fun.

Min-Ji: I'd be excited about (taking) any job, even a low-paying one, as long as it's something I'd enjoy doing. My friend Ben told me about a position as a sales representative for a pharmaceutical company. I'm really interested in (finding) out more about it.

Carmen: That would be a good job for you. You'd be good at (selling.)

B Complete the conversation. Use gerunds.

Edith: Thanks for ____letting____ me know about the teacher assistant job.
(let)

Kevin: I'm glad you're interested in ____applying____ for it. You've been talking about
(apply)

____going____ back to school to become a teacher for a long time.
(go)

Edith: I'm not looking forward to ____calling____ the school office to get more
(call)

information about the job. I'm terrible at ____talking____ to strangers. I'm always
(talk)

concerned about ____not making____ a good impression.
(not make)

Kevin: You'll be fine. The first person that you'll talk to is the secretary, Mrs. Leshem.

Don't be afraid of ____asking____ her anything you want. She's really nice.
(ask)

Discuss job-related skills and abilities

Getting Started   5 minutes

- Say: *You've learned about infinitives and gerunds after verbs. In this lesson you'll learn about gerunds that are the object of a preposition.*

- Review *preposition* and *object of the preposition.* Explain: *Prepositions are words such as in, on, of, about, and* between. *The object of a preposition is a noun or noun phrase that comes after a preposition.*

- On the board, write: *I'm not interested in watching sports on television.* Explain: *In this sentence, the object of the preposition* in *is the gerund* watching.

- Copy the sentences from the grammar chart onto the board.

- Point to each sentence and ask the class: *What is the preposition? What is the object of the preposition?* Circle the preposition and underline the object of the preposition in each sentence.

Presentation   15 minutes

Gerunds as objects of prepositions

- Read the first Grammar Watch note. Point to the first sentence on the board and ask: *Can we say: I'm thinking about to apply for a position at a hair salon?* (No. Use a gerund after a preposition.)

- Draw a two-column chart on the board with the headings *Adjective + Preposition* and *Verb + Preposition.*

- Say: *Sometimes the gerund comes after a verb and a preposition. Other times the gerund comes after an adjective and a preposition.* Point to the example sentences. Ask: *Is this an adjective + preposition phrase or a verb + preposition phrase?* Elicit the correct response from the class and write the phrases (*thinking about, worried about*) under the correct headings.

- Read the adjective + preposition and verb + preposition phrases in the grammar chart and have the class repeat.

- Read the second Grammar Watch note. Before students look at the lists on page 281, ask them if they can think of other adjective + preposition or verb + preposition phrases to add to the two lists on the board.

Expansion: Grammar Practice

- Play a game. Divide the class into groups of eight, if possible.

- Have the students in each group take turns coming to the board to write sentences using the phrases in the grammar chart. Each student in a group can write only one sentence.

- Give a time limit. Go over the sentences and make necessary corrections. The group that comes up with the most correct sentences wins.

Controlled Practice   20 minutes

1   PRACTICE

A Read the conversation between...

- Read the first line of the dialogue. Ask: *Do you see a gerund? What phrase does it come after?* Write *concerned about getting* on the board.

- Have students complete the exercise alone. Walk around and provide help as needed.

- Check answers. Choose students to read the lines of dialogue and say which phrases they underlined.

- Pair students and have them practice reading the dialogue.

B Complete the conversation. Use...

- Have students work alone or in pairs to complete the exercise.

- While students are working, walk around and provide help as needed.

- Have a pair of students read the dialogue. Write the answers on the board. If there is a mistake, point to it and ask the class: *Is this correct?* or *Do you agree?* Make corrections as needed.

Expansion: Grammar Practice

- Have students write sentences using five verb + preposition phrases and five adjective + preposition phrases, all followed by gerunds. Above-level students can write more.

Lesson 5 Discuss job-related skills and abilities

2 PRACTICE

Complete each conversation. Use...

- Read the phrases in the box.
- Have an above-level student read item 1 with you. Make sure students understand that they need to write gerunds.
- Have students work in pairs.
- Give a time limit. Walk around and provide help as needed.
- Have pairs of students read the conversations. Write the answers on the board. Make corrections as needed.

Communicative Practice   20 minutes

Show what you know!

STEP 1. Choose a job. Complete...

- Have students work alone or with a partner to think of a job and complete the sentences.
- *Optional:* You may want to brainstorm as a class and write job titles on the board to help students choose.

STEP 2. GROUPS. Discuss the jobs you chose.

- Form similar-ability groups. Have each group select a timekeeper and a reporter.
- Model the activity by talking about your job, for example, *A teacher . . . must be good at explaining ideas; is responsible for checking students' progress; is used to making lesson plans; sometimes worries about not having enough time.*

- Give a time limit. Remind students to use gerunds, when possible.
- Walk around and provide help as needed.
- Have the reporter from each group share the group's sentences.

■ MULTILEVEL INSTRUCTION for Show what you know!

Pre-level Have groups choose one job and complete the exercise together.

Above-level Have each student in the group choose a different job, complete the sentences, and share ideas with the group.

■ Expansion: Speaking Practice

- Write the following phrases on the board: *be good at, believe in, be capable of,* and *care about.*
- Choose a somewhat uncommon job, for example, dog walker, lifeguard, or food taster, and have students use the phrases to talk about the qualifications or skills needed for the job, for example: *A dog walker must be good at controlling dogs. A lifeguard must be capable of rescuing people.*

Progress Check

Can you . . . discuss job-related skills and abilities?

Say: *We have practiced talking about job-related skills and abilities. Now, look at the question at the bottom of the page. Can you discuss job-related skills and abilities? Write a checkmark in the box.*

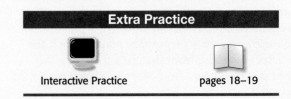

Extra Practice	
Interactive Practice	pages 18–19

PRACTICE

Complete each conversation. Use each phrase in the box once. Use gerunds.

> answer questions about benefits
> ~~apply for the teacher assistant job~~
> get your application materials
>
> not have a certificate
> send my application and résumé today
> solve problems

1. **Margaret:** Hello. I'm interested in _applying for the teacher assistant job_.

   Receptionist: OK. Please fill out this application.

2. **Antonio:** I want to apply for a job as an auto mechanic, but I'm worried about
   _____ not having a certificate _____. Do I need to get training?

   Receptionist: Yes. You need a Certificate of Completion from a vocational training

   program for a job with us.

3. **Interviewer:** If you're good at _____ solving problems _____ and have a

   desire to learn, we'll give you on-the-job training.

   Fernando: That's great. Thanks.

4. **Ibrahim:** I'd like to discuss the benefits the company offers.

   Receptionist: I'm sorry. You'll have to talk to Joan Leshem, but she's away from her

   desk. She's responsible for _____ answering questions about benefits _____.

5. **Receptionist:** You can go to our website and get the job application there.

   Silvio: Thank you. I'm planning on _____ sending my application and résumé today _____.

   Receptionist: We look forward to _____ getting your application materials _____.

Show what you know! Discuss job-related skills and abilities

STEP 1. Choose a job. Complete the sentences about the job you chose.

A/An _____
       (name of job)

- must be good at _____.
- is responsible for _____.
- is used to _____.
- sometimes worries about _____.

STEP 2. GROUPS. Discuss the jobs you choose.

*Can you...*discuss job-related skills and abilities? ☐

Reading

1 BEFORE YOU READ

A CLASS. Discuss. What is the meaning of the word *discrimination*? What types of discrimination might occur at work?

B GROUPS. Who decides which questions employers can and cannot ask during a job interview?

C Read the title and the headings for each section of the article. Predict. What is the main idea of the article?

2 READ

CD1 T22

Listen and read the article. Was your prediction about the main idea correct? What is a problem that sometimes happens at job interviews?

http://www.getandkeepajob.com

Get and Keep a Job   Home   Interviews   Résumés

Do I Really Have to Answer That?

Imagine this. You're at a job interview. You're nervous, but everything is going well. Then the employer asks, "I see you're not wearing a wedding ring. Are you planning to get married soon?"

For years, job applicants have complained about employers who ask for information that isn't related to work skills or experience, such as the question above about marital status. Here's what the experts say about questions that are too personal and maybe even **illegal**.

Interview Do's and Don'ts

U.S. **anti-discrimination** laws forbid some questions but allow others. For example, an interviewer cannot ask, "How long have you lived in the U.S.?" But she can ask, "What is your current address and phone number?" It's against the law to ask, "How much do you weigh?" Instead, an interviewer should explain a job's physical requirements and find out if you're capable of doing the work.

Other questions, such as "If you could be any animal, what animal would you like to be?" or "What's your favorite book?" are legal but shouldn't be part of an interview. They confuse applicants and don't relate directly to worker qualifications.

Answers to Inappropriate Questions

So what should you do if you find yourself in front of an interviewer who is asking **inappropriate** questions?

Some people answer them because they feel it's the best way to get a job. Job experts recommend that applicants respond to every question—but with information that shows they can meet the job requirements. For example, a good reply to "Do you live far from here?" is "I'm a responsible employee. I always come to work on time." Applicants who refuse to answer illegal and inappropriate questions should know that the company probably won't offer them a position, but in the end, it might not be the best place to work.

Before you decide what to do, ask yourself two questions: "How much do I want the job?" and "What kind of boss am I looking for?"

Read about job interview questions

Getting Started   5 minutes

1 BEFORE YOU READ

A CLASS. **Discuss. What is the meaning...**

- Write the word *discrimination* on the board.
- Group students. Tell them not only to define discrimination but also to think of examples.
- Give a time limit. Walk around and provide help as needed.
- Call on students to define *discrimination* and give examples. Write their ideas on the board.

Possible answers: Some types of discrimination that might occur at work are: not hiring a person because of his or her ethnic background, not promoting a person because of his or her gender or age.

> ### Language Note
>
> *Discrimination* is the unfair treatment of a person or group because of their race, religion, color, age, social class, gender, marital status, sexual orientation, or disability.

B GROUPS. **Who decides which questions...**

- Ask: *Do you think it's legal in a job interview to ask someone how old he or she is?* Poll the class and have students explain their opinions.
- Explain that according to U.S. law, it's illegal to ask certain questions in a job interview, for example, it is illegal to ask people how old they are. Ask the class: *Can you think of other questions that are illegal to ask?*

> ### Culture Connection
>
> The following are questions an employer can legally ask: *Do you have a green card? Which languages do you speak? Are you over the age of eighteen? What hours can you work? How many days of work did you miss last year?* In contrast, it is illegal to ask the following questions: *Are you a U.S. citizen? What is your native language? How old are you? Do you have children? Do you have any health problems?*

C **Read the title and the headings...**

- Define vocabulary as needed: *do's and don'ts: things people should and should not do; inappropriate: not fitting, suitable, or correct (behavior)*
- Have volunteers say their predictions about the main idea. Write them on the board. Ask the class if they agree.

Answer: The article is about what to do in a job interview if an interviewer asks questions that are illegal or inappropriate.

Presentation   15 minutes

2 READ

Listen and read the article.

- Play CD 1, Track 22. Ask students to listen to and read along with the article.
- When students have finished reading, point to students' predictions on the board and ask: *Were your predictions correct?* Have a volunteer restate the main idea.
- Read the second question in the directions. To answer this question, students must read the second heading in the article and infer the answer. If students are having difficulty, have them reread the heading. Then ask the question again.

Answer: The interviewer sometimes asks questions that are inappropriate.

Expansion: Speaking Practice

- Some interview questions are legal but nevertheless inappropriate. An example from the reading is *What's your favorite book?* Questions about an interviewee's clothing, hairstyle, etc. are also inappropriate. Ask students to give additional examples of inappropriate interview questions.

Controlled Practice   20 minutes

3   CHECK YOUR UNDERSTANDING

Ⓐ Complete the sentences. Circle...

- Have students compare answers with a partner.
- Call on students to read the questions and answers. Write the answers on the board.

Reading Skill: **Using Details to Understand Important Ideas**

- Read the Reading Skill.
- Define details. Say: *Details are pieces of information that support or develop a main idea so that we can understand it better. Facts, examples, reasons, stories, numbers, and names are all types of details.*

Ⓑ Read the Reading Skill. Then circle...

- Read choice a. Ask: *Does the writer tell any stories about himself or herself?* Give students time to look back at the article and find the answer (*no*).
- Repeat with the remaining choices. Have students underline examples of interview questions.

  Expansion: Reading Practice for 3B

- Have students make two lists in their notebooks: examples of appropriate questions from the reading and examples of inappropriate questions.

Ⓒ GROUPS. Discuss. Why is it important...

- Form cross-ability groups.
- Have the groups share their answers.

4   WORD WORK

A prefix is a group of letters...

- Write on the board: *illegal, inappropriate,* and *anti-discrimination.*
- Read item 1 and have students answer chorally.
- Read item 2 and have students answer chorally.

  Expansion: Word Work

- Have students think of other words beginning with the prefixes *il-, in-,* and *anti-*. Write them on the board and define if necessary.

Communicative Practice   20 minutes

Show what you know!

STEP 1. Think about job interviews in...

- Have students from the same country of origin work together, if possible.
- Give a time limit for talking. Circulate and provide help as needed.

  MULTILEVEL INSTRUCTION for STEP 1
  Pre-level Have students write one question employers can ask and one they can't.
  Above-level Have students write three or more questions employers can and can't ask.

STEP 2. GROUPS. Discuss. How are...

- If possible, form groups with students from different countries of origin.
- Model a possible response, for example, *In the U.S., an employer can't ask you if you're married, but in [country] they can.*
- Make a two-column chart on the board with the headings *Similar* and *Different*. Have students make a similar chart in their notebooks.
- As students are talking, encourage them to take notes in their chart.
- To wrap up, have students use their notes to make sentences about similarities and differences between job interviews the U.S. and their countries of origin. Take notes on their sentences in the chart on the board.

Extra Practice

Interactive Practice   pages 20–21

A **Complete the sentences. Circle the correct answers.**

1. An interviewer cannot ask about your _____.
    a. (marital status)   b. address   c. work skills

2. U.S. anti-discrimination laws say that an interviewer can ask _____.
    a. how long you've been in the U.S.   c. (what kind of experience you have
    b. how much you weigh

3. Employment specialists suggest that applicants _____ during an interview.
    a. (answer all the questions   c. ask the interviewer two questions
    b. complain about illegal questions

B **Read the Reading Skill. Then circle the answer that best completes the statement.**

The author of the article gives details by _____.

a. telling personal stories   c. providing numbers
b. using names of people and places d. (including examples)

> **Reading Skill:** Using Details to Understand Important Ideas
>
> Look for details to help you understand an author's ideas more completely.

C **GROUPS. Discuss. Why is it important for job applicants to ask themselves "How much do I want the job?" and "What kind of boss am I looking for?"**

A prefix is a group of letters added to the beginning of a word to change its meaning. Look at the boldfaced words in the article. Complete the sentences.

1. The prefixes *il-* in *illegal* and *in-* in *inappropriate* mean _____ not _____.

2. The prefix *anti-* in *anti-discrimination* means _____ against _____.

Show what you know!   Discuss job-interview questions

STEP 1. Think about job interviews in your country. List questions employers can and can't ask.

STEP 2. GROUPS. Discuss. How are the interview dos and don'ts in the U.S. similar to and different from those in your country?

Listening and Speaking

1 BEFORE YOU LISTEN

CLASS. Discuss.

1. What questions do employers ask applicants during a job interview?
2. Have you ever been on a job interview? What questions were you asked?

2 LISTEN

CD1 T23

A 🔊 **Kyong-Mo Lee is interviewing Steve Santos for a job at Capital Express Delivery Services. Listen. What position is Steve applying for?**

CD1 T23

B 🔊 **Read the questions. Listen to the job interview again. Then answer the questions.**

1. What is Steve's job now?
   a. truck driver
   b. supermarket manager
   c. dispatcher

2. What kind of license does he have?
   a. chauffeur's license
   b. bus driver's license
   c. commercial driver's license

3. What is one reason that Steve wants to leave his job at Trends Supermarket?
   a. He wants a job closer to home.
   b. He wants different work hours.
   c. He wants more money.

4. What is one reason that Steve wants to be a dispatcher some day?
   a. He wants to work indoors.
   b. He enjoys solving problems.
   c. He is tired of his current job.

C **GROUPS. Discuss. Do you think Steve made a good impression? Why or why not?**

Getting Started   5 minutes

1 BEFORE YOU LISTEN

CLASS. **Discuss.**

- Read the first question. Elicit students' answers and write them on the board.

Possible answers: What is your previous experience? Where have you worked before? Are you a team player? Why do you want to work here? How did you hear about this job? What shift do you want to work? Can you use a computer?

- Read the second question. Call on volunteers to answer. If students mention a question that is written on the board, place a checkmark next to the question.

Presentation   10 minutes

2 LISTEN

🅐 💿 **Kyong-Mo Lee is interviewing...**

- Have students look at the photo. Ask: *How does Kyong-Mo Lee look? What is his job? How does Steve look? Is this a good way to dress for a job interview?*
- Play CD 1, Track 23. If students need extra support, tell them they may read the Audio Script as they listen.
- Have a student answer the question. Ask the class: *Do you agree?*

Answer: Steve is applying for a job as a truck driver.

> **Culture Connection**
>
> Personal appearance is important in making a good impression at a job interview. Applicants are expected to dress neatly in clothing appropriate for the job. Clothing should be clean and ironed. Both women and men should avoid loud colors, revealing clothing, or heavy cologne. Women should wear minimal jewelry and makeup.

Controlled Practice   5 minutes

🅑 💿 **Read the questions. Listen...**

- Have students read the questions before listening. Encourage them to predict the answers.
- Play Track 23 again. Have students listen and answer the questions.
- Have students compare answers with a partner.
- Check answers. Call on students to read each question and answer. Write the answers on the board.

Communicative Practice   10 minutes

🅒 GROUPS. **Discuss. Do you think...**

- Define *to make a good impression.* Say: *To make a good impression is to cause somebody to have positive ideas about you.*
- Form similar-ability groups. Have each group choose a reporter.
- Give a time limit for discussion.
- Play Track 23 again, if necessary. Have students listen specifically for characteristics that would cause Steve to make a good (or bad) impression. Have students take notes.
- Have each group's reporter share their group's answers with the class. Write Steve's characteristics on the board.

▬ **MULTILEVEL INSTRUCTION for 2C**

Pre-level Have students give one reason why Steve made a good (or bad) impression.

Above-level Have students give all the reasons why Steve made a good (or bad) impression.

▬ **Expansion: Speaking Practice for 2C**

- Form cross-ability pairs. Have students look at the list of characteristics on the board and say which ones they possess.
- Provide a model. For example, *Steve is good with technology. I'm good with technology, too.*
- Have each student report on one characteristic that he or she shares with Steve.

Presentation   5 minutes

3 CONVERSATION

Pronunciation Watch

- Write a familiar multisyllabic name on the board. Ask the class: *How do you say this name?* After the class answers, repeat the name and clap your hands on the stressed syllables. Then say: *What if I say it like this?* Repeat the name but clap and stress the wrong syllables. (Students will probably laugh.)
- Read the Pronunciation Watch note.
- Write on the board the names of famous people. Say the names with incorrect stress. Have the class repeat the names with correct stress.

Teaching Tip

When speaking to students, try to use natural pronunciation. Avoid overenunciating or slowing down too much. If it is necessary to simplify your speech, use simpler vocabulary and syntax and avoid slang.

A 🔘 **Listen to the words. Notice...**

- Play CD 1, Track 24. Have students listen.
- Play Track 24 again. Have students listen and repeat.

Controlled Practice   10 minutes

B 🔘 **Listen to these words. Put...**

- Copy all six words onto the board. Point to *control*. Ask: *How do we pronounce this word?* Say the word and place a dot over the second syllable.
- Play CD 1, Track 25. Have students listen and complete the exercise.
- Have volunteers come to the board to put a dot over the stressed syllable.
- Call on students to say the words.

C 🔘 **Steve Santos's job interview...**

- Play CD 1, Track 26. Have students listen and read along silently.
- Ask: *What is the most important thing Steve has learned? Is Steve a calm person?*

4 PRACTICE

A **PAIRS. Practice the conversation.**

- Form cross-ability pairs and have students take turns reading each role.
- Have students switch partners and practice again.
- Walk around and listen as students are practicing. Take notes on errors with word stress.
- Say the incorrect forms you wrote in your notes. Have the class repeat them correctly.
- Ask volunteers to perform the conversation.

Communicative Practice   15 minutes

B **PAIRS. Discuss.**

- Walk around and provide help as needed.
- Read each question. Call on volunteers to answer.

Teaching Tip

Encourage students to offer contrasting opinions and answers by asking questions such as *Who has a different answer?* or *Who disagrees?*

C **ROLE PLAY. PAIRS. Role-play...**

Teaching Tip

While pairs are performing role plays, use the scoring rubric for speaking on page T-xiii to evaluate each student's vocabulary, grammar, fluency, and how well he or she completes the task. You may want to review the completed rubric with the students.

- Form similar-ability pairs. Have students switch roles and practice again.
- Have volunteers role-play their conversation.

Extra Practice

Interactive Practice

3 CONVERSATION

CD1 T24

A 💿 **Listen to the words. Notice the stressed syllable in each word. Then listen again and repeat.**

Pronunciation Watch

In words with more than one syllable, one syllable is stressed. The stressed syllable sounds louder than other syllables and has a strong, clear vowel sound.

•　　　　　　　•　　　　　　•　　　　　　•
general　　　im**por**tant　　　de**liv**ery　　　**su**permarket

CD1 T25

B 💿 **Listen to these words. Put a dot (•) over the stressed syllable.**

　　•　　　　　　•　　　　　　　•　　　　　•　　　　　　　•　　　　　　•
1. control　　2. interesting　　3. experience　　4. interview　　5. responsible　　6. absolutely

CD1 T26

C 💿 **Steve Santos's job interview with Kyung-Mo Lee continues. Listen and read.**

Mr. Lee:　I have a general question. What's the most important thing you've learned from your work experience?

Mr. Santos:　Oh, that's an interesting question! Let me think. I've learned a lot! Sometimes things happen that you don't expect; for example, when there's bad weather or something goes wrong with a delivery. I learned a long time ago that I can't control everything—especially not the weather—but I can control my response. There's no reason to get upset with things you can't control.

Mr. Lee:　So, do you think you stay calm under pressure?

Mr. Santos:　Yes. Absolutely. Everyone who knows me thinks I'm a really calm person.

4 PRACTICE

A PAIRS. **Practice the conversation.**

B PAIRS. **Discuss.**

1. Do you think Mr. Santos gave a good answer to Mr. Lee's question about what he's learned from his work experience? Why or why not?

2. Imagine that you are being interviewed for a job. How would you answer that question?

C ROLE PLAY. PAIRS. **Role-play a job interview.**

Student A: You are the interviewer. Ask, "What's the most important thing you've learned from your work experience?"

Student B: You are the job applicant. Use the answer you discussed in Exercise B.

Grammar

Simple past and present perfect		
	Simple past	Present perfect
	Steve **learned** a long time ago that he can't control everything.	Steve **has learned** a lot from his work experience.
	Steve **worked** at Grand Supermarkets from 2001 to 2006.	Steve **has worked** for Trends Supermarkets since 2006.
	When **did** you **start** working there?	How long **have** you **been** a driver?

········ **Grammar Watch**

- Use the simple past for actions, feelings, or situations that occurred at a specific time in the past.
- Use the present perfect for actions, feelings, or situations that occurred at an indefinite time in the past.
- Use the present perfect with *for* or *since* to show that an action, feeling, or situation started in the past and continues up to now.

1 PRACTICE

A Read the information about Li's work history. Underline six examples of the simple past. Circle five more examples of the present perfect.

I've lived in the U.S. since 2000, and I've been lucky with finding work. I've had a few different jobs at CDS Drugtores. My first job there was as a stock clerk. Next I worked as a cashier. But then I got a job in the pharmacy department, and I really liked it. I've always liked working with people and I was good in chemistry in school, so I decided to become a pharmacist. I've just enrolled in a program at the university. I haven't started my classes yet, but I hope to get a job as a pharmacist in the future.

B Two managers are talking about an employee. Complete the sentences. Use the present perfect.

Bob: How long ___has Dan worked___ here?
                    (Dan/work)

Jim: Since 2006. He ___has been___ one of our best employees since he
                    (be)

started here. He won the Employee of the Month award three times in the

last three years.

Bob: Is it true that he ___has had___ the highest sales in the company for
                    (have)

the last two years?

Jim: Yes, and he's also very dependable. He ___hasn't missed___ a day's work in
                    (not miss)

the last two years. And he's easygoing and calm. He ___has never raised___
                    (never/raise)

his voice.

Getting Started   5 minutes

- Say: *In this lesson we're going to learn about the simple past and the present perfect.*

- Ask the class: *Who has a job?* Select a student who raised his or her hand and ask: *When did you start your job?* Write the student's answer on the board. For example, *[John] started his job in March 2007.* Underline *started*. Circle *March 2007*.

- Ask the class: *How long has [John] had his job?* Elicit an answer with *for* and write it on the board, for example, *[John] has had his job for [two] years.* Underline *has had*. Circle *for*.

- Ask *[John]: Have you thought about getting another job?* Write: *[John] has thought about getting another job.* Underline *has thought*.

- To reinforce, ask another student the same set of questions.

Presentation   15 minutes

Simple past and present perfect

- Read the first Grammar Watch note. Point to the sentence *[John] started his job in March 2007.* Ask: *When did [John] start his job?* (March 2007). Explain: *If we know the specific time when something happened, we use the simple past.*

- Read the second note. Point to the sentence *[John] has thought about getting another job.* Ask: *Do we know when [John] thought about getting another job?* (no) Explain: *We use the present perfect when we don't know when something happened in the past. The time is indefinite.*

- Read the third note. Point to the sentence *[John] has had his job for [two] years.* Ask: *Does [John] have his job now?* (yes). Explain: *The action started in the past and continues until now, so we use the present perfect.*

- Read the sentences in the grammar chart. After each sentence, ask: *Why do we use the simple past (present perfect)?* Have students restate the Grammar Watch rules.

Language Note

In some languages it is correct to say the equivalent of *He has seen a doctor this morning.* Explain that in English the simple past must be used with a specific time in the past.

- Write on the board: *say, walk, learn,* and *write.* Elicit the past participle of each verb (*said, walked, learned,* and *written*).

- Have the class conjugate an irregular verb in the present perfect. For example, using the verb *write,* follow the pattern: T: *I have written. You . . .* Ss: *have written.* T: *He or she . . .* Ss: *has written.*

- Do another conjugation in the negative, for example, *I haven't written. You haven't written,* etc.

Expansion: Grammar Practice

- Explain that English verbs have three forms: present, past, and past participle. Sometimes the past and past participle are the same, for example, *I worked, I have worked.* Sometimes the past and past participle are different, for example, *I saw, I have seen.*

Controlled Practice   20 minutes

1   PRACTICE

A   Read the information about...

- Write the first sentence on the board. Ask: *How many verbs does the sentence have? What are they? Are they in the simple present or present perfect?*

- Circle *'ve lived* and *'ve been.* Ask: *Why is the present perfect correct in this sentence?* (The first verb shows an action that started in the past and continues up to now. The second verb shows a situation that occurred at an indefinite time in the past.)

- Have students complete the exercise alone.

- Check answers. On the board, write the following headings: *Simple past* and *Present perfect.* Call on students to read the sentences in the passage and say which words they underlined or circled.

- Write the verbs under the correct headings. Make corrections as needed.

B   Two managers are talking...

- Have students work alone or in pairs.

- While students are working, walk around and provide help as needed.

- Check answers. Have two students read the dialogue. Write the verb forms on the board.

- Confirm answers by asking the class: *Is this correct? Why is the (simple past / present perfect) correct?*

2 PRACTICE

Unscramble the sentences. Put...

- Read item 1 with the class. Ask: *How do we decide which verb form to use?* (Check the time expression.)
- Have the class do item 2 together.
- Have students continue working alone or in pairs. Give a time limit. Walk around and provide help as needed.
- Check answers. Have six students write sentences for items 3 to 8 on the board. Have other students read the sentences and say if they are correct. If there is an error, elicit corrections from the class.

▬ Expansion: Speaking Practice for 2

- Have students "interview" Dan Miller, Raquel Hernandez, and Michael Shen from Exercise 2.
- Divide students into three groups. Assign a different "interviewee" to each group.
- Have each group write several interview questions for its interviewee, for example: (for Dan Miller) *How did you win your award?* (for Raquel Hernandez) *How did you injure your back?* (for Michael Shen) *Why haven't you returned the interviewer's phone calls?*
- Bring the class together. Choose three above-level students to play the roles of Dan Miller, Raquel Hernandez, and Michael Shen.
- Have volunteers perform the interviews for the class.

Communicative Practice   20 minutes

Show what you know!

GROUPS. Discuss.

- Give a time limit for discussion.
- Walk around and provide help as needed.
- To wrap up, call on students to share their answers with the class.

▬ Expansion: Speaking Practice for Show what you know!

- Form cross-ability pairs to practice an interview. Have the lower-level student interview the higher-level student, using the questions in the box.
- Have volunteers perform the interview for the class.

Progress Check

Can you . . . describe previous work experience and duties?

Say: *We have practiced describing previous work experience and duties. Now look at the question at the bottom of the page. Can you describe previous work experience and duties? Write a checkmark in the box.*

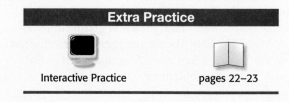

Extra Practice	
Interactive Practice	pages 22–23

PRACTICE

Unscramble the sentences. Put the words in order. Use the present perfect or the simple past. More than one order may be possible.

Dan Miller

1. (win / last week / Dan / his third Employee of the Month Award)

   Dan won his third Employee of the Month Award last week.

2. (since 2006 / an outstanding employee / Dan / be)

   Dan has been an outstanding employee since 2006.

Raquel Hernandez

3. (her back / Raquel/ two months ago / injure)

   Raquel injured her back two months ago.

4. (since her injury occurred / She / work / not)

   She hasn't worked since her injury occurred. (*or* She has not worked . . .)

5. (I / for five years / Raquel / know)

   I've known Raquel for five years. (*or* I have known . . .)

Michael Shen

6. (arrive late for his interview / Michael / last week)

   Michael arrived late for his interview last week.

7. (interested in the job / He / during the interview / seem/not)

   He didn't seem interested in the job during the interview. (*or* He did not seem . . .)

8. (He / since last Tuesday / not / the interviewer's phone calls / return)

   He hasn't returned the interviewer's phone calls since last Tuesday. (*or* He has not returned . . .)

Show what you know!   Describe previous work experience and duties

GROUPS. Discuss.

1. What is your current job? How long have you had the job?
2. What other jobs have you had?
3. Which job has been the best job for you? Why?

Can you... describe previous work experiences and duties? ☐

Writing

1 BEFORE YOU WRITE

A CLASS. Discuss. What is the purpose of a cover letter? How is a cover letter different from a résumé?

B Read the writing model.

Writing Tip

Do not include unnecessary information in a cover letter.

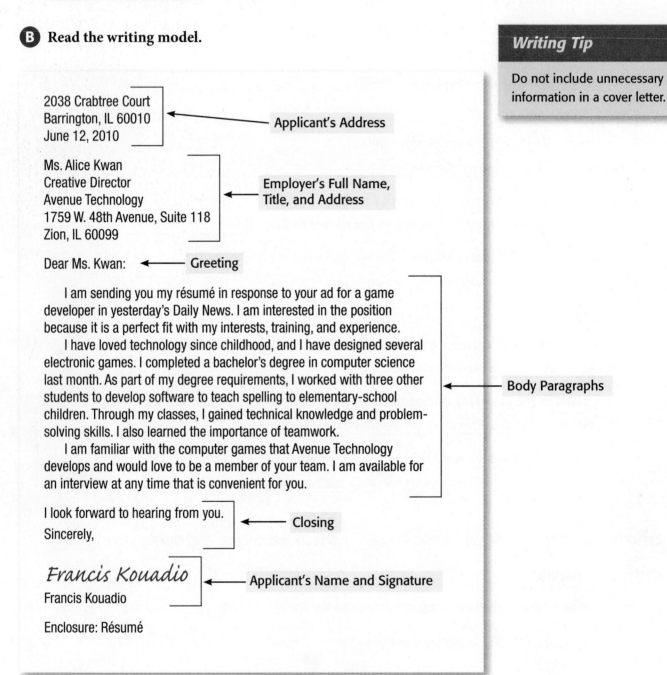

2038 Crabtree Court
Barrington, IL 60010 ← **Applicant's Address**
June 12, 2010

Ms. Alice Kwan
Creative Director
Avenue Technology ← **Employer's Full Name, Title, and Address**
1759 W. 48th Avenue, Suite 118
Zion, IL 60099

Dear Ms. Kwan: ← **Greeting**

I am sending you my résumé in response to your ad for a game developer in yesterday's Daily News. I am interested in the position because it is a perfect fit with my interests, training, and experience.

I have loved technology since childhood, and I have designed several electronic games. I completed a bachelor's degree in computer science last month. As part of my degree requirements, I worked with three other students to develop software to teach spelling to elementary-school children. Through my classes, I gained technical knowledge and problem-solving skills. I also learned the importance of teamwork. ← **Body Paragraphs**

I am familiar with the computer games that Avenue Technology develops and would love to be a member of your team. I am available for an interview at any time that is convenient for you.

I look forward to hearing from you. ← **Closing**
Sincerely,

Francis Kouadio ← **Applicant's Name and Signature**
Francis Kouadio

Enclosure: Résumé

Getting Started   5 minutes

1 BEFORE YOU WRITE

A CLASS. Discuss. What is the purpose of...

- On the board, write the following headings: *Résumé* and *Cover Letter*.
- Ask: *What information do we find in a résumé?* If necessary, have students look at the résumé on page 30 and name the parts. (*Objective, Qualifications, Related Experience,* and *Education*). Write them below the heading *Résumé* on the board.
- Point to *Cover Letter* and ask: *What is the purpose of a cover letter? What information is in a cover letter? How is a cover letter different from a résumé?* Write students' ideas on the board.

Possible answers: In general, the purpose of a cover letter is to get the employer's attention and make him or her see why you should be given a personal interview. A few ways in which a cover letter is different from a résumé: a résumé gives comprehensive information about a job applicant's qualifications, work experience, and education, while a cover letter emphasizes those things in an applicant's background that are relevant to the position he or she is seeking; a résumé usually takes a neutral tone, while a cover letter should reflect the applicant's personality and enthusiasm; a résumé uses incomplete sentences while a cover letter uses complete sentences and follows the rules of grammar and usage, etc.

- Ask: *Has anyone ever written a cover letter? What information did you include in it?*

Presentation   15 minutes

B Read the writing model.

- Tell the class they're going to read a cover letter from Francis Kouadio (whose model résumé they saw in Lesson 3).
- Hold up your book. Read the labels designating the parts of the cover letter (*applicant's address, employer's name,* etc.) and point to them in your book. Have students find them in their own books.
- Ask questions to clarify the content of each section. For example: *What information is in the applicant's address? Who is Alice Kwan? What is her title? What is the proper greeting to use in a cover letter? What are the two parts of the closing? Why does the applicant write his name twice?*
- Ask questions to focus students' attention on the format of the letter. For example: *Is the employer's name on the left or on the right? Which parts of the letter are double-spaced? Which parts are single-spaced? Which lines are indented? What punctuation comes after the greeting? After Sincerely?*
- Read the body of the letter out loud as students read silently.

Language Note

Always use *Ms.* when addressing a woman in the cover letter because it avoids the issue of marital status.

Writing Tip: **Cover Letter Content**

- Read the Writing Tip.
- Discuss what is meant by *unnecessary information.* Remind students that legally they are not required to give information about their race, religion, age, ethnicity, and so on.
- Ask: *What other information should not be included in the cover letter?* Elicit, for example, family information.

C **PAIRS. Answer the questions.**

- Form pairs or small groups. Encourage students to underline the parts of the cover letter that answer the questions.
- Check answers.

Answers: 1. The job is a perfect fit with his interests, training, and experience. 2. his résumé

D **What kind of information...**

- Reread the first paragraph with the whole class. Ask: *What information does the first paragraph contain? In general, what should you write in the first paragraph of a cover letter?* Do the same for each paragraph of the letter.
- Form cross-ability pairs. Tell pairs to reread the other paragraphs and write the kind of information that belongs in each.
- Call on students to share their answers. Write them on the board next to the numbers 1, *2*, and *3*.

Answers: The first paragraph of Francis Kouadio's letter tells what job he is applying for and how he learned about it. The second paragraph explains why he is interested in the position and describes the elements of his experience and education that make him well qualified for it. The third paragraph expresses his enthusiasm for the company and indicates that he is available for an interview.

Controlled Practice   20 minutes

2 **THINKING ON PAPER**

A **BRAINSTORM. Read the résumé that you...**

- If your class does not have Internet access, bring (or have students bring) newspapers to class and have students use the want ads to choose a job.
- Choose an ad to use as a model for Exercise B. Pretend that you are going to apply for this job.

B **Plan and organize the body paragraphs...**

- Copy the oval Y chart onto the board.
- Read the section heads out loud. Ask: *What does this mean?* Elicit examples of words and phrases for each category. Write them on the board.
- Read the ad you chose in Exercise A. Say: *I'm going to apply for this job.*
- Fill in the chart with your interests, education, and skills. (The information can be invented.)

- Have students copy the chart. Suggest that they write at least two items in each section.
- Have two or three volunteers write their charts on the board. Check them for appropriate language and make corrections as needed.
- Explain that students will use these notes to write the body of their cover letter.

Communicative Practice   20 minutes

3 **WRITE**

Write a cover letter for the job...

- Help students get organized. They will need the writing model on page 42, the outline of the body of the letter from Exercise 1D, their ad, and their notes.

Language Note

The language in a cover letter should be formal. It should not use slang or contain personal questions about the employer.

4 **CHECK YOUR WRITING**

- Read the questions in the checklist. Show how they correspond to the parts of the writing model.
- Have students read their letter and check off the items in the checklist.
- Collect papers and make corrections as needed in letter format, use of infinitives, gerunds, verb forms, and the contents of the letter.

Teaching Tip

You may want to collect student papers and provide feedback. Use the scoring rubric for writing on page T-xiv to evaluate each student's vocabulary, grammar, mechanics and how well he or she has completed the task. You may want to review the completed rubric with the students.

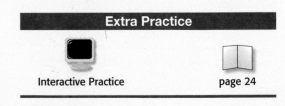

Extra Practice

Interactive Practice   page 24

C PAIRS. Answer the questions.

1. Why does Francis think he is the best person for the game developer position?

2. An *enclosure* is something inside an envelope (or an electronic file) along with a letter. What is the enclosure with Francis Kouadio's letter?

D What kind of information is in the first body paragraph of Francis Kouadio's cover letter? the second paragraph? the third paragraph?

2 THINKING ON PAPER

A BRAINSTORM. Read the résumé that you prepared for Exercise 3C on page 31. Then use a newspaper, the Internet, or your networking skills to find a job that you would like to apply for.

B Plan and organize the body paragraphs of a cover letter for the job you want. Organize your ideas in a chart like this.

Qualifications

Interests and Personal Qualities

Skills

Education and Experience

3 WRITE

Write a cover letter for the job you want to apply for. Use your brainstorming ideas and the information in your chart. Look at the writing model for an example.

Writing Tip

If you don't know the name of the person you are writing to, use *To Whom It May Concern:* as a greeting.

4 CHECK YOUR WRITING

☐ Did you include the date, your address, the employer's address, and your name and signature?

☐ Did you tell how you heard about the job?

☐ Did you explain why you think you're the best person for the job?

☐ Did you use correct capitalization, punctuation, and spelling?

1   REVIEW

For your grammar review, go to page 246.

2   ACT IT OUT   What do you say?

STEP 1. CLASS. Review what you learned on pages 30–31 about preparing a résumé.

STEP 2. ROLE PLAY. PAIRS. Role-play this situation. Use the résumé you wrote for Exercise 3C on page 31.

Student A: You are an employment specialist at a career center. You are meeting with a client who has visited you several times before. She brought her résumé today for you to look at. You are giving her advice on ways to improve it.

Student B: You are a jobseeker. You need help with your résumé, so you brought a copy of it to the career center. Ask the employment specialist for advice and suggestions.

3   READ AND REACT   Problem-solving

STEP 1. GROUPS. Read about Usman's problem.

Usman Amir has a job interview at 9:00 this morning. It is now 8:15. It will take him at least thirty minutes to drive to the interview. Usman needs an extra copy of his résumé to take to the interview, but he just discovered that his printer isn't working.

STEP 2. GROUPS. What is Usman's problem? Discuss a solution. List three things that he can do.

4   CONNECT

For your Planning for Learning, go to page 257.
For your Team Project, go to page 264.

Which goals can you check off? Go back to page 25.

 Go to the CD-ROM for more practice.

1 REVIEW

Turn to page 246 for the Grammar Review.

2 ACT IT OUT

STEP 1. CLASS. Review what you learned...

- Direct students to look back at pages 30 and 31. Call on volunteers to list what should be included on a résumé.

STEP 2. ROLE PLAY. PAIRS. Role-play...

- Have students look at the photo. Ask: *Where are the people? How are they dressed? What are they doing? What are they looking at? What is their relationship?*
- Read the role descriptions.
- Discuss with the class: *What kind of problem might Student B have with his or her résumé?* (the objective or another part is missing; the format is incorrect; the objective is not specific; the writer has listed only one or two qualifications; the qualifications are written as complete sentences; the experience section is not in chronological order, etc.)
- Model the role play with an above-level student. Play the role of Student A. You can begin like this: *Hello [name]. It's good to see you again. How can I help you today?*
- Form cross-ability pairs.
- Have students write out their dialogues. Walk around and provide help as needed.
- Tell students to practice out loud at least twice.
- Have volunteers perform their role play.

> **Teaching Tip**
>
> While pairs are performing, use the scoring rubric for speaking on page T-xiii to evaluate each student's vocabulary, grammar, fluency, and how well he or she completes the task.

3 READ AND REACT

STEP 1. GROUPS. Read about Usman's problem.

- Read while students follow along silently. To check comprehension, ask: *What is Usman's problem?*

STEP 2. GROUPS. What is Usman's problem?...

- Form cross-ability groups and have students choose a timekeeper, a note taker, and a reporter. The note taker writes down the group's solutions.
- Give a time limit for discussion.
- Have the reporter from each group share the group's solutions. Write them on the board.
- Have students vote on the best solution.

Possible answers: 1. He can phone the interviewer saying he will be late, then go to a copy shop to print the extra copy. 2. He can e-mail the résumé to the interviewer, then phone, explain his problem, and ask the interviewer to print out his résumé.

Expansion: Speaking Practice for STEP 2

- Form cross-ability pairs.
- Have students role-play a phone conversation between Usman and an employment specialist. Usman explains the problem with his résumé. The specialist suggests a solution, using the list on the board.
- Have volunteers perform their phone conversation.

4 CONNECT

Turn to page 257 for the Planning for Learning Activity and page 264 for the Team Project. See page T-xi for general notes about teaching these activities.

Progress Check

Which goals can you check off? Go back to page 25.

Ask students to turn to page 25 and check off any remaining goals they have reached. Call on students to say which goals they will practice outside of class.

 Go to the CD-ROM for more practice.

If your students need more practice with the vocabulary, grammar, and competencies in Unit 2, encourage them to review the activities on the CD-ROM.

3 Community Life

CD 1
Tracks 27–37

Interactive Practice
Unit 3

Workbook
Unit 3

Unit Overview

Goals
- See the list of goals on the facing page.

Grammar
- Participial adjectives
- *Wish* in the present and future
- Verb + object + infinitive

Pronunciation
- Pronunciation of unreleased final stop consonants
- Weak and blended pronunciation of *to*

Reading
- Read an article about community gardens
- *Reading Skill:* Making inferences

Writing
- Write a paragraph about your neighborhood

Life Skills
- Give and follow directions

Preview
- Say the unit title. Ask: *What do you think this unit will be about?*
- Hold up your book or have students look at their books. Set the context by asking the preview questions. You can also ask: *What do you see in the photo? What are the people doing? What kind of neighborhood is this? Does your neighborhood look like this?*

Unit Goals
- Point to the Unit Goals. Have students read them silently.
- Tell students they will be studying these goals in Unit 3.
- Say each goal and explain unfamiliar vocabulary as needed, for example, *festival: a large celebration; issues: problems or topics that people care about.*
- Tell students to circle one or more goals that are very important to them. Call on several volunteers to say the goals they circled.
- Write a checkmark (✓) on the board. Say: *We will come back to this page again. You will write a checkmark next to the goals you learned in this unit.*

Community Life

Preview

Read the title. What's important in a community? What's *most* important?

UNIT GOALS

- [ ] Talk about cultural festivals and traditions
- [ ] Describe feelings about a neighborhood
- [ ] Give and follow directions
- [ ] Describe community issues
- [ ] Talk about making changes in a community
- [ ] Discuss ways to improve a community
- [ ] Identify community problems
- [ ] Express feelings about a neighborhood

Listening and Speaking

1 BEFORE YOU LISTEN

CLASS. Look at the picture. What kind of festival do you think this is? Are festivals like this a tradition in your home country?

2 LISTEN

CD1 T27

A Mali Prem and Eric Torres are talking about a Thai Festival. Listen. Who is going to the festival?

CD1 T27

B Read the questions. Then listen to the conversation again. Circle the correct answers.

1. What does the festival celebrate?
   a. the first day of spring
   b. Thai Independence Day
   c. Thai New Year's Day

2. What does Mali say about the food at the festival?
   a. It's spicy.
   b. It's amazing.
   c. It's cheap.

3. What do some children do at the festival?
   a. play games
   b. drink water
   c. throw water

C GROUPS. What things are common in your culture that people from other cultures might find surprising?

Talk about cultural festivals and traditions

Getting Started
5 minutes

1 BEFORE YOU LISTEN

CLASS. Look at the picture. What kind...

- Hold up your book and point to the photo or have students look at their books. Read the questions and have volunteers answer.

Presentation
10 minutes

2 LISTEN

A 💿 **Mali Prem and Eric Torres...**

- Have students look at the photo. Ask: *Who are the speakers? Where are they from? How old are they? Where are they? What is their relationship?*
- Remind students to listen specifically for the answer to the question. It is not necessary to understand every word.
- Play CD 1, Track 27.
- Have students compare answers with a classmate.
- Call on a volunteer to answer the question.

Answer: Mali and Eric are going to the festival.

Controlled Practice
10 minutes

B 💿 **Read the questions. Then listen...**

- Have students read the questions and predict the answers.
- Play Track 27 again.
- Call on students to read the questions and answers. Write the letters of the answers on the board.
- If students have difficulty answering a question, play the corresponding part of the recording again.

Culture Connection

The Thai New Year festival is called *songkram*. It is usually celebrated for three days, beginning on April 13. Thai people celebrate by eating traditional foods, thoroughly cleaning their homes, and visiting their temples and bringing food to the monks, as well as by participating in a variety of customs involving water—especially throwing water on one another! These same customs are followed by many immigrants living in Thai neighborhoods in the U.S.

Communicative Practice
10 minutes

C GROUPS. **What things are common...**

- Give an example from a U.S. perspective. For example, many immigrants and visitors to the U.S. are surprised that Americans eat turkey and pumpkin pie on Thanksgiving. Ask the class: *Which American customs surprised you when you first arrived?*
- If possible, group students from different countries.
- Give a time limit for discussion.
- While students are talking, walk around and provide help as needed.
- To wrap up, select a number of students and ask: *What was the most surprising thing you learned in your group's discussion?*

Expansion: Speaking Practice for 2C

- Have students prepare short oral reports about New Year customs and celebrations in their cultures.
- On the board, write topics associated with New Year celebrations, for example, *date and season, food, clothing, gifts, greetings, home customs, religious customs,* and *other customs.*
- Have students from the same culture work together. Have them divide up the topics so that each student reports on one aspect of the holiday. Pre-level students can report on simpler aspects of the New Year holiday, such as the date and season, food, or gifts. Above-level students should report on the more complex aspects of the holiday, such as home and religious customs.
- Give a time limit for preparation. While students are working, walk around and provide help as needed.
- Bring the class together. Have each group do a report to the class.

Presentation 10 minutes

3 CONVERSATION

Pronunciation Watch

- On the board, write: *tip, cab, hat, sad, book,* and *leg.* Say: *I'm going to say each word two ways. Tell me what you notice about the last sound.*
- Say each word twice, first pronouncing the final consonant very strongly and the second time pronouncing it naturally with a short, quiet sound.
- Elicit from the class the difference between the first and second pronunciations.
- Read out loud the Pronunciation Watch note.
- To reinforce, say each word again, pronouncing the final consonant naturally with a short, quiet sound.
- Have students repeat each word after you.

> **Language Note**
>
> Final stops /p/, /b/, /t/, /d/, /k/, and /g/ are unreleased at the ends of words. In other words, they are pronounced with no release of air. In the student book this is described as *short, quiet pronunciation.*

Ⓐ Listen to the words. Notice...

- Play CD 1, Track 28. Have students listen.
- Play Track 28 again. Have students listen and repeat.
- Call on students to say each word. Make corrections as needed.

Ⓑ Mali and Eric talk after...

- Play CD 1, Track 29. Have students listen and read along silently.
- *Optional:* Have above-level students listen with their books closed.
- Check comprehension. Ask: *What did Eric think of Thai Town? When is Thai Town busy? Is Eric going to come back?*
- Have students underline the final /p/, /b/, /t/, /d/, /k/, and /g/ sounds. Have them listen to the conversation again and notice the short, quiet pronunciation.

Controlled Practice 10 minutes

4 PRACTICE

Ⓐ PAIRS. Practice the conversation.

- Form cross-ability pairs and have students take turns reading each role.
- Have students switch partners and practice again.
- Listen as students practice. Take notes on students' pronunciation of final stops.
- If necessary, model the pronunciation of the final stops and have the class repeat.
- Ask volunteers to perform the conversation.

Communicative Practice 10 minutes

Ⓑ MAKE IT PERSONAL. GROUPS. Discuss.

- Define *diverse.* Say: *A diverse neighborhood has people of different races, ages, and religions.*
- Read question 1. Tell about your neighborhood.
- Read question 2 and draw a chart on the board. Label the column heads *Common Culture, Diverse Culture.* Label the rows *Advantages, Disadvantages.*
- Tell students to talk about the advantages and disadvantages of living in common-culture neighborhoods and diverse neighborhoods.
- Form groups. Give a time limit.
- Have volunteers share their answers to question 1 with the class.
- Have volunteers share their answers to question 2. Write students' ideas in the chart on the board.

> **Teaching Tip**
>
> Encourage students to offer contrasting opinions and answers by asking questions such as *Who lives in a different kind of neighborhood? Who has a different answer? Who disagrees?*

Extra Practice

Interactive Practice

---

3 CONVERSATION

CD1 T28

A 🔘 **Listen to the words. Notice the short, quiet pronunciation of the underlined consonant sounds. Then listen again and repeat.**

sho**p**	grea**t**	a**t** nigh**t**	bore**d**	thin**k**
chea**p**	bes**t**	foo**d**	ba**ck**	perfe**ct**

> **Pronunciation Watch**
>
> The sounds /p/, /b/, /t/, /d/, /k/, and /g/ often have a short, quiet pronunciation at the end of a word.

CD1 T29

B 🔘 **Mali and Eric talk after the festival. Listen and read.**

Mali: So what did you think of Thai Town?

Eric: It's pretty amazing. It has so many restaurants and shops. Is it always so crowded?

Mali: Mostly at night and on the weekends. A lot of people come to eat and shop.

Eric: The things in the stores looked really interesting. I'm usually bored by shopping, but I'd like to come back and check out the crafts.

Mali: Great. I'll tell you about the best restaurants where the food is cheap.

Eric: Perfect!

4 PRACTICE

A PAIRS. **Practice the conversation.**

B MAKE IT PERSONAL. GROUPS. **Discuss.**

1. What kind of neighborhood do you live in? Is it a neighborhood like Thai Town where people share a common language and culture, or is it a diverse neighborhood?

2. Which is better—a neighborhood where people share a common language and culture, or a diverse neighborhood?

3. Make two charts: one for neighborhoods where people share a common culture and one for diverse neighborhoods. List advantages and disadvantages for each.

Grammar

Participial adjectives

It's pretty **amazing**.	I'm **amazed** at all the restaurants and shops.
Shopping is **boring**.	Eric is usually **bored** by shopping.

Grammar Watch

- Adjectives ending in -*ing* and -*ed* refer to feelings. Use an -*ing* adjective to describe the cause of a feeling. Use an -*ed* adjective to describe a feeling experienced by a person. *See page 281 for a list of* -ed *and* -ing *(participial) adjectives.*

- Some adjectives, like *worried* and *relieved*, have only -*ed* forms.

- Prepositions often follow -*ed* adjectives: *Eric is bored by shopping*. (*See page 281 for a list of* -ed *adjectives* + *prepositions*).

1 PRACTICE

A Mark the boldfaced adjectives *F* (feeling experienced by a person) or *C* (cause of the feeling).

Because life in a new country is **exciting** [C] but difficult, immigrants often live in neighborhoods with people from their homeland. That way, when they're **worried** [F] about food, schools, or medical care, or when they feel **confused** [F] about something that happens at work or school, they can find help. If it becomes too **frustrating** [C] to speak English, there's always someone who can speak their native language. Besides, at the end of a long hard day, it's simply more **relaxing** [C] to be in a place that seems like home.

B Complete the conversation between Laila Kassim and Maria Ruiz. Use the prepositions *about, at, of,* or *with*. More than one answer is sometimes possible.

Laila: I'm worried _about_ my children. I can't let them play outside.

Maria: I understand. My husband and I moved to our neighborhood about a month ago. At first, I was excited _about_ having American neighbors. But that changed quickly. I'm surprised _at / about_ how busy people are all the time.

Laila: I know what you mean. But I have a happy story. When my sister first moved, she was nervous _about_ bothering the American family next door. She was embarrassed _about / by_ her English, and they didn't seem very helpful. But then the children started playing together, and everything changed. Now she's thrilled _at / about / with_ the great relationship she has with her neighbors.

Getting Started   5 minutes

- Introduce the grammar point with a short anecdote. You could, for example, tell a story about a movie that you loved but a companion disliked. Include in your story sentences such as *The special effects were amazing; I thought the movie was really exciting, but my friend was so bored she fell asleep.*
- As you are telling the story, write the *-ing* and *-ed* words on the board.
- Point to the words on the board and say: *In this lesson we're going to look at adjectives that end in -ing and -ed.*

Presentation   15 minutes

Participial adjectives

- Copy the grammar chart onto the board. Read the sentences and underline the participial adjectives.
- Read the first Grammar Watch note. Point to the sentences in the chart with *-ing* participles and ask: *What's the cause of the feeling?* (all the restaurants and shops) Then point to the sentences with *-ed* participles and ask: *Which person has the feeling in this sentence?* (I)
- Read the second note. Elicit sentences with *worried* and *relieved*. Ask students: *When do you feel worried? When do you feel relieved?* Write students' sentences on the board.
- Read the third note and point to the sentences in the chart with *amazed at* and *bored by*. Ask students if they know any other *-ed* adjectives followed by prepositions. If necessary, cue them by saying *interested . . . (in), surprised . . . (by), worried . . . (about).*

Expansion: Grammar Presentation

- Have students look at the list of *-ed* adjectives + prepositions on page 281. Give them a time limit, such as two minutes, to examine the list and memorize as many combinations as possible.
- Divide students into teams. Say an *-ed* adjective from the list. Have students call out the preposition. Award one point to the first team to call out the correct preposition.

Controlled Practice   20 minutes

1 PRACTICE

A Mark the boldfaced adjectives...

- Read the first sentence. Ask: *What is exciting? What is the cause?* (life in a new country)
- Have students continue working alone or in pairs. While they are working, walk around and provide help as needed.
- Check answers. If it is necessary to clarify an answer, ask: *What is the cause of the feeling?* or *Who is experiencing the feeling?*
- Write the boldfaced words and the answers, *C* or *F*, on the board.

B Complete the conversation between...

- Read the first sentence. Ask: *Is there another preposition we can use here?* (no)
- Remind students they can consult the list on page 281 if necessary.
- Have students work alone or in pairs. While they are working, walk around and provide help as needed.
- Have a pair of volunteers read the conversation. Write the adjectives and the prepositions on the board. For each item, ask: *Is there another preposition we can use here?* If yes, write it on the board as well.

Expansion: Speaking Practice for 1B

- Form cross-ability pairs. Have pairs make sentences using the answers on the board from Exercise 1B.
- Call on students to read their sentences to the class. Make corrections as needed.
- To make the activity more challenging, tell students to write a conversation using as many of the items as they can.
- Have pairs perform their conversation for the class.

2 PRACTICE

Ⓐ Read the sentences about...

- Read item 1. Ask: *Why is* disappointed *correct?* (It describes the way Maria feels.)
- Have students work alone or in pairs.
- Write the numbers *2* through *5* on the board. Call up students to write the answers. Point to each item and ask: *Is this correct?* If there is an error, elicit the correction and write it on the board.

■ Expansion: Speaking Practice for 2A

- Discuss the cultural aspects of items 2 and 3. Read item 2 and ask: *Why doesn't the neighbor wait for an answer? When people say* How are you? *in the U.S., are they really asking about your health?*
- Read item 3. Ask: *In the U.S., is it polite to ask someone about his or her age? Is it polite in your culture?*
- Ask: *What other topics should you not ask about in the U.S.?* (how much money people make and how much they paid for things such as their house, etc.)
- Have volunteers share their ideas with the class.

Ⓑ Complete the sentences with...

- Read the first sentence and point out that although the story is in the past, the *-ed* and *-ing* forms do not change.
- Have students complete the exercise alone or in pairs. Walk around and provide help as needed.
- Have students compare answers with a partner.
- Call on students to read the sentences with the answers they filled in. Write them on the board. Point to each item and ask the class: *Is this correct?* Elicit corrections as needed.

Communicative Practice   20 minutes

Show what you know!

STEP 1. Check (✓) three adjectives to describe...

- As an example, say how you feel about your own neighborhood, for example, *I'm encouraged by the friendliness of my neighbors.* Write the sentence on the board.

■ MULTILEVEL INSTRUCTION for STEP 1

Pre-level Have students write just one or two sentences.

Above-level Have students write more than three sentences.

STEP 2. GROUPS. Discuss.

- Form cross-ability groups. Have each group select a timekeeper, a note taker, and a reporter.
- For item 1, tell students to share their sentences from Step 1. For item 2, the note taker should write down each student's answer.
- Give a time limit.
- Walk around as students are talking and provide help as needed.
- To wrap up, reporters should say how many people in their group were happy and unhappy and describe their classmates' reasons.
- Create a chart on the board with the headings *Happy* and *Unhappy*. As reporters are speaking, write their reasons in the proper column.

■ Expansion: Speaking Practice for STEP 2

- Tell students to remain in groups.
- Have them look at the reasons in the *Unhappy* column on the board.
- Have them discuss solutions to the problems and say what advice they would give to a person with this problem.
- Have a representative from each group choose one problem and share the group's solution.

Progress Check

Can you . . . describe feelings about . . .

Say: *We have practiced describing feelings about a neighborhood. Now, look at the question at the bottom of the page. Can you describe feelings about a neighborhood? Write a checkmark in the box.*

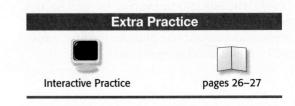

Extra Practice	
Interactive Practice	pages 26–27

A Read the sentences about Maria's feelings. Circle the correct adjectives.

1. Maria didn't find what she expected when she moved to a new neighborhood. Maria was (disappointed)/ disappointing.

2. One of Maria's neighbors always says, "Hello. How are you?" but never waits for an answer. Maria is (confused)/ confusing and wonders why.

3. Maria asked one of her neighbors her age. Later she found out that it's not OK to ask that question. Maria felt (embarrassed)/ embarrassing.

4. Maria wanted to know more about Laila's sister. She thought that the sister's experience was **interested** /(interesting.)

5. Laila's sister's experience gave Maria some hope. She was (encouraged)/ encouraging about the possibility of getting to know her neighbors.

B Complete the sentences with the *-ed* or *-ing* form of the verb in parentheses.

Crime was increasing in the neighborhood, and everyone felt ___frightened___.
(frighten)

People were also ___worried___ about the trash and litter problem. They said they
(worry)

were ___frustrated___ that the streets were so dirty. People were ___tired___ of
(frustrate)   (tire)

complaining, but the situation was ___depressing___. There was a special meeting at
(depress)

City Hall. The meeting was ___encouraging___. Everyone felt ___satisfied___ that the
(encourage)   (satisfy)

city council was starting to make improvements.

Show what you know!   Describe feelings about a neighborhood

STEP 1. Check (✓) three adjectives to describe how you feel about your
neighborhood. Then write statements about your feelings.

☐ worried   ☐ frightened   ☐ excited   ☐ bored
☐ frustrated   ☐ encouraged   ☐ satisfied   ☐ other: _____

I'm excited about the different backgrounds of my neighbors.

STEP 2. GROUPS. Discuss.

1. Share your ideas from Step 1.

2. How many people in your group are happy in their neighborhood? How many are unhappy? What are the reasons?

Can you… describe feelings about a neighborhood?   ☐

Life Skills

1 BEFORE YOU LISTEN

CLASS. Many community centers in the U.S. have after-school programs for children and teens. Discuss.

1. What kinds of activities do they offer?

2. Which activities are the most popular for young children? Which are popular among teenagers?

2 LISTEN

CD1 T30

A 🔊 The director of the Hanson Park Community Center is returning a call to a parent. Listen to their conversation and take notes. What kinds of classes does the after-school program offer?

1. reading _____

2. gymnastics _____

3. swimming _____

4. basketball _____

5. tennis _____

CD1 T30

B 🔊 Read the statements. Then listen to the conversation again. Write *T* (true) or *F* (false). Correct the false statements.

__T__ 1. The Hanson Park Community Center offers tutoring in reading every day.

__F__ 2. The Hanson Park Community Center is located in ~~a building downtown~~. Hanson Park

__F__ 3. The Hanson Park Community Center is open from 3 P.M. to ~~9~~ 7 P.M.

__F__ 4. Mrs. Suarez ~~will~~ can't enroll her daughter in the art classes.

__F__ 5. Mrs. Suarez thinks her daughter will be interested in taking ~~swimming~~ tennis lessons.

__F__ 6. To enroll children in classes, parents should ~~mail a letter to the director of after-school classes.~~ come to the center and fill out an application.

__T__ 7. Classes at the Hanson Park Community Center are free.

Getting Started   5 minutes

- Write *community center* on the board. (Alternately, if your school's neighborhood has a community center, write the name of the center on the board.)
- Ask about students' experience, for example: *Is there a community center in your neighborhood? Where is it located? Do you go there? How often? What kinds of activities do you do there?*

1   BEFORE YOU LISTEN

CLASS. Many community centers in the...

- Read question 1 and write students' answers on the board.
- Read question 2 and elicit answers. Write *C* next to activities that are popular for children and *T* next to those that are popular with teens.
- Follow up by asking: *Which activities do you do? Which ones do your children or your teenagers do?*

▬▬ **Expansion: Speaking Practice for 1**

- Ask the following additional questions: *Which additional activities would you like your community center to offer? What hours is your center open? Are the hours convenient for you? What do you like the best about your center? What don't you like?*

Presentation   10 minutes

2   LISTEN

A 🔘 **The director of the Hanson Park...**

- Explain *take notes*. Students should listen specifically for five kinds of classes and write one on each line. Remind students it is not necessary to understand every word.
- Play CD 1, Track 30.
- Have students compare their notes with those of a classmate.
- Ask the class: *How many kinds of classes did you hear mentioned?* If students weren't able to hear all five, play the recording again.
- Elicit the answers from the class and write them on the board.

Controlled Practice   25 minutes

B 🔘 **Read the statements. Then listen...**

- Have students read the statements silently and predict whether they are true or false.
- Play Track 30 again.
- Have students complete the exercise alone or in pairs.
- Check answers. Call on students to read each statement and say whether it is true or false. If it is false, ask the student to correct it. Write the answers on the board.

▬▬ **Expansion: Listening Practice for 2B**

- Write the following questions on the board: *Which sport does Mrs. Suarez think her daughter will like? What are the center's hours? How can Mrs. Saurez sign up her daughter for classes? How much does it cost?*
- Play the second part of Track 30 again.
- Call on students to read the questions and say the answers.

3 PRACTICE

A Look at the map. Look at the compass...

- Draw a large compass on the board and write in *N, S, E,* and *W.* Say: *This is a compass. It shows directions.*
- Have students answer the question. Write *North, South, East,* and *West* on the compass on the board.

Expansion: Listening Practice for 3A

- On the compass on the board, fill in *Northeast, Northwest, Southeast,* and *Southwest.*
- Figure out the directions in your classroom. Point to the north and say: *This is north.*
- Have the class stand up. Tell students you will say a direction and they should turn and face the direction you say.
- Practice all the directions on the compass.

B Jenna Smith, the director...

- Write the following terms on the board: *drive north, make a right, make a left, travel east,* and *cross-street.*
- Say: *These expressions are used for giving directions. Which verbs do you see?* (*drive, make, travel*) *What's another way of saying* make a right *or* make a left? (turn right, turn left) *What is a cross-street?* (the nearest street that crosses the street a place is located on)
- Play the first three speaking turns of CD 1, Track 31. Stop and ask: *How does the woman ask for directions?* (Can you give me directions to the center?) Write *the woman's* question on the board. Play the segment again if necessary.
- Play the entire Track 31. Watch students to see if they are able to mark the route on their maps.
- Play Track 31 again if necessary. This time, stop the recording after each segment of Jenna's directions and ask the class: *Where are you now?* Then play the next segment.
- If students are struggling, hold up your book, play the recording, and trace the route while students watch. Then play the recording again and have students trace the route in their own books.
- At the end of the recording, ask the class: *Where are you?* (at 1200 Hanson Park Drive)

C Look at the map. Circle...

- Have students complete the exercise alone.
- Have them compare answers with a partner.
- Call on students to read the sentences and state the answer. Write the answers on the board.

Communicative Practice   20 minutes

D ROLE PLAY. PAIRS. Role-play these situations.

Teaching Tip

While pairs are performing role plays, use the scoring rubric for speaking on page T-xiii to evaluate each student's vocabulary, grammar, fluency, and how well he or she completes the task. You may want to review the completed rubric with the students.

- Read the role descriptions. Clarify that students will both ask and give directions.
- Pair students of similar ability. Give them a time limit for practicing both role plays.
- Walk around and provide help. Take notes on errors involving asking and giving directions.
- Have volunteers perform one of their role plays.

MULTILEVEL INSTRUCTION for 3D

Pre-level Review the Audio Script from Exercise 3B. Have students read it twice in pairs, switching roles. Then have them write scripts for their role plays, using the Audio Script from Exercise 3B as a model.

Above-level Have students ask for directions to other locations on the map (not just the Hanson Park Community Center).

Progress Check

Can you . . . give and follow directions?

Say: *Look at the question at the bottom of the page. Can you give and follow directions? Write a checkmark in the box.*

Extra Practice
Interactive Practice	pages 28–29

3 PRACTICE

A Look at the map. Look at the compass rose. What do the letters *N*, *E*, *W*, and *S* stand for?

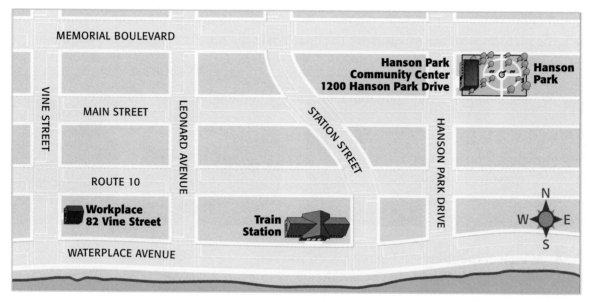

B Jenna Smith, the director of Hanson Park Community Center, is giving a parent directions to the center. Listen and mark the route on the map.

C Look at the map. Circle the correct words. (If necessary, listen to Jenna Smith's directions again.)

1. The parent should go **north** / **south** on Vine Street to get to the Hanson Park Community Center.

2. The director tells the parent to drive **east** / **west** on Route 10.

3. The Hanson Park Community Center is **northwest** / **northeast** of her workplace.

4. The nearest cross-street to the Hanson Park Community Center is **Hanson Park Drive** / **Memorial Boulevard.**

D ROLE PLAY. PAIRS. Role-play these situations.

1. **Student A:** You need directions to the Hanson Park Community Center from your home. You live on Memorial Boulevard between Vine Street and Leonard Avenue.
   Student B: Look at the map and give directions.

2. **Student B:** You need directions to the Hanson Park Community Center from your home. You live on Waterplace Avenue by the train station.
   Student A: Look at the map and give directions.

Can you...give and follow directions? ☐

Listening and Speaking

1 BEFORE YOU LISTEN

A Match the pictures with the words from the box. Write the numbers next to the words.

___2___ graffiti   ___4___ a pothole   ___1___ garbage   ___3___ a vacant lot

1

2

3

4

B CLASS. Which of the things in Exercise A do you see on your way to school? Where do you see them? Do you think they are problems? Why or why not?

2 LISTEN

CD1 T32

A Jamil Hadad and Linlin Yang work at the same company. Listen. What's the topic of their conversation?

CD1 T32

B Read the statements. Then listen to the conversation again. Write *T* (true) or *F* (false). Correct the false statements.

___F___ 1. Last week, the garbage truck ^never^ came ~~to~~ ~~Linlin's house on schedule~~.

___T___ 2. Both Linlin and Jamil have a problem with their garbage pick-up.

___F___ 3. ^Teenagers^ ~~The fast-food restaurants~~ throw their garbage in the vacant lot.

___F___ 4. Linlin and Jamil agree that it's ^not^ OK for teenagers to hang out in the ^vacant lot^ ~~park~~.

___T___ 5. Linlin is upset because there aren't enough after-school programs.

C PAIRS. Discuss. Linlin says that the trash in the vacant lot is a *health hazard*. What does she mean?

Getting Started 5 minutes

1 BEFORE YOU LISTEN

A Match the pictures with...

- Say: *We're going to talk about problems that exist in some communities.*
- Say each word or phrase and have students repeat.
- Have students do the exercise.
- Go over the answers. Say the number of the picture and have the class say the problem.

B CLASS. Which of the things...

- Say the number of each picture and its corresponding word(s). Ask: *How many people see this problem on the way to school?*
- Call on volunteers to answer the questions.

▬ Expansion: Speaking Practice for 1B

- Ask: *Are there any other problems that you see on your way to school?*
- Have volunteers answer the question. Write their responses on the board.

Presentation 15 minutes

2 LISTEN

A Jamil Hadad and Linlin Yang work...

- Have students look at the photo. Ask: *Who are the speakers? What is their relationship? Where are they? What are they doing?*
- Remind students to listen specifically for the answer to the question. It is not necessary to understand every word.
- Play CD 1, Track 32.
- Call on a volunteer to answer the question.

Answer: The topic is problems in their neighborhood.

Controlled Practice 20 minutes

B Read the statements. Then...

- Do item 1 with the class. Remind students that if part of a statement is false, they should strike out that part and write the correction above the line.
- Have students read the remaining statements silently and predict whether they are true or false.
- Play Track 32 again.
- Have students complete the exercise alone or in pairs.
- Check answers. Call on students to read each statement and say whether it is true or false. If it is false, ask the student to correct it. Write the answers on the board.
- If students have difficulty answering a question, play the corresponding part of the recording again.

C PAIRS. Discuss. Linlin says that...

- Write the word *hazard* on the board. Elicit the meaning from the class. (*A hazard is something dangerous.*)
- Have students turn to their neighbors and discuss the question. Give a time limit.
- Ask: What is a health hazard? *Why is trash a health hazard?* Call on volunteers to answer.

Answer: A health hazard is something that has the potential to harm people. Trash is a health hazard because it contains not only bacteria but also hazardous objects such as broken glass and sharp pieces of metal.

▬ Expansion: Speaking Practice for 2C

- Ask: *What are some other health hazards in a community? Why are they dangerous?*
- Write students' responses on the board.

3 CONVERSATION

 Jamil and his wife Maryam are...

- Play CD 1, Track 33. Have students listen and read along silently.
- Check comprehension. Ask: *What is Linlin's problem? Do Jamil and Maryam have the same problem? What do Linlin and Jamil wish? What does Maryam wish?*

4 PRACTICE

A PAIRS. **Practice the conversation.**

- Form cross-ability pairs and have students take turns reading each role.
- Have students switch partners and practice again.
- Ask volunteers to perform the conversation.

■■ MULTILEVEL INSTRUCTION for 4A

Pre-level Have students practice with the same partner.

Above-level Have students continue the conversation with three or four more exchanges, using their own ideas.

Communicative Practice 20 minutes

B PAIRS. **Use the conversation as...**

> **Teaching Tip**
> While pairs are performing role plays, use the scoring rubric for speaking on page T-xiii to evaluate each student's vocabulary, grammar, fluency, and how well he or she completes the task. You may want to review the completed rubric with the students.

- Model a role play with an above-level student, using Wish List 1. For example, A: *I had lunch with _____ the other day . . . We talked about . . . We both wish there were more educational programs . . .*
- Pair students of similar ability and have them role-play a similar conversation using the items from one of the Wish Lists.
- Call on pairs of students to perform their role play.

■■ MULTILEVEL INSTRUCTION FOR 4B

Pre-level Have students choose items from the same Wish List.

Above-level Have students choose items from any of the Wish Lists or substitute their own ideas.

■■ Expansion: Speaking Practice for 4B

- Have students write a real Wish List of activities they would like to have in their communities.
- Pair students. Have them role-play conversations using their Wish Lists.
- Call on pairs of students to perform their role plays.

C MAKE IT PERSONAL. **Think about...**

STEP 1. GROUPS. **Discuss.**

- Form cross-ability groups. Have each group select a timekeeper, a note taker, and a reporter. The note taker should write down the group's ideas and rankings.
- Give a time limit.
- While students are talking, walk around and provide help as needed.
- Have each group's reporter write the group's list on the board.

Answer: 1. Community services include community centers and their programs; libraries; services for the elderly, handicapped, homeless, and needy; city-sponsored youth sports and recreation programs; parks and swimming pools; literacy and English classes, and more.

STEP 2. CLASS. **Share your results. Which...**

- Look at the lists on the board. With the help of the class, select the three services that are listed most often and circle them.
- Have the class discuss why these three are the most important.

Extra Practice

Interactive Practice

---

3 CONVERSATION

CD1 T33

Jamil and his wife Maryam are talking. Listen and read.

Jamil: I had lunch with Linlin at work today. She has a problem with the garbage pickup. They don't pick up the garbage at her house on schedule.

Maryam: Oh, yeah? The same problem we have.

Jamil: Yeah. And I told her about our problem with the vacant lot. We both wish there were more after-school programs in the community.

Maryam: Do you mean activities for young children?

Jamil: That would be good, but we also need sports for teens.

Maryam: Do you know what I wish?

Jamil: No. What?

Maryam: I wish they had a swimming pool.

4 PRACTICE

A PAIRS. Practice the conversation.

B PAIRS. Use the conversation as a model to make similar conversations. Use the information in the wish lists.

Wish List 1	Wish List 2	Wish List 3
educational programs	services for senior citizens	concerts
homework help	health and fitness classes	movies and art shows
computer classes	free hot lunches for anyone over 65	a chess club

C MAKE IT PERSONAL. Think about community services.

STEP 1. GROUPS. Discuss.

1. List six important community services.
2. Which community services are the most important? Number them from *1* (most important) to *6* (least important).

STEP 2. CLASS. Share your results. Which are the three most important community services?

Grammar

Wish in the present and future

I **wish**	(that) we **had** a swimming pool in this community.
We **wish**	(that) the Sanitation Department **would come** to our neighborhood.
I **wish**	(that) there **were** more after-school programs at the community center.

Grammar Watch

- Use *wish* + simple past to talk about things that you want to be true now, but that are not true.
- Use *wish* + *could* or *would* (not *can* or *will*) to talk about things that you hope will be true in the future.
- Use *were*, instead of *was*, after *wish*.

1 PRACTICE

A Some people are not satisfied with the services at their public library. Circle the verb *wish*. Underline the verb in the *wish* clauses.

Carlos: We (wish) the library opened earlier in the morning.

John: I (wish) it didn't close at 4:00 P.M. on Fridays.

Millie: I (wish) the movie selection at the library were better. I (wish) the movies weren't so old. How about some new releases?

Yusef: I don't have a computer. I (wish) the library would get more computers.

B A local newspaper interviewed people about problems with traffic. Complete the sentences with the correct form of the verbs.

Tim: The traffic is getting worse. I wish I ___didn't need___ a car.
  (not need)

Gladys: I just wish there ___were___ more free parking downtown.
  (be)

Andre: The streets are in bad condition. I wish the city ___would fix___ the potholes.
  (fix)

Julio: I wish that people ___wouldn't drive___ so fast.
  (not drive)

Bo: We need more stop signs. I wish we ___had___ a stop sign on every corner.
  (have)

Getting Started   5 minutes

- Ask the class: *Is there something about our classroom that you don't like?* Elicit two to three answers, for example: *Our classroom doesn't have an Internet connection. Our classroom is noisy. Our classroom doesn't have windows.*
- Write students' sentences on the board. Then point to each sentence, read it, and follow up with *I wish . . .*, for example: *I wish our classroom had an Internet connection. I wish it weren't noisy. I wish our classroom had windows.*
- Say: *In this lesson we're going to use* wish *to talk about changes we would like to make in our communities.*

Presentation   15 minutes

Wish in the present and future

- Copy the grammar chart onto the board. Read the sentences. Circle *wish* and underline the boldfaced verbs.
- Read the first Grammar Watch note. To clarify, point to the first sentence on the board and ask: *Does this community have a swimming pool?* (no) Say: *Our community doesn't have a swimming pool, but I wish we had one.*
- Read the second note. Read the second sentence on the board and ask: *Does the Sanitation Department come to our neighborhood?* (no) Say: *It doesn't come, but we wish it would come.*
- Read the third note. Point to the third sentence on the board. Ask: *Are there enough after-school programs at the community center?* (no) Say: *There aren't enough after-school programs. I wish there were more.*

Controlled Practice   25 minutes

1 PRACTICE

A Some people are not satisfied...

- Have a student read the first sentence. On the board, write *wish* and circle it. Write and underline *opened.*
- Have students continue working alone or in pairs. While they are working, walk around and provide help as needed.
- Check answers. Call on students to read the remaining sentences and say which words they underlined. Write them on the board. Point to each answer and ask: *Is it a present or future verb?*

B A local newspaper interviewed people...

- Read the first sentence.
- Have students complete the remaining items. While students are working, walk around and provide help as needed.
- Have students compare answers with a partner.
- To check answers, assign students to be Gladys, Andre, Julio, and Bo. Have them read their sentences. Write the answers on the board. If a student makes an error, ask the class: *Is this correct?* Elicit the correction from the class.

2 PRACTICE

Jack's family is talking at the...

- Read the directions.
- Read Jack's line and then the example. Review the grammar if needed. Ask: *Why is* there were *correct?* (Because we use *were* with *wish* to talk about things we want to be true now, but that are not true.)
- Have students work alone or in pairs. Give a time limit. Walk around and provide help as needed.
- Write the numbers *2* through *7* on the board. Call on students to write the answers on the board. Point to each item and ask the class: *Is this correct?* If there is an error, elicit the correction from the class and write it on the board.

Communicative Practice   15 minutes

Show what you know!

STEP 1. Complete these two sentences about...

- Provide models. Form two sentences about your own neighborhood.
- Remind students to use *wish* + the simple past to talk about now and *wish* + *would* or *could* to talk about the future.
- While students are writing, walk around and provide help as needed.

STEP 2. GROUPS. Tell each other...

- Have each group select a timekeeper, a note taker, and a reporter.
- Give a time limit.
- Have each member of the group read his or her sentences. The note taker should write down each person's wishes.
- Tell groups to choose three wishes to present to the whole class.

STEP 3. CLASS. Share your wishes. What...

- Each group's reporter should tell the class about the three wishes his or her group has chosen.
- Write the wishes on the board.
- Note which three wishes are repeated most often and circle them. If no wishes are repeated, have the class vote on three wishes for their neighborhood.

■ **Expansion: Writing Practice for Show what you know!**

- Write several topics on the board, for example, *job, home, family,* and *health.*
- Tell students to write two sentences about each topic using *wish.*
- Provide models, for example: *I wish I didn't work on Saturdays. I wish my house had four bedrooms. I wish my parents lived near me. I wish I were a good athlete.*
- Pair students and have them share and discuss their sentences.
- Collect the sentences. Correct errors with the use of *wish.*

Progress Check

Can you...talk about making changes in...
Say: *We have practiced talking about making changes in a community. Now, look at the question at the bottom of the page. Can you talk about making changes in a community? Write a checkmark in the box.*

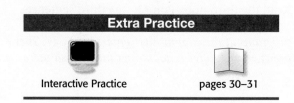

Extra Practice
Interactive Practice   pages 30–31

Jack's family is talking at the dinner table. Read what they're saying. Then rewrite each person's opinion as a wish. More than one answer is possible.

Jack: I think we need a hospital in the neighborhood.

Fran: The streets are so noisy. What do you think, Jason?

Jason: I agree, but public transportation is the biggest problem for me. The buses should run more frequently—every ten minutes would be great.

Carol: Well, I'd just like to be able to go to the park more often!

Sarah: I want swings and slides in the playground.

Mark: I'd like a place to play baseball. How about you, Uncle David?

David: A baseball field is a good idea, Mark, but I don't know why this family complains so much.

1. Jack wishes _____there were_____ a hospital nearby.

2. Fran wishes the streets _____weren't_____ so noisy.

3. Jason wishes the buses _____ran_____ every ten minutes.

4. Carol wishes she _____could go_____ to the park more often.

5. Sarah wishes the playground _____had_____ more equipment.

6. Mark wishes _____there were_____ a baseball field in the neighborhood.

7. David wishes his family _____didn't complain_____ so much.

Show what you know!   Talk about making changes in a community

STEP 1. **Complete these two sentences about your neighborhood.**

I wish _____ now.

I wish _____ in the future.

STEP 2. GROUPS. **Tell each other your wishes.**

STEP 3. CLASS. **Share your wishes. What three neighborhood changes were the most common?**

Can you... talk about making changes in a community? ☐

Reading

1 BEFORE YOU READ

A CLASS. Discuss. Are there community gardens in the area where you live? Who plants these gardens?

B Read the title and the headings in the article. Predict. What is the main idea?

2 READ

CD1 T34

Listen and read the article. Was your prediction about the main idea correct? What is the author's opinion about community gardens?

Green Is the Way to Go

by Jo Atkinsen,
Freelance Contributor

Today, communities around the U.S. are going green. For some, that means paying attention to the **environment** by recycling or controlling pollution. But others are turning their neighborhoods green by planting community gardens.

Green Brings Benefits

A growing number of government and community leaders point out that gardening is a great way to improve the appearance of a neighborhood and the **value** of homes and businesses. It also unites neighborhood residents. Research at Texas A & M University and the University of Illinois shows that city areas with more green have less crime.

One Neighborhood's Story

Norris Square in Philadelphia is a neighborhood that has benefited from a community garden. In the 1980s, Norris Square was known for its **run-down** buildings and vacant lots filled with trash. Then a group of Puerto Rican women planted vegetables and flowers in one vacant lot. Soon there was also an outdoor kitchen and colorful murals showing rural life in Puerto Rico.

The Las Parcelas Community Garden became a place of beauty and a source of fresh food for Norris Square **residents**. It also became a source of neighborhood **pride**. Soon people were working together to do home repairs, clean up other vacant lots, remove graffiti, and plant more trees and flowers throughout the neighborhood.

Today, instead of fights in the park, there are festivals. Instead of **abandoned** cars along the streets, there are trees. People can now enjoy a neighborhood that is cleaner, safer, and more beautiful.

Plant Your Own Seeds

If you want to start a community garden in your area, you can get information from the Community Gardening Association at www.communitygarden.org.

Read about community involvement

Getting Started

1 BEFORE YOU READ

Ⓐ CLASS. Discuss. Are there...

- Have students look at the photo. Ask: *What kind of garden is this? Where do you think this is? Is there a garden like this near your home?*
- On the board, write *community garden*. Ask: *What is a community garden?* If students do not know, explain: *A community garden is an area owned by the city where residents of a neighborhood are allowed to plant their own garden.*
- Have volunteers share their answers with the class.

▬▬ Expansion: Speaking Practice for 1A

- With the class, discuss the advantages and disadvantages of having your own garden. Write students' ideas on the board in a two-column chart.

Ⓑ Read the title and the headings...

- On the board, write *go green*. Say: *Many cities, businesses, schools, and families are going green these days. What do you think that means?* (taking steps to control pollution, planting more trees and flowers in public areas, using less energy, and recycling)
- Have students look at the title and headings. Call on students to share their predictions about the main idea. Write their ideas on the board.

Answer: The main idea of the article is that neighborhoods are going green by planting community gardens.

Presentation

2 READ

🎧 Listen and read the article. Was your prediction...

- Note: Do not pre-teach the boldfaced vocabulary. The items are practiced in Exercise 4.
- Play CD 1, Track 34. Ask students to listen and read along with the article.
- When students have finished reading, point to the main-idea predictions on the board and ask: *Were your predictions correct?* Have a volunteer restate the main idea.
- Call on volunteers to state the author's opinion about community gardens. Since the article does not say what the author's opinion is, students must infer that it is positive. Ask: *How do you know?* Have students find words and phrases in the text that give a positive impression, for example: *a place of beauty, fresh food,* and *a source of pride.*

Answer: The author thinks that community gardens bring many benefits to the neighborhoods that have them.

- As a follow-up, have students listen as they read the article again.

Controlled Practice   20 minutes

3 CHECK YOUR UNDERSTANDING

Ⓐ Complete the sentences. Circle...

- Have students work alone to complete the exercise.
- Have students compare answers with a partner.
- Call on students to read the questions and answers. Write the answers on the board.

Reading Skill: **Making Inferences**

- Read the Reading Skill. Explain that an inference is the same as a logical guess.
- Explain that in order to make logical guesses, readers must use their knowledge and look for clues in the text. This kind of reading is often called *reading between the lines.*
- Point out that students practiced making an inference when they answered the question about the author's opinion in Exercise 2.

Ⓑ Read the Reading Skill. Then answer...

- Have students read the article again. Tell them to underline information (any clue) that helps them answer the question.
- Take a vote. Ask: *How many people think crime probably increased? decreased? stayed the same? How do you know?*

Answer: Crime probably decreased. The article says, "Research at Texas A&M . . . shows that city areas with more green have less crime." We know that the green areas in Norris Square increased, so the crime should have decreased.

- Go through the text and have students say which information they underlined.

4 WORD WORK

Find these boldfaced words in the article. Circle...

- Explain that both of the definitions given for each word are in the dictionary, but only one is correct in the context of the article. Students need to read the sentence—and sometimes the whole paragraph—in which a word appears before they choose their answer.

- Do the first item with the class. Read the first paragraph out loud. Ask: *What does* environment *mean in this paragraph? How do you know?* (Clues are the words *recycling* and *pollution*.)
- Have students complete the remaining items and compare answers with a partner.
- Call on students to say the answers.

Communicative Practice   15 minutes

Show what you know!

GROUPS. Discuss. Would you like to start...

- Write *Community Garden* in the center of the board. Below and to each side, write the words *For* and *Against.*
- With the class, brainstorm one reason for and one reason against starting a community garden.
- Have students continue working in groups. Have them choose a timekeeper, a note taker, and a reporter.
- Give a time limit. While students are talking, walk around and provide help as needed.
- Have reporters share their group's ideas with the class. Write the reasons for and against on the board.

Community Building

If there is a community garden near your school and it is feasible to leave the premises, take your class on a field trip to the garden. Arrange a tour if possible.

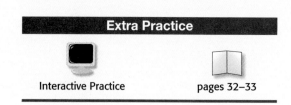

Extra Practice

Interactive Practice   pages 32–33

3 CHECK YOUR UNDERSTANDING

A Complete the sentences. Circle the correct answers.

1. Residents of Norris Square planted the Las Parcelas Community Garden in _____.
   (a. a lot)   b. a park   c. a building

2. Norris Square residents started the Las Parcelas Community Garden in _____.
   a. the 1970s   (b. the 1980s)   c. the 1990s

3. Members of the community _____ in the Las Parcelas Community Garden.
   a. planted fruit trees   (b. built an outdoor kitchen)   c. painted grafitti

B Read the Reading Skill. Then answer the question.

Did crime probably increase, decrease, or stay the same in Norris Square because of the Las Parcelas Community Garden? Explain.

> **Reading Skill:** Making Inferences
>
> If an author doesn't give information directly, use what you read to make a logical guess about what is probably true.

4 WORD WORK

Find these boldfaced words in the article. Circle the definition that matches the meaning in the article.

1. environment
   (a. the natural world)   b. the people and things around you

2. value
   a. the importance of something   (b. the money something is worth)

3. run-down
   (a. in very bad condition)   b. very tired and not healthy

4. residents
   a. doctors in training   (b. people who live in a particulat place)

5. pride
   a. a feeling that you are better than others   (b. a feeling of satisfaction)

6. abandoned
   (a. not being used or taken care of)   b. illegally parked

Show what you know! Talk about community involvement

GROUPS. Discuss. Would you like to start a community garden? List reasons for and against starting a garden.

Listening and Speaking

1 BEFORE YOU LISTEN

A PAIRS. You are going to listen to a discussion at a city council meeting. The council members use the following words. Match the words with the definitions.

_d_	1. convince	a.	make the size or amount of something larger
_c_	2. urge	b.	say who someone is or what something is
_b_	3. identify	c.	try hard to persuade someone to do something
_a_	4. increase	d.	persuade; get someone to agree
_f_	5. investigate	e.	make the size or amount of something smaller
_e_	6. reduce	f.	try to find out the truth about something

B CLASS. Look at the picture. What is the purpose of the ad?

Community Policing.

Making a Difference in Your Neighborhood.

2 LISTEN

CD1 T35

A Clara Ramos is a city council representative. She is answering Hugo Lopez's questions. Listen to their conversation. What are Clara Ramos and Hugo Lopez talking about?

CD1 T35

B PAIRS. Read the questions. Listen to the conversation again. Then answer the questions.

1. What did Clara Ramos ask the mayor and the chief of police to do?

2. What answer did she receive?

3. How can neighborhood residents help the police?

4. Why is there usually less crime as a result of community policing?

C PAIRS. Read this quote: "Safety is the responsibility of everyone in the community, not just the police." Who would probably make the statement, Clara Ramos or Hugo Lopez? Explain.

COUNCILMEMBER · SEVENTH DISTRICT

Getting Started — 5 minutes

1 BEFORE YOU LISTEN

Ⓐ PAIRS. You are going to listen...

- Write *city council* on the board. Explain: *A city council is a group of people who supervise and make decisions about the operations of a city. The members of the council represent different areas (districts) of the city. They are elected by the people who live in that area.*
- Read the list of words and have students repeat. Point out that all the words are verbs.
- Repeat item 1 and read definition d.
- Form cross-ability pairs and have them complete the exercise.
- Check answers. Say the number of the item. Have the class say the letter of the definition.

Expansion: Vocabulary Practice for 1A

- Pair students. Assign each pair a number from 1 to 6. Tell students to form a sentence using the word corresponding to their assigned number.
- Go around the room and have one student from each pair say the pair's sentence. Make oral corrections as needed.
- Follow up by having students write sentences using the items.

Ⓑ CLASS. Look at the picture. What...

- Read the text on the sign in the picture. Ask: *What is community policing?* (Residents work together with police to make their neighborhood safer through activities such as Neighborhood Watch, citizen patrols, neighborhood newsletters, alley cleanups, etc.)
- Ask: *Where can you see an ad like this?* (on the side of a bus, on the bulletin board at a community center, supermarket, or local newspaper)
- Call on volunteers to give their idea about the purpose of the ad.

Answer: The purpose of the ad is to get people interested in community policing.

Presentation — 10 minutes

2 LISTEN

Ⓐ 💿 Clara Ramos is a city council...

- Play CD 1, Track 35. Have students listen for the answer to the question.
- Call on students to share their answers.

Answer: They're talking about how community policing can help provide better protection against crime in the community.

Controlled Practice — 10 minutes

Ⓑ 💿 PAIRS. Read the questions. Listen...

- Play Track 35 again. Have students listen for the answers to the questions.
- Call on students to answer the questions. For questions 1 and 2, replay the recording if necessary. For questions 3 and 4, have volunteers share their opinions.

Answers: 1. She asked them to provide more patrol officers. 2. The answer was no, but instead, the district is going to expand its community policing program. 3. They can help identify problems and find solutions. 4. because the community can help the police identify problems before they occur.

Ⓒ PAIRS. Read this quote: "Safety is..."

- Provide questions to help students infer the answer. For example, write the following questions on the board: *Who mentions the community-policing program, Clara or Hugo? Did Hugo like the idea right away?*
- Have students look at the Audio Script on page 287.
- Pair students and have them answer the questions on the board and in their book.
- Have volunteers answer the question about who made the statement and explain their choice.

Answer: Clara Ramos would probably make the statement because she supports community policing.

Expansion: Speaking Practice for 2C

- Ask: *Do you agree with the quote? Why or why not?*
- Call on students to share their answers.

Presentation   10 minutes

3 CONVERSATION

Pronunciation Watch

- On the board, write: *I like to walk on the beach. Let's go to the beach this evening. Do you need to leave work early?* Say the sentences. Ask: *What do you notice about the word to?* (*To* is pronounced *ta.*)
- On the board, write: *Do you want to see a movie tonight? My brother and I are going to catch the midnight show.* Say the sentences. Ask: *What do you notice about want to and going to?* (They are pronounced *wanna* and *gonna.*)
- Read the Pronunciation Watch note. Point out that *to, want to,* and *going to* are not stressed.

A Listen to the phrases and...

- Read the first item. Stress the words *like* and *come.* Do not stress *to.*
- Play CD 1, Track 36. Have students listen.
- Play Track 36 again. Have students repeat.

B Eva Lopez is talking with her...

- Play CD 1, Track 37. Students listen and read along silently.
- Check comprehension. Ask: *What does the neighborhood need, according to Eva? What does Hugo suggest? What is Hugo going to do tonight? What does Eva want to do?*

Controlled Practice   10 minutes

4 PRACTICE

A PAIRS. Practice the conversation.

- Form similar-ability pairs and have students take turns reading each role.
- Have students switch partners and practice again.
- Take notes on instances when students forget to use the relaxed pronunciation of *to.*
- Practice the items in your notes with the class as follows: T: *I heard _____. It should be _____.* Have the class repeat the correct form.
- Ask volunteers to perform their conversations.

MULTILEVEL INSTRUCTION for 4A

Pre-level Have students practice several times with the same partner.

Above-level Have Student A read his or her part and Student B respond without looking at the conversation. Have students switch roles.

Communicative Practice   15 minutes

B PAIRS. Do you think Eva will...

- Read the last two lines of the conversation in Exercise 3B with an above-level student.
- Give students a time limit for discussion.
- Take a class vote. Ask: *How many think Eva will attend the meeting? Why do you think so? How many think Eva will not attend? Why?*

C PROBLEM-SOLVING. Think about...

STEP 1. Read about Hugo. What is...

- Read the paragraph or pair students and have them read it together.
- Check comprehension. Ask: *What did Hugo see? Does he know the young men?*

STEP 2. GROUPS. Discuss possible solutions to...

- Group students and have them choose a timekeeper, a note taker, and a reporter. The note taker keeps the list of solutions the group proposes.
- Give a time limit. Provide help as needed.
- Call on reporters to share their group's solution. Write all suggested solutions on the board. Then have the whole class vote on the best one.

Expansion: Speaking Practice for 4C

- Write additional discussion questions on the board, for example: *Does your neighborhood have community policing? What activities do community members participate in? Do you participate? What experiences have you had?*
- Discuss as a whole class or in small groups.

Extra Practice

Interactive Practice

---

3 CONVERSATION

Pronunciation Watch

The word *to* usually has a short, weak pronunciation. In conversation, *want to* is often pronounced "wanna" and *going to* is often pronounced "gonna."

CD1 T36

A Listen to the phrases and sentences. Notice the weak pronunciation of *to*. Then listen again and repeat.

to come with me   I'd like you to come with me.

to make a difference   This is our chance to make a difference.

want to ("wanna")   We want to ("wanna") have better services.

going to ("gonna")   Now you're going to ("gonna") tell me to go to the meeting.

CD1 T37

B Eva Lopez is talking with her husband Hugo one week after the city council meeting. Listen and read.

Eva: You know what this neighborhood needs? More streetlights, especially in the school parking lot.

Hugo: If you really feel that way, Eva, why don't you do something about it?

Eva: Now you're going to tell me to go to the community-policing meeting, aren't you?

Hugo: The meeting is tonight at 7:30. I'd like you to come with me.

Eva: Not tonight. I'm working on the community newsletter.

Hugo: You can work on the newsletter another night. This meeting is important. It's our chance to make a difference.

4 PRACTICE

A PAIRS. Practice the conversation.

B PAIRS. Do you think Eva will attend the community-policing meeting? Explain.

C PROBLEM-SOLVING. Think about neighborhood problems.

STEP 1. Read about Hugo. What is his problem?

Hugo Lopez saw several young men in his neighborhood breaking windows and writing graffiti on the wall at the community center. They live in the Southland neighborhood, so he knows them and their families well.

STEP 2. GROUPS. Discuss possible solutions to the problem. Make a list. Then decide on the best solution.

Grammar

Verb + object + infinitive		
We don't **want**	**the city**	**to take away** services.
He **urged**	**us**	**not to believe** everything we hear.

········· **Grammar Watch**

- An infinitive is *to* + base form of the verb. To make a negative infinitive, use *not* + *to* + base form of the verb.
- With verb + object + infinitive, use object pronouns (*me, you, him, her, it, us, them*).

1   PRACTICE

A **Read the conversation from a community-policing meeting. Circle the verb, draw a line under the object, and draw two lines under the infinitive.**

Officer: My Name is Officer Brown. As part of our community-policing effort, I (urge) you to check on neighbors who might need help.

Mrs. Soliz: My neighbor, Mrs. Soto, is eighty years old. I always (ask) her to call if she needs anything, but she (tells) me not to worry. What should I do?

Officer: Continue what you're doing. And, please, if you notice any change in her daily routine, try to find out what's going on.

Mrs. Soliz: I've noticed that some senior citizens are too trusting. They open the door when strangers knock. I've (told) Mrs. Soto not to do that.

Officer: That can be a problem. We have a safety class for seniors at the community center. We (teach) them to ask for identification even when they've made a call for service. We (remind) them not to open their doors until they know it's safe.

B **Cross out the noun object in each sentence. Then change the noun object to a pronoun object.**

1. The mayor doesn't want ~~the sanitation workers~~ to go on strike. *them*

2. The community-policing program encourages ~~the residents in our neighborhood~~ to work with the police. *them*

3. Community council members urge ~~residents~~ not to miss meetings. *them*

4. The police expect ~~my neighbors and me~~ to report anything unusual. *us*

5. Tell ~~Mrs. Soto~~ not to leave her door unlocked. *her*

6. Please ask ~~Mr. Lee~~ to check on ~~Mrs. Soto~~ once or twice a week. *him* *her*

Getting Started · 5 minutes

- Write on the board: *I want to find a job.* Ask the class: *What is the verb?* (want) *What is the infinitive?* (to find)
- Using a different color, insert *my brother* between *want* and *to* in the sentence above. Ask the class: *What's the difference between the sentences?* (The second sentence has an object. It changes the meaning. In the first sentence, the speaker wants to find a job. In the second sentence, the speaker wants a different person—his or her brother—to find a job.)
- Say: *In this lesson, we're going to practice sentences that have the structure verb + object + infinitive.*

Presentation · 10 minutes

Verb + object + infinitive

- Copy the grammar chart onto the board. Read the sentences. Circle the verbs, draw a line under the objects, and draw two lines under the infinitives.
- Explain *urge.* Say: *To urge means to suggest something very strongly. For example, if you have a high fever, I urge you to see a doctor.*
- Read the first Grammar Watch note. Point to the infinitives in the examples.
- Read the second note. Point to *us* in the second example. Point to *the city* in the first example and explain that the object can also be a noun.

> **Language Note**
> Other verbs that can be followed by an object and an infinitive include *ask, advise, tell, teach, remind, encourage, expect,* and *warn.*

Expansion: Grammar Practice

- Write several scrambled sentences on the board, for example: *expects / on time / The teacher / us / our homework / to complete,* and *Parents / the truth / their children / encourage / always / to tell,* and *to speak / I / the teacher / more slowly / asked.*
- Pair students and have them unscramble the sentences. Have them raise their hands when they are ready.
- Call on different students to say the unscrambled sentences.

Controlled Practice · 25 minutes

1 PRACTICE

A Read the conversation from a...

- Read the first two sentences and copy the example on the board.
- Have students complete the exercise alone or in pairs. Walk around and provide help as needed.
- Ask the class: *How many verbs did you circle? What's the first one?* Elicit each verb + object + infinitive. Circle and underline the appropriate words.

Expansion: Speaking Practice for 1A

- Pair students and have them read the conversation.
- Remind students to use the relaxed pronunciation of *to.*
- Call on pairs to perform the conversation for the class.

B Cross out the noun object in each...

- Read item 1. Ask: *Why is* them *correct?* (It replaces *the sanitation workers*—third person plural)
- Have students complete the exercise alone or in pairs. Walk around and provide help as needed.
- Write the numbers *2* through *6* on the board. Have students come up and write the crossed-out noun and the pronoun that replaces it, as in the example.
- Call on students to read the sentences with the pronouns out loud.

Expansion: Grammar Practice for 1B

- Have students circle the verbs in Exercise 1B.
- Tell them to make a list of verbs that can be followed by verb + object + infinitive, beginning with the verbs they circled in Exercises 1A and 1B.
- Ask the class if they know other verbs that belong on the list. Elicit an example sentence with each correct verb. Have students add each verb to their list.

Identify community problems

2 PRACTICE

A Captain Liu is telling an officer...

- Write *street smart* on the board. Explain: *A street-smart person takes steps to avoid being the victim of a crime.*
- Read the first three sentences, which include the example.
- Have students complete the exercise alone or in pairs. Walk around and provide help as needed.
- Call on individuals to read the sentences. Write the answers on the board.
- Point out new verbs that are followed by object + infinitive (*advise, warn*)

B Complete the sentences about...

- Read item 1. Ask: *What are some other ways we could complete the sentence?*
- Have students complete the exercise alone or in pairs. Walk around and provide help as needed.
- Write the numbers *2, 3,* and *4* on the board. Call on several students to write their answers on the board.
- Make corrections as needed.

Communicative Practice   20 minutes

Show what you know!

STEP 1. GROUPS. Identify a problem in...

- With the class, identify problems in the neighborhood where your school is located. Write the problems on the board.
- Group students and tell them to choose one of the problems on the board for their discussion. Have them choose a timekeeper, a note taker, and a reporter. The note taker should record the group's ideas.
- Give a time limit. While students are talking, walk around and provide help as needed.

STEP 2. CLASS. Share your ideas.

- Make a large three-column chart on the board with the headings: *Problem, Who Can Help, What To Say.*
- Have reporters share their group's ideas with the class. First they should report on the problem their group discussed. Then they should say whom they would talk to and what they would say.
- Write a summary of all the reports in the chart on the board.

■■■■ **Expansion: Writing Practice for STEP 2**

- Have students write a letter to the person whom they'd talk to, using the ideas summarized in the chart on the board.

Progress Check

Can you . . . identify community problems?

Say: *We have practiced identifying community problems. Now, look at the question at the bottom of the page. Can you identify community problems? Write a checkmark in the box.*

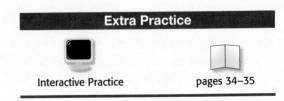

Extra Practice

Interactive Practice   pages 34–35

A Captain Liu is telling an officer about a class he wants her to give on street safety. Complete each sentence with an object pronoun and the correct form of the verb.

Prepare a list of "street smart" tips. Teach the people to follow the four basic rules. Also tell ___*them to stay away*___ from areas like parking
(stay away)
lots and alleys that are empty or poorly lit. Remind ___them not to carry___ lots of cash. Advise
(not carry)
___them to be___ careful with their wallets. Just last week I saw a man who was
(be)
a target for crime. I warned ___him not to keep___ his wallet in his back pocket.
(not keep)

B Complete the sentences about ways to improve safety. Include an object + infinitive.

1. All city parks close at 11:00 P.M., but there are people in Southland Park all night.

   The police should tell ___*them to go home*___.

2. Women and senior citizens are often easy targets. Why don't we organize special

   self-defense classes, like karate? The classes will teach ___them to defend themselves___.

3. The vacant lot across from the park is full of litter. Let's talk to Mrs. Hyer, the owner of

   the lot. We can ask ___her to clean up the lot___.

4. Mr. Torres likes walking his dog late at night. Someone should tell

   ___him to be alert___.

Show what you know! Identify community problems

STEP 1. GROUPS. **Identify a problem in the neighborhood where you attend school. Discuss.**

- Who can you talk to in order to find a solution to the problem?
- What will you say to get help?

STEP 2. CLASS. **Share your ideas.**

Can you...identify community problems? ☐

Writing

A GROUPS. Communities can create a sense of belonging. Discuss.

1. What is an *outsider*? Why is it important NOT to feel like an outsider?
2. What can people do to feel like part of their community?

B Read the writing model. What is a *block party*? What is the author's opinion of block parties?

A Block Party That Made a Difference

In July 2008, I went to my first block party. My husband and I were living in a new neighborhood, and we felt like outsiders. Then came the big event. I had no idea a block party could be such a great experience. First of all, the party was fun. The city closed our street to traffic, and everyone came out. There were games for children, music for teens and adults, and food for everyone. Best of all, I really got a chance to talk to some of my neighbors. That brings me to the second reason I liked the block party: I learned a lot about my neighborhood. I found out about the best places to shop and eat. I heard about programs and services at the library and the community center. I also found out about neighborhood volunteer projects, like cleaning up the park and delivering hot meals to senior citizens. You may already know the last reason I am a big fan of block parties. My husband and I made some good friends that day, and we now feel like part of the community. A few weeks after the block party, I started volunteering in the neighborhood, and yes, I am on the planning team for this year's event.

C PAIRS. Answer the questions.

1. Why was the block party fun?
2. How did the block party change the author's life?
3. Would you like to attend a block party? Explain.

> **Writing Tip**
>
> Details are important in your writing. Examples are an excellent way to give details.

D What is the second reason the author likes block parties? Draw one line under the author's reason. What are three examples that give details about her second reason? Write *1*, *2*, and *3* next to each example.

E GROUPS. Compare your answers.

Express feelings about your neighborhood

Getting Started   5 minutes

1   BEFORE YOU WRITE

Ⓐ GROUPS. Communities can create...

- Write *teacher, manager, gardener,* and *outsider* on the board. Ask the whole class: *What does -er at the end of a word mean?* (a person) *What is an outsider?* (a person who does not belong to a particular group)
- Form cross-ability groups. Give a time limit. While students are talking, walk around and provide help as needed.
- Bring the class together. Call on volunteers to answer the questions.

Possible answers: 1. It's important NOT to feel like an outsider because that's an unpleasant feeling. People need to get services and feel supported in their community. 2. People can introduce themselves to their neighbors, become involved in community projects, and go to community events.

Presentation   15 minutes

Ⓑ Read the writing model. What is...

- Read the model out loud as students read along silently.
- Tell students to read the paragraph again and underline the information that answers the questions.
- Have a volunteer answer the first question.

Answer: A *block party* is a party for all the people who live on a block or in a neighborhood. The city closes a street and all the neighbors come out. There are games, music, and food.

- Have another volunteer answer the second question. Since this is an inference question, ask the student: *How do you know?*

Answer: The author has a very positive opinion. She says she had fun, she learned a lot about her neighborhood, and she made some good friends at the party.

Ⓒ PAIRS. Answer the questions.

- Read the first question and ask the class: *How many reasons does the writer give?* (three) *Which words help you identify them?* (first, second, last)
- Pair students and give a time limit for talking. Walk around and provide help as needed.
- Call on students to read the questions and say their answers.

Answers: 1. There were games, music, and food, and the writer got to talk to her neighbors. 2. She learned a lot about the neighborhood and made good friends. Now she feels like part of the community, and she has started volunteering in the neighborhood.

Ⓓ What is the second reason...

- Have students work alone. Give a time limit.

Answers: A line should be drawn under "I learned a lot about my neighborhood." The three examples are: 1. "I found out about the best places to shop and eat." 2. "I heard about programs and services at the library and the community center." 3. "I also found out about neighborhood volunteer projects, like cleaning up the park and delivering hot meals to senior citizens."

Ⓔ GROUPS. Compare your answers.

- Have students compare the sentence they underlined in Exercise D and the sentences they numbered.
- Bring the class together and check answers.

Writing Tip: Using Details

- Read the Writing Tip. Ask: *Why are details important?* (They illustrate the main ideas. They make writing more interesting and easier to remember.)
- Have students underline the first reason in the model paragraph. Ask: *How many details support this reason?* (five) *What are they?* (everyone came out; there were games for children; there was music for teens and adults; there was food for everyone; and the writer got a chance to talk to her neighbors) *Can you write two details in the same sentence?* (yes) *How can you connect them?* (with *and* or commas) *Which words connect the different details?* (*and, best of all*)

Controlled Practice 20 minutes

2 THINKING ON PAPER

A BRAINSTORM. Think about the neighborhood...

- Remind students that when they brainstorm, they should try to think of a lot of ideas. Later they will choose the ones they want to write about.
- As an example, ask the class to name things they like about their neighborhood and things they dislike. Write the items on the board.
- Give a time limit. While students are writing, walk around and provide help as needed.
- Pair students and have them share their charts with each other.
- Have students share their likes and dislikes with the class. Make two lists on the board.

B Decide whether you...

- Demonstrate the activity. Select one of the likes or dislikes on the board. Have students think of one reason and two (or more) details to support the reason. Write students' ideas in the form of an outline.
- Have students complete the exercise alone. Give a time limit. While students are working, walk around and provide help as needed.
- Pair or group students and have them share their outlines with one another.

▬ MULTILEVEL INSTRUCTION for 2B

Pre-level Have students give just one reason and provide two details to support their point of view.

Above-level Have students give more than two details to support the reasons for their point of view. Alternately, have them write about one thing they like and one thing they dislike, supporting each with reasons and details. Tell them to separate the two parts of their paragraph with the transition *On the other hand*.

Communicative Practice 20 minutes

3 WRITE

Write a paragraph about what you like...

- Say: *Now use the outline you wrote in Exercise 2B to write your paragraph. It's OK to change or add ideas while you are writing.*
- Review paragraph format. Remind students to give their paragraph a title, indent the first line, and begin each sentence with a capital letter.
- Encourage students to use the unit grammar: participial adjectives, *wish* in the present and future, and verb + object + infinitive phrases.

4 CHECK YOUR WRITING

> **Teaching Tip**
>
> You may want to collect student papers and provide feedback. Use the scoring rubric for writing on page T-xiv to evaluate each student's vocabulary, grammar, mechanics and how well he or she has completed the task. You may want to review the completed rubric with the students.

- Read the questions in the checklist. Say: *These questions will help you write a better paragraph.*
- Have students read their paragraphs and check off the questions in the checklist. Alternately, have them revise their paragraphs according to the items in the checklist.
- Collect papers. Make corrections as needed in paragraph format, participial adjectives, *wish* in the present or future, verb + object + infinitive phrases, and the items in the writing checklist.

▬ Expansion: Writing Practice

- Have students rewrite their paragraphs.
- Pair students and have them read their paragraphs to each other.
- Have volunteers read their paragraphs to the class.

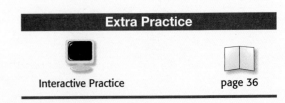

Extra Practice	
Interactive Practice	page 36

2 THINKING ON PAPER

A BRAINSTORM. **Think about the neighborhood where you live. What do you like about the neighborhood? What do you dislike? Organize your reasons in a chart like this.**

Things I Like in My Neighborhood	Things I Dislike in My Neighborhood
A.	A.
B.	B.

B **Decide whether you want to write about what you like or what you dislike about your neighborhood. Plan and organize your paragraph. Give reasons for your like (or dislike). Give examples that support your reasons.**

What I Like or (Dislike) Most About My Neighborhood: _____

  A. Reason: _____

     1. _____

     2. _____

  B. Reason: _____

     1. _____

     2. _____

3 WRITE

Write a paragraph about what you like or dislike most about your neighborhood. Use the information in your plan. Look at the writing model for an example.

4 CHECK YOUR WRITING

☐ Did you state the main idea, or subject, of your paragraph?

☐ Did you use words like *first, second,* and *third* to signal your reasons?

☐ Did you give examples to provide details?

☐ Did you use correct capitalization, punctuation, and spelling?

1 REVIEW

For your grammar review, go to page 247.

2 ACT IT OUT What do you say?

STEP 1. CLASS. Review the conversation on page 59 (CD1, Track 37).

STEP 2. ROLE PLAY. PAIRS. Role-play this situation.

Student A: You are organizing a spring clean-up in the neighborhood park next Saturday. Explain the reasons that the spring clean-up is a good idea. Try to convince Student B to help.

Student B: You have Saturday off and you have a lot to do. You don't have time to go to the spring clean-up. Explain your reasons.

3 READ AND REACT Problem-solving

STEP 1. GROUPS. Read about Lydia's problem.

Until recently, Lydia's neighborhood was an immigrant community, and residents shared the same language and culture. However, the area is changing. There are a lot of new residents who are not from Lydia's home culture. Lydia no longer feels at home in her community. She is afraid that these and other changes will make it difficult for her and her family to continue living in the neighborhood.

STEP 2. GROUPS. What is Lydia's problem? Discuss a solution. List three things that she and her family can do to solve the problem.

4 CONNECT

For your Community-Building Activity, go to page 258.
For your Team Project, go to page 265.

Which goals can you check off? Go back to page 45.

 Go to the CD-ROM for more practice.

1 REVIEW

Turn to page 247 for the Grammar Review.

2 ACT IT OUT

STEP 1. CLASS. Review the conversation...

- Play CD 1, Track 37. Have students listen as they read the script on page 59.

STEP 2. ROLE PLAY. PAIRS. Role-play this situation.

> **Teaching Tip**
>
> While pairs are performing role plays, use the scoring rubric for speaking on page T-xiii to evaluate each student's vocabulary, grammar, fluency, and how well he or she completes the task. You may want to review the completed rubric with the students.

- Have students look at the illustration. Ask: *Where are the people? What are they doing?*
- Read the role descriptions.
- Model the role play with an above-level student. Play the role of Student B. Student A can begin like this: *I'm organizing a spring cleanup in the park next Saturday.*
- Tell students to practice out loud at least twice.
- Have volunteers role-play for the class.

▬ MULTILEVEL INSTRUCTION FOR 2

Pre-level Have students write their dialogue. Tell Student A to give just one reason why the cleanup is a good idea. Tell Student B to give one reason why he or she cannot participate.

Above-level Have students practice without notes. Tell Student A to give three reasons why the cleanup is important or why Student B will benefit from participating. Have Student B give three reasons why he or she cannot participate.

3 READ AND REACT

STEP 1. GROUPS. Read about Lydia's problem.

- Read the paragraph while students follow along silently.

STEP 2. GROUPS. What is Lydia's problem?...

- Form groups of three or four. Have each group choose a timekeeper, a note taker, and a reporter.
- Give a time limit for discussion.
- Walk around and provide help as needed.
- Have the reporter from each group share the group's ideas. Write all the ideas on the board.
- Have the class vote on the best solution.

▬ Expansion: Speaking Practice for STEP 2

- Ask students if they have had a similar experience and how they dealt (or are dealing) with it.
- If students don't have a similar experience, have students share their opinions about whether this would be a problem for them. If so, how would they deal with it?

4 CONNECT

Turn to page 258 for the Community-Building Activity and page 265 for the Team Project. See page T-xi for general notes about teaching these activities.

Progress Check

Which goals can you check off? Go back to page 45.
Ask students to turn to page 45 and check off any remaining goals they have reached. Call on students to say which goals they will practice outside of class.

▬ Go to the CD-ROM for more practice.

If your students need more practice with the vocabulary, grammar, and competencies in Unit 3, encourage them to review the activities on the CD-ROM.

4 On the Job

CD 1
Tracks 38–51

Interactive Practice
Unit 4

Workbook
Unit 4

Unit Overview

Goals

- See the list of goals on the facing page.

Grammar

- Phrasal verbs
- Negative *yes/no* questions
- Indirect instructions, commands, and requests

Pronunciation

- Stress in phrasal verbs
- Weak and strong pronunciation of auxiliary verbs

Reading

- Read an employee handbook
- Read an article about reducing workplace injuries
- *Reading Skill:* Recognizing restatements

Writing

- Write a memo to a supervisor

Life Skills

- Interpret information about employee benefits

Preview

- Say the unit title. Ask: *What does* on the job *mean?*
- Hold up your book or have students look at their books. Set the context by asking the preview questions. You can also ask: *Where are the people? What's their job? What are they doing?*

Unit Goals

- Point to the Unit Goals. Have students read the goals silently.
- Tell students they will be studying these goals in Unit 4.
- Say each goal and explain unfamiliar vocabulary as needed. For example: *Supervisor: a boss or manager; the person who checks an employee's work. Employee benefits: things that employees get in addition to their salary, such as health insurance and vacation. Injury: physical damage to the body. Performance review: A written evaluation of an employee's work. Memo: short for memorandum; a short, written communication with information or instructions for employees.*
- Tell students to circle one or more goals that are very important to them. Call on several volunteers to say the goals they circled.
- Write a checkmark (✓) on the board. Say: *We will come back to this page again. You will write a checkmark next to the goals you learned in this unit.*

On the Job

Preview

Read the title. Why are the people shaking hands? What do you think they are saying?

UNIT GOALS

☐ Communicate with supervisors and co-workers

☐ Interpret information about employee benefits

☐ Check your understanding of a situation at work

☐ Talk about common workplace injuries

☐ Ask and answer performance review questions

☐ Follow work-related instructions

☐ Write a memo to a supervisor

Listening and Speaking

1 BEFORE YOU LISTEN

A CLASS. Sandra Duval is a new teller at People's Bank. It's her first day at work. Discuss. How do you think Sandra feels?

CD1 T38
B Read and listen to the words. Which ones have you seen or heard before?

> automatically   endorse   firsthand   observe   procedure

CD1 T38
C Listen again and repeat.

2 LISTEN

CD1 T39
A Sandra is talking to Robert Stamov, her manager at the bank. Listen to the first part of their conversation. How does Sandra feel about having to observe Robert? Why?

CD1 T40
B Read the statements. Then listen to the whole conversation. Write *T* (true) or *F* (false). Correct the false statements.

___F___ 1. Sandra will receive on-the-job training from Robert for ~~two weeks~~. *one week*

___F___ 2. Robert explains how to ~~cash~~ a check. *deposit*

___T___ 3. Robert explains the procedure for personal bank accounts.

___T___ 4. The bank's customers deposit checks more often than cash.

___T___ 5. The amount on the check and the deposit slip must be the same.

C Sandra says, "I'm a little nervous, but I'll get over it." What does she mean? What does the phrase *get over it* mean?

D PAIRS. Sandra asked Robert a lot of questions. Is it a good idea to ask so many questions on the first day of a job? Explain.

Communicate with supervisors and co-workers

Getting Started   5 minutes

1 BEFORE YOU LISTEN

A CLASS. Sandra Duval is a new teller...

- Have students look at the photo in their books. Ask: *Who are the people? How old are they? What is their relationship? What do you think they're talking about?*
- Ask students if they remember their first day at work. How did they feel? How do they think Sandra Duval feels?

Possible answer: Sandra probably feels nervous. She may also feel happy and excited.

B Read and listen to the words...

- Play CD 1, Track 38. Have students listen and circle the words they know.
- Call on students to define the words and say them in sentences. For example: *Automatically: done by machine, without human effort. Endorse: to write one's name on the back of a check. Firsthand: To see or experience directly, not through a book or another person. Observe: to watch without intervening. Procedure: a way of doing something.*

C Listen again and repeat.

- Play Track 38 again. Have students listen and repeat.
- Call on students to say each word. Correct pronunciation as needed.

Presentation   10 minutes

2 LISTEN

A Sandra is talking to Robert Stamov...

- Play CD 1, Track 39. Have students listen.
- Have students discuss the questions with a classmate.
- If necessary, play Track 39 again for students to check their answers.
- Call on students to share their answers.

Answer: Sandra feels positive about observing Robert. She thinks it will be helpful to observe the bank's procedures before she actually follows them.

Controlled Practice   10 minutes

B Read the statements...

- Have students read the statements silently and predict if they are true or false.
- Play CD 1, Track 40.
- Pair students and have them decide on answers.
- Check answers. Call on students to read each statement and say if it is true or false. If it is false, ask the student to correct it. Write the answers on the board.

C Sandra says "I'm a little nervous,..."

- Write *get over it* on the board.
- Have a volunteer answer the questions.

Answer: Sandra means that soon she won't be nervous anymore. *Get over it* means to recover (from an illness) or feel better.

- Have other students form sentences about their own experiences, using *get/got over it.*

D PAIRS. Sandra asked Robert...

- Pair students and give them a time limit for discussion.
- Call on a volunteer to answer the question. Ask the class: *Does anyone disagree?* or *Does anyone have a different opinion?*

Teaching Tip

After a student has expressed an opinion, you can encourage further discussion by asking *Does anyone disagree?* or *Who has a different idea?*

Presentation   5 minutes

3 CONVERSATION

Pronunciation Watch

- On the board, write: *1. Lena put away her clothes. 2. Lena put her clothes away. 3. Lena put them away.*
- Read the Pronunciation Watch note.
- Read the sentences on the board. Clap on the stressed verbs and nouns (shown in italics). (1. *Lena put away* her *clothes*; 2. *Lena put* her *clothes away*; 3. *Lena put* them *away*)

Ⓐ 🔊 Listen to the sentences....

- Play CD 1, Track 41. Have students listen.
- Play Track 41 again. Have students listen and repeat.
- Say *Sentence 1*. Point to various students and have them say the words with correct stress. To correct errors, model the correct pronunciation and have the student repeat.
- Repeat for the rest of the sentences.

Controlled Practice   15 minutes

Ⓑ 🔊 Read the sentences. Put a dot...

- Do item 1 with the class. Repeat the rule if necessary: Pronouns are not stressed.
- Have students complete the remaining items, working alone or in pairs.
- Play CD 1, Track 42. Have students listen and check their answers.
- Call on students to read the sentences aloud. Correct errors as needed. Write the stressed words in each item on the board.

Ⓒ 🔊 Sandra is talking to Jason...

- Play CD 1, Track 43. Have students listen and read along silently.
- *Optional:* You may want to have above-level students listen with their books closed.
- Check comprehension. Ask: *Is Sandra learning quickly or slowly? What does Sandra need to find out about? When is the meeting? What is it about?*

4 PRACTICE

Ⓐ PAIRS. Practice the conversation.

- Form pairs. Have them read the conversation once, then switch roles and practice again.
- Walk around and listen as students are practicing. Take notes on pronunciation errors. Select a few key errors and correct as follows: *T: I heard _____. What should it be?* Elicit the correct form. Have the class repeat.
- Ask volunteers to perform their conversation for the class.

Communicative Practice   15 minutes

Ⓑ MAKE IT PERSONAL. Think about your...

STEP 1. GROUPS. What do you expect...

- With the class, read the example. Explain: If you get an orientation to a place, you become familiar with it. For example, you learn the location of the lunchroom, the copy machine, the restrooms, etc.
- Form groups. Have them choose a timekeeper, note taker, and reporter. Give a time limit. As students are talking, walk around and provide help as needed.

STEP 2. CLASS. Share your ideas.

- Have each reporter share the group's list with the class. Write all the responses on the board.
- Survey the class. Point to each response on the board and ask: *How many people did this on their first day at a new job?*
- Select a few key pronunciation errors. Say the incorrect pronunciation. Elicit the correct pronunciation and have the class repeat.

Extra Practice

Interactive Practice

CD1 T41

A 🔘 Listen to the sentences. Notice the stressed words. Then listen again and repeat.

Fill out the form.   Fill the form out.   Fill it out.

Pronunciation Watch

In most phrasal verbs, both the verb and particle can be stressed. If there is a noun object, the noun may be stressed instead of the particle. If there is a pronoun object, the pronoun is not stressed.

CD1 T42

B 🔘 Read the sentences. Put a dot (•) over the words in the underlined sections that would be stressed. Then listen and check your answers.

1. Let me know if I can help you out.
2. I'm a little nervous, but I'll get over it.
3. Turn the computer off before you leave.
4. I already turned it off.
5. There's a lot to learn, but you're picking it up quickly.

CD1 T43

C 🔘 Sandra is talking to Jason, another teller. Listen and read their conversation.

Sandra: There sure is a lot to learn for this job.

Jason: There *is* a lot to learn, but you're picking it up quickly. Let me know if there's any way I can help you out.

Sandra: Thanks, Jason. Right now, I need to find out about my health benefits.

Jason: You're in luck. There's a meeting tomorrow to discuss our health plan.

Sandra: Oh, yeah. I forgot. What time is the meeting?

Jason: Two o'clock. But you should check with Robert.

4 PRACTICE

A PAIRS. Practice the conversation.

B MAKE IT PERSONAL. Think about your first day at a new job.

STEP 1. GROUPS. What do you expect to do? Make a list of four things.

> 1. Get an orientation to the building.

STEP 2. CLASS. Share your ideas.

Grammar

Phrasal verbs

Separable phrasal verbs	Inseparable phrasal verbs
Fill out the deposit slip completely. **Fill** the deposit slip **out** completely. **Fill** it **out** completely.	I'll **get over** my nervousness. I'll **get over** it.

Grammar Watch

- A phrasal verb consists of a verb + a **particle**. Particles are words such as *up, down, on, off, after, by, in,* and *out.*

- For **inseparable phrasal verbs**, the verb and the particle must stay together.

- For **separable phrasal verbs**, the verb and the particle can stay together or be separated.

- Many phrasal verbs can take **objects** (nouns or pronouns). When the object of a separable phrasal verb is a noun, the object can come before or after the particle. When the object is a pronoun, the object must come before the particle.

- Inseparable phrasal verbs sometimes have two particles, for example, *get along with.*

- *See page 282-283 for a list of phrasal verbs and their meanings.*

1 PRACTICE

Read the conversation. Underline the phrasal verbs. Then write the correct phrasal verb next to each definition.

Robert: When the bank closes, there's still quite a bit of work for the tellers. Most evenings you'll work until 6:00. At the end of the day, don't <u>turn off</u> your computer or other equipment until we've <u>put together</u> our final report for the day. It's important that we have an exact record of all transactions.

Sandra: What if there's a problem and I can't <u>figure</u> it <u>out</u>?

Robert: For now, you'll <u>talk it over</u> with me or another teller. If we see any problems, we'll <u>point</u> them <u>out</u>. But I'm not worried. You're doing an excellent job.

Sandra: Thanks. You can <u>count on</u> me to do my best.

1. _____turn off_____ = stop

2. _____talk over_____ = discuss

3. _____count on_____ = depend on

4. _____put together_____ = assemble

5. _____figure out_____ = solve a problem

6. _____point out_____ = indicate, show

Getting Started   5 minutes

- Review the concept of phrasal verbs. On the board, write: *On workdays, I get up at 7 A.M. 2. I eat lunch at 12:30.* Ask: *What's the verb in each sentence?* Elicit *get up* and *eat* and underline them. Explain: *Eat is a regular verb. It is one word. Get up is a phrasal verb. It consists of a verb + a particle. Particles are prepositions or adverbs.*

- Ask students if they know any other phrasal verbs. List them on the board.

- Say: *In this lesson we're going to learn more about phrasal verbs.*

Presentation   15 minutes

Phrasal verbs

- Copy the grammar chart onto the board. Read the first Grammar Watch note. Point to the chart and ask: *Which words are particles?* Elicit *out* and *over* and circle them.

- Say: *There are two kinds of phrasal verbs, separable and inseparable.*

- Read the second and third Grammar Watch notes. Point to the sentences in the *Separable phrasal verbs* column of the chart. Read the first two sentences to show that the verb and particle can be separated.

- Point to the first sentence in the *Inseparable phrasal verbs* column. Explain that *get over* is like one word. You cannot put any other words between *get* and *over.*

- Read the fourth note. Point to the last sentence in the *Separable* column. Highlight the word *it.* Then ask: *Can we say* fill out it*? (no)*

- Point to the last sentence in the *Inseparable* column. Highlight the word *it.* Ask: *Can we say* get it over*? (no)*

- To reinforce, write the following sentences in a list on the board: *1. Please turn off the light. 2. Please turn the light off. 3. Please turn it off. 4. Please turn off it. 5. Last night I ran into an old friend. 6. Last night I ran into him. 7. Last night I ran him into. 8. Last night I ran a friend into.*

- Pair students. Say: *Some sentences are correct. Some sentences are not correct English. Decide which sentences are incorrect.*

- *Optional:* Provide a hint. Say: *Three sentences are incorrect.* (Sentences 4, 7, and 8 are incorrect.)

- Check answers. Say the number of each sentence and ask the class: *Is it correct or incorrect?* For the incorrect items, ask the class to explain why they are incorrect.

- Read the fifth note. Ask students if they can think of any other three-word phrasal verbs, for example, *drop out of, get out of,* and *look out for.*

 Expansion: Grammar Practice

- Play a game. Write selected phrasal verbs from the lists on pages 282–283 on two sets of index cards, one with verbs and the other with particles.

- Form groups of four or five. Give each group both sets of cards. Have students shuffle the cards. Then have the students in each group make up phrasal verbs by matching the words on the two sets of index cards. Tell them they can use the verbs and particles more than once.

- Give a time limit.

- Have each group write their phrasal verbs on the board. Have students check for correctness, using the list in the Appendix. The group that comes up with the most correct phrasal verbs wins.

Controlled Practice   20 minutes

1 PRACTICE

Read the conversation. Underline...

- Read Robert's first speaking turn. Ask the class: *What does* turn off *mean?* Direct students to item 1.

- Have students complete the exercise. Walk around and provide help as needed.

- Check answers. Then go over the list and have the class say if each verb is separable or inseparable. Elicit all possible ways of saying each sentence.

Expansion: Speaking Practice

- Form cross-ability pairs and have students practice reading the conversation. The pre-level student should read the part of Sandra.

- Remind students about the proper pronunciation of phrasal verbs.

- While students are practicing, walk around and correct errors in pronunciation.

- Have volunteers perform the conversation for the class.

2 PRACTICE

Ⓐ Unscramble the sentences. Put the words...

- Read the example. Tell students that if a verb is separable, they should write the sentence in two ways. If they are not sure whether a verb is separable or inseparable, they should consult the lists on pages 282–283.
- Have students work alone or in pairs.
- Write the numbers *2* through *5* on the board. Call up students to write the sentences.
- Have other students read the sentences on the board. If there is an error, have students correct it.

Ⓑ Circle the object in each sentence. Then...

- Read the example.
- Have students complete the exercise.
- Write the numbers *2* through *5* on the board. Call on students to write the sentences with pronouns on the board.
- Call on students to read the sentences and make corrections as needed.

▮▮▮ Expansion: Writing Practice for 2B

- Have students write two-line dialogues using the phrasal verbs in Exercise 2B. For example, A: *Did you remember to turn off your computer? B: Yes, I turned it off. A: Can you point out the teacher? B: No, I can't point her out. She's not here.*

Communicative Practice   20 minutes

Show what you know!

ROLE PLAY. PAIRS. Role-play this situation....

Teaching Tip

While pairs are performing, use the scoring rubric for speaking on page T-xiii to evaluate each student's vocabulary, grammar, fluency, and how well he or she completes the task.

- Read the role descriptions.
- Review the meanings of the verbs in the box. Pair students and assign each of them a verb. Have them look up the meaning, if necessary, on pages 282–283 and write a sentence about somebody's first day at work using the verb.
- Have students write their sentences on the board. Read them and make corrections as needed.
- On the board, write A: *What are my job responsibilities? B: You need to . . . You have to . . . You should . . .* Tell students they can use these phrases in their dialogues. They can also get ideas by listening again to the conversation on CD 1, Track 40 and by reading again the conversations in Exercise 3C, page 67; and Exercise 1, page 68.
- Suggest that students decide where their conversation will take place (an office, a factory, a restaurant, etc.).
- Model the role play with an above-level student. Play the role of Student B. Include three phrasal verbs from the list.
- Have students write out their dialogues.
- Tell students to practice out loud at least twice.
- Have volunteers role-play for the class.

▮▮▮ MULTILEVEL INSTRUCTION for Show what you know!

Pre-level Have students write a short conversation using just one or two phrasal verbs each. Suggest that they use the conversation in Exercise 1, page 68 as a model.

Above-level Have each speaker use two to three phrasal verbs in their conversation and write an outline instead of a script.

Progress Check

Can you . . . communicate with supervisors and co-workers?

Say: *Look at the question at the bottom of the page. Can you communicate with supervisors and co-workers? Write a checkmark in the box.*

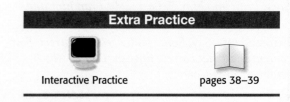

Extra Practice

Interactive Practice   pages 38–39

A Unscramble the sentences. Put the words in order. More than one answer is possible.

1. filled / The customer / out / the form

   The customer filled the form out. OR: _The customer filled out the form._

2. the new employee / out / We / with her first assignment / to help / offered   We offered to help out the new employee with her first assignment. (or We offered to help the new employee out with her first assignment.)

3. he'll / over / He's / about the new schedule, / it / get / but / upset

   He's upset about the new schedule, but he'll get over it.

4. me / on time / count / the job / can / You / on / to do

   You can count on me to do the job on time.

5. talk / should / with your manager / over / that problem / You

   You should talk over that problem with your manager. (or You should talk that problem over with your manager.)

B Circle the object in each sentence. Then, on notepaper, rewrite each sentence using an object pronoun (*it, them, her*, or *him*).

1. Be sure to turn off (your computer) before you leave.

   Be sure to turn it off before you leave.

2. Can you point out (the new employees)?   Can you point them out?

3. Their accountants figured out (the problem.)   Their accountants figured it out.

4. The managers put (this plan) together.   The managers put it together.

5. She can count on (her co-workers.)   She can count on them.

Show what you know!   Communicate with supervisors and co-workers

ROLE PLAY. PAIRS. **Role-play this situation. Use the phrasal verbs in the box.**

Student A: You are starting a new job. Discuss your responsibilities with your supervisor.

Student B: You are Student A's supervisor, and it is his or her first day on the job. Discuss Student A's job responsibilities.

count on	figure out	find out	get over	help out	pick up
point out	put together	take over	talk over	turn off	turn on

Can you...communicate with supervisors and co-workers? ☐

Life Skills

1 READ AN EMPLOYEE HANDBOOK

A CLASS. New employees often receive a handbook on the first day of work. Discuss. What kind of information is usually included in an employee handbook?

B Read part of a company's employee handbook. Which benefits are probably different for part-time employees?

ACE Computer Solutions

Employee Benefits Overview

Welcome to Ace! We are pleased to provide you with information about your employment here. (Note: This information applies only to full-time employees.)

PAYROLL: All employees are paid bi-weekly, that is, at the end of every 2 weeks.

HOURS: The normal workday is 8 hours with one hour for lunch. You are expected to work Mon.–Fri.

OVERTIME: Here at Ace, we work overtime only when necessary. Full-time employees are allowed to work a maximum of 10 hours of overtime per week. The company pays employees one and one-half times their hourly rate for overtime work. Supervisors must approve all overtime.

PAID TIME OFF (PTO): After 90 days of service, you are eligible for PTO:

• *Sick leave:* 10 paid sick days per year. Please note that if you are out sick longer than 2 days, you must supply a doctor's note describing the nature of the illness and saying that you can return to work.

• *Vacation:* Vacation days are based on length of service (less than 5 years = 10 days per year; 5–10 years = 15 days per year; 11–19 years = 20 days per year; 20 or more years = 24 days per year).

• *Personal days:* You are allowed 5 personal days per year. If possible, please get permission from your supervisor at least 10 business days in advance.

• *Holidays:* Ace is closed on these holidays: New Year's Day, Martin Luther King Jr. Day, Memorial Day, Independence Day, Labor Day, Thanksgiving, and Christmas.

Getting Started   5 minutes

1 READ AN EMPLOYEE HANDBOOK

A CLASS. New employees often receive...

- Survey the class. Ask: *How many of you received an employee handbook on your first day at work?*
- Call on students who raised their hands. Ask: *Did you read it? What kind of information did it include?* List students' answers on the board.
- If no one has received an employee handbook, brainstorm with the class on the information that is probably included.

Answer: An employee handbook may include any or all of the following information: a welcome statement, history of the company, names of company executives, how to contact the human resources department, hiring policies, orientation for new employees, employee classifications, hours, and schedules, pay policies, benefits, vacations and time off, information about performance reviews, workplace dress code and expected behavior, health and safety issues, drugs and alcohol warnings, antidiscrimination information, information about sexual harassment, procedure for making a complaint, and procedure for terminating employment.

Presentation   15 minutes

B Read part of a company's...

- With the class, do a preliminary survey of the reading. Ask questions about the title and main headings. For example: *Which company does the employee handbook come from?* (ACE Computer Solutions) *What are the four main topics on this page?* (payroll, hours, overtime, *and* paid time off) *What is PTO?* (paid time off) *Which topics are included in paid time off?* (sick leave, vacation, personal days, *and* holidays)
- Give students a time limit for reading.
- While students are reading, walk around and provide help as needed.
- Repeat the question in the directions and elicit answers from students. List answers on the board.

Answer: The following benefits are probably different for part-time employees: hours, overtime, sick leave, vacation, and personal days.

Culture Connection

The Family and Medical Leave Act is a law that guarantees employees up to twelve workweeks of unpaid leave during any twelve-month period for the birth and care of a new baby or adopted child or for the care of an immediate family member with a serious medical condition.

Controlled Practice   20 minutes

2 PRACTICE

Ⓐ Read the questions. Circle...

- Read the directions.
- Have students complete the exercise. Give a time limit. While they are reading, walk around and provide help as needed.
- Say an item number and have the class call out the letter of the correct answer. Make corrections as needed.

Communicative Practice   20 minutes

Ⓑ GROUPS. Discuss.

- Form cross-ability groups. Have each group choose a timekeeper, a note taker, and a reporter. The note taker should list students' responses to questions 2 and 4.
- Give a time limit for discussion. While students are talking, walk around and provide help as needed.
- Go over the questions with the class. Have volunteers share their ideas regarding questions 1 and 3. Have reporters share their group's answers to questions 2 and 4.

Possible answers: 1. Ace has very good benefits. It allows ten sick days and ten vacation days for all employees. 2. (See list of typical information in Employee Handbook on page T-70.) 3. because overtime is expensive for the company 4. People take personal days to take care of sick relatives, to get married, to attend family functions such as funerals, to take care of business matters, to be with their children when school is closed or if their babysitter is sick.

▇ Expansion: Speaking Practice

- Form groups of four to five students. Have them go over each section of the Ace Employee Benefits Overview and compare their benefits with those of Ace. If students do not have a job, they can speak about a previous job they had in the U.S., or they can talk about benefits that are typical for people with their occupation in their home country.

Progress Check

Can you . . . interpret information about employee benefits?

Say: *We have practiced interpreting information about employee benefits. Now, look at the question at the bottom of the page. Can you interpret information about employee benefits? Write a checkmark in the box.*

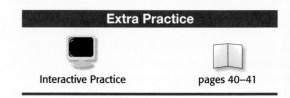

Extra Practice	
Interactive Practice	pages 40–41

A Read the questions. Circle the correct answers.

1. How many times a month do Ace employees usually receive a paycheck?
   a. one
   b. two
   c. four

2. How many hours do full-time Ace employees normally work a day?
   a. seven
   b. eight
   c. ten

3. Imagine you're an Ace employee. You were home sick for four days. What do you have to do before you go back to work?
   a. get permission from your supervisor
   b. see a doctor
   c. notify a co-worker

4. Justin, an Ace employee, has been with the company for thirteen years. How many vacation days can he take?
   a. ten
   b. fifteen
   c. twenty

5. Silvia, another Ace employee, wants to take a personal day on her birthday, June 30. What is the last day she can ask for permission from her supervisor?
   a. May 30
   b. June 1
   c. June 16

6. Which is NOT a paid holiday for Ace employees?
   a. Presidents' Day
   b. Memorial Day
   c. Labor Day

B GROUPS. Discuss.

1. Do you think that Ace has good employee benefits? Explain.

2. This page is only a small part of an employee handbook. What other information do most employee handbooks include?

3. Why do you think Ace doesn't want employees to work overtime for more than ten hours?

4. What are some reasons employees take personal days?

Can you...interpret information about employee benefits? ☐

Listening and Speaking

1 BEFORE YOU LISTEN

CLASS. **Look at the picture of the doctor, the resident (someone who has almost finished training as a doctor), and the nurse.**

1. What job duties do you think each person has?
2. The resident is holding a patient's chart. What kind of information is in a patient's chart?

2 LISTEN

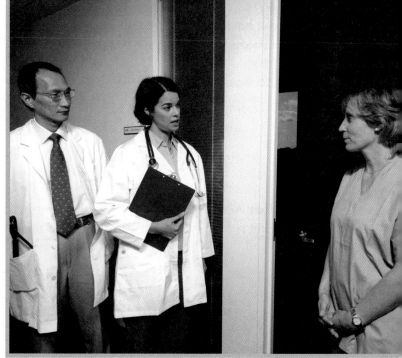

CD1 T44

A 📀 **Listen to two conversations at a hospital. A doctor and a resident are a talking to a nurse. What kind of nurse is Carolina— responsible or not responsible? Explain.**

CD1 T44

B 📀 **Listen again to the first conversation. Complete the statements. Choose the correct words.**

1. The resident doesn't see Mr. Cordova's **chart** /(**vital signs**)

2. The nursing assistant probably (**forgot to write**)/ **wrote** Mr. Cordova's vital signs in the chart.

3. Carolina **remembers to write** / (**offers to take**) Mr. Cordova's vital signs.

CD1 T45

C 📀 **Read the statements. Listen again to the second conversation. Write T (true) or F (false). Correct the false statements.**

__T__ 1. Mrs. Worth had a gall bladder operation yesterday.

   start walking
__F__ 2. Mrs. Worth needs to ~~wait for a while before she walks~~.

   not
__F__ 3. The nurses have ∧ helped Mrs. Worth to walk.

   not
__F__ 4. There are ∧ a lot of nurses on duty on Carolina's floor.

   will
__F__ 5. Carolina ~~doesn't~~ have time to help Mrs. Worth.

Getting Started   5 minutes

1   BEFORE YOU LISTEN

CLASS. Look at the picture...

- Ask: *What do you think: Which person is a doctor? Which one is a nurse? How do you know? What do you think they are talking about?*
- Elicit the job duties of full doctors, residents, and nurses and list them on the board.

Answers: 1. Doctors treat patients, prescribe medications, perform procedures, and supervise residents. **Residents** also treat patients, prescribe medications, and perform procedures, but they do so under the supervision of a full doctor. **Nurses** take care of patients and give them medicine as prescribed by a doctor or resident.

2. A patient's chart contains the patient's medical history, a list of medications the patient is taking, allergies, insurance information, and personal information.

> **Culture Connection**
>
> Both *full* doctors (in hospitals they are called *attending* physicians) and residents are licensed medical doctors. Residents are doctors who have recently finished medical school and who are still doing on-the-job training in a hospital. An attending physician is one who has finished residency and who has an established medical practice. Attending physicians supervise residents, and they are the ones who have ultimate responsibility for patients.

Presentation   10 minutes

2   LISTEN

A **Listen to two conversations...**

- Write the following terms on the board: *vital signs (vitals)*, *gall bladder*, and *procedure*. Tell students that they will hear these terms in the conversations. Point to each item and ask if anyone knows what they mean. If not, provide the definitions: *vital signs: a patient's blood pressure, temperature, and pulse; gall bladder: the small organ that stores bile from the liver, necessary for the digestion of food; procedure: a medical treatment that follows a series of steps, such as an operation.*
- Play CD 1, Track 44. Remind students to listen for clues that tell whether the nurse is responsible or not.
- Call on volunteers to say if they think the nurse is responsible or not. Ask them to explain their answer.

Answer: She is responsible. She is going to take the vital signs of one patient and help another patient to walk.

Controlled Practice   10 minutes

B **Listen again to the first...**

- Have students read the questions silently and predict the answers.
- Play CD 1, Track 44.
- Call on students to answer the questions.

C **Read the statements. Listen again...**

- Have students read the statements silently and predict if they are true or false.
- Play CD 1, Track 45.
- Pair students and have them compare answers.
- Call on students to read each item and say if it is true or false. If it is false, ask the student to correct it. Write the answers on the board.

Presentation 10 minutes

3 CONVERSATION

Pronunciation Watch

- Write on the board: *They have eaten; You can go now; I couldn't see her;* and *Did you lock the door?*
- Explain that *have, can, couldn't,* and *did* are *auxiliary verbs.* (*Auxiliary* verbs support main verbs.)
- Read the Pronunciation Watch note.
- Read the sentences on the board. Except for *couldn't,* these auxiliaries are all *unstressed.*

A Listen to the sentences...

- Play CD 1, Track 46. Have students listen.
- Play Track 46 again. Have students repeat.
- Have a student read each item.

Controlled practice 10 minutes

B Listen to the sentences. Circle the words...

- Play CD 1, Track 47. Have students listen and circle.
- Call on students to read the sentences with the correct word. Have the class repeat.

▮▮ Expansion: Pronunciation Practice

- Write *I can swim* and *I can't swim* on the board.
- Say each sentence and clap on the stressed words (*swim* in sentence 1; *can't swim* in 2). Ask: *What's the difference between* can *and* can't? (*Can* isn't stressed; *can't* is. Also, in connected speech, the vowel in *can* is shortened to schwa; in *can't,* the full vowel is pronounced.) Say the sentences again. Underline *swim* and *can't swim.*
- Write sentences with *can* and *can't* on the board. Say the sentences randomly. Have students say either *can* or *can't* after each sentence.
- Pair students. Have Student A say the sentences and Student B respond *can* or *can't.*

C Two nurses are talking at the...

- Define *on call. When it is a doctor's turn to work, the doctor is* on call *or available to be called if needed.*
- Play CD 1, Track 48. Have students listen and read.

4 PRACTICE

A PAIRS. Practice the conversation.

- Form pairs and have students read the conversation in Exercise 3C. Then have them switch roles and read again.
- Have pairs perform the conversation for the class.

Communicative Practice 15 minutes

B ROLE PLAY. PAIRS. You are co-workers...

> **Teaching Tip**
>
> While pairs are performing role plays, use the scoring rubric for speaking on page T-xiii to evaluate each student's vocabulary, grammar, fluency, and how well he or she completes the task. You may want to review the completed rubric with the students.

- Write the following terms on the board and elicit definitions: *Supply closet: the place in a hospital where supplies are stored; bandages: strips of fabric that are wrapped around an injury or wound; in charge of: to be responsible for something; stock (verb): to replace needed supplies.*
- Pair students of similar ability for practice.
- Have volunteers role-play their conversations.

▮▮ MULTILEVEL INSTRUCTION FOR 4B

Pre-level Allow students to read both parts before speaking.

Above-level Have the speakers suggest two ways to solve the problem.

Extra Practice

Interactive Practice

CONVERSATION

CD1 T46

A 🔘 **Listen to the sentences. Notice that the /t/ sound is often very quiet at the end of negative contractions. Then listen again and repeat.**

Pronunciation Watch

Auxiliary verbs (such as *have*, *can*, and *could*) usually have a strong pronunciation, with a clear vowel sound, in negative contractions and at the end of a sentence. They have a weak pronunciation, with a short, quiet vowel sound, when they come before another word in a sentence.

Can't she see Mr. Singer?   Yes, she **can**. She can see him today.

Couldn't he wait?   Yes, he **could**. He could wait until tomorrow.

Haven't they taken her out of bed?   Yes, they **have**.   Where have they taken her?

CD1 T47

B 🔘 **Listen to the sentences. Circle the words you hear.**

1. **Has** / (**Hasn't**) Mrs. Worth been out of bed?
2. (**Did**) / **Didn't** the nurse take her vital signs?
3. (**Could**) / **Couldn't** we look at her chart?
4. **Have** / (**Haven't**) any of the nurses walked with her?
5. I **can** / (**can't**) help her right now.

CD1 T48

C 🔘 **Two nurses are talking at the nurse's station. Listen and read.**

Valerie: Carolina, Mr. Singer would like to talk with Dr. Paige. Have you seen her?

Carolina: I don't think she's on call today. Wasn't she on call last night?

Valerie: I don't know. I was pretty sure she was on the schedule for today.

Carolina: Let me check. See. She was here last night. Dr. Garcia is on duty today. Can't he see Mr. Singer?

Valerie: He could, but Dr. Paige is her doctor. Mr. Singer really wants to talk to her. He wants to know the results of his recent tests.

Carolina: Well, in that case, tell him that Dr. Paige will be in tomorrow. Couldn't Mr. Singer wait until then?

Valerie: I think so. I'll explain that to him.

4 **PRACTICE**

A **PAIRS. Practice the conversation.**

B **ROLE PLAY. PAIRS. You are co-workers at Greenville General Hospital. Read your part, but don't read your partner's part. Solve the problem.**

Student A: You're looking for some bandages in the supply closet. A co-worker told you that Student B had put them in there. Speak to Student B about the bandages.

Student B: You aren't in charge of the bandages. Another person stocks them in the supply closet.

Grammar

Negative *yes/no* questions

Questions	Responses
Didn't the nurse take Mr. Cordova's vital signs this morning?	No, she didn't. They're not on the chart.
Haven't they tried to take her down the hall?	Yes, they have. They walked with her last night.

Grammar Watch

- Negative *yes/no* questions begin with negative forms of *be* or negative forms of auxiliary verbs, like *do*, *did*, *have*, *can*, *will*, and *should*. Use contractions in negative questions.
- Use negative *yes/no* questions to check information that you think is true.
- Use short answers to respond to negative questions. Answer with *yes* if the information is true and *no* if it is not true.

1 PRACTICE

A Match the questions that fast-food workers ask one another with the answers.

__b__ 1. Didn't you train for the cashier job?

__e__ 2. Didn't he give you the schedule you wanted?

__a__ 3. Don't most of the workers get along?

__c__ 4. Aren't the uniforms ready?

__d__ 5. Hasn't payroll given you your paycheck?

a. Yes, they do. They're good friends.

b. No, I didn't. I trained to take orders.

c. No, they're not. They're at the cleaners.

d. No, they haven't, and I need it now!

e. No, he didn't. I'm working nights again.

B Unscramble the questions. Put the words in the correct order.

1. they / about the schedule change? / you / tell / didn't

   Didn't they tell you about the schedule change?

2. yet? / arrived / hasn't / the cleaning crew

   Hasn't the cleaning crew arrived yet?

3. about that? / won't / complain / the customers

   Won't the customers complain about that?

4. get / part-time employees / don't / health insurance?

   Don't part-time employees get health insurance?

Getting Started   5 minutes

- Introduce negative *yes/no* questions by asking about information students know. For example, ask: *Isn't [student's name] from Mexico?* If students are confused by the negative contraction, nod your head up and down or shake it side to side to indicate the correct answer and have students say *yes* or *no*. Expand, for example: say: *Yes, she is* or *No, he isn't.*

- Write two questions and two responses—one affirmative and one negative—on the board. Say: *In this lesson we'll learn how to use negative yes/no questions.*

Presentation   15 minutes

Negative *yes/no* questions

- Copy the grammar chart onto the board. Circle the negative auxiliaries in the questions. Read the questions and answers.

- Read the first Grammar Watch note. Elicit the negative forms of all the auxiliaries in the note; for example, *T: Do, Ss: Don't. T: Can, Ss: Can't. T: Did, Ss: Didn't,* etc.

- Say: *Now let's talk about the meaning of negative yes/no questions.* Point to the first example in the grammar chart. Ask: *What does the speaker believe? Did the nurse take Mr. Cordova's vital signs or not?* (yes) Point to the second example and ask: *What does the speaker believe? Have they tried to take her down the hall or not?* (yes) Read the second Grammar Watch note.

- Read the third note. Point again to the first example and the answer. Ask: *What does* No, she didn't *mean?* (The speaker in the question assumed something that wasn't true. In fact, the nurse didn't take Mr. Cordova's vital signs.) Point to the second example and ask: *What does* Yes, they have *mean?* (The speaker in the question assumed correctly. They have taken her down the hall.)

Language Note

- Tell students that negative *yes/no* questions have two other meanings. On the board, write: *1. Don't you like it?* and *2. Aren't you ready yet?*

- Bring a funny item of clothing or accessory (for example, a hat or huge sunglasses) to class. Put on the item. When students begin to smile or laugh, point to sentence 1 and, in a surprised tone of voice ask: *What's the matter? Don't you like it?* Repeat the question and say: *I asked a negative yes/no question. Why? How did I feel?* (surprised).

- Say: *[female student's name] and [male student's name] are going to a movie together. [female student's name] is getting annoyed because [male student's name] isn't ready, and they're going to be late. She says: Aren't you ready yet?* Ask: *How does the woman feel?* (annoyed, impatient, angry) Say: *That's right. We use negative yes/no questions to show that we are angry, impatient, or annoyed.*

Controlled Practice   20 minutes

1   PRACTICE

Ⓐ Match the questions...

- Do item 1 with the class. Read the question. Have the class read the answer. Ask: *Why does the first speaker say* didn't? *What does the speaker believe?* (that the second speaker trained to be a cashier) *Was the first speaker correct?* (no)

- Tell students to complete the exercise alone or in pairs. Walk around and provide help as needed.

- Have students compare answers.

- Call on pairs of students to read the questions and answers. Write the answers on the board.

- *Optional:* You many want to call on students to say what the speaker believes in each question before completing the exercise.

Ⓑ Unscramble the questions. Put...

- Do item 1 with the class.

- Have students complete the exercise. Walk around and provide help as needed.

- Have students compare answers.

- Call on students to write answers on the board. Have other students say if they are correct.

2 PRACTICE

Ⓐ Write negative questions. Use...

- Do the first item with the class.
- Tell students to complete the exercise alone or in pairs. Walk around and provide help as needed.
- Have students compare answers.
- Call on students to write the questions on the board. Have other students say if they are correct.

Ⓑ Read each response. Then write...

- Look at item 1 with the class. Instruct students to read the answer first, then write a question starting with a negative auxiliary. Remind students that a negative *yes/no* question can have either a positive or a negative answer.
- Have students complete the remaining items.
- Call students up to the board to write the questions. Have the class correct as needed.

Communicative Practice   20 minutes

Show what you know!

ROLE PLAY. PAIRS. Role-play a conversation...

> **Teaching Tip**
>
> While pairs are performing role plays, use the scoring rubric for speaking on page T-xiii to evaluate each student's vocabulary, grammar, fluency, and how well he or she completes the task. You may want to review the completed rubric with the students.

- Have the class practice forming negative *yes/no* questions, using the items in the box. For example, *Haven't you gotten your building pass? Haven't you watched the training video?*
- Read the role descriptions. Explain that Student A is an experienced employee, and Student B is a new employee.

- Do a model role play with an above-level student. Play the role of Student A. Imagine a situation in which Student B tells Student A about a problem he or she has doing one of the things listed. For example, Student B hasn't had time yet to watch the training video.
- Form cross-ability pairs. Instruct students to choose one of the items in the box, and then create a scenario to match.
- Have students practice their role plays at least twice. While they are practicing, walk around and provide help as needed.
- Have pairs perform their role plays for the class. Take note of errors with negative *yes/no* questions.
- Go over the errors you noted. Say the incorrect form; have the class make the correction.

■■■ **MULTILEVEL INSTRUCTION for**
        Show what you know!

Cross-ability Have the above-level student play the role of Student A. Have the pre-level student play the role of Student B.

Progress Check

Can you . . . check your understanding of a situation at work?

Say: *We have practiced checking our understanding of a situation at work. Now, look at the question at the bottom of the page. Can you check your understanding of a situation at work? Write a checkmark in the box.*

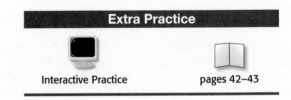

Extra Practice	
Interactive Practice	pages 42–43

A Write negative questions. Use the prompts and the correct form of the verb.

1. _____Didn't you clock in_____ yet?
   (you / did clock in)

2. _____Can't I work_____ the morning shift instead?
   (I / can work)

3. _____Didn't you bring_____ your uniform?
   (you / did bring)

4. _____Shouldn't we close up_____ soon?
   (we / should close up)

5. _____Haven't you taken_____ your break yet?
   (you / have taken)

6. _____Shouldn't they clean_____ the counters?
   (they / should clean)

B Read each response. Then write a negative *yes/no* question that one co-worker asked another. Use the words in parentheses.

1. **A:** Haven't you finished the report yet_____? (you / finish the report / yet)

   B: No, I haven't. I'm still working on it.

2. **A:** Didn't he tell his supervisor about the problem? (he / about the problem / tell his supervisor)

   B: No, he didn't. He didn't want her to know.

3. **A:** Shouldn't we prepare for the meeting_____? (we / prepare / for the meeting)

   B: Of course we should. The director will be there.

4. **A:** Can't they hire more workers for the holiday_____? (they / for the holiday season / hire more workers)

   B: No, they can't. They're already over budget.

Show what you know! Check your understanding of a situation at work

ROLE PLAY. PAIRS. Role-play a conversation between two employees at work.

Student A: You are talking to a new employee. That employee is having difficulty meeting one of the requirements described below. Find out what his or her problem is. Use one of the phrases in the box.

Student B: You are the new employee. Answer Student A's question about the difficulty you are having.

get your building pass	establish your work hours
read the safety manual	try on your safety equipment
watch the training video	arrange to receive your paycheck

Can you...check your understanding of a situation at work? ☐

Reading

1 **BEFORE YOU READ**

A CLASS. A company's *fulfillment center* stores products in a warehouse and then packs them and sends them to customers. Discuss. What kinds of injuries can happen at a fulfillment center?

B CLASS. Adjustable computer screens and adjustable tables are two examples of *ergonomic* work equipment. What is the meaning of *ergonomic*?

2 **READ**

CD1 T49

Listen and read the article. What is the main idea?

Another Way to Stay Healthy

It is sometimes known as RSI (repetitive stress injury), RMI (repetitive motion injury), or MSD (musculoskeletal disorder). The name may change, but the problem remains the same. All of us here at We Pack, We Ship (WPWS) must be careful at work. We are all **at risk** of suffering from work-related injuries.

WPWS has always been concerned about the health and well-being of our **associates**. We realize how serious RSI can be. The severe pain caused by RSI often makes it necessary for employees to miss work and lose income. In order to reduce the amount of missed work time due to RSI, one year ago we formed the Safety Committee. The committee's **recommendations** have already led to several steps to control RSI. The first improvements were made in the office, where we created comfortable and well-lit workspaces for the office staff. Each workstation has ergonomic furniture, and all computers include an adjustable monitor and an ergonomic keyboard.

WPWS Safety Committee members discuss ways to avoid workplace injuries.

And good news for the warehouse staff, too! We're reorganizing the space so that workers can reach merchandise more easily and use machines to move heavy materials whenever possible. Other changes include conveyor belts that carry boxes from packing stations to the shipping area and adjustable tables that allow packers to avoid unnecessary bending, lifting, and twisting.

The Safety Committee has announced that it will be offering a series of workshops on ways to decrease our chances of developing carpal tunnel syndrome, tendonitis, and other **debilitating** RSIs. The workshops will provide training on the correct use of tools and equipment and the best ways to complete various tasks. The workshops will also teach exercises to keep us strong and healthy. The committee members haven't yet decided on the schedule of workshops, so look for more information in next month's newsletter.

Getting Started   5 minutes

1 BEFORE YOU READ

A CLASS. A company's *fulfillment center*...

- Write *fulfill* on the board. Say the word in a sentence, for example *I asked the school secretary for a new printer cartridge, and I hope she will fulfill my request.* Elicit the meaning (*to carry out a request*).
- Read the directions and ask students to repeat the definition of *fulfillment center*. Ask if anyone has ever worked at such a place.
- Call on students to answer the question and list their answers on the board.

Possible answers: You can injure your back lifting heavy objects. You can be injured by articles that fall off the shelves. You can be injured using machinery.

> **Language Note**
>
> In a company, the *fulfillment process* includes all the steps involved in fulfilling a customer's order, for example: warehousing, finding the item ordered, packaging it, and shipping it. In companies that do e-commerce, the process also includes maintaining online inventories, processing new accounts, and maintaining databases of customers.

B CLASS. Adjustable computer screens...

- Define *adjustable* (*able to be adjusted*). Ask: *Are your desks adjustable? Is there anything you use every day that is adjustable?* (*car seats, baby strollers, headsets for mp3 players,* etc.)
- Read the directions. Write *ergonomic* on the board.
- Call on students to share their ideas. Use them to build a definition of *ergonomics*.

Answer: *Ergonomics* is the study of how the design of equipment affects how well people can use it and do their work. Equipment that is *ergonomic* allows a person to work comfortably and to avoid injury while working.

> **Language Note**
>
> *Ergonomics* comes from the Greek word *ergon*, meaning *work*, and *-nemein* meaning *manage*. The word was coined in 1950.

Presentation   20 minutes

2 READ

Listen and read the article. What is...

- Have students look at the photograph. Ask questions to establish context. For example: *Who are the people? Where are they? What are they doing? What is WPWS?*
- Read the title out loud. Ask the class what they think the article is about. Write their predictions.
- Note: Do not preteach the boldfaced items. They will be taught in Exercise 4.
- Play CD 1, Track 49. Ask students to listen and read along with the article.
- When students have finished reading, point to the predictions on the board and ask: *Were your predictions correct? What is the main idea?*

Answer: The article is about avoiding workplace injuries.

Expansion: Speaking Practice

- Explain *carpal tunnel syndrome* and *tendinitis*. Point to the underside of your wrist and say: Carpal tunnel syndrome *is a medical condition in which a person gets a lot of pain or weakness in the wrist.* Next, explain that tendons are structures that connect muscles to bones. For example, there are tendons in your fingers, and a large tendon (the Achilles tendon) in your heel. Point to these areas and say: Tendinitis *is inflammation or pain in a tendon.*
- Ask students: *What jobs or activities can cause carpal tunnel syndrome or tendinitis? Is this a problem in your job? Have you ever had either of these conditions? What did you do about it?*

Controlled Practice   20 minutes

3 CHECK YOUR UNDERSTANDING

Ⓐ Complete the sentences. Circle...

- Read item 1. Tell students to read rapidly to find answer (d). Remind them not to read every word. Have them hold up their books and point to the place where they found the answer.
- Have students complete the remaining items.
- Check answers. Call on students to read the sentences and say the correct answers.

Reading Skill: **Recognizing Restatements**

- Read the Reading Skill. Explain that writers often repeat important information, using different words. Good readers are able to distinguish between a restatement and new information and read more quickly or slowly, as needed.
- Point out two sentences in the first paragraph: *All of us here at We Pack, We Ship must be careful at work. We are all at risk of suffering from work-related injuries.*

Ⓑ Read the Reading Skill. Then match...

- Demonstrate that sentence b is a restatement of sentence 1. Write sentence 1 on the board like this: *The first / improvements / were made / in the office.* Have students compare sentence 1 with sentence b. Ask: *Which word in sentence b is similar to the first? (began) Which phrase is similar to improvements? (changes to make work conditions better)* Explain: *A restatement expresses the same basic concepts as the original sentence, although it is different from it.*
- Have students complete items 2 and 3 and compare answers with a partner.
- Check answers. If students have difficulty, divide sentences 2 and 3 into concepts and match each concept with similar information in sentences *c* and *a* respectively.

4 WORD WORK

Find the boldfaced words...

- Remind students that *guessing from context* means reading a word or phrase in a sentence or paragraph and using the information surrounding the unknown word or phrase to guess what it means.
- Do item 1 with the class. Have students reread the sentence with the phrase *at risk*. Tell students to substitute the phrases *in danger, protected from,* and *afraid* and choose the one that makes sense in the sentence.
- Have students do the remaining items alone or in pairs.
- Have volunteers say the answers and explain how they guessed the meaning. Make corrections as needed.

Communicative Practice   15 minutes

Show what you know!

GROUPS. Make a list...

- Have students reread the last paragraph of the article, which gives general ideas about what the workshops will include. If students need help with the task, instruct them to think of specific examples of tools, equipment, and activities for avoiding or treating specific medical conditions or problems. Elicit one example from the class and write it on the board. Ask students to say how the example could possibly reduce RSIs.
- Form cross-ability groups. Have them select a timekeeper, a note taker, and a reporter. Give a time limit for discussion.
- While students are talking, walk around and provide help as needed.
- Have each group's reporter share the group's list.

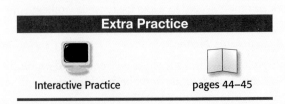

Extra Practice

Interactive Practice   pages 44–45

3 CHECK YOUR UNDERSTANDING

A Complete the sentences. Circle the correct answers.

1. We Pack, We Ship (WPWS) created the Safety Committee to _____.
   a. write a safety handbook
   b. make sure employees knew the rules
   c. save the company money
   d. improve employees' attendance *(circled)*

2. Tendonitis is a type of _____.
   a. RSI *(circled)*
   b. ergonomic equipment
   c. exercise
   d. safety procedure

3. Employees can get a safety-workshop schedule _____.
   a. on page 6 of the newsletter
   b. in next month's newsletter *(circled)*
   c. from the Safety Committee right now
   d. at packing stations

B Read the Reading Skill. Then match each statement to one that has the same, or almost the same, meaning.

__b__ 1. The first improvements were made in the office.

__c__ 2. We created comfortable, well-lit spaces for the office staff.

__a__ 3. Each workstation has ergonomic furniture.

a. Tables and chairs help employees work quickly and easily.
b. Changes to make work conditions better began in the office.
c. We made the work areas relaxing and bright.

> **Reading Skill:**
> Recognizing Restatements
>
> When you read, look for information that the author repeats or explains again with different words.

4 WORD WORK

Find the boldfaced words in the article. Guess their meanings from context. Choose the best definition.

1. **at risk**   a. in danger *(circled)*   b. protected from   c. afraid
2. **associates**   a. managers   b. customers   c. co-workers *(circled)*
3. **recommendations** a. improvements   b. suggestions *(circled)*   c. problems
4. **debilitating**   a. causing anger   b. causing weakness *(circled)*   c. frightening

Show what you know! Talk about common workplace injuries

GROUPS. Make a list of three activities that will probably take place at the workshops that the Safety Committee is planning. How can those workshop activities help reduce RSIs?

Listening and Speaking

1 BEFORE YOU LISTEN

CLASS. **Many companies give their employees regular performance reviews. Discuss.**

1. Why are performance reviews important?
2. Why are performance reviews especially important for new employees?

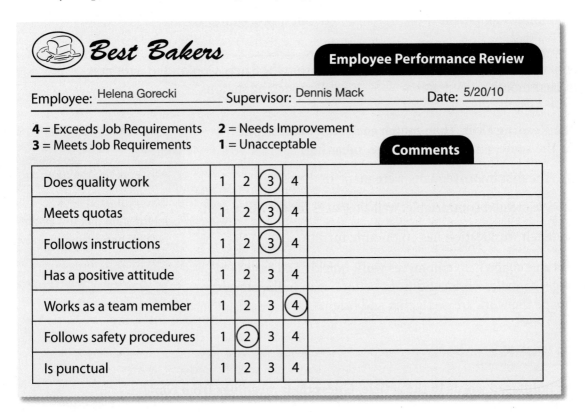

Best Bakers   **Employee Performance Review**

Employee: _Helena Gorecki_   Supervisor: _Dennis Mack_   Date: _5/20/10_

4 = Exceeds Job Requirements   **2** = Needs Improvement
3 = Meets Job Requirements   **1** = Unacceptable

Comments

Does quality work	1	2	(3)	4	
Meets quotas	1	2	(3)	4	
Follows instructions	1	2	(3)	4	
Has a positive attitude	1	2	3	4	
Works as a team member	1	2	3	(4)	
Follows safety procedures	1	(2)	3	4	
Is punctual	1	2	3	4	

2 LISTEN

CD1 T50

A Dennis Mack is a supervisor at Best Bakers. He is giving a performance review to Helena Gorecki, a new employee. Listen. Then look at the Employee Performance Review. In which category of job requirements does Helena need improvement?

CD1 T50

B Listen again. Circle the numbers in the performance review above, based on what Tim says. He hasn't yet covered all the categories.

C PAIRS. Compare your answers.

Getting Started   5 minutes

1 | BEFORE YOU LISTEN

CLASS. Many companies give their employees...

- Have students look at the blank Employee Performance Review sheet from Best Bakers. Ask questions to assess students' experience with performance reviews. For example: *What is this form? What is a performance review? Who gives the review? Who gets it? How often? Have you ever had one?*

- Define the following terms as needed: *exceed: go beyond or above; meet: satisfy or do what is required; quota: the minimum number or amount that is required; punctual: on time.*

- Read and discuss the questions with the class.

Possible answers: 1. Performance reviews are important because they give employees feedback about their job performance and ways they can improve. 2. Performance reviews are especially important for new employees because there is so much new to learn and because both employers and employees need to know early on if an employee is suitable for the job.

Presentation   15 minutes

2 | LISTEN

A **Dennis Mack is a supervisor...**

- Have the class look at the photo on page 79. Ask: *Where are Dennis and Helena?* (in an office) *What are they talking about?* (They're probably talking about her performance review.)

- Play CD 1, Track 50. Play it again if necessary.

- Call on a volunteer to answer the question. Ask the class: *Is that correct?* or *Do you agree?*

Answer: Helena needs improvement in following safety procedures.

Controlled Practice   20 minutes

B **Listen again. Circle the numbers...**

- Have students read the review form and predict the answers.

- Play CD 1, Track 50. Have students circle the numbers on the form as they listen.

C PAIRS. Compare your answers.

- As a follow-up, say each item in the performance review and have the class call out the number. Play all or part of the recording again, as needed.

Expansion: Speaking Practice

- Form cross-ability pairs and have them do a two-minute role play in which Helena tells a friend about her good performance review. The higher-level partner should play the role of Helena and should summarize the evaluation, including the item in which Helena needs improvement. The lower-level partner should play the role of the friend.

Teaching Tip

While pairs are performing role plays, use the scoring rubric for speaking on page T-xiii to evaluate each student's vocabulary, grammar, fluency, and how well he or she completes the task. You may want to review the completed rubric with the students.

3 CONVERSATION

Listen and read this part...

- Play CD 1, Track 51. Have students listen and read silently.

4 PRACTICE

A PAIRS. Practice the conversation.

- Form cross-ability pairs and have students read the conversation in Exercise 3. Tell them to take turns reading each role.
- Have students switch partners and practice again.
- Walk around and listen as students are practicing. Provide help as needed.
- Ask volunteers to perform the conversation for the class.

Communicative Practice   20 minutes

B ROLE PLAY. PAIRS. Role-play this situation. Use...

> **Teaching Tip**
>
> While pairs are performing role plays, use the scoring rubric for speaking on page T-xiii to evaluate each student's vocabulary, grammar, fluency, and how well he or she completes the task. You may want to review the completed rubric with the students.

- Model the activity with an above-level student. Play the role of the supervisor.
- Form cross-ability pairs.
- Give a time limit for speaking. Walk around and provide help as needed.
- Have volunteers role-play their interview for the class.

▬ MULTILEVEL INSTRUCTION for 4B

Cross-ability Have pre-level students play the role of the employee. Have above-level students play the role of the supervisor.

▬ Expansion: Speaking Practice

- Have the same pairs do another role play. This time, the supervisor gives a very different review: The parts of the job that were good before will be bad, and vice versa.

Extra Practice

Interactive Practice

---

3 CONVERSATION

CD1 T51

Listen and read this part of Helena's review.

Dennis: First of all, I want you to know that we're happy in general with your work.

Helena: Oh, thank you!

Dennis: Yes, the quality of your work is very good. And you're meeting your quotas, which is really important. I gave you a "3" in both categories.

Helena: Thank you. I understand how important it is to get all the packages out on time.

Dennis: Exactly. And you're good at following instructions. I gave you a "3" there, too.

Helena: Sometimes I have to ask for clarification.

Dennis: That's great. You should always ask if you're not sure. It's better to ask than to do the wrong thing.

Helena: OK. Good.

4 PRACTICE

A PAIRS. **Practice the conversation.**

B ROLE PLAY. PAIRS. **Role-play this situation. Use the conversation as a model.**

Student A: You are a supervisor at Best Bakers. You are giving a performance review to one of your employees. Fill out the Employee Performance Review form before you begin. Make up the information.

Student B: You are an employee at Best Bakers. You are meeting with your supervisor to discuss your performance review. Respond to your supervisor's comments.

Grammar

Indirect instructions, commands, and requests

Direct speech	Indirect speech		
	Reporting Verb	**Object**	**Indirect Request**
"Ask a question if you're not sure."	He **said**		**to ask** a question if **we're** not sure.
"Leave your earrings and rings at home."	She **told**	**us**	**to leave our** earrings and rings at home.
"Please don't wear jewelry on the job."	She **asked**	**them**	**not to wear** jewelry on the job.
"Wear shoes that will protect your feet."	Company policy **requires**	**us**	**to wear** shoes that will protect **our** feet.

Grammar Watch

- When direct instructions, commands, and requests change to the indirect form, the verb changes to the infinitive form. Pronouns may also change to preserve the original meaning of the speaker.
- Use reporting verbs, such as *advise, ask, instruct, order, say, tell,* and *warn,* to introduce indirect instructions, commands, and requests.
- Most verbs that report indirect instructions, commands, and requests have an object. However, the verb *say* does not.

1 PRACTICE

Read the statements about performance reviews. Circle the reporting verbs. Underline the indirect requests and commands.

1. My supervisor (asked) me to speed up my production. I'm not meeting my quotas.

2. He also (told) me to think about safety and cleanliness. He specifically (asked) me to keep my work area cleaner.

3. My manager (told) me not to take such long breaks. She (said) to limit my breaks to twenty minutes.

4. She (reminded) me to wash my equipment at the end of my shift.

5. My boss (warned) me not to be late again or I might lose my job.

6. My supervisor (asked) me to check my work more carefully.

7. At the start of my review, my boss (told) me to relax.

Follow work-related instructions

Getting Started

5 minutes

- Give the class a simple command, for example, *Stand up.* Ask: *What did I tell you to do?* (You told us to stand up.) Next, ask: *What did I say to do?* (You said to stand up.) Finally, ask: *What did I ask you to do?* (You asked us to stand up.) Write all three sentences on the board.
- Say: *These sentences are examples of indirect instructions, commands, and requests.*

Presentation

15 minutes

Indirect instructions, commands, and requests

- Copy the sentences from the grammar chart onto the board. Point to the sentences in the left-hand column. Say: *These are direct statements. Somebody said these exact words, so we use quotation marks.* Write a pair of quotation marks on the board.
- Read the first Grammar Watch note. Ask: *Which four reporting verbs are used in the grammar chart?* Elicit these verbs and write them on the board: *say, tell, ask,* and *require.*
- Add the verbs *advise, instruct, order,* and *warn* to the four verbs already on the board. Point to the third example sentence (*Please don't wear jewelry . . .*) and have students form an indirect statement using each verb. (*The boss advised us / instructed us / ordered us / warned us not to wear . . .*)
- Read the sentences in indirect speech. Then ask: *What comes after each reporting verb?* (*say +* infinitive, *tell / ask / require +* object + infinitive). To reinforce, read the first Grammar Watch note.
- Tell students to notice how possessive pronouns change when we switch from direct to indirect speech. Point to the second statement in direct speech, and say to a student: *Leave your earrings and rings at home.* Then turn to the class and say: *Change the sentence to indirect speech with a possessive pronoun. What did I tell her?* (You told her to leave <u>her</u> earrings and rings at home.) Then address the same student and ask: *What did I tell you?* (You told me to leave <u>my</u> earrings and rings . . .)
- Demonstrate with another example from the chart. Say to a student: *Wear shoes that will protect your feet.* Then turn to the class and say: *What did I ask him to do?* (You asked him to wear shoes that will protect <u>his</u> feet.) Repeat with a group of students, telling them to wear shoes, and ask: *What did I ask them to do?* (You asked them to wear shoes that will protect <u>their</u> feet.)

Language Note

The verb *warn* is usually used in the negative to talk about something with dangerous or unwanted consequences, for example, *The teacher warned us not to cheat on the test.*

Expansion: Grammar Practice

- On the board, write the verbs *say, tell,* and *ask.* Point to one verb and give the class a command, for example, *Open your books.* Have the class use the verb you are pointing to and respond with indirect speech, for example: *The teacher told us to open our books* or *The teacher said to open our books* or *The teacher asked us to open our books.*
- After giving the class several commands, call on an above-level student to give the commands.
- Turn the activity into a game. Have all students stand up. Direct the command to one student, for example, *Stand on one foot.* The student must respond by carrying out the command and by stating the correct indirect statement. For example, the student will stand on one foot and say, *The teacher told me to stand on one foot.* If the student makes a mistake, he or she must sit down. Continue playing until just one student is standing.

Controlled Practice

20 minutes

1 PRACTICE

Read the statements about performance...

- Read the example with the class. Pantomime a circle in the air and say: *Ask is the reporting verb.* Pantomime underlining something and say: *to speed up is an indirect request.*
- Have students complete the exercise alone or in pairs.
- While students are working, walk around and provide help as needed.
- Select students to come to the board, copy the sentences, and circle and underline the appropriate words and phrases.
- Confirm answers by asking the class: *Is this correct?* Correct errors as needed.

2 PRACTICE

Felix attended classes on office...

- Read the first procedure in the list of e-mail procedures. Ask: *What is the implied subject of this sentence?* (you). Then have students look at the corresponding item in the exercise below. Ask: *What happened to the pronoun* you? *How did it change? Why?* (It changed to *us* because Felix is reporting on what the instructor said.)

- Read the second procedure and do item 2 with the class. Provide help as needed. Write the answers on the board.

- Have students continue working alone or in pairs. Give a time limit. Walk around and provide help as needed.

- Check answers. Have students write sentences 3 to 7 on the board. Have other students read the sentences and say if they are correct. If there is an error, elicit corrections from the class.

Communicative Practice   20 minutes

Show what you know!

PAIRS. Give instructions for a simple...

- Model the activity. Give the class instructions for how to check voice mail. Write the following steps on the board: *1. Press the Play button on the answering machine. 2. Listen to the messages. 3. Press the Delete button to erase the messages after you hear them.*

STEP 1. Student A: Write...

- Have the class model Step 1 by writing the steps to complete the procedure.

STEP 2. PAIRS. Student A: Read...

- Have an above-level student model Step 2 by reading the instructions to the class, using indirect speech. For example, *[teacher's name] said to press the Play button . . . Then, [he or she] said to listen to the messages. Finally, [he or she] told us to press the Delete button . . .*

- Have the class write the instructions, using indirect speech.

STEP 3. CLASS. Student B: Describe...

- Have a student model Step 3 by describing the procedure, using indirect speech.

- Pair students of similar ability. Tell them to repeat Steps 1–3.

- Encourage students to use a variety of reporting verbs. Write the following verbs on the board: *say, tell, ask, require, instruct, order, advise,* and *warn.*

- Walk around and provide help as needed.

- Call on several students to describe the procedures they heard.

▆▆ MULTILEVEL INSTRUCTION for Show what you know!

Pre-level Have students write directions for a simple process involving just three or four steps, such as how to mail a package, answer the phone, open up the office or business in the morning, or close up the office at night.

Above-level Have students describe a process with more steps and harder vocabulary, such as how to use a copy machine, order new office equipment, set up a meeting, or check inventory.

Progress Check

Can you . . . follow work-related instructions?
Say: *We have practiced following work-related instructions. Now, look at the question at the bottom of the page. Can you follow work-related instructions? Write a checkmark in the box.*

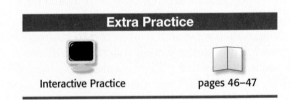

Extra Practice
Interactive Practice   pages 46–47

PRACTICE

Felix attended classes on office procedures. Read the notes he took about using office e-mail. Then change the direct commands into indirect instructions and requests.

E-mail Procedures

1. Click on the program icon to open the program.
2. Enter your password when prompted. Don't share your password with anyone.
3. Enter the e-mail address of the person you're writing to in the "To" section.
4. Don't forget to complete the "Subject" line.
5. Compose your message in the open section below "Subject."
6. Click on "Send" after completing the e-mail.
7. Remember, log out once you're done so that your privacy is protected.

---

1. The teacher told _us to click on the program icon_ to open the program.

2. He told _____us to enter our password_____ when prompted and warned

   _____us not to share our password_____ with anyone.

3. Next he said __to enter the e-mail address of the person__ in the "To" section.

4. He reminded _____us not to forget to complete_____ the "Subject" line.

5. He then instructed _____us to compose our messages_____ in the open section below "Subject."

6. He told _____us to click on "Send"_____ after completing the email.

7. Finally, he advised __us to remember to log out once we're done__ to protect our privacy.

Show what you know! Follow work-related instructions

PAIRS. Give instructions for a simple procedure, such as how to use a copy machine or how to check voice mail.

STEP 1. Student A: Write the steps to follow to complete the procedure.

STEP 2. PAIRS. Student A: Read the instructions to Student B. Student B: Write the instructions.

STEP 3. CLASS. Student B: Describe the procedure using indirect instructions.

Can you... follow work-related instructions? ☐

Writing

1 BEFORE YOU WRITE

A CLASS. Have you ever written a memo to your supervisor at work? Why did you write the memo? What happened after your supervisor read the memo?

B GROUPS. Why is it important to be concise and clear in a memo to a supervisor?

C Read the writing model. What problem does Lev Shepel describe? How many solutions does he offer?

> ### Writing Tip
>
> Most memos are short. They contain language that is direct and clear. The purpose of a memo is usually stated in the first paragraph. Information is often presented in a list instead of a paragraph.

Memo   **ILEA Furniture**

To: Henry Avalos, Warehouse Manager
From: Lev Shepel, Delivery Associate
Date: 6/17/10
Re: Improving Furniture Delivery Times

The purpose of this memo is to offer several simple solutions to the problem of late furniture deliveries.

In my last performance review, you pointed out that over 50% of my deliveries were behind schedule. I believe that other drivers are having similar problems with their deliveries because of the following reasons:
- increased traffic along our delivery routes
- poorly planned delivery routes
- road construction in many areas.

We can't control traffic or road conditions, but we can take these steps to increase on-time deliveries:
- install GPS (navigational systems) to help drivers get around traffic jams and avoid construction delays
- plan delivery routes so that drivers spend less travel time going from one delivery location to the next.

Thank you for considering my suggestions. I hope that you will allow me to present my ideas at our staff meeting next week.

D PAIRS. Answer the questions.

1. Why do you think Lev Shepel is worried about the problem of late furniture deliveries?
2. How can GPS help to solve the problem that Lev describes?
3. What does Lev want his supervisor to do?

E Another driver at Ilea Furniture also wrote a memo. His subject line was "Deliveries." Why is Lev's subject line better?

Write a memo to a supervisor

Getting Started 5 minutes

1 BEFORE YOU WRITE

A CLASS. Have you ever written...

- Write *memo* on the board. Ask the class: *What is a memo?* Elicit the meaning or explain: *A memo (short for memorandum) is a written communication from one person to other persons in an organization.*
- Call on various students to answer the questions and share their experiences.

B GROUPS. Why is it important...

- Form groups and have them choose a reporter.
- Give a time limit for discussion.
- Have reporters share the group's answer to the question.

Answer: Supervisors are usually very busy, so they don't have time to read long memos.

Writing Tip: Composing Memos

- Read the Writing Tip out loud. Point out that the purpose of the memo is explicitly stated in the first paragraph of the memo.
- Have students find the two lists in the memo. Ask students what information is presented in each list. *(reasons for late deliveries, solutions to the problem)*

Presentation 15 minutes

C Read the writing model. What problem...

- Have students look at the model. Ask questions to help them find key information in the memo. Ask: *Who is the memo written to?* (Henry Avalos, Warehouse Manager) *Who is it from?* (Lev Shepel, Delivery Associate) *When was it written?* (June 17, 2010) *What does* re *mean?* (about) *What is the memo about?* (It's about improving delivery times.)
- Have students read the memo. Instruct them not to worry about unfamiliar vocabulary but rather to read in order to find the answers to the questions.
- Go over the answers to the questions.

Answer: The problem is late furniture deliveries. Lev proposes two solutions.

- Direct students' attention to the organization of the memo. On the board, write: *purpose, problem and causes, solutions,* and *conclusion.* Say each part and have students point to the paragraph that discusses each topic.

D PAIRS. Answer the questions.

- Check that students know what *GPS* means. Explain: GPS *means* global positioning system. *It helps you to know where you are when you're driving.* Find out how many students have a GPS in their cars and how often they use it.
- Form pairs and have them answer the questions. Give a time limit.
- Check answers. Have students read the part of the memo that helped them to answer each question.

Answers: 1. He is worried about getting a negative performance review. 2. GPS can help drivers get around traffic jams and avoid construction delays. 3. He wants his supervisor to allow him to present his ideas at the next staff meeting.

Expansion: Speaking Practice

- Have a higher-level student play the role of Lev Shepel. The other students are Lev's co-workers. Everyone is at the staff meeting where Lev is presenting his suggestions. Lev presents the problem, the causes, and his solutions. Other students ask questions.

E Another driver at Ilea Furniture...

- Form pairs and have them discuss the answer to the question. Give a time limit.
- Call on students to share their ideas.

Answer: Lev's subject is more specific. It hints at the problem (slow furniture delivery times) and Lev's purpose (to suggest ways to solve the problem).

Write a memo to a supervisor

Controlled Practice   20 minutes

2   THINKING ON PAPER

Ⓐ BRAINSTORM. Think about problems...

- Guide students to brainstorm about problems at their workplaces. List the problems on the board.
- If students don't have jobs, tell them to think about their last job, write about an imaginary job, or sit with a student who has a job now.
- Group students and have them share their lists. Encourage them to add ideas to their lists based on their conversation with their classmates.

Ⓑ Choose one of your problems. Plan...

- Tell students to look at the list they created in Exercise A and choose one problem to write their memo about.
- Have students brainstorm about the reasons and solutions for the problem. (It is not necessary to have three reasons and three solutions for each problem, but items should be bulleted.) Remind students to list ideas in phrases, not complete sentences.
- Pair students and have them share their ideas.

Communicative Practice   20 minutes

3   WRITE

Write a memo about the most important...

- Read the items in the checklist in Exercise 4. After each item, ask: *Did Lev Shepel do this in the writing model?* Tell students to use these questions, the model, and their lists from Exercise 2B to guide their writing.
- Have students write in class. Walk around and provide help as needed.

4   CHECK YOUR WRITING

- Have students read their memos and check off the questions in the checklist.
- Collect the memos and correct them. Return papers to their writers and have students write a final draft.

Teaching Tip

You may want to collect student papers and provide feedback. Use the scoring rubric for writing on page T-xiv to evaluate each student's vocabulary, grammar, mechanics and how well he or she has completed the task. You may want to review the completed rubric with the students.

Teaching Tip

You may wish to experiment with having students read and comment on one another's writing (peer editing). If you and your students are comfortable with this idea, make copies of the checklist in Exercise 4 and give one to each student. Collect students' memos and redistribute them. Instruct students to read the memo they received and check off the items in the checklist to the best of their ability. You may also wish to instruct them to write a positive or encouraging comment to the writer at the bottom of the checklist. Have students return memos and checklists to the writers. Give writers time to rewrite their memos or make corrections based on the comments of their peers.

Expansion: Writing Practice

- Use errors from students' papers to review capitalization, punctuation, and spelling. Copy sentences with errors onto a handout or overhead transparency. (You may or may not wish to underline the part of the sentence containing an error.) Pair or group students and have them correct the errors. Then check items with the whole class.

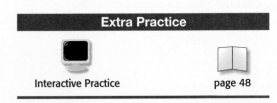

Extra Practice

Interactive Practice   page 48

2 THINKING ON PAPER

(A) BRAINSTORM. Think about problems you have at work. Make a list in a chart like this.

Problems That My Supervisor Should Know About
1.
2.
3.
4.

(B) Choose one of your problems. Plan and organize your own memo. Write the reasons for the problem and ideas for solutions in a chart like this.

Most Important Work Problem: _____	
Reasons for the Problem	My Ideas for Solutions
•	•
•	•
•	•

3 WRITE

Write a memo about the most important problem where you work.
Use the information in your plan. Look at the writing model for an example.

4 CHECK YOUR WRITING

☐ Did you include a clear subject line?

☐ Did you state your purpose in your first paragraph?

☐ Did you present your reasons and solutions as a list in order to make your memo easy to read?

☐ Did you use correct capitalization, punctuation, and spelling?

---

1 REVIEW   For your grammar review, go to page 248.

2 ACT IT OUT   What do you say?

STEP 1. CLASS. Review the conversation on page 66 (CD1, Track 40).

STEP 2. ROLE PLAY. PAIRS. Role-play this situation.

Student A: You are a new employee at a credit-card customer service center. You would like more information about employee benefits. Your manager gave you the Employee Handbook, but you received so much information that you are confused. You have decided to talk to an experienced co-worker.

Student B: You have worked at the customer service center for three years. You want to help your new co-worker. Look back at the Employee Handbook on page 70 for ideas of what to explain.

3 READ AND REACT   Problem-solving

STEP 1. GROUPS. Read about Raquel's problem.

Ariana Cordeiro works at a large hotel. Last week, Ariana's manager changed her work schedule. Ariana used to work from 4:00 P.M. to midnight, but now she has to work the day shift—from 8:00 A.M. to 4:00 P.M. With her new schedule, Ariana can't go to her English class. She also has a problem with child care.

STEP 2. GROUPS. What is Ariana's problem? Discuss a solution. List three things that she can do.

4 CONNECT   For your Planning for Learning, go to page 258.
For your Team Project, go to page 266.

Which goals can you check off? Go back to page 65.

 Go to the CD-ROM for more practice.

Show what you know!

1 REVIEW

Turn to page 248 for the Grammar Review.

2 ACT IT OUT

STEP 1. CLASS. Review the conversation on...

- Play CD 1, Track 40. If necessary, direct students to the Audio Script on page 287.

STEP 2. ROLE PLAY. PAIRS. Role-play this situation.

> **Teaching Tip**
>
> While pairs are performing role plays, use the scoring rubric for speaking on page T-xiii to evaluate each student's vocabulary, grammar, fluency, and how well he or she completes the task. You may want to review the completed rubric with the students.

- Have students look at the photo. Ask: *What is the man looking at? How does he feel?*
- Read the role descriptions.
- With the class, compose the two opening lines of the role play and write them on the board. For example: *A: Hi _____ [student name]. Do you have time to answer some questions for me? I need more information about employee benefits. B: No problem! What do you want to know?*
- Similarly, with the class, compose the two closing lines of the role play and write them on the board.
- Model a role play with an above-level student. Play the role of Student B.
- Pair students of similar ability.
- Tell students to practice out loud at least twice.
- Have volunteers role-play for the class.

▰▰ MULTILEVEL INSTRUCTION for 2

Pre-level Have students talk about one or two benefits only, for example, overtime and sick leave. Allow them to write out or take notes on their dialogue and use the script to practice several times before performing without it.

Above-level Have Student B talk about a mistake that he or she made concerning benefits when he or she first started working at the company.

3 READ AND REACT

STEP 1. GROUPS. Read about Ariana's problem.

- Read the directions while students follow along.

STEP 2. GROUPS. What is Ariana's problem?...

- Form groups of three or four. Have each group choose a timekeeper, a note taker, and a reporter.
- Tell students to use indirect speech (*I advise her to speak to her manager*, etc.)
- Have the reporter from each group share the group's solutions. List them on the board.
- Have the class vote on the best solution.

▰▰ Expansion: Speaking Practice

- Pair students and have them role-play a conversation between Ariana and a friend. Ariana tells the friend her problem, and the friend suggests solutions, using the ideas discussed in Step 2.

4 CONNECT

Turn to page 258 for the Planning for Learning Activity and page 266 for the Team Project. See page T-xi for general notes about teaching these activities.

Progress Check

Which goals can you check off? Go back to page 65.

Ask students to turn to page 65 and check off any remaining goals they have reached. Call on students to say which goals they will practice outside of class.

▰ Go to the CD-ROM for more practice.

If your students need more practice with the vocabulary, grammar, and competencies in Unit 4, encourage them to review the activities on the CD-ROM.

Safe and Sound

Classroom Materials/Extra Practice

CD 1
Tracks 52–63

Interactive Practice
Unit 5

Workbook
Unit 5

Unit Overview

Goals

- See the list of goals on the facing page.

Grammar

- Present real conditionals
- Adverb clauses of time
- Expressing degrees of certainty

Pronunciation

- Intonation and pauses in sentences with two clauses
- Pronunciation of /i/ (as in *eat*) and /ɪ/ (as in *it*)

Reading

- Read about preparing for natural disasters
- *Reading Skill:* Identifying an author's purpose

Writing

- Write a plan for an emergency situation

Life Skills

- Interpret an evacuation map
- Talk about planning for a hurricane

Preview

- Say the unit title. Explain: *Safe* means away from/out of danger. *Sound* means whole, unharmed. *Safe and sound* is an old expression used when someone has escaped or avoided a dangerous situation, for example, *After the tornado, the baby was found in the bathtub, safe and sound.*
- Hold up your book or have students look at their books. Have students look at the picture. Read the preview question. You can also ask: *What is happening? How does the American Red Cross help people? What are some examples of disasters?*

Unit Goals

- Point to the Unit Goals. Have students read them silently.
- Tell students they will be studying these goals in Unit 5.
- Say each goal and explain unfamiliar vocabulary as needed, for example, *prevent: take action so that an unwanted or dangerous situation does not occur; in case of: if something happens.*
- Tell students to circle one or more goals that are very important to them. Call on several volunteers to say the goals they circled.
- Write a checkmark (✓) on the board. Say: *We will come back to this page again. You will write a checkmark next to the goals you learned in this unit.*

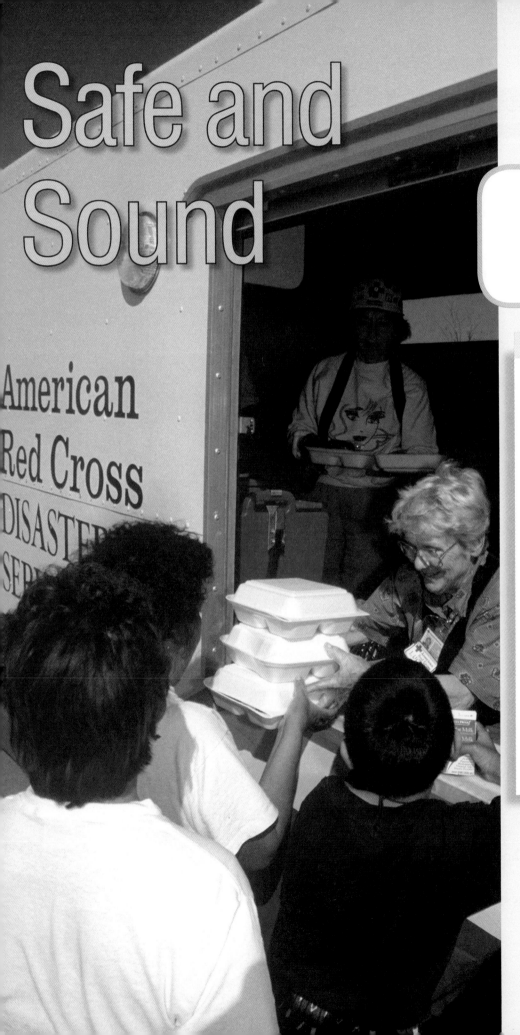

Safe and Sound

Preview

Read the title. Look at the picture. Why do these people need help?

UNIT GOALS

- ☐ Identify ways to prevent fires

- ☐ Talk about what to do in case of fire

- ☐ Talk about dangerous weather

- ☐ Discuss weather reports

- ☐ Talk about planning for a hurricane

- ☐ Interpret an evacuation map

- ☐ Communicate in a 911 emergency

- ☐ Write a plan for an emergency situation

Identify ways to prevent fires

Listening and Speaking

1 BEFORE YOU LISTEN

A CLASS. Discuss. What do you think the people in a fire-safety class want to learn?

B GROUPS. Find a *smoke alarm, a CO₂ detector,* and a *fire extinguisher* in the picture. How does each device help with safety in a home?

2 LISTEN

A CD1 T52
Lt. Tyrone Jefferson is teaching the first of four fire-safety classes. Listen. What is the focus of tonight's class?

B CD1 T52
Read the statements. Then listen again. Write *T* (true) or *F* (false) based on Lt. Jefferson's instructions. Correct the false statements.

___F___ 1. Lt. Jefferson will first talk about fire safety
                kitchen
        in the ~~bedroom~~ and then discuss fire safety
        in other parts of the home.

___T___ 2. Cooking is the main cause of fires in homes
        in the U.S.

___T___ 3. It's probably a good idea to wear a shirt with
        short sleeves when you're cooking.

___F___ 4. If food catches fire, you should ~~throw water on it~~. put a lid on it.

___T___ 5. If the phone rings in another room, Lt. Jefferson suggests that you ignore it.

___F___ 6. Children should always be in the kitchen when you're cooking.

C PAIRS. What is one question that you would like to ask Lt. Jefferson?

Getting Started   5 minutes

1 BEFORE YOU LISTEN

A CLASS. Discuss. What do you think...

- Inform students that they're going to hear a teacher talking to students in a fire-safety class. Read and discuss the question in the student book. You can also ask: *Where can people take a fire safety class?* (in a community center) *Who teaches such a class?* (usually a firefighter) *Would you like to take such a class? Why?*

B GROUPS. Find a *smoke alarm*...

- Have students look at the photo and find the objects. If students do not know what a fire extinguisher looks like, for example, use the photo to teach them. You can also point to the smoke alarm in your classroom.
- Group students and give a time limit for discussion.
- Call on volunteers to answer the questions.

Answers: The objects are, from left to right, smoke alarm, two fire extinguishers, and a carbon monoxide detector. A smoke alarm sounds when there is smoke and/or fire; fire extinguishers can be used to put out small fires before they become large; the alarm in a carbon monoxide detector sounds if carbon monoxide, a dangerous gas, is present.

Culture Connection

Most states have laws requiring homes and apartments to have smoke detectors. Some states allow battery-operated devices. Others require hard-wired ones. All battery-operated devices should be checked regularly to make sure the battery works. Everyone should know how to check the batteries and replace them if necessary.

Community Building

Put students in pairs. Have them check your school building for fire safety. For example, some students can find out the location of all fire extinguishers. Others can check the smoke alarms in each room and inform the office about any that need new batteries. Others can bring in maps of the facility and show the class the location of all emergency exits.

Presentation   10 minutes

2 LISTEN

A Lt. Tyrone Jefferson is teaching...

- Instruct students to listen for the word *focus* and to raise their hands when they hear the answer to the question.
- Play CD 1, Track 52.
- Call on a student to answer the question.

Answer: Tonight's focus is fire prevention.

Controlled Practice   10 minutes

B Read the statements. Then listen...

- Have students read the statements silently and predict if they are true or false.
- Play Track 52 again.
- Have students compare their answers with those of a classmate.
- Call on students to read each item and say if it is true or false. If it is false, ask the student to correct it. Write the answers on the board.
- Statement 3 is an inference question. After a student gives the answer, ask: *How do you know? What did you hear?* (Lt. Jefferson says to keep clothing away from fire while one is cooking.)
- Note: Item 5 is an inference question. Lt. Jefferson says, "never leave the kitchen while food is still cooking on the stove."

C PAIRS. What is one question...

- Go around the room and have students read their questions. List them on the board.

◼ Expansion: Speaking Practice for 2C

- Group students and have them discuss the answers to the questions on the board.

Presentation   10 minutes

3 CONVERSATION

Pronunciation Watch

- Write a sentence with two clauses on the board, for example, *When you leave the room, please turn out the light.* Explain that the sentence has two clauses that are separated by a comma.
- Read the sentence. Pause slightly between the clauses. Ask the class: *What did you hear after the word* room? (a pause) *What did you hear at the end of the sentence?* (the voice goes down)
- Read the Pronunciation Watch note.

> **Language Note**
>
> If the dependent clause (beginning with *if* or *when*) is the second clause in the sentence, there is no comma—and no pause—between the clauses.

A Listen to the sentences. Notice...

- Play CD 1, Track 53. Have students listen.
- Play Track 53 again. Have students repeat.
- Select students to repeat the sentences again. Make sure they pause between clauses.

Controlled Practice   10 minutes

B Read the sentences. Add a comma...

- Read item 1 with a pause between the two clauses. Have students repeat.
- Have students work alone or in pairs.
- Play CD 1, Track 54. Have students check their answers.
- Call on students to repeat the sentences.

C Lt. Jefferson is asking the class...

- Play CD 1, Track 55. Have students listen and read along silently.
- Check comprehension. Ask: *How can cigarettes cause fires? If you live with a smoker, how can you prevent a fire?* (You can ask smokers to smoke outside.)

4 PRACTICE

A PAIRS. Practice the conversation.

- Form cross-ability pairs and have students take turns reading each role.
- Have students switch partners and practice again.
- Ask volunteers to perform the conversation.

Communicative Practice   15 minutes

B PAIRS. Discuss. Talk about...

- With the class, look at the illustrations and go over vocabulary as needed.
- Pair students. Have them discuss why the situations in the illustrations are dangerous. Tell them to list other situations that can cause fires.
- Go over each question and have students share their answers.

C MAKE IT PERSONAL. Talk about fire safety.

STEP 1. GROUPS. Discuss...

- Form groups. Make sure each group has a timekeeper, a note taker, and a reporter.
- Give a time limit. While students are talking, walk around and provide help as needed.
- Have the note taker write down the group's ideas.

STEP 2. CLASS. Share your ideas.

- Have reporters share their group's ideas. List them on the board.

Expansion: Speaking Practice

- In groups, have students discuss ways to improve fire safety in and around the school.
- *Optional:* Take notes on students' ideas, type them up, and have students present their suggestions to your school administration. Ask a member of the administration to report back to the class.

Extra Practice

Interactive Practice

3 CONVERSATION

Pronunciation Watch

When there is more than one clause in a sentence, each clause usually has its own intonation. When you start a sentence with a clause that begins with *if* or *when*, let your voice go up or down a little and pause at the end of that clause.

CD1 T53

A Listen to the sentences. Notice the intonation. Then listen again and repeat.

If we want to keep our home safe, / what do you recommend?

When you're in the kitchen, pay attention to what you're doing.

CD1 T54

B Read the sentences. Add a comma where the voice should go up or down a little and pause. Then listen again and check your answers.

1. If a pan of food catches fire, put a lid over it.
2. When you finish cooking, remember to turn off the stove and oven.
3. If you have children, you should be extra careful.
4. If you use a space heater, don't put it too close to your bed.
5. When you leave the room, don't forget to blow out the candle.

CD1 T55

C Lt. Jefferson is asking the class questions. Listen and read.

Lt. Jefferson: Let's continue talking about how to prevent home fires. Can anyone think of other possible dangers?

Mr. Sokolov: Cigarettes can be a cause of fires, right?

Lt. Jefferson: That's correct, especially if people smoke in bed.

Mr. Sokolov: A fire can also start if a smoker leaves a cigarette burning in an ashtray.

Lt. Jefferson: Right again.

Mr. Sokolov: So, if we live with someone who smokes and we want to keep our home safe, what do you recommend?

Lt. Jefferson: One thing you can do is to ask smokers to smoke outside.

4 PRACTICE

A PAIRS. Practice the conversation.

B PAIRS. Discuss. Talk about situations that can cause fires. Use the ideas in the pictures or your own ideas.

C MAKE IT PERSONAL. Think about fire safety.

STEP 1. GROUPS. Discuss. What are some ways to improve fire safety in your own home?

STEP 2. CLASS. Share your ideas.

Grammar

Present real conditionals

If clause	Result clause
If a pan of food **catches** fire,	**put** a lid over it and **turn** the stove off.
If you **have** children,	you **should be** extra careful.
If you **don't have** a smoke detector,	your home **isn't** safe.
If we **want** to keep our home safe,	what **do** you **recommend**?

Grammar Watch

- Present real conditional sentences describe true situations that occur under real or possible conditions. They are also used to give instructions or advice under these conditions.

- Conditional sentences can begin with either the *if* clause or the result clause. Use a comma between the clauses only when the *if* clause comes first: *If you have children, you should be extra careful.* BUT: *You should be extra careful if you have children.*

- For present real conditional questions, use question word order only in the result clause.

1   PRACTICE

Read the poster that Lt. Jefferson used during his class on fire safety.
Draw one line under the *if* clause and two lines under the result clause.

What to Do in CASE of FIRE

- If you see smoke coming under the door, don't open the door! Don't open the door if it is very hot or warm! Go to another exit.

- If the door is cool, open it slowly.

- If there is smoke along your escape route, drop to the floor and crawl on your hands and knees below the smoke.

- If you are trapped, close the doors between you and the fire. If you can get to a phone, dial 911 and ask for the fire department. If you can't reach a phone, go to a window and signal for help with a sheet or a flashlight.

Getting Started 5 minutes

- On the board, write *If we hear a fire alarm . . .* Ask the class: *If we hear a fire alarm, what should we do?* (We should leave the building, etc.) Write the answer(s) on the board.
- Circle the word *if*. Point to the sentences on the board and say: *Sentences with* if *are called conditional sentences.*
- Point to the *if* clause and say, *This part of the sentence is called the* if *clause.* Point to the other clause and say: *This part of the sentence is called the result clause.*
- If you think your students will benefit from further explanation, you can point out that each clause has a subject and a verb. If a clause begins with a command, the implied subject is *you.*

Presentation 10 minutes

Present real conditionals

- Copy the grammar chart on the board. Circle the word *if* in each sentence. Underline the verbs. Read each sentence out loud as students follow along.
- Read the first Grammar Watch note. Point to the underlined verbs and ask: *What is the time of these sentences?* (present) Point to the first sentence and ask: *Is it possible for a pan to catch fire?* (yes) Summarize by saying: *These sentences are called* real conditionals *because it's possible for the situation to happen.*
- Read the second note. Circle the comma in each of the example sentences. Then have students read each sentence with the clauses in reverse order. As they say each sentence, erase the comma and adjust the capital letters, for example, *Put a lid over it and turn the stove off if a pan of food catches fire.*
- Read the third note. Point to the last example sentence. Read the *if* clause. Write *S* above the subject (*we*) and *V* above the verb (*do, want*). Then point to the result clause and do the same (*you, recommend*).

Controlled Practice 15 minutes

1 PRACTICE

Read the poster that Lt. Jefferson...

- Have students look at the poster. Read the first sentence.
- Have students complete the exercise. Walk around and provide help as needed.
- Have students compare answers.
- Go over the answers. Read each sentence clause by clause. Have students respond by saying *If clause* or *Result clause.*

Expansion: Grammar Practice

- Type ten to twelve present real conditional sentences on a piece of paper, with the *if* clauses in one column and the result clauses in the other column. For example: *If you go out / don't leave candles burning. You should buy a fire extinguisher / if you don't have one.* Make copies of the page and cut the clauses into strips.
- Distribute the strips among the students. (If you have more students than strips, have students work in pairs.)
- Have students mingle and find the classmate whose clause logically combines with theirs to make a sentence. Have students write their sentences on the board.
- Call on students to read the sentences and correct errors as needed.

Controlled Practice   15 minutes

2   PRACTICE

A Combine the two clauses...

- Read the answer to item 1. Circle *if* and the comma. Then call a student to the board to rewrite the sentence with the clauses in reverse order.

- Have students continue working alone or in pairs. Give a time limit. Walk around and provide help as needed.

- Have students come to the board and write the sentences. Correct errors as needed.

- *Optional:* Have students rewrite their answers, reversing the order of the clauses.

B PAIRS. These statements about fire safety...

- Read item 1. Ask: *What are some other ways we could complete this sentence?* (*ask somebody,* etc.).

- Form cross-ability pairs. While students are working, walk around and provide help as needed.

- For items 2 through 5, have two or three students per item come to the board and write their sentences. Have students write complete sentences so that you can check commas and capital letters.

Communicative Practice   15 minutes

Show what you know!

STEP 1. GROUPS. What should you do...

- On the board, draw a two-column chart with the headings *Should* and *Shouldn't*.

- Ask the class: *What's one thing you should do if there's a fire?* (You should leave your home immediately.) *What's one thing you shouldn't do?* (You shouldn't open a door if it is hot.) Write the examples in the chart.

- Remind students that they can write both positive and negative sentences.

- Form groups. Have them select a timekeeper, a note taker, and a reporter. The note taker writes students' ideas in a chart like the one on the board.

- Give a time limit. While students are working, walk around and provide help as needed.

STEP 2. CLASS. Share your ideas.

- Have reporters share their group's ideas. Write them in the chart on the board.

▬▬ Expansion: Speaking Practice

- Ask students if they have ever experienced a fire at home or at work. Ask: Which things in the chart did you do or not do? If there's a fire in the future, will you do anything differently? Call on volunteers to share their experiences and answer the questions on the board.

Progress Check

Can you . . . talk about what to do in case of fire?

Say: We have practiced talking about what to do in case of fire. Now, look at the question at the bottom of the page. Can you talk about what to do in case of fire? Write a checkmark in the box.

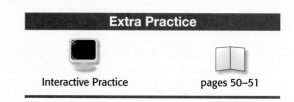

Extra Practice	
Interactive Practice	pages 50–51

A Combine the two clauses to make a conditional sentence about fire safety. Keep the clauses in the same order and add *if* to one clause. Include a comma if necessary.

1. (a fire occurs / leave your home immediately)

   If a fire occurs, leave your home immediately.

2. (you have small children / tell them not to hide under a bed in case of fire)

   If you have small children, tell them not to hide under the bed in case of fire.

3. (family members can't escape by themselves / make plans to help them)

   If family members can't escape by themselves, make plans to help them.

4. (don't open a door / it is hot to the touch)

   Don't open a door if it is hot to the touch.

5. (your clothes catch fire / drop to the floor and roll back and forth)

   If your clothes catch fire, drop to the floor and roll back and forth.

B PAIRS. These statements about fire safety at work are false. Make changes to each underlined result clause so that each statement will be true.

1. If you don't know where the fire exits in your building are, ~~don't worry~~. *find out*

2. If you hear the fire alarm, ~~don't leave your work area until firefighters arrive.~~ *leave your work area and get out of the building*

3. ~~Get~~ your coat and other personal belongings ʌ if you don't have them with you. *Leave* *behind*

4. If you work on the 10th floor, take the ~~elevator~~ to exit the building. *stairs or fire escape*

5. ~~Keep walking forward~~ if you see smoke. *Drop to the floor and crawl on your hands and knees*

Show what you know!   Talk about what to do in case of fire

STEP 1. GROUPS. What should you do if there's a fire at home or at work? Make a list stating what you should and shouldn't do in case of fire.

STEP 2. CLASS. Share your ideas.

Can you...talk about what to do in case of fire? ☐

Reading

1 BEFORE YOU READ

A CLASS. What happens during an earthquake?

B Skim the title, the first paragraph, and the last paragraph of the article. Predict. What is the main idea of the article?

2 READ

CD1 T56

 Listen and read the article. What three things should be part of a good earthquake emergency plan?

What You *Don't Know* May *Hurt* You

Many of us have the wrong idea when it comes to earthquakes. Unfortunately, our **misconceptions** may affect the way that we prepare—or even worse, do not prepare—for this very dangerous natural disaster.

Belief #1: In the U.S., earthquakes happen only on the West Coast, in states like California. Although scientists cannot predict earthquakes, research shows that earthquakes can happen anywhere, anytime. That's why it's important to have an earthquake emergency plan. The first step in your plan should be to make your home safe. For example, use the bottom shelves of cupboards and bookcases for items that are heavy or breakable. Make sure that heavy furniture and electronic equipment, like television sets, won't fall during an earthquake.

DUCK

COVER

HOLD

Belief #2: The safest place to be during an earthquake is in a doorway. In most buildings today, an inside wall is safer than a doorway. It's even better to get under a piece of furniture such as a table or a desk. As part of your emergency plan, practice "duck, cover, and hold."

Belief #3: After the shaking of an earthquake stops, the danger is over. Earthquakes can cause serious damage, so even after a quake, the situation will remain dangerous. Your emergency plan should include **evacuation routes** so that you and your family can have a safe way to leave your home after the shaking has ended. Also learn about work and school emergency plans, and agree on a place where the family can meet when it's safe to be outdoors.

Don't be **fooled** by these or other common misconceptions. Plan, prepare, and practice so that you'll be ready when an earthquake occurs.

Getting Started   5 minutes

1   BEFORE YOU READ

A CLASS. **What happens during...**

- The question can be interpreted in several ways. To clarify, ask: *What happens to the earth during an earthquake?* (It shakes). *What happens as a result?* (Buildings fall down, bridges collapse, roads get cracks in them, etc.)

B **Skim the title, on the first paragraph,...**

- Remind students that skimming is fast reading to get a general idea about something. Tell them not to worry about unfamiliar vocabulary. Instead, they should focus on words and information they *can* understand and use it to predict the main idea.
- Give students one to two minutes to skim.
- Call on volunteers to share their predictions. Write them on the board.

Answer: The article is about misconceptions that affect how people prepare for an earthquake.

Presentation   15 minutes

2   READ

 Listen and read the article. What...

- Play CD 1, Track 56. Ask students to listen and read along with the article.
- When students have finished reading, point to students' predictions from Exercise 1B on the board and ask: *Was your prediction correct?* Have a volunteer restate the main idea.
- Call on different students to say one thing that should be part of a good earthquake emergency plan. Have each student read the sentence in the text that contained the answer.

Answer: Making your home safe. Practicing "duck, cover, and hold." Planning evacuation routes.

Controlled Practice   20 minutes

3 CHECK YOUR UNDERSTANDING

***Reading Skill:* Identifying an Author's Purpose**

- Read the Reading Skill.
- Ask: *Why is it important to know the author's purpose?* (It can help you decide if you want to read something or not. It will also affect how quickly you read and how much you pay attention. For example, if the purpose is to entertain, you can read quickly. But if the purpose is to persuade, it's important to read carefully and remember that you're reading somebody's opinion and that your opinion may be different.)

Ⓐ Read the Reading Skill. Then...

- Survey the class. Ask: *How many people think the purpose is to persuade? Why do you think so?* Repeat with the other answer choices.

Language Note

The following language provides clues that the author's purpose is to persuade: . . . *it's important to have an earthquake emergency plan;* . . . *practice "duck, cover, and hold"; Your emergency plan should include . . . ; Also learn about . . . ; Don't be fooled . . . ; Plan, prepare, and practice . . .*

Ⓑ Complete the sentences. Circle...

- Check answers with the class.
- Item 3 requires an inference. Ask the class: *How do you choose the correct answer?*

Ⓒ PAIRS. Why is it a good idea...

- Ask the class: *What does* duck *mean here? Is it a noun?* (no) *Is it a verb?* (yes)
- Demonstrate and explain *duck, cover, and hold: Duck: bend down. Cover: get under a heavy piece of furniture. Hold: hold onto it and stay where you are until the shaking ends.*
- Have students answer the question, referring to the article, for example: *The article says people should get under a piece of furniture and shouldn't leave their homes until the shaking has stopped.*

Answer: to protect yourself from falling objects.

4 WORD WORK

Find the boldfaced words in the...

Teaching Tip

Review the following strategies that students can use to guess the meaning of unfamiliar words: (1) Read the entire sentence in which an unfamiliar word occurs for clues to the word's meaning; (2) Read the sentence before and/or after the one with the unfamiliar word for clues; (3) Use knowledge of prefixes and suffixes to figure out a word's meaning. Demonstrate the third strategy as follows:

- Work with the class to figure out the meaning of *misconception*. First, tell them to think of other *words* that begin with this prefix, for example, *mistake, misplace,* and *misread.* Ask: *What does* mis- *mean?* (wrong)
- Next, ask: *What word do you see inside* misconception? (concept) *What is a* concept? (an idea) *So what does* misconception *mean?* (a wrong idea)
- Pair students and have them try to figure out the remaining items.
- Call on students to share their definitions. Ask them which clues they used to help them guess.

Communicative Practice   20 minutes

Show what you know!

STEP 1. PAIRS. Discuss. What kinds...

- Have students share their answers. Make a list of natural disasters on the board.

STEP 2. What can you do...

- Have students discuss what they can do to prepare for the natural disasters in Step 1.
- Make a list of students' ideas on the board.

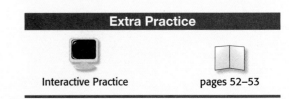

Extra Practice

Interactive Practice   pages 52–53

3 CHECK YOUR UNDERSTANDING

A Read the Reading Skill. Then complete this statement. Circle the correct answer.

In this reading, the author's purpose is to _____.
a. persuade   b. entertain   (c.) inform

> **Reading Skill:** Identifying an Author's Purpose
>
> Think about an author's objective or purpose. Is it to *entertain* you by telling a story? Is it to *inform* you by giving facts? Is it to *persuade* you to agree with a specific opinion?

B Complete the sentences. Circle the correct answers.

1. To prepare for an earthquake, you should put heavy items and items that can break _____.
   a. under a table   (b.) on a low shelf   c. in a doorway

2. As part of your earthquake plan, you should _____.
   a. find out when the next earthquake will happen
   b. read several books about preparing for an earthquake
   (c.) include a way to leave your home during the earthquake

3. The author probably thinks that some people _____.
   a. are not afraid of earthquakes
   (b.) are not prepared for earthquakes
   c. don't know anything about earthquakes

C PAIRS. Why is it a good idea to "duck, cover, and hold" during an earthquake?

4 WORD WORK

Find the boldfaced words in the article. Use the context to figure out the meaning of each word. Write the meaning.

1. misconceptions _wrong ideas_

2. evacuation routes _a safe way to leave your home_

3. fooled _misled, confused_

Show what you know!   Talk about preparing for natural disasters

STEP 1. PAIRS. Discuss. What kinds of natural disasters like earthquakes, tornadoes, or floods occur in the area where you live?

STEP 2. What can you do to prepare for them?

Listening and Speaking

1   BEFORE YOU LISTEN

A CLASS. Discuss. What do you know about hurricanes? What do you know about tornadoes?

B GROUPS. Read the hurricane warning. What do the boldfaced words mean?

"**Meteorologists** at the **National Weather Service** have issued a severe weather **warning**. People who live in **coastal** areas should be prepared to **evacuate** their homes and go to a safe inland location. **Tides** will be high, and rain will be extremely heavy. Residents in areas near rivers and lakes should be prepared for **floods**."

2   LISTEN

CD1 T57

A Henry Ponce is the host of the radio show *Know Your World*. His guest today is meteorologist Dr. Kay Wilkins. Listen to the first part of their conversation. When does hurricane season in the Atlantic Ocean officially start and finish?

Starts: June 1   Finishes: November 30

WEEKEND FORECAST

SAT   SUN

79°

CD1 T58

B Read the questions. Then listen to the whole conversation. Circle the correct answers.

1. What is <u>not</u> a danger of hurricanes?
   a. wind and rain   b. high waves   c. fires

2. Where do hurricanes generally cause the greatest damage?
   a. inland   b. on the coast   c. over water

3. Where do hurricanes get their power?
   a. inland   b. on the coast   c. over water

CD1 T58

C What is the difference between a hurricane watch and a hurricane warning?

STEP 1. Listen to the conversation again.

STEP 2. GROUPS. Discuss the difference.

D GROUPS. Discuss.

1. Which hurricanes have you either heard about or experienced personally?

2. How did the hurricane affect peoples' lives?

3. What can people do to prepare for a hurricane?

Talk about dangerous weather

Getting Started   5 minutes

1 BEFORE YOU LISTEN

A CLASS. Discuss. What do you know...

- Make a two-column chart on the board with the headings *Tornadoes* and *Hurricanes*. Take notes on students' responses.

B GROUPS. Read the hurricane warning...

- Read the paragraph.
- Divide the class into groups. Assign one word or phrase to each group. Have them use a dictionary or the Internet to find out what the terms mean. (Note: When using the Internet, students should type in *What is X?* If *X* is more than one word, they should put it in quotation marks, for example, *What is the "National Weather Service"?*)
- Instruct students to read the paragraph, inserting the definition of their word to make sure the definition they chose is logical.
- Write the boldfaced words on the board. Call up students to write the definitions.

Answers: 1. **meteorologists:** scientists who study weather. 2. **National Weather Service:** The U.S. government agency responsible for weather forecasting 3. **warning:** a sign or statement that something bad is coming 4. **coastal:** near ocean or large body of water 5. **evacuate:** leave quickly in an emergency 6. **tides:** the rise and fall of the ocean every twelve hours 7. **flood:** a very large amount of water that has overflowed its source and now covers an area that is normally dry

- Have students read the paragraph again.

Presentation   5 minutes

2 LISTEN

A Henry Ponce is the host...

- Ask: *Who is the woman in the photo?*
- Tell students to listen for the answer and not worry about words they don't know.
- Play CD 1, Track 57. For extra support, students may read the Audio Script on page 288 as they listen.
- Call on a volunteer to answer the question.

Answer: Starts: June 1 Finishes: November 30

Teaching Tip

Teach students how to listen for specific information. For example, if a question begins with *When*, instruct students to listen for time words such as months, seasons, or years. If a question includes the name of a place, students should listen carefully for the name.

Controlled Practice   10 minutes

B Read the questions. Then listen...

- Have students read the questions silently and predict the answers.
- Play CD 1, Track 58.
- Call on students to read the questions and answers.
- If students are having difficulty with one question, replay the segment of the listening passage that answers the question. Have students repeat what they heard, and then answer the question again.

C What is the difference between...

STEP 1. Listen to the...

- Play Track 58 again. Instruct students to listen specifically for the words *watch* and *warning*.

STEP 2. GROUPS. Discuss the...

- Have students form groups to discuss the differences.

Answer: Hurricane watch: an announcement from the National Weather Service that there is a possibility of a hurricane in the next thirty-six hours. **Hurricane warning:** an announcement that a hurricane is expected to arrive in the next twenty-four hours.

Communicative Practice   10 minutes

D GROUPS. Discuss.

- Form groups. Try to put a student in each group who has either experienced a hurricane or who knows something about hurricanes. Have groups select a timekeeper, a note taker, and a reporter.
- Have reporters share their group's answers.

Lesson 4 Talk about dangerous weather

Presentation 10 minutes

3 CONVERSATION

Two friends are talking about...

- Play CD 1, Track 59. Have students listen and read along silently.
- *Optional:* Have above-level students listen with their books closed.
- Check comprehension. Ask: *What is a flood watch?* (There is a possibility of flooding based on current forecasts.) *What is the National Weather Service predicting?* (three more inches of rain) *What are the speakers going to do?* (keep checking the weather reports for updates)

Controlled Practice 10 minutes

4 PRACTICE

A PAIRS. **Practice the conversation.**

- Form cross-ability pairs and have students take turns reading each role.
- Have students switch partners and practice again.
- Walk around and listen as students are practicing. Provide help as needed.
- Ask volunteers to perform the conversation for the class.

Language Note

It pays to . . . is an idiomatic use of the verb *pay* that has nothing to do with money. It means that an action is smart, beneficial, or worthwhile. *It pays to be prepared* means that the speakers will benefit if they take steps to prepare themselves before the storm arrives.

MULTILEVEL INSTRUCTION for 4A

Pre-level Have students practice several times with the same partner.

Above-level Have students add two or three speaking turns to the conversation in the book. For example, they could talk about steps they will take to prepare for the coming storm.

Communicative Practice 10 minutes

B MAKE IT PERSONAL. **Think about your...**

STEP 1. GROUPS. **Describe an experience...**

- Form groups and have them choose a timekeeper.
- Point out that bad weather can include both cold and heat as well as weather phenomena such as hurricanes, windstorms, etc.
- Give a time limit for the activity. Have group members figure out how much time each student has to speak. The timekeeper should keep track.

STEP 2. CLASS. **Share your experiences.**

- Ask volunteers to repeat their stories for the whole class.

Extra Practice

Interactive Practice

3 CONVERSATION

CD1 T59

Two friends are talking about the weather. Listen and read.

Man: Can you believe this weather?

Woman: It's been really bad lately. Now there's a flood watch.

Man: I know. I heard it on the radio before I left home this morning.

Woman: The National Weather Service says there could be three more inches of rain. There's a severe weather watch that lasts until midnight.

Man: Wow...this could be very dangerous.

Woman: Yeah. It's probably a good idea to keep checking the weather report for updates.

Man: You're right. On days like today, it pays to be prepared.

4 PRACTICE

A PAIRS. **Practice the conversation.**

B MAKE IT PERSONAL. **Think about your experiences in bad weather.**

STEP 1. GROUPS. **Describe an experience that you have had in bad weather.**

STEP 2. CLASS. **Share your experiences.**

Grammar

Adverb clauses of time

Adverb clause (time)	Main clause
When there is the possibility of a hurricane in the next 36 hours,	the National Weather Service issues a hurricane watch.
As soon as you hear the warning,	make sure that your emergency preparations are complete.
Before I left home this morning,	I heard about the flood watch.
Until the weather service cancels the storm watch,	you should check the weather report regularly.
After they hit land,	hurricanes lose strength.

1 PRACTICE

A Read the sentences about thunderstorms.
Underline the adverb clauses.

1. <u>After lightning flashes in the sky</u>, you hear the sound of thunder.
2. The sky usually turns dark <u>before a thunderstorm begins</u>.
3. <u>When there's a thunderstorm</u>, you should not stand under a tree.
4. Get inside a building or a car <u>as soon as you see lightning</u>.
5. You should stay inside <u>until the thunderstorm ends</u>.

Grammar Watch

- Adverb clauses of time tell when one action happened in relation to another action.
- Sentences can begin with the adverb clause or the main clause. Don't use a comma between the clauses when the adverb clause comes at the end. *Hurricanes lose strength after they hit land.*

B Complete the paragraph about weather forecasting. Use *when, before, until,* or *after*.

_____When_____ scientists predict storms quickly and correctly, they save lives. __Before / Until__ they had technology to help them do their job, meteorologists worked slowly. Their work became easier and faster __when / after__ they began using computers. Today, weather forecasters give up to thirty minutes' advance warning __before__ a tornado actually arrives. As a result, people have time to find a safe place to stay __until__ the storm is over. For example, __when__ powerful tornadoes passed through Oklahoma in 1999, only 44 people died. However, 695 people lost their lives and 2,000 more were injured in 1925 because the tornadoes went through just a few minutes __after__ they received the tornado warning.

Getting Started   5 minutes

- On the board, write: *It always rains after I wash my car.*
- Say: *Let's look at this sentence. It has two clauses.* Circle the word *after*. Underline the clause that follows. Say: *This clause starts with a time word. It's an* adverb clause. Draw two lines under the clause beginning with *It.* Say: *This clause starts with the subject. It's the* main clause.

Presentation   10 minutes

Adverb clauses of time

- Copy the grammar chart on the board.
- Read the first Grammar Watch note. Then read each sentence in the grammar chart and ask: *Did the events happen at the same time, or did one event happen first? Which event happened first?* Write *1* above the first event and *2* above the second one. (In the first sentence, the two events occur at the same time. In the others, however, one event occurs before the other.)
- Summarize the previous step. On the board, write: *As soon as—1; Before—2; Until—2; After—1.* Explain, for example: *The clause with* after *happened first. The clause with* before *happened second,* etc.
- Read the second Grammar Watch note. Point out that the comma rule for sentences with adverb clauses is the same as the rule for sentences with *if* clauses (Lesson 2).

Language Notes

- *After* and *Before* are used when the actions in the two clauses are sequential.
- *As soon as* and *after* are both used with the action that happens first. However, *as soon as* means that the second action follows the first more immediately.
- *When* is used when the two actions are simultaneous. However, *when* can also be a synonym for *after*, for example, *After / As soon as / When you leave, close the door.*
- *Until* is used when the action in the other clause continues up to the occurrence of the action in the clause with *until*.

Controlled Practice   15 minutes

1 PRACTICE

A Read the sentences about...

- Read the example. If necessary, define *lightning* (a bright flash of light that occurs in the sky during a storm); *flash* (to shine brightly for a moment); *thunder* (the loud sound that occurs after a flash of lightning during a storm)
- Have students work alone or in pairs.
- Check answers. Say the sentence number. Have students say which words they underlined.

B Complete the paragraph about...

- Explain *weather forecasting.* (the science of trying to predict the weather)
- Remind students to read each sentence and figure out which action happens first. This will help them choose the correct adverb.
- Have students work alone or in pairs.
- Read the paragraph sentence by sentence and have students call out the adverb that fits in each blank. If students are confused, have them decide if the actions are simultaneous (happening at the same time), almost simultaneous, or sequential (happening one after the other). If sequential, have students say which event happens first.

■ Expansion: Grammar Practice for 1B

- Write sentences about your daily routine on the board. Use each adverb from the lesson once. For example: *As soon as I get out of bed, I make coffee. When the coffee is ready, I pour it into a cup. Before I eat breakfast, I feed my dog. After I eat breakfast, I brush my teeth. I read the newspaper until it's time to leave.*
- In each sentence, have students come to the board and write *1* above the activity that occurs first and *2* above the activity that occurs second.
- Have students write their own sentences about their routines. While students are working, walk around and provide help as needed.
- Pair students and have them read their sentences to each other.
- Select students to write their sentences on the board. Go over them with the class.

Discuss weather reports

Controlled Practice   15 minutes

2 PRACTICE

A Read the following facts about...

- Read item 1. Remind students that *when* can mean *after*.
- Have students complete the items, working alone or in pairs.
- Go over the answers.

B Combine the two sentences...

- Define *radar*. (a method that uses radio waves to find the position of things such as planes) Use it in a sentence: *The police can also use radar to determine how fast a car is going.*
- Ask students to share what they know about radar. In particular, ask if anyone knows how the military uses radar.
- Read item 1 with the class.
- Have students complete the items, working alone or in pairs.
- Have students write the sentences on the board. Go over them with the class. In each sentence, write *1* above the first event and *2* above the second.
- Have students transpose the clauses in each sentence, giving alternate answers, for example: 1. When they wanted to know the location of planes and ships, the military used radar during World War II.

Communicative Practice   15 minutes

Show what you know!

Watch a weather report...

- Download a short weather report from the radio, television, or an Internet site (see weather.yahoo.com or The Weather Channel). As needed, prepare a list of technical terms and definitions. Also prepare a set of comprehension questions.
- Go over the vocabulary with the class and write the comprehension questions on the board.
- Read the weather report to the class. Call on students to answer the questions.

- Read the weather report again and have students take notes.
- Have students write sentences describing the weather report, using adverb clauses of time. Have students write the sentences on the board. Correct errors as needed.
- Download another short weather report; if possible, use an update of the earlier report so that vocabulary will be recycled.
- Read the report several times and have students take notes.
- Have an above-level student report the information that he or she heard, using adverb clauses of time.
- Pair students. Have them make sentences describing the weather report. Remind them to use adverb clauses of time.
- Have several students write their sentences on the board. Correct as needed.

▬▬ MULTILEVEL INSTRUCTION for Show what you know!

Pre-level Have students listen specifically for one piece of information, such as the high and low temperatures.

Above-level Have students listen for as much information as they can.

Progress Check

Can you . . . discuss weather reports?

Say: *We have practiced discussing weather reports. Now, look at the question at the bottom of the page. Can you discuss weather reports? Write a checkmark in the box.*

Extra Practice	
Interactive Practice	pages 54–55

A Read the following facts about tornadoes. Decide which of the events in brackets occurred first. Mark one event *1* (occurred earlier) and the other event *2* (occurred later).

1.   2   1
   [Tornadoes occur] [when cold, dry air from Canada meets warm, moist air from the Gulf of Mexico.]

2.   1   2
   [After the winds of a tornado begin to turn in a circular direction,] [they move faster and faster.]

3.   2   1
   [Before a tornado arrives in an area,] [you will usually hear a loud warning siren.]

4.   2   1
   [Until scientists learned some basic facts about tornadoes,] [they had trouble predicting them.]

5.   1   2
   [When the violent winds of a tornado hit buildings,] [serious structural damage often occurs.]

6.   1
   [Weather Service personnel use weather radar to confirm a potential tornado]
                          2
   [before they issue a tornado warning.]

B Combine the two sentences with the adverb in parentheses. Include a comma if necessary.

1. The military used radar during World War II. / They wanted to know the location of planes and ships. (when) *The military used radar during World War II when they wanted to know the location of planes and ships.*

2. Radar worked well. / There was bad weather. (until) Radar worked well until there was bad weather.

3. It began to rain or snow. / Radar operators noticed that something strange happened with their equipment. (as soon as) As soon as it began to rain or snow, radar operators noticed . . .

4. Scientists began to use radar to look at weather. / The war ended. (after) Scientists began to use radar to look at weather after the war ended.

5. Modern tools like radar were used to predict the weather / Forecasting was much less reliable than it is today. (before) Before modern tools like radar were used to predict the weather, forecasting was much less reliable . . .

Show what you know!   Discuss weather reports

Watch a weather report on television or on the Internet. Take notes about the information the meteorologist gives. Describe what happened during the weather report to a partner. Use adverb clauses of time.

Can you... discuss weather reports? ☐

Talk about planning for a hurricane

Life Skills

1 INTERPRET AN EVACUATION MAP

A What supplies would you need for a hurricane or other natural disaster? List items for each category at the right.

☐ water
☐ food
☐ first aid supplies
☐ personal care items
☐ child care supplies
☐ cleaning supplies
☐ communication devices
☐ documents

B PAIRS. Discuss. Are you prepared? Which items do you already have? Which ones do you need to get? What other supplies would be useful?

C CLASS. Look at the map. In what areas are hurricanes especially dangerous? Why is it important for people to know how to interpret an evacuation map?

2 PRACTICE

A Look at the map. Circle the correct answers.

1. What color are the evacuation routes?
   a. red   b. blue   c. tan   (d.) green

2. You live in Miami Beach. A major hurricane is coming, and you need to evacuate. In which direction do you need to go in order to evacuate?
   a. northeast   (b.) northwest   c. southeast   d. southwest

3. You live in Miami-Dade County on SW 136th Street, west of State Highway 997. In which direction do you need to go in order to evacuate?
   (a.) east, then north   b. east, then south   c. west, then north   d. west, then south

4. You live in the Florida Keys. Which two routes can you take to evacuate?
   a. Card Sound Road and U.S. Highway 41   (c.) U.S. Highway 1 and Card Sound Road
   b. U.S. Highway 1 and State Highway 994   d. U.S. Highway 1 and U.S. Highway 41

B In which direction do most evacuation routes travel from Miami-Dade County? Why?

C GROUPS. Think about what you learned earlier about hurricanes. How will you prepare for a coming hurricane? Make a list.

1. listen for hurricane watch   3. gather emergency supplies

2. listen for hurricane warning   4. know your evacuation route

Getting Started   10 minutes

1 INTERPRET AN EVACUATION MAP

Ⓐ What supplies would you need...

- Write the categories on the board. Go over them with the class, defining terms as needed, for example, say: personal care items *includes such things as a toothbrush, shampoo, etc.*
- Elicit items in each category and write examples on the board. For example, for *water*, students could indicate the quantity they need to prepare, such as *five gallons.*

Possible answers: water—five gallons per person; food—canned meats, beans, tuna, fruits, and vegetables; first-aid supplies—bandages, gauze, antibiotics; personal care items—toothbrush, toothpaste, soap; child care supplies—diapers, baby food; cleaning supplies—bleach, rags, sponges; communication devices—portable radio, cell phone and charger; documents—copies of birth certificates, driver's licenses, passports.

Ⓑ PAIRS. Discuss. Are you prepared?

- Pair students. Have them look at the list on the board and answer the questions.
- Go around the room and have each student share one item he or she has and one item he or she needs to get.
- Ask the class about additional useful supplies and list them on the board.

Presentation   10 minutes

Ⓒ CLASS. Look at the map. In what areas...

- Define *areas* by giving students several choices. For example, ask: *Are hurricanes more dangerous near the coast or inland? Are they more dangerous outdoors or indoors?* Call on volunteers to answer.

Answer: Hurricanes are more dangerous in coastal areas.

- Review the meaning of *evacuation route* (first presented in Lesson 3). Have students look at the map. Say: *This map shows evacuation routes for Miami-Dade County in southern Florida.*
- Call on volunteers to answer the second question.

Answer: It's important for people to know how to interpret an evacuation map so that they can leave the area quickly when a hurricane is coming.

Controlled Practice   20 minutes

2 PRACTICE

Ⓐ Look at the map. Circle the correct answers.

- Have students look at the map legend. Ask: *What color are the evacuation routes?* (green)
- You may choose at this point to go over the abbreviations and symbols used in maps. See Expansion on page T-97.
- Have students answer the questions alone or in pairs.
- To check answers, have students hold up their books and point to the evacuation routes.

▬▬ **Expansion: Speaking Practice**

- Have pairs of students ask and answer questions about evacuation routes using the present real conditional, as follows: A: *If you live on Palm Drive in Miami-Dade, what is your evacuation route?* B: *Go west on Palm Drive. Then go north on South Highway 997 or northeast on South Highway 826.*

Ⓑ In which direction do most...

- Have students look at the map again. Ask if anyone knows the answer. (*north and west, because the hurricanes usually come from the south or the east*)
- Ask: *Where is it more dangerous in a hurricane—on the coast, or inland? So why do the evacuation routes travel north and west?* (to get away from the coast)

Communicative Practice   20 minutes

Ⓒ GROUPS. Think about what you learned...

- With the class, think of an example and write it on the board, for example, *Make sure there is gas in the car.*
- Form groups. Make sure each group has a timekeeper, a note taker, and a reporter. The note taker should write down the group's ideas.
- Give a time limit. While students are talking, walk around and provide help as needed.
- Have the reporter from each group share the group's list of ideas. Write all ideas on the board.

▨ Expansion: Map Study

- Students may need help understanding some of the abbreviations on the map. Write the following abbreviations on the board: *Hwy, Rd, Ave, Dr, St, Blvd, USHY, STHY,* and *INTL.*

- Call on students to provide the corresponding words. (*highway, road, avenue, drive, street, boulevard, United States highway, state highway,* and *international*) Have students work in pairs to find the abbreviations on the map.

- Direct students' attention to the compass rose on the map. Elicit the directions *North, South, West, East, Northeast, Southeast, Southwest,* and *Northwest.* Have students work in pairs to find abbreviations for the directions on the map, for example, *N, SW,* etc.

Progress Check

Can you . . . talk about planning for a hurricane?

Say: *We have practiced talking about planning for a hurricane. Now, look at the question at the bottom of the page. Can you talk about planning for a hurricane? Write a checkmark in the box.*

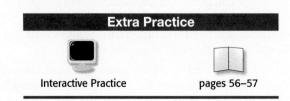

Extra Practice

Interactive Practice   pages 56–57

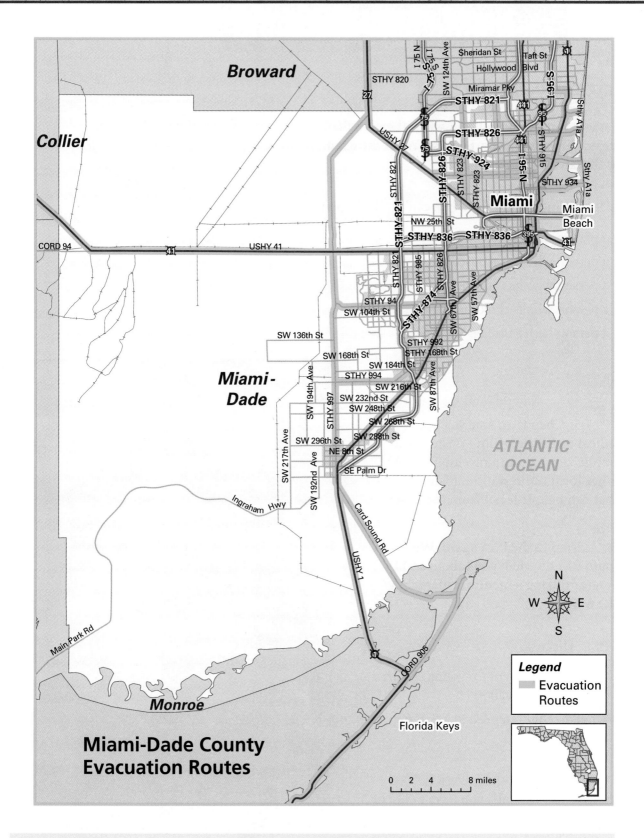

Miami-Dade County
Evacuation Routes

Broward

Collier

Miami-Dade

Monroe

Florida Keys

ATLANTIC OCEAN

Miami

Miami Beach

I 75 N
I 75 S
STHY 820
Sheridan St
Hollywood Blvd
SW 124th Ave
Miramar Pky
STHY-821
441
I-95-S
STHY 821
STHY-826
441
27
75
USHY 27
STHY-826
STHY-924
STHY 823
STHY 823
I-95-N
STHY A1a
75
STHY 821
STHY-821
STHY 934
NW 25th St
STHY-836
STHY-836
395
STHY A1a
CORD 94
USHY 41
41
STHY 821
STHY 985
STHY 826
SW 57th Ave
41
STHY 94
SW 104th St
STHY-874
SW 67th Ave
SW 136th St
STHY 992
STHY 168th St
SW 168th St
SW 184th St
STHY 994
SW 87th Ave
SW 194th Ave
SW 216th St
STHY 997
SW 232nd St
SW 248th St
SW 268th St
SW 296th St
SW 288th St
NE 8th St
SW 217th Ave
SE Palm Dr
SW 192nd Ave
Ingraham Hwy
Card Sound Rd
USHY 1
Main Park Rd
CORD 905
1
I-95 915

N
W E
S

0 2 4 8 miles

Legend
Evacuation Routes

Listening and Speaking

1 BEFORE YOU LISTEN

A CLASS. You should call 911 when there's a life-threatening emergency. Discuss. What are examples of life-threatening emergencies?

Hello. 911. What's your emergency?

B PAIRS. Which of these people can't talk? Explain.

- ☐ a person who is bleeding
- ☑ a person who is unconscious
- ☐ a person who has allergies
- ☑ a person who is choking
- ☐ a person with a broken leg

2 LISTEN

CD1 T60

A Iris Chen is an emergency medical technician (EMT). She made a public-service announcement (PSA) for her local radio station. Listen. What can people learn from the PSA?

CD1 T60

B Listen to the PSA again. What should you do when you talk to a 911 operator during a medical emergency? Take notes.

C PAIRS. Discuss.

1. Why is it important for young children to know how to call 911?

2. What do children need to know to place a 911 call?

D MAKE IT PERSONAL. PAIRS. Describe any 911 calls you have made or have heard about.

Getting Started   5 minutes

1 BEFORE YOU LISTEN

A CLASS. **You should call 911...**

- Write *life-threatening emergency* on the board. Ask the class to define the term. If they need help, explain: life-threatening *means a serious condition that could kill you, such as a heart attack.* Ask: *What are some other life-threatening emergencies?* (poisoning, stroke, bleeding, injury, etc.)

B PAIRS. **Which of these...**

- Read the five choices. Define terms, for example, *unconscious: unable to see, hear, or feel what is happening as a result of an accident or injury.*
- Check the answers. Call on volunteers to explain.

> **Teaching Tip**
>
> If a speaking activity is short, pair students who are sitting near each other. For longer activities, use index cards with students' names to form pairs.

Presentation   5 minutes

2 LISTEN

A **Iris Chen is an emergency medical...**

- Define *public-service announcement* by explaining: PSAs *are similar to advertisements, but the speaker isn't trying to sell anything. Their purpose is to give the public useful or interesting information about events or services in their community.*
- Have students look at the photo. Ask: *What is Ms. Chen wearing? What does she do in her job?*
- Play CD 1, Track 60.
- Have students answer the question.

Answer: People can learn how to prepare for an emergency. They can also learn what information the 911 operators need.

> **Culture Connection**
>
> According to the Federal Communications Commission, a public-service announcement is *any announcement for which no charge is made and which promotes programs, activities, or services of federal, state, or local governments (e.g., army recruitment, sale of bonds, etc.) or the programs, activities, or services of nonprofit organizations (e.g., United Way, Red Cross blood donations, etc.) and other announcements that serve community interests.*

Controlled Practice   5 minutes

B **Listen to the PSA again...**

- Play Track 60 again. Have students take notes.
- Have students compare notes with a partner.
- Call on students to share their answers. Write the answers on the board.

Answers: Stay calm; speak slowly; explain the emergency briefly; give information about anyone who is bleeding, unconscious, or not breathing; give the location of the emergency; answer the operator's questions; don't hang up until the operator tells you to.

Communicative Practice   10 minutes

C PAIRS. **Discuss.**

Answers: 1. Children may be alone with an adult who becomes injured or ill. 2. They need to be able to describe the emergency and give information about their location.

■ **Expansion: Listening Practice for 2C**

- Write the following questions on the board:
  1. According to the speaker, where should people put their phone number and the 911 number? 2. What information should callers give the 911 operator in an emergency? 3. Why is it important for 911 callers not to hang up until the operator tells them to?
- Have students listen again to Track 60.
- Have them answer the questions with a partner.
- Check answers with the class.

D MAKE IT PERSONAL. PAIRS. **Describe any...**

- If possible, put one student in each pair who has had experience with a 911 call.

Presentation   5 minutes

3 **CONVERSATION**

Pronunciation Watch

- Write the words *clean, feel, fit,* and *quick* on the board. Ask students to read each word. Ask: *What's the vowel sound in this word? How do we spell that sound?* (ea *or* ee *for* /i/; i *for* /ɪ/)
- Read the Pronunciation Watch.
- Explain the tense versus lax pronunciation of /i/ and /ɪ/, respectively. Say: *To pronounce* /i/, *stretch your lips and smile. Say* eat. *To pronounce* /ɪ/, *relax your lips. Say* it.

A 🔘 **Listen to the words. Notice...**

- Play CD 1, Track 61. Have students listen.
- Play Track 61 again. Have students repeat.

Controlled Practice   5 minutes

B 🔘 **Listen and circle the word...**

- Play CD 1, Track 62. Have students listen and circle the words.
- Check answers. Repeat the words again if needed.

■■ **Expansion: Listening Practice for 3B**

- On the board, write: *1. eat 2. it*
- Pair students. Tell them to take turns saying and listening to words in Exercise 3B. The speaker chooses one of the words. The listener holds up one finger if the speaker says a word with /i/ and two fingers if the speaker says a word with /ɪ/.
- If listeners are having trouble identifying the correct sound, make sure speakers are pronouncing the words correctly. Remind speakers to smile when they say /i/ and relax their lips when they say /ɪ/.

Presentation   5 minutes

C 🔘 **Pattama Somsiri is talking...**

- Have students look at the photo. Ask: *Who is Pattama? How does she look? Why?*
- Play CD 1, Track 63. Have students listen and read along silently.

Controlled Practice   10 minutes

4 **PRACTICE**

A PAIRS. **Practice the conversation.**

- Form cross-ability pairs and have students take turns reading each role.
- Have students switch partners and practice again.
- Listen as students are practicing. Take notes on errors with the pronunciation of /i/ and /ɪ/.
- Ask volunteers to perform the conversation.
- Go over the pronunciation errors in your notes. Say the incorrect forms and have the class repeat them correctly.

Communicative Practice   10 minutes

B ROLE PLAY. PAIRS. **Role-play this...**

> **Teaching Tip**
>
> While pairs are performing role plays, use the scoring rubric for speaking on page T-xiii to evaluate each student's vocabulary, grammar, fluency, and how well he or she completes the task. You may want to review the completed rubric with the students.

- Model the role play with an above-level student. Play the role of Student B. You can begin like this: *911 operator. Can I have your name?* Also ask for the caller's address and phone number and what the problem is.
- Form pairs. Have students practice several times.
- Have volunteers role-play their conversation.

■■ **MULTILEVEL INSTRUCTION for 4B**

Cross-ability Have higher-level students play the role of Student B. Have lower-level students play the role of Student A.

Extra Practice

Interactive Practice

3 CONVERSATION

CD1 T61

A Listen to the words. Notice the underlined vowel sound in each group of words. Then listen again and repeat.

/i/	/ɪ/
eat	it
breathe	will
bleeding	minutes

CD1 T62

B Listen and circle the word you hear.

1. (eat)/ it   2. (feel)/ fill   3. leave /(live)   4. (seat)/ sit   5. steal /(still)

CD1 T63

C Pattama Somsiri is talking to a 911 operator. Listen and read.

Operator: Ma'am, I have your address and phone number. The ambulance will be there in a few minutes.

Pattama: OK…but what should we do until it arrives?

Operator: Is your sister still having trouble breathing?

Pattama: Yes, but my husband is helping her. He took a first-aid class last year, so he must know what to do.

Operator: Your sister may be having an allergic reaction.

Pattama: Well, she's allergic to nuts, but she was eating chocolate cake when the problem started. There weren't any nuts in the cake, so that couldn't be the problem.

Operator: If the cake is from a bakery, there might be nuts in it. I'll tell the EMTs about your sister's allergy.

4 PRACTICE

A PAIRS. Practice the conversation.

B ROLE PLAY. PAIRS. Role-play this conversation. It takes place during an emergency 911 call.

Student A: You are at home. You just walked into the living room and found your grandfather on the floor. He is unconscious, but he's breathing. You know that your grandfather has a heart problem. You call 911. Answer the 911 operator's questions.

Student B: You are a 911 operator. You just received an emergency medical call. Find out who the victim is and where he is. Ask if the person is breathing or bleeding. Also ask if the caller can put the victim in a comfortable position.

Grammar

Expressing degrees of certainty

There weren't any nuts in the cake, so that	**can't** **couldn't**	be the problem.
A 911 call	**could** **may** **might**	save the life of someone you love.
In an emergency, some people	**may not** **might not**	be thinking clearly.

My husband took a first-aid class, so he **must** know what to do.

She didn't have an allergic reaction, so the cake **must not** contain any nuts.

Could it be an allergic reaction?

Grammar Watch

- Use *can't* or *couldn't* to show that something is almost impossible.
- Use *could, may (not),* and *might (not)* to show that something is possible but NOT certain.
- Use *must* to show that something is almost certainly true. Use *must not* to show that something is almost certainly NOT true.
- Use *could* (not *may* or *might*) for questions.

1 PRACTICE

Mrs. Johnson fell down the stairs in her home. Decide which sentence shows more certainty. Circle your answer.

1. a. Mrs. Johnson's leg may be broken
    b. Mrs. Johnson's leg must be broken.

2. a. She might be in a lot of pain right now.
    b. She must be in a lot of pain right now.

3. a. She could need medical attention.
    b. She must need medical attention.

4. a. She may not be close enough to the phone to call 911.
    b. She couldn't be close enough to the phone to call 911.

5. a. There might not be anyone else at home with Mrs. Johnson.
    b. There couldn't be anyone else at home with Mrs. Johnson.

Getting Started   5 minutes

- Arrange with a fellow teacher or an administrator to knock on your classroom door. Ask: *Who could that be? What do you think?* Have students guess. Then open the door and let students see if their guess was correct.
- Say: *When [name] knocked on the door, I asked a question. Who remembers what it was?* Elicit the question and write it on the board.
- Ask: *What does* could *mean in this sentence?* (possibility)
- Set the context of the lesson. Say: *In this lesson we'll learn how to use* could *and other modals to talk about degrees of certainty or possibility.*

Language Note

Many modals have more than one meaning. *Could* and *couldn't* are potentially confusing because they're used to talk about ability in the past (*When I was fifteen I couldn't drive*) as well as possibility in the present (*Who could that be? It could be Jane. I know she's here today. It couldn't be Max because he's at work.*) In addition, *could* is used both in present and past questions, but with different meanings: *Could you swim when you were five?* (past ability) *Could this shirt belong to Ed?* (possibility in the present)

Presentation   10 minutes

Expressing degrees of certainty

- Draw a horizontal line across the board. Above the line on the left, write *0%*. In the center of the line, write *50%*. On the right end, write *99%*.
- Explain: *When we talk about degrees of certainty, we're talking about the possibility that something will or will not happen.*
- Read the first Grammar Watch note. Then read the corresponding example. Ask: *How certain is it that the nuts are the problem? Is it impossible, possible, or almost certain?* (impossible) Write *can't* and *couldn't* beneath the horizontal line on the board, under *0%*.
- Read the second note. Then read the corresponding examples. Ask: *How certain is it that a 911 call will save someone's life?* (possible but not certain) *How certain is it that in an emergency, people don't think clearly?* (possible but not certain) Write *could, may (not),* and *might (not)* under *50%* on the line.

- Read the third note. Then read the corresponding examples. Ask: *How certain is it that the woman's husband knows what to do?* (quite certain) *How certain is it the woman that the cake doesn't contain nuts?* (almost certain) Write *must* and *must not* under *99%* on the line.
- Read the fourth note and the corresponding example. Say: *We use* could *in questions about possibility.*

Language Note

Can't and *couldn't* are used to talk about something that is nearly impossible. But the affirmative *could* is used to indicate possibility, for example, *It could rain.*

▬▬ Expansion: Grammar Practice

- Write a set of sentences with the modals from the lesson, one sentence per modal. For example: *It can't be twelve o'clock already. I just started working! / My friends and I could go to a movie tonight. / I might not be able to go to school tomorrow. / The teacher must know what this word means. / The man is asking for directions. He must not live around here. / It might rain tonight.*
- Make multiple sets of the sentences. Cut the sentences into strips and mix them up.
- In class, divide students into small groups. Give one set of strips to each group.
- Instruct students to read the sentences and divide them into three groups: Impossible, Possible, and Almost Certain.

Controlled Practice   10 minutes

 PRACTICE

Mrs. Johnson fell down the stairs...

- Do item 1 with the class. Point to the horizontal line on the board and ask: *Which is more certain,* may *or* must? (*must*)
- Have students work in pairs to complete the remaining items.
- While students are working, walk around and provide help as needed.
- Check answers.

Controlled Practice   15 minutes

2   PRACTICE

Complete the conversation between...

- Have students read the items in the box and label them *I* (*impossible*), *P* (*possible*), or *AC* (*almost certain*). (*couldn't be = I; could have, may be, might be able to, might not know = P; must be coming = AC*)
- Read the example item with the class.
- Have students continue working alone or in pairs. Walk around and provide help as needed.
- Check answers.

▬▬ Expansion: Speaking Practice for 2

- Pair students and have them practice reading the conversation.
- Call on one or more pairs to perform the conversation for the class.

Communicative Practice   20 minutes

Show what you know!

STEP 1. Read the suggestions...

- Read the suggestions in the students' book.
- Give students two to three minutes to write their own suggestions.

STEP 2. GROUPS. Discuss...

- Give a time limit for discussion.
- Walk around and provide help as needed.
- To wrap up, call on students to share their suggestions and explanations with the class.

▬▬ Expansion: Writing Practice

- Form groups of three or four. Instruct them to choose three suggestions and write a public-service announcement on what to do after a 911 call. As a model, have them refer to the script for Lesson 7, Exercise 2A (see page 289).
- Have one person from each group read the group's PSA to the class. Have students take notes on the suggestions in each PSA.
- After all PSAs are read, ask students which ideas they found to be helpful.

Progress Check

Can you . . . communicate in a 911 emergency?

Say: *We have practiced communicating in a 911 emergency. Now, look at the question at the bottom of the page. Can you communicate in a 911 emergency? Write a checkmark in the box.*

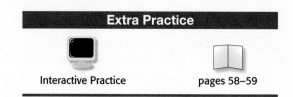

Extra Practice	
Interactive Practice	pages 58–59

Complete the conversation between an EMT and a 911 operator. Use the phrases in the box.

couldn't be   could have   ~~may be~~   might be able to   might not know   must be coming

Operator: I have a caller on the line. He's reporting a bicycle accident.

It sounds like there _____*may be*_____ serious injuries.

EMT: Can you give me the location of the accident?

Operator: I have no phone number or street address on my computer screen.

That means the call _____must be coming_____ from a cell phone.

EMT: Did you ask the caller for the information?

Operator: Yes, but there's a problem. I think he's a tourist. He _____might not know_____

exactly where he is. He says he's at the north end of Centennial Park, but that

_____couldn't be_____ the correct location. The north section of the park is closed.

EMT: How about the police? We _____might be able to_____ get information from

the officer in the area.

Operator: The police have already been contacted.

EMT: Great. Please tell the caller not to move the victims. They _____could have_____

broken bones.

Show what you know!   Communicate in a 911 emergency

STEP 1. Read the suggestions about what to do after a 911 call. Then write your own suggestion.

- Have someone wait outside until the emergency team arrives.
- Turn on an outside light, even during the day.
- Stay with the injured person and reassure him or her that help is on the way.

- _____

STEP 2. GROUPS. Discuss the suggestions. Explain why it's important to follow each suggestion.

Can you...communicate in a 911 emergency? ☐

Writing

1 BEFORE YOU WRITE

A CLASS. Where can you find information about what to do during an earthquake or other emergency situation?

B Read the writing model. How did the writer learn what to do during an earthquake?

An Earthquake Survival Guide

I just moved to California, so I've never lived through an earthquake. However, I talked to members of my family who have been here for many years. I learned about their emergency plan and what to do during and after an earthquake. First, if you're outside, move away from buildings or other things that can fall on you. If you're inside, stay there. Get under a table, desk, or other large piece of furniture and hold on. After the shaking ends, carefully check for injuries and damage to your home. Give first aid and turn off the water, electricity, and gas if necessary. Then take your emergency supplies and leave the building. When you're outside, be careful. There may be dangers such as falling bricks or pieces of broken metal and glass. If the members of your family are not all with you, go to the meeting place that you agreed on. Call one family member who doesn't live in the earthquake area to let them know you're OK. Finally, work with your neighbors. Together, you can help those who need it and survive until life returns to normal. Earthquakes are frightening, but I feel better knowing what to expect.

C PAIRS. Answer the questions.

1. What should you do if you're outside during an earthquake?
2. If you're at home, what's the first thing you should do after the earthquake ends?
3. Why should you call a family member who lives in another city or state after an earthquake instead of calling a family member who lives nearby?
4. Why is the author glad that he learned what to do during and after an earthquake?

D Write 1–5 to show the order of steps in "An Earthquake Survival Guide."

___2___ When it's safe, take your emergency supplies and leave your house.

___4___ Go to the place where you agreed to meet your family.

___5___ Finally, work with your neighbors so that you can help one another.

___1___ Give first aid if there are any injuries.

___3___ Watch out for things like falling bricks when you're outside.

Writing Tip

When you write about how to do something, put the steps in a logical order.

Getting Started   5 minutes

 BEFORE YOU WRITE

A CLASS. **Where can you find...**

- Elicit answers and write them on the board.
- Follow up by asking: *Which of these sources of information have you used? When? Why?* Call on volunteers to answer.

Answer: friends, family, the Internet, community and government agencies, etc.

Presentation   15 minutes

B **Read the writing model...**

- Read the model out loud as students read silently.
- Have students answer the question.

Answer: The writer talked to family members who have lived in California for many years.

C PAIRS. **Answer the questions.**

- Form pairs or small groups. Encourage students to underline the parts of the writing model that answer the factual questions or that give clues to inference questions.
- Give a time limit.
- Walk around and provide help as needed.
- Check answers. Call on students to read the questions and say the answers.

Answers: 1. Move away from things that can fall on you. 2. Check for injuries and damage to your home. 3. because phone service may be unreliable in your area after an earthquake 4. He feels better knowing what to expect.

Writing Tip: Using Sequential Order

- Read the Writing Tip.
- Define *sequential order* as the order in which events or steps in a process occur, from first to last.

D Write *1 through 5* **to show the order of steps...**

- Instruct students to find and underline the five steps in the writing model, then number them in sequential order.

Expansion: Writing Practice for 1D

- Have students read the paragraph again and circle the time words that show sequence of events (*first, after, then, when, finally*)
- Ask questions to help students identify the basic organization of the paragraph. First, ask: *Which sentences are the introduction? (the first three sentences) What information do they give? (They tell how the writer learned what to do during an earthquake.) Which sentences tell what to do during the earthquake? (sentences 4, 5, and 6) How is this part organized? (from outside to inside) What is the topic of the next part of the paragraph? (what to do after the shaking ends) What's next? (what to do after you leave the building) What's the last step? (work with your neighbors)*
- As you ask the questions above, outline the topics on the board. Have students copy the outline into their notebooks. They can use it as a guide for their own writing.
- Ask questions to help students see the writer's craft, that is, the way a well-written paragraph is composed, for example: *Is it necessary to begin every sentence with a time word? (no) Are all sentences the same length? (no) Do all sentences use the same grammar? (no)* Have students find examples of sentences with different syntax (for example, some sentences contain adverbial clauses of time, while others do not).

Write a plan for an emergency situation

Controlled Practice 20 minutes

2 THINKING ON PAPER

Ⓐ RESEARCH. Find out what to do...

- If students get their information from people they know, remind them to take detailed notes of the conversation.
- Try to pick up disaster-preparedness brochures from your local Red Cross or community center.
- If students use the Internet to get information, have them use the search term [X] *preparedness* (where [X] is the type of disaster). A good site for students to consult is the American Red Cross. Have students print a copy of the Internet page they consult.

Ⓑ Plan and organize your paragraph...

- Copy the chart onto the board. Add more steps if necessary. Model the activity with the class, using a disaster that does not normally occur in the region where you live.
- Explain the steps in your preparedness plan. As you speak, write the steps and details on the board. Have students copy them into their notebooks.
- Have students fill in the chart with notes on their disaster. While students are working, walk around and provide help as needed.

Communicative Practice 20 minutes

3 WRITE

Ⓐ Write a paragraph about...

- While students are writing, walk around and provide help as needed.
- Pair students and have them read their introductions to each other.

Ⓑ Complete your paragraph about...

- Remind students to try to use the unit grammar: present real conditionals, adverb clauses of time, and modals to express degrees of certainty.
- While students are writing, walk around and provide help as needed.

4 CHECK YOUR WRITING

Teaching Tip

You may want to collect student papers and provide feedback. Use the scoring rubric for writing on page T-xiv to evaluate each student's vocabulary, grammar, mechanics and how well he or she has completed the task. You may want to review the completed rubric with the students.

- Read the questions in the checklist.
- Have students read their paragraph and check off the items in the checklist.
- If students are unable to check something off because they left it out, or if they want to rewrite part of their paragraph, encourage them to do so.
- Collect papers and correct them. Make corrections as needed in content and the unit grammar.

Expansion: Writing Practice for 4

- Have students rewrite their paragraphs in class. Then pair students and have them read their paragraphs to each other.

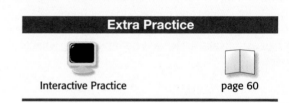

Extra Practice

Interactive Practice   page 60

A RESEARCH. Find out what to do during and after a tornado, blizzard, flood, wildfire, or other natural disaster. Ask someone who has had personal experience or ask your teacher how to get information at the library or on the Internet.

B Plan and organize your paragraph in a chart like this. Write your steps in time order.

What to Do During and After a _____	
Steps	**Details**
Step 1	
Step 2	
Step 3	

3 **WRITE**

A Write an introduction that explains how you learned about your topic. Look at the writing model for an example.

B Complete your paragraph about what to do during and after a natural disaster. Use the information in your plan. Look at the writing model for an example.

4 **CHECK YOUR WRITING**

☐ Did you include an introduction?
☐ Did you list specific steps in time order?
☐ Did you include a conclusion?
☐ Did you use correct capitalization, punctuation, and spelling?

1 REVIEW   For your grammar review, go to page 249.

2 ACT IT OUT   What do you say?

STEP 1. CLASS. Review the conversations on pages 86 and 87 (CD1, Tracks 52 and 55).

STEP 2. ROLE PLAY. PAIRS. Role-play this situation.

Student A: You just took a fire-safety class at the local community center. You are visiting your cousin. Tell your cousin what you learned. Include information about how to prevent a fire in the home and what to do if there is a fire emergency.

Student B: You want to learn about fire safety. You know that your cousin just took a fire-safety class at the community center. You want to know if you should take the course. Ask questions about it. You're especially worried about fires because several members of your family smoke.

STEP 3. PAIRS. Talk about fire safety at home and at work.
Use the ideas from your role play or your own ideas.

3 READ AND REACT   Problem-solving

STEP 1. Read about the problem.

You are beginning to prepare emergency supplies to be ready for a hurricane, an earthquake, or other disaster. However, the items that you need are expensive. Next month you'll be able to buy more supplies, but this month you can spend only $50 on your emergency items.

STEP 2. GROUPS. Decide which emergency supplies to buy this month. Use the price list. Explain your choices.

ITEM	PRICE
First-Aid Kit	$18.95
Radio	$24.98
Flashlight	$9.99
Batteries	$9.29 a pack
Water	$1.50 per gallon
Canned Fruit, Vegetables, Beans	average $1.25 each
Rain Ponchos	$10 each
Sleeping Bags	$24.99
Medicine	$50
Other:	

4 CONNECT   For your Organizing and Planning for Learning, go to page 259.
For your Team Project, go to page 267.

Which goals can you check off? Go back to page 85.

 Go to the CD-ROM for more practice.

Show what you know!

1 REVIEW

Turn to page 249 for the grammar review.

2 ACT IT OUT

STEP 1. CLASS. Review the conversations...

- Pair students and have them reread the conversation in Exercise 3C, page 87.
- Have them restate the fire safety tip in the conversation. Write it on the board.

STEP 2. ROLE PLAY. PAIRS. Role-play this...

> **Teaching Tip**
>
> While pairs are performing, use the scoring rubric for speaking on page T-xiii to evaluate each student's vocabulary, grammar, fluency, and how well he or she completes the task.

- Read the role descriptions.
- Model the role play with an above-level student.
- Pair students. Tell them to begin by listing the fire safety tips they will include in their role play.
- Have them practice out loud at least twice.
- Have volunteers role-play for the class.

■■■ MULTILEVEL INSTRUCTION for STEP 2

Pre-level Have students write out their dialogue. Tell them to include one tip for preventing a fire and one step to take if there is a fire emergency.

Above-level Have students practice without notes. Tell them to include all the tips they can think of for preventing fires and dealing with a fire emergency.

STEP 3. PAIRS. Talk about fire safety...

- Make a chart on the board with the headings *Fire Prevention* and *Fire Emergency*. Elicit one example in each category and write it on the board.
- Form groups of three to four students. Have them choose a timekeeper, a note taker, and a reporter. The note taker should copy the chart and use it to take notes on the group's discussion.
- Have the reporters share the items from their group's discussion. Write the tips on the board.

3 READ AND REACT

STEP 1. Read about the problem.

- Read the problem out loud. Give students time to look at the list of items and prices.

STEP 2. GROUPS. Decide which emergency...

- Form cross-ability groups and have students choose a timekeeper, a note taker, and a reporter. The note taker should write down the group's ideas.
- Give a time limit for discussion.
- While students are talking, walk around and provide help as needed.
- Have reporters write the group's list and prices on the board, showing that their total does not exceed $50.00.

■■■ Expansion: Speaking Practice for STEP 2

- Tell students to imagine that the next month they also have only $50.00 to spend on supplies. Have them decide which additional supplies they will buy.
- Have groups share their lists with the class.

4 CONNECT

Turn to page 259 for your Organizing and Planning for Learning Activity and page 267 for your Team Project. See page T-xi for teaching tips for these activities.

Progress Check

Which goals can you check off? Go back to page 85.

Ask students to turn to page 85 and check off any remaining goals they have reached. Call on students to say which goals they will practice outside of class.

■ Go to the CD-ROM for more practice.

If your students need more practice with the vocabulary, grammar, and competencies in Unit 5, encourage them to review the activities on the CD-ROM.

Moving In

Classroom Materials/Extra Practice

CD 1
Tracks 64–75

Interactive Practice
Unit 6

Workbook
Unit 6

Unit Overview

Goals

- See the list of goals on the facing page.

Grammar

- Expressing expectation and permission
- Tag questions with *be*
- Tag questions with *do* as an auxiliary verb
- Reported speech

Pronunciation

- Intonation in tag questions
- Intonation in exclamations

Reading

- Read about why people move
- *Reading Skill:* Distinguishing an author's main ideas from details

Writing

- Write a letter of complaint

Life Skills

- Interpret a lease

Preview

- Hold up your book or have students look at their books. Set the context by asking the preview questions. You can also ask: *Where are the people? Why? What do you think the woman is pointing at?*

Unit Goals

- Set the context of the unit by asking questions about housing and how to find a place to live, for example, *Where do you live—in a house, an apartment, or somewhere else? How did you find the place where you live?*

- Hold up your book or have students look at their books. Read the title and ask the preview questions if you have not already done so. You can also ask: *What do you think will happen next?*

- Point to the Unit Goals. Have students read them silently.

- Tell students they will be studying these goals in Unit 6.

- Say each goal and explain unfamiliar vocabulary as needed, for example, *tenant: a person who rents a house or apartment; lease: a contract between a tenant and a landlord; landlord: the person who owns a house or apartment that tenants are renting.*

- Tell students to circle one or more goals that are very important to them. Call on several volunteers to say the goals they circled.

- Write a checkmark (✓) on the board. Say: *We will come back to this page again. You will write a checkmark next to the goals you learned in this unit.*

Moving In

Preview

Read the title. What are these people doing? What do you think they are talking about?

UNIT GOALS

- ☐ Identify tenant responsibilities
- ☐ Interpret a lease
- ☐ Talk about landlord responsibilities
- ☐ Check that information is correct
- ☐ Talk about moving
- ☐ Discuss problems with neighbors
- ☐ Write about a housing problem

Listening and Speaking

1 BEFORE YOU LISTEN

CLASS. When you rent a house or an apartment, you are responsible for certain things. Discuss.

1. What are some tenant responsibilities? Make a list.
2. Tenants often have to give the landlord a *security deposit* when they move in. What is a security deposit for?

2 LISTEN

CD1 T64

A  Jessica is talking to her mother. Listen to the first part of their conversation. What is the conversation about?

CD1 T64

B Read the statements. Then listen again. Write *T* (true) or *F* (false). Correct the false statements.

_T__ 1. Each roommate will have her own bedroom.

_F__ 2. The rent is ~~$1,100~~. $1,200

_F__ 3. They have to pay for ~~water~~ and electricity. gas

_F__ 4. The security deposit is ~~two~~ month's rent. one

CD1 T65

C Listen to the whole conversation. How does Jessica's mother feel about Jessica's moving out?

a. excited   b. annoyed   (c.) worried

CD1 T65

D Read the statements. Listen again. Check all the things Jessica's mother mentions.

☑ Jessica and her roommates may damage the apartment.

☐ They may not be safe.

☐ They may have problems with the building manager.

☑ They may have noisy neighbors.

E PAIRS. Do you think parents and grown children should live together, very near each other, or farther away? Explain.

Getting Started   5 minutes

 1   BEFORE YOU LISTEN

CLASS. When you rent a house...

- Write the word *tenant* on the board and call on a student to define it.
- Read question 1 and list answers on the board.

Possible answers: Pay rent on time, put garbage and recyclables in designated cans, keep the hallways clear, report problems with the apartment.

- Call on students to answer question 2.

Answer: A security deposit encourages renters to take good care of their unit because if they damage it, the landlord can keep all or part of the deposit.

Presentation   10 minutes

 2   LISTEN

A 🔘 **Jessica is talking to her...**

- Have students look at the picture. Ask: *Who is talking? Who is listening? How does Jessica look?*
- Play CD 1, Track 64. Have students listen.
- Call on students to answer the question.

Answer: They are talking about Jessica's new apartment.

> **Culture Connection**
>
> In the U.S. young people usually move out of their parents' home after they finish high school. If they go away to college, they usually live in a dormitory with other students. If they get a job or go to college locally, they may rent an apartment with roommates.

Controlled Practice   10 minutes

 B 🔘 **Read the statements. Then...**

- Have students read the statements silently and predict if they are true or false.
- Play Track 64 again.
- Call on students to read each item and say if it is true or false. If it is false, ask the student to correct it. Write the answers on the board.

C 🔘 **Listen to the whole conversation. How...**

- Say the answer choices. Have students pantomime the meanings with facial expressions.
- Play CD 1, Track 65.
- Survey the class. Ask: *How many people chose answer a? answer b? answer c?* Confirm the correct answer and ask: *How did you know?* List the clues on the board. If necessary, replay the recording.

D **Read the statements. Listen...**

- Play Track 65 again. Instruct students to check the statements as they listen.
- Read each statement and have students raise their hands if they checked it.
- Discuss the statements that the class disagrees about. If necessary, play the recording again.

Communicative Practice   10 minutes

E **PAIRS. Do you think parents...**

- Have one or more students share their opinions with the class.

▬▬ **Expansion: Speaking Practice for 2E**

- On the board, make a grid consisting of three columns and two rows. Across the top, write the headings *Live Together, Live Near Each Other,* and *Live Far Away.* Along the side, write *Advantages* and *Disadvantages.*
- Group students and have them discuss the advantages and disadvantages of each living arrangement. Each group should select a timekeeper, a note taker to copy the grid and take notes on the group's ideas, and a reporter.
- Give a time limit for discussion.
- Have the reporter from each group summarize the advantages and disadvantages that the group discussed.
- Have the class vote. Ask: *Imagine you are eighteen years old. You have just finished high school. Where would you prefer to live—with your family, near your family, or far away from your family?*
- Call on volunteers to explain their vote.

Presentation   5 minutes

 CONVERSATION

 Jessica is talking to her new...

- Play CD 1, Track 66. Have students listen and read along silently.
- Check comprehension. Ask: *How many parking spaces will Jessica and her roommates have? What does Jessica mean when she says* I guess we'll have to take turns? *Who is* we? *What is* a permit? *Where are tenants supposed to park? Where are visitors supposed to park? Why can't they park in the lot?*

Controlled Practice   10 minutes

4 **PRACTICE**

A PAIRS. **Practice the conversation.**

- Form pairs. Have them practice the conversation. Then have them switch roles and practice again.
- Walk around and listen as students are practicing. Provide help as needed.
- Ask volunteers to perform the conversation.

Communicative Practice   10 minutes

Teaching Tip

While pairs are performing role plays, use the scoring rubric for speaking on page T-xiii to evaluate each student's vocabulary, grammar, fluency, and how well he or she completes the task. You may want to review the completed rubric with the students.

- Point to each illustration and ask: *What do you see? What does the sign say? What does it mean?*
- Choose one situation and model a role play with an above-level student. Play the role of Student B, the landlord. Student A can begin like this: *Hello, [name]. I forgot to ask you: Is smoking allowed in the hallways?*

- Form cross-ability pairs.
- Tell students to practice out loud at least twice.
- Have volunteers perform their role play.

▬▬ MULTILEVEL INSTRUCTION for 4B
Cross-ability Have the higher-level student play the role of Student B.

Culture Connection

Recycling is becoming more and more common in the U.S. Many homes and apartments are required to have separate containers for garbage, grass and plant refuse, and recyclables. Some places require people to sort their recyclables into categories: paper, glass, and metal.

▬▬ Expansion: Speaking Practice for 4B

- Have students discuss the rules shown in the illustrations. On the board, write: *What is the rule where you live? Do you think it is fair?*
- Group students. Give a time limit for discussion. Walk around and provide help as needed.
- Call on volunteers to share their answers to the questions.

Extra Practice

Interactive Practice

3 CONVERSATION

CD1 T66

Jessica is talking to her new landlord, Harry. He is telling her about the building rules. Listen and read.

Jessica: I forgot to ask you: Does the apartment come with parking?

Harry: Yes, each tenant is allowed one parking space.

Jessica: Oh, then I guess we'll have to take turns. Where's the parking lot?

Harry: Behind the building. You can park in spot number 11. Make sure to hang this permit on your mirror. That way I know it's yours.

Jessica: Thanks. What if I have visitors?

Harry: Visitors aren't allowed to park in the tenant lot. If they do, their cars will be towed away. They have to park in the street. We have strict rules so no one will take the tenants' spots.

Jessica: OK.

4 PRACTICE

A PAIRS. Practice the conversation.

B ROLE PLAY. PAIRS. Look at the pictures. Role-play situations 1, 2, and 3. Use the conversation as a model.

Student A: You are a tenant.

Student B: You are the landlord. Tell the tenant each building rule.

Grammar

Expressing obligation, expectation, and permission

Tenants	are	**required to**	recycle glass, metal, and paper.
		supposed to	be considerate of their neighbors.
Tenants	are not	**allowed to**	smoke in the hallways.
		permitted to	have pets.
Are	visitors	**allowed**	to park in this lot?

Grammar Watch

- Use *be required to* when you talk about obligations, or things that people must do.
- Use *be supposed to* when you talk about expectations, or things that people should do.
- Use *be allowed / be permitted to* when you talk about permission, or things that people may do (things that are not against the rules).
- *Be permitted to* means the same thing as *be allowed to*, but it is more formal.

1 PRACTICE

Read the apartment building rules. Circle the tenant responsibilities that show obligations. Underline the expressions that merely show expectation. Use a double underline below the expressions that show permission.

480 Cumberland Drive

- Tenants are required to pay their rent on the first of the month.
- Tenants who pay their rent late are required to pay a late fee of $25.
- Tenants are not supposed to make noise in their apartments after 10:00 P.M.
- Tenants are not allowed to keep bicycles or strollers in the hall. They are supposed to keep them in their apartments.
- Tenants are permitted to use the laundry room only between the hours of 8 A.M. and 10 P.M.

Getting Started   5 minutes

- Write the word *responsibilities* on the board. Draw a circle around it and four spokes from the edge of the circle outward. On each spoke, write: *am required to, am supposed to, am not allowed to,* and *am not permitted to.*

- Talk about your job responsibilities. For example, say: *In every job, employees have responsibilities. Here are some responsibilities that I have in my job: First, I am supposed to arrive on time. Second, I am required to take attendance at every class. Third, I'm not allowed to photocopy chapters of books. And fourth, I'm not permitted to cancel class without telling my boss.*

- Point to each expression on the board as you say it.

- On the board, write: *be (not) + (supposed/required/ allowed/permitted) + to + verb.* Say each expression and point to the corresponding part of the formula.

- Ask students to repeat your responsibilities. Point to each spoke on the wheel.

- Say: *In this lesson, we will learn how to use these four expressions to talk about tenants' responsibilities.*

Presentation   10 minutes

Expressing obligation, expectation, and permission

- Copy the grammar chart onto the board

- Read out loud the first Grammar Watch note. Then read the first example on the chart. Say: *Tenants are required to recycle glass, metal, and paper. It means that there is a rule that people must follow.* Have students rephrase the sentence with *must.*

- Read out loud the second note and second example. Explain that it means that there is a rule that people should follow. Have students rephrase the sentence using *should.*

- Read out loud the third note. Explain that the negative forms of *allowed to* and *permitted to* express *prohibition,* that is, that people *can't* do something. Read the third and fourth examples. Have students rephrase the sentences with *can't.*

- Read the fourth note. Explain that *more formal* means that something is used more often in writing rather than in speaking.

- Read the last example. Have the class change the other sentences into questions.

- To conclude, ask: *Which sentence talks about obligation?* (the first) *Which one talks about expectation?* (the second) *Which sentences talk about prohibition?* (the third and fourth) *Which one asks about permission?* (the last)

- Remind students that subjects and verbs must agree. To practice, point to an example sentence on the board. Change the subject and have students complete the sentences correctly. For example: T: *You . . .* Students: *are supposed to recycle glass, metal, and paper.* T: *I . . .* Students: *am required to pay a security deposit.*

■ **Expansion: Grammar Practice**

- On the board, write the following incomplete sentences: *1. Landlords are _____ keep the building clean. (should) 2. Landlords are _____ fix broken plumbing. (must) 3. Landlords are _____ raise the rent without giving notice. (can't) 4. Landlords are _____ force tenants to move without notice. (can't)*

Answers: 1. supposed to 2. required to 3. not permitted / allowed to 4. not permitted / allowed to

- Pair students. Tell them to fill in the blanks with expressions from the chart. They should use each expression once.

Controlled Practice   10 minutes

1 PRACTICE

Read the apartment building rules. Circle...

- Read the rules out loud. Explain vocabulary as needed, for example, *stroller: a chair with wheels, used for pushing babies around.*

- Ask: *Does the first sentence talk about obligation or expectation?* (obligation)

- Walk around and provide help as needed.

- Check answers. Have students say which words they circled, underlined, or double underlined. Have them say if the meaning is obligation, expectation, or permission.

■ **Expansion: Grammar Practice**

- Form pairs consisting of Student A and Student B. Have Student A read the first apartment building rule. Tell Student B to restate it using *should, must / have to, can,* or *can't.* Have students switch roles on the second item. Continue taking turns until the end of the list.

Identify tenant responsibilities

Controlled Practice   15 minutes

2   PRACTICE

Ⓐ Complete the rules. Use the correct...

- Read item 1. To reinforce the structure, repeat each word in the blank and point to the formula on the board. Then ask: *What is the meaning here: Is it obligation, expectation, prohibition, or permission?*

- Have students complete the exercise, working alone or in pairs. Walk around and provide help with vocabulary as needed. For example: *late fee: a fine or penalty imposed when someone pays his or her rent or a bill late; common areas: in an apartment building, the areas outside of people's apartments, such as the entryway, lobby, laundry room, garage, etc., that everyone in the building uses; dispose of: throw away; lease term: the length of time that the lease is for.*

- Write the numbers *2* through *10* on the board. Call up students to write the answers.

- Have other students read the sentences and say if they are correct or incorrect. If there is an error, have students correct it.

> **Teaching Tip**
>
> To guide students to correct errors, try the following techniques: 1. Point to the whole item containing the error and ask the class, *What's wrong here?* 2. Point to the specific incorrect word and have the class make the correction. 3. Read or say an item, stopping right before the incorrect word. Then pause, indicating to students that the next word is the one they need to correct.

Communicative Practice   20 minutes

Ⓑ GROUPS. Look at the rules...

- Define *reasonable* as *something that is fair and that people are usually willing to do.*

- Form groups.

- Instruct students to look at the list of items in Exercise A and discuss each one in turn. Or to save time, have students take turns discussing the items. For example, Student 1 discusses item 1, Student 2 discusses item 2, etc.

- Give a time limit for discussion. While students are talking, walk around and provide help as needed.

- To conclude, ask the class: *Which items are unreasonable, in your opinion? Why?*

▇▇ MULTILEVEL INSTRUCTION for 2B

Pre-level Have students answer question 1 only. Have them read an item out loud and then say *This is true where I live* or *This is not true where I live.*

Above-level Have students read the items and then discuss questions 1 and 2 together.

Show what you know!

CLASS. Discuss tenant responsibilities...

- Instruct the class to think from the point of view of a building manager.

- Call on students to provide tenant responsibilities, and write them on the board.

- Discuss as a class the relative importance of each item on the board. Encourage students to politely disagree and to support their opinions.

- Finally, have students vote on the responsibilities and tally the votes on the board. Rank the top five according to the vote tally.

Progress Check

Can you . . . identify tenant responsibilities?

Say: *We have practiced identifying tenant responsibilities. Now, look at the question at the bottom of the page. Can you identify tenant responsibilities? Write a checkmark in the box.*

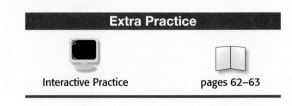

Extra Practice
Interactive Practice   pages 62–63

A Complete the rules. Use the correct form of one of the phrases in the box. More than one answer may be possible.

> (not) be permitted to   (not) be required to   (not) be supposed to

1. Tenants _are not permitted to_ make changes to the apartment.

2. No one _____is permitted to_____ smoke in the building.

3. If the rent is paid late, the tenant _____is required to_____ pay a late fee of $20.00.

4. Tenants _____are not permitted to_____ entertain guests in the common areas of the apartment building. No one _____is permitted to_____ have parties after 10 P.M.

5. New tenants _____are required to_____ move in between the hours of 10 A.M. and 6 P.M.

6. Tenants _____are required to_____ keep the front door of the building locked at all times.

7. Tenants _____are supposed to_____ give three month's notice if they plan to move out.

8. All tenants _____are required to_____ dispose of garbage in trash containers.

9. Tenants _____are supposed to_____ put glass, cans, and paper in the green recycling containers.

10. Tenants _____are required to_____ return all keys at the end of their lease term.

B GROUPS. Look at the rules in Exercise A. Discuss.

1. If you ever rented an apartment, which rules were true where you lived?

2. Do you think the rules are reasonable or unreasonable? Explain.

Show what you know!   Identify tenant responsibilities

CLASS. Discuss tenant responsibilities from the point of view of a building manager. What are the five most important things that tenants should be required to do? Number them from 1 to 5, with 1 being the most important and 5 being the least important.

Can you...identify tenant responsibilities?   ☐

Life Skills

1   INTERPRET A LEASE

A   **GROUPS.** When people rent an apartment or a house, they usually sign a *lease*. The lease describes the tenant's and landlord's rights and responsibilities. What things do you think leases include? Make a list.

B   **CLASS.** Read the first part of the lease. Does the lease decribe any of the things you mentioned?

2   READ

Look at the lease again. Complete the sentences. Circle the correct answers.

1. _____ is going to live in the apartment.
   a. Vaslav Nowak
   b. Anita Cruz *(circled)*

2. The lease is for _____.
   a. one year *(circled)*
   b. five months

3. The rent is _____ per month.
   a. $1,500 *(circled)*
   b. $1,000

4. The rent is due on _____.
   a. April 1
   b. the 5th day of each month *(circled)*

5. The landlord _____ the security deposit after the tenant moves out if the apartment is damaged or dirty.
   a. can keep *(circled)*
   b. must return

6. The _____ has to pay for damage caused by normal everyday use.
   a. landlord *(circled)*
   b. tenant

PARTIES: The parties to this agreement are: _Vaslav Novak_, herein referred to as LANDLORD, and _Anita Cruz_, herein referred to as TENANT.
TERM: This agreement is to begin on _April 1_, _2009_, and is:

___ month-to-month

✔ an agreement for the specific term of _12_ months, ending on _April 1, 2010_.

1. RENT: Rent: _$1,500_/month. Rent is payable in advance by the _5th_ day of each month, and will be delivered to _Vaslav Novak, 1000 Center St., Apt 40B, Mountain View, CA 94040_.

2. SECURITY DEPOSIT: Tenant has paid to landlord, and landlord acknowledges receipt of _$1,500_ as a cleaning and security deposit. The landlord may keep all or any part of this deposit upon termination of this rental agreement for any of the following reasons:
   i) to cover unpaid rent owed to the landlord
   ii) to pay the cost of repairing any damage to the premises resulting from abuse, misuse, or neglect, not including normal wear and tear.

| Getting Started | 5 minutes | Controlled Practice | 10 minutes |

1 INTERPRET A LEASE

Ⓐ GROUPS. When people rent an apartment...

- Write *lease* on the board. Ask: *What is a lease?* (an agreement or contract between a landlord and a tenant) *What is the purpose of a lease?* (to protect the rights of both the tenant and the landlord)
- Survey the class. Ask: *How many of you live in an apartment? Do you have a lease?*
- Call on students who have a lease to say what kinds of information their lease includes. List responses on the board.

Possible answers: The starting and ending dates of the lease, the rent, the security deposit, the landlord's responsibilities in the building, the building rules that the tenant agrees to follow.

Presentation   10 minutes

Ⓑ CLASS. Read the first part...

- Tell students they are going to read the first part of the lease without using a dictionary. Explain that they should try to guess the meaning of unfamiliar words. To illustrate, read the first line of the agreement out loud. Ask the class: *What does* parties *mean in this case? Does it mean celebration?* (no) *Does it mean* people? (yes) *Which people?* (Vaslav Novak and Anita Cruz or the landlord and the tenant)
- Have students read.
- Refer the class to the items you listed on the board in Exercise 1. Point to each one and ask: *Does the lease talk about this? Where?* Have students read the part of the lease that corresponds to each item on the board. Have them define pertinent vocabulary, using the context if possible.

Controlled Practice   10 minutes

2 READ

Ⓑ Look at the lease again. Complete...

- Again, encourage students to guess the meaning of words they don't know. The items in the exercise can help. For example, after students do item 2, they should be able to figure out that a *term* is a period of time.
- Tell students to underline the part of the lease that gives the answer to each question.
- Have students complete the items. Then have them compare answers with a partner.
- Call on volunteers to say the answers.

▮▮▮ MULTILEVEL INSTRUCTION for 2B

Cross-ability Pair proficient readers with weaker readers. Have students take turns reading sections of the lease out loud. The higher-level student can help the lower-level student with reading.

▮▮▮ Expansion: Speaking Practice for 2B

- Put students in groups. Make sure each group has one or more students who have signed a lease on their apartment. Have students compare the lease in their book with their actual leases. Ask the following questions: *1. Who is your landlord? 2. When did your lease begin? 3. What is the term of your lease? 4. How much is the rent? When is it payable? 5. How much is your security deposit? What does it cover? 6. If you want to terminate your lease, how far in advance do you need to tell your landlord? 7. If you damage the premises accidentally, are you required to pay for repairs?*

Presentation
10 minutes

3 PRACTICE

Ⓐ Read the second part of the lease. What...

- Have students read the words in capital letters. Ask: *What does* shall *mean?* (will) *What information is in the section that starts* The landlord shall? (things the landlord is required to do) *What information is in the section that starts* The tenant shall? (things the tenant is required to do)
- Have students continue reading.
- Have students answer the question.

Answers: who pays for the utilities, rules about pets, landlord's responsibilities, and tenant's responsibilities

Controlled Practice
10 minutes

Ⓑ Read the statements. Write...

- Do item 1 with the class. Read the item and ask the class if it is true or false. When students answer, ask: *How do you know?* Have students read the part of the lease that provides the answer.
- Have students complete the exercise alone or in pairs.
- Check answers.

Communicative Practice
15 minutes

Ⓒ GROUPS. Before you sign a lease,...

- Point out the word *terms* in the instructions. It means *rules*. Ask: *What did the word* term *mean in the lease?* (a period of time) Remind students that the same word can have different meanings, depending on the context.
- Group students.
- Give a time limit for discussion. While they are talking, walk around and provide help as needed.
- Go over the questions with the whole class.

Possible answers: 1. You might not be able to move when you want to. 2. You might not be able to have your friends or relatives live with you. 3. You might be stuck in an apartment because you can't get out of the lease.

Culture Connection

When reading legal documents, it is important to read and understand every word (this is called *reading the fine print*) before signing anything. Even people who speak English as their first language will often have a lawyer read a legal document and advise them before they sign it.

■■ MULTILEVEL INSTRUCTION for 3C

Cross-ability Pair proficient readers with weaker readers. Have students take turns reading sections of the lease out loud. The higher-level student can help the lower-level student with reading.

Progress Check

Can you . . . interpret a lease?

Say: *We have practiced interpreting a lease. Now, look at the question at the bottom of the page. Can you interpret a lease? Write a checkmark in the box.*

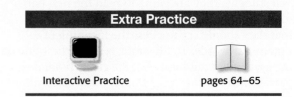

Extra Practice	
Interactive Practice	pages 64–65

A Read the second part of the lease. What does it descibe?

B Read the statements. Write *T* (true) or *F* (false). Correct the false statements.

_F_ 1. The landlord pays for ~~electricity and~~ water.

_T_ 2. The landlord is required to make sure appliances work and fix them if they break.

_F_ 3. Both ~~the landlord and~~ the   is   required   tenant ~~are supposed~~ to keep the apartment clean and safe.

_T_ 4. The tenant is not supposed to make changes to the apartment without permission.

_F_ 5. The tenant is not allowed to   and   smoke in the hallways, ~~but~~ is not allowed to smoke in his or her apartment.

_F_ 6. The tenant is not allowed to use the laundry room after ~~8~~ P.M.   10

3. UTILITIES: The tenant agrees to pay for all utilities except __water__, which shall be paid by the landlord.

4. PETS: Tenants shall not keep a pet on the premises.

5. THE LANDLORD SHALL:
   i) keep the public areas in a clean and safe condition.
   ii) keep the appliances in the rental unit in good working order.
   iii) paint the rental unit every three years.
   iv) supply a smoke alarm and CO detector in each rental unit.

6. THE TENANT SHALL:
   i) pay rent promptly when due.
   ii) keep the rental unit in a clean, safe, and habitable condition.
   iii) place garbage and refuse in the containers provided.
   iv) park only in the parking spot provided in the tenants' parking lot.

7. THE TENANT SHALL NOT:
   i) alter the premises (for example, paint) without permission of the landlord.
   ii) smoke on the premises.
   iii) use the laundry facilities between the hours of 10 P.M. and 8 A.M.

C GROUPS. Before you sign a lease, it's important to read it carefully. Don't sign it if you don't agree with the terms (rules). Discuss what problems might occur if you didn't know the answers to the following questions.

1. How long is the lease for?
2. Who will be living in the apartment (whose names will be on the lease)? Can other family members or other roommates be added later?
3. Can you get out of the lease if you need to move early, for instance, because of a job change or a family emergency?

Can you...interpret a lease? ☐

Listening and Speaking

1   BEFORE YOU LISTEN

GROUPS. Where can you go if you have a problem with your landlord? What agencies in your community might provide free assistance?

2   LISTEN

CD1 T67

A Manuel Rodríguez is a guest on *This Week,* a radio talk show. Listen to the first call. What kind of questions does Manuel answer?

CD1 T67

B Read the statements. Then listen to the first call again. Write *T* (true) or *F* (false). Correct the false statements.

   _F_   1. Manuel is a ~~tenant with a problem~~. *tenant rights lawyer*

   _T_   2. The caller wants his landlord to install new smoke detectors in his apartment.

   _T_   3. The caller's smoke detectors aren't working.

   _F_   4. The caller hasn't called his landlord ~~yet~~ to complain about his problem.

   _T_   5. Manuel tells the caller to send a letter to his landlord.

CD1 T68

C Listen to the second call. Circle the word or phrase that best completes each statement.

1. The caller's landlord wants **(to raise her rent)** / **her to move**.
2. The caller's landlord **(is not allowed to)** / **is not going to** raise the rent right now.
3. The caller's lease is up **one year** / **(six months)** from now.
4. The caller **sometimes** / **(never)** pays her rent late.
5. The caller will probably **sign a new lease** / **(look for a new apartment)** when her lease is up.

D **GROUPS.** Discuss. Why does Manuel ask the second caller if she has ever damaged the apartment or paid her rent late?

Getting Started   5 minutes

1 BEFORE YOU LISTEN

GROUPS. **Where can you go...**

- If possible, tell about a time when you or someone you know had a problem with a landlord. Tell which person, agency, or organization you or they contacted in order to resolve the problem.
- Read the directions. Define *agency* as *a government or private organization that provides a service*
- Form groups of three or four. Tell them to appoint a note taker who will list the group's ideas.
- Have a representative from each group come to the board and write the group's list.
- Ask: *Which answers were given by more than one group? What is the best way for tenants to get help, in your opinion?*

Culture Connection

Most cities have an agency that specializes in resolving landlord-tenant conflicts. To find such an agency on the Internet, type the name of your city and *tenant's rights, resources for tenants,* or *housing department.* Another resource for low-income renters is the legal aid society or foundation.

Presentation   5 minutes

2 LISTEN

A Manuel Rodriguez is a guest...

- Explain *radio talk show* as *radio programs that allow listeners to call in and share their ideas on a particular topic.* Ask: *Do you enjoy listening to talk shows? Which ones?*
- Explain *tenant rights lawyer* as *a lawyer who specializes in helping tenants when they have problems with their landlords.*
- Play CD 1, Track 67. Remind students to listen specifically for the answer to the question.
- Call on students to share their answers.

Answer: He answers questions about tenant law in Texas.

Controlled Practice   10 minutes

B **Read the statements. Then listen...**

- Have students read the questions and predict the answers.
- Play Track 67 again.
- Call on students to answer the questions and correct false statements.

C **Listen to the second call. Circle...**

- Have students read the items before listening. Answer questions about vocabulary as needed.
- Define *in effect*: *describes a condition that is still true.*
- Play CD 1, Track 68.
- Call on students to share their answers.

Communicative Practice   10 minutes

D GROUPS. **Discuss. Why does Manuel...**

- Form groups, each with a timekeeper.
- Give a time limit for discussion.
- To wrap up, call on each group to share the group's answer to the question.

Answer: If she has done either of these things, the landlord has a right to break the lease.

Expansion: Speaking Practice for 2D

- Ask students if they have ever had either of the problems described by the two callers. If so, what did they do to resolve the problem?

Expansion: Writing Practice for 2D

- With the class, brainstorm other landlord-tenant problems that they'd like to ask Manuel. For example, say: *Your kitchen faucet leaks. You called the landlord a week ago and so far no one has come to fix it. You want to know if you can call a plumber yourself and give the bill to the landlord.* List the ideas on the board.
- Form groups of three. Have them practice reading the Audio Script on page 289 for Exercises 2A, 2B, and 2C.
- Instruct students to write a conversation between a third caller and Manuel. They can choose an idea from the board and use the Audio Script as a model for their conversation.

Presentation   10 minutes

3 CONVERSATION

Pronunciation Watch

- On the board, write several sentences with tag questions, for example: *You live in a house, don't you? Ping is married, isn't she? Samuel doesn't have a job, does he?*
- Read each sentence and have the class repeat. Ask: *What does your voice do at the end of the sentence?* (It goes up.)
- Explain: *The question at the end of the sentence is called a* tag. *Questions with tags are called* tag questions.
- Read the Pronunciation Watch note.

Ⓐ Listen to the sentences. Notice...

- Play CD 1, Track 69. Have students listen.
- Play Track 69 again. Have students listen and repeat.

Ⓑ Lisa Ming is calling...

- Play CD 1, Track 70. Have students listen and read silently.
- *Optional:* Have above-level students close their books while they listen.
- Check comprehension. Ask: *What problem does Lisa report? What is the landlord going to do? What is Lisa concerned about?*

Controlled Practice   5 minutes

4 PRACTICE

Ⓐ PAIRS. Practice the conversation.

- Form pairs and have students read the conversation in Exercise 3B. Have them switch roles and read again.
- Walk around and listen as students are practicing. Provide help as needed.
- Have pairs perform the conversation for the class.

Communicative Practice   15 minutes

Ⓑ ROLE PLAY. PAIRS. Role-play this situation....

> **Teaching Tip**
>
> While pairs are performing role plays, use the scoring rubric for speaking on page T-xiii to evaluate each student's vocabulary, grammar, fluency, and how well he or she completes the task. You may want to review the completed rubric with the students.

- Read the roles. If necessary, explain *locksmith: a person who fixes and installs locks.*
- Model the role play with an above-level student. Play the role of Student A. You can begin like this: *Hello, [name]? This is [name] in apartment [number and letter]. I'm calling because . . .*
- Pair students of similar ability. Tell students to practice out loud at least twice.
- Have volunteers perform their role play.

■■■ MULTILEVEL INSTRUCTION for 4B

Pre-level Have students write out their conversation and practice several times.
Above-level Have students practice without writing a script. You can also tell them to practice twice, switching roles the second time.

Ⓒ MAKE IT PERSONAL. GROUPS. Discuss.

- Form groups of three or four. Give a time limit.
- Have volunteers share their answers with the class.

> **Community Building**
>
> Ask students to share their knowledge about community resources for helping tenants in disputes with landlords. For example, ask them for the names of any such organizations, where they're located, what kinds of problems they can help with, and what they charge.

Extra Practice

Interactive Practice

3 CONVERSATION

CD1 T69

A 🔊 Listen to the sentences. Notice the intonation of the tag questions. Then listen and repeat.

aren't you?   You're going to stay there with him, **aren't** you?

is he?   The repairman isn't there yet, **is** he?

doesn't he?   He has to replace the smoke detectors, **doesn't** he?

does she?   Your landlord doesn't pay for water, **does** she?

CD1 T70

B 🔊 Lisa Ming is calling her building manager. Listen and read.

Max: Hello?

Lisa: Hi. This is Lisa Ming in Apartment 5F.

Max: Oh, hi, Lisa. What can I do for you?

Lisa: We don't have any hot water in the bathroom. Could you send someone over?

Max: Sure, I'll call the plumber right now. Will you be at home?

Lisa: No, I'm leaving for work in a few minutes.

Max: Then, is it OK with you if I let the plumber in?

Lisa: Yes, …but you're going to stay there with him, aren't you?

Max: Yes, I will.

Lisa: Because I don't want any strangers in our apartment while we're out.

Max: Don't worry. I'll be there while he does the work.

Lisa: Thanks, Mr. Cove.

4 PRACTICE

A PAIRS. Practice the conversation.

B ROLE PLAY. PAIRS. Role-play this situation. Use the conversation as a model.

Student A: You are a tenant. The lock on the door of your building is broken, and anyone can walk in. You ask the building manager to take care of the problem.

Student B: You are a building manager. You will send a locksmith to fix the door right away.

C MAKE IT PERSONAL. GROUPS. Discuss.

1. Did you or someone you know ever have a problem with a building manager? What was the problem?

2. What did you or that person do? What did the building manager do?

Grammar

Tag questions with *be*	
Affirmative statement	Negative tag
The repairman **is** on his way,	**isn't** he?
You**'re going to stay** there,	**aren't** you?
Negative statement	Affirmative tag
The repairman **isn't** there yet,	**is** he?
The landlord **wasn't** at home,	**was** he?

Tag questions with *do* as an auxiliary verb	
Affirmative statement	Negative tag
You **called** the landlord,	**didn't** you?
He **has to** replace the smoke detectors,	**doesn't** he?
Negative statement	Affirmative tag
Your landlord **doesn't pay** for water,	**does** she?
The repairman **didn't come** yet,	**did** he?

Grammar Watch

- Use tag questions to check that information is correct or when you are not sure the other person will agree.
- Use negative tags with affirmative statements. Use affirmative tags with negative statements.

1 PRACTICE

A Match the beginnings of the sentences with the endings.

__f__ 1. You called the landlord,   a. is there?

__d__ 2. You didn't see mice in the apartment,   b. doesn't he?

__e__ 3. The plumber fixed the sink,   c. is he?

__b__ 4. The landlord has to paint the lobby,   d. did you?

__a__ 5. There isn't any lead paint in the apartment,   e. didn't he?

__c__ 6. The plumber isn't in the basement,   f. didn't you?

B Complete the sentences. Circle the correct words.

1. You checked the lease, **did** / (**didn't**) you?
2. The landlord wasn't in the office, (**was**) / **wasn't** he?
3. You're going to sign the lease, **are** / (**aren't**) you?
4. The building manager takes care of all the repairs, **does** / (**doesn't**) he?
5. You sent a letter to the landlord, **did** / (**didn't**) you?
6. There isn't any damage in your apartment, (**is**) / **isn't** there?
7. The landlord is responsible for keeping the building safe, **is** / (**isn't**) she?
8. The landlord and the plumber are finished with the work, **are** / (**aren't**) they?

Check that information is correct

Getting Started — 5 minutes

- Write two sentences from Lesson 4, Exercise 3A on the board. For example: *The repairman isn't there yet, is he? He has to replace the smoke detectors, doesn't he?* Focus attention on the form of tag questions. Point to the examples and explain: *Tag questions consist of a statement and a short question called a tag. The tag consists of* be *or* do *and a subject.*
- Demonstrate the rising intonation of the tag. Read the examples and have students repeat. Ask: *Does your voice go up or down at the end?* (up)
- Say: *In this lesson, we'll learn about tag questions with* be *and* do.

Presentation — 15 minutes

Tag questions with *be*; Tag questions with *do* as an auxiliary verb

- Copy the grammar charts onto the board
- Read the sentences and have students repeat. (Note: This lesson deals only with tags that have rising intonation. Make sure to pronounce all the tags consistently.)
- For tags with *be*, draw a line from each boldfaced verb to the matching boldfaced auxiliary. Elicit the rule. Ask: *If the main verb is* be, *what verb is used in the tag?* (be)
- Similarly, draw lines from the main verbs to the auxiliaries in the *do* chart. Ask: *If the verb isn't* be, *what verb do we use in the auxiliary?* (a form of *do*)
- Circle the subjects in the statements and the subjects of the tags. Explain that they agree in number.
- Read the first Grammar Watch note. Rephrase: *We use tags in conversation when we think something is true or correct but we want to make sure.*
- Read the second note. Illustrate by pointing to the verbs and tags in the chart. As you point, remind students: *Affirmative statement, negative tag. Negative statement, affirmative tag.*

▬▬▬ **Expansion: Grammar Practice**

- Say a few statements about the students in the class. Use *be* and *do* and have the class provide the tags, for example: *José is a gardener . . . (isn't he?) Amelia has two children . . . (doesn't she?) Sonya isn't working now . . . (is she?) Tina and Sandra aren't sisters . . . (are they?)*

- *Optional:* Have students change the sentences in the chart from singular to plural.
- *Optional:* Play a game. Instruct students to write four present-time statements on a piece of paper. Two should be affirmative and two should be negative. Encourage students to use a variety of subjects (singular and plural). Pair students and have them exchange papers. Students should read their partners' sentences and attach matching tags.

Controlled Practice — 15 minutes

1 PRACTICE

Ⓐ Match the beginnings of the sentences...

- Do item 1 with the class. To guide students toward the correct answer, ask: *Is the main verb* be *or something else? Will the tag use* be *or* do? *Is it present or past?*
- Clarify vocabulary as needed, for example, mice *is the plural of* mouse, lead paint *is paint with lead, a dangerous chemical.*
- Instruct students to work alone or in pairs.
- Call on students to say the answers.
- Read all the sentences and tags and have the class repeat after you. Check that students are using correct intonation.

Ⓑ Complete the sentences. Circle...

- Read the example with the class. Remind students that a positive statement requires a negative tag and vice versa.
- Instruct students to work alone or in pairs.
- Call on students to read the sentences. Have the whole class repeat each item. Check for correct intonation of the tag.

▬▬▬ **Expansion: Grammar Practice for 1B**

- On the board, write tag questions with errors, for example: *The apartment is too cold, doesn't it? Sam forgot to take out the trash, doesn't he? You didn't call the landlord, don't you? The refrigerator is broken, is it?*
- Pair students and have them correct the errors.
- Have students write the corrected sentences on the board.

Controlled Practice   10 minutes

2 PRACTICE

Complete the conversations...

- Do item 1 with the class.
- Have students complete the remaining items, working alone or in pairs.
- While students are working, walk around and provide help with vocabulary as needed.
- Play CD 1, Track 71.
- Check answers. If students missed any items, lead them through the steps of choosing the correct tag. That is, ask: *Is the main verb* be *or something else? Will the tag use* be *or* do*? Is it present or past?*

Communicative Practice   15 minutes

Show what you know!

ROLE PLAY. PAIRS. Role-play this situation. Ask...

> **Teaching Tip**
> While pairs are performing role plays, use the scoring rubric for speaking on page T-xiii to evaluate each student's vocabulary, grammar, fluency, and how well he or she completes the task. You may want to review the completed rubric with the students.

- Read the directions, roles, and example.
- Have the class turn to pages 110–111 and reread the lease. Elicit another sample tag question and response and write it on the board.
- Form cross-ability pairs and have students work together to write the five tag questions.
- Instruct students to practice their role play at least twice.
- Have volunteers perform their role play for the class.

■ MULTILEVEL INSTRUCTION

Pre-level Have students play the role of Student A and ask the tag questions they wrote in the previous activity.

Above level Have students play the role of Student B and answer the tag questions according to the information in the lease.

Progress Check

Can you . . . check that information is correct?

Say: *We have practiced checking that information is correct. Now, look at the question at the bottom of the page. Can you check that information is correct? Write a checkmark in the box.*

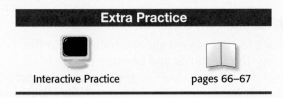

Extra Practice

Interactive Practice   pages 66–67

CD1 T71

Complete the conversations with tag questions. Then listen and check your answers.

1. **A:** What's wrong, Li An?

   B: The landlord kept our security deposit because the carpet has stains on it.

   A: Oh … but we didn't stain the carpet, ___did we___?

2. **A:** The landlord charged us for damage to the living room wall.

   B: But why? The living room wall isn't damaged, ___is it___?

3. **A:** Let's get started. You cleaned the kitchen, ___didn't you___?

   B: Yes, this morning. What else do we need to do?

4. **A:** You didn't like the apartment we saw this morning, ___did you___?

   B: Yes I did. I liked it very much!

5. **A:** That apartment would be perfect for us! What did you think?

   B: I liked it, too. But it's kind of expensive, ___isn't it___?

   A: The rent *is* a little high. But the landlord pays for gas and electricity, ___doesn't he or she___?

Show what you know!   Check that information is correct

ROLE PLAY. PAIRS. **Role-play this situation. Ask and answer questions, using information in the lease on pages 110–111.**

Student A: You are interested in an apartment. Make up a list of five tag questions for the landlord.

Student B: You are the landlord. Answer the tenant's questions.

Student A: *The lease is for one year, isn't it?*
Student B: *Yes, it is.*

Can you… check that information is correct? ☐

Reading

1 BEFORE YOU READ

GROUPS. **What are some reasons that people choose to move to a new city or town?**

2 READ

CD1 T72

 Listen and read the article. Does it mention the reasons you guessed?

Americans on the Move

Ann Kramer is unusual. She was born and raised in Long Beach, California, and now lives there with her husband and children. Why is she unusual? Because these days, one in three Americans moves to a state different from where he or she was born. Why are so many Americans on the move?

One of the biggest reasons people **relocate** is to find jobs. When businesses close and jobs **disappear** in an area, people move. In recent years, people have moved away from places like Detroit, Buffalo, and Cleveland. Factories in these cities have closed, and hundreds of thousands of jobs have been lost. On the other hand, the population of Atlanta has grown because big companies like Home Depot and Coca Cola have created many new jobs there.

Another reason people move is the rising cost of cities. People have to live in places they can afford. As prices rise in some neighborhoods, people move to cheaper areas. In Harlem in New York and Logan Square in Chicago, some **lower-income** residents are moving away because rents are too high. As rents continue to rise in expensive cities like New York and San Francisco, more of the original populations may leave.

A third reason people move is **assimilation**. For example, 100 years ago, there were strong Italian communities in New York City, such as Little Italy in Manhattan. About 90 percent of the people who lived there were Italian and most spoke Italian or Sicilian. There were Italian newspapers, clubs, theaters, and Catholic churches. The children of these Italian immigrants stayed in the community. But gradually, the grandchildren of these immigrants became more fully part of American society. As this happened, the third generation started to move away. Now, many Italians have moved out of Manhattan to suburbs all over New Jersey and Long Island.

As Americans move out of one community and into another, they enrich the places they pass through. Stamford, Connecticut, was once home to Irish and Italian immigrants. Now families from Argentina, Uruguay, Poland, and Haiti live there. Fifty-four languages are spoken in the city public schools. The constant movement of Americans through cities and suburbs mixes classes, languages, and cultures, and continues to change the American landscape.

Getting Started · 10 minutes

1 BEFORE YOU READ

GROUPS. **What are some reasons...**

- Elicit one reason from the class and write it on the board, for example, *Some people move to find a better job.*
- Put students in groups of three or four. Tell them to choose a timekeeper, a note taker, and a reporter. Ask them to brainstorm reasons. Give them a time limit for discussion.
- Call on reporters to give their group's answers. List the reasons on the board.

Possible answers: to be closer to family or friends, to be closer to place of work, for the climate, for the lifestyle and attractions of the area, etc.

Presentation · 15 minutes

2 READ

 Listen and read the article. Does...

- With the class, read the title of the article. Explain that *on the move* is an idiom that means something is moving or changing.
- Play CD 1, Track 72. Ask students to listen and read along with the article.
- Tell students to look for the reasons people move. Tell them to place a checkmark next to reasons found both on the board and in the article.
- Note: This part of the lesson focuses on main ideas. Do not preteach the boldfaced vocabulary. The words will be taught in Exercise 4.
- When students have finished reading, turn to the list of reasons on the board, point to each one and ask: *Is this reason in the article? Where?* Have students read out loud the sentences in the article that correspond to the reasons on the board.
- To wrap up, ask and discuss: *Does the article mention any reasons that are not on the board? Are there any reasons on the board that are not in the article?*

> **Teaching Tip**
>
> In English writing, information is normally organized from the general to the specific. The most general sentence, which gives the main idea, is often (but not always) the first sentence of a paragraph. Therefore, to get a quick idea about the content of an article, students should read the first paragraph and then the first sentence of each subsequent paragraph.

Controlled Practice 20 minutes

3 CHECK YOUR UNDERSTANDING

Reading Skill: **Distinguishing an Author's Main Ideas from Details**

- Read the Reading Skill.
- Ask: *Which sentence gives the main idea?* (Why are so many Americans on the move?) Point out that in an article with several paragraphs, the main idea is usually in the first paragraph. The main idea is then developed in the paragraphs that follow.
- Tell students to circle the connecting words that introduce each reason (*one of the biggest reasons, another reason, a third reason*). Explain that writers use connectors like these to help readers recognize and remember the details that support the main idea.

PAIRS. Read the article again. Answer...

- Form cross-ability pairs. The above-level student should help the pre-level student with vocabulary.
- Have students write their answers to the questions. For question 1, students should rewrite the question as a statement. For question 2, they should list the three reasons introduced by the connecting words they circled above. For question 3, they should choose one detail within each of the three paragraphs that provide the reasons why Americans move.
- Have each pair of students compare answers with another pair.
- Go over answers with the whole class.

MULTILEVEL INSTRUCTION FOR 3

Pre-level For question 3, have students underline the details in the text on page 116.

Above-level For question 3, have students take notes on the details in the space on page 117. Then have them add one more detail that they know about from their experience.

4 WORD WORK

Find the boldfaced words...

- On the board, write *re-* and *dis-*. Ask students to say words that begin with these syllables (use the word *prefixes* if your students are familiar with it). Ask: *What does* re- *mean?* (again) *What does* dis- *mean?* (opposite of) Tell students that they can use prefixes to help them guess the meanings of words they don't know.
- Tell students they can also use *suffixes* to help them guess. Suffixes tell the part of speech of a word. For example, in the word *assimilation,* the *-tion* ending identifies the word as a noun. A noun can be a person, place, thing, or concept.
- Do item 1 with the class. Have students reread the first sentence of the second paragraph. Ask: *Which word in paragraph 1 has the same meaning as* relocate? (*move*)
- Pair students and have them do the exercise. Tell them not to use a dictionary. Instead, they should find each item in the text, read the sentence in which it appears, and guess what it means.
- Have volunteers say the answers and explain how they guessed the meaning. Correct as needed.

EXPANSION: Vocabulary Practice

- Select other words from the text and have students use the context to guess what they mean. Possible words to select are *residents, suburbs,* and *enrich.*

Communicative Practice 15 minutes

Show what you know!

GROUPS. Discuss.

- On the board, create a chart with the headings *Positive* and *Negative.* Tell students to discuss both positive and negative reasons for moving.
- Form groups of three or four. Have each group select a timekeeper, a note taker, and a reporter. The note taker should copy the chart from the board and take notes.
- Give a time limit for discussion.
- Have each group's reporter share the group's positive and negative reasons for moving.

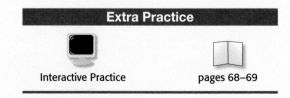

Extra Practice

Interactive Practice pages 68–69

3 CHECK YOUR UNDERSTANDING

PAIRS. Read the article again. Answer the questions.

1. What is the main idea of the article?

   These days many Americans are on the move.

2. What are the author's answers to the question "Why are so many Americans on the move?"

   a. to find jobs

   b. the rising cost of cities

   c. assimilation

3. Find one detail for each answer the author gives.

   a. businesses close

   b. prices are rising, for example, rents

   c. people become more fully part of American society

4 WORD WORK

Find the boldfaced words in the article. Figure out their meaning from context. Then write the definitions.

1. relocate move

2. disappear go away, leave

3. lower-income having less money

4. assimilation to become a part of

Show what you know! Talk about moving

GROUPS. Discuss.

1. Have you ever moved? Why did you move? Were your reasons for moving described in the article?

2. What are some of the things that happen when people move to a new community?

Listening and Speaking

1 BEFORE YOU LISTEN

GROUPS. Discuss.

1. What kinds of problems can people have with their neighbors?
2. If you have a problem with a neighbor, what can you do?
   Who should you talk to?

2 LISTEN

CD1 T73

A Oscar and Marta live in an apartment building. They are talking about their neighbors. Listen to their conversation. What is the problem?

CD1 T73

B Read the statements. Then listen to the conversation again. Circle the correct answers.

1. Oscar and Marta **know** /(**don't know**) the neighbors well.
2. The neighbors were (**rude**)/ **polite** when Marta asked them to be quiet.
3. (**Oscar**)/ **Marta** is very angry about the situation.
4. Marta wants to call the **police** / (**building manager.**)
5. It **is permitted** /(**is not permitted**) to make noise in the building after 10 P.M.
6. Oscar and Marta decide to call the **police** /(**building manager.**)

C GROUPS. Discuss. What should Oscar and Marta do about their neighbors?

D MAKE IT PERSONAL. PAIRS. Have you ever had a problem with your neighbors? Describe your experience.

Lesson 7 Discuss problems with neighbors

Getting Started 5 minutes

1 BEFORE YOU LISTEN

GROUPS. Discuss.

- Model answers to the questions. Tell about a problem you or someone you know had with a neighbor and what you or the other person did about it.
- Form groups. Give a time limit for discussion.
- Have several volunteers share their answers. Write them on the board under the headings *Types of Problems* and *Solutions*.

Possible answers: 1. People have problems when neighbors make noise frequently, when they don't keep the property neat and clean, when they're nosy, etc. 2. You should talk to your neighbor to make him or her aware of the problem. If that doesn't work and if the neighbor is breaking a building rule, you can talk to your building manager or landlord. If those things don't work, you may want to move out!

Presentation 5 minutes

2 LISTEN

A **Oscar and Marta live...**

- Hold up your the book and point to the picture or have students look in their own books. Ask: *Who are the speakers? Where are they? How do they look? (annoyed or upset) Why? Can you guess what the conversation will be about?*
- Play CD 1, Track 73.
- Ask: *What is the problem with the neighbors? Was your guess correct?* Call on volunteers to answer.

Answer: The problem is that their neighbors are noisy.

Controlled Practice 10 minutes

B 🖸 **Read the statements. Then listen...**

- Tell students to read the statements silently and predict the answers.
- Play Track 73 again. Have students circle the answers.
- Write the numbers *1* through *6* on the board. Call on students to read the statements and say the correct answers. Have them explain how they chose their answers.
- If necessary, play the recording again. Have students raise their hands when they hear the answer to a question. Stop the recording and ask students to repeat what they heard.

Communicative Practice 10 minutes

C **GROUPS. Discuss. What should...**

- Put students in small groups. Tell them to choose a timekeeper, a note taker, and a reporter.
- Point to the list of solutions already on the board. Remind students they can choose one of these solutions or think of something different.
- Give a time limit for discussion.
- While students are talking, walk around and provide help as needed.
- Have reporters share their group's solution(s). Add any new solutions to the list on the board.

■■■ Expansion: Speaking Practice for 2C

- Read each solution on the board and have students vote on the best one. Then call on one or more students to explain why the solution with the most votes is indeed the best.

D **MAKE IT PERSONAL. PAIRS. Have you ever...**

- Try to pair students so that each pair contains someone who has had a problem with neighbors.
- Have students discuss their experiences. Circulate and provide help as needed.

Lesson 7 Discuss problems with neighbors

Presentation   10 minutes

3 CONVERSATION

Pronunciation Watch

- Before class, locate several facts that will evoke a strong reaction from the class. For example, go to the website for the Guinness Book of World Records and find some facts there. The point is to elicit expressions such as *Wow!* or *That's amazing!* from the students.

- Write the expressions on the board. Repeat them and ask: *What does my voice do?* Elicit the fact that it rises quite high and then falls.

- Read the Pronunciation Watch note. Explain that *strong feeling* can be positive or negative, for example, surprise, joy, shock, or disgust.

A   **Listen to the sentences. Notice...**

- Play CD 1, Track 74. Have students listen.
- Play Track 74 again. Have students listen and repeat.

B   **Two neighbors are talking. Listen...**

- Write the word *exterminator* on the board. Ask: *What does an exterminator do?* (kills insects and other pests) Say: *This word is in the conversation. What do you think the conversation will be about?*

- Play CD 1, Track 75. Have students listen and read along silently.

- Check comprehension. Ask: *What did Maria see? Where did she see it? Where did it come from? Who is she going to call?*

Controlled Practice   5 minutes

4 PRACTICE

A **PAIRS. Practice the conversation.**

- Form pairs and have students read the conversation in Exercise 3B. Tell them to take turns reading each role.

- Walk around and listen as students are practicing. Notice their pronunciation of expressions of strong feeling (*Oh, no! That's horrible!*) Correct if needed.

- Ask volunteers to perform the conversation for the class.

Communicative Practice   15 minutes

B **ROLE PLAY. PAIRS. Role-play this situation....**

> **Teaching Tip**
> While pairs are performing role plays, use the scoring rubric for speaking on page T-xiii to evaluate each student's vocabulary, grammar, fluency, and how well he or she completes the task. You may want to review the completed rubric with the students.

- Read the role descriptions. Discuss with the class: *How can Student B find out who has been parking in his or her space?* (knock on the neighbors' doors and ask them if they know who owns the car; get the license number and call the DMV to find out who the owner is; or report the problem to the landlord)

- Form cross-ability pairs.
- Tell students to practice out loud at least twice.
- Have volunteers perform their role play.

C **PROBLEM-SOLVING.**

STEP 1. Read the problem. Think...

- Read the situation and clarify vocabulary.
- Instruct students to think about the problem by themselves and make a list of solutions.

STEP 2. GROUPS. Discuss the problem...

- Group students and have them share the solutions they wrote down in Step 1.

- Have a representative from each group tell the class which solution the group voted the best. List all solutions on the board.

- Have the class vote on the best solution among those on the board.

Expansion: Speaking Practice for STEP 1

- Ask if anyone has ever had a problem similar to Pedro's and what they did to solve it.

Extra Practice

Interactive Practice

3 CONVERSATION

CD1 T74

A Listen to the sentences. Notice the intonation. Then listen and repeat.

Oh, no!   That's horrible!   It's disgusting!

CD1 T75

Pronunciation Watch

To show strong feeling, make your voice go up very high and then fall.

B Two neighbors are talking. Listen and read.

Maria: I saw a mouse in the laundry room last night!

Rosa: Oh, no! That's horrible! Li Ping told me that she had mice in her building, too.

Maria: She did? It must be the construction next door. She said they were repairing the pipes.

Rosa: Come to think of it, there's some construction here, too, in the basement near the laundry room. I bet that's why there are mice.

Maria: Ugh! I can't stand mice! I'm going to call the landlord. I'll ask him to call the exterminator.

4 PRACTICE

A PAIRS. Practice the conversation.

B ROLE PLAY. PAIRS. Role play this situation. You are neighbors in the same apartment building.

Student A: A neighbor has parked in your parking spot three times this week, and you have had to park your car in the street. Tell Student B about your problem.

Student B: Tell Student A to find out who has been parking in the spot. Then tell Student A to talk to that neighbor and ask him or her to stop parking there.

C PROBLEM-SOLVING.

STEP 1. Read the problem. Think of a few possible solutions.

One of Pedro's neighbors, Leo, leaves for work very early in the morning. Leo's co-worker picks him up at 4:00 A.M. Many mornings, the co-worker honks his horn to let Leo know he's waiting. The horn wakes Pedro up, and he can never go back to sleep.

STEP 2. GROUPS. Discuss the problem. Share ideas about solving it. Vote on the best solution.

Grammar

Reported speech

Direct speech	Reported speech				
Lidia said, "You're too noisy."	Lidia	said			they were too noisy.
Lidia told her neighbor, "Your car is in my parking spot."		told	her neighbor	(that)	his car was in her parking spot.
The landlord said, "I'll fix it tomorrow."	The landlord	said			he would fix it tomorrow.

Grammar Watch

- Use reported speech to tell what a speaker says without using the exact words.
- In both direct and reported speech, the verb *tell* takes an object. The verb *say* does not.
- In formal English, when the reporting verb is in the past, the verb in the reported speech is often also in the past. In informal English, the verb in the reported speech does not change to the past, especially when speech is reported soon after it is spoken: *Lidia said they're too noisy.*
- Pronouns and possessives in reported speech usually change to keep the speaker's original meaning.
- *See page 283 for additional changes in verb tenses, pronouns, and possessives in reported speech.*

1   PRACTICE

A Read the advice column questions from two tenants. Underline the reported speech.

Q: One of my neighbors smokes all the time. I told him that <u>smoking wasn't allowed in the building</u>. I also told him that <u>my children are getting sore throats</u>. He said <u>he would stop</u>, but I can still smell smoke from his apartment. What should I do?

Q: The ceiling in our bathroom leaks every time our upstairs neighbors take a shower. The building manager said <u>he would send a plumber</u>, but it's been three days. I told my neighbors that <u>they should call, too</u>. They said <u>they did</u>, but <u>nothing has happened.</u> What should I do?

B Complete the statements. Use *said* or *told*.

My friend Inez called me last week. She was really upset. She ___told___ me that her neighbor had bought two big dogs. She ___said___ the dogs were always running in the halls. When they saw her, they jumped on her. She ___said___ she was terrified. I ___told___ her that she should complain to the landlord, but she ___said___ that she didn't like to complain. I ___told___ her I would call the landlord for her, but she ___said___ she would work it out.

Getting Started 5 minutes

- Ask a simple question, for example, *When did you move to [name of city]?*
- Call on several students to answer the question. Write the answers on the board in quotation marks, for example, "I moved last March."
- Next, write *[name of student] said* _____ _____. *Ask the class: What did [name of student] say? ([name of student] said he moved to [name of city] last March.)* Write this sentence on the board without quotation marks.
- Point to the first response. Say: *This kind of answer is called* direct speech. *When we write it, we use quotation marks.*
- Point to the second response. Say: *This kind of response is called* reported speech. *When we write it, we don't use quotation marks.*
- Say: *In this lesson, we'll learn about the differences between direct speech and reported speech, and you'll practice using reported speech.*

Presentation 10 minutes

Reported speech

- Copy the grammar chart onto the board.
- Read the sentences. Ask: *Do the sentences with direct speech repeat the speaker's exact words?* (yes) *What about the sentences with reported speech?* (no)
- Read the first Grammar Watch note. Point to the two sides of the grammar chart and say: *The information in the two types of statements is the same, but the words are not exactly the same.*
- Point to the verbs *said* and *told* in the examples. Ask: *What comes after* said? *What comes after* told? (*Told* is followed by an object.) Then read the second Grammar Watch note.
- Read the first and second examples in the Direct Speech column. For each sentence, ask the class: *What is the time of the direct statement?* (present) *What is the time of the reported statement?* (past) Make sure students notice the tense change. Then read the third Grammar Watch note. Point out that the first two examples in the chart follow the rule for formal, or written English.
- Read the third example. Circle and draw a line from *'ll* in the direct statement to *would* in the indirect one. Explain: *'ll changes to* would *in indirect speech when the reporting verb is in the past.*

- Read the fourth note. Point out that in the first example, the direct *you* changes to the indirect *they*. In the second example, the direct *your* changes to the indirect *his*. In the third example, the direct *I* changes to the indirect *he*.
- Point out that in reported speech, the *that* before the reported statement is optional.

Expansion: Grammar Practice

- Make a four-column chart on the board. In the first column, write several nouns, such as *The teacher* and *My mother*. In the second column, write *say* and *tell*. In the third column, write *me, him,* and the names of two students. In the fourth column write two or three sentences with verbs in the present or past tense, for example, *He was late / I am too noisy.*
- Point to elements from each column and have students build reported statements, for example, *The teacher told Miguel he was late. / My mother said I am too noisy.*

Controlled Practice 15 minutes

1 PRACTICE

A Read the advice column questions...

- Tell students that Q means *question*. A real advice column would also have an *A*, meaning *answer*.
- Read the example.
- Have students complete the exercise.
- Check answers.

Culture Connection

Advice columns are very popular in the U.S. Most newspapers have an advice column to help people with their personal problems. There are also many advice columns on the Internet. Some of them are specialized, for example, advice columns that deal with medical questions, home improvement, finance, etc.

B Complete the statements. Use...

- Read the first three sentences. Remind students that *told* is followed by an object.
- Have students work alone or in pairs.
- Have students read the completed sentences. Correct errors as needed.

Controlled Practice   15 minutes

2 PRACTICE

Ⓐ Read the tenants' problems. Rewrite...

- Read the directions. Remind students that in informal English, they don't need to change the verbs in the reported statement to the past.
- Do item 1 with students.
- Have students complete the exercise. Then have them compare answers with a partner.
- Write the numbers 2 through 5 on the board. Call on students to write their sentences on the board.
- Have other students read the sentences on the board and say if they are correct. If there are errors, have students try to correct them.

Ⓑ Complete the paragraph about...

- Read the directions. Remind students that in formal English, they need to change the verbs in the reported statement to the past. Also remind them that *will* changes to *would* in reported speech.
- Do the example with students.
- Have students complete the exercise. Then have them compare answers with a partner.
- Have students read the sentences with the verbs filled in. Write them on the board. Correct errors as needed.

Communicative Practice   15 minutes

Show what you know!

PAIRS. Talk about a problem...

- Model the activity. Talk about a problem you had with a neighbor and what you did or said. Also say how you resolved the problem.
- Pair students. Give a time limit for discussion. While students are talking, walk around and provide help as needed.
- Call on volunteers to share their answers with the class.

▬▬ Expansion: Speaking Practice

- Tell pairs of students to choose one of the problems they discussed and role-play a conversation about it.

Progress Check

Can you . . . discuss problems with neighbors?

Say: *We practiced discussing problems with neighbors. Now, look at the question at the bottom of the page. Can you discuss problems with neighbors? Write a checkmark in the box.*

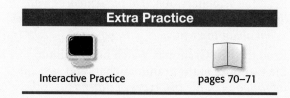

Extra Practice
Interactive Practice   pages 70–71

2 PRACTICE

A Read the tenants' problems. Rewrite them using *said* and informal English.

1. **Ivan:** "My neighbors' kids get up early and play and wake my wife and me up."

   Ivan said that his neighbors' kids get up early and play and wake his wife and him up.

2. **Victoria:** "The hallway in our building always smells of strong cooking odors from the restaurant next door."

   Victoria said that the hallway in her building always smells of strong cooking odors from the restaurant next door.

3. **Adina:** "My neighbors have visitors at 2:00 and 3:00 in the morning, and they sometimes ring my doorbell by accident."

   Adina said that her neighbors have visitors at 2:00 and 3:00 in the morning, and they sometimes ring her doorbell by accident.

4. **Ming:** "We live right near a fire station, and the sirens wake our kids up all the time."

   Ming said they live near a fire station, and the sirens wake their kids up all the time.

5. **Ibrahim:** "My neighbor parks her car in my space almost every weekend."

   Ibrahim said that his neighbor parks her car in his space almost every weekend.

B Complete the paragraph about Sara's problem. Use the verbs in parentheses. Use formal English.

Last week, I spoke to the building manager about two problems. The first is with the front door. I told him that it ___didn't close___ properly and that this ___was___ a dangerous
(not close)   (be)
situation. He said he ___knew___ about the problem. I told him that he ___needed___
(know)   (need)
to install an automatic lock. He said he ___would look___ into it. The second problem is with
(look)
the nightclub down the block. It closes late, and people make a lot of noise when they leave. The
manager said he ___was___ sorry but that he ___wasn't able___ to do anything about it.
(be)   (not be able)

Show what you know! Discuss problems with neighbors

PAIRS. Talk about a problem you have had with a neighbor. Use reported speech.

1. What did your neighbor do? What did you do or say?
2. How did you resolve the problem?

Can you...discuss problems with neighbors? ☐

Write a letter of complaint

Writing

1 BEFORE YOU WRITE

A CLASS. When a tenant has a problem in his or her apartment, he or she often writes a letter of complaint to the landlord to describe the problem. Why is writing a letter a good idea?

B GROUPS. Have you ever written a letter of complaint to a landlord? What did you complain about? What happened next?

C Read the writing model. Underline the complaint in the letter. Circle the solution to the problem.

> ### Writing Tip
>
> When you write a letter of complaint, clearly state the problem and ask for a solution to the problem.

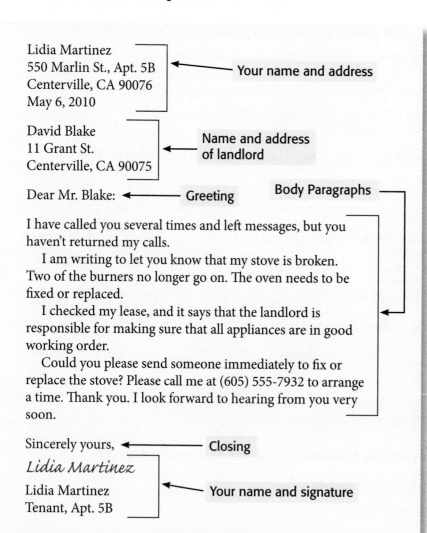

Lidia Martinez
550 Marlin St., Apt. 5B
Centerville, CA 90076
May 6, 2010

→ Your name and address

David Blake
11 Grant St.
Centerville, CA 90075

← Name and address of landlord

Dear Mr. Blake: ← Greeting

Body Paragraphs

I have called you several times and left messages, but you haven't returned my calls.

I am writing to let you know that my stove is broken. Two of the burners no longer go on. The oven needs to be fixed or replaced.

I checked my lease, and it says that the landlord is responsible for making sure that all appliances are in good working order.

Could you please send someone immediately to fix or replace the stove? Please call me at (605) 555-7932 to arrange a time. Thank you. I look forward to hearing from you very soon.

Sincerely yours, ← Closing

Lidia Martinez

Lidia Martinez
Tenant, Apt. 5B

← Your name and signature

Getting Started   5 minutes

1 BEFORE YOU WRITE

A CLASS. When a tenant...

- Ask the class: *What does* complain *mean, as in the sentence* I complained to my landlord about my noisy neighbors? Explain that *a letter of complaint* is a letter in which you formally complain about a problem and ask that the problem be corrected.
- Read the directions.
- Call on volunteers to answer the question. List students' reasons on the board.

Possible answer: It's good to write a letter because then you have a record of your complaint.

B GROUPS. Have you ever written...

- Ask students to raise their hands if they have written a letter of complaint. (It is likely that few, if any, students will have written such a letter.) Have the other students form groups with those students. The students who have written letters should tell about their experience. The other members of the group should ask questions.
- Give a time limit for discussion.
- (Note: If just one or two students have written a complaint letter, have the whole class interview them. If no student has written such a letter, tell the class about a real letter that you have written or describe an imaginary one. Explain what the letter was about, why you wrote it, and what kind of response you got.)

Presentation   15 minutes

Writing Tip: **Writing a Complaint**
Read the Writing Tip. Emphasize that you have a much better chance of getting your problem solved if you ask for a solution than if you just complain about the problem.

C Read the writing model. Underline...

- Instruct students to read the body of the letter, underline the complaint, and circle the solution. Explain that the complaint is the problem that the writer wants the landlord to fix or resolve, and the solution is the action that the writer wants the landlord to take.
- Give a time limit for reading.
- Call on students to say which parts of the letter they underlined and circled.

Answers:
Underline: my stove is broken
Circle: The oven needs to be fixed or replaced.

▬▬ Expansion: Parts of a Formal Letter

- With the class, look at the letter of complaint and name all the parts, beginning with the writer's name and address at the top and concluding with the writer's name and signature at the bottom.
- Go over each body paragraph. Ask students: *What is this paragraph about?*
- Read the last sentence of the letter and the closing. Point out that these parts of the letter should be formal and very polite.

Controlled Practice   20 minutes

2   THINKING ON PAPER

A BRAINSTORM. Think about problems...

- Brainstorm one or two problems with the class and write them on the board.
- Have students choose two other problems and write them in their books. If they don't have real problems, tell them to write invented ones.
- Have students share their lists with one or two classmates.

B Choose one problem. Think...

- Copy the diagram onto the board and model the task. Ask one student to name a problem. Ask the class to provide solutions. Write the class's ideas on the diagram. Point out that the diagram should contain ideas, not complete sentences. (Note: It is not necessary to include four solutions. Include as many as the class suggests.)
- Allow students to work alone, in pairs, or in groups. Give a time limit.
- As students are working, circulate and help them think of solutions, if necessary.
- Have several volunteers copy their diagrams on the board. Point to each diagram and ask the class: *How many have had a similar problem? Did you try one of these solutions? Did it work?*

Communicative Practice   20 minutes

3   WRITE

Write your own letter of complaint. Focus...

- Remind students to include a problem and one or more solutions.
- Have students include the first paragraph of the writing model only if it is true. Otherwise, they can begin their letter with the second paragraph.
- While students are writing, walk around and provide help as needed. Make sure that they are following correct letter form.

■ MULTILEVEL INSTRUCTION for 3

Pre-level Have students write one sentence about the problem and one sentence about the solution.

Above-level Have students include more than one solution or write several sentences about one solution.

4   CHECK YOUR WRITING

Teaching Tip

You may want to collect student papers and provide feedback. Use the scoring rubric for writing on page T-xiv to evaluate each student's vocabulary, grammar, mechanics and how well he or she has completed the task. You may want to review the completed rubric with the students.

- Read the questions in the checklist.
- Have students read their paragraphs and check off the questions in the checklist.
- Collect papers and correct them. Make corrections as needed in paragraph format, content, and the items in the writing checklist.

■ Expansion: Writing Practice

- Have students rewrite their letters in class, incorporating your comments. Then pair students and have them read their letters to each other.

Extra Practice

Interactive Practice   page 72

A BRAINSTORM. Think about problems you might have in your house or apartment. Write a list of problems.

Problem A: _____

Problem B: _____

B Choose one problem. Think of possible solutions. Plan and organize your letter. Organize your ideas like this.

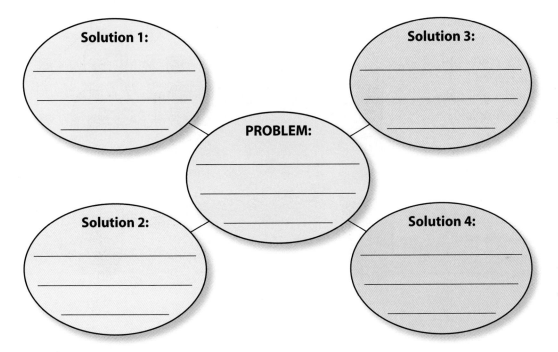

Solution 1:
_____
_____
_____

Solution 3:
_____
_____
_____

PROBLEM:
_____
_____
_____

Solution 2:
_____
_____
_____

Solution 4:
_____
_____
_____

3 **WRITE**

Write your own letter of complaint. Focus on one problem and its solution. Use the information in your plan. Look at the writing model for an example.

4 **CHECK YOUR WRITING**

☐ Did you clearly explain the problem?

☐ Did you ask for a specific solution?

☐ Did you include your name, address, and phone number?

☐ Did you use correct capitalization, punctuation, and spelling?

1 REVIEW

For your grammar review, go to page 250.

2 ACT IT OUT   What do you say?

STEP 1. CLASS. Review the conversation on page 119 (CD1, Track 75).

STEP 2. ROLE PLAY. PAIRS. Role-play this situation.

Student A: You are a tenant. The lobby in your apartment building has not been painted in twenty years, and the carpeting is ripped and stained. You meet a neighbor in the lobby and complain about the problem.

Student B: You are Student A's neighbor. Listen to Student A's complaints about the lobby and discuss what to do.

3 READ AND REACT   Problem-solving

STEP 1. Read about Gustavo's problem.

Gustavo moves into a new apartment that is closer to his place of work. He doesn't know anyone in the building. He would like to get to know his neighbors, but he finds them unfriendly.

STEP 2. GROUPS. What is Gustavo's problem? Discuss a solution. List three things that he can do.

4 CONNECT

For your Self-Evaluation Activity, go to page 259.
For your Team Project, go to page 268.

Which goals can you check off? Go back to page 105.

 Go to the CD-ROM for more practice.

Show what you know!

1 REVIEW

Turn to page 250 for the Grammar Review.

2 ACT IT OUT

STEP 1. CLASS. **Review...**

- Play CD 1, Track 75. Have students listen as they read the script on page 119.
- Tell them to read the conversation with a partner.
- Have volunteers perform the conversation for the class.

STEP 2. ROLE PLAY. PAIRS. **Role-play this...**

Teaching Tip

While pairs are performing role plays, use the scoring rubric for speaking on page T-xiii to evaluate each student's vocabulary, grammar, fluency, and how well he or she completes the task. You may want to review the completed rubric with the students.

- Have students look at the illustration. Ask: *Where is the woman? What is the problem? What should she do?*
- With the class, discuss: *What are some ways that the building manager might respond?* (He could agree to fix the problem immediately; he could say that he will send someone to fix it; he could refuse to the fix the problem because it was caused by the tenants' carelessness; or he could say that the problem is not his responsibility because it is not covered in the lease.)
- Pair students. Instruct them to choose roles and practice at least twice.
- While students are practicing, walk around and provide help as needed.
- Call on pairs to perform for the class.

3 READ AND REACT

STEP 1. **Read about Gustavo's problem.**

- Read the problem. Tell students to think about a solution to Gustavo's problem.

STEP 2. GROUPS. **What is Gustavo's problem?...**

- Put students in groups of three or four. Tell them to choose a timekeeper and a reporter.
- Give a time limit for discussion. While students are talking, walk around and provide help as needed.
- When time is up, call on the reporters to share their group's solution. Write all solutions on the board.

MULTILEVEL INSTRUCTION for STEP 2

Pre-level While other students conduct a discussion of the pros and cons of each solution, have pre-level students listen. Then have them vote on the best one.

Above-level Have students conduct a discussion of the pros and cons of each solution and write the pros and cons on the board. Then have the class vote on the best solution.

4 CONNECT

Turn to page 259 for the Self-Evaluation Activity and page 268 for the Team Project. See page T-xi for teaching tips for these activities.

Progress Check

Which goals can you check off? Go back to page 105.

Ask students to turn to page 105 and check off any remaining goals they have reached. Call on students to say which goals they will practice outside of class.

 Go to the CD-ROM for more practice.

If your students need more practice with the vocabulary, grammar, and competencies in Unit 6, encourage them to review the activities on the CD-ROM.

7 Behind the Wheel

Classroom Materials/Extra Practice

CD 2
Tracks 2–15

Interactive Practice
Unit 7

Workbook
Unit 7

Unit Overview

Goals
- See the list of goals on the facing page.

Grammar
- *Would rather* and *would prefer* to express preferences
- Embedded *wh-* questions
- Embedded *yes/no* questions
- Past perfect statements, questions, and answers

Pronunciation
- Using stress and intonation for content words
- Pronunciation of *had, would,* and *'d*

Reading
- Discuss consumer-protection laws
- Reading Skill: Using visuals

Writing
- Write about a good or bad purchase

Life Skills
- Talk about buying car insurance

Preview
- Have students look at the photo. Say the unit title. Ask: *What do you think this unit will be about?*
- Ask the preview questions. You can also ask: *How many people own a car? What kind? What do you like and dislike about it?*

Unit Goals
- Point to the Unit Goals. Have students read them silently.
- Tell students they will be studying these goals in Unit 7.
- Say each goal and explain unfamiliar vocabulary as needed, for example, *maintenance: the upkeep or care of property or equipment; consumer: someone who buys goods or services; purchase: to pay money for, to buy.*
- Tell students to circle one or more goals that are very important to them. Call on several volunteers to say the goals they circled.
- Write a checkmark (✓) on the board. Say: *We will come back to this page again. You will write a checkmark next to the goals you learned in this unit.*

Behind the Wheel

Preview

Read the title. How much does it cost to buy and own a car? What are some things that car owners have to spend money on?

UNIT GOALS

- [ ] Talk about things to consider when buying a car
- [ ] Describe preferences in cars
- [ ] Talk about buying car insurance
- [ ] Discuss car maintenance and repairs
- [ ] Discuss consumer-protection laws
- [ ] Describe a car accident
- [ ] Write about a good or bad purchase

Listening and Speaking

1   BEFORE YOU LISTEN

When you buy a car, you need to consider a lot of factors. Read the list of factors. Which ones are most important to you?

vehicle type = sedan, convertible, SUV, minivan, pickup, etc.
make and model = Ford Focus, Honda Civic, Toyota Corolla, etc.
safety features = seat belts, air bags, antilock brakes, etc.
optional features = CD player, power steering, air-conditioning sunroof, etc.
mileage = the total distance a car has traveled
gas mileage = miles per gallon (mpg) of gasoline
reliability = how well a car works; dependability
warranty = a written promise to fix or replace a product that doesn't work

2   LISTEN

A   CD2 T2   **Listen to the first part of Mark and Eva Ortega's conversation. What type of car do they want to buy? Why?**   a used car, because it is less expensive

B   CD2 T3   **Read the statements. Then listen to the whole conversation. Write *T* (true) or *F* (false). Correct the false statements.**

___T___ 1. Mark and Eva think it's important for a car to have a warranty.

___T___ 2. They want to buy a car with power steering.

___F___ 3. They ~~don't~~ care about air-conditioning.

___F___ 4. They agree that front airbags are _^not enough to make a car safe.

___F___ 5. Mark and Eva have ^{not}_^agreed they want a red car.

Talk about things to consider when buying a car

Getting Started

1 BEFORE YOU LISTEN

When you buy a car, you need to consider...

- Have students read the items and definitions. Make sure that students understand the difference between *mileage* and *gas mileage*. Define *power steering (a steering system that makes it easy to turn the wheel of a car), SUV (Sport utility vehicle—a car with a large, boxy shape, designed for driving off the road), pickup (a kind of small truck).*
- Answer other questions about vocabulary. Elicit additional examples of vehicle type, make and model, optional features, and safety features.
- Tell students to imagine they are shopping for a car. Have them choose the two factors that are most important to them.
- Go around the room and have each student name the two items he or she picked.

Presentation

2 LISTEN

A **Listen to the first part...**

- Have students look at the photo. Ask: *Who are the speakers? How old are they? Where are they?*
- Remind students that it is not necessary to understand every word in the conversation. They should listen specifically for the answers to the questions.
- Play CD 2, Track 2. Have students compare answers with a classmate.
- Call on volunteers to share questions with the whole class.

Controlled Practice
20 minutes

B **Read the statements. Then listen...**

- Have students read the statements and predict the answers.
- Play CD 2, Track 3. Have students compare answers with a partner.
- Call on students to read the statements and answers out loud.
- If students have difficulty with an answer, play the corresponding part of the recording again.

3 CONVERSATION

 Read and listen to Mark and Eva's conversation...

- Play CD 2, Track 4. Have students listen and read along silently.
- Check comprehension. Ask: *What kind of car are Mark and Eva looking at? How much does it cost? How many miles does it have? Who was the previous owner? What are Mark and Eva going to do?*

MULTILEVEL INSTRUCTION for 3

Pre-level Give students time to read the Audio Script before listening.

Above-level Have students listen with their books closed.

4 PRACTICE

A GROUPS. Practice the conversation.

- Form groups of three and have students take turns reading each role.
- As needed, explain: I can let you have it for *means* I will sell it to you for (this price); There are (number) miles on the car *means* The car has been driven (number) miles.
- Walk around and listen as students are practicing. Provide help as needed.
- Ask volunteers to perform the conversation for the class.

Communicative Practice   20 minutes

B MAKE IT PERSONAL. Think about...

STEP 1. What are the three most important factors...

- Read the items. Explain vocabulary as needed.
- Have students rank the items, working alone.
- Form pairs. Have students compare answers with a partner.

STEP 2. CLASS. Share your results. Explain...

- Call on volunteers to share their answers and explain their choices. Ask questions to involve the whole class, for example, *Do you agree? Who has a different answer?*
- Read each item in Step 1 and have students vote on the one they think is most important.

C GROUPS. Imagine that you want to buy a used car...

- With the class, look at each picture. Ask students to describe what they see.
- Form groups. Give a time limit for discussion.
- Call on volunteers to say which car they chose and why they chose it.

Expansion: Speaking Practice for 4C

- On the board, write: *What make and model of car do you own now? Which cars have you owned in the past? Which factors helped you decide to buy these cars?*
- Put students in groups of four or five. Instruct them to look at the factors in Exercise 4B as they discuss the questions on the board.
- While students are talking, walk around and provide help as needed.
- To wrap up, take a class survey. Ask each student the model of their most recent car. Find out which car model is the most popular.

Extra Practice

Interactive Practice

CONVERSATION

CD2 T4

Read and listen to Mark and Eva's conversation with a salesperson at Tri-State Motors.

Salesperson: So, you're looking at the 2005 Ford Focus. It's a great little car, isn't it? I can let you have it for just under $9,000.

Mark: We've checked prices for this make and model. I think we can get the car for less.

Salesperson: I might be able to get you a lower price. I'll talk to my manager.

Eva: I see there are 58,000 miles on the car. How many previous owners have there been?

Salesperson: Just one. She drove the car mostly for shopping. Our mechanics have inspected the car. It's in excellent condition. Would you like to take a test drive? I can go get the keys for you.

Mark: Thanks, but not right now. We'd rather look at some other cars first.

4 PRACTICE

A GROUPS. Practice the conversation.

B MAKE IT PERSONAL. Think about the important factors in buying a car.

STEP 1. What are the three most important factors in buying a car? Write *1* (most important), *2*, and *3*.

_____ make and model   _____ gas mileage   _____ purchase price

_____ safety   _____ reliability   _____ other: _____

STEP 2. CLASS. Share your results. Explain your choices.

C GROUPS. Imagine that you want to buy a used car. Look at the pictures. Which car would you most like to have? Why?

Describe preferences in cars

Grammar

Would rather and *would prefer* to express preferences

Statements			
Mark and Eva **would rather**	**buy**	a compact	**than** a full-size car.
Mark and Eva **would prefer**	**buying**	a small car	(**to** a full-size car).
	to buy	a small car.	
They**'d rather not**	**have**	a large vehicle.	
They**'d prefer not**	**having**	a big car.	

Questions			
A: **Would** you **rather**	**drive**	a minivan	**than** an SUV?
B: Yes, I **would**.			
A: **Would** you **prefer**		a Ford	**to** a Toyota?
B: No, I **wouldn't**.			

Grammar Watch

- *Would rather* and *would prefer* both express preference.

- Use the base form of the verb after *would rather*. Use an infinitive or a gerund after *would prefer*. The infinitive is more common than the gerund.

- When comparing nouns with *would rather*, use *than* between the two nouns. When comparing nouns with *would prefer*, use *to* between the two nouns.

1 PRACTICE

I'd rather drive a sports car than a minivan any day!

Raul

I like this car, but I'd rather not drive a two-door model. And I'd really prefer a blue car to a yellow one.

2005 Hybrid
$10,999
Great Gas Mileage

Marina

I want a safe car, and I'd prefer not to spend money on car repairs.

Yuan

Look at the pictures. Check (✓) the statements that are true.

_✓_ 1. Raúl doesn't want to drive a minivan.

_✓_ 2. Marina is looking for a four-door car.

_____ 3. Marina really likes yellow cars.

_✓_ 4. Yuan wants a reliable car.

_____ 5. Yuan and Raúl like the same kinds of cars.

Getting Started   5 minutes

- Write several pairs of related items on the board (or use pairs of pictures), for example: *1. peaches, pears; 2. blue, orange; 3. soccer, baseball.*

- Select a student and interview him or her. Point to each pair of items and ask, for example: *Which fruit do you like better? Which color do you like more? Which sport do you like to play?*

- Compare the student's preferences with your own. Use *prefer* and *would rather*. For example: *Jorge likes to eat peaches, but I prefer pears. Jorge likes the color blue, but I prefer orange.* Write the sentences on the board.

- Repeat with another student. This time have the class form the comparisons, for example: T: *Marta likes pears.* Ss: *I prefer peaches* or *I would rather eat peaches.* Write a few more sentences with *prefer* and *would rather* on the board.

- Say: *In this lesson we'll learn how to express preferences with* prefer *and* would rather.

Presentation   25 minutes

Would rather and would prefer to express preferences

- Copy the grammar chart onto the board. Underline the boldfaced words.

- Read the first Grammar Watch note. Then read the first two statements. After each statement, ask the class: *Which thing do Mark and Eva like better?*

- Read the second Grammar Watch note. Then read all the sentences with *would rather.*

- Read the third Grammar Watch note and all the sentences with *would prefer.*

- Point out the contractions. Say each pronoun and *would* and have students say the contracted form, for example: T: *I would;* Ss: *I'd.* Ask: *Can we use a contraction if the subject is a noun?* (no)

Language Note

The sentence *Mark and Eva would prefer buying a small car to a large one* can also be expressed as *Mark and Eva would prefer buying a small car to buying a large one.* When you make comparisons with *would prefer* followed by a gerund, repetition of the gerund in the comparison is optional.

Expansion: Grammar Practice

- On index cards, write pairs of similar items, for example, in the categories of foods, sports, TV shows, types of music, seasons, colors, etc. Each card will have a pair of related items on it, such as *cat/dog.* Try to make one card per student.

- Distribute the cards among the students.

- Have students stand up and mingle. Classmates should form pairs consisting of Student A and Student B. Student A should show his or her card to Student B and make a sentence using *would rather* or *would prefer,* for example, *I'd rather have a dog than a cat.* Student B should agree or disagree, for example, *Me too. / Not me. I'd rather have a cat.*

- The pair should repeat the process, this time speaking about the items on Student B's card. Student B should speak first and Student A should agree or disagree.

- After the pair has spoken about both cards, students should swap cards, then each student should move on and speak with another classmate.

- Allow enough time for four or six swaps.

- Have several students write sentences on the board. Have other students read the sentences and correct errors as needed.

Controlled Practice   20 minutes

1   PRACTICE

Look at the pictures. Check....

- Pair students and have them look at the art. Tell them to take turns reading the speech balloons.

- Read the first item with the class. Ask: *Which picture matches the statement?*

- Have students complete the remaining items, working in pairs. While they are working, walk around and provide help as needed.

- Check answers. Read each sentence and have students say *check* or *no check* and which photo gave them the answer: left, right, or middle.

Expansion: Grammar Practice for 1

- Have students paraphrase each speech balloon. For example, if the speech bubble uses *would prefer,* have students restate it with *would rather.*

2 PRACTICE

Ⓐ Circle the correct words.

- Explain that *FYI* means *for your information* and *SUV* means *sport utility vehicle*.
- Remind students that *would rather* is followed only by the base form and *would prefer* is followed by an infinitive, gerund, or noun. In the comparison, *would rather* uses *than* and *would prefer* uses the gerund.
- Read the first sentence with the class and go over the first item.
- Have students complete the remaining items on their own, then compare answers with a partner.
- Go over the answers. Call on students to read the sentences with the correct words. Correct errors as needed.

Ⓑ Complete the conversation. Use...

- Read the example.
- Tell students to complete the exercise on their own.
- Have students compare answers with a classmate.
- Go over the answers. Read the conversation and have students call out the missing words.

Expansion: Speaking Practice for 2B

- Form groups of three. Instruct students to practice reading the conversation.
- Have students switch roles and practice again.
- Call on volunteers to read the conversation for the class.

MULTILEVEL INSTRUCTION for 2B

Cross-ability Have the higher-ability students help the lower-ability students with pronunciation.

Communicative Practice   15 minutes

Show what you know!

STEP 1. Write the make and model...

- Remind students that they saw this vocabulary in Lesson 1.
- Ask: *What is your dream car? What make and model of car would you prefer owning? Why?*
- Have students write their answers, working alone.

STEP 2. Groups. Discuss your choices.

- Form groups.
- Instruct students to read their answers and reasons from Step 1 and discuss each one in turn. Encourage them to politely agree and disagree.
- Give a time limit for discussion. While students are talking, walk around and provide help as needed.

Expansion: Speaking Practice for STEP 2

- Have students call out the make and model of a car they would not buy and write these names on the board.
- Have students discuss the list of cars on the board.

Progress Check

Can you . . . describe preferences in cars?
Tell students to look at the question at the bottom of the page and write a checkmark in the box.

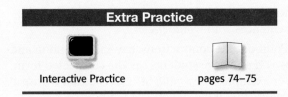

Extra Practice
Interactive Practice   pages 74–75

A Circle the correct words.

Auto FYI

by Art Jeffers, Columnist

When it's time for your next car, truck, or SUV, where (would you rather) / would you prefer get your information? People don't always agree on the best way to become a smart auto shopper.

Some car buyers would prefer **read** / (reading) *Consumer Reports* and the *Kelley Blue Book*. Others would rather (use) / **to use** the consumerreports.org and kbb.com websites **to** / (than) spend hours looking at books and magazines.

Another group of car buyers would rather (learn) / **learning** from personal experience (than) / **to** read what the experts have to say. They (would rather) / **would prefer** do research by talking to friends and by paying attention to the cars they see on the road.

So, what about you? Would you prefer relying on your personal experience **to** / (than) using a website? Or would you rather (follow) / **following** the advice of experts? Whatever you do, get as much information as possible before you buy your next vehicle.

B Complete the conversation. Use *would rather (not)*, *would prefer (not)*, *would you rather*, or *would you prefer*.

Raúl: I love sports cars. I know they're expensive, and most people _would rather not_ spend that much on a car. But I don't care. I _would rather_ spend the money and drive a really cool car. How about you, Marina? What kind of car _would you prefer_ having?

Marina: A hybrid. I like the combination of a gas engine and an electric motor with a battery. I _would prefer not_ going to the gas station if I can avoid it.

Raúl: Hey, Yuan, how about you? What kind of car _would you rather_ drive?

Yuan: A safe car. I _would rather not_ have to worry about having an accident. I _would prefer_ having a car with a good safety record to anything else.

Show what you know! Describe preferences in cars

STEP 1. Write the make and model of the car you would prefer. Write three reasons.

STEP 2. GROUPS. Discuss your choices.

Can you...describe preferences in cars? ☐

Life Skills

1   READ A CAR INSURANCE RENEWAL NOTICE

CLASS. All drivers in the U.S. must have car insurance and must carry insurance identification cards in their vehicles. Discuss.

1. Why is car insurance so important?

2. What information is given in the identification card at the right?

3. The words *premium* and *deductible* appear on all insurance policies. What do these terms mean?

State.com	Phone Number: 1-800-188-5514
	NEW YORK STATE INSURANCE IDENTIFICATION CARD

Policy Number	Effective Date	Expiration Date
0528-73-66-05	12/18/2008 (12:01 A.M.)	06/18/2009 (12:01 A.M.)

Applicable with respect to the following Motor Vehicle.

GILBERT, LAURA S.	2004	JEEP	GRCHER LAR
1 SHADY LN.	Year	Make	Model
WHITE PLAINS, NY 10606			

Name & Address of issuer.	1J4GW48S64743281
STATE CAR INSURANCE COMPANY	Vehicle identification Number
ONE STATE PLAZA	Company Code: 639
Washington, DC 20076-0001	

2   PRACTICE

A   **Once or twice a year, car owners are required to renew their car insurance. Read this part of an insurance renewal notice.**

B   **Read the questions. Circle the correct answers.**

1. Who is Tom Russo?
   a. the insurance agent   (b.) the car owner

2. How long is the policy for?
   a. a month   (b.) a year

3. How much does the policy cost a year?
   a. $126.00   (b.) $1,512.00

4. How much does the owner pay before the insurance company begins to cover any expenses?
   (a.) $500.00   b. $126.00

State   *Car Insurance*

Renewal Notice

Name of Insured
Tom Russo

Policy Number
12 4356 995 42

Policy Period
June 1, 2009–May 31, 2010

Vehicle Description: 2008 Ford Explorer
Deductible: $500
Monthly Premium: $126

Your agent is:
Josefina Blanco
Phone: (201) 555-2299
E-mail: jblanco@state.com

3   TALK ABOUT BUYING CAR INSURANCE

CLASS. Discuss.

1. How could you find out about car insurance?

2. What types of questions would you ask?

Getting Started   5 minutes

 1 READ A CAR INSURANCE RENEWAL NOTICE

CLASS. All drivers in the U.S....

- Have students look at the insurance card. If you have a real card, bring it to class and pass it around.
- Read the questions and call on volunteers to answer.
- Discuss with the class: *What other information appears on an auto insurance card?*

Culture Connection

Most states require drivers to have auto insurance in case of an accident involving injury to persons or damage to property. Auto insurance laws and rates differ from state to state.

Presentation   5 minutes

2 PRACTICE

Ⓐ Once or twice a year, car owners are required...

- Write the words *renew* and *renewal* on the board. Ask: *What do these words mean?* If necessary, point out that the prefix *re-* means *again*.
- Read through the renewal notice with the class.

Language Note

The following terms may be found on an auto insurance renewal notice: *insured: the person named in the policy; policy: the contract between the insured person and the insurance company, which describes the details of the person's insurance; period: an amount of time; vehicle: a car, truck, or motorcycle; agent: the insurance company employee who writes a client's policy.*

Controlled Practice   5 minutes

Ⓑ Read the questions. Circle...

- Have students answer the questions. Then have them compare answers with a partner.
- Go over answers with the whole class.

Communicative Practice   15 minutes

3 TALK ABOUT BUYING CAR INSURANCE

CLASS. Discuss.

- Read each question and call on volunteers to answer.
- List students' responses on the board. For question 2, suggest that students can ask questions corresponding to the information in the renewal notice above.

▬▬ **Expansion: Role Play for 3**

Teaching Tip

While pairs are performing role plays, use the scoring rubric for speaking on page T-xiii to evaluate each student's vocabulary, grammar, fluency, and how well he or she completes the task. You may want to review the completed rubric with the students.

- Have students role-play a conversation between an insurance agent and a prospective customer. The customer can ask the questions from item 2. The agent can answer using information from the renewal form above, for example: Customer: *How much is the deductible?* Agent: *$500.00.*

Controlled Practice   20 minutes

4 PRACTICE

Ⓐ 🎧 **Tom's co-worker Amy is planning...**

- Before listening, have students review the answers to Exercise 3, item 1. Say: *Let's see if the information in the listening matches your ideas.*
- Play CD 2, Track 5. Have students take notes.
- Have students compare answers with a partner.
- Call on individual students to say the answers.
- If students have difficulty answering a question, play the corresponding part of the recording again.

Ⓑ **PAIRS. What are some things...**

- If possible, pair students who have auto insurance with students who don't. You can also form larger groups centered around a student who has insurance.
- Have students complete the activity. Students who have insurance should share their experience.

Ⓒ 🎧 **Now Amy and Tom are talking about...**

- Explain *insurance quote: On the basis of a customer's answers to a set of questions, an insurance agent informs the customer how much his or her policy will cost.*
- Play CD 2, Track 5.
- Have students review their answers to Exercise B Then have them compare answers with a partner.
- Go over the answers with the whole class. If students have difficulty with any items, replay the part of the recording that provides the answer to the item.

Ⓓ 🎧 **Tom mentions several things...**

- Have students predict the answers. List their predictions on the board.
- Play CD 2, Track 6 and have students take notes.
- Check answers. Point to the items on the board and ask: *Were your predictions correct?*

■■ **MULTILEVEL INSTRUCTION for 4D**

Pre-level Have students listen for at least one thing that can raise a person's insurance premiums.

Above-level The instructions for the activity ask students to list three things that can raise premiums. The speaker, Tom, actually mentions six (some are implied.) Have students listen for as many factors as possible.

Communicative Practice   10 minutes

Ⓔ **CLASS. Discuss.**

- Read item 1. Then read each item in Exercise B. Ask students to raise their hands if they checked it.
- Call on one above-level student to explain why insurance companies want to know this information.
- Read item 2. Take a class vote. Ask: *Who thinks it's fair?* Have students raise their hands.
- Call on several speakers to explain their reasons. List the reasons on the board.
- Ask: *Does anyone have a different opinion?* Call on students to raise their hands.

Progress Check

Can you . . . talk about buying car insurance?

Say: *We have practiced talking about buying car insurance. Now, look at the question at the bottom of the page. Can you talk about buying car insurance? Write a checkmark in the box.*

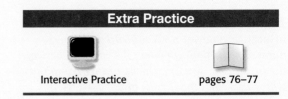

Extra Practice	
Interactive Practice	pages 76–77

A 🔊 Tom's co-worker Amy is planning to buy her first car. Listen to their conversation. Tom and Amy mention three ways to find out about car insurance. What are they? Take notes.

1. from a friend
_____

2. on the Internet
_____

3. in the yellow pages (of the telephone book)
_____

B PAIRS.   What are some things that insurance companies ask when you want to get a quote, or price estimate, for car insurance? Check (✓) the information companies probably ask about.

☐ annual salary   ☐ type of car (year, make, and model, etc.)
☐ age   ☐ safety features
☐ marital status   ☐ when you bought the car
☐ checking account number   ☐ estimated number of miles you will drive each year

C 🔊 Now Amy and Tom are talking about getting a quote. Listen. Were your predictions in Exercise B correct? Change your answers if necessary.

D 🔊 Tom mentions several things that affect a person's car insurance. Listen again. List three things that can raise insurance premiums.

1. the kind/ type of car
_____

2. safety features
_____

3. how many miles per year you will drive
_____
   (*also:* age and marital status)

E CLASS. Discuss.

1. Look back at the things you checked in Exercise B. Why do you think insurance companies want to know about these things?

2. Do you think it's fair for some drivers to pay higher premiums than others? Explain.

Can you...talk about buying car insurance?   ☐

Listening and Speaking

1 BEFORE YOU LISTEN

A Read the tips from a website about car maintenance and repairs.

B CLASS. Discuss.

1. What do the boldfaced words in the tips mean?

2. What can car owners do to keep their cars in good condition?

2 LISTEN

CD2 T7

A Jake Alexander is the host of the radio show *All Things Auto*. Listen. In his opinion, what is his number one car-care tip?

don't delay

CD2 T7

B Read the questions. Then listen to Jake Alexander again. Circle the correct answers.

1. How often should you change the oil in your car?
   a. once a week
   b. once a month
   c. once every three months

2. How often should you check your car's tires?
   a. once a week
   b. once a month
   c. once every three months

3. Where can you find out how much air to put in your tires?
   a. under the hood
   b. under the car
   c. in your owner's manual

4. What color is engine coolant?
   a. green or brown   b. green or yellow   c. red or black

5. What happens when you do regular car maintenance?
   a. You save money.   b. You spend more.   c. You drive more.

File   Edit   View   Favorites   Tools   Help

Back   Search

Address http://www.CarCare4All.com

CarCare4All

A tire's **tread** becomes worn either because it has been used for a long time or because it doesn't have enough air.

Car Maintenance Tips

In addition to gas, don't forget the other things that you must put into your car. **Oil** keeps your car's engine running well. **Engine coolant** keeps the engine from getting too hot. Other **fluids** that you should check and add to your car when necessary are **transmission fluid** and **brake fluid**. And then there's the **washer fluid**. After all, you need to see out your windows. Finally, remember that the **air pressure**, or amount of air in your tires, is important. Also keep in mind that what goes in sometimes comes out, so be on the lookout for **leaks**.

Getting Started 10 minutes

1 BEFORE YOU LISTEN

Ⓐ Read the tips from a website...

- Have students read silently. Then form cross-ability groups.
- Tell students to define as many terms as possible.
- Give a time limit for discussion. Walk around and provide help as needed.
- Go over all the terms with the whole class. Have a volunteer say what each boldfaced item is. If no one knows, provide the definition yourself.

MULTILEVEL INSTRUCTION for 1A

Cross-ability In each group, have an above-level student read the passage out loud while pre-level students read silently. Above-level students should also help other group members by defining the vocabulary.

Ⓑ CLASS. Discuss.

- Say the phrase *in good condition.* Have students repeat. Explain: *Something is working properly when it is in good condition.*
- Have students look at the boldfaced items in the website tips and repeat them. Point out that the vowel sounds in *tread* and *leak* are different although they use the same spelling. Tell them to form sentences about those items. For example, for *oil,* they can say: *You should check the oil in your car regularly.*
- List students' answers on the board.

Presentation 5 minutes

2 LISTEN

Ⓐ 💿 Jake Alexander is the host...

- Remind students to listen specifically for the answer to the question. It is not necessary to understand every word.
- Play CD 2, Track 7.
- Call on a volunteer to answer the question. Note: The answer is *Don't delay. Do it today.* Students may not know the word *delay.* Explain as needed: *Don't delay means* don't postpone or waste time.

Controlled Practice 5 minutes

Ⓑ 💿 Read the questions. Then listen...

- Have students read the questions and predict the answers.
- Play Track 7 again. Have students listen and circle the correct answers.
- Have students complete the exercise alone or in pairs.
- Check answers. If students have difficulty answering a question, play the corresponding part of the recording again.

Presentation
20 minutes

3 CONVERSATION

Pronunciation Watch

- On the board, write: *I'd like to buy a new car. Maybe I'll get a Honda.* Read both sentences, stressing the last word of each sentence. Ask students: *Which word has the strongest stress?* (the last one) *What happens to the intonation?* (It rises, then falls.) Say the sentences again and have students repeat.
- Read the Pronunciation Watch note.

Language Note

Typically, the word with the heaviest stress is the last <u>content</u> word (that is, noun, verb, adjective, or -*ly* adverb) of a sentence or clause—not necessarily the last word. In the sentence, *I'd like to buy a new car,* the word *car* gets the heaviest stress. In contrast, in the sentence, *I'd like to buy a blue one,* the heaviest stress falls on the word *blue* because the last word, *one,* is a pronoun, and pronouns typically do not receive heavy stress.

A **Listen to the sentences. Notice...**

- Play CD 2, Track 8. Have students listen.
- Play Track 8 again. Have students listen and repeat.

Teaching Tip

Suggest that students close their books when they are listening to items in a pronunciation lesson. Listening without reading will help students focus on the sound.

B **Listen to these sounds...**

- Write the words *squeal, squeak,* and *ping* on the board.
- Play CD 2, Track 9. Have students listen. Point to the words on the board as they are explained in the audio.

C **Lester is calling an auto repair shop...**

- Play CD 2, Track 10. Have students listen and read along silently.

- Check comprehension. Ask: *What is the problem with Lester's car? When does the mechanic tell him to bring it in?*

Controlled Practice
5 minutes

4 PRACTICE

A **PAIRS. Practice the conversation.**

- Form pairs of similar ability and have students practice reading at least twice. They should practice reading both roles.
- Walk around and listen as students are practicing. Correct errors in sentence stress.
- Ask volunteers to perform the conversation.

■■■ **MULTILEVEL INSTRUCTION for 4A**

Pre-level Have students practice the same role several times.

Above-level After students read the conversation in the book, have them close their books and practice again without reading.

Communicative Practice
15 minutes

B **MAKE IT PERSONAL. What do you know...**

STEP 1. Write four car-care tips.

- Have students work alone or in pairs.

STEP 2. CLASS. Share your car-care tips.

- Go around the room and have students share their tips. Have them write each new tip on the board.
- Read the sentences and correct errors as needed.

■■■ **Expansion: Speaking Practice for STEP 2**

- Have an Ask the Expert session in your class. First, find out if any of your students work as mechanics or if they are good at car repairs. Designate that person as the expert. Have other students ask the expert about car maintenance or car repair.

Extra Practice

Interactive Practice

3 CONVERSATION

Pronunciation Watch

Use stress and intonation to show which word in a clause or sentence is the most important. Make your voice go up on that word and make the vowel extra long. The most important word is often the last word in a clause or sentence.

CD2 T8

A Listen to the sentences. Notice how the stress and intonation highlight the most important word. Then listen again and repeat.

Can you tell me what the **prob**lem is?

When I looked under the **car** this morning, I noticed a dark **stain**.

You might have an **oil** leak.

I'll see you to**mo**rrow, then.

CD2 T9

B Listen to these sounds: a squeal, a squeak, and a ping. Have you ever heard any of these sounds in a car?

CD2 T10

C Lester is calling an auto repair shop. Listen and read.

Mechanic: Osman's Auto Repair. How can I help you?

Lester: I want to know if I can bring my car in tomorrow.

Mechanic: Sure. Can you tell me what the problem is?

Lester: When I looked under the car this morning, I noticed a dark stain.

Mechanic: You might have an oil leak. Bring the car in tomorrow morning, and we'll take a look at it. We open at 7:00 A.M.

Lester: Thanks. I'll see you tomorrow, then.

4 PRACTICE

A PAIRS. Practice the conversation.

B MAKE IT PERSONAL. What do you know about car maintenance?

STEP 1. Write four car-care tips.

STEP 2. CLASS. Share your car-care tips.

Grammar

Embedded *wh-* Questions

Direct question	Embedded *wh-* question		
What is the problem?	Can you tell me	**what**	**the problem is**?
Why does the "Check Engine" light go on?	Could you explain	**why**	**the "Check Engine" light goes on**?
When did the noises start?	I don't know	**when**	**the noises started**.
What time will my car be ready?	I wonder	**what**	**time my car will be ready**.
How much will the repairs cost?	I want to know	**how**	**much the repairs will cost**.

1 PRACTICE

Grammar Watch

- Use embedded questions to ask for information politely or to express information about which you are uncertain.
- Put embedded questions inside questions such as *Do you know…?* inside statements such as *I don't know….* and
- Use statement word order (subject + verb) for most embedded questions.

A Read the conversation. Underline three embedded *wh-* questions.

A: Do you know if the car will be ready tomorrow?

B: Yes, it will. I'm a little worried. I don't know how much the repairs are going to cost.

A: I can't believe you didn't get a written estimate from the mechanic! He should tell you what it's going to cost before he begins work on your car.

B: Of course you're right. I don't know why I didn't think of that.

B Complete the conversation. Put the words in the correct order to form questions—both direct and embedded.

Katy: Do you know <u>where the receipt from the mechanic is</u> ?
(is/the/receipt/where/the/from/mechanic)

Doug: I don't remember <u>what I did with it</u> when I came home.
(it/with/what/did/I)

Katy: Mark, please tell me. <u>Where is that receipt</u> ?
(is/where/receipt/that)

Doug: It's probably in my wallet. Can you tell me <u>why it is so important</u> ?
(so/why/it/is/important)

Katy: I want to know <u>how much coolant the mechanic put</u> in the radiator.
(coolant/how much/the/put/mechanic)

Doug: <u>Why do you need to know that</u> ?
(do/need/you/know/to/why/that)

Katy: There's steam coming from the hood. I want to find out <u>what the problem is</u>. Maybe he put in too much coolant,
(the/is/what/problem)
or not enough.

Getting Started   10 minutes

- On the board, write this mini-dialogue: *Mechanic: What's the problem? Car owner: I don't know.*
- Point to the mechanic's question. Ask the class: *What did the mechanic ask the customer?* Write: *The mechanic asked the customer* and have students complete the statement. Students are likely to say: *The mechanic asked the customer what is the problem.* Write this incorrect response on the board. Then, very obviously, erase the word *is* and write it at the end of the sentence. Read the corrected sentence and have the class repeat.
- Point to the customer's answer. Ask: *What doesn't the customer know?* Write: *The customer doesn't know* and elicit *what the problem is* and write it on the board. Again, make it obvious that the verb is attached at the end of the sentence.
- Underline the embedded question and say: *A question that comes after another question or statement is called an* embedded question. *Embedded* means inside.

Language Note

In embedded clauses, the word order is subject + verb. Sometimes this means the verb will be the last word in the clause, for example, *Can you tell me what the problem* is? But if the sentence ends with a prepositional phrase or an adverb, the verb precedes them, for example: *I don't know what I did with my keys.*

Presentation   15 minutes

Embedded *wh-* questions

- Copy the items from the grammar chart onto the board. Read the direct questions and the corresponding embedded questions. Explain that *I wonder* means *I would like to know the answer to something.*
- Read the first Grammar Watch note. Point out that adding *please* makes a question even more polite, for *example, Can you please tell me what time it is?*
- Read the second Grammar Watch note. Say: *In other words, we can put one question inside another question.* Have students look at the first two examples. Point to the items on the left and say: *These are direct questions.* Then point to the embedded questions. Point out that *Can you tell*

me and *Could you explain* are also questions, so the embedded questions have question marks at the end.
- Read the third note. Then have students look at the third and fourth examples. Say: *We can also put a question inside statements.* Explain that *I don't know* and *I wonder* are statements; therefore, the statements with the embedded questions end with a period.

Expansion: Grammar Practice

- Remind students that embedded questions are polite, so we often use them when we're speaking with strangers. Tell the class to imagine that they are waiting for a bus at a crowded bus stop. Have them write on a slip of paper a direct question they might ask a stranger, for example, *What time is it? Which bus goes downtown?* or *Has the number 10 bus already come?*
- Collect the slips and put them into a box or hat.
- Call students to the front of the room. Have them pull a slip out of the hat and form an embedded question with it, for example, *Can you tell me what time it is?*
- Have another student answer with *I don't know,* for example, *Sorry, I don't know what time it is.*

Controlled Practice   10 minutes

1 PRACTICE

Ⓐ Read the conversation. Underline...

- Read the example with the class.
- Have students do the exercise.
- Call on students to read the embedded questions they underlined.

Ⓑ Complete the conversation. Put the words...

- Read the example. Remind students that the verb in the embedded question comes after the subject.
- Have students complete the remaining items. While they are working, walk around and provide help as needed. Note: The sixth item is not an embedded question.
- Have students compare answers with a partner.
- Have students come to the board and write the questions. Correct errors as needed.

Presentation   10 minutes

Embedded *Yes/No* Questions

- Copy the items from the grammar chart onto the board. Read the direct questions and the corresponding embedded questions. Explain that *if* and *whether* mean the same thing, though *whether* is more formal.

> **Language Note**
>
> *If* and *whether* are similar in meaning but somewhat different in usage. *Whether* can be used with the phrase *or not*, for example, *I don't know whether I need new tires or not* and *I don't know whether or not I need new tires.*

- Tell students that all the information from the Grammar Watch notes on page 134 is also true for embedded *yes/no* questions. The punctuation and word order are also the same.

> **Expansion: Grammar Practice**
>
> - Make a two-column chart on the board. In the left column, write *Can you tell me, Do you know, I don't know,* and *I wonder.* In the right column write four or five *yes/no* questions, for example, *Does the car need oil? Is the tire pressure too low? Has the bus come yet? Can I take my bicycle on the bus?*
> - Have students form embedded questions by choosing one item from the left column and one item from the right. Have them write their sentences on the board.
> - Read the sentences on the board and correct any errors.

Controlled Practice   5 minutes

2 PRACTICE

A Circle one embedded *yes/no* question...

- Have students look at the practice on page 134 and complete the exercise.
- Ask them which embedded question they circled. (*Do you know if the car will be ready tomorrow?*)

B Pilar is shopping in an auto parts store. Change...

- Read the example. Remind students that the verb in the embedded question comes after the subject.
- Have students complete the remaining items.

C Correct the mistakes in the embedded questions...

- Read the example.
- Have students complete the remaining items.

Communicative Practice   10 minutes

Show what you know!

CLASS. What other things do you want to know...

- Do an example with the class. Ask an embedded question, for example, *Can someone tell me where I can buy leather seat covers?* Call on one person to answer.
- Have each student write one embedded question.
- Call on students to ask and answer the questions.

> **Community Building**
>
> - Invite a professional mechanic to be a guest speaker in your class.
> - Before class, have students write questions they would like to ask the speaker. For example, students could ask the speaker about his or her job, about the parts of a car or car repair in general, or about a specific problem they have or have had with a particular car.

Progress Check

Can you . . . discuss car maintenance and repairs?

Say: *We have practiced discussing car maintenance and repairs. Now, look at the question at the bottom of the page. Can you discuss car maintenance and repairs? Write a checkmark in the box.*

Extra Practice

Interactive Practice   pages 78–79

Embedded *Yes/No* Questions

Direct question	Embedded *Yes /No* question		
Does my car need an oil change?	Can you tell me		**my car needs an oil change?**
Can I bring my car in tomorrow?	I want to know	**if** **whether**	**I can bring my car in tomorrow.**
Did they fix the problem?	Do you know		**they fixed the problem?**

2 PRACTICE

A Circle one embedded *Yes/No* question in Exercise 1A.

B Pilar is shopping in an auto parts store. Change the direct questions in parentheses to embedded questions. Include a period or a question mark.

Pilar: Can you tell me _if you have windshield wipers for a 2006 Honda Accord?_
(Do you have windshield wipers for a 2006 Honda Accord?)

Salesperson: Yes, ma'am, we do. They're in Aisle 6.

Pilar: Do you know _____ if they are on sale? _____
(Are they on sale?)

Salesperson: I'm not sure _____ if the sale ended yesterday. _____ I'll find out.
(Did the sale end yesterday?)

Pilar: Could you also find out _____ if I will need a special bulb for the turn signal? _____
(Will I need a special bulb for the turn signal?)

C Correct the mistakes in the embedded questions about car maintenance and repairs.

1. He wants to know ~~does~~ [if] the car ~~need~~ [needs] new brakes.

2. They asked whether ~~was it~~ [it was] safe to drive with a damaged tire.

3. Can you tell me ~~does~~ [if] the engine ~~need~~ [needs] more coolant?

4. We wonder ~~that~~ [if] the leak is coming from the radiator[?]~~.~~

5. The mechanic wasn't sure ~~did~~ [if] they ~~have~~ [had] the parts he needed to repair my car.

Show what you know! Discuss car maintenance and repairs

CLASS. What other things do you want to know about car maintenance and repairs? Write some embedded questions. Then take turns asking and answering them.

Can you...discuss car maintenance and repairs? ☐

Reading

1 BEFORE YOU READ

PAIRS. Look at the title and the headings for each section of the article. Predict. What is the article about?

2 READ

CD2 T11

Read and listen. Was your prediction correct? What do you think a "lemon" is? What happened to Shawn Chastain?

A Sour Purchase Turns Sweet

When Shawn Chastain came home with his new SUV, he thought he had bought the car of his dreams. Shawn had recently become a new father, and it was important for him to have a safe, **reliable** vehicle for his family. However, in just a few months, his dream turned into a nightmare when the "Check Engine" light came on and never went off. Shawn's SUV was a lemon.

No one knew what the problem was.

As soon as the trouble started, Shawn followed the procedures in his warranty. He took his SUV to the dealership where he had made his purchase, but the mechanics there couldn't figure out why the "Check Engine" light was on. They made several repairs, but nothing solved the problem, and Shawn wondered if his vehicle was safe. Shawn kept written records of what

happened on each of his trips to the dealership—all six of them! Then he decided it was time to contact the Texas Department of Transportation (TexDOT).

TexDOT provided a solution.

In Texas, if a vehicle is a lemon, the manufacturer must repair it, replace it, or buy it back. However, the owner has **responsibilities**, too.

According to TexDOT officials, Shawn Chastain gave them the proof they needed to **enforce** the Texas law. He

had kept a complete record of all his **interactions** with the manufacturer and dealer, including all repair orders, letters, and phone calls. Because of Shawn's careful record-keeping, TexDOT was able to reach an agreement with the manufacturer.

Shawn's problem caused him months of **aggravation**, but he finally got satisfaction. In the end, the manufacturer bought back his SUV. Thanks to that money, Shawn and his family finally own a car they can trust.

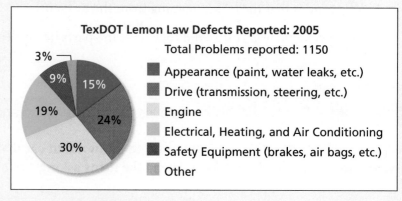

TexDOT Lemon Law Defects Reported: 2005

Total Problems reported: 1150

- 15% — Appearance (paint, water leaks, etc.)
- 24% — Drive (transmission, steering, etc.)
- 30% — Engine
- 19% — Electrical, Heating, and Air Conditioning
- 9% — Safety Equipment (brakes, air bags, etc.)
- 3% — Other

Getting Started   10 minutes

1 BEFORE YOU READ

- Read the lesson title. If necessary, define *consumer* as *someone who buys goods or services.*
- Define *consumer protection laws* as *laws that protect consumers against, for example, dangerous or defective products, fraud, and credit card theft.*

PAIRS. Look at the title...

- Read the title. Ask the class: *What kind of taste is sour? Is it good or bad? Is a* sour purchase *good or bad? What does* turn *mean here? (change) What does the title mean, in other words?* (a bad purchase changed into a good one)
- Read the two subheadings. On the basis of this information, ask students: *What information is in the article?* (a problem and a solution)
- Say: *If you look at the title and the headings, what do you think the article is about?* List students' predictions on the board.

   Expansion: Reading Practice for 1

- Have students look at the article's title, headings, and art. Based on this information, have them write two questions they would like the article to answer, for example: *What was the* sour purchase? *Who made the purchase? What is* TexDOT? *What does the art show? What is a* lemon law? *What is a* defect?
- Call on students to share their questions. Write them on the board.
- Explain that asking questions about a text provides a purpose for reading and helps people to read faster, with better concentration.

Presentation   15 minutes

2 READ

Ⓐ 💿 **Read and listen. Was your prediction...**

- Have students read silently. Give a time limit, but extend the reading time if necessary.
- Point to the predictions on board and ask: *Were your predictions correct?* Have a volunteer restate the topic of the article.
- Tell students they are going to do an exercise to improve reading fluency. Play CD 2, Track 11. Have students read along as they listen to the audio.
- Call on students to answer the other questions. Elicit the definition of a *lemon.* Have students provide examples, if possible.

Answer: A lemon is a car that has problems.

- Have another student answer the question about Shawn Chastain.

Possible answers: Shawn kept a complete record of all interactions with the manufacturer and dealer. Because of this, the TexDOT was able to help him solve his car problems.

- Call on students to answer the questions from the Expansion activity.

Controlled Practice   15 minutes

3 CHECK YOUR UNDERSTANDING

A Complete the statements. Circle...

- Have students do the exercise. Give a time limit.
- Have them compare answers with a partner.

Reading Skill: Use Visuals

- Read the *Reading Skill*. Explain that *visual* means *something we can see*. Visuals include charts, graphs, photos, and illustrations—all non-text items that accompany a reading.
- *Charts* tend to present information in the form of tables, with columns and rows. *Graphs* can take other shapes, for example, a pie chart, a bar graph, a line graph, a pictograph, etc.

B Read the Reading Skill. Then look at the pie chart...

- Look at the pie chart with the class. Ask: *What is the pie chart about?* (the number of lemon law defects that were reported to the Texas Department of Transportation in 2005)
- Hold up your book and point to the pie chart. Say: *This is called a* pie chart.
- Point to the key. Say: *This is called the* key. *It explains the colors and the parts of the pie chart.*
- Pair students and have them answer the questions.
- As a follow-up, have students form sentences about the percentage of defects shown in the pie chart.

4 WORD WORK

Find the boldfaced words...

- On the board write *discuss/discussion*. Point to the first word and ask: *What's the part of speech—the grammar—of this word?* (verb) Then point to the second word and ask again: *What's the part of speech of this word?* (noun) *How do you know?* (The *-ion* ending shows that the word is a noun.) Explain that endings that identify a word's part of speech, or grammar, are called *suffixes*.

- Make a three-column chart on the board with the headings *Adjective, Verb,* and *Noun.* Read each boldfaced word in the text and have students say in which column it belongs. Circle the suffixes.
- Elicit other words that end with the same suffixes.
- Form cross-ability pairs. Have students find the boldfaced words in the text, read the sentence in which they appear and guess what they mean.
- Have students work together to circle the correct words. Go over the answers.

▬▬ **MULTILEVEL INSTRUCTION for 4**
Cross-ability Have the above-level student help the lower-level student use the context to guess the meaning of the boldfaced words.

▬▬ **Expansion: Vocabulary Practice for 4**

- Have students write sentences using the words in Exercise 4 and the other boldfaced words from the reading (*reliable, enforce, record, interaction,* and *aggravation*).
- For each word, call on several students to share their sentences with the whole class.

Communicative Practice   20 minutes

Show what you know!

- Have students find information about lemon laws in their own state.
- Direct them to sources of information about lemon laws. In addition to their state's DMV website, they can also consult a lawyer who specializes in consumer protection cases, an insurance agent, their state's Department of Consumer Affairs, and the Internet in general (students can do a search for *state name + lemon law*).
- Have students work in teams to locate the answers and report their findings to the class.

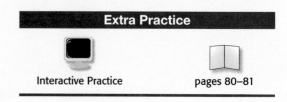

Extra Practice

Interactive Practice   pages 80–81

3

CHECK YOUR UNDERSTANDING

A Complete the statements. Circle the correct answers.

1. Shawn Chastain was worried about _____.
   a. the appearance of his SUV   (b.) the safety of his SUV   c. the speed of his SUV

2. Shawn Chastain used the Texas lemon laws _____.
   (a.) as soon as his problems started
   b. before he went to TexDOT
   c. after he had given the dealer many opportunities to fix his SUV

3. Shawn took the money that he received from the manufacturer and probably _____.
   a. got another SUV in the same make and model
   (b.) did research before he bought another vehicle
   c. repaired his SUV

B Read the Reading Skill. Then look at the pie chart on page 136 and answer the questions.

> **Reading Skill:** Use Visuals
>
> Use charts, graphs, and other visuals to learn important facts.

1,150

1. What was the total number of problems reported to TexDOT?

2. What was the most common problem reported? What percentage of defects were related to safety equipment?

engine problems, 9 percent

4

WORD WORK

Find the boldfaced words in the article and guess their meanings from the context. Then complete the sentences using the correct forms of those words. Circle the correct words.

1. TexDOT decided it was the manufacturer's (**responsiblity**) / **responsible** to buy back Shawn's car.

2. (**Reliablility**) / **Reliable** is an important factor to consider when buying a new or used car.

3. Many cars have an **interaction** / (**interactive**) navigational system that gives drivers directions.

4. The Department of Transportation is responsible for the (**enforcement**) / **enforce** of certain laws.

Show what you know!   Discuss consumer-protection laws

Research lemon laws or other consumer-protection laws in the state where you live. Report to the class. Make sure your report describes
- what the law covers,
- what the manufacturer must do according to the law,
- whether the consumer has any responsibilities according to the law.

Listening and Speaking

1   BEFORE YOU LISTEN

PAIRS. Nora Peters and Frank Liu were involved in a fender bender (a car accident that isn't very serious). What do you think probably happened?

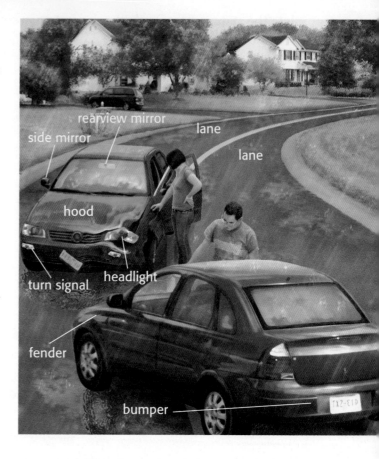

2   LISTEN

CD2 T12

A   Listen. Why did the accident happen? Check (✓) the cause.

- ☐ a. Nora was talking on her cell phone.
- ☐ b. Frank didn't put on his turn signal.
- ☐ c. Nora was speeding.
- ☑ d. Frank saw Nora's car too late.

CD2 T12

B   Listen to Nora and Frank's conversation again. Then answer the questions.

1. Was anyone hurt in the accident?   no
2. Why did Nora want to find her cell phone?   to call the police
3. Does Frank have insurance? How do you know?   yes, he has an insurance card
4. What advice did Nora get from her insurance agent?   take pictures of the damaged cars

CD2 T12

C   Listen to the conversation again. What four things did Nora and Frank go back to get from their cars?

1. cell phone
2. insurance card
3. registration
4. driver's license

D   GROUPS. Discuss. What do you think Nora and Frank do next?

Getting Started   5 minutes

 BEFORE YOU LISTEN

PAIRS. Nora Peters and Frank Liu were...

- Have students look at the picture. Say each car part and have the class repeat.
- Pair students and have them answer the question.
- Bring the class back together and call on volunteers to explain the function and importance of each car part.

Presentation   5 minutes

 LISTEN

A 💿 **Listen. Why did the...**

- Ask the class if anyone has been involved in a *fender bender*. Say: *A fender bender is a minor car accident.* Refer students to the illustration on page 138. Point out the fender. Have the student describe the accident and what happened afterwards. If students cannot provide an example, tell of an incident from your own experience.
- Remind students to listen for the answer to the question. They do not need to understand every word.
- Play CD 2, Track 12.
- Have students choose their answer and compare with a partner.
- Play Track 12 again, if necessary.
- Call on a student to say the answer. Ask the class: *Is that correct?*

Controlled Practice   10 minutes

B 💿 **Listen to Nora and Frank's...**

- Have students read the questions and predict the answers before listening.
- Play Track 12 again.
- Call on students to answer the questions. Replay the recording if necessary.

> **Teaching Tip**
>
> In exercises that ask students to listen for multiple pieces of information, you can simplify the task for pre-level students by asking them to listen specifically for just one.

C 💿 **Listen to the conversation again...**

- Play Track 12 again.
- Call on students to say the answers. Write them on the board.

Communicative Practice   10 minutes

D GROUPS. Discuss. **What do you think Nora...**

- Form groups. Have each group choose a timekeeper, a note-taker, and a reporter.
- Give a time limit for discussion. While students are talking, walk around and provide help as needed.
- Have each group's reporter share the group's answers to the questions.

Expansion: Speaking Practice for 2D

- Write the following questions on the board. *In an accident, what should you do if . . . 1. someone is injured? 2. the other driver refuses to show you his or her driver's license? 3. the other driver starts shouting at you? 4. the other driver is drunk? 5. you discover that your vehicle registration or insurance information is not in your car? 6. you do not have a cell phone with a camera?*
- Form groups. Have students discuss the questions.
- Have students share their ideas with the class.

Presentation   10 minutes

3 CONVERSATION

Pronunciation Watch

- On the board, write: *I'd like to go to the bank this afternoon. / At 5 P.M., I'd already finished work.* Point to *I'd* in the two sentences. Ask: *What does the 'd mean in the first sentence?* (would) *What does the 'd mean in the second sentence?* (had)
- Say the two sentences. Ask: *Does I'd sound the same or different in the two sentences?* (the same)
- Read the Pronunciation Watch note. Point out that pronouns with *'d* are not normally stressed. Therefore, it's hard to hear the *'d*.

A **Listen to the sentences. Notice...**

- Play CD 2, Track 13. Have students listen.
- Play Track 13 again. Have students listen and repeat.

Controlled Practice   10 minutes

B **Listen to the sentences. Circle...**

- On the board, write: *1. She/She'd; 2. He/He'd; 3. He/He'd; 4. We/We'd; 5. They/They'd.*
- Play Track 14. Stop after item 1 and elicit the answer from students.
- Play the rest of Track 14. Have students complete the exercise.
- Check answers.

4 PRACTICE

A **Nora is talking to an officer. Listen and read...**

- Play Track 15. Have students listen and read along silently.
- Check comprehension. Ask: *What does Nora need to fill out? Which documents does the officer ask to see? Where did the accident happen? Had anything unusual happened before the accident?*

B **PAIRS. Practice the conversation.**

- Form pairs and have students take turns reading each role.
- Take notes on pronunciation errors involving features that have been taught so far.
- Go over pronunciation errors. Have the class repeat the correct form.
- Ask volunteers to perform the conversation.

Communicative Practice   10 minutes

C **ROLE PLAY. PAIRS. Role-play this situation.**

> **Teaching Tip**
>
> While pairs are performing role plays, use the scoring rubric for speaking on page T-iii to evaluate each student's vocabulary, grammar, fluency, and how well he or she completes the task. You may want to review the completed rubric with the students.

- Read the role descriptions.
- With the class, make a list of questions the police officer might ask. Write them on the board.
- Model the activity with an above-level student. Have the student play the role of the police officer.
- Form cross-ability pairs. Tell them to practice at least twice.
- Give a time limit. Walk around and provide help as needed.
- Have volunteers role play their conversation.

MULTILEVEL INSTRUCTION for 4C

Cross-ability Have the higher-level student play the role of Student A (the driver). Have the lower-level student play the role of Student B (the police officer) and use the questions on the board.

Extra Practice

Interactive Practice

CD2 T13

A 🔘 **Listen to the sentences. Notice that the pronoun +'d is pronounced as only one syllable. Then listen again and repeat.**

Pronunciation Watch

Had and *would* usually have a short, weak pronunciation when used with another verb. After a pronoun, use the contraction *'d* for either *had* or *would*.

'd = would   **I'd** rather drive a small car.

               We'd prefer a safe car.

'd = had   **He'd** started changing lanes.

               She'd already checked her car.

CD2 T14

B 🔘 **Listen to the sentences. Circle the words you hear.**

1. **(She)** / She'd slowed down because of the rain.
2. **He** / **(He'd)** already started moving into the right lane.
3. **(He)** / He'd left his cell phone in the car.
4. **We** / **(We'd)** prefer to buy from a dealer.
5. **They** / **(They'd)** like the red car.

CD2 T15

A 🔘 **Nora is talking to an officer. Listen and read. What does the officer ask to see?**

Officer: What can I do for you?

Nora: My name is Nora Peters. I was just involved in a car accident.

Officer: You'll have to fill out an accident report. Can I see your driver's license, vehicle registration, and insurance card?

Nora: Certainly. Here they are.

Officer: Thank you. Now, exactly where did the accident happen?

Nora: On Center Street, near Ashland Avenue.

Officer: Had anything unusual happened before the accident?

Nora: Not really. It was raining, and I had just slowed down. …

B PAIRS. **Practice the conversation.**

C ROLE PLAY. PAIRS. **Role-play this situation.**

Student A: You are talking to a police officer about a car accident. Tell the officer when, where, and how the accident happened. Describe the damage to your car.

Student B: You are a police officer at the Green Avenue Police Station. Get personal information and details about the accident that Student A was involved in.

Grammar

Past perfect statements

Nora **had** just **started** to slow down when she saw Frank's car.

Frank **hadn't noticed** the car coming from the opposite direction when he started to make his turn.

Past perfect questions and answers

A: **Had** Nora **looked** at the damage to her car before she talked to Frank?
B: Yes, she **had**.

A: When Frank and Nora called the police station, **had** they already **taken** pictures?
B: No, they **hadn't**.

A: Where **had** Frank **left** his cell phone?
B: He**'d left** it in his car.

Grammar Watch

Use the past perfect to show time order in the past. The past perfect shows that one action happened earlier than the other.

*Frank **had started** moving into the left lane before he saw Nora.*

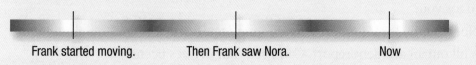

| Frank started moving. | Then Frank saw Nora. | Now |

1 PRACTICE

There was an accident on Center Avenue yesterday evening. Read the sentences. Decide which action happened first and which one happened second. Mark the earlier action *1* and the later action *2*.

                                    1   2
1. Sarah Miller had just gone into her favorite video store when she heard a loud crash.

            2   1
2. She rushed out of the store. There had been a car accident at the corner.

        1   2
3. Sarah had left her cell phone at home, so she went back to the store to call 911.

                2   1
4. One of the drivers was yelling that another driver hadn't used his turn signal.

                2   1
5. When Sarah came out of the store, all the drivers had gotten out of their cars.

Lesson 8 Describe a car accident

Getting Started

- On the board, write: *Judy entered the cafeteria. Sam left.* Write *1* above *entered* and *2* above *left*. Ask: *How can we make one sentence that shows this order of events?* Elicit one or more of the following sentences: *When Judy entered the cafeteria, Sam left; Sam left after (when) Judy entered the cafeteria; As soon as Judy entered the cafeteria, Sam left.* Write these sentences on the board.

- Erase *1* and *2* and write them again, reversing the order. Again ask: *How we can make one sentence showing this order of events?* Students may respond with *Sam left before Judy entered the cafeteria.* If so, write this sentence on the board. Then say: *Here's another way of saying the same thing.* On the board write: *By the time Judy entered the cafeteria, Sam had left.*

- Underline *had left* and say: *This is the past perfect tense. It consists of* had (not) + *past participle.* Write the formula on the board.

Presentation
15 minutes

Past perfect statements, questions, and answers

- Read the Grammar Watch note.

- Copy the grammar chart onto the board. Read each sentence and have students tell you which event happened (or didn't happen) first. Write *1* above the past perfect verb.

- Circle the adverbs *when* and *before*. Explain that the past perfect is often used in sentences with an adverb clause and a main clause.

- Point to the first example. Explain that *just* emphasizes that the first event occurred shortly before the second one.

- Focus on the question with *already*. Explain that the past perfect is often used to emphasize that one event was finished (or not) before another event happened.

- In the questions, remind students of the word order: *had* + subject + past participle, for example, *Had Nora looked . . . ?*

Controlled Practice
15 minutes

1 PRACTICE

There was an accident on Center Avenue...

- Read item 1 with the class.

- Have students complete the exercise alone or in pairs. Walk around and provide help as needed.

- Have students compare answers with a partner.

- Check answers. For each item, have students say which word they marked with *1* and which word they marked with *2*.

Expansion: Grammar Practice for 1

- On a slip of paper, have each student write down an activity he or she did yesterday, for example, *talked to my mother, got gas,* or *walked my son to school.*

- Collect the slips and put them into a box or hat.

- On the board, write: *I had just _____ when _____.*

- Have students take turns picking a slip out of the box and forming a sentence using the formula on the board. For example, if the slip says *talked to my mother,* the student could say *I had just talked to my mother when my father called.*

- Model one or two examples.

- Remind students to use the past participle, not the past, with *had just*. However, the verb in the main clause should be in the past.

Lesson 8 Describe a car accident

2 PRACTICE

A Match the clauses to describe...

- Read item 1.
- Have students complete the exercise.
- Have them compare answers with a partner.
- Check answers. Have students read the complete sentences.

B Complete the conversations. Use...

- Read the example with an above-level student.
- Have students complete the exercise alone or in pairs. Walk around and provide help as needed.
- Call on pairs of students to read the completed items. Make corrections as needed.

Expansion: Speaking Practice for 2B

- Pair students and have them practice reading the conversations. Then have them switch roles.
- Call on pairs to perform the conversations in front of the class.

Communicative Practice   20 minutes

Show what you know!

GROUPS. Discuss. Talk about a car accident...

STEP 1. Describe what happened. Remember...

- Tell students to take out a piece of paper and list the events just before, during, and after their accident. Tell them to include five or six events. If students have not had an accident, tell them to imagine one.
- Demonstrate by telling about an accident you have had. For example, *I had just stopped at a red light when a truck ran into me. The truck pushed my car into the intersection. Unfortunately, there was a pedestrian in the crosswalk right in front of my car . . .*
- Form groups. Have students use their notes to tell about their accidents.

STEP 2. Ask and answer questions...

- As each student is telling about his or her accident, members of the group should ask questions with *who, what, when, where, why,* and *how* to elicit more details about what happened.

Expansion: Speaking Practice for Show What You Know

- On the Internet you can find photographs of car accidents. (Do a search for *car crashes*.) Find some photos that are not violent. Make copies of several accidents for the class.
- Group students and give each group a photo. Have them invent stories describing what happened just before, during, and after the accident.
- Have a representative from each group show the photo and repeat the story for the class.

Progress Check

Can you . . . describe a car accident?

Say: *We have practiced describing a car accident. Now, look at the question at the bottom of the page. Can you describe a car accident? Write a checkmark in the box.*

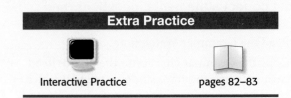

Extra Practice	
Interactive Practice	pages 82–83

A Match the clauses to describe what happened before a number of car accidents.

1. __d__ It had rained,

2. __e__ It was 10:00 P.M.,

3. __f__ Lucy had dropped her cell phone,

4. __b__ Bob Park moved into the left lane,

5. __c__ Victoria Gomez had stepped on the gas

6. __a__ Kim Truong didn't stop at the intersection

a. because she hadn't seen the red light.

b. but he hadn't used his turn signal.

c. right before she saw the cars in front of her.

d. and the roads were wet.

e. but the streetlights hadn't come on yet.

f. so she reached down to get it.

B Complete the conversations. Use the past perfect.

1. **A:** What happened to your car?

   B: I had an accident last week. I ____had____ just ___pulled___ onto the highway
   (pull)
   when a truck ran into me.

   A: That's terrible! Did anyone get hurt?

   B: The truck driver had minor injuries because he __had not remembered__ to put on his seatbelt.
   (not remember)

   A: ___Have___ you ever ___had___ an accident before?
   (have)

   B: Yes. I was in a fender bender last year.

2. **A:** Felix and I were in an accident yesterday.

   B: Oh, no! Is everyone all right?

   A: Fortunately, no one got hurt. But you know, Felix is a terrible driver.

   B: I agree. ___Had___ you ever ___driven___ with him before?
   (drive)

   A: No, I ___had not___. Yesterday was the first time—and the last!
   (not have)

Show what you know! Describe a car accident

GROUPS. Discuss. Talk about a car accident that you have been involved in or seen.

STEP 1. Describe what happened. Remember to use the past perfect to show time order in the past.

STEP 2. Ask and answer questions about the accidents.

Can you...describe a car accident? ☐

Write about a good or bad purchase

Writing

1 BEFORE YOU WRITE

A GROUPS. Discuss.

1. What is a *major purchase*?

2. What major purchases have you made? Make a list.

B CLASS. Share your lists.

C Read the writing model. Why was the writer's purchase a good one?   The car is safe and reliable.
The writer did a lot of research.

Down with Buyer's Remorse!

Some people suffer from buyer's remorse. They make major purchases quickly and then wonder if they did the right thing. I'm different. I shop carefully and feel good about my decision afterward. I recently used my shopping skills to buy an incredible used car. First, I did research on several different websites and looked at ads in the local newspaper. I knew that I would rather have a four-door than a two-door model, but I checked the prices for both. I also found out about important safety features. Next, I did more research to learn about repair costs and gas mileage. I decided to look for a small hybrid. Several weeks later, I found exactly what I wanted, but I didn't buy it immediately. I asked my brother's mechanic to inspect it, and I used the VIN (vehicle identification number) to see if the car had ever been in an accident. Finally, I was ready to buy. The car wasn't cheap, but I got a good deal. My new car is safe, reliable, and fun to drive. Besides, it's cute and saves me a lot of money on gas. I have absolutely no regrets.

Writing Tip

Use time words and phrases to signal the steps in a process.

D PAIRS. Answer the questions.

1. What is *buyer's remorse*?   when a buyer makes a quick purchase and then realizes it may have been a bad decision

2. What did the writer do before buying a car?   a lot of research and checking

3. Why does the writer like her new car?   It is safe and fun.

E List four time words or phrases that the writer used to signal the steps in her process of buying a car.

1. ___first___

2. ___next___

3. ___several weeks later___

4. ___finally___

Write about a good or bad purchase

Getting Started

1 BEFORE YOU WRITE

A GROUPS. Discuss.

- Read the questions and give an example for question 2. For example, say: *My last major purchase was a new refrigerator.*
- Group students. Have them choose a note-taker to write down their responses.

Presentation

B CLASS. Share your lists.

- Have a representative from each group read the group's list of major purchases.

C Read the writing model. Why was...

- Read the model out loud while students follow along silently. Tell them not to worry about unfamiliar vocabulary but rather to focus on finding the sentences that answer the question.
- Call on volunteers to answer the question.

D PAIRS. Answer the questions.

- Have students read the paragraph again, silently this time, and answer the questions.
- Have them compare answers with a partner.
- Go over the questions with the class. Note that the definition of *buyer's remorse* is given in the second sentence of the paragraph.

Writing Tip: Using Time Words

- Read the Writing Tip.
- Ask the class: *What are some common time signals?* (First, Next, Finally, etc.) Write them on the board.
- Point out that time signals are usually followed by a comma.

E Find four time words or phrases...

- Have students circle the time expressions, then list them in their books.
- Go over the answers.

▮▮ Expansion: Speaking Practice for E

- Pair students. Instruct them to talk about a recent process or sequence of events, such as cooking something or their previous evening's routine. Tell them to use at least four time expressions.

Write about a good or bad purchase

Controlled Practice   20 minutes

2   THINKING ON PAPER

Ⓐ BRAINSTORM. Think about your recent...

- Remind students that when they brainstorm, they should try to think of a lot of ideas. Later they will choose the one they want to write about.
- Pair students and have them share their charts with each other.

Ⓑ Choose one purchase to describe. Plan...

- Demonstrate the activity. Select a purchase you made and list on the board the steps you followed. Then explain.
- Have students complete the steps. While they are working, walk around and provide help as needed.
- Pair or group students and have them share their notes with one another.

■■ MULTILEVEL INSTRUCTION for 2B
Pre-level Have students write four steps or fewer.
Above-level Have students write four steps or more. Tell them they can use the time expressions in their book or substitute others.

Communicative Practice   20 minutes

3   WRITE

Write a paragraph about your good purchase...

- Say: *Now use your notes from Exercise 2B to write your paragraph. It's OK to change or add ideas while you are writing.*
- Review paragraph format. Remind students to give their paragraph a title, indent the first line, begin each sentence with a capital letter, and double-space the lines.
- Encourage students to use the past perfect tense.
- Have students write in class.

4   CHECK YOUR WRITING

- Read the questions in the checklist.
- Have students read their paragraphs and check off the questions in the checklist. Alternately, have them revise their paragraphs according to the items in the checklist.
- *Optional:* Pair students. Have them read each other's papers and check them for the items in Exercise 4.

Teaching Tip

When doing peer editing, give the editors a specific list of criteria to check for. You can organize the criteria in increasing order of complexity to match your students' ability. At the most basic level, have students check one another's papers for formatting features: presence or absence of a title, margins, double-spacing, and indenting. At the next level, students can check basic punctuation such as capital letters and periods. The next level can include grammar points that have been taught and that students are expected to know. The highest level of peer editing can address content issues such as the clarity of supporting details, the organization of information, and the use of connectors.

Teaching Tip

You may want to collect student papers and provide feedback. Use the scoring rubric for writing on page T-xiv to evaluate each student's vocabulary, grammar, mechanics, and how well he or she has completed the task. You may want to review the completed rubric with the students.

Extra Practice

Interactive Practice   page 84

A BRAINSTORM. Think about your recent purchases—both large and small. Create a chart like this to record your ideas.

My Good Purchases	My Bad Purchases

B Choose one purchase to describe. Plan and organize your ideas in the space below. Use time words to show the order of the steps in your buying process.

My Best or Worst Purchase: _____

What I did right or what I did wrong

Step 1: First, _____

Step 2: Next, _____

Step 3: Then _____

Step 4: Finally, _____

3 WRITE

Write a paragraph about your good or bad purchase. Use your ideas and the steps you listed above. Use the writing model as an example.

4 CHECK YOUR WRITING

☐ Did you describe a good (or a bad) purchase?

☐ Did you clearly state your main idea?

☐ Did you use time words to show the order of the steps in your buying process?

☐ Did you use correct capitalization, punctuation, and spelling?

1 REVIEW

For your grammar review, go to page 251.

2 ACT IT OUT — What do you say?

STEP 1. **Review the conversation on page 139 (CD 2, Track 15).**

STEP 2. ROLE PLAY. GROUPS.
Role-play this situation.

Student A: You are the driver of a large SUV. You had just started backing out of a parking space when you heard a loud crashing noise. You hadn't seen the small car that was waiting for another parking space.

Student B: You are the driver of a compact car. You were waiting for a parking space when a large SUV backed into you. You are angry that the SUV damaged the passenger's side door of your car.

Student C: You are a police officer who was patrolling the neighborhood. Find out what the problem is. After the drivers give you the details of the accident, tell them that they must go to the police station to complete an accident report.

3 READ AND REACT — Problem-solving

STEP 1. GROUPS. **Read about Maria's problem.**

María Campos is having a problem with the brakes on her car. She's not sure how much the repairs will cost, but she knows brake work is usually expensive and she doesn't have the money right now. She paid $500 to have her car repaired last month and $900 for car repairs four months ago. María lives far from her job, so she can't walk to work. She needs to decide what to do about her car.

STEP 2. GROUPS. **What is Maria's problem? Discuss a solution. Give reasons to explain your decision.**

4 CONNECT

For your Planning for Learning go to page 260.
For your Team Project, go to page 269.

Which goals can you check off? Go back to page 125.

 Go to the CD-ROM for more practice.

1 REVIEW

Turn to page 251 for the Grammar Review.

2 ACT IT OUT

STEP 1. Review the conversation...

- Play CD 2, Track 15. If necessary, direct students to the script on page 139.

STEP 2. ROLE PLAY. GROUPS. Role-play this...

Teaching Tip

While pairs are performing role plays, use the scoring rubric for speaking on page T-xiii to evaluate each student's vocabulary, grammar, fluency, and how well he or she completes the task. You may want to review the completed rubric with the students.

- Have students look at the illustration. Ask: *Where is this? Who are the people? What happened?*
- Read the role descriptions. Work with the students to flesh out the details of the role play. For example, ask: *How does Student A feel? What will he or she say? How about Student B? Who will probably speak first?*
- Model the role play with two above-level students. Play the role of Student A or B. The police officer should speak first. For example, the officer can say: *What's the problem here?*
- Remind students to try to use the unit grammar in their role play.
- Tell students to practice out loud at least twice.
- Have volunteers role-play for the class.

MULTILEVEL INSTRUCTION for 2

Pre-level Have students play the role of the police officer. Tell them to begin by asking what the problem is. They should listen to the other speakers, then tell them to come to the police station to fill out a report.

Above-level Have students play the role of Student B. Tell them to act angry, even when Student A tries to apologize and exchange information.

3 READ AND REACT

STEP 1. GROUPS. Read about Maria's problem.

- Read the paragraph while students follow along silently.

STEP 2. GROUPS. What is Maria's problem?...

- Form groups of three or four. Have each group choose a timekeeper, a note taker, and a reporter.
- Give a time limit for discussion.
- Walk around and provide help as needed.
- Have the reporter from each group share the group's ideas. Write all the ideas on the board.
- Have the class vote on the best solution.

Expansion: Speaking Practice for STEP 2

- Ask students if they have had a similar experience and how they dealt with it.

4 CONNECT

Turn to page 260 for the Planning for Learning Activity and page 269 for the Team Project. See page T-xi for classroom management tips for these activities.

Progress Check

Which goals can you check off? Go back to page 125.

Ask students to turn to page 125 and check off any remaining goals they have reached. Call on students to say which goals they will practice outside of class.

 **Go to the CD-ROM for more practice.**

If students need more practice with the vocabulary, grammar, and competencies in Unit 7, encourage them to review the activities on the CD-ROM.

How Are You Feeling?

8

Classroom Materials/Extra Practice

CD 2
Tracks 16–26

Interactive Practice
Unit 8

Workbook
Unit 8

Unit Overview

Goals

- See the list of goals on the facing page.

Grammar

- Present perfect continuous
- *Such . . . that* and *so . . . that*
- *Should, ought to, had better,* and *must*

Pronunciation

- Words that begin with groups of consonants (consonant clusters)
- Stress in words ending in *-ical, -ity, -tion, -ize,* and *-ate*

Reading

- Discuss preventive health practices
- Reading Skill: Scanning a list for details

Writing

- Describe a personal experience with healthcare

Life Skills

- Interpret and complete a health insurance form

Preview

- Have students look at the picture. Read the unit title. Ask: *What do you think this unit will be about?*
- Ask the preview questions. You can also ask: *What is the doctor holding? What is around the doctor's neck? What is the patient wearing? Does he look sick?*

Unit Goals

- Point to the Unit Goals. Have students read them silently.
- Tell students they will be studying these goals in Unit 8.
- Say each goal and explain unfamiliar vocabulary as needed, for example, *personnel: the people who work at a place; symptoms: signs of an illness as experienced by a patient; risk: the danger that an injury or loss will occur.*
- Tell students to circle one or more goals that are very important to them. Call on several volunteers to say the goals they circled.
- Write a checkmark (✓) on the board. Say: *We will come back to this page again. You will write a checkmark next to the goals you learned in this unit.*

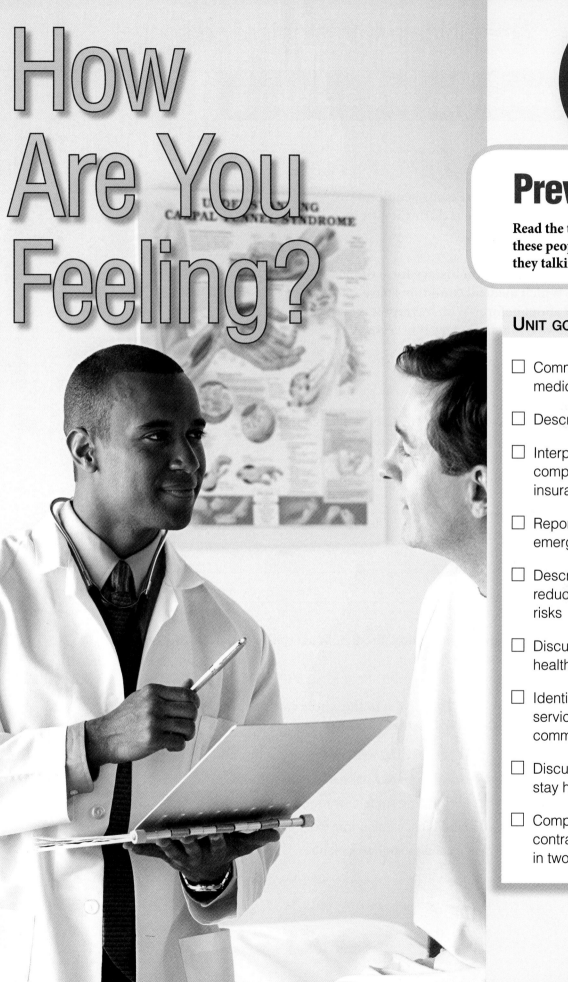

How Are You Feeling?

8

Preview

Read the title. Who are these people? What are they talking about?

UNIT GOALS

- ☐ Communicate with medical personnel

- ☐ Describe symptoms

- ☐ Interpret and complete a health insurance form

- ☐ Report a medical emergency

- ☐ Describe ways to reduce your health risks

- ☐ Discuss preventive health practices

- ☐ Identify health-care services within the community

- ☐ Discuss ways to stay healthy

- ☐ Compare and contrast health care in two places

Listening and Speaking

1 BEFORE YOU LISTEN

A CLASS. **What are some reasons people go to see a doctor? What happens during a visit to the doctor?**

B PAIRS. **Read the medical history form on page 147. Which medical conditions have you heard about before? Which symptoms do you know? Use a dictionary if necessary.**

2 LISTEN

CD2 T16

A **Irma Garcia is a patient at the City Center Clinic. She is talking to Dr. Kim. Listen to the first part of their conversation. What four symptoms has Mrs. Garcia been experiencing? Take notes.**

1. _She can't sleep._____

2. _She has a lot of congestion._____

3. _She can't breathe well._____

4. _Her body hurts. / She feels achy._____

B **Think about Mrs. Garcia's symptoms. Predict. What will Dr. Kim say she has? What will be the doctor's diagnosis?**

CD2 T17

C **Read the statements. Then listen to the whole conversation. Write _T_ (true) or _F_ (false). Correct the false statements.**

_F_ 1. Mrs. Garcia hasn't been feeling well for the past six weeks.

_F_ 2. Dr. Kim thinks that Mrs. Garcia has a bad cold.

_T_ 3. Mrs. Garcia has been eating some new foods lately.

_T_ 4. Mrs. Garcia's daughter just came home from college.

_T_ 5. Mrs. Garcia may be allergic to houseplants.

Lesson 1 Communicate with medical personnel

Getting Started   10 minutes

1 BEFORE YOU LISTEN

A CLASS. What are some reasons...

- Read each question and call on students to answer. List students' answers on the board in separate columns.
- For the first question, try to elicit the word *prevention* or other terms that pertain to avoiding illness before it happens, for example, *well-baby visit*. Also try to elicit *treatment*.

B PAIRS. Read the medical history form...

- Define *symptoms*. As an example, ask: *What are the symptoms of a cold?* (runny nose, sneezing, cough, temperature, and headache)
- Pair students and have them go over the conditions and symptoms. Tell them they may use a bilingual dictionary to look up items if necessary.
- Go over the conditions and symptoms. Elicit definitions or translations.

Presentation   10 minutes

2 LISTEN

A Irma Garcia is a patient...

- Have students look at the photo. Ask: *What symptoms might Mrs. Garcia be having? What do you think her problem is?*
- Remind students to listen specifically for the answer to the question. It is not necessary to understand every word.
- Play CD 2, Track 16.
- Have students compare answers with a classmate.
- Call on a volunteer to answer the question.

B Think about Mrs. Garcia's symptoms. Predict...

- Make sure students understand that *diagnosis* means *the identification of a medical condition after tests and a doctor's evaluation of symptoms*.
- Ask: *What do you think Mrs. Garcia's problem could be?* List students' predictions on the board.

Controlled Practice   10 minutes

C Read the statements. Then listen...

- Have students read the statements silently and predict whether they are true or false.
- Play CD 2, Track 17.
- Have students complete the exercise and compare answers with a partner.
- Check answers. Call on students to read each statement and say whether it is true or false. If it is false, ask the student to correct it. Write the answers on the board.
- Refer back to students' guesses in Exercise B. Ask: *What was the doctor's diagnosis? Was your prediction correct?*

Expansion: Speaking Practice

- Talk about allergies. Ask such questions as: *Who has an allergy? What are you allergic to? What are your symptoms?* and *If you have an allergic reaction, how do you treat it?*

Presentation · 10 minutes

3 CONVERSATION

Pronunciation Watch

- On the board, write: *stop, plant, predict, blood,* and *stroke.* Say each word.
- Point to each letter and say *consonant* or *vowel.* After you do the first couple of words, have students join in and label each sound with you.
- Circle the consonant clusters (*st, pl, pr,* and *bl*).
- Read the Pronunciation Watch note.
- *Optional:* Tell the class that groups of consonants are called *consonant clusters.*
- Say each word again and have students repeat.

Ⓐ 💿 Listen to the words. Notice...

- Play CD 2, Track 18. Have students listen.
- Play Track 18 again. Have students listen and repeat.
- Call on students to say each word. Correct as needed.

> **Teaching Tip**
>
> Speakers of such languages as Spanish and Farsi have difficulty pronouncing initial clusters with *s,* for example, *sleep* and *stop.* They tend to insert a schwa before the cluster. To correct this error, have students take a deep breath and make a hissing sound. Then have them say the rest of the word, for example, *sssssstop.* Next, have them say the word with the cluster in phrases such as *Don't stop,* and *Go to sleep.*

Ⓑ 💿 Irma Garcia is talking with the...

- Play CD 2, Track 19. Have students listen and read silently.
- *Optional:* Have above-level students listen with their books closed.
- Check comprehension. Ask: *Is Mrs. Garcia's prescription ready? How much medicine is Mrs. Garcia supposed to take every day? What are the possible side effects? What should she do if she has a problem?*

Controlled Practice · 10 minutes

4 PRACTICE

Ⓐ PAIRS. Practice the conversation.

- Form cross-ability pairs and have students take turns reading each role.
- Have students switch partners and practice again.
- Go over errors in the pronunciation of consonant clusters. Say the incorrect form and have students repeat with correct pronunciation.

Ⓑ MAKE IT PERSONAL. Keep track of your...

- Explain *keep track of* (to know and update).

STEP 1. Fill out a medical history form...

- Repeat the definition of any condition or symptom.
- Have students fill out the medical history form only if they feel comfortable doing so. Keep in mind that medical information is confidential. Students who do not feel comfortable doing this activity should be allowed to pass.

> **Culture Connection**
>
> In some states, people with pre-existing medical conditions such as diabetes or cancer can be denied medical insurance. For this reason, many people with such conditions may be reluctant to talk about their health or to put anything on paper.

Communicative Practice · 10 minutes

STEP 2. GROUPS. Discuss why it's important...

- Form groups. Give a time limit for discussion. While students are talking, walk around and provide help as needed.
- Call on volunteers to share their answers.

Extra Practice

Interactive Practice

3 CONVERSATION

CD2 T18

A 🎵 **Listen to the words. Notice the groups of consonant sounds. Then listen and repeat.**

Pronunciation Watch

Many words and syllables begin with a group of consonant sounds. We say the consonants in a group closely together.

sneezing	**st**omachache	**cl**inic	**dr**owsiness
sleepiness	**str**oke	**qu**estion	**pr**e**scr**iption

CD2 T19

B 🎵 **Irma Garcia is talking with the pharmacist at a drugstore. Listen and read.**

Irma Garcia: Excuse me. My name is Irma Garcia. Is my prescription ready yet?

Pharmacist: Let me check. Have you been waiting long?

Irma Garcia: About half an hour, I guess.

Pharmacist: I'm sorry. I have the prescription right here. Did Dr. Kim talk to you about this medication?

Irma Garcia: She told me to take one tablet daily.

Pharmacist: Did she explain the possible side effects, such as sleepiness?

Irma Garcia: Yes, and she told me that the medicine could also cause dry mouth.

Pharmacist: OK. Be sure to read the information on the label and follow the directions. Please give your doctor a call if you have any problems.

4 PRACTICE

A **PAIRS. Practice the conversation.**

B **MAKE IT PERSONAL. Keep track of your medical history.**

STEP 1. Fill out a medical history form like the one above. List other details of your medical history, such as immunizations, surgeries, medications, etc. Use this information the next time you go to the doctor.

STEP 2. GROUPS. Discuss why it's important to know your own medical history and the medical history of family members.

City Center Clinic	**New Patient—Medical History**

Name:_____

Address:_____

Phone #:_____

E-mail Address:_____

Medical Conditions (Check all that apply.)

	You	A Family Member
High blood pressure	☐	☐
High cholesterol	☐	☐
Heart disease	☐	☐
Diabetes	☐	☐
Stroke	☐	☐
Cancer	☐	☐
Allergies	☐	☐

Symptoms (Check all that you have been experiencing in the past six months.)

☐ tiredness	☐ vomiting
☐ sleeplessness	☐ nausea
☐ sneezing	☐ stomachache
☐ coughing	☐ headache
☐ congestion	☐ chest pain
☐ dizziness	☐ weakness in arms or legs
☐ aches and pains	☐ numbness in feet

Grammar

Present perfect continuous		
Statements		
I**'ve been sneezing** a lot lately.		
This **has been going on**	*for*	about two weeks.
I **haven't been feeling** well	*since*	my daughter came home.

Grammar Watch

- Use the present perfect continuous to show that an action started in the past and is still going on.
- To show how long an action has been going on, use the present perfect continuous with *for* + the length of time, or *since* + the time the action began.

Questions	Short answers
A: **Has** Mrs. Garcia **been feeling** tired recently?	B: Yes, she **has**.
A: **Have** you **been eating** any new kinds of food?	B: No, I **haven't**.
A: What **have** Mrs. Garcia and her husband **been doing** lately?	B: They**'ve** both **been working** in the family business.

1 PRACTICE

A Read these waiting room conversations. Underline the present perfect continuous.

1. **Receptionist:** It's nice to see you. Have you been feeling better since your last visit?
   Mr. Jackson: Yes, I have. My arm hasn't been hurting at all. I'm just here for a follow-up.

2. **Ms. Weber:** I've been seeing Dr. Kim for two years. Have you been coming here long?
   Mr. Owolabi: No. My wife made this appointment for me. I've been getting sleepy at work lately.

3. **Nurse:** Dr. Kim will see you now, Mrs. Garcia. I hope you haven't been waiting too long.
   Mrs. Garcia: I've been here about fifteen minutes, but that's OK. I've been reading an interesting article about allergies. Maybe I'll finish it after I see the doctor.

B Dr. Kim is talking to a new patient, Charles Owolabi. Circle the correct words.

Dr. Kim: Good afternoon, Mr. Owolabi. What brings you here today? Has / (Have) you been having some health problems?

Mr. Owolabi: I've been feeling very tired (for) / since the past few months.

Dr. Kim: You have / (Have you) been experiencing any other symptoms?

Mr. Owolabi: Yes, I **am** / (have). I'm a carpenter, and I sometimes get cuts on my hands at work. The cuts **been** / (have been) taking longer to heal.

Dr. Kim: You wrote here that there's a history of diabetes in your family.

Mr. Owolabi: That's right. My grandmother was diabetic, and so is my mother. She **is taking** / (has been taking) insulin **for** / (since) 2005.

Getting Started · 10 minutes

- Think of an imaginary person with a mysterious medical condition. Describe the symptoms for the class and say how long they have been going on. Let students ask you questions and then "diagnose" the condition. You could say, for example: *My cousin Vince has a strange medical condition. Since Christmas, he's been sneezing and coughing all the time. He's also been having trouble sleeping. He has a lot of congestion at night. He never had these problems before. What do you think his problem is?*

- Once students have made their diagnoses, review the symptoms. On the board, write: *He's been sneezing and coughing since Christmas. He's also been having trouble sleeping.*

- Underline the present perfect continuous verbs. On the board, write: has/have + been + *present participle*. Say: *This verb form is called the* present perfect continuous.

Presentation · 15 minutes

Present perfect continuous

- Copy the grammar chart onto the board. Read the sentences and underline the present perfect continuous verbs. Circle *for* and *since*.

- Read the first Grammar Watch note. Point to each example and ask if the action is still happening or is happening now. For example, point to the first example and ask: *Is the speaker still sneezing a lot?* (*yes*)

- Read the second note. Point to the second and third examples. Illustrate them with diagrams like the following:

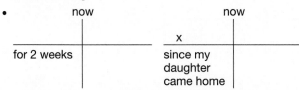

Reinforce the fact that *for* refers to the duration of the action. *Since* refers to the beginning point of the action.

- Read the questions and short answers. Point out the word order in the questions: *Has/have + subject + been + present participle.* Also point out that the short answers use *has, hasn't, have,* or *haven't.*

Language Note

- The present perfect continuous can only be used with action verbs. With non-action (stative) verbs, English uses the present perfect. Contrast *Joe has been dating Beth for two years* with *Joe has known Beth for two years.*

- With some action verbs, both the present perfect and the present perfect continuous are used interchangeably. Contrast *I've lived in this house for ten years* with *I've been living in this house for ten years.* However, with most verbs, the present perfect continuous is used more frequently to talk about an activity that began in the past, continues until now, and will continue into the future.

Controlled Practice · 15 minutes

1 PRACTICE

Ⓐ Read these waiting room conversations...

- Choose six students to read the lines of dialogue.
- Have students underline the present perfect continuous as they listen.
- Call on students to say the parts of the sentences that they underlined.

Ⓑ Dr. Kim is talking to a new patient...

- Do the first item with the class.
- Have students work alone or in pairs.
- Have a pair of volunteers read the conversation with the answers they circled. Write the answers on the board. Elicit corrections as needed.

▇▇▇ Expansion: Speaking Practice for 1B

- Have students look at the list of symptoms on page 149.
- Pair students and have them role-play a conversation between a patient and a nurse. The nurse is taking the patient's medical history.
- Model the role play with an above-level student. For example: Nurse: *Are you experiencing any symptoms?* Patient: *Yes, I'm tired all the time, and I have chest pains.* Nurse: *How long have you been . . .*
- Have volunteers perform their role play.

2 PRACTICE

Mrs. Garcia and Dr. Kim are talking about...

- Read the example. Review the grammar if needed.
- Have students do the exercise alone or in pairs. Walk around and provide help as needed.
- Have students read the lines with the answers. Write the answers on the board.

Communicative Practice   20 minutes

Show what you know!

STEP 1. Many students suffer from stress...

- Introduce *stress*. Ask: *What is stress?* (a feeling of pressure, tension, anxiety, or nervousness) *Is stress a problem for you?*
- Read the list of symptoms. Have students repeat. Define vocabulary as needed.
- Have students check their symptoms and fill in any other symptoms they are experiencing.
- Ask the class about any other symptoms they listed. Write them on the board.

STEP 2. GROUPS. Talk about any symptoms...

- Form groups. Have each group select a timekeeper, a note taker, and a reporter. The note taker should write down the group's responses to Step 1.
- Give a time limit. Walk around as students are talking and provide help as needed.
- To wrap up, have reporters share their group's answers to Step 1.

Community Building

Demonstrate some relaxation or guided imagery techniques that you know, or obtain a CD or DVD of techniques from the library. With the class, discuss the relationship between stress and relaxation. *(Relaxation techniques lower the level of the stress hormone cortisol in the brain, they make us feel more alert, and they enhance our mood.)* Then try the techniques.

Progress Check

Can you . . . describe symptoms?

Say: *We have practiced describing symptoms. Now, look at the question at the bottom of the page. Can you describe symptoms? Write a checkmark in the box.*

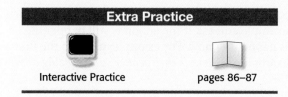

Extra Practice

Interactive Practice   pages 86–87

PRACTICE

Mrs. Garcia and Dr. Kim are talking about Mrs. Garcia's allergy. Complete their conversation. Use the present perfect continuous.

Dr. Kim: Good morning, Mrs. Garcia. How ___*have*___ you ___*been doing*___
(do)
since I saw you last month?

Mrs. Garcia: Great! I __'ve been sleeping__ much better. The congestion in
(sleep)
my nose is gone, and I ___haven't been coughing___ at night.
(not/cough)

Dr. Kim: ___Have___ you ___been taking___ your medicine regularly?
(take)

Mrs. Garcia: Yes. I __'ve been following__ your instructions, Dr. Kim.
(follow)

Dr. Kim: ___Has___ the medication ___been causing___ any side effects?
(cause)

Mrs. Garcia: No. Everything ___has been going___ perfectly.
(go)

Dr. Kim: And your daughter?

Mrs. Garcia: Well, she ___has been working___ in the garden lately. She gave all
(work)
her houseplants away when she learned about my allergy!

Show what you know! Describe symptoms

STEP 1. **Many students suffer from stress. Check (✓) any symptoms of stress that you have been experiencing.**

☐ get headaches

☐ feel dizzy

☐ have stomachaches

☐ have difficulty sleeping

☐ get frequent colds

☐ other: _____

STEP 2. **GROUPS. Talk about any symptoms of stress that you have been experiencing. Share ideas about things that can relieve stress.**

Can you...describe symptoms? ☐

Life Skills

1 INTERPRET AN INSURANCE ENROLLMENT FORM

CLASS. Discuss. Many companies in the U. S. offer health insurance coverage to their employees.

1. What is health insurance?
2. Why is health insurance important?

2 READ

Read part of a health insurance enrollment form. Find and underline these words:
dependent, divorce, enroll in, spouse, waive.

ABLE Phone Company   **Health Insurance Enrollment Form**

Open Enrollment Period: You must <u>enroll in</u> your health insurance plan within one month of your date of hire. You can make changes only during the first two weeks of January or the last two weeks of October.

Section 1: Employee Information

Name (first, last) *Patricia Noon*   Social Security Number *123-45-6789*
Address *112 East Street*   ☐ Male ☒ Female Birthdate *11/20/1980*
City, State, Zip *Middletown, CT 06457*   Marital Status ☐ Single ☒ Married
Phone Number *860-555-3263*   Employment Status ☒ Full-Time ☐ Part-Time
Starting Date *January 5, 2010*

Section 2: Type of Enrollment: Select (x) one.
☐ <u>Waive</u> (I do not wish to enroll in the company plan.)
☒ Enroll
☐ Change (I want a different type of plan.)

Section 3: Members Covered: Indicate who you wish to cover.
☒ Self   ☒ <u>Spouse</u>   ☒ <u>Dependent</u>(s)

Name (first, last) of all others to be covered   Birthdate
<u>Spouse</u> *John Noon*   04/25/1979
<u>Dependent</u> *Maria Noon*   12/03/2007
<u>Dependent</u>
<u>Dependent</u>

Section 4: Reason(s) for Changing Type of Plan (Mark all that apply.)
☐ New Employee ☐ Marriage ☐ <u>Divorce</u> ☐ Birth ☐ Change of <u>Spouse</u>'s Employment

---

Getting Started   10 minutes

 1 **INTERPRET A HEALTH INSURANCE ENROLLMENT FORM**

CLASS. Discuss. Many companies...

- Read the questions and call on students to answer.

Possible answers:

1. Health insurance is a form of insurance that provides payment of benefits for covered sickness or injury.

2. Health insurance protects you and your dependents from the risk of uncertain or expensive medical bills. Without health insurance, you may not be able to afford expensive medical services. Health insurance pays for services that you use often.

▬▬ **Expansion: Speaking Practice for 1**

- Ask the class: *How many of you have health insurance through your work?*

- Select students who have insurance and ask: *Who is covered—just you, or members of your family as well? Do you have to pay a monthly premium? How much is it?*

- Note: The topic of health insurance can be sensitive. If you suspect this topic may upset some students, skip this activity.

> **Culture Connection**
>
> According to the National Coalition on Health Care, nearly 46 million Americans, or 18 percent of the population under age 65, did not have health insurance in 2007. The majority of the uninsured—80 percent—were native or naturalized American citizens. While the majority of Americans who have insurance receive it through their jobs, the percentage of people (workers and their families) with employment-based health insurance has dropped from 70 percent in 1987 to 62 percent in 2007.

Presentation   15 minutes

2 **READ**

Read part of a health insurance enrollment form....

- With the class, survey the enrollment form. Read each section heading and ask: *What is this section about?*

- Explain that *open enrollment period* means *the time when employees are allowed to enroll in the insurance plan or change their insurance coverage.*

- Have students read the form. Give a time limit, but extend the time if necessary. Remind them that they do not need to understand every word.

- Remind them to underline the words listed in the directions.

Controlled Practice   15 minutes

3 WORD WORK

Match the words you underlined...

- Remind students to look at the words in context before selecting their definitions. For example, they should see that *dependent* is a noun in this case, not an adjective. More specifically, it's a noun that refers to a person.
- Have students do the exercise.
- Go over the answers.

▇▇ Expansion: Vocabulary Practice for 3

- Have students write each word from Exercise 3 in an original sentence. Call on students to read their sentences for the class.

4 CHECK YOUR UNDERSTANDING

A Look at the enrollment form again....

- Have students do the exercise alone or in pairs.
- Go over the answers.

▇▇ Expansion: Writing Practice for 4A

- Have students fill out the insurance plan enrollment form with their own information.
- Pair students and have them talk about the information they wrote in each section, for example, for Section 1, *My name is _____. My address is _____. My employment starting date is (was) _____.*
- Note: Tell students <u>not</u> to write their real Social Security numbers on the form!

Communicative Practice   20 minutes

B PAIRS. Discuss.

- Pair students and give a time limit for discussion.
- Explain that *waive* means *to give up a right or benefit that someone doesn't need or want.*
- Call on volunteers to share their answers.

C CLASS. Discuss.

- In response to the question in item 1, elicit information about free or low-cost clinics from students who have used them. Write the names and addresses of such resources on the board.
- In response to the first question in item 2, have students raise their hands if their home countries have government-provided health care. Call on students to describe the system in their countries.
- Have students raise their hands if they think the U.S. government should pay for health care. As a class, list some points for and against health care being paid for by the U.S. government.

Culture Connection

An organization called Cover the Uninsured is working to assist people who do not have health insurance and to bring about legislation that will make insurance available to everyone.

▇▇ Expansion: Speaking Practice for 4C

- Have a debate about the pros and cons of government-provided health insurance. Divide students into two teams, pro and con. Have teams list all the reasons why the government (as opposed to employers) should or should not be responsible for people's health insurance.
- Have each team choose a spokesperson to present the team's arguments.
- Have the class listen to both sides of the issue and vote on the "winner" of the debate.

Progress Check

Can you . . . interpret and complete a health insurance form?

Say: *We have practiced interpreting and completing a health insurance form. Now, look at the question at the bottom of the page. Can you interpret and complete a health insurance form? Write a checkmark in the box.*

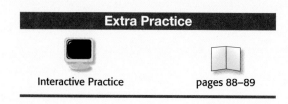

Extra Practice

Interactive Practice   pages 88–89

3 WORD WORK

Match the words you underlined in the form with their definitions.

___b___ 1. dependent   a. the end of a marriage

___a___ 2. divorce   b. a person for whom you provide food, clothing, housing

___c___ 3. enroll in   c. officially join

___e___ 4. spouse   d. choose not to have or do something

___d___ 5. waive   e. a husband or wife

4 CHECK YOUR UNDERSTANDING

A **Look at the enrollment form again. Complete the sentences with information from the form.**

1. The employees at ABLE Phone Company can change their health insurance plan

   during the months of ___January___ and ___October___.

2. Patricia's Social Security number is ___123-45-6789___.

3. Patricia was born on ___11/20/1980___.

4. Patricia has been working at the company since ___January 5, 2010___.

5. Patricia's husband's name is ___John___. ___Maria___ is her daughter's name.

6. Patricia was 27 when her daughter was born. Her husband was ___28___ years old.

B **PAIRS. Discuss.**

1. Patricia is expecting her second child in December. When do you think she should change her health insurance plan?

2. One of Patricia's co-workers is going to waive his health benefits. What are some possible reasons for his decision?

C **CLASS. Discuss.**

1. Some companies offer health insurance to their employees, but many do not. What can people do when their company doesn't help pay for health insurance?

2. In some countries, the government pays for people's health care. Is that true in your country? Should the government pay for health care in the U.S.? Explain.

Can you...interpret and complete a health insurance form? ☐

Listening and Speaking

1 BEFORE YOU LISTEN

A Some medical conditions are serious or could become serious. These emergencies require a 911 call for an ambulance. Check (✓) the situations that you think are medical emergencies.

☐ sneezing and coughing ☐ a stroke

☐ a stomachache ☐ a heart attack

☐ a broken leg ☐ congestion

B GROUPS. Compare answers. Discuss. What are some situations that would NOT require a 911 call?

2 LISTEN

CD2 T20

A Listen to the 911 call. What kind of medical emergency do you think the caller is describing?

a. broken arm b. heatstroke c. heart attack

CD2 T20

B Read the questions. Then listen to the conversation again. Circle the correct answers.

1. Which statement best describes the condition of the caller's husband?
   a. He is conscious and in no pain.
   b. He is conscious and sweating badly.
   c. He is unconscious.

2. What ongoing condition is the caller's husband taking medication for?
   a. diabetes b. high blood pressure c. pain

3. Why is the caller's husband having difficulty breathing?
   a. He is overweight. b. He is diabetic. c. He is having chest pain.

4. Which statement best describes the caller?
   a. She is calm. b. She is frightened. c. She is angry.

C GROUPS. Discuss. In your opinion, did the 911 operator handle the call well? Why or why not?

Report a medical emergency

Getting Started — 10 minutes

Have students look at the photo. Ask: *What kind of vehicle is this?* (an ambulance) *What do you call a person who works in this vehicle?* (a paramedic) *What kind of knowledge does this person need in order to do the job?* (how to treat shock, stop bleeding, immobilize a broken bone, start an IV, give injections, etc.)

1 BEFORE YOU LISTEN

A Some medical conditions are serious...

- Define *emergency* as *a condition that, if untreated, could lead to serious injury or death.*
- Read through the list. Have students repeat the items. Provide definitions as needed.
- Have students do the exercise.

Culture Connection

In some cultures, a stomachache is regarded as a serious medical condition. Some Japanese workers, for example, will stay home from work if they have a stomachache. In contrast, few Americans regard this condition as serious, and most employers would frown upon a worker missing work for this reason.

B GROUPS. Compare answers. Discuss....

- Say each item in Exercise 1A and have students raise their hands if they think it is an emergency.
- Elicit additional conditions that would not require a 911 call.

Presentation — 5 minutes

2 LISTEN

A Listen to the 911 call. What kind...

- Define *heatstroke* as *a very serious medical condition in which the body stops working normally because of exposure to high temperatures.*
- Play CD 2, Track 20.
- Call on a volunteer to answer the question. Ask the class if they agree. Ask: *What information helped you to choose the correct answer?* (chest pains)

Controlled Practice — 5 minutes

B Read the questions. Then listen...

- Have students read the questions and predict the answers.
- Play Track 20 again.
- Have students do the exercise alone or in pairs.
- Check answers. If students have difficulty answering a question, play the corresponding part of the recording again.

Communicative Practice — 5 minutes

C GROUPS. Discuss. In your opinion,...

- Ask: *Who thinks the operator handled the call well? Why?* Call on volunteers to reply.
- Ask if anyone has an opposite opinion. Have that person explain his or her answer.

Culture Connection

When someone makes a 911 call, it is customary for the operator to stay on the line with the caller until the ambulance arrives.

Presentation 5 minutes

3 CONVERSATION

 A man has just called 911. Listen and read.

- Play CD 2, Track 21. Have students listen and read along silently.
- *Optional:* Have above-level students listen with their books closed.
- Check comprehension. Ask: *What is the woman's problem? When did it start? What was her first symptom? What does the operator tell the man to do at the end? Why?*

Controlled Practice 5 minutes

4 PRACTICE

Ⓐ PAIRS. Practice the conversation.

- Form cross-ability pairs and have students take turns reading each role.
- Instruct students that the 911 operator should remain calm, while the caller should act upset.
- Walk around and listen as students are practicing.
- Ask volunteers to perform the conversation for the class.

███ **MULTILEVEL INSTRUCTION for 4A**

Cross-ability Have pre-level students read the role of the caller. Have above-level students read the role of the operator.

Communicative Practice 25 minutes

Ⓑ GROUPS. Discuss.

- Read the first question and discuss it with the class.
- Form groups and have them discuss the second question. Give a time limit. Walk around while students are talking and provide help as needed.
- Have several students describe their experiences calling 911. Ask: *Why did you call? What did the operator tell you to do? Do you think calling 911 was the right thing to do in that situation?*

Ⓒ ROLE PLAY. PAIRS. Role-play this situation...

- Read the role descriptions and the suggested situations.
- Plan a model role play with the class. First, have students select the medical emergency. Elicit possible symptoms. List those on the board. Then elicit a list of questions that 911 operators normally ask. List those as well.
- Role-play the situation with an above-level student. Play the role of Student B.
- Pair students of similar ability and have them role-play a similar conversation.
- Call on pairs of students to perform their role play for the class.

███ **MULTILEVEL INSTRUCTION for 4C**

Pre-level Have students role-play using the information on the board.

Above-level Have students choose an emergency not listed in the book, for example, a child has been bitten by a dog, someone fell off a ladder and hit his head, a woman has gone into labor, or someone is in shock after eating peanuts.

Extra Practice

Interactive Practice

CD2 T21

A man has just called 911. Listen and read.

911 Operator:	911. What's your emergency?
Caller:	It's my wife. Her legs are so weak that she can't walk.
911 Operator:	Is your wife conscious, sir? Can she talk?
Caller:	She's conscious, but she can't speak.
911 Operator:	Can I have your exact address, please?
Caller:	1175 West Hampton Street, Apartment 12-B.
911 Operator:	Thank you, sir. Now, can you tell me when the symptoms began?
Caller:	Just a few minutes ago. At first, she had a bad headache. Then she couldn't stand up.
911 Operator:	Everything will be OK, sir. I know it's hard in a situation like this, but stay calm. The paramedics are on their way. Please stay on the line.

4 | PRACTICE

A PAIRS. **Practice the conversation.**

B GROUPS. **Discuss.**

1. Why did the 911 operator continue talking to the caller until the paramedics arrived?

2. Have you ever placed a 911 call? Describe the situation.

C ROLE PLAY. PAIRS. **Role-play this situation about a medical emergency. Use one of the ideas below or your own idea.**

- A family member may have food poisoning.

- A co-worker may have broken an arm or a leg.

- A friend or family member is bleeding heavily.

- A child has swallowed dish detergent or other cleaning fluid.

Student A: A family member, friend, or co-worker has just had a medical emergency, and you call 911. Tell the 911 operator what has happened and describe the person's condition and symptoms. Follow the instructions of the 911 operator.

Student B: You are a 911 operator and Student A calls you about a medical emergency. Listen as Student A describes the condition of the person who needs medical attention. Ask questions to find out information you need to know. Give Student A instructions about how best to handle the situation.

Grammar

Such . . . that and *so . . . that*	
It was **such** a terrible situation	**that** the caller couldn't remain calm.
The man had **such** serious symptoms	**that** his wife called 911.
His legs are **so** weak	**that** he can't walk.
You got to the ER **so** quickly	**that** we were able to give you excellent care.
He has **so many** vague symptoms	**that** it's difficult to say what the problem is.
I was in **so much** pain	**that** I couldn't move.

Grammar Watch

- Use *such* with nouns.
- Use *so* with adjectives or adverbs.
- Use *so many* with plural nouns. Use *so much* with non-count nouns. *See page 284 for a list of non-count nouns.*

1 PRACTICE

A Read this information from a medical website. Circle the examples of *such . . . that* and *so . . . that*. Underline the clauses beginning with *that*.

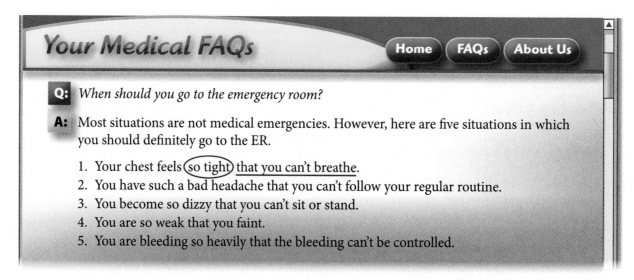

Your Medical FAQs   Home   FAQs   About Us

Q: *When should you go to the emergency room?*

A: Most situations are not medical emergencies. However, here are five situations in which you should definitely go to the ER.

1. Your chest feels (so tight) that you can't breathe.
2. You have such a bad headache that you can't follow your regular routine.
3. You become so dizzy that you can't sit or stand.
4. You are so weak that you faint.
5. You are bleeding so heavily that the bleeding can't be controlled.

B Six months ago Charles Owalabi's doctor told him he was at risk for diabetes. Read what Charles has done since then. Unscramble the sentences on notepaper.

1. worried / I / that / was / so / diabetes / I / might get / that I went on a strict diet.

   I was so worried that I might get diabetes that I went on a strict diet.

2. relief / It's / a / such / that my blood tests are normal now.

3. these days / eating / healthy foods / I'm / such / that I feel like a new person.

4. weight / so / I've / much / In fact, / lost / that people don't recognize me.

5. health problems / many / so / can / other / Diabetes / lead to / that it can be dangerous.

Describe ways to reduce your health risks

Getting Started · 10 minutes

- On the board, make two lists with the headings *Reasons* and *Results*. Under *Reasons*, write: *It was cold.* Under *Results*, write: *The water in our pipes froze.*
- Ask the class: *How can we combine these two short sentences into one longer sentence?* (Because it was cold, the water in our pipes froze. It was cold; therefore, the water in our pipes froze.) Try to elicit *It was so cold that the water in our pipes froze.* If no one offers this sentence, write: *It was _____ cold _____ the water in our pipes froze.* If students are unable to fill in the blanks, provide the answers.
- Under *Reasons*, write: *It was a cold day.* Again ask: *How can we combine the two short sentences into one longer one?* (It was such a cold day that the water in our pipes froze.)
- Underline *so . . . that* and *such . . . that*. Say: *In this lesson, you'll learn how to use* so *and* such + that *to talk about reasons and results.*

Presentation · 10 minutes

Such . . . that and so . . . that

- Copy the grammar chart onto the board.
- Read each sentence and ask students: *What comes after* such? (adjective + noun) *What comes after* so? (adjective or adverb)
- Read the Grammar Watch notes as a follow-up.

Controlled Practice · 20 minutes

1 PRACTICE

A Read this information from a medical website....

- Read the website's question, answer, and example. Ask the class: *What is the reason?* (chest is tight) *What is the result?* (can't breathe)
- Have students do the exercise.
- Pair students and have them compare answers. For each, have them identify the reason and the result.
- Call on volunteers to give you the reasons and the results.

B Six months ago, Charles Owalabi's...

- Read the example.
- Have students complete the exercise on their own.
- Have students compare answers with a classmate.
- Go over the answers with the class.

Answers:

1. I was so worried that I might get diabetes that I went on a strict diet.
2. It's such a relief that my blood tests are normal now.
3. I'm eating such healthy foods these days that I feel like a new person.
4. In fact, I've lost so much weight that people don't recognize me.
5. Diabetes can lead to so many other health problems that it can be dangerous.

2 PRACTICE

A A doctor wrote a letter to her local...

- Before starting the exercise, make sure students understand that *family practice* means *a medical practice that provides general care for people of all ages, as opposed to a specialization like pediatrics, dermatology, surgery,* etc.
- Read the first sentence with the class.
- Have students do the exercise alone.
- Have students compare answers with a partner.
- Go over the answers by having different students read the text with the filled-in words. Correct errors as needed.

B Read these reasons for not getting...

- Introduce the exercise by asking: *How often do you exercise? Do you think you exercise enough? If not, why not?*
- Read the directions and item 1.
- Have students do the exercise.

Answers:

1. I'm so busy that I don't have time to exercise.
2. Gyms are so expensive that I can't afford to go to one.
3. Exercising is so boring that it's hard for me to keep doing it.
4. I'm so tired when I come home from work that I just want to eat and go straight to bed.
5. I have so many chores on the weekend that I can't find the time to work out.
6. I haven't exercised in such a long time that I'll never be able to get back into shape.
7. I was in such pain the last time I worked out that I never want to do it again.

- Call on seven students to write the combined sentences on the board. Have other students read the sentences and correct errors as needed.

Communicative Practice 20 minutes

███ **Expansion: Speaking Practice for 2B**

- Pair students and have them talk about the last time they or a family member were sick. Instruct them to use *so . . . that* and *such (a) . . . that* to describe their illness. For example: *The last time I had a cold, I was so tired that I couldn't get out of bed. I sneezed so hard that my glasses flew off my face.*

Show what you know!

STEP 1. GROUPS. Discuss.

- Read the questions with the class and elicit one sample response to each.
- Group students and have them select a timekeeper, a note taker, and a reporter.
- Give a time limit. While students are writing, walk around and provide help as needed.

STEP 2. CLASS. Share your ideas.

- Have students share their answers to question 1 orally.
- For question 2, have representatives from each group come to the board and write two of the excuses that the group came up with.
- Have class members read the sentences on the board and correct errors as needed.

Progress Check

Can you . . . describe ways to reduce your health risks?

Say: *We have practiced describing ways to reduce your health risks. Now, look at the question at the bottom of the page. Can you describe ways to reduce your health risks? Write a checkmark in the box.*

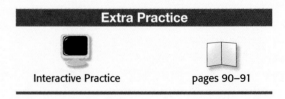

Extra Practice
Interactive Practice   pages 90–91

A A doctor wrote a letter to her local newspaper. Complete the letter with *so*, *such*, or *so many*.

Dear Editor,

Your recent article on healthy living raised ___such___ an important issue that I left copies in my waiting room for my patients. Many of them complain that they have ___so many___ responsibilities at work that they have no time to eat healthy meals or get exercise. However, as your article points out, we can all make small changes ___so___ easily that there is no excuse not to.

Small changes can lead to big benefits. Let's take breakfast as an example. Medical experts say that breakfast is ___such___ an important meal that no one should skip it. But thousands of children start their school day on empty stomachs. This has become ___such___ a serious problem that many schools now serve breakfast. And what about adults? Why are ___so many___ of us still skipping breakfast? We say we're ___so___ busy that we don't have time for breakfast. Well, it's time to find the time! This idea seems ___so___ simple that everyone should understand it.

B Read these reasons for not getting enough exercise. Combine the sentences on notepaper using *such … that, so … that, so much … that,* or *so many … that.*

1. I'm busy. I don't have time to exercise.
   I'm so busy that I don't have time to exercise.
2. Gyms are expensive. I can't afford to go to one.
3. Exercising is boring. It's hard for me to keep doing it.
4. I'm tired when I come home from work. I just want to eat and go straight to bed.
5. I have chores on the weekend. I can't find the time to work out.
6. I haven't exercised in a long time. I'll never be able to get back into shape.
7. I was in pain the last time I worked out. I never want to do it again.

Show what you know! Describe ways to reduce your health risks

STEP 1. GROUPS. Discuss.

1. What are the two most important things a person can do to stay healthy?
2. What are five excuses people use for not exercising or eating a healthy diet? Make a list. Use *so . . . that* and *such . . . that* where possible.

STEP 2. CLASS. Share your ideas.

Can you…describe ways to reduce your health risks? ☐

Reading

Overweight Population in the U.S.

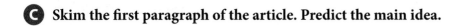

1 **BEFORE YOU READ**

A CLASS. **Look at the graph. Discuss. What information does it show?**

B **Study the definitions.**

life expectancy = the length of time that a person will probably live
decrease your chances = lessen the possibility
significant = large enough to be important
obesity = the condition of being too overweight, especially in a way that is dangerous
dramatically = noticeably

C **Skim the first paragraph of the article. Predict the main idea.**

2 **READ**

CD2 T22

 Read and listen. Was your prediction correct?

The Long and Short of It

People in the U.S. have been living longer and longer. Consider this: In 1900, the average American lived to the age of 47. In 1950, the average lifespan was 68. In 2007, **life expectancy** was 77.9. So, what would it take to live to the age of 100? Some experts believe that we can find the answer if we look at the leading causes of death.

What the Numbers Say
The Centers for Disease Control and Prevention (CDC) is part of the U.S. Department of Health and Human Services. Recent CDC statistics show that heart disease, cancer, and stroke are the top three causes of death in the U.S. For every 100,000 people, 210.3 people died from heart disease, 184 died from cancer, and 47 died as a result of a stroke in 2005. That's the bad news. The good news is the number of deaths from heart disease, cancer, and stroke declined from 2004 to 2005 and the number could continue to drop.

What We Should Do
Researchers feel that doctors are getting better at diagnosing and curing diseases. They also say disease prevention is important, and that's where there's more bad news-good news. According to the CDC, 34 percent of people in the U.S. who are twenty or older are overweight. However, if we can control our weight, we have a better chance of keeping our blood pressure low and a better chance of avoiding heart disease and stroke. A healthy weight can also help prevent certain kinds of cancer.

A Weighty Issue

• If you are overweight, losing a small amount of weight (even 10 percent of your current weight) will help **decrease your chances** of having health problems such as high blood pressure or Type 2 diabetes.

• Statistics from 2003–2004 and 2005–2006 showed no **significant** increase in the number of U.S. adults who were overweight. However, **obesity** is still a problem in this country.

• It is not just adults who have weight problems. The number of children and teens in the U.S. who are overweight has gone up **dramatically** since the 1970s.

In short, genetics certainly plays a role in how long we'll live, but the research is clear. The genes we receive from our parents are just part of the story. Modern medicine and what we do to prevent disease can make a big difference in whether or not we live to be 100.

Getting Started   5 minutes

- Read the lesson title and define *preventive health practices* as *actions people can take to avoid getting sick.*
- Ask students what they and their family members do to avoid getting sick, for example, *get enough sleep, exercise, go to the dentist, get vaccinated,* and *have regular checkups.*

Presentation   20 minutes

1 BEFORE YOU READ

Ⓐ CLASS. Look at the graph. Discuss. What...

- Help students to read the graph. Ask: *What is the title of the graph? What years does it cover? What do the colors mean? What are the numbers on the left?*
- Help students to interpret the information. Ask: *What trend, or change over time, does the graph show?* (The percentage of overweight people in all age groups grew between the periods of 1976–80 and 2003–04.)

Ⓑ Study the definitions.

- Say the terms and have students repeat them.
- Have students read the definitions.

▮▮ Expansion: Vocabulary Practice for 1B

- Tell students to close their books.
- Read the definitions to the students and call for volunteers to give you the words.

Ⓒ Skim the first paragraph of the article. Predict...

- Remind students that the main idea of an article is often found in the last sentence of the first paragraph.
- Have students read the first paragraph.
- Call on students to state their predictions. Write them on the board.

▮▮ Expansion: Reading Practice for 1C

- Have students survey the article more fully. First, read the title. Ask the class: *What is it?* (life span or life expectancy)
- Have students look at the subheads. Ask them to predict what second section (*statistics about the leading causes of death*) and third section (*what people can do to reduce their chances of early death*) are about.

2 READ

 Read and listen. Was your prediction correct?

- Have students read the complete article silently.
- Ask: *What was the article about? Which prediction on the board was correct?*
- Play CD 2, Track 22. Have students listen to the article as they read along.
- Tell students that reading while listening improves their fluency because it doesn't allow them to stop and reread passages.

Language Note

The long and short of it is an expression meaning *the sum or the gist of something.* If you have told the long and the short of it, you have told it all. The title of the reading is a play on words.

Controlled Practice   20 minutes

3 CHECK YOUR UNDERSTANDING

Reading Skill: Scanning a List for Details

- Read the Reading Skill. Remind students that *scanning* means *reading quickly for specific information.* Say: *When people scan, their eyes move quickly over the page until they find the information they want. Then they stop reading.*

Ⓐ Read the Reading Skill. Then read the...

- Do item 1 with the class. Instruct students to find the information as quickly as possible, then answer the question. (*F*)
- Give a time limit.
- Have students compare answers with a partner.
- Go over the answers. Have students correct the false statements.

> **Teaching Tip**
>
> Give a time limit for scanning activities. This will encourage students to read more quickly.

Ⓑ Complete the sentences. Circle the correct...

- Have students scan the article and underline the answers to the questions.
- Go over the questions and answers.

Ⓒ Look again at the graph on page 156. Circle...

- Explain the difference between *percentage* and *percent.* Say: *Percentage is a noun, as in* the percentage of X. *Percent is an adjective; it is used with a number, as in* 15 percent.
- Form cross-ability pairs and have students do the exercise together.
- Check answers.

▅▅ MULTILEVEL INSTRUCTION for 3C

Cross-ability Have above-level students help pre-level students read the sentences with statistics.

4 WORD WORK

GROUPS. *Genetics* is the study of genes. What...

- Ask students if they know what genes are. Define *gene* as *the microscopic material inside cells that determines our characteristics.*
- Form groups to list inherited characteristics. Have each group choose a timekeeper, a note taker, and a reporter.
- Give a time limit for discussion. While students are talking, walk around and provide help as needed.
- Have the reporter from each group share the group's list of characteristics. Write them on the board.

Communicative Practice   15 minutes

Show what you know!

GROUPS. Discuss.

- Read the questions.
- Form groups.
- Give a time limit for discussion. While students are talking, walk around and provide help as needed.
- To wrap up, have volunteers share their answers to the questions.

> **Community Building**
>
> • Organize (or have students organize) a healthy activity that your students can do together, such as a hike, a bike ride, or a run on the beach.
>
> • Have a guest come to your class to talk about ways to cook more healthfully, for example, replacing lard and butter with vegetable oil, reducing meat consumption, and cutting down on salt and sugar.

Extra Practice

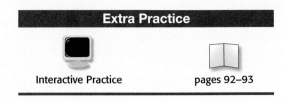

Interactive Practice   pages 92–93

A Read the Reading Skill. Then read the statements. Write *T* (true) or *F* (false). Scan the bulleted items on page 156 to find your answers.

Read information in a bulleted list quickly to look for details such as facts and numbers.

___F___ 1. You must decrease your weight by at least 20 percent to improve your health.

___T___ 2. Being overweight can cause high blood pressure and Type 2 diabetes.

___F___ 3. There were a lot more overweight adults in the U. S. in 2006 than in 2004.

___F___ 4. The number of overweight children and teens has increased since the 1960s.

B Complete the sentences. Circle the correct answers.

1. In 1950, the average American lived to the age of _____.
   a. 47   (b.) 68   c. 77.9

2. In 2005, the number of people in the U.S. who died from heart disease, cancer, and stroke _____.
   a. increased   (b.) decreased   c. stayed the same

3. Since the 1970s, the number of overweight children and teens has _____.
   (a.) increased   b. decreased   c. stayed the same

4. People who are overweight probably have _____.
   a. low blood pressure   (b.) high blood pressure   c. a low risk for cancer

C Look again at the graph on page 156. Circle the statement that is NOT true.

   a. From 2003 to 2004, more than 15 percent of children ages 6 to 11 were overweight.
   b. From 1976 to 1980, 5 percent of children ages 2 to 5 and 5 percent of teens were overweight.
   (c.) The percentage of overweight adults in the U.S. increased more than any other group between the two time periods shown.

4 WORD WORK

GROUPS. *Genetics* is the study of genes. What is a *gene*? List some characteristics that parents pass on to their children through genes.

Show what you know!   Discuss preventive health practices

GROUPS. Discuss.

1. Do you have a healthy lifestyle? Does the information in the article make you want to change your lifestyle? Explain.

2. What other things can people do to live healthfully?

Listening and Speaking

1 BEFORE YOU LISTEN

A GROUPS. What kinds of immunizations have you had? Why did you get these vaccinations?

B PAIRS. Look at the picture of a health fair. Discuss.

1. What types of services might a health fair provide?
2. Why would people go to a health fair instead of to a doctor?

2 LISTEN

CD2 T23

A A radio news anchor is reading a public service announcement (PSA). Listen. What is the purpose of the announcement?

CD2 T23

B Read the questions. Listen to the PSA again. Then answer the questions.

1. According to state law, who must get specific vaccinations?
2. When is the immunization deadline for school children?
3. In addition to immunizations, what can children ages 5 to 12 get at the health fair?
4. What time does the health fair start on Saturday? What are the hours on Sunday?

C GROUPS. Answer the questions.

1. Which immunizations are required in schools where you live? (Look on the school district's website.)
2. Why do you think immunizations are required for all first-time students?
3. Where in your community can children can get their immunizations? (Ask the parents in your group, or check on the school district's website.)

Getting Started

10 minutes

Read the lesson title. Ask the class: *What do you expect to learn in this lesson?*

1 BEFORE YOU LISTEN

A GROUPS. What kinds of immunizations...

- Say the words *immunizations* and *vaccinations*. Have students repeat. Illustrate the meaning of the words by pantomiming giving yourself an injection.
- Write and say the names of common immunizations such as *influenza, mumps, measles, chicken pox, rubella, polio, diphtheria, tetanus, hepatitis, whooping cough (pertussis)*, and *tuberculosis*. Explain or translate terms as needed.
- Form groups and have students discuss the questions.

B PAIRS. Look at the picture of a health...

- Have students look at the picture. Read the text on the sign in the picture. Ask: *What kind of event is this?*
- Read the first question. Call on students to answer.
- Pair students and have them discuss question 2.
- To wrap up, ask if any of the students have ever attended a health fair.

Presentation

5 minutes

2 LISTEN

A A radio news anchor is reading...

- Review the definition of *public service announcement: a noncommercial radio or television advertisement that provides information for the benefit of the public.*
- Play CD 2, Track 23.
- Pair students and have them answer the question.
- Play the recording again if necessary.
- Have students answer the question. Ask: *What words or information helped you choose the correct answer?*

Controlled Practice

15 minutes

B Read the questions. Listen to the PSA...

- Have students read the questions and predict the answers.
- Play Track 23 again. Have students take notes on the answers to the questions.
- Call on students to answer the questions.

Answers: 1. students entering school for the first time and for students in pre-school programs, kindergarten, grade 5, and grade 9. 2. no later than September 15. 3. free medical checkups 4. 10:00 A.M.; noon until 6:00 P.M.

Culture Connection

Depending on the state they live in, children are required to have some or all of the following immunizations before they can start school: mumps, measles, chicken pox, rubella, polio, diphtheria, tetanus, hepatitis, whooping cough (pertussis), and tuberculosis. Adults need periodic booster shots of some immunizations, such as tetanus and tuberculosis. Annual influenza vaccinations are recommended for both children and adults. Travelers to some countries need additional immunizations against certain diseases, such as yellow fever and malaria.

C GROUPS. Answer the questions.

- For question 1, do an Internet search for *[state name] required immunizations.*
- For question 3, try searching for *[name of school district] immunizations.*
- Form groups. Try to have a parent of school-age children in each group.
- Have students share their answers to question 3.

Expansion: Reading Practice for 2C

- Have students find the addresses, web addresses, and phone numbers of all the resources they listed in Exercise 2C. Type up the list and distribute it.

Presentation

10 minutes

3 CONVERSATION

Pronunciation Watch

- On the board, write the suffixes *-ical, -ity, -tion, -ize* and *-ate*. Write two examples for each.
- Ask students to pronounce the words. Underline the syllable they stress.
- Say: *Let's see if you're right.* Read the Pronunciation Watch note. Then point to each word on the board and ask: *Was your pronunciation correct?*

A 🔘 **Listen to each word. Notice the stress....**

- Play CD 2, Track 24. Have students listen.
- Play Track 24 again. Have students listen and repeat.

B 🔘 **Put a dot (•) over the stressed syllable...**

- Do item 1 together. Write the word on the board. Ask students how to pronounce it. Place a dot over the syllable they stress.
- Form cross-ability pairs. Have them do the exercise.
- Play CD 2, Track 25. Have students listen and check their answers.

C 🔘 **A mother has called the nurse...**

- Play CD 2, Track 26. Have students listen and read silently.
- Check comprehension. Ask: *Why is the mother calling? What grade will the daughter be in next year? What is the mother going to do?*

Controlled Practice

5 minutes

4 PRACTICE

A **PAIRS. Practice the conversation.**

- Form pairs and have students take turns reading each role.
- Take notes on pronunciation errors.
- Practice the items in your notes with the class as follows: T: *I heard _____. It should be _____.* Have the class repeat the correct form.
- Ask volunteers to perform the conversation.

Communicative Practice

15 minutes

B **ROLE PLAY. PAIRS. Role-play this situation.**

Teaching Tip

While pairs are performing role plays, use the scoring rubric for speaking on page T-xiii to evaluate each student's vocabulary, grammar, fluency, and how well he or she completes the task. You may want to review the completed rubric with the students.

- Before class, research places that offer free dental exams for schoolchildren. Then find out if your state is one of those that require schoolchildren to have a dental exam. If it is not, explain that some states have this requirement and that more and more states are following this trend.
- With the class, discuss places that offer free dental exams for schoolchildren. List them on the board.
- Read the role descriptions.
- Model the role play with an above-level student. Play the role of the nurse. Begin the conversation by greeting the parent and asking how you can help. The parent should show you the letter he or she received and explain why he or she thinks it is unfair.
- Form cross-ability pairs. Have students practice their role play at least twice.
- Have volunteers perform their role play.

Culture Connection

As of September 2007, only seven states and the District of Columbia required dental checkups for children in some grades. However, this trend appears to be growing.

▬▬ MULTILEVEL INSTRUCTION for 4B

Cross-ability Have the lower-level student play the role of Student A (the parent). The higher-level student should play the role of Student B (the nurse).

Extra Practice

Interactive Practice

3 CONVERSATION

CD2 T24

A Listen to each word. Notice the stress. Then listen again and repeat.

Pronunciation Watch

In words that end in *-ical*, *-ity*, and *-tion*, stress the syllable just before the ending. In words that end in *-ize* and *-ate*, the stress is usually two syllables before the ending.

mḛdical   oḇésity   immuniẓation   ḭmmunize   commṵnicate

CD2 T25

B Put a dot (•) over the stressed syllable in each word. Then listen and check your answers.

1. examin̊ation   2. ph̊ysical   3. commu̇nity   4. spec̊ialize   5. particḭpate

CD2 T26

C A mother has called the nurse at her daughter's school. Listen and read.

Nurse:	Good morning. This is Nurse Doyle speaking. How can I help you?
Mother:	Good morning. I received a letter about my daughter. It says that she should get a medical check-up.
Nurse:	What grade will your daughter be in when school starts?
Mother:	Fifth grade.
Nurse:	I see. Then your daughter must see a doctor. State law requires all fifth-grade students to have a physical examination. And your daughter's immunizations must be up to date, too.
Mother:	OK. Then I guess I'd better make a doctor's appointment.
Nurse:	Yes, and you'd better do it soon. We must receive the results of the medical exam and the list of immunizations no later than September 15th. That's the deadline.

4 PRACTICE

A PAIRS. Practice the conversation.

B ROLE PLAY. PAIRS. Role-play this situation.

Student A: You are a parent. You don't have medical or dental insurance. You received a letter from your child's school. It says that your second grader cannot go to class until he or she has gone to a dentist. You think the requirement to have a dental exam is unfair because you can't pay for the exam.

Student B: You are a school nurse. You must talk to any parent who received a letter saying that his or her child needs to go to the dentist before that child can come back to school. The dental exam is a state requirement for all students in the second grade. Suggest some places that might provide dental treatment free of charge.

Grammar

Should, ought to, had better, and must

For more information, you **should** visit the Radio WDKM website.

School officials say that parents **should not** wait until the last minute.

Parents **ought to** have their children immunized now.

I**'d better** make a doctor's appointment soon, or I'll miss the deadline.

You**'d better not** forget. It's very important.

Your daughter's immunizations **must** be up to date. It's a requirement.

A: Should I make an appointment today?   **B:** Yes, you **should**.

Grammar Watch

- Use *should* or *ought to* for advice, suggestions, and opinions.
- Use *had better* (*'d better*) for strong advice or suggestions.
- Use *must* when something is required or necessary.
- For negative meanings, use *should not* (*shouldn't*) and *had better not* (*'d better not*).
- Use *should* in questions.

---

1 PRACTICE

A Two co-workers are talking about the importance of getting a flu shot. Read their conversation. Underline the examples of *should, ought to, had better,* and *must*.

A: I think that everyone <u>should</u>¹ get a flu shot.

B: I agree, but the company <u>ought to</u> give us the shots for free.

A: You'd <u>better</u>² not say that too loudly. You <u>should</u>¹ be grateful that we can get the vaccine for just $10.

B: You're right. It's a good deal, especially for someone like me.

A: Why especially for someone like you?

B: I'm over fifty, and I have heart disease. They say that anyone over the age of fifty or with medical conditions like heart disease or diabetes <u>should</u> get a flu shot every year. It's already September 24. I'd <u>better</u>² go to Smithson's soon.

A: Don't forget to take your ID card. The announcement says that you <u>must</u>³ have an employee ID to get the $10 price.

> **Attention Employees!**
>
> Flu shots will be available for all MRC Tire Company employees at Smithson's drugstores during the month of September. Show your employee ID card to get the special price of $10.

B Look at the examples you underlined. For each example, write: *1* (advice, suggestion, opinion), *2* (strong advice, strong suggestion), or *3* (requirement).

Getting Started   10 minutes

- On the board, draw the following continuum:

  Advisable _____ Necessary

- Say: *This lesson is about ways to stay healthy. One way to stay healthy is to get a flu shot.* Point to the word *Advisable* and say: *For some people, getting a flu shot is advisable; that means it's a good idea.* Elicit other examples. *(college students, parents, teenagers, the elderly).* Write the examples on the board. Then say: *These people* <u>should</u> *get a flu shot.*

- Point to the word *Necessary* and say: *For other people, getting a flu shot is necessary; it's required for their work. Who are those people?* (health-care workers, soldiers, and day-care workers) Write these groups on the right side of the board. Then say: *These people* <u>must</u> *get a flu shot. It's required.*

- To conclude, say: *In this lesson, we'll learn how to use the modals* should, shouldn't, had better, had better not, *and* must *to talk about things that are advisable or necessary for good health.* Write the five modals on the board.

Presentation   15 minutes

Should, ought to, had better, and *must*

- Copy the grammar chart onto the board. Read the first three sentences. Ask: *What do* should, should not, *and* ought to *mean?* (a suggestion or advice) Note: *Ought to is pronounced* awdda.

- Read the first Grammar Watch note. Emphasize that *should* and *ought to* are similar in meaning, but *should* is used more often. Note: In North America, *ought to* is used only in the affirmative.

- Read the two sentences with *'d better* and *'d better not.* Read the second Grammar Watch note. Explain *strong advice.* Say: *We use* had better *when we think the advice or suggestion is urgent or there will be serious consequences if the advice is not followed.*

- Read the sentence with *must* and the third Grammar Watch note. Explain that in conversation people rarely use *must*; normally they use *have to. Must* is used for official or legal requirements, for example, *Children must be immunized before they can attend school.* Read the fourth Grammar Watch note. Read the second and fifth sentences.

- Read the last sentence and the last note. Explain that only *should* is used to ask for advice or a recommendation.

■■■ **Expansion: Grammar Practice**

- Explain the difference between *should not* and *had better not*: Should not *is used for giving advice.* Had better not *is used to give a warning.* (The implication is that if the listener does an action, there will be a negative consequence.

- Write the following sentences on the board, and have students fill in the blanks with *should not* or *had better not*: 1. You _____ forget your keys again. I won't be here later to let you in. 2. Students _____ eat in class. 3. I _____ stay out late tonight. I have a huge exam tomorrow. 4. We _____ park here. We might get a ticket. 5. You _____ leave your wet socks on the floor.

Controlled Practice   20 minutes

1 PRACTICE

Ⓐ **Two co-workers are talking about...**

- Have students look at the illustration. Ask: *What's this?* (an announcement on a bulletin board)

- Read the directions and the example. Note: Students should not pay attention to the *1* over *should* until Exercise B.

- Have students complete the exercise.

- Go over the text line by line and have students say which words they underlined.

Ⓑ **Look at the examples you underlined...**

- Have students look at the example. Ask: *What does* should *indicate in this sentence?* (an opinion)

- Have students complete the exercise alone.

- Go back over the underlined items and have students say what number they assigned to each. Be sure to ask what each numbered word means.

- Pair students and have them practice reading the conversation. Then have them switch roles.

- Call on volunteers to read the conversation.

■■■ **Expansion: Speaking Practice for 1B**

- Write the following questions on the board, and have students discuss in pairs: *1. Do you get a flu shot every year? 2. Why or why not? 3. If you get a flu shot, who pays for it? 4. How much does it cost? 5. Do you think the cost is reasonable?*

2 PRACTICE

Ⓐ Unscramble the sentences on notepaper. Put...

- Read item 1 with the class.
- Have students do the exercise.
- Have students compare answers with a partner.

Answers:

1. Children and adults should have annual medical checkups.
2. Everyone ought to get seven to eight hours sleep.
3. Adults had better find time to reduce stress in their lives.
4. Older people should not give up an active lifestyle.
5. We must take steps to protect our health.

- Call on students to write their sentences on the board. Have other students read the sentences and correct as needed.

Ⓑ Read the health article from the...

- Read the title. Ask: *What do you think this article will be about?* (Kids should learn about healthy habits at a young age.)
- Remind students that modals are followed by the base form of the verb (the verb without *to*) except for *ought to*.
- Read the opening paragraph. Have students explain the error.
- Have students do the exercise.
- Pair students and have them go over their corrections together.
- Go over the corrections with the whole class.

▮▮ MULTILEVEL INSTRUCTION for 2B

Cross-ability Have above-level students help pre-level ones find and correct the errors in the reading passage.

Communicative Practice   15 minutes

Show what you know!

STEP 1. GROUPS. Discuss advice, suggestions,...

- Group students and instruct them to write five sentences, using each modal from the lesson (*should, ought to, had better, had better not,* and *must*) once.
- Give a time limit. While students are working, walk around and provide help as needed.
- For each modal, select two students to write their sentences on the board.
- Call on students to read the sentences on the board and correct errors as needed.

STEP 2. CLASS. Which three ideas...

- Have the class look at the sentences on the board. Tell students to choose the idea they think is most helpful. Point to each sentence and have students vote. Circle the three items that get the most votes.

Progress Check

Can you . . . discuss ways to stay healthy?

Say: *We have practiced discussing ways to stay healthy. Now, look at the question at the bottom of the page. Can you discuss ways to stay healthy? Write a checkmark in the box.*

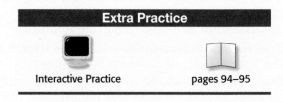

Extra Practice	
Interactive Practice	pages 94–95

PRACTICE

A Unscramble the sentences on notepaper. Put the words in order.

1. annual / should / medical / Children / and / have / checkups / adults
   Children and adults should have annual medical checkups.

2. sleep / get / Everyone / seven to eight / ought to / of / hours

3. had better / their / find time / to / stress / in / lives / Adults / reduce

4. people / should / active / give up / an / Older / lifestyle / not

5. must / We / to / health / take steps / protect / our

B Read the health article from the Radio WDKM website. Find and correct six mistakes with *should, ought to, had better,* and *must.* The first mistake has been corrected for you.

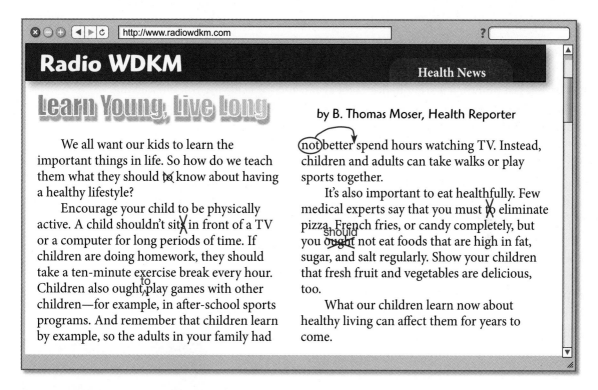

Show what you know! Discuss ways to stay healthy

STEP 1. GROUPS. Discuss advice, suggestions, recommendations, or requirements for good health. Record your ideas on the board. Use full sentences.

STEP 2. CLASS. Which three ideas are most helpful? Take a vote.

Can you...discuss ways to stay healthy? ☐

Writing

1   BEFORE YOU WRITE

A GROUPS. People sometimes have illnesses, injuries, or other health issues that require visiting a doctor or going to a hospital. What experiences have you had with medical personnel? Make a list.

B PAIRS. Describe one of your experiences. Use words that make the experience vivid, that is, words that express what it was like.

C Read the writing model. Underline the words that express what the experience was like for the writer.

A Visit to the Doctor

Last summer I fell on the sidewalk and sprained my ankle. After a week, it felt better. But last month, it started to hurt a lot again, and I was having trouble walking. I went to the clinic, but the doctor there said that I needed to see an orthopedist and recommended Dr. Nemec. I couldn't get an appointment until the next week. I was very worried and sat nervously in the waiting room. My ankle ached with pain, and I could barely put any weight on it. I limped into Dr. Nemec's examining room. It was cold, and I shivered while waiting to see her. Everything in the room was bright white or metal, and there was a lot of medical equipment that I did not recognize. What would this doctor do to me with all those machines?

When Dr. Nemec walked into the office, she smiled warmly. Her soft voice and firm but gentle manner immediately put me at ease. She examined me very thoroughly but without hurting me. She pressed gently where my ankle hurt and explained what she was going to do. Dr. Nemec was reassuring and competent, and this made all my fear—and even some of the pain—go away. I knew that everything would be all right.

Writing Tip: Using Sensory Details

When you write a personal narrative, use sensory details to help the reader see, hear, feel, smell, or taste what you are describing. Sensory details appeal to the reader's five senses.

D PAIRS. Answer the questions.

1. How does the writer feel before he sees the doctor? Circle the details that let you know.

2. How does the writer feel while and after the doctor examines him? Underline the details that let you know.

3. Find sensory details in the writing model. Which senses do they appeal to?

Getting Started   10 minutes

Tell students that in this lesson, they will write a narrative, or story, about their personal experience with health care. They will learn to use sensory details in their writing to make their narrative come alive and be interesting. Elicit the meaning of *sensory details (details that appeal to the senses of sight, hearing, touch, smell, and taste).*

1 BEFORE YOU WRITE

A GROUPS. People sometimes have...

- Ask: *What kinds of health issues would you go to the doctor for?* Write students' answers on the board.
- Point to each item on the board and identify any items the class thinks doesn't require a doctor or hospital visit. Erase any health issue that the class agrees shouldn't be on the list.
- Read the question. Tell students to make their own list.

Presentation   10 minutes

B PAIRS. Describe one of your...

- Ask students if they themselves have gone to the doctor for any of the health issues listed on the board. Note: If students are hesitant to share, shift the discussion to a personal experience of your own that you can share. Describe the experience, giving details on how you felt at the time, what you saw, what you heard, etc.
- Encourage one or two above-level students to relate their own experience visiting a doctor, going to a hospital, or waiting in an emergency room. Ask questions to elicit details that relate to the senses.

Controlled Practice   20 minutes

C Read the writing model...

- Give students time to read the writing model.
- Have them underline the words and phrases that enable them to picture in their minds the writer's feelings while in the waiting room and his descriptions of the examining room as well as of the doctor.
- Have students compare their answers.
- Call on students to read out loud the language they underlined. Ask them to say what sense—sight, sound, touch, smell, taste—each word or phrase appeals to.

D PAIRS. Answer the questions.

- Have students scan the reading to answer the questions.

Possible answers:

1. Circle *very worried, sat nervously, ached with pain, cold,* and *shivered.*

2. Underline *put me at ease, reassuring,* and *made my fear and pain all go away.*

3. Answers could include: *ached with pain* (touch); *barely put any weight on it, limped, cold,* (touch); *shivered* (sight and feeling); *bright white* and *metal* (sight); *warmly* (sight); *soft voice* (hearing); *firm but gentle manner* (touch), *press gently* (touch).

- Have students compare their answers.
- Go over the answers with the class.

Writing Tip: **Using Sensory Details**

- Read the tip.
- Write these column heads on the board: *see, hear, feel, smell, taste.*
- Elicit at least three examples of adjectives for each column. For concrete examples, remind them to look around the classroom and notice every sound, sight, and smell around them.

▬▬▬ Expansion: Writing practice for D

- Put students into pairs. Have them write 3–5 sentences describing how they feel right now and what they see, hear, and smell around the classroom. Encourage them to use the adjectives on the board.
- Call on students to share their sentences.

2 THINKING ON PAPER

BRAINSTORM. Think about your...

- Copy the chart on the board.
- As an example, ask the class to imagine that they were in an emergency room of a hospital. Have them close their eyes as you ask these questions: *What do you see? Look at the people's faces. How do you think they're feeling? What other things do you see? What do you hear? What do you smell?* Write the questions on the board. Write students' answers in the appropriate row in the chart.
- Tell students to skip "Taste" if it's not appropriate.
- Now have students complete the chart. Remind them to ask themselves questions to help them imagine or remember the situation.

Communicative Practice   20 minutes

3 WRITE

In a personal narrative...

- Tell students to read the writing model again. Then have them read the instructions in Exercise 3.
- Give students a few minutes to think of a health-care experience to write about.
- Have students write in class. Encourage them to use some of the sensory details they wrote in Exercise 2.

■■ MULTILEVEL INSTRUCTIONS for 3

Pre-level Have the pre-level students write individual sentences about the topic instead of paragraphs. Remind students to use the questions on the board to help them with ideas.

Above-level Have the above-level students write two or more paragraphs.

4 CHECK YOUR WRITING

- Read the questions in the checklist.
- Have students read their paragraphs and check off the questions in the checklist. Alternately, have them revise their paragraphs according to the items in the checklist.
- Collect papers. Make corrections as needed in paragraph format, grammar, and the items in the checklist.

■■ Expansion: Writing Practice for 4

- Have students rewrite their paragraphs.
- Pair students and have them read their paragraphs to each other.
- Have volunteers read their paragraphs to the class.

Teaching Tip

You may want to collect student papers and provide feedback. Use the scoring rubric for writing on page T-xiv to evaluate each student's vocabulary, grammar, mechanics, and how well he or she has completed the task. You may want to review the completed rubric with the students.

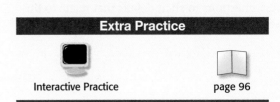

Extra Practice

Interactive Practice   page 96

2 THINKING ON PAPER

BRAINSTORM. Think about your experiences with health care. Choose one of your experiences to write about. Use the sensory-details chart below to list details that make your experience vivid.

Sensory details	
Sight	
Hearing	
Touch	
Smell	
Taste	

3 WRITE

In a personal narrative, a writer tells a story about a personal experience. Write a personal narrative about an experience you had with health care. Use the writing model as an example. Include the details from your chart to make your description come alive.

4 CHECK YOUR WRITING

☐ Did your narrative describe a personal experience you had with health care?

☐ Did you include sensory details to help the reader see, hear, feel, smell, or taste what you described?

☐ Did you use correct capitalization, punctuation, and spelling in your narrative?

1 REVIEW

For your grammar review, go to page 252.

2 ACT IT OUT   What do you say?

STEP 1. Review the conversation on page 159 (CD2, Track 26).

STEP 2. ROLE PLAY. PAIRS. Role-play this situation.

Student A: You recently moved to a new city with your daughter, who has just started fourth-grade. You're at the City Center Clinic with your daughter because she has been having stomachaches. You talk to the person next to you, who tells you that all fifth-grade students in your state must have a medical exam.

Student B: You're at the City Center Clinic with your son because he needs to get the medical exam required for all fifth-grade students. You tell this to the person next to you. When you hear that this person's daughter is suffering from stomachaches, you tell him or her that your son had stomachaches when he started his new school.

3 READ AND REACT   Problem-solving

STEP 1. GROUPS. Read about the problem.

We all know that diet plays an important role in preventing heart attacks, strokes, and some kinds of cancer. However, it is often difficult to make healthy changes in the way we eat. Why do people find it so hard to eat a healthy diet?

STEP 2. Keep a record of all the food that you eat for 24 hours. Bring your "food diary" to class.

STEP 3. Discuss. What are one or two changes that each member of your group can make to have a better diet? Give advice and explain your reasons.

4 CONNECT

For your Community-Building Activity, go to page 260.
For your Team Project, go to page 270.

Which goals can you check off? Go back to page 145.

 Go to the CD-ROM for more practice.

1 REVIEW

Turn to page 252 for the Grammar Review.

2 ACT IT OUT

STEP 1. Review the conversation...

- Play CD 2, Track 26. If necessary, direct students to the script on page 159.

STEP 2. ROLE PLAY. PAIRS. Role-play this situation.

> **Teaching Tip**
>
> While pairs are performing role plays, use the scoring rubric for speaking on page T-xiii to evaluate each student's vocabulary, grammar, fluency, and how well each student completes the task. You may want to review the completed rubric with the students.

- Have students look at the illustration. Ask: *Who are the people? Where are they? What are they doing? How do they look?*
- Read the role descriptions. Then have students read them silently.
- Make an outline of the role play with the class. Ask questions to elicit ideas from the students. For example, ask: *Who probably speaks first? What does he or she say? What do the speakers talk about first? What does Student A ask about? How does Student B answer? How does the conversation end?*
- Model the role play with an above-level student. Play the role of Student B.
- Remind students to try to use the unit grammar in their role play.
- Tell students to practice at least twice.
- Have volunteers role-play for the class.

▬▬ MULTILEVEL INSTRUCTION for 2

Pre-level Have students do a shorter version of the role play. They can speak only about the stomachache, for example. They can also write a script of their role play before speaking.

Above-level Have students practice without notes and improvise on the situation as much as they want. For example, they can ask each other where they come from and how long they have lived in the area and which schools their children attend.

3 READ AND REACT

STEP 1. GROUPS. Read about the problem.

- Read the paragraph out loud while students follow along silently.
- Form small groups and have them discuss the question. Give a time limit.
- Call on volunteers to answer the question.

STEP 2. Keep a record of all the food you eat...

- Suggest that students keep a record either by time of day, by meal, or by food category such as meat, fruit, drinks, etc.

STEP 3. Discuss. What are one or two changes...

- Form groups. Have students show their food diaries to their classmates.
- Tell classmates to give suggestions using *should(n't)* or *had better (not)*.

4 CONNECT

Turn to page 260 for the Community-Building Activity and page 270 for the Team Project. See page T-xi for classroom management tips for these activities.

Progress Check

Which goals can you check off? Go back to page 145.

Ask students to turn to page 145 and check off any remaining goals they have reached. Call on students to say which goals they will practice outside of class.

CD-ROM Practice

 Go to the CD-ROM for more practice.

If students need more practice with the vocabulary, grammar, and competencies in Unit 8, encourage them to review the activities on the CD-ROM.

Partners in Education

Classroom Materials/Extra Practice

CD 2
Tracks 27–38

Interactive Practice
Unit 9

Workbook
Unit 9

Unit Overview

Goals
• See the list of goals on the facing page.

Grammar
• Adverb clauses of reason
• Infinitives and adverb clauses of purpose
• Adjective clauses: Relative pronoun as subject and object of the clause
• Past modals: Expressing degrees of certainty about the past
• Expressing advice or opinions about the past

Pronunciation
• Pronunciation of past modals

Reading
• Talk about after-school programs
• Reading Skill: Distinguishing fact from opinion

Writing
• Write a letter to the editor

Life Skills
• Interpret and respond to a report card
• Discuss school safety

Preview
• Say the unit title and have students look at the photo. Ask: *What does* partners *mean? Who are the partners in this picture? Which other people could be partners in education?*
• Read the preview question. You can also ask: *Do you have children? What grades are they in? Have you ever gone to their school? How often do you talk to their teachers? What are some ways that parents can get involved in their children's school?*

Unit Goals
• Point to the Unit Goals. Have students read them silently.
• Tell students they will be studying these goals in Unit 9.
• Say each goal and explain unfamiliar vocabulary as needed, for example, *personnel: the people who work somewhere; correspond with: communicate with by phone, mail, or e-mail; editor: the person who manages part or all of a newspaper.*
• Tell students to circle one or more goals that are very important to them. Call on several volunteers to say the goals they circled.
• Write a checkmark (✓) on the board. Say: *We will come back to this page again. You will write a checkmark next to the goals you learned in this unit.*

Partners in Education

Preview

Read the title. Why is it important for parents to be involved in their children's education?

UNIT GOALS

- [ ] Discuss a student's progress

- [ ] Talk about parents' involvement in school

- [ ] Interpret and respond to a report card

- [ ] Talk with school personnel

- [ ] Talk about improving schools

- [ ] Talk about after-school programs

- [ ] Discuss school safety

- [ ] Write a letter to the editor

Listening and Speaking

1   BEFORE YOU LISTEN

A GROUPS. In many places in the U.S., the school system has three levels: elementary school, middle school, and high school. Discuss. How are the schools organized in the area where you live?

B GROUPS. The word *grade* has two meanings. What is its meaning in each of these sentences?

1. My daughter is in the second **grade**.
    ^ level

2. Her **grade** on the spelling test was an A.
    ^ mark

2   LISTEN

CD2 T27

A Mrs. Adamski is talking to Mr. Bowman, the guidance counselor at her children's school. Listen to the first part of their conversation. Then circle the correct answer.

Mr. Bowman made the appointment with Mrs. Adamski because _____.
a. her son is having some problems with his grades
b. her son will start high school this fall
c. he wants her daughter to be a better student
d. he wants to help her daughter go to college

B PAIRS. Now listen to the whole conversation. Predict. Why does Mr. Bowman say it's time for Monica to start thinking about college?

CD2 T28

C Read the statements. Then listen to the whole conversation. Write *T* (true) or *F* (false). Correct the false statements.

_F_ 1. Monika is ~~already~~ *not* making plans to go to college.

_T_ 2. Monika might be able to get a scholarship to go to college.

_F_ 3. Mrs. Adamski ~~doesn't want~~ *wants* her daughter to go to college.

_T_ 4. There are special classes to help students prepare for college.

_T_ 5. Mrs. Adamski will bring her husband on her next visit to the guidance office.

D PAIRS. Was your prediction correct? What did Mr. Bowman mean by "Yes and no"?

Lesson 1 Discuss a student's progress

Getting Started

1 BEFORE YOU LISTEN

A GROUPS. In many places in the U.S.,...

- Write the three levels of school in a list on the board. Have students say which grades comprise each level in your area.
- Write the grades next to the levels. For example, in many places elementary school consists of kindergarten to fifth grade. Next to *elementary school* write *K–5*.

Expansion: Speaking Practice for 1A

- Add the ages of students at each level to the information on the board. For example, elementary-school students are typically five to ten or eleven years old.

B GROUPS. The word *grade* has two meanings....

- Call on students to answer the question.
- Ask the class: *How many of you have children in school? What grades are they in?* Go around the room and have students answer.
- Ask: *What grade did you get on the last test?* Call on volunteers to answer.

Presentation
10 minutes

2 LISTEN

A Mrs. Adamski is talking to Mr. Bowman...

- Have students look at the photo. Say: *The woman is Mrs. Adamski. The man is Mr. Bowman. Where are they?* (at school)
- Remind students to listen specifically for the answer to the statement. It is not necessary to understand every word.
- Play CD 2, Track 27.
- Call on a volunteer to answer.

B PAIRS. Now listen to the whole conversation....

- Explain *yes and no*. Say: *The answer* yes and no *means that the previous speaker said or asked something that was partly right and partly wrong. For example, if a class asks a teacher,* Did you read our paragraphs? *and the teacher answers* Yes and no, *she might mean that she read some but not all of the paragraphs.*
- Play the first half of the conversation again. Have students listen specifically for Mrs. Adamski's question at the end. Ask the class: *What did Mrs. Adamski ask?* (She asks, *College? Monika is only thirteen years old. College is a long way off.*)
- Have students guess what Mr. Bowman meant when he said *yes and no*. Write their guesses on the board.
- Put students in pairs. Read the directions.
- Play the rest of the conversation. Ask a volunteer to answer the question. Play the end of the conversation again if necessary.

Controlled Practice
10 minutes

C Read the statements. Then listen...

- Have students read the statements silently and predict whether they are true or false.
- Play CD 2, Track 28.
- Have students do the exercise.
- Check answers. Call on students to read each statement and say whether it is true or false. If it is false, ask the student to correct it.

D PAIRS. Was your prediction correct? What...

- Ask: *What did Mr. Bowman mean when he said* yes and no?
- Have students raise their hands if their prediction was correct.

Presentation   15 minutes

3 CONVERSATION

A 🖸 **Listen to the sentences. Notice...**

- On the board, write a sentence with both stressed and unstressed words. For example, *I have a meeting after school with my daughter's teacher.*
- Say: *I'm going to read the sentences. Tell me which words are stressed.* (If necessary, remind students that stressed words are louder, higher, and spoken more clearly than unstressed words.) Read the sentences, stressing the words *meeting, school, daughter's, and teacher.*
- Point to each word and have students tell you if it is stressed or not. Repeat the sentences as needed.
- Read the sentences again and have students repeat.
- Explain the pronunciation rule as follows: *Important words, such as nouns, verbs, adjectives, and adverbs, are normally stressed. Pronouns, prepositions, and articles are normally short and weak (not stressed). These words often have a very short, quiet vowel sound.*
- Play CD 2, Track 29. Have students listen.
- Play Track 29 again. Have students listen and repeat.
- Call on students to say the sentences.

B 🖸 **Mrs. Adamski is at a middle-school...**

- Play CD 2, Track 30. Have students listen and follow silently.
- Check comprehension. Ask: *Who is Mr. Manning? What do Mrs. Adamski and Mr. Manning talk about? Why? What does Mr. Manning suggest? Does Mrs. Adamski like the suggestion?*

C **CLASS. Discuss. What is a...**

- Read the first question and have students share ideas. If necessary, ask specific questions such as *What do teachers do at a parent-teacher conference? What do parents do?* (Teachers talk to parents about their child's progress or work at school. Parents listen and ask specific questions about their child's work and behavior at school.) Write students' ideas on the board.
- Discuss the difference between the two events.

Controlled Practice   5 minutes

4 PRACTICE

A PAIRS. **Practice the conversation.**

- Form cross-ability pairs and have students take turns reading each role.
- Take notes on students' pronunciation of stressed and unstressed words.
- Using your notes, correct pronunciation errors.

▬ MULTILEVEL INSTRUCTION

Cross-ability Have the lower-level student read the part of Mrs. (or Mr.) Adamski. Have the above-level student play the role of Mr. (or Mrs.) Manning.

Communicative Practice   10 minutes

B MAKE IT PERSONAL. GROUPS. **Discuss...**

- Read the directions.
- Group students so that each group has one or more parents of children enrolled in school.
- To conclude, have a few students share their experiences with the class.

▬ Expansion: Speaking Practice for MAKE IT PERSONAL

- Have students role-play a parent-teacher conference. The roles can be as follows:

Student A: You are meeting with your child's science teacher. Your child enjoys doing the science experiments, but he or she didn't do well on the last science test. The teacher makes a suggestion. Ask for more information.

Student B: You are a science teacher. You are meeting the parent of one of your students. The student enjoys your class but did not do very well on the last test. Make a suggestion to the parent.

Extra Practice

Interactive Practice

3 CONVERSATION

CD2 T29

A Listen to the sentences. Notice the stress on the information that is different in the second sentence in each conversation. Then listen and repeat.

A: Her daughter has problems with her grades.
B: No, her son has problems with his grades.

A: Her daughter is sixteen years old.
B: No, her daughter is thirteen years old.

Pronunciation Watch

Use stress to highlight information that is new or different, which is often the last important word in a clause or sentence. To correct or disagree with something, highlight the information that is different.

CD2 T30

B Mrs. Adamski is at a middle school parent-teacher conference. Listen and read the conversation.

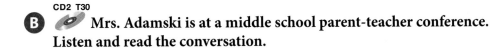

Mr. Manning:	I'm so glad you could come to talk about your son. I'm Mr. Manning, Robert's math teacher.
Mrs. Adamski:	It's nice to meet you. Robert says he's having some problems with math.
Mr. Manning:	Well, Robert is a great kid, and he seems to enjoy the class. But, yes, I think he needs a little help.
Mrs. Adamski:	I saw his last test. He got a 70. I think it was because he didn't study enough.
Mr. Manning:	That's possible. Since he's having some trouble, it would be good for Robert to have a tutor.
Mrs. Adamski:	That sounds like a good idea. Will it be expensive?
Mr. Manning:	No! We have a free after-school program. Students help each other. It's peer tutoring.

C CLASS. Discuss. What is a parent-teacher conference? What is Parent-Teacher Night? How are these events different?

4 PRACTICE

A PAIRS. Practice the conversation.

B MAKE IT PERSONAL. GROUPS. Discuss. Have you had any experiences talking to teachers or other school personnel — either for your child or for yourself? Share your experiences.

Grammar

Adverb clauses of reason	
Main clause (result)	Adverb clause (reason)
I'd like Monika to start planning now	**because** she is one of our best students.
I want Robert to get some tutoring	**since** he is having some trouble in math.

> **Grammar Watch**
>
> Use a comma between the clauses when the adverb clause comes first: *Since he is having some trouble, I want Robert to get some tutoring.*

1 PRACTICE

A Read the statements from parents about Parent-Teacher Night. Draw one line under the reason. Draw two lines under the result.

1. "I always go to Parent-Teacher Night because I like the personal contact with my child's teachers."

2. "It's important to find out what the teachers are really like since my child spends so much time with these people every day."

3. "Since there's a chance to talk one-on-one with the teachers, I can ask about ways for my daughter to improve."

4. "Because our children's education is very important to us, my husband and I want to participate in school activities."

5. "I enjoy Parent-Teacher Night because it gives me a chance to meet other parents."

B Read the statements from teachers about Parent-Teacher Night. Combine the sentences using either *because* or *since*. Don't change the order of the clauses.

1. I'm happy to see parents at Parent-Teacher Night. It means they care.

   I'm happy to see parents at Parent-Teacher Night because it means they care.

   OR *I'm happy to see parents at Parent-Teacher Night since it means they care.*

2. I want parents to help their children at home. I always explain my requirements.

   Since I want parents to help their children at home, I always explain my requirements.

3. The teachers feel happy and proud. Most parents show a lot of respect for them.

   The teachers feel happy and proud because most parents show a lot of respect for them.

4. Parents don't always know what's going on at school. Children don't tell them.

   Parents don't always know what's going on at school because children don't tell them.

5. Home-school communication is important. Parents and teachers should talk often.

   Since home-school communication is important, parents and teachers should talk often.

Getting Started   10 minutes

- Define *Parent-Teacher Night* (also called *Back-to-School Night* or *Open House* in some places). Say: *Parent-Teacher Night is an evening when parents can go to their children's school, see their children's classrooms, and meet their children's teachers.*
- Ask: *How many of you have attended Parent-Teacher Night at your child's school?* Have students raise their hands. Select several students and ask: *Why do you go?* Use students' answers to compose sentences with *because*. Write them on the board. For example: *I go to Parent-Teacher Night because I want to meet my child's teacher.*
- Explain: *In English, the word* since *has the same meaning as* because. Model a sentence with *since* instead of *because*. Then have students read the sentences, substituting *since* for *because*.
- Underline each clause of the sentences on the board and circle the words *because* and *since*. Point to the main clause and say: *This part of the sentence is called the* main clause *or* independent clause *because we can put a period after it.* Then point to the dependent clause and say: *This part of the sentence is called an* adverb clause. *It has a subordinating conjunction followed by a subject and a verb.* Say: *In this lesson we'll learn how to make sentences that talk about reasons and results.*

Presentation   10 minutes

Adverb clauses of reason

- Copy the grammar chart onto the board. Read the sentences. Point out that *because* and *since* come at the beginning of the clause that gives the reason or cause. The main clause gives a result, or effect.
- Tell students that one way to determine which clause is the reason clause is to see which clause answers the question *Why?*
- Read the Grammar Watch note. Rewrite one of the example sentences on the board with the clause at the beginning of the sentence.

Expansion: Writing Practice for Grammar

- Have students rewrite the sentences that were created in Getting Started, reversing the order of the clauses, adjusting punctuation, and inserting a comma.
- While students are writing, walk around and provide help as needed.

Controlled Practice   10 minutes

1 PRACTICE

Ⓐ Read the statements from parents about...

- Read item 1. To reinforce meaning, ask: *What is the reason?* (The speaker likes the personal contact with her child's teachers.) *What is the result?* (The speaker goes to Parent-Teacher Night.)
- Have students do the exercise alone or in pairs. While they are working, walk around and check answers. Provide help as needed.

Ⓑ Read the statements from teachers about...

- Using the example, model these steps in completing the exercise: First, have students identify the reason clause (the one that answers the question *Why?*). Then, have them write the sentence, inserting *because* or *since* before the reason. Finally, have them check the punctuation, inserting a comma if the reason clause is first.
- Have students do the exercise. While they are writing, walk around and provide help as needed.
- Call students to the board to write the sentences.
- Call on other students to read the sentences on the board and make corrections as needed.

Expansion: Speaking Practice for 1B

- Have students discuss their reasons for making certain decisions regarding their or their children's schooling. Write these questions on the board: *1. Where do your children go to school? 2. Why did you choose to send them there? 3. Have you ever made an appointment to speak to your children's teacher or the principal of your children's school? 4. Why? 5. (For students who do not have children) Why are you attending this school or this class?*
- Form groups. Tell students to take turns asking and answering the questions.
- Instruct students to use *because* and *since* in their answers.
- Give a time limit for discussion. While students are talking, walk around and provide help as needed.

Presentation   10 minutes

Infinitives and adverb clauses of purpose

- On the board, write: *I came to class early to talk with my teacher privately.* Read the sentence. Ask: *What is the main clause?* (I came to class early) Underline it twice. Then ask: *What is the adverb clause?* (to talk with my teacher privately) Underline it once.

- Say: *This sentence is like the sentences you saw on page 168 because it has a main clause and an adverb clause. However, the meaning of this sentence is different. Instead of a reason and a result, this sentence talks about a* purpose *and a result. A* purpose *is like a goal.*

- Explain: *We can use* to *to signal a purpose.*

- Ask: *Does anybody know another way to say this sentence?* (I came to class early so that I could talk with my teacher privately.) Point out that *so that* can also be used to talk about a purpose.

- Read the Grammar Watch notes.

Language Note

It is important to distinguish between infinitives of purpose and infinitives that are objects of verbs or adjective phrases (such as *It's important to . . .*). Infinitives of purpose can be expanded to *in order*; for example, *I need a large pot (in order) to cook this chicken.* Sentences with infinitives of purpose can also be rephrased with *so that*, for example, *I need a large pot so that I can cook this chicken.*

Controlled Practice   10 minutes

2 PRACTICE

Ⓐ Read part of the introduction...

- After reading the directions, remind students that they should only underline the infinitives of purpose. They should not underline infinitives that are objects of verbs or adjective phrases. Have students look at the first sentence. It contains an infinitive of purpose, whereas the infinitive in the second sentence does not.

- Have students do the exercise.

- Check answers with the whole class.

Ⓑ Use *to* or *so that* to complete each school rule.

- Read item 1.

- Have students do the exercise and compare answers with a classmate.

- Go over answers.

▬▬ Expansion: Speaking Practice for 2B

- Have students say certain school rules and requirements. List them on the board.

- Put students in pairs or groups. Have them discuss the purpose of the rules and requirements. Remind them to use *to* or *so that*.

- Have students share their ideas and write sentences with *to* or *so that* on the board.

- Call on students to read the sentences on the board. Correct errors as needed.

Communicative Practice   10 minutes

Show what you know!

GROUPS. Discuss. Do you think it is important...?

- Form groups. Try to make sure that each group has one or more members who have children in school.

- Have each group choose a timekeeper, a note taker, and a reporter. The note taker should record students' answers to the second question.

- Give a time limit for discussion.

- Call on reporters to share their group's answer to the second question.

Progress Check

Can you . . . talk about parents' involvement in school?

Say: *We have practiced talking about parents' involvement in school. Now, look at the question at the bottom of the page. Can you talk about parents' involvement in school? Write a checkmark in the box.*

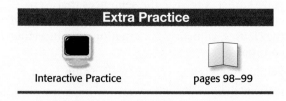

Extra Practice	
Interactive Practice	pages 98–99

Infinitives and adverb clauses of purpose

Main clause (result)	Adverb clause or infinitive (purpose)
You took off time from work	**to** meet with me.
I'll bring my husband	**so that** we can both talk to you.

Grammar Watch

- In the infinitive, *to* is followed by the base form of the verb.
- *So that* is followed by a subject and a verb.

2 PRACTICE

A Read part of the introduction to the West Apollo Elementary School Parents' Guide. Underline the infinitives and clauses that talk about purpose.

West Apollo Elementary School publishes this handbook to provide useful information for parents. It is especially important for you to look at the School Rules on page 8 so that you will understand West Apollo's policies and procedures. In addition, you should pay close attention to the calendar on page 11 so that you can make plans for days when school is closed. See the list of school personnel on page 10 to become familiar with our staff.

B Use *to* or *so that* to complete each school rule.

1. You must provide the name and phone number of a family member _so that_ the school can contact someone in case of emergency.

2. West Apollo Elementary School doors will be locked at 7:45 A.M. _to_ protect the safety of our students.

3. If your child misses school, you must provide a written note _to_ explain the absence.

4. Cell phones are not permitted in school _so that_ classes are not disrupted.

5. Fire drills are conducted _so that_ everyone is prepared if there is ever a real fire in school.

Show what you know! Talk about parents' involvement in school

GROUPS. Discuss. Do you think it is important for parents to be involved in their children's schooling? Why? In what ways can parents get involved?

Can you... talk about parents' involvement in school? ☐

Life Skills

1 READ A CHILD'S REPORT CARD

A CLASS. Discuss.

1. How often do children receive report cards?

2. What kind of information normally appears on a report card?

3. What type of grading systems can be used?

B PAIRS. Read part of Manuel Medina's fifth-grade report card. Study the headings. Help each other with new vocabulary.

2 PRACTICE

A Read the statements. Write *T* (true) or *F* (false). Correct the false statements.

___T___ 1. Manuel was absent more often than he was late.

___T___ 2. The lowest grade on Manuel's report card is in social science.

___F___ 3. Manuel has a C in two classes.

___T___ 4. Manuel has done well on all computer assignments.

___F___ 5. Manuel's grade in science is a 70.

Reporting Period 1

Student Name: Manuel Medina
Teacher Name: A. Brown

Days Absent: 3
Days Late: 1

Academics	Total Grade	Comments
English Language Arts	78	Needs to improve writing. Needs to read more
Mathematics	98	Excels in all aspects of math
Science	72	Has trouble with science vocabulary
Social Science	70	Difficulty with reading affects ability to perform well on tests
Computer	95	Has done an excellent job on all computer assignments
Habits & Attitudes		
Work Habits		
Follows directions		
Completes all class and homework assignments	X	Needs to turn in homework regularly and on time
Social Habits		
Works well in groups	X	Needs to participate in group activities
Shows respect for others		
Is responsible and reliable		

Assessment Key	
90–100 = A (Excellent)	69–60 = D (Poor)
80–89 = B (Good)	Below 60 = F (Failing)
79–70 = C (Average)	X = needs improvement

B PAIRS. Answer the questions.

1. What are Manuel's two best classes? mathematics, computer

2. Which academic skill does Manuel need to improve the most? reading

3. Which "Habits & Attitudes" does Manuel need to improve? turn in homework, participate in group activities

Getting Started   5 minutes

If necessary, define *report card* as a *document that schools send out several (usually two to four) times a year to inform parents of their children's progress in academic skills and behavior.*

Presentation   10 minutes

1 READ A CHILD'S REPORT CARD

A CLASS. **Discuss.**

- Read each question and call on students to answer. If students don't know the answers, share information from your own experience.

Answers:

1. Two to four times a year (or quarterly).
2. Letter grade, numerical grade, and either *pass* or *fail* next to each subject as well as attendance. The report card also includes comments from teachers.
3. See Culture Connection.

Culture Connection

Numerous grading systems are used in the U.S. Examples are letter grades (*A, B, C, D,* and *F*), percentage scores, *Pass / Not Pass,* and comments (*Excellent / Good / Fair / Needs Improvement* or *Excellent / Satisfactory / Unsatisfactory*). Different systems may be used at different grade levels; for example, some school districts may use a comment system for elementary schools and letter grades for high school.

B PAIRS. **Read part of Manuel Medina's...**

- Read the title with the whole class. Ask: *What does* Reporting Period 1 *mean?* (the first report card of the year, which is sent out in late November)
- Have students look at the Assessment Key at the bottom. Explain: *The key explains the meaning of the grades in the report card.*
- Form cross-ability pairs. Have them read the rest of the report card together.

Controlled Practice   15 minutes

2 PRACTICE

A **Read the statements. Write *T* (true) or...**

- Have students remain with their partners from Exercise 1B and do the exercise together.
- Check answers. Call on students to read each statement, say whether it is true or false, and correct the false statements.

■■■ **MULTILEVEL INSTRUCTION for 2A**
Cross-ability Have the high-level student help the lower-level student with vocabulary.

B PAIRS. **Answer the questions.**

- Have students switch partners and answer the questions.
- Go over the answers with the whole class.

■■■ **Expansion: Speaking Practice for 2C**

- Discuss with the whole class. Say: *Imagine that Manuel is your child. Do you think it is a problem that Manuel doesn't participate in groups? Are you worried about his academic skills? Why or why not?*

Communicative Practice 30 minutes

3 PRACTICE

GROUPS. Discuss. What should a parent do...?

- With the class, define a *low grade* as generally *a grade lower than a C or a score lower than 70 percent.* Define a *failing grade* as *a grade of F or a score lower than 60 percent.*

- Form groups. Have each group select a note taker and a reporter. The group should think of various actions a parent could take, for example, meet with the child's teacher, get a tutor, talk to the child. The note taker should write them down.

- Have the reporter from each group report on the group's ideas.

- Ask volunteers what they would do if they were in this situation.

4 READ

A Read the note that Manuel's mother sent...

- Form cross-ability pairs. Have students read the note and discuss the question together.

- Discuss the question with the whole class.

▰▰▰ **MULTILEVEL INSTRUCTION for 4A**

Cross-ability Have the lower-level student read Ms. Medina's note out loud. Have the higher-level student help with pronunciation and vocabulary.

B Now read Ms. Brown's note to Ms. Medina...

- Form different pairs. Again, have students read the note and discuss the question together.

- Discuss the question with the whole class.

C Read both notes again. Then answer the questions.

- Have students do the exercise alone.

- Have them compare answers with a classmate.

- Go over the answers with the class.

Answers:

1. She should call Ms. Brown to arrange the day and time for the meeting.

2. In the evening, so Ms. Medina doesn't have to miss work.

3. They're going to discuss ways to help Manuel read more.

5 WRITE

Write a note to your child's teacher about...

- Tell students their note should have two parts: a description of the problem, and a request for a meeting.

- If possible, have them write their notes in class. While students are writing, walk around and provide help as needed.

- Pair students and have them read their note to their partner.

- Collect the notes. Correct spelling and punctuation.

- Have students write a clean draft of their notes.

▰▰▰ **Expansion: Writing Practice for 5**

- Collect students' notes. Mix them and hand them out randomly to the class.

- Have each student write a response to the note they received, using Ms. Brown's note as a model.

Progress Check

Can you . . . interpret and respond to a report card?

Say: *We have practiced interpreting and responding to a report card. Now, look at the question at the bottom of the page. Can you interpret and respond to a report card? Write a checkmark in the box.*

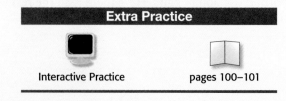

Extra Practice

Interactive Practice   pages 100–101

3 PRACTICE

GROUPS. Discuss. What should a parent do if a child receives a low or failing grade on a report card?

4 READ

A Read the note that Manuel's mother sent to his teacher, Ms. Brown, after reading his report card. Why did she write the note?

B Now read Ms. Brown's note to Ms. Medina. How does she respond to Ms. Medina's request for a conference? She says yes.

> Dear Ms. Brown,
>
> My husband and I looked at Manuel's report card yesterday. We are concerned about his grades in social science, science, and English. We have been trying to get him to read more, but it is difficult.
>
> Could we have a conference to talk about how to help him? I would prefer to meet in the early evening after work, but I can be available almost anytime.
>
> Thank you for your help.
>
> Sincerely,
>
> Bertha Medina

Dear Ms. Medina,

Thank you for contacting me about Manuel's grades.

I would be happy to meet to discuss ways to help Manuel read more. I can be at the school in the evening so you don't have to miss work. Please call me at 310-555-9904 to set up a day and time for our conference.

Sincerely,

Arlene Brown

C Read both notes again. Then answer the questions.

1. What does Ms. Medina need to do now to arrange a meeting with Ms. Brown?
2. Are Ms. Medina and Ms. Brown going to meet in the morning, afternoon, or evening? Why?
3. What are Ms. Medina and Ms. Brown going to discuss?

5 WRITE

Write a note to your child's teacher about something you would like to discuss. If you don't have children, write a note to your English teacher about your own learning. Use Ms. Medina's note as a model.

Can you...interpret and respond to a report card? ☐

Listening and Speaking

1 BEFORE YOU LISTEN

A Discuss. If you were enrolling a child in a new school, what would you want to find out about the school?

B GROUPS. In some school districts, parents have to prove that their family lives in that district. Why? What things can they use to show their home address?

2 LISTEN

CD2 T31

A Mr. Lopez is talking to the secretary at West Apollo Elementary School. Listen to the first part of their conversation. Why is Mr. Lopez at school with his daughter? to enroll her

CD2 T31

B Listen to the first part of the conversation again. Answer the questions.

1. Why is Marta changing schools? she moved to a different home

2. How many days of school has Marta missed? 3 days

3. What grade is Marta in? second grade

CD2 T32

C Read the questions. Listen to the whole conversation. Then circle the correct answers.

1. What does Mr. Lopez use to prove his address?
   a. his lease   b. a phone bill   c. an electric bill

2. What other information did Mr. Lopez bring with him?
   a. an emergency contact form   b. Marta's school-bus schedule   c. Marta's health records

3. What information does the secretary give Mr. Lopez?
   a. a list of school rules   b. a medical form   c. a list of school supplies

4. When will Marta begin school?
   a. today   b. next week   c. no information

Lesson 4 Talk to school personnel

Getting Started
10 minutes

1 BEFORE YOU LISTEN

Ⓐ Discuss. If you were enrolling a child...

- Define *enrolling* as *signing up or registering a child for school.*
- Elicit questions that students would ask and write them on the board.

Ⓑ GROUPS. Discuss. In some school districts,...

- Form groups. Try to make sure there are parents of schoolchildren in each group.
- Give a time limit for discussion.
- Call on students to share their answers with the whole class.

Culture Connection

In most cities, schools are funded by property taxes, that is, taxes that are paid by homeowners. Children normally attend school in the district where they live.

Presentation
5 minutes

2 LISTEN

Ⓐ Mr. Lopez is talking to the secretary...

- Have students look at the photo. Ask: *Who do you think the speakers are? Where are they? What do you think they are doing?*
- Remind students to listen specifically for the answer to the question. It is not necessary to understand every word.
- Play CD 2, Track 31.
- Call on a volunteer to answer the question.

Controlled Practice
20 minutes

Ⓑ Listen to the first part of the...

- Play CD 2, Track 31.
- Have students do the exercise.
- Call on students to answer the questions.

Ⓒ Read the questions. Listen...

- Have students read the questions and predict the answers.
- Play CD 2, Track 32. Have students answer the questions.
- Check answers. If students are unable to answer a question, play that section of the recording again.

Lesson 4 Talk to school personnel

3 CONVERSATION

 Mr. Lopez continues to speak...

- Play CD 2, Track 33. Have students listen and read along silently.
- *Optional:* Have above-level students listen with their books closed.
- Check comprehension. Ask: *What is Mr. Lopez's first question? What does he need to do? What else does he want to do? What day is good for him?*

4 PRACTICE

A **PAIRS. Practice the conversation.**

- Form cross-ability pairs and have students take turns reading each role.
- Walk around and listen as students are practicing.
- Ask volunteers to perform the conversation for the class.

▮ MULTILEVEL INSTRUCTION for 4A

Pre-level Have students practice with the same partner.

Above-level Have students continue the conversation with three or four more exchanges, using their own ideas.

Communicative Practice 25 minutes

B **ROLE PLAY. PAIRS. Role-play this situation.**

- Read the role descriptions and define vocabulary as needed, for example, *guidance counselor: the person at a school who helps students and parents make decisions about students' education and their future.*
- Using the conversation in Exercise 3 as a model, role-play the call with an above-level student. Play the role of the school secretary.
- Pair students of similar ability. Have them choose a situation and practice their role play at least twice.
- Call on pairs of students to perform their role play for the class.

▮ MULTILEVEL INSTRUCTION for 4B

Pre-level Have students write a script for a conversation that follows the model of the conversation in Exercise 3. Have them practice reading the script several times. Then have them role-play without using their script.

Above-level Have Student A (the parent) choose the reason for the call without informing Student B (the secretary). This will make the role play more authentic.

C **MAKE IT PERSONAL. GROUPS. Schools...**

- Form groups. Have each group select a timekeeper, a note taker, and a reporter. The note taker should write down the group's answer to question 3.
- Give a time limit. While students are talking, walk around and provide help as needed.
- Have each group's reporter share the group's answer to question 3.

Extra Practice

Interactive Practice

CD2 T33

Mr. Lopez continues to speak with the school secretary. Listen and read.

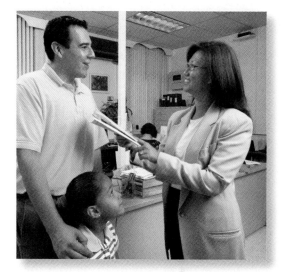

Mr. Lopez: I have a question.

Secretary: Certainly.

Mr. Lopez: I heard that there's a free lunch program. Is that true?

Secretary: Yes. We have a free lunch program for students who need financial assistance.

Mr. Lopez: That's great. What do I need to do?

Secretary: Here's an application. You'll need to fill it out, and you'll need to provide documents that show income.

Mr. Lopez: No problem. One more thing.

Secretary: Sure.

Mr. Lopez: I'd like to talk with my daughter's teacher. Would that be possible?

Secretary: Yes, but you'll need to make an appointment.

Mr. Lopez: OK. Wednesday is best for me.

Secretary: First, let me get your daughter's name again and the teacher's name.

4 PRACTICE

A PAIRS. **Practice the conversation.**

B ROLE PLAY. PAIRS. **Role-play this situation.**

Student A: You are a parent. Call the school. Choose one of the reasons below for your call. Use the information below.

Student B: You are the school secretary. Answer the parent's questions. Also help the parent make an appointment.

Reasons for the call

a. You want information about the breakfast program, and you want to speak to the principal.

b. You want information about after-school programs, and you want to speak to your child's teacher.

c. You want information about the school calendar, and you want to speak to the guidance counselor.

C MAKE IT PERSONAL. GROUPS. **Schools have many different programs for students. Discuss.**

1. What kinds of school programs do you know about?

2. When and where do these programs take place?

3. What other programs do you think schools ought to have?

Grammar

Adjective clauses: Relative pronoun as subject of the clause

Main clause	Adjective clause	
	Relative pronoun—Subject	Verb (+ Object)
We have a free lunch program for students	**who/that**	need financial assistance.
I brought an electric bill,	**which/that**	has my name and address on it.

1   PRACTICE

Grammar Watch

- Use *who* for people.
- Use *which* for things.
- Use *that* for both people and things.

A   Read the paragraph. Underline the adjective clauses. Circle the person or thing that the adjective clauses give information about.

     The Parent-Teacher Association is an (organization) which works on both the national and local levels. At the local level, parents and other family members meet to share (ideas) that can improve student learning. The PTA members also work on special projects. For example, they sometimes sell candy, cookbooks, or tickets to a dance to earn (money) which can help the school buy new computers. In some cases, the money is used to pay (guest) (speakers), who come to the school to teach students for a day. The local PTA does a lot of good, and it gives the (people) who participate in its activities a feeling of belonging to the community.

B   Complete the sentences with *who* or *which*.

1. Schools in the U.S. have programs, ___which___ help parents get involved in their children's education.

2. Parents ___who___ know what their children are doing in school can help them do better.

3. Parent-teacher conferences are important meetings ___which___ give parents one-on-one time with school personnel.

4. Parents can ask for a translator ___who___ speaks their language.

5. Guidance counselors ___who___ work at the school can request meetings with parents.

Getting Started   5 minutes

- On the board, write the following incomplete sentences: *1. My children go to a school that . . . , 2. I prefer teachers who . . . ,* and *3. I love gifts, which I receive from . . .*

- Ask: *What is special about your or your children's school? What kind of teachers do you prefer? What kind of gifts do teachers love?* Use the answers students give to complete the sentences with adjective clauses.

- Underline the adjective clause in each sentence. Double-underline the relative pronouns. Circle the noun that they modify.

- Explain: *The underlined parts of the sentence are called* adjective clauses. Who, that, *and* which *are called* relative pronouns. *Adjective clauses give information about the nouns before them. In this lesson we'll learn about adjective clauses.*

Presentation   10 minutes

Adjective clauses: Relative pronoun as subject of the clause

- Copy the sentences from the grammar chart onto the board. Write each sentence with just one relative pronoun. Read the sentences aloud.

- Point to each sentence and ask: What is the adjective clause in this sentence? Which noun does it modify?

- Read the Grammar Watch notes. Point to the first sentence in the grammar chart and circle *students.* Say: *Students are people. In this sentence, both* who *and* that *are correct.*

- Point to the second example sentence. Say: *An electric bill is a thing, so we use* that *or* which *in the adjective clause.*

- Circle the relative pronouns in the examples. Say: *These words are the subjects of the clauses.* Point to the first example and ask: *Who needs financial assistance?* (students)

- Point out that in sentences with adjective clauses, the verb in the adjective clause must agree with the noun that the clause modifies: *We have a free lunch program for* students *who* need *financial assistance. I brought an* electric bill *that* has *my name and address on it.*

- Point out that an adjective clause can also come in the middle of a sentence: *Parents* who work during the day *can ask for meetings in the evening.*

Language Notes

- Adjective clauses that give defining information about the noun they modify are called *restrictive clauses.* Restrictive clauses are not set off with commas, for example, *Our school district is looking for teachers who can teach advanced science courses.* In contrast, clauses that do not give defining information about the noun they modify are called *nonrestrictive clauses.* They are set off with commas, for example, *Mr. Costa, who teaches advanced science courses, is a popular teacher.*

- In North American English, restrictive clauses that describe things or ideas can begin with either *that* or *which.* However, nonrestrictive clauses can only start with *which.*

- *That* is far more common than *which* in restrictive clauses.

Controlled Practice   10 minutes

1 PRACTICE

A Read the paragraph. Underline the...

- Read the example. Suggest that students underline the adjective clauses first, then circle the noun they modify.

- Have students do the exercise.

- Call on students to read the clauses they underlined and to say which words they circled.

B Complete the sentences with *who* or *which.*

- Have students restate the rules for using *who, that,* and *which.*

- Read item 1. Have students complete the exercise.

- Check answers. Have students say which additional relative pronoun would be correct in each item.

Expansion: Speaking Practice

- Have students play a definitions game. Instruct them to think of a person, place, or animal and write a description of it, using an adjective clause.

- Have each student read his or her description. The class should call out the person, place, or animal being described.

Presentation   10 minutes

Adjective clauses: Relative pronoun as object of the clause

- Copy the sentences from the grammar chart onto the board. Underline the adjective clauses. Double-underline the relative pronouns.
- Remind students that in subject clauses, *who* or *that* is the subject of the clause. It is followed by a verb. Repeat one of the examples from the grammar chart.
- Point to the object-pattern examples and explain that, in contrast, in object clauses, the relative pronoun is followed by a subject and a verb.
- For most classes, this description of the difference between subject clauses and object clauses will suffice. If your students request a more detailed explanation, proceed as follows:
  1. Write the first example as two simple sentences: *1. I need a phone number. 2. I can call it.*
  2. Say: *Sentences with adjective clauses have two clauses. Let's suppose that they start out as two simple sentences. Notice the object in the second sentence. (Circle it.) To make a sentence with an adjective clause, we combine the two simple sentences into one sentence. In the second sentence, we replace the object* it *with* that *or* which, *and we put the relative pronoun after* phone number.
  3. Repeat the process with the second example.
- Read the Grammar Watch note. Have the students look at the examples again and say each sentence in three ways.

Controlled Practice   10 minutes

2 PRACTICE

A Read the letter to parents in West...

- Read the example with the class. Make sure students understand what to circle, underline, and double underline.
- Read the items and clarify vocabulary.
- Have students do the exercise individually or in pairs.
- Call students up to the board and have them mark the items. Make corrections as needed.

B Read the sentences. Cross out the relative...

- Read item 1 with the class. Ask: *Can we cut the relative pronoun in this sentence?* (no) *Why not?* (It is the subject of the clause. A verb comes after it.)
- Have students do the exercise alone or in pairs.
- Go over the answers. Have the class say all possible ways of forming each sentence.

Expansion: Speaking Practice

- Play the definitions game again, but this time have students use adjective clauses with object relative pronouns. Tell them to use object clauses in their definitions. For example, *It's a tool (that) people use to cut hair. It's an instrument (that) you hang on the wall, and it tells the time.*
- Have students read their definitions, and have the class guess what the item is.

Communicative Practice   15 minutes

Show what you know!

GROUPS. Discuss.

- Form groups. Have them choose a timekeeper, a note taker and a reporter. The note taker should write down the group's ideas.
- Give a time limit for the discussion.
- Have the reporters share their group's ideas. Write them on the board.
- As a follow-up, point to each idea and have students raise their hands if they have helped or are helping their child's school in this way.

Progress Check

Can you . . . talk about improving schools?

Say: *We have practiced talking about improving schools. Now, look at the question at the bottom of the page. Can you talk about improving schools? Write a checkmark in the box.*

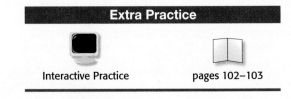

Extra Practice

Interactive Practice   pages 102–103

Adjective clauses: Relative pronoun as object of the clause		
Main clause	**Adjective clause**	
	Relative pronoun — Object	Subject + Verb
I need a phone number	**(which/that)**	we can call.
You're the person	**(who/that)**	I spoke with.

2 PRACTICE

A Read the letter to parents in West Apollo School District. Underline the relative pronouns. Circle the person or thing the relative pronoun refers to. Double underline the subject and the verb that follow the relative pronoun.

Dear Parent:

Please become involved in our schools! Here are examples of (things) that <u>you can do</u>.

1. Volunteer to go on one of the many (field trips) which <u>our students make</u>.

2. Find time to coach a sports team. Think about the future (athletes) that <u>you can help</u>.

3. Help organize (a multi cultural night) that <u>students, parents, and teachers can attend</u>.

Remember: Everything that <u>you do</u> helps all our children.

B Read the sentences. Cross out the relative pronoun if it can be omitted.

1. Silvia is the kind of mother who likes to be involved in her children's education.

2. Are there things ~~which~~ I can do to help my son with his schoolwork?

3. The project ~~that~~ Mrs. Bentley assigned shouldn't take more than an hour.

4. Parents should talk to their children about the work ~~that~~ they're doing in class.

5. Charlie told his mother the name of the teacher who helped him.

Show what you know! Talk about improving schools

GROUPS. Discuss.

What are at least five things parents can do to help their children's school? Take notes.

Can you...talk about improving schools? ☐

Reading

1 BEFORE YOU READ

A CLASS. What did you do after school when you were a child? If you are a parent, what do your children do after school?

B GROUPS. After-school programs need to pay for the teachers and supplies. The words below can be used to talk about money. Discuss their meanings.

cuts   budget   reduce   eliminate

2 READ

A Look at the highlighted quote. What do you predict the author will say about after-school programs?

CD2 T34

B Read and listen. Was your prediction correct? What does Meg Reitz think of after-school programs?

Commentary   MEG REITZ

What's the Real Cost of Cutting After-School Programs?

Because they have to make cuts in the annual budget, local school board officials are discussing whether or not to continue **funding** for after-school programs. As far as I can see, there should be no discussion about whether or not to continue paying for them. After-school programs are essential.

Today's parents, both mothers and fathers, have jobs, and they work long hours. So who's taking care of the kids until Mom or Dad gets home? A major benefit of after-school programs is safety. They keep young people **occupied**, and busy children usually stay out of trouble. However, after-school programs are more than a babysitting service. They provide educational, cultural, and personal advantages.

> *". . . after-school programs cost money, but they're worth every dollar."*

Research has shown that students who participate in after-school programs have a better attitude, and as a result, they attend class regularly, get better grades, and have an increased chance of graduating from high school. Also, after-school programs allow time for art, music, and hands-on learning in math and technology. They can offer field trips to concerts, museums, and places that show the history of our city.

In after-school programs, young people can learn about themselves, too. They may find out what they're really interested in and decide on a future career. While they're having fun doing a science project or preparing for a dance performance, students can develop their creativity and communication skills. And many programs give students the chance to work together on a team.

Sure, after-school programs cost money, but they're worth every dollar. Besides, help is available. Our school board can ask for **support** from local business groups and apply for funds from the government. There's no good reason to reduce or eliminate programs that benefit our children.

Lesson 6   Read about after-school programs

Getting Started 5 minutes

Read the lesson title. Tell the class that in this lesson, they will read a magazine article that expresses the writer's opinion about after-school programs.

1 BEFORE YOU READ

Ⓐ CLASS. What did you do after school...

- Go around the room and call on students to answer the questions.

Ⓑ GROUPS. After-school programs need...

- On the board write the sentences from the reading containing the target words: *Because they have to make cuts in the annual budget, local school board officials are discussing whether or not to continue funding for after-school programs,* and *There's no good reason to reduce or eliminate programs that benefit our children.* Read the sentences out loud.
- Encourage students to guess the meanings of the words. Write their guesses on the board.
- Have them look up the meanings of the words and compare them with their guesses.

Presentation 25 minutes

2 READ

Ⓐ Look at the highlighted quote. What...?

- Hold up your book and show students the highlighted quote. Read it aloud.
- Have students guess what the author's opinion about after-school programs is. Write their predictions on the board.

Ⓑ 💿 Read and listen. Was your prediction...

Note: Do not pre-teach the boldfaced vocabulary. The items are practiced in Exercise 4.

- Ask: *What is a commentary?* (an article in which someone comments, or states his or her opinion about a question or issue)
- Read the title. Ask: *What do some people want to do?* (cut after-school programs) *What does the author want?* (not to cut them)
- Have students read silently, without using dictionaries. Give a time limit, but allow more time to read if necessary.
- When time is up, point to students' predictions on the board and ask: *Was your prediction correct?*
- Call on volunteers to state the author's opinion.
- As a final step, play CD 2, Track 34 as students read and listen.

Read about after-school programs

3 CHECK YOUR UNDERSTANDING

Reading Skill: Distinguishing Fact from Opinion

- Read the Reading Skill.
- Bring in a newspaper and show students the editorial page. Explain that the editorial page has letters and commentaries on events in the news.
- Discuss the difference between a fact and an opinion, and give examples of language associated with each. A *fact* is something that can be proven to be true. Facts can be supported by observation, by science, or by numbers. An *opinion* is someone's belief. Opinions can be identified, for example, by verbs such as *believe, think, suppose,* and *imagine*; by adjectival phrases such as *It's important, essential,* and *crucial*; and by words that have positive or negative connotations, for example, an *articulate* politician versus a *slick* politician.

Controlled Practice   15 minutes

A Read the statements. Write *F* (fact)...

- Explain that in this case, *F* means *fact,* not *false.*
- Read item 1 with the class.
- Have students do the exercise.
- Check answers. Ask students how they know whether the statement is a fact or an opinion.

B Complete the sentences.

- Have students complete the sentences.
- Check answers.

C GROUPS. Discuss. The title of the reading...

- Explain that the word *cost* can refer to money, but it can also mean *harmful effects.*
- Have students go through the reading and underline the benefits of after-school programs.
- Put students in groups. Instruct them to discuss what harmful things would happen if the benefits they underlined were taken away.

Expansion: Writing Practice

- Have students rewrite each of the author's main points (the benefits of after-school programs, according to the author) in their own words.

4 WORD WORK

Find the boldfaced words in the article and...

- Do the first item with the class. Have a student read the sentence in which *funding* appears. Tell students to read the next sentence and select the word that has the same meaning. *(paying)*
- Have students complete the remaining items and compare answers with a partner.
- Call on students to say the answers.

MULTILEVEL INSTRUCTION

Cross-ability Have above-level students work with pre-level students to define the terms.

Communicative Practice   15 minutes

Show what you know!

GROUPS. Discuss an after-school program...

- With the class, make a list of types of after-school programs. For example, there are programs at schools, in community centers, and at parks. Most cities also have after-school sports.
- Form groups. Try to include in every group a person with children.
- Give a time limit for discussion.
- To wrap up, have volunteers share their knowledge with the whole class.

Community Building

If possible, go with your students to visit an after-school program on your school campus or at a nearby park or community center. Alternately, have students research an after-school program in your area.

Extra Practice

Interactive Practice   pages 104–105

3 CHECK YOUR UNDERSTANDING

A Read the statements. Write *F* (fact) or *O* (opinion).

Reading Skill: Distinguishing Fact from Opinion

When you read, be careful to distinguish between facts and opinions. A fact is something that can be proven, or is true. An opinion is what someone believes or thinks.

__F__ 1. School board officials are discussing whether or not to fund after-school programs.

__O__ 2. It's important to keep after-school programs.

__F__ 3. Students in after-school programs get better grades.

__F__ 4. After-school programs cost money.

__O__ 5. After-school programs are worth the cost.

B Complete the sentences.

1. Student safety after school is often a problem because _students are not occupied—or don't_ _have much to do—and parents are not home_.

2. Students who participate in after-school programs are more likely to _have a better attitude,_ _attend class regularly, get better grades, and graduate_.

3. After-school programs often provide opportunities for students to work directly with _people and projects related to their future careers_.

4. Money for after-school programs often comes from _local business groups and_ _the government_.

C GROUPS. Discuss. The title of the reading asks a question. Based on what the author says, what is the answer to that question?

4 WORD WORK

Find the boldfaced words in the article and guess their meaning from the context. Write a synonym for each word.

1. funding __money__   2. occupied __busy__   3. support __help__

Show what you know!   Talk about after-school programs

GROUPS. Discuss an after-school program that you know about. What are the advantages of the program?

Discuss school safety

Listening and Speaking

1 | BEFORE YOU LISTEN

CLASS. What makes a school safe? What can school officials do to improve student safety?

2 | LISTEN

CD2 T35

A The West Apollo Elementary School principal is talking to a group of parents, teachers, and community leaders. Listen. What does she want them to do? contribute ideas

Student Safety Matters

CD2 T35

B Read the questions. Listen to the principal again. Then circle the correct answers.

1. Before this evening, how many times had the committee met?
   a. none   b. one   c. two

2. How many improvements does the mayor want each school to make?
   a. three   b. four   c. five

3. Which places are **NOT** mentioned?
   a. classrooms   b. playgrounds   c. parking lot

Discuss school safety

Getting Started   10 minutes

Read the lesson title. Ask the class: *Does your children's school have a safety plan? What do you know about it?*

1 BEFORE YOU LISTEN

CLASS. **What makes a school safe? What can...**

- Read the first question and have students share ideas. If necessary, ask such specific questions as: *What makes a school safe physically?* (fences, fire alarms, etc.) *What role does communication play in making a school safe?* (For example, in the event of a disaster, the school should have a plan in place for contacting parents.)

- Read the second question. If necessary, ask students to think about specific areas of safety such as playground safety, accident prevention, disaster prevention, antiterrorism, drug prevention. You may want to list these topics on the board.

Presentation   10 minutes

2 LISTEN

Ⓐ **The West Apollo Elementary School...**

- Have students look at the illustration. Ask them to point out the school principal. Inform students that the other people in the picture—the parents, teachers, and community leaders—are an *advisory committee*, a group whose job is to work with the principal to make the school safer. Note: An advisory committee advises someone—in this case the principal—but does not have the authority to actually make changes.

- Play CD 2, Track 35.

- Have students answer the question. If they can't, tell them to listen for the word *assist*, which means *help*. Play the recording again.

Controlled Practice   5 minutes

Ⓑ **Read the questions. Listen...**

- Play Track 35 again. Have students listen for the answers to the questions.

- Check answers. Play the recording again if necessary.

Presentation 10 minutes

3 CONVERSATION

Pronunciation Watch

- On the board, write: *1. We should have left earlier. 2. We shouldn't have stayed out late. 3. We could have taken the bus. 4. I couldn't have met you last night.* and *5. It must have rained.*
- Tell students they will learn the grammar of past modals in Lesson 8. For now, quickly explain the implied meanings of the sentences: *1. We didn't leave early. 2. We stayed out late. 3. We didn't take the bus. 4. It was not possible for me to meet you last night.* and *5. I guess that it rained (probably because the streets are wet.)*
- Read the Pronunciation Watch note. Explain that the first word of the modal is stressed.
- Read the sentences on the board. Tell students to focus on the pronunciation of the past modals.

A 🔘 **Listen to the sentences. Notice...**

- Play CD 2, Track 36. Have students listen.
- Play Track 36 again. Have students listen and repeat.

Controlled Practice 10 minutes

B 🔘 **Listen to the sentences. Circle...**

- Play CD 2, Track 37. Have students listen and fill in the missing words.
- Check answers.
- Play the recording again as needed.

Expansion: Speaking Practice

- Have students say the sentences aloud to a partner after they fill them in.

C **Two parents on the safety advisory...**

- Play CD 2, Track 38. Have students listen and read along silently.
- Check comprehension. Ask: *Why was Parent A disappointed? What does the playground need, according to the parents? What happened on the playground last week? What did the teachers do?*

4 PRACTICE

A **PAIRS. Practice the conversation.**

- Form cross-ability pairs. Have them practice the conversation twice.
- Correct mispronunciations of past modals.
- Ask volunteers to perform their conversation.

▬▬▬ MULTILEVEL INSTRUCTION for 4A

Cross-ability Have the lower-level student read the part of Parent B. Have the higher-level student read the role of Parent A and take care to pronounce past modals correctly.

Communicative Practice 15 minutes

B **MAKE IT PERSONAL. GROUPS. Imagine you...**

- Form groups. Tell students to discuss why the items on the checklist are important. Have them add other items.
- Go over the items with the whole class. Call on students to say why they are important.
- Ask students which items they checked and added to the checklist. (These items will differ according to the location of your school. For example, schools in California must all have safety procedures in case of earthquakes.)

Community Building

Invite a guest speaker to talk to your class about a safety issue that concerns the students in your class. In high-crime areas, for example, the speaker might talk about ways to keep safe while traveling to and from school.

Extra Practice

Interactive Practice

CD2 T36

A 🔘 **Listen to the sentences. Notice the pronunciation of the past modals. Then listen and repeat.**

The teachers **should have** ("should of") stopped the fight.

They **shouldn't have** ("shouldn't of") allowed it to start.

You **must have** ("must of") heard about the plan.

When you say past modals such as *may have, must have, might have, should have, shouldn't have, could have,* and *couldn't have,* link the two words together and pronounce them as one word. *Have* usually sounds like *of* (or *a* in fast speech).

CD2 T37

B 🔘 **Listen to the sentences. Circle the words you hear.**

1. I **should have / (shouldn't have)** told her about the problem.
2. The teachers **(could have)/ couldn't have** stopped the fight.
3. They **(should have)/ shouldn't have** talked to the parents.
4. My son **could have / (couldn't have)** been involved in the fight.
5. You **(should have)/ shouldn't have** gone to the meeting.

CD2 T38

C 🔘 **Two parents on the safety advisory committee are talking. Listen and read.**

Parent A: I was disappointed in our meeting tonight. I think we should have talked much more about playground safety.

Parent B: I agree. Too many kids get hurt on the school playground.

Parent A: Right. We need good-quality equipment. I'm not sure the swings and slides we have now are of good quality.

Parent B: And the children need better supervision. Who is watching them on the playground?

Parent A: I don't know. My son told me there was a fight last week. Nobody did anything about it. The teachers should have stopped it.

Parent B: Stopped it? The teachers shouldn't have allowed it to start!

4 **PRACTICE**

A **PAIRS. Practice the conversation.**

B **MAKE IT PERSONAL. Discuss ideas about school safety.**

GROUPS. Imagine you are members of a school safety committee. Which three things are the most important for safety? Use the list below. Add your own ideas.

☐ knowing what to do in case of fire   ☐ knowing what to do in case of bad weather

☐ supervising students on the playground   ☐ protecting students on the Internet

☐ making sure students do not use cell phones   ☐ other: _____

Grammar

Past modals: Expressing degrees of certainty about the past				
Subject	Modal	Have	Past participle	
They	**may (not)** **might (not)** **must (not)** **could (not)**	**have**	noticed	the problems.

· · · · · · **Grammar Watch**

- Use *may (not) have, might (not) have,* or *could have* to show that you are not certain that something happened.

- Use *must have* to show that you are almost certain that something has happened.

- Use *must not have* to show that you are almost certain that something has NOT happened.

- Use *cannot have, could not have (can't have, couldn't have)* to show that you are certain that something has NOT happened.

1   PRACTICE

A **Read the conversation between a student and teacher. Underline the past modal phrases.**

Admir: Ms. Lee, I can't find my bike helmet. I <u>might have left</u> it here. Did you see it?

Ms. Lee: No, I'm sorry. I didn't. <u>Could</u> you <u>have left</u> it at home?

Admir: No, I was wearing it this morning.

Ms. Lee: Well, that's good. You should wear it whenever you ride. Maybe you left it in the cafeteria.

Admir: Oh, you're right! I got breakfast this morning. I <u>must have left</u> it there.

B **Complete the sentences. Use *may have, may not have, must have,* or *couldn't have.***

1. **A:** Where is Mr. Chen?

   B: He was out yesterday, so he _____may not have_____ heard about the safety meeting.

2. **A:** The superintendent of schools was here. She looked very pleased.

   B: She _____must have_____ noticed the safety signs.

3. **A:** I'm not sure the safety committee checked the equipment on the playground.

   B: They _____couldn't have_____ been there yet. There are still no seats on the swings!

4. **A:** Did you see Victor at the meeting?

   B: He _____may have_____ been there, but I didn't see him.

Getting Started   5 minutes

- Draw a continuum on the board. Label it *Degrees of Certainty*. From left to right or top to bottom, write *50%*, *95%*, and *100%*. Next to (or under) *50%*, write *may (not) have, might (not) have, could have*; next to (or under) *95%*, write *must (not) have*; and next to (or under) *100%*, write *cannot have, could not have*.

- Write one or two examples on the board. For example, *1. You must have heard about the plan. 2. Your children might have talked to you.* Underline the past modals and say: *These are past modals. In this lesson, we'll learn how to use them to talk about degrees of certainty about the past. For example, in the first sentence, the speaker is almost sure you heard about the plan. In the second sentence, the speaker thinks it is possible, but not certain, that your children talked to you.*

- Help students notice the form of past modals: modal (+ optional *not*) + *have* + past participle. Write the formula on the board.

Presentation   15 minutes

Past Modals: Expressing degrees of certainty about the past

- Copy the affirmative forms of the sentences from the grammar chart onto the board.

- Read the first, second, and fourth sentences aloud. Say the negative form of each sentence as well. Point to *50%* on the illustration on the board and read the first Grammar Watch note. Reiterate that *may have, might have,* and *could have* are similar in meaning. However, *could not have* does not mean 50 percent certainty. (It means 100 percent).

- Read the third example (*They must (not) have . . .*) Point to *95%* on the illustration on the board and read the second and third notes. Explain that *95%* means *almost certain.*

- Write on the board: *They could not have noticed the problems.* Point to *100%* and read the last note. Reiterate that *100%* means *you are certain something did not happen because it is impossible.*

Teaching Tip

Could have and *couldn't have* are potentially confusing because the affirmative form has the meaning of 50 percent certainty, while the negative form has the meaning of 100 percent.

Controlled Practice   10 minutes

1   PRACTICE

Ⓐ Read the conversation between a student...

- Read the example.
- Have students do the exercise.
- Check answers. Have students read the clauses they underlined.

Ⓑ Complete the sentences. *Use may have,...*

- Clarify the directions: Students should use each modal once.
- Remind students to use *may have* or *may not have* if the speaker is uncertain, *must have* if the speaker is almost certain, and *couldn't have* if the speaker is certain.
- Have students do the exercise in pairs.
- Call on pairs to read the items. Write the answers on the board. Correct as needed.

Expansion: Grammar Practice

- Write the following conversations between two family members on the board. *1. A: Where's my library book? It's not here. B: Hmm. I'm not sure. Mom _____ returned it to the library. 2. A: Why doesn't Annie answer her phone? I've been trying to call her all day. B: She _____ remembered to take her cell phone with her. 3. A: Where's the car? B: It's not here? Your brother _____ taken it. 4. A: We're out of milk. B: Mom _____ gone to the store yet. 5. A: I just called Dad's office. He's not there. B: Well, it's only four o'clock. He _____ left yet.*

- Have students fill in the blanks with all possible modals. Discuss the meanings of the different possibilities. (Best answers: 1. *may/might/could have* 2. *must not have* 3. *must have* 4. *must not have* 5. *couldn't/can't have*)

- Pair students and have them practice each conversation twice, switching roles.

Lesson 8 Discuss school safety

Presentation   5 minutes

Expressing advice or opinions about the past

- Copy the grammar chart onto the board.
- Read the first sentence. Ask: *Did the teacher stop the fight?* (no) Read the first Grammar Watch note. Say: Advisable in the past *means something was a good idea, but it didn't happen.* Should have *shows that the speaker is sorry the action did not happen.*
- Read the second sentence and the second note. Say: Not advisable in the past *means the action was not a good idea, but it happened, and the speaker is sorry it happened.*

Controlled Practice   10 minutes

2 PRACTICE

Some children behaved in unsafe ways...

- Read item 1. Ask: *How does the speaker feel about the children's action?* (The speaker disapproves or thinks it was a bad idea.)
- Have students complete the exercise.
- Call students to the board to write the answers.
- Have other students read the sentences on the board and say if they are correct.

Expansion: Grammar Practice

- On the board write the following conversation between two parents or use an overhead transparency. Have students fill in the blanks with past modals. *A: The lighting in this parking lot is so much better. They _____ installed new lighting. B: Looks like it. I think they _____ made some other changes, too. A: Really? Like what? B: Well, I heard they have two teachers monitoring the playground at all times. I think some parents _____ complained that there wasn't enough supervision. A: That's a good change. They _____ done it a long time ago, actually. B: I know. But it's good that they're fixing things now.* (Answers: *must have, may / might have, must have / might have / may have, should have*)
- Have students fill in the blanks in all possible ways. Discuss their choices.
- Have students practice reading the conversation in pairs. Call on volunteers to perform the conversation for the class.

Communicative Practice   15 minutes

Show what you know!

STEP 1. Read about Tuan's problem.

- Have students write a sentence using each of the past modals *must have, may have,* and *might have.*

STEP 2. PAIRS. Discuss Tuan's problem. Use...

- Pair students.
- Have a person from each pair write one possible cause on the board.
- Have the class read the sentences on the board. Tell students to write down as many sentences as they can telling what Tuan's parents should have done.
- Have a student from each pair write one sentence on the board expressing an opinion about what Tuan's parents should have done.

STEP 3. GROUPS. Share your ideas.

> ### Culture Connection
>
> Injuries caused by carrying heavy backpacks are a growing problem among American schoolchildren. Problems include pain in the shoulders, neck, and back; fatigue; incorrect posture; improper development of back muscles; and even fractures of the spine. Experts recommend that children should carry no more than 15 percent of their body weight in their backpacks, but studies have shown that many children carry as much as 25 pounds (possibly 40 to 50 percent of their body weight) of books and supplies to and from school.

Progress Check

Can you . . . discuss school safety?

Say: *We have practiced discussing school safety. Look at the question at the bottom of the page. Can you discuss school safety? Write a checkmark in the box.*

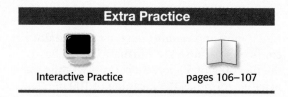

Extra Practice

Interactive Practice   pages 106–107

Expressing advice or opinions about the past				
Subject	Should (not)	Have	Past participle	
A teacher	**should**	**have**	stopped	the fight.
The teachers	**shouldn't**	**have**	allowed	it to start!

2 PRACTICE

Some children behaved in unsafe ways on the bus. Write sentences saying what they should have or shouldn't have done.

1. The children played loud music. _They shouldn't have played loud music._

2. They didn't wear their seat belts. They should have worn their seat belts.

3. They ran up and down the aisle. They shouldn't have run up and down the aisle.

4. They put their heads out the windows. They shouldn't have put their heads out the window.

5. They didn't show respect for the driver. They should have shown respect for the driver.

6. They got out of their seats. They shouldn't have gotten out of their seats.

7. They didn't listen to the bus driver. They should have listened to the bus driver.

8. They threw candy wrappers in the aisle. They shouldn't have thrown candy wrappers in the aisle.

Show what you know! Talk about school safety

Nine-year-old Tuan Le was having terrible back pains. The doctor said that the problem was Tuan's backpack.

STEP 1. Read about Tuan's problem.

STEP 2. PAIRS. Discuss Tuan's problem. Use past modals to answer the following questions.

1. What was the cause of Tuan's back pain? List as many possible causes as you can.

2. What should Tuan's parents have done? List anything that might have helped.

STEP 3. GROUPS. Share your ideas.

Can you...talk about school safety? ☐

Writing

1 BEFORE YOU WRITE

A GROUPS. **Parents sometimes disagree with decisions that their local school districts make. What can they do when this happens?**

B **Many newspapers encourage their readers to write *letters to the editor*. In a letter to the editor the writer expresses his or her feelings about an important topic. Underline three words that show how the person who wrote the letter below feels about the additional in-service days in the West Apollo School District.**

Letter to the Editor:

As working parents of two young children, my wife and I were <u>surprised</u> and <u>upset</u> when we found out that the number of teacher in-service days (when teachers get training) in the West Apollo School District had increased from three to five days per year. As you know, when teachers have in-service days, the children are off from school.

I believe that students benefit from the work their teachers do during in-service. However, I am <u>concerned</u> about children whose parents cannot take time off from their jobs or pay for extra child care on the additional in-service days. One possible solution is for the school district to organize special activities for students on these days.

Non-teaching staff, such as classroom aides, could supervise these activities in the school cafeteria or gymnasium. A second possible solution would involve direct cooperation among parents. With careful planning, they could almost certainly find a stay-at-home mother, a grandparent, or another responsible family member to take care of small groups of children. The children could go to a different home on each in-service day so that everyone contributes to the child care.

I plan to talk to the principal of our children's school and to the president of my local PTA about this important issue as soon as possible. All parents should do the same.

C PAIRS. **Answer the questions about the letter.**

1. What is an advantage of teacher in-service days?
2. What is a disadvantage of teacher in-service days?
3. Do you agree or disagree with the writer? Explain.

Writing Tip

When a letter or an essay includes more than one paragraph, it's important to put similar information together. What kind of information did the writer put in the first paragraph? In the second paragraph? In the last paragraph?

Write a letter to the editor

Getting Started   10 minutes

- If necessary, define *a letter to the editor* as *a letter that a newspaper reader can send to the newspaper in which he or she expresses an opinion about issues in the news.*
- Explain that all letters are read, though only a few get published in the paper.
- Bring in a copy of a newspaper and show students the letters to the editor page.

1   BEFORE YOU WRITE

Ⓐ GROUPS. Parents sometimes disagree...

- To help focus students' thinking, provide examples of recent decisions that your local school board has made. Ask students if they approve or disapprove of these decisions.
- Form groups. Have them choose a timekeeper, a note taker, and a reporter and discuss answers to the question.
- Give a time limit. While students are talking, walk around and provide help as needed.
- To wrap up, have the reporter from each group share the group's ideas.

Presentation   20 minutes

Ⓑ Many newspapers encourage their readers...

- Read the letter out loud as students read silently.
- Point out the salutation *Letter to the Editor.*
- Tell students to look for the adjectives that describe the writer's feelings. *(surprised, upset, concerned)*
- Have students read the letter again silently.
- Call on students to say which words they underlined. Ask: *Do these words show the writer's positive or negative feelings?* (negative)

Ⓒ PAIRS. Answer the questions about the letter.

- Read question 1. As a clue, tell students to look for a word that means *advantage (benefit).*

Answer: Students benefit from the work their teachers do during in-service.

- Read question 2. Ask students to predict where they will find the answer *(following the word* However)

Answer: Some parents do not have money to pay for babysitters on those days.

- Pair students and have them answer questions 1 and 2. Then have them discuss question 3.

Answers will vary.

- Discuss question 3 with the whole class. You can also ask students if they agree with the writer's suggested solutions.

Writing Tip: **Keeping Similar Information Together**

- Read the Writing Tip.
- Ask: *How did the letter writer organize the information?*
- Elicit answers and write them on the board in the form of an outline. For example: *I. Statement of the problem; II. Why it is a problem* (the disadvantages)*; III. Solutions; IV. The writer's plan of action / recommendation.*
- Note: In the writing model, both the problem and solutions are discussed in the second paragraph. You may want to suggest that students write four short paragraphs, discussing the disadvantages in the second, and the solutions in the third.
- Have students copy the outline into their notebooks. Tell them they will need it when they do Exercise 3.

Expansion: Writing Practice for 1C

- Reiterate the information in the Writing Tip. Then point out that often, the different sections of a piece of writing are separated by transitions.
- Have students go through the letter and circle the transitions *However, One possible solution,* and *A second possible solution.*

Controlled Practice   10 minutes

2   THINKING ON PAPER

Ⓐ BRAINSTORM. Think about a decision...

- Copy the brainstorming chart onto the board.
- Choose a decision that was recently made in your school or district. Use this decision as a model. (If you are unfamiliar with a real example, choose a hypothetical one. Examples could be a decision to require students to wear uniforms, to ban cell phones from campus, to close the cafeteria, to remove junk food from vending machines).
- With students, brainstorm and take notes on the positive and negative results. Write ideas in the chart, not full sentences.

Ⓑ Choose the negative result that is the...

- Follow through with the example you introduced in Exercise 2A. For example, if the problem is the decision to ban cell phones, the biggest negative result might be that students and parents are unable to reach one another.
- Copy the graphic organizer onto the board. Write the model problem in the center. With the class, brainstorm as many solutions as possible. (It can be more or fewer than four.) For example, students might be allowed to carry cell phones, but if the phone rings during class a teacher can confiscate it. Another solution might be to require students to leave phones in lockers. A third might be that students must deposit phones in a basket on the teacher's desk at the beginning of each class.
- Form pairs or groups. Have students discuss the pros and cons of each suggested solution. Have them choose the two best solutions.
- Call on volunteers to say which two solutions they chose. Have them explain their reasons.
- Have students select their own problem and brainstorm their own solutions, using the graphic organizer.
- Have them share their ideas with a partner or partners.

Communicative Practice   20 minutes

3   WRITE

Write your own letter to the editor...

- Have students take out the outline you did of the model letter in the Writing Tip after Exercise 1C.
- Say: *Use the outline to write your letter. It's OK to change or add ideas while you are writing.*
- Read the checklist items in Exercise 4. Tell students to use them as a guide while they are writing.
- Encourage students to use the unit grammar: adverb clauses of reason and purpose; infinitives of purpose; adjective clauses; and past modals.
- Have students write in class.

▨ MULTILEVEL INSTRUCTION for 3

Pre-level Give students the option of providing just one solution to the problem they chose. They can shorten or omit the advantages or disadvantages.

Above-level Have students write four paragraphs. They should include the advantages and disadvantages of the decision as well as two or more solutions.

4   CHECK YOUR WRITING

- Have students read their paragraphs and check the boxes in the checklist. Alternately, have them revise their paragraphs according to the items in the checklist.
- Collect papers. Make corrections as needed in paragraph format, grammar, and the items in the writing checklist.

▨ Expansion: Writing Practice for 4

- Have students rewrite their paragraphs.
- Pair students and have them read their paragraphs to each other.
- Have volunteers read their paragraphs to the class.

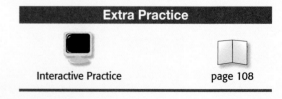

| **Extra Practice** |
| Interactive Practice | page 108 |

2 THINKING ON PAPER

A BRAINSTORM. Think about a decision in your child's school or in the school you are attending that you are unhappy about. Organize your ideas in a chart like this.

Decision I disagree with: _____	
Positive results	Negative results

B Choose the negative result that is the biggest problem. Think of solutions to that problem. Organize your ideas like this.

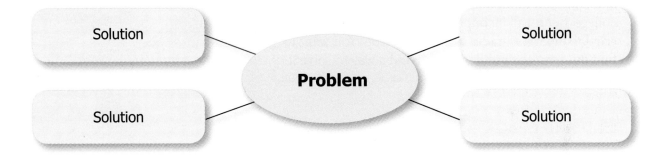

3 WRITE

Write your own letter to the editor about a recent school decision that you did not agree with. Focus on the problem you chose in Exercise 2B and two solutions to that problem. Use the writing model as an example.

4 CHECK YOUR WRITING

☐ Did you explain the decision and explain the reasons that it is a problem?

☐ Did you give possible solutions?

☐ Did you describe the actions you would take?

☐ Did you group similar ideas together?

☐ Did you use correct capitalization, punctuation, and spelling?

1   REVIEW   For your grammar review, go to page 253.

2   ACT IT OUT   What do you say?

STEP 1. Review the conversation on page 167 (CD2, Track 30).

STEP 2. ROLE PLAY. PAIRS. Role-play this situation.

Student A: You are a parent who thinks that school is important. You know that your son's grades have fallen since he got a job. You want your son to succeed in school, but you also want him to work to make money. You are talking to your son's math teacher.

Student B: You are a high school math teacher. You are talking to the parent of one of your favorite students. You think that his/her son should go to college, but it will be impossible for him to get a scholarship if his grades continue to drop. You want to find out what the problem is and find a way to solve it.

3   READ AND REACT   Problem-solving

STEP 1. GROUPS. Consider the problem.

You are a group of parents who live in the same neighborhood. Your children attend the same middle school. One of the parents just told you how many times she has gone to the school recently for events such as a PTA meeting, a parent-teacher night, and a student safety meeting. She also mentioned that there is going to be a family barbecue at the school next Friday evening. Some other parents in the group never received information about any of these events.

STEP 2. GROUPS. Discuss. What are the possible reasons that some of the parents didn't receive information from their children's school? What should the parents do?

4   CONNECT   For your Self-Efficacy Activity, go to page 261.
For your Team Project, go to page 271.

Which goals can you check off? Go back to page 165.

 Go to the CD-ROM for more practice.

Show what you know!

1 REVIEW

Turn to page 253 for the Grammar Review.

2 ACT IT OUT

STEP 1. Review the conversation...

- Play CD 2, Track 30. If necessary direct students to the script on page 167.

STEP 2. ROLE PLAY. PAIRS. Role-play...

> **Teaching Tip**
>
> While pairs are performing role plays, use the scoring rubric for speaking on page T-xiii to evaluate each student's vocabulary, grammar, fluency, and how well he or she completes the task. You may want to review the completed rubric with the students.

- Have students look at the illustration. Ask: *Who are the people? Where are they? What are they talking about?*
- Read the role descriptions.
- With the class, brainstorm about some solutions to the problem. List them on the board.
- Model the role play with an above-level student. Play the role of the teacher. You can begin like this: *Thank you for coming to see me, [name]. I wanted to talk to you about [child's] grades.* Include one or more of the solutions suggested by the students.
- Remind students to try to use the unit grammar in their role play.
- Tell students to practice out loud at least twice.
- Have volunteers perform their role-play.

3 READ AND REACT

STEP 1. Consider the problem.

- Read the problem out loud while students read silently.
- To check comprehension, ask: *What is going to happen next Friday evening? What is the problem?*

STEP 2. GROUPS. Discuss. What are the...

- Form groups of three or four. Have each group choose a timekeeper, a note taker, and a reporter. The note taker should write down the reasons and actions that the group proposes.
- Give a time limit for discussion. Walk around and provide help as needed.
- Have the reporter from each group share the group's ideas. List the solutions on the board.
- Have students vote on the best solution.

▬ Expansion: Speaking Practice for STEP 2

- Ask students if they have had a similar experience and how they dealt (or are dealing) with it.

4 CONNECT

Turn to page 261 for the Self-Efficacy Activity and page 271 for the Team Project. See page T-xi for classroom management tips for these activities.

Progress Check

Which goals can you check off? Go back to page 165.

Ask students to turn to page 165 and check off any remaining goals they have reached. Call on students to say which goals they will practice outside of class.

 Go to the CD-ROM for more practice.

If students need more practice with the vocabulary, grammar, and competencies in Unit 9, encourage them to review the activities on the CD-ROM.

Safety First

Classroom Materials/Extra Practice

CD 2
Tracks 39–49

Interactive Practice
Unit 10

Workbook
Unit 10

Unit Overview

Goals
- See the list of goals on the facing page.

Grammar
- *Make / have / let / get* + Verb
- Reflexive pronouns
- *Could you / I . . . ? / Why don't you / I . . . ? / Would you mind . . . ?*

Pronunciation
- Auxiliary verbs
- The letter *o*

Reading
- Talk about workplace safety
- *Reading Skill:* Looking for words that signal time order

Writing
- Write about ways to improve workplace safety

Life Skills
- Interpret and complete an accident report

Preview
- Say the unit title and have students look at the picture. Ask: *What do you think this unit will be about?*
- Ask the preview questions. You can also ask: *What is happening in the photo? What safety measures do you see? Do you think this is a safe workplace?*

Unit Goals
- Point to the Unit Goals. Have students read them silently.
- Tell students they will be studying these goals in Unit 10.
- Say each goal and explain unfamiliar vocabulary as needed for example, *progress report: an oral or written report from an employee to a manager or a worker to a customer detailing the progress of a project so far; accident report: a report concerning the details of an accident occurring at work or on a job site; promotion: the elevation of a worker from a lower-level position to a higher-level one.*
- Tell students to circle one or more goals that are very important to them. Call on several volunteers to say the goals they circled.
- Write a checkmark (✓) on the board. Say: *We will come back to this page again. You will write a checkmark next to the goals you learned in this unit.*

Safety First

10

Preview

Read the title. What types of accidents can occur at work?

UNIT GOALS

- ☐ Give a progress report

- ☐ Talk about work requirements

- ☐ Discuss workplace safety

- ☐ Talk about preventing accidents at work

- ☐ Interpret and complete an accident report

- ☐ Recognize requirements for promotions

- ☐ Make requests, suggestions, and offers at work

- ☐ Write about ways to improve workplace safety

Listening and Speaking

1   BEFORE YOU LISTEN

A   GROUPS. Which things are most important to employers? Speed (how fast employees work)? Quality (how good employees' work is)? Make a list of things an employer wants or expects from an employee.

B   When people or companies need to build something, they often hire a *contractor* to manage the project. The contractor often hires *subcontractors*. Look at the picture of a contractor and a subcontractor. What tasks do you think each person does?

2   LISTEN

A   CD2 T39   Sam is a contractor. He is talking to his subcontractor, Oleg. Oleg is making kitchen cabinets for Sam. Listen to their conversation. What is the problem?   The wood did not arrive on time. The cabinets are not ready.

B   CD2 T39   Read the statements. Then listen to the conversation again. Write *T* (true) or *F* (false). Correct the false statements.

                                                                  yesterday

_F_   1. The wood arrived from the supplier ~~a week ago~~.

_F_   2. Sam's work on this kitchen is ~~one~~ *two* week*s* late.

_F_   3. Oleg ~~didn't call~~ *called* Sam to tell him about the problem.

_F_   4. Oleg ~~needs~~ *doesn't need* to finish so work can be done on the counters.

_T_   5. Sam wants Oleg to hurry.

_F_   6. Sam and Oleg ~~don't~~ care about quality.

C   GROUPS. Sam is upset because Oleg has not finished his work. Discuss.

1. What could Oleg have done differently?

2. What could Sam have done differently?

Getting Started　5 minutes

1 BEFORE YOU LISTEN

A GROUPS. Which things are most important...

- Form groups. Have them choose a timekeeper, a note taker, and a reporter to write down the group's ideas.
- Give a time limit. While students are talking, walk around and provide help as needed.
- Have the reporter from each group share the group's list. Write the responses on the board.

B When people or companies need...

- Have students look at the photo and answer the question. Ask students to say what they see in the picture that supports their guess.

Culture Connection

A contractor's job is to manage a building project. Besides hiring the workers, the contractor is also responsible for obtaining permits and meeting all the legal requirements of the project. Contractors must be licensed and they must have insurance. Subcontractors are independent workers who are hired by the contractor to work on a specific project. They can have specific skills, such as carpentry or plumbing. Subcontractors are also required to be licensed and insured.

Presentation　10 minutes

2 LISTEN

A Sam is a contractor. He is talking to...

- Have students look at the photo. Ask: *Which man is the contractor, and which one is the subcontractor? Where are they?*
- Remind students to listen specifically for the answer to the question in the Student Book. It is not necessary to understand every word.
- Play CD 2, Track 39.
- Have students compare answers with a classmate.
- Call on a volunteer to answer the question.

Controlled Practice　10 minutes

B Read the statements. Then listen...

- Read item 1 with the class.
- Have students read the questions and predict the answers.
- Play Track 39 again. Have students answer the questions.
- Call on students to read the questions and answers. If an answer is false, have students correct it.
- If students have difficulty answering a question, play the corresponding part of the recording again.

C GROUPS. Sam is upset because Oleg...

- Briefly review the structure and meaning of the past modal *could have* + past participle. Say: Could have *is used to talk about possibility in the past.*
- Form groups. Have them choose a timekeeper, a note taker, and a reporter to write down the group's ideas.
- Give a time limit. While students are talking, walk around and provide help as needed.
- To wrap up, have the reporter from each group share the group's ideas. Have them use *could have* + past participle.

Expansion: Speaking Practice for 2C

- Discuss the following questions with the class: *Have you ever done any building or remodeling on your home? If so, who did the work for you? Was the work completed on time? If not, what caused the delay?*

Presentation   10 minutes

3   CONVERSATION

A 🖸 **Sam is doing work...**

- Define terms as needed, for example, *supplier: the company or business that sells a particular product, such as sinks; back order: an order or part of an order of goods waiting to be filled because it is not currently available.*
- Play CD 2, Track 40. Students listen and read silently.
- *Optional:* You may want to have above-level students listen with their books closed.
- Check comprehension. Ask: *What is the name of the building manager? What is the name of Sam's subcontractor? What is the problem? Why can't Sam use a different supplier?*

Controlled Practice   10 minutes

B **PAIRS. Practice the conversation.**

- Form cross-ability pairs and have students take turns reading each role.
- Have students switch partners and practice again.
- Walk around and listen as students are practicing. Provide help as needed.
- Ask volunteers to perform the conversation for the class.

▬ MULTILEVEL INSTRUCTION for 3B

Cross-ability Have the lower-level student read the part of Jan.

Communicative Practice   15 minutes

C **ROLE-PLAY. PAIRS. Role-play this situation....**

- Read the role descriptions.
- Discuss the situation with the class. Have them decide when the remodel was supposed to be finished; how many bathrooms the subcontractor has finished; how far behind he is; and when he now expects to finish the job.
- Model the role play with an above-level student. Play the role of Student A. Have Student B begin the conversation. For example: B: *Hello, [name]? This is [name]. Listen, I'm calling because I need a progress report on the bathroom remodeling. My tenants are getting upset . . .*
- Have students write out their dialogues if necessary. Walk around and provide help as needed.
- Tell students to practice out loud at least twice.
- Have volunteers perform their role-play for the class.

D **MAKE IT PERSONAL. GROUPS. Talk about...**

- Ask the class: *What are some ways that employers pressure employees to work faster?* List students' ideas on the board.
- Form groups. Give a time limit for discussion. While students are talking, walk around and provide help as needed.
- Call on volunteers to share their answers.

Extra Practice

Interactive Practice

3 CONVERSATION

CD2 T40

A Sam is doing work at an apartment building. He called the building manager to give her a progress report. Listen and read.

Sam: Jan? This is Sam Baker. I wanted to give you a progress report on the work we're doing on the kitchens at 215 River Road.

Jan: Oh, good. I was just going to call you.

Sam: Well, here's the thing. I just spoke to Kurt, my subcontractor, and he's running a little behind schedule—but we're doing everything we can.

Jan: How much behind schedule? What's the problem?

Sam: Five sinks are on backorder. We got the supplier to rush the order, but we won't get them until next Monday.

Jan: Can you find a different supplier?

Sam: I had Kurt check around, and it doesn't look like anyone else has what we need. I'll have him check some other places, and I'll get back to you.

Jan: Call me tomorrow.

B PAIRS. Practice the conversation.

C ROLE PLAY. PAIRS. Role-play this situation.

A building manager has hired you to remodel twelve bathrooms in an apartment building.

Student A: You are a contractor. Your subcontractor is having problems. He is supposed to remodel one bathroom every two days, but he is behind schedule.

Student B: You are the building manager. Tenants are upset because the schedule for remodeling their bathrooms keeps changing. You want a progress report.

D MAKE IT PERSONAL. GROUPS. Talk about your own job experiences or those of people you know. Discuss.

1. Is there a lot of pressure on the job to work fast?
2. Is there a lot of pressure to do quality work?
3. Is it easy or difficult to make employers happy?

Grammar

Make/have/let/get + Verb			
I	**made**	Kurt	**check** around.
	had	Boris	**call** you from the van.
You need to	**let**	the counter guy	**measure** the space.
We	**got**	the supplier	**to rush** the order.
We	**didn't get**	the supplier	**to rush** the order.

· · · · · · · · Grammar Watch

- Use *make* when someone requires another person to do something.
- Use *have* when someone asks another person to do something.
- Use *let* when someone allows another person to do something.
- Use *get* when someone persuades another person to do something, *get* is followed by the infinitive instead of the base form.

1 PRACTICE

A Read the first sentence. Then underline the correct noun or pronoun to make the second sentence true.

1. The manager had me drive the forklift.
   The manager / (I) drove the forklift.

2. Our boss let us go home early on July 3.
   Our boss / (We) went home early on July 3.

3. The supervisor made them work faster.
   The supervisor / (They) had to work faster.

4. Pam got Mei-Ling to work the night shift.
   Pam / (Mei-Ling) changed her shift.

B Complete the instructions for supermarket cashiers. Use the verbs in the box. Use one verb twice.

> get   have   let   make

1. If the customer has a store card, ____have____ her give you the card before you start scanning items.

2. If you need to check the price of an item, ____get____ your bagger to find the information, so you can continue helping the customer.

3. Always ____let____ the customer take her time getting her money out. Never ____make____ the customer hurry.

4. If the customer is paying by credit card, don't forget to ____have____ him or her sign the receipt.

Getting Started   10 minutes

- Ask for a student volunteer to help you demonstrate the grammar.
- Hand the student a mop or a broom and tell the student to clean the floor (or a similar task). In a voice that makes it clear you are pretending, say: *You have to clean this floor before you go out.* Pause and then say: *The parent made the teenager clean the floor.* Write *make* on the board.
- Have the student pretend to cut your hair. Say: *I didn't cut my own hair. I had [name] do it.* Write *have* on the board.
- Offer the student your textbook (or another object). Say: *Would you like to borrow my book?* Hand the book to the student. Then say: *I let [name] borrow my book.* Write *let* on the board.
- Finally, ask the student to perform a classroom task such as erasing the board. Say: *Could you please erase the board for me? I don't have time.* After the student does it, say: *I got [name] to erase the board.* Write *get* on the board.
- Point to the four verbs on the board. Tell the class: *We'll learn about these verbs in this lesson.*

Presentation   20 minutes

Make / have / let / get + Verb

- Copy the sentences from the grammar chart onto the board. Divide each sentence into two parts: the first noun + verb, and the second noun + verb. Point and explain: *The subject of the sentence is the doer of the first verb. The object of the sentence is the doer of the second verb. In all the sentences, the subject causes* (makes, has, lets, gets) *the object to do something.*
- Have students look at all the examples. Ask: *What do you notice about* get? (It's followed by object + infinitive, whereas *make, have,* and *let* are followed by object + base form.)
- Read the first sentence and the first Grammar Watch note. Explain that with *make*, the subject requires, forces, or compels the object to perform an action. The object has no choice.
- Read the second sentence and the second Grammar Watch note. Say: *We often use* have *to talk about services or tasks that other people do for us.* Provide other examples.

- Read the third sentence and the third Grammar Watch note. Say: Let *means* allow *or* permit.
- Read the fourth example and the fourth Grammar Watch note. Say: Get *means* persuade.

> **Language Note**
>
> The four verbs *make, have, let,* and *get* are often called *causative* verbs. In all sentences with these verbs, the subject causes (by means of force, permission, or persuasion) the object to perform some kind of action.

Expansion: Grammar Practice

- Repeat the mini-role plays from Getting Started. As you perform each action, say each sentence with a verb. Emphasize the verbs as shown.
- Have students respond with *make, have, let,* or *get,* as follows: 1. T: *I required [name] to sweep the floor.* Ss: *You* made *[name] sweep the floor.* 2. T: *I paid [name] to cut my hair.* Ss: *You* had *[name] cut your hair.* 3. T: *I allowed [name] to borrow my book.* Ss: *You* let *[name] borrow your book.* 4. T: *I persuaded [name] to erase the board.* Ss: *You* got *[name] to erase the board.*

Controlled Practice   15 minutes

1 **PRACTICE**

Ⓐ Read the first sentence. Then underline...

- Read the first sentence out loud. Ask: *Who drove the forklift?*
- Have students do the exercise.
- Check answers.

Ⓑ Complete the instructions for supermarket...

- Have students look at the photo. Ask: *What is the woman doing?*
- Read the first sentence.
- Have students complete the exercise.
- Check answers. Have students paraphrase sentences to show comprehension. For example, *get your bagger to . . .* means *persuade the bagger to . . .*

2 PRACTICE

Ⓐ Read what each person said. Then state...

- Define *foreperson* as *a worker who is in charge of other workers.*
- Read the example. Tell students to watch out for similar pronoun shifts in the other items in the exercise.
- Write the following on the board: *Supervisor: You can take an extra fifteen minutes for lunch today.* ➔ *The supervisor let . . .*
- Have students complete the sentence *The supervisor let us (the employees) take an extra fifteen minutes for lunch today.* Point out the shift in person from *you* to *us* or *employees* when the sentence is transformed from the supervisor's exact words to a report of what the supervisor said.
- Have students work alone or in pairs.
- Check answers. Have students write the sentences on the board. Have other students read the sentences and make corrections as needed.

Ⓑ Rewrite the new sentences on notepaper...

- Clarify the task. The object nouns are the nouns following the first verb. Put another way, they are the performers of the second action.
- Do the first item with the class as an example: *The supervisor had* them *turn off their machines at night.*
- Have students complete the activity in pairs.
- Check answers.

Communicative Practice 15 minutes

Show what you know!

STEP 1. GROUPS. What things has an...

- Read the list of items. Instruct students to place a checkmark next to the items that their employer (present or past) asked or allowed them to do.
- Form groups. Instruct students to explain, describe, or elaborate on each item that they checked.

■■■ MULTILEVEL INSTRUCTION for STEP 1

Pre-level Have students speak only about the items on the list.

Above-level Have students add items to those on the list, including something that their employer got them to do, for example, *work overtime* or *work on a weekend.*

STEP 2. PAIRS. Do any of these issues pose...

- Pair students and have them discuss the issue they chose.
- While students are talking, walk around and provide help as needed.
- Have volunteers tell the class about their problems. Have the class discuss solutions, for example, *quit the job, speak to the boss, write a letter to the company president,* and *try to repair the problem.*

Progress Check

Can you . . . talk about work requirements?

Say: *We have practiced talking about work requirements. Now, look at the question at the bottom of the page. Can you talk about work requirements? Write a checkmark in the box.*

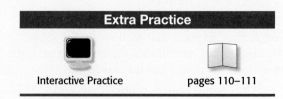

Extra Practice

Interactive Practice　　　　　pages 110–111

PRACTICE

A Read what each person said. Then state what the person wanted or allowed, using the verb in parentheses.

Supervisor: All employees must turn off their machines at night.

(*have*) The supervisor _had the employees turn off their machines at night._

Foreperson: Harry, remember to clean off your shoes.

(*make*) The foreperson _made Harry clean off his shoes._

Boss: You can use the company van this weekend.

(*let*) My boss _let me use the company van on the weekend._

Rafael: Sandra and Ben, please work until the job is finished.

(*get*) Rafael _got Sandra and Ben to work until the job was finished._

Manager: New workers, please don't ask questions until the training is over.

(*not let*) The manager _did not let the new workers ask questions until the training was over._

Jocelyn: Dan, I want you to meet all the people working on the site.

(*have*) Jocelyn _had Dan meet all the people on the site._

B Rewrite the new sentences on notepaper, changing any object nouns to pronouns.

Show what you know! Talk about work requirements

STEP 1. GROUPS. What things has an employer asked or allowed to you to do at work? Discuss the ideas below or your own ideas.

- have you work late
- have you work on weekends
- make you wait for your paycheck
- make you work overtime

- make you work in unsafe conditions
- let you take several breaks
- let you leave work early
- let you try a new procedure

STEP 2. PAIRS. Do any of these issues pose problems for you? Choose one issue to discuss. What can you do to solve this problem?

Can you...talk about work requirements? ☐

Lesson 3 Discuss workplace safety

Reading

1 BEFORE YOU READ

CLASS. Look at the pictures. Where have you seen these things? Why are they important?

exit door

fire extinguisher

sprinkler system

2 READ

CD2 T41

Read and listen. What did the Triangle Shirtwaist Factory fire make the American public realize? Many workplaces were unsafe.

---

http://www.onthejobsafety.com

Triangle Shirtwaist Factory Fire

On March 25, 1911, fire broke out in the Triangle Shirtwaist Factory in New York City. Inside the factory, the workers were all women, some only 15 years old. Some of them got out. But on the 9th floor, there were only two exit doors. One exit was filled with smoke. The other exit door was locked. The workers on that floor were trapped. One hundred and forty-eight workers were killed.

The Triangle Shirtwaist Factory fire made the newspaper headlines. People were **outraged** to learn of the working conditions there, in which women and children of 12 or 13 years old worked fourteen-hour shifts during a 60- to 72-hour workweek in dangerous and **unsanitary** conditions. The Triangle Shirtwaist Factory was typical of many unsafe workplaces in the early twentieth century. In factories, mills, and mines, workers, including children, worked long hours on dangerous machines with no clean air to breathe. In these workplaces, people were injured and sometimes even killed.

After the fire, the **public** became more aware of these conditions and asked the government to make workplaces safer. Workers organized into powerful **unions** that fought for safer conditions. Conditions improved gradually. But it wasn't until 1970 that the government created the Occupational Safety and Health Administration (OSHA). The purpose of OSHA is to prevent injuries and deaths in the workplace by enforcing rules for safety and health. For example, each workplace has to have a sprinkler system, fire extinguishers, and at least two exit doors. OSHA **inspectors** visit workplaces regularly to make sure companies follow the rules.

Today, if a company does not follow safety rules, it has to pay a fine. Workers can complain to OSHA about unsafe conditions. Thanks in part to OSHA, conditions for workers in the U.S. are now much safer than they used to be.

Getting Started   5 minutes

 BEFORE YOU READ

CLASS. Look at the pictures. Where...

- Hold up your book, point to each picture, and ask: *What is this?* (emergency exit, sprinkler system, and fire extinguisher)
- Have students say where these items are located in your classroom or school.
- Have volunteers answer the questions.

Presentation   15 minutes

 READ

Read and listen. What did the...

- Note: Do not pre-teach the boldfaced vocabulary. The items are practiced in Exercise 4.
- Have students look at the photo. Ask: *What do you see? When do you think the photo was taken? Why do you think it was taken?*
- Have students read silently without using dictionaries.
- Give a time limit, but allow more time to read if necessary.
- When time is up, call on volunteers to answer the question. Have them read the sentence in which the answer is found. Hint: The article does not use the word *realize*. Students should look for other words *(learn, aware)* to find the answer.
- As a final step, play CD 2, Track 41 as students read and listen.

Expansion: Reading Practice

- In Unit 9, students learned the concept of unity— that a paragraph should have one main idea. Pair students. Assign each pair one paragraph from the reading. Instruct them to find the main idea of the paragraph.
- Call on students to say the main idea of each paragraph in their own words. Take notes on the main ideas in the form of an outline on the board.

Teaching Tip

Having students outline the main ideas of a reading text helps them to see the global organization of the text.

Controlled Practice 20 minutes

3 CHECK YOUR UNDERSTANDING

Reading Skill: **Looking for Words that Signal Time Order**

- Read the Reading Skill.
- Have students skim the article again and highlight the dates and time expressions that show time order.

A Read the Reading Skill. Then read...

- Tell students to look at the words they highlighted as they do the exercise.
- Check answers.

B PAIRS. Discuss.

- Pair students and have them answer as many questions as possible.
- Share answers with the whole class. Have students share what they know about worker unions and OSHA.

Culture Connection

OSHA, the Occupational Safety and Health Administration, is part of the U.S. Department of Labor. It was created in 1970 for the purpose of preventing workplace injuries. The agency oversees a wide range of regulations pertaining to, for example, the use of protective equipment (such as hard hats), permissible levels of hazardous materials, the use of guards on moving machine parts, air quality in work spaces, procedures for handling contagious materials (such as viruses), and more.

4 WORD WORK

Find the boldfaced words in the article...

- Say the words and have students repeat.
- Form cross-ability pairs. Have students find the words and use the context to define them. Then have them do the exercise.
- Call on students to say the answers. Have students say the clues that helped them figure out the meaning of each word.

MULTILEVEL INSTRUCTION for 4

Cross-ability Have pre-level students find the words and read the sentences in which they appear. Then have above-level students help them guess what the words mean and do the exercise.

Communicative Practice 20 minutes

Show what you know!

STEP 1. Are working conditions safe...

- Ask the class to name a job that that is still dangerous today, for example, *coal miner.*
- Have students think of other dangerous jobs and write them down.

STEP 2. GROUPS. Share your lists. What can...

- Form groups.
- Have students take turns talking about the items on their list. Instruct them to explain why the jobs they listed are dangerous and then to figure out what can be done to minimize the danger.

Expansion: Reading Practice for Show what you know!

- Have students do an Internet search for *most dangerous jobs.* For example, according to MSN Money, the most dangerous job in America—measured in terms of number of fatalities—is a timber cutter.
- Have them print out the lists they find. In class, have them compare the Internet lists with their own lists.
- Go over the items on one of the Internet lists and find out if any students have performed any of those jobs.

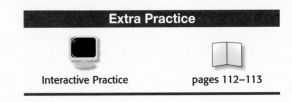

Extra Practice	
Interactive Practice	pages 112–113

3 CHECK YOUR UNDERSTANDING

A Read the Reading Skill. Then read the article again. Number the sentences below in chronological (time) order.

Reading Skill: Looking for Words That Signal Time Order

When you read, look for dates and words such as *before*, *after*, *next*, and *finally* that show sequence.

_2_ People asked the government to make factories safer.

_3_ The government created OSHA.

_4_ Conditions in factories have become much safer.

_1_ The Triangle Shirtwaist Factory fire occurred.

B PAIRS. Discuss.

1. Describe the working conditions in factories in the early twentieth century.
2. Why were so many workers killed in the 1911 Triangle Shirtwaist Factory fire?
3. What kinds of worker unions do you know? What do these unions do?
4. What are some of the safety rules OSHA has introduced?

4 WORD WORK

Find the boldfaced words in the article and guess their meaning from the context. Then use them to complete the sentences.

> outraged   unsanitary   public   union   inspector

1. The American ___public___ was ___outraged___ about working conditions in factories.

2. Many workers joined the ___union___ because they wanted better working conditions.

3. The OSHA ___inspector___ told the factory management to clean up the factory floor because it was ___unsanitary___.

Show what you know!   Discuss workplace safety

STEP 1. Are working conditions safe for all workers today? What are some jobs that are still dangerous? Make a list.

STEP 2. GROUPS. Share your lists. What can be done to make these jobs safer?

Listening and Speaking

1 BEFORE YOU LISTEN

CLASS. What is this machine? What are some of the safety hazards (dangers) of working with a machine like this?

2 LISTEN

CD2 T42

A Asad works on a printing press. He has a new co-worker, Claudia. Listen to their conversation. What is Asad worried about?

Claudia's safety

CD2 T42

B Read the statements. Then listen to the conversation again. Write *T* (true) or *F* (false). Correct the false statements.

__T__ 1. The workers are not supposed to wear loose-fitting clothes or jewelry when they operate the press.

__F__ 2. Claudia didn't go to the safety training.
       went

__F__ 3. The company didn't give Claudia a safety training manual.
       gave

__F__ 4. Claudia didn't read the safety training manual.

__F__ 5. Claudia read the safety training manual, but she didn't understand it all.
       remember

__F__ 6. Asad sometimes does a safety check of his equipment before he starts.
       always

__F__ 7. Asad told Claudia to keep her hands on the machine.
       away from

CD2 T42

C Listen again. How does Asad do a safety check? What are some other things you might want to check?

Getting Started   5 minutes

1   BEFORE YOU LISTEN

CLASS. What is this machine? What...

- Students may not know the term *printing press*. Write it on the board. Have students answer the questions. You can also ask: *Where can you find a machine like this? What is it used for? How does it work? What is the man wearing on his ears? Why do you think he's wearing them?*

Presentation   5 minutes

2   LISTEN

A   Asad works on a printing...

- Have students look at the photos. Ask: *Who is the man? Where is he? What problem might he be having?*
- Tell students to read the question. Then have them look at the photo again. Tell them to predict the answer.
- Remind students to listen specifically for the answer to the question. It is not necessary to understand every word.
- Play CD 2, Track 42.
- Call on a volunteer to answer the question. Ask students: *Was your prediction about the conversation correct?*

Controlled Practice   15 minutes

B   Read the statements. Then listen...

- Do item 1 with the class.
- Have students read the remaining statements silently and predict whether they are true or false. Define terms as needed, for example, *jewelry: accessories such as necklace, bracelet, etc.; manual: a book of instructions.*
- Play Track 42 again.
- Have students complete the exercise alone or in pairs.
- Call on students to read each statement and say whether it is true or false. If it is false, ask the student to correct it. Write the answers on the board.
- If students have difficulty answering a question, play the corresponding part of the recording again.

C   Listen again. How does Asad...

- Instruct students to listen for three steps in the safety check.
- Play Track 42 again.
- Check the answers to the first question.

Answer: Asad makes sure the guards are all on the machine. He makes sure not to be wearing long sleeves or jewelry. He keeps his hands a safe distance from the rollers.

- With the class, discuss the second question.

Talk about preventing accidents at work

Presentation 10 minutes

3 CONVERSATION

Pronunciation Watch

- On the board, write the following phrases. *1. stand up, 2. ask Allan, 3. pick apples,* and *4. give advice*
- Say each phrase. Say to students that final consonants join clearly to words beginning with vowels. Draw a linking curve from the *d* to the *u* in the first example, and repeat the phrase *stand up*. Draw a linking curve from the *k* to the *A* as you repeat the second phrase. Draw a linking curve from the *k* to the *a* in the third phrase, as you repeat it. Cross out the *e* in *give*, then draw a linking curve from the *v* to the *a* in the fourth phrase as you repeat it.
- Read the Pronunciation Watch note.
- Read the sentences again and have students repeat.

A 🔘 **Listen to the sentences. Then listen...**

- Play CD 2, Track 43. Have students listen.
- Play Track 43 again. Have students listen and repeat.

Controlled Practice 15 minutes

B 🔘 **Read the sentences. Draw a line...**

- Do item 1 with the class.
- Play CD 2, Track 44. Have students do the remaining items.
- Play Track 44 again. Check answers.

C **Asad and Claudia are continuing...**

- Play CD 2, Track 45. Have students listen and read silently.
- *Optional:* Have above-level students listen with their books closed.
- Check comprehension. Ask: *What happened to Luis? What is Claudia going to do?*

4 PRACTICE

A **PAIRS. Practice the conversation.**

- Form cross-ability pairs.
- Walk around and listen as students are practicing. Listen to make sure students are linking end consonants with beginning vowels correctly.
- Go over pronunciation errors as needed. Say: *I heard _____. What's the correct pronunciation?*
- Ask volunteers to perform the conversation for the class.

▬▬ MULTILEVEL INSTRUCTION for 4A

Pre-level Have students read the role of Claudia.

Above-level Have students read the role of Asad.

Communicative Practice 10 minutes

B **MAKE IT PERSONAL. GROUPS. Discuss.**

- Answer the questions yourself. Tell students about your experience.
- Form groups. Give a time limit for discussion. While students are talking, walk around and provide help as needed.
- Call on volunteers to share their answers with the whole class.

Extra Practice

Interactive Practice

3 CONVERSATION

Pronunciation Watch

The words in a sentence are usually pronounced together without stopping. Link a consonant sound at the end of one word to a vowel sound at the beginning of the next word without stopping.

CD2 T43

A 🔊 **Listen to the sentences. Then listen and repeat.**

He was out of work for a month.

That's awful.

I'll go back and read it again.

Good idea.

Do you have any questions?

CD2 T44

B 🔊 **Read the sentences. Draw a line (⌣) to show where a consonant sound is linked to a following vowel sound. Then listen and check your answers.**

1. These machines are dangerous.

2. Don't wear a bracelet when you're operating the press.

3. I'll take it off right now.

4. Make sure the guards are all on the machine.

CD2 T45

C 🔊 **Asad and Claudia are continuing their conversation. Listen and read.**

Asad: You know, Luis cut himself badly last year and couldn't work for a month.

Claudia: Oh! That's awful!

Asad: I know. So that's why I want to be sure everyone is taking safety precautions.

Claudia: You're right. I think I'll go back and read the safety manual again. Maybe I'll make notes to myself to help me remember.

Asad: Good idea. There are some useful pointers in the manual. I don't want you to injure yourself.

4 PRACTICE

A PAIRS. Practice the conversation.

B MAKE IT PERSONAL. GROUPS. Discuss.

1. Have you ever worked in a dangerous workplace? What were the safety hazards?

2. What did you do to keep yourself safe?

Grammar

Reflexive pronouns

Subject pronoun		Reflexive pronoun	
I		**myself**	
You (singular) You (plural)		**yourself** **yourselves**	
He	hurt	**himself**	at work.
She		**herself**	
We		**ourselves**	
They		**themselves**	

········· **Grammar Watch**

- Use a reflexive pronoun when the subject and object of a sentence refer to the same people.
- Remember: If the subject and object are different, use an object pronoun: *The supervisor helped her at work.*
- You can also use a reflexive pronoun to emphasize that someone or some group did something alone. *By* is sometimes added: *I installed the safety equipment (by) myself.*
- See page 284 for a list of verbs that can be used with reflexive pronouns.

1 PRACTICE

Read what a nurse's aide wrote about her first day at work. Circle the reflexive pronouns and underline the nouns they refer back to.

My first day at work was OK, but I made a couple of mistakes. I was helping patients with their breakfast because some <u>patients</u> can't feed (themselves). First, I helped <u>a</u> <u>patient</u> who couldn't hold her glass of juice by (herself) and <u>I</u> spilled it all over (myself)! It was embarrassing! Then I had to help another patient with his bandage. I know that when you work with sick people <u>you</u> have to protect (yourself), but <u>I</u> forgot to put on my latex gloves to keep (myself) safe. Later I helped bathe <u>a patient</u> who couldn't wash (himself). This time, I remembered to wear my gloves!

Talk about preventing accidents at work

Getting Started   5 minutes

- Tell a story about the first time you did something by yourself in a foreign country for example, go to the post office, use a pay phone, or ride a bus. Start by saying *I want to tell you about the first time I _____ by myself.* Tell what you did and how you felt.
- Call on volunteers to tell similar stories about their experiences in the U.S. After each anecdote, write on the board: *[name] [verb] by herself/himself.*
- Say: Myself, himself, *and* herself *are called* reflexive pronouns. *In this lesson we'll learn how we use these pronouns.*

Presentation   20 minutes

Reflexive pronouns

- Copy the grammar chart onto the board. Read the sentences. Have students repeat.
- Read the first and second Grammar Watch notes. In the examples, circle each subject and each reflexive pronoun. Point out that they refer to the same person, for example, *I* and *myself*.
- Do a quick drill. Erase the reflexive pronouns. Read the subject pronouns and have students respond with the reflexive pronoun.
- Read the third note, which deals with the meaning of reflexive pronouns. To reinforce, ask questions and have students respond with a reflexive. Then have the class restate the response. For example: A: *[name,] did [name] help you with your homework?* B: *No, I did it by myself.* Ss: *She did it by herself.* A: *[name,] did someone drive you to class?* B: *No, I drove myself.* Ss: *She drove herself (to class.)*
- Write the following on the board: *Johanna drove Kurt to class.* Ask: *Can we use a reflexive in this sentence?* (no) *Why?* (because the subject and object are different people)

Expansion: Grammar Practice

- Select verbs from the list on page 284 and write them on slips of paper. Give one slip to each student. Tell students to create a sentence using the verb and a reflexive pronoun, for example, *I told myself to do a safety check before operating the equipment.*
- Have students stand up and mingle. As they meet a classmate, they should say the sentence they created and listen to their classmates' sentence. Then they should switch slips of paper, and each student should create a new sentence using the new verb. Remind students to use subjects other than *I* in some of their sentences.
- Have students mingle and switch papers as many times as time permits.
- At the end, collect all the slips. Call out each verb and have a volunteer say a sentence with it.

Controlled Practice   15 minutes

 PRACTICE

Read what a nurse's aide wrote about her first day...

- Read the passage. Define words as needed, for example, *bandage: a covering for a wound; latex: material used for making gloves.*
- Read the example with the class.
- Have students do the exercise.
- Check answers. Have students say which words they circled and underlined.

Talk about preventing accidents at work

2 PRACTICE

A Complete the conversations. Circle...

- Remind students that we can only use the reflexive when the subject and object are the same person.
- Read item 1 with the class.
- Have students complete the exercise and compare answers with a partner.
- Check answers.
- Have students read the items in pairs. Call on volunteers to read them for the class.

B Complete the sentences with the correct...

- Read item 1 with the class.
- Have students do the exercise and compare answers with a partner.
- Check answers.

Communicative Practice   20 minutes

Show what you know!

STEP 1. Answer the questions.

- Model answering each question with information about yourself.
- Have students take notes on their answers. While students are working, walk around and provide help as needed.

STEP 2. GROUPS. Ask one another the...

- Form small multilevel groups.
- Instruct students to ask and answer the questions in a circular fashion. For example, Student A reads the first question and Student B answers; Student B reads the second question and Student C answers; etc.
- If possible, students should explain their answers, not answer just *yes* or *no*.
- While students are talking, walk around and provide help as needed.

▬▬ MULTILEVEL INSTRUCTION for STEP 2

Pre-level Have students ask and answer the questions in the book. Tell them they may give short answers if they are unable to explain.

Above-level When the group has finished answering all the questions in the book, have students ask two or three additional questions using reflexives.

Progress Check

Can you . . . talk about preventing accidents at work?

Say: *We have practiced talking about preventing accidents at work. Now, look at the question at the bottom of the page. Can you talk about preventing accidents at work? Write a checkmark in the box.*

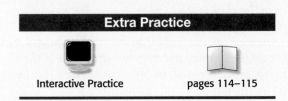

Extra Practice
Interactive Practice   pages 114–115

A Complete the conversations. Circle the correct words.

1. **A:** Wang burned **him /** (**himself**) on the bread oven today. I feel bad. I should have warned (**him**) / **himself** that the oven was really hot.

   B: Don't blame **you /** (**yourself.**) It was an accident.

2. **A:** Can you move those wires out of the way? People might trip on (**them**) / **themselves** and hurt **them /** (**themselves.**)

   B: OK, I will.

3. **A:** Never operate this forklift by **you /** (**yourself.**) Someone else should always be nearby in case you have an accident.

   B: I know. The supervisor already told (**me**) / **myself** that.

B Complete the sentences with the correct reflexive pronouns.

1. Salma is a deli worker. When she slices meat, she is careful not to cut ___*herself*___.

2. Ironworkers often work high up on bridges and tall buildings. They take special care to keep ___themselves___ safe on the construction site.

3. The scaffold rope broke, and Hakeem lost his balance, but he kept ___himself___ from falling.

4. The company doesn't want us to injure ___ourselves___ on the machines.

5. You shouldn't use a tall ladder by ___yourself___. You should have someone hold it.

6. I have to attend the course so I don't hurt ___myself___ on the new equipment.

Show what you know! Talk about preventing accidents at work

STEP 1. **Answer the questions.**

1. Have you ever hurt yourself on the job? What happened?
2. Do you know other people who have hurt themselves on the job? What happened?
3. If you hurt yourself at work, do you tell your boss? Why?
4. Do you do everything you can to keep yourself safe at work? Explain.

STEP 2. **GROUPS. Ask one another the questions and explain your answers.**

Can you. . . talk about preventing accidents at work? ☐

Life Skills

1   READ AN ACCIDENT REPORT

When people have an accident at work, they often fill out an accident report. What kind of accident did Charles have? He fell from a ladder.

Employee's Report of Work-related Injury   To be completed immediately after the accident and submitted to your supervisor

Employee Name: _Charles Beaumont_   ID Number: _5673472_

Male [X]   Female [ ]   Date of Birth: _4/16/80_   Marital Status: _M_

Home Address: _18 Center Street Apt. 6B, Mountain View, CA 94040_
    Street   City   ZIP Code

Home Phone No. _650-555-4827_   Cell Phone No. _650-555-1029_

Job Title: _Roofer_

Employment Start Date: _5/1/2008_

Date of Accident: _2/25/10_

Location of Accident: _200 Blossom Ln., Mountain View, CA_

Describe in detail how the accident occurred:

> I was repairing the roof of a barn. The ladder gave way because the ground was soft. I fell backwards approximately 35 feet to the ground.

(Describe the work you were engaged in, describe how the injury occurred, and explain the cause.)

Part of body injured: _lower back_
(be specific—example: right middle finger, left ankle, upper back)

Type of injury: _sprain_
(example: sprain, burn {degree of burn}, contusion, sutured)

Was medical treatment sought? If so: _Dr. Lao, 524 Filmore Street, Mountain View, CA 94040_   _650-555-1122_
        Name and Address of Medical Provider   Phone Number

No. of days missed from work: _3_

Return to work date (as stated by physician): _3/3/10_

Type of leave used: _sick days_

No. of days worked with restrictions: _0_

Name of witness (es): _Mike Cabrera_   Phone No. _650-555-8304_

Was safety equipment provided? Yes [X] No [ ]

Was safety equipment used? Yes [X] No [ ]

Signature of employee: _Charles Beaumont_   Date: _3/3/10_

Questions? Call 650-555-9827

Interpret and complete an accident report

Getting Started   10 minutes

- Explain that in case of an accident at most workplaces, workers will be required to fill out an accident report form for insurance purposes.
- If you have ever had to fill out such a form, tell the class about your experience.
- Ask the class if anyone has ever had to fill out such a form. Have them tell the class about their experience.

Presentation   15 minutes

1 READ AN ACCIDENT REPORT

When people have an accident at work...

- Have students read the accident report.
- Call on a student to answer the question.
- Ask additional comprehension questions. For example, *Which part of his body did Charles injure? How many days of work did he miss? Did he use safety equipment?*

MULTILEVEL INSTRUCTION for 1

Cross-ability Have the above-level student help the pre-level student with vocabulary as they read the form together.

Expansion: Speaking Practice for 1

- According to the accident report, Charles fell 35 feet backwards, yet he only sprained his back and missed three days of work. Discuss: 1. *What kind of injury would you expect in the case of a person falling 35 feet? 2. Why wasn't Charles injured any worse? 3. Have you ever witnessed a similar accident?*

Interpret and complete an accident report

Controlled Practice   15 minutes

2 PRACTICE

A Read the report again. Then answer...

- Have students answer the questions in complete sentences.

B PAIRS. Compare your answers.

- Have students compare answers with a partner. If partners have different answers, they should look back at the report together and determine which answer is correct.

Expansion: Writing Practice for 2A

- Write the numbers *1* through *8* on the board. Call up students to write their answers on the board.
- Have other students read the sentences and state if they are correct.
- Correct errors as needed.

Communicative Practice   20 minutes

C GROUPS. Discuss.

- Form groups. If possible, make sure at least one person in each group is employed.
- Have groups choose a timekeeper.
- Give a time limit for discussion. While students are talking, walk around and provide help as needed.
- To wrap up, call on students who work to explain the procedures that are followed at their job in case of an injury.

Community Building

Have students who work bring in sample blank accident report forms from their job and share them with the class.

D MAKE IT PERSONAL. **Imagine that you...**

- With the class, brainstorm some accidents that could happen at work. List them on the board.
- Have students choose one of the accidents on the board or use their own idea and fill in the report form.

Expansion: Speaking Practice for D

- Put students in groups. Have them share their accident reports and answer their classmates' questions. Encourage students to use their imagination when talking about their accidents.
- Call on volunteers to tell the class about their "accidents."

Progress Check

Can you . . . interpret and complete an accident report?

Say: *We have practiced interpreting and completing an accident report. Now, look at the question at the bottom of the page. Can you interpret and complete an accident report? Write a checkmark in the box.*

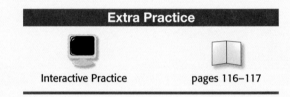

Extra Practice	
Interactive Practice	pages 116–117

A Read the report again. Then answer the questions.

1. Where does Charles Beaumont live and work?

   Mountainview, CA

2. What does he do?

   He is a roofer.

3. How old is he?

   (calculate using current year)

4. How did the accident happen?

   A ladder broke and he fell.

5. What was his injury?

   He hurt his lower back.

6. What doctor did he see?

   Dr. Lao

7. How long did he stay out of work?

   3 days

8. Who saw the accident?

   Mike Cabrera

B PAIRS. Compare your answers.

C GROUPS. Discuss.

1. Why is it important to fill out an accident report form?
2. Is it good for the employer? Is it good for the employee? Explain your answers.
3. If you work, what procedures do you follow at your workplace when you have an accident or injure yourself?

D MAKE IT PERSONAL. Imagine that you had an accident at a job. Complete the accident report form on page 275. Make up the details.

Can you...interpret and complete an accident report? ☐

Listening and Speaking

1 BEFORE YOU LISTEN

GROUPS. What are reasons that a manager gives an employee a raise (more money) or a promotion (higher-level job)? Make a list.

2 LISTEN

CD2 T46

A Lisa works at Parcel Movers, a package-delivery service. She is talking to her manager, Don. Listen to their conversation. What good news does Don give her? What is one reason he gives?

CD2 T46

B Read the sentences. Then listen to the conversation again. Circle the correct answers.

1. Lisa started working as a sorter _____ ago.
   a. three months
   (b.) six months
   c. six years

2. Don says that Lisa is an _____ worker.
   (a.) efficient
   b. innovative
   c. inaccurate

3. When there is a lot of work to do, Lisa _____.
   a. works faster
   b. asks for help
   (c.) helps her co-workers

4. Don offers Lisa _____.
   (a.) a promotion
   b. a safety training course
   c. advice about lifting packages

5. Tomorrow Lisa is supposed to _____.
   (a.) meet with Don
   b. meet with her new supervisor
   c. attend a training program

C **GROUPS.** Think about the reasons Lisa has been promoted. Does your job or a job you know about have the same requirements for promotion? What do people need to do to get promoted?

Getting Started · 10 minutes

1 · BEFORE YOU LISTEN

GROUPS. What are reasons that a manager...

- Write the words *raise* and *promotion* on the board. Ask students to define them and share their experiences. For example, you can ask: *Who got a raise or promotion recently?*
- Form groups. Have them select a timekeeper, a note taker, and a reporter to write down the group's reasons.
- Give a time limit. While students are talking, walk around and provide help as needed.
- Have the reporter from each group share the group's list.

Presentation · 5 minutes

2 · LISTEN

 Lisa works at Parcel Movers,...

- Make sure students understand *package delivery service.* (FedEx, UPS, etc.)
- Play CD 2, Track 46. Have students listen for the answers to the questions.
- Call on students to answer the questions. Play the recording again if necessary.

Controlled Practice · 5 minutes

B **Read the sentences. Then listen...**

- Have students read the questions and predict the answers before listening.
- Define a *sorter* as *a person who divides items (like packages) into similar categories.* For example, packages might be sorted according to ZIP code.
- Play Track 46 again.
- Have students do the exercise.
- Call on students to give the answers.

Communicative Practice · 10 minutes

C **GROUPS. Think about the reasons Lisa...**

- With the class, review the reasons why Lisa was promoted. *(She's efficient, accurate, helpful, safe, and conscientious.)* Play CD 2, Track 46 again if necessary.
- Form groups. Give a time limit for discussion. While students are talking, walk around the room and provide help as needed.
- Have volunteers answer the questions.

Expansion: Speaking Practice for 2C

- Have students tell about a person at their work who was recently promoted. Ask students why they think that person was chosen. If necessary, prompt students by asking questions that use the same vocabulary as the conversation. For example, *Is [the person who was promoted] efficient/conscientious/helpful? Does he or she follow safety procedures? Do other workers respect this person?*

Presentation
10 minutes

3 CONVERSATION

Pronunciation Watch

- Write the following sentence on the board. Underline the letter *o* in each word: *The job was done two weeks ago.*
- Instruct students to listen to the sentence and answer the question: *Are the* o *sounds pronounced the same or differently?* (differently) Read the sentence slowly several times.
- Say the words *job, done,* and *ago* in isolation. Exaggerate the vowels. Have students repeat.
- Read the Pronunciation Watch note.

> ### Language Note
>
> The words *no, ago,* and *promoted* have a long, rounded *o,* /ou/, sound. In the words *job, not,* and *operate,* the *o* is transcribed as /ɑ/. Finally, in the words *other, done,* and *company,* the *o* is pronounced /ʌ/.

A 🔘 **Listen to the words. Notice...**

- Play CD 2, Track 47. Have students listen.
- Play Track 47 again. Have students listen and repeat.

Controlled Practice
10 minutes

B 🔘 **Listen to the words. Notice...**

- Copy the chart from Exercise A onto the board.
- Read the word *only.* Ask the class: *Does it sound like* no, job, *or* other? [no] Write it in the first column on the chart.
- Play CD 2, Track 48. Have students do the exercise.
- Check answers. Say each word. Have students hold up one finger if it belongs in column 1, two fingers if it goes in column 2, and three fingers if it goes in column 3.

C 🔘 **Kay and Luis are talking about their...**

- Explain difficult vocabulary as needed.
- Play CD 2, Track 49. Have students listen and read silently.
- Check comprehension. Ask: *How long has Kay been working at the company? Is she a good employee? What is the problem? What does Luis suggest?*

4 PRACTICE

A **PAIRS. Practice the conversation.**

- Form pairs and have students take turns reading each role.
- Have students switch partners and practice again.
- Take notes on errors in the pronunciation of words with o.
- Review the pronunciation errors in your notes. Have the class repeat the correct form.
- Ask volunteers to perform the conversation.

■■■ **Expansion: Speaking Practice for 4A**

- Have students role-play a conversation between Kay and her manager. To begin, Kay should knock on her manager's door and ask if the manager has time to talk to her. Then she should repeat the things she told Luis: how long she's been with the company and her good work habits. The manager should reply, either explaining why Kay hasn't received a promotion or agreeing that Kay deserves one and will get it soon.
- Pair above-level students with lower-level students. The above-level student should play the part of the manager.

Communicative Practice
10 minutes

B **PROBLEM-SOLVING. GROUPS. Kay...**

- Form groups. Have them select a timekeeper, a note taker, and a reporter.
- Give a time limit for the discussion.
- Have reporters share their groups' ideas.

Extra Practice

Interactive Practice

3 CONVERSATION

Pronunciation Watch

The letter *o* can spell several different vowel sounds.

CD2 T47

A 🔊 **Listen to the words. Notice the pronunciation of the underlined letters. Then listen again and repeat.**

no	job	other
ago	not	done
promoted	operate	company
only	stop	doesn't
don't	problem	come

CD2 T48

B 🔊 **Listen to the words. Notice the pronunciation of the underlined letters. Write each word in the correct column in the chart in Exercise A.**

1. only   2. stop   3. don't   4. doesn't   5. come   6. problem

CD2 T49

C 🔊 **Kay and Luis are talking about their jobs at Parcel Movers. Listen to their conversation.**

Kay: You know, I've been working here for five years now, and they still haven't promoted me.

Luis: Wow, that's too bad. Do you have any idea why not?

Kay: Not really. I think I'm a good employee.

Luis: You don't come to work late, do you?

Kay: No, I come in on time every day. And I work hard. I don't think my manager likes me.

Luis: Why don't you ask for a transfer? You could come and work in our operations department. My manager is demanding but very supportive. And I think there's an opening.

Kay: I don't know. Maybe. Tell me more about the department. What's it like?

4 PRACTICE

A **PAIRS. Practice the conversation.**

B **PROBLEM-SOLVING. GROUPS. Kay doesn't think her manager likes her. Discuss.**

1. What might be some other reasons that Kay didn't get a promotion?

2. What do you think Kay should do?

Make requests, suggestions, and offers at work

Grammar

Could you/I . . . ? / Why don't you/I . . . . ? / Would you mind . . . ?

Questions				Affirmative answers	Negative answers
Could	I	talk	to you?	Yes, of course. Sure. No problem.	Sorry, I'm busy. Sorry, I can't.
Could	you	work	overtime tonight?		
Why don't	you	ask	the supervisor?	Good idea.	I don't think that's a good idea.
Why don't	I	help	you with that?	Thanks.	That's OK, I don't need any help.
Would you mind	working		on Saturday?	Not at all.	I'm sorry, but I can't. I'd rather not.

Grammar Watch

- Use *Could I/you* and *Would you mind* to make polite requests for permission or help.
- Use *Why don't you . . .* to make suggestions.
- Use *Why don't I . . .* to make offers.
- When someone makes a request with *Would you mind*, use a negative answer, *Not at all,* to say you agree to the request.

1 PRACTICE

A Match the requests or suggestions with the correct response.

__b__ 1. Could I take a break now? ☐R

__g__ 2. Could you show me how to use this ladder? ☐R

__e__ 3. Why don't we clean up now? ☐S

__a__ 4. Would you mind saying that again? ☐R

__d__ 5. Why don't I help you with that box? ☐O

__c__ 6. Why don't you finish it tomorrow? ☐S

__f__ 7. Why don't I start that for you? ☐O

a. Not at all. I said, put on your protective glasses.

b. No problem. You've been working a long time.

c. It's due today.

d. Thanks a lot.

e. Good idea.

f. Great. I'll finish later.

g. Sure. You hold it this way.

B Look at Exercise A again. Is each question a *request* (R), a *suggestion* (S), or an *offer* (O)?

Getting Started   10 minutes

- On the board, write a two-column chart with the headings *Questions* and *Answers*. In the *Questions* column, list *Could you . . . ?* and *Could I . . . ?*
- Ask questions that will elicit both positive and negative responses. For example, ask a student *Could I use your pencil?*
- Next, ask questions that will most likely elicit negative responses. These can be humorous. For example: *Could you buy me a flat-screen TV?*
- Next, write the phrases *Why don't you . . .* and *Why don't I . . .* in the *Questions* column. Ask the class: *Who has a problem?* Call on a student to state a (nonserious) problem. Respond with *Why don't you . . .* Ask another student to name a problem. Offer to help with *Why don't I. . . .*
- Point to the chart and say: *We'll learn about these questions and responses in this lesson.*

Presentation   20 minutes

Could you/I...? / Why don't you/I...?...

- Read the first example in the Grammar chart. Say: Could I *is a polite way of asking for permission.* Give another example.
- Read the second example. Explain: Could you *is a polite way of asking somebody to do something.* Give another example.
- Read the affirmative and negative answers for the questions with *Could you/I.* Explain: *These are polite ways of saying* yes *or* no *to requests.*
- Read the sentence with *Why don't you.* Explain: *We use* Why don't you *to give a suggestion or advice.* Point to the responses and say: *These are polite ways of agreeing or disagreeing with a suggestion.*
- Read the sentence with *Why don't I.* Explain: *This is a polite way of offering to help somebody.* Point to the responses and say: *These are polite ways of accepting or turning down an offer.*
- Finally, read the sentence with *Would you mind.* Say: Would you mind *is a way of asking for something. It's followed by a gerund.* Point to the responses. Say: Not at all *means you agree to help.* I'm sorry *means you can't help.*
- Read all the Grammar Watch notes.

Language Note

Students are often confused by *Would you mind* because the response is counter intuitive; that is, a *no* answer means that the person agrees, and a *yes* answer means the person refuses!

Expansion: Grammar Practice

- Make a set of *yes/no* cards, one card for each student. Write *yes* on half of the cards and *no* on the other half. Shuffle the cards and place them on your desk.
- Divide the class into five groups. Each student in group 1 will write a request with *Could I* on a strip of paper. Each student in group 2 will write a request with *Could you,* each student in group 3 will write a suggestion with *Why don't you,* and so on.
- Collect all the strips and put them into a container.
- Call students up to the front of the room one by one. Each student will draw a strip out of the container and hand it to you. You will read the question on the strip. The student takes a *yes/no* card from the top of the deck and responds.
- For example, suppose a student draws a strip which says *Could I borrow $100?* and the student draws a card that says *yes.* An appropriate reply would be *Sure you can, Yes, of course,* or *No problem.*

Controlled Practice   10 minutes

1 PRACTICE

Ⓐ Match the requests or suggestions...

- Read the requests and suggestions. Have students match the request or suggestion with the correct response. Do item 1 as an example.
- Have students complete the exercise. Make sure students understand they should ignore the boxes following the questions until they do Exercise 1B.
- Check answers.
- Pair students and have them take turns reading the questions and responding appropriately.

Ⓑ Look at Exercise 1A again. Is each question...

- Do item 1 with the class as an example.
- Have students identify the meaning of each question.
- Check answers.

2 PRACTICE

Complete the questions with the correct...

- Read the expressions in the box.
- Do item 1 with the class as an example. Remind students that some items have more then one correct answer.
- Have students complete the exercise in pairs.
- Check answers.
- Form pairs and have them read the dialogues. Then have them switch roles and read again.
- Call on one pair to read each item out loud.

Communicative Practice   20 minutes

Show what you know!

ROLE PLAY. PAIRS. Role-play these situations.

> **Teaching Tip**
>
> While pairs are performing role plays, use the scoring rubric for speaking on page T-xiii to evaluate each student's vocabulary, grammar, fluency, and how well he or she completes the task. You may want to review the completed rubric with the students.

- Model one of two of the situations with an above-level student. For example: A: *Excuse me, Bob. I forgot my glasses. Could I borrow yours?* B: *No problem* or *Sorry, I'm using them now.*
- Form cross-ability pairs.
- Have students alternate making requests, suggestions, or offers and responding. Remind them to use the target grammar.
- After pairs have practiced all the items, have different pairs perform each situation for the class.

MULTILEVEL INSTRUCTION for ROLE PLAY

Cross-ability Have the higher-level student initiate the request or suggestion. Have the lower-level student respond.

Progress Check

Can you . . . make requests, suggestions, and offers at work?

Say: *We have practiced making requests, suggestions, and offers at work. Now, look at the question at the bottom of the page. Can you make requests, suggestions, and offers at work? Write a checkmark in the box.*

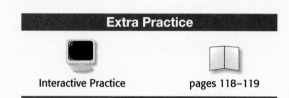

Extra Practice	
Interactive Practice	pages 118–119

Complete the questions with the correct expressions in the box. You will use some expressions more than once.

> Could I Could you Why don't I Why don't you Would you mind

1. **A:** _____Why don't I_____ get that down for you?
   B: Thanks. I'd appreciate that.

2. **A:** _____Would you mind_____ working on Sunday?
   B: I'm sorry, but I can't. I'm going to a wedding.

3. **A:** _____Could you_____ answer the phones for me for a couple of minutes?
   B: Sure. No problem.

4. **A:** _____Could I_____ borrow your copy of the safety manual?
   B: I'm sorry. I don't have it. I lent it to Sam.

5. **A:** _____Why don't you_____ tell your supervisor your idea?
   B: I'm already planning to. I'll talk to her tomorrow.

6. **A:** _____Would you mind_____ moving those boxes away from the exit?
   B: Not at all. They're a safety hazard where they are.

7. **A:** _____Why don't you_____ carry a bottle of water with you so you don't get thirsty?
   B: Good idea. It's really hot out here.

Show what you know!   Make requests, suggestions, and offers at work

ROLE PLAY. PAIRS. Role-play these situations. Take turns making requests or suggestions.

- You work in a clothing factory. You see a coworker using a sewing machine while wearing a long-sleeved sweater. Suggest that your coworker take off her sweater.
- You are a construction worker. You forgot to bring your protective glasses to work. Ask your supervisor if you can borrow his extra pair of glasses.
- You are a delivery driver. You don't feel well. Ask another driver to cover your shift for you.
- You work in a warehouse. Your back hurts, and you are unable to finish unpacking a shipment on time. A co-worker offers to help you.

Can you...make requests, suggestions, and offers at work? ☐

Writing

1 BEFORE YOU WRITE

A GROUPS. Sometimes workers have good ideas for making improvements at their workplaces. Discuss. What are some ways that workers can make their suggestions known to their bosses?

B Read the writing model. What is Lorenzo Herrera writing about? Who is he probably writing to?

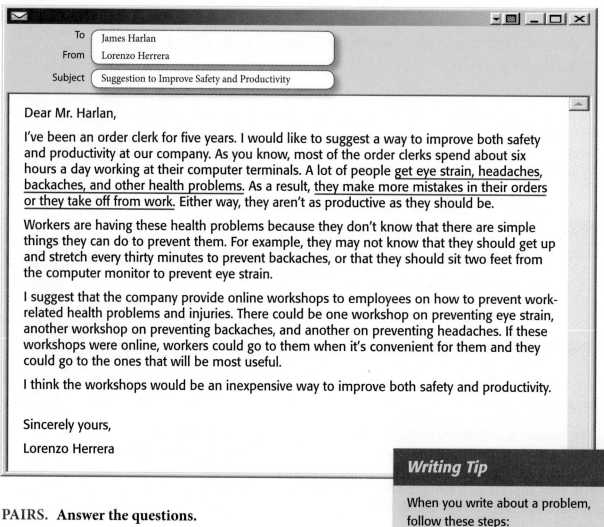

To   James Harlan

From   Lorenzo Herrera

Subject   Suggestion to Improve Safety and Productivity

Dear Mr. Harlan,

I've been an order clerk for five years. I would like to suggest a way to improve both safety and productivity at our company. As you know, most of the order clerks spend about six hours a day working at their computer terminals. A lot of people get eye strain, headaches, backaches, and other health problems. As a result, they make more mistakes in their orders or they take off from work. Either way, they aren't as productive as they should be.

Workers are having these health problems because they don't know that there are simple things they can do to prevent them. For example, they may not know that they should get up and stretch every thirty minutes to prevent backaches, or that they should sit two feet from the computer monitor to prevent eye strain.

I suggest that the company provide online workshops to employees on how to prevent work-related health problems and injuries. There could be one workshop on preventing eye strain, another workshop on preventing backaches, and another on preventing headaches. If these workshops were online, workers could go to them when it's convenient for them and they could go to the ones that will be most useful.

I think the workshops would be an inexpensive way to improve both safety and productivity.

Sincerely yours,

Lorenzo Herrera

Writing Tip

When you write about a problem, follow these steps:

1. identify the problem
2. explain the cause
3. suggest a solution

C PAIRS. Answer the questions.

1. What is happening at the writer's workplace?
2. Why does the writer think workers are getting injured?
3. What suggestions does the writer make to his supervisor?

Write about ways to improve workplace safety

Getting Started

1 BEFORE YOU WRITE

A GROUPS. Sometimes workers have good...

- Read the question aloud. Elicit one suggestion from the whole class, for example, the workplace could have a suggestion box.
- Put students in groups. Have them choose a timekeeper, a note taker, and a reporter.
- Give a time limit. While students are talking, walk around and provide help as needed.
- Have the reporter from each group share the group's ideas. Make a list on the board.

Presentation

B Read the writing model. What is...

- Read the model out loud as students read silently.
- Tell students to read the paragraph again and underline the information that answers the questions.
- Call on students to answer the questions.

C PAIRS. **Answer the questions.**

- Pair students and have them answer the questions.
- Go over the questions and answers with the whole class.

Answers:

1. Order clerks are sitting too long in front of computers.

2. They experience eye strain, headaches, backaches, and other health problems.

3. Workers should get up and stretch every thirty minutes, they should sit two feet from the computer monitor, and the company should provide online workshops to inform workers how to stay safe.

■■■■ MULTILEVEL INSTRUCTION for 1C

Cross-ability For question 1, have above-level students help pre-level students to identify not only the problem for the workers (*workers have health problems*) but also the resulting problem for the company (*workers make mistakes or take time off from work*).

Writing Tip: Identifying Problem, Cause, and Solution

- Read the Writing Tip.
- Ask: *In the writing model, are the three topics in the same paragraph, or is each one in a separate paragraph?* (separate) *How does the writer conclude the letter?* (with the advantages of his suggestion)

D Read the writing model again. Underline...

- Review the steps in the Writing Tip if necessary.
- Pair students and have them follow the directions.
- Go over the answers with the class.

Expansion: Writing Practice for 1D

- Write the following questions on the board:
  1. What do you think of Lorenzo's proposed solution?
  2. Can you think of other solutions?
- Have students discuss the questions in pairs.

Controlled Practice   15 minutes

2   THINKING ON PAPER

A BRAINSTORM. Think about potential...

- With the class, define each word in the box. Have students define or demonstrate the terms. If possible, have them use the words in sentences. Allow students to translate or use a dictionary.
- Have each student write down one or more potential hazards in his or her workplace, home, or school.
- Have them compare notes with a partner.
- Alternately, have the class brainstorm together. Write students' ideas on the board.

B Choose one of the safety issues...

- Copy the graphic organizer on the board and do a model brainstorm with the class. For example, falls are a potential problem at your school because the entryway gets slippery after it rains.
- Elicit solutions from the students and write them on the graphic organizer. For example, the school could install nonslip carpeting in the entry area; an overhang could be installed outside the building so that students could remove their wet coats outside; and the entryway could be paved with nonslip stone or cement.
- Have students think of solutions to the hazard they picked in Exercise A and write possible solutions on the graphic organizer.

MULTILEVEL INSTRUCTION

Pre-level Have students think of one problem and one possible solution.

Above-level Have students think of one problem and several possible solutions. Have them write about the advantages and disadvantages of each solution and choose the best one.

Communicative Practice   20 minutes

3   WRITE

Write an e-mail to a supervisor about an idea...

- Read the directions. Remind students to write the problem, cause, and solution(s) in separate paragraphs. Also remind them to write a concluding sentence.
- Review letter format.
- Encourage the students to use polite expressions for making requests, suggestions, and offers.
- Have students write in class.

4   CHECK YOUR WRITING

- Have students read their paragraphs and check the questions in the checklist. Alternately, have them revise their paragraphs according to the items.

Teaching Tip

You may want to collect student papers and provide feedback. Use the scoring rubric for writing on page T-xiv to evaluate each student's vocabulary, grammar, mechanics, and how well he or she has completed the task. You may want to review the completed rubric with the students.

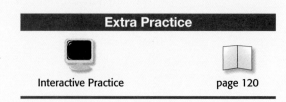

Extra Practice

Interactive Practice   page 120

D Read the writing model again. Underline the sentences in which Lorenzo identifies the problems, circle the sentences that explain the causes, and star (★) the sentence that suggests a solution.

2 THINKING ON PAPER

A BRAINSTORM. Think about potential safety-related problems at your school or workplace. Use the words in the box to get ideas.

> burns   clutter   cuts   exits   falls   hazards   poisons   strain

B Choose one of the safety issues you thought of. Think of solutions to that problem. Organize your ideas in a diagram like this.

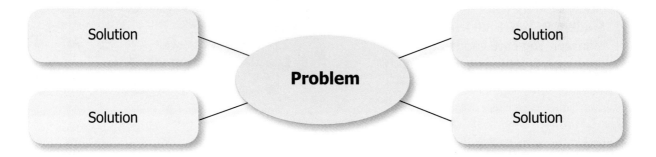

Solution | Solution

Problem

Solution | Solution

3 WRITE

Write an e-mail to a supervisor about an idea to improve safety at your school or your workplace. Use the writing model as an example.

4 CHECK YOUR WRITING

☐ Did you identify the problem and explain the causes?

☐ Did you suggest a solution?

☐ Did you use correct capitalization, punctuation, and spelling?

1 REVIEW

For your grammar review, go to page 254.

2 ACT IT OUT What do you say?

STEP 1. Review the conversation on page 198 (CD2, Track 46).

STEP 2. ROLE PLAY. PAIRS. Role-play this situation.

Student A: You've worked at your job for five years. You're hoping to get a promotion to supervisor.

Student B: You're Student A's manager. You have good news! Student A is getting a promotion.

3 READ AND REACT Problem-solving

STEP 1. Read the problem.

Sometimes workers have accidents in the kitchen at Mangia Pizza. Last week a pizza cook slipped on some tomato sauce that had spilled on the floor. She was wearing sandals and a tank top. She fell against the pizza oven and burned her arm. And yesterday, a prep cook slipped on a piece of cheese and crashed into another kitchen worker, who was slicing onions. That worker cut himself with his knife.

STEP 2. GROUPS. What is the problem? Discuss a solution. How can the workers at Mangia Pizza prevent accidents in the future?

4 CONNECT

For your Self-Evaluation Activity, go to page 261.
For your Team Project, go to page 272.

Which goals can you check off? Go back to page 185.

 Go to the CD-ROM for more practice.

Show what you know!

1 REVIEW

Turn to page 254 for the Grammar Review.

2 ACT IT OUT

STEP 1. Review the conversation.

- Replay the conversation from page 198 (CD 2, Track 46).

STEP 2. ROLE PLAY. PAIRS. Role-play this situation.

> **Teaching Tip**
>
> While pairs are performing role plays, use the scoring rubric for speaking on page T-xiii to evaluate each student's vocabulary, grammar, fluency, and how well he or she completes the task. You may want to review the completed rubric with the students.

- Read the role descriptions.
- Model the role play with an above-level student. Play the role of Student B. You can begin the conversation like this: *Could you come into my office for a minute, [name]? There's something I want to discuss with you.*
- Remind students to try to use the unit grammar in their role play.
- Tell students to practice at least twice.
- Have volunteers role-play for the class.

■■■ MULTILEVEL INSTRUCTION for 2

Pre-level Have students play the role of Student A. Give them the responses to use for their conversation, but give them out of order: *I try my best. / Oh, wow! That's great! / Thank you. I'm really excited to have this opportunity. / Oh, sure. / Is everything OK? / Oh, thanks! Great! / Thank you. / Well, safety is important. / Thanks. We're all part of a team.* Tell them to use these as responses. They should practice reading the script several times. Then they should try to role-play without reading.

Above-level Have students practice without notes. Tell Student B to give three reasons why he or she is promoting Student A.

3 READ AND REACT

STEP 1. Read the problem.

- Read the paragraph while students follow along silently.
- Have students restate the two accidents.

STEP 2. GROUPS. What is the problem? Discuss...

- Form groups of three or four. Have each group choose a timekeeper, a note taker, and a reporter.
- Give a time limit for discussion. Walk around and provide help as needed.
- Have the reporter from each group share the group's ideas. Write all the ideas on the board.

■■■ Expansion: Speaking Practice for STEP 2

- Ask students if they have had a safety problem at their workplace. Ask them how they dealt with it.

4 CONNECT

Turn to page 261 for the Self-Evaluation Activity and page 272 for the Team Project. See page T-xi for classroom management tips for these activities.

Progress Check

Which goals can you check off? Go back to page 185.

Ask students to turn to page 185 and check off any remaining goals they have reached. Call on students to say which goals they will practice outside of class.

■ Go to the CD-ROM for more practice.

If students need more practice with the vocabulary, grammar, and competencies in Unit 10, encourage them to review the activities on the CD-ROM.

Know the Law!

Classroom Materials/Extra Practice

CD 2
Tracks 50–59

Interactive Practice
Unit 11

Workbook
Unit 11

Unit Overview

Goals
- See the list of goals on the facing page.

Grammar
- Past continuous for interrupted action
- Passives: Present passive and simple past passive
- Adverb clauses of condition and contrast

Pronunciation
- Weak pronunciation of *is, are, was,* and *were*

Reading
- Talk about DNA evidence
- Reading Skill: Understanding longer sentences

Writing
- Write about different legal systems

Life Skills
- Identify people in a courtroom

Preview
- Say the unit title and have students look at the art. Ask: *What do you think this unit will be about?*
- Read the preview questions and elicit students' answers. As needed, provide background on the picture. Say: *This is a photo of a trial, which is the legal process for determining if a person accused of a crime is guilty or innocent. The person who supervises at a trial is called a* judge. *In a criminal trial, the person accused of a crime is called a* defendant. *There are two sides in a trial and each side is represented by lawyers. A group of twelve citizens, called a* jury, *listens to the lawyers and ultimately decides if the defendant is guilty or innocent. The judge's job is to make sure that all laws and procedures are followed.*
- As you explain the terms above, write them on the board. Encourage students to copy them into their vocabulary notebooks.

Unit Goals
- Point to the Unit Goals. Have students read them silently.
- Tell students they will be studying these goals in Unit 11.
- Say each goal and explain unfamiliar vocabulary as needed, for example, *misdemeanor: a crime that is not serious; courtroom: the place where trials are held; DNA: the genetic material that determines all our characteristics.*
- Tell students to circle one or more goals that are very important to them. Call on several volunteers to say the goals they circled.
- Write a checkmark (✓) on the board. Say: *We will come back to this page again. You will write a checkmark next to the goals you learned in this unit.*

Know the Law!

Preview

Read the title. Look at the picture. Where are these people? What are they doing?

UNIT GOALS

- ☐ Identify misdemeanors

- ☐ Talk about legal problems

- ☐ Identify people in a courtroom

- ☐ Describe what happens in a courtroom

- ☐ Talk about DNA evidence

- ☐ Discuss traffic laws

- ☐ Write about different legal systems

Listening and Speaking

1 BEFORE YOU LISTEN

A **PAIRS.** Look at the signs. They warn against misdemeanors, or crimes that are not very serious. What does each sign mean?

B **GROUPS.** Discuss. Are the actions in the signs illegal in other countries?

2 LISTEN

A CD2 T50 David is telling his cousin Solange about an experience he and his daughter had. Listen to the conversation. What happened to David and his daughter?

B CD2 T50 Read the statements. Listen to the conversation again. Then write *T* (true) or *F* (false).

> **UNDER 18 CURFEW**
> **SUN–THURS**
> **10:00 PM–6:00 AM**
> **FRI–SAT**
> **11:00 PM–6:00 AM**

___F___ 1. David's daughter got a fine for littering in the park.

___T___ 2. The police called David shortly after 10 P.M.

___T___ 3. The city has a 10 P.M. curfew for all teenagers.

___F___ 4. Caroline and her friends were on their way to the movies at 10:15 P.M.

___F___ 5. One of Caroline's friends was robbed.

___T___ 6. David and Solange didn't know about the curfew.

C **GROUPS.** Discuss. Do you think that a 10 P.M. curfew for teenagers is a good idea? Why or why not?

Getting Started — 5 minutes

- Choose three activities that are misdemeanors in your area and write them on the board. For example, *1. driving a car without front and back license plates; 2. drinking alcoholic beverages at the beach;* and *3. failing to get a license for a dog.*
- Ask students: *Which of these activities are illegal? (all of them)* Say: *These activities are illegal, but they are not serious crimes. They are called misdemeanors.*

Presentation — 10 minutes

1 BEFORE YOU LISTEN

A PAIRS. Look at the signs. They warn...

- Write the word *misdemeanors* on the board. Say it and have students repeat.
- Ask students to give additional examples of misdemeanors that they know about.
- Ask students to define *loitering* (standing around without any obvious purpose) and *littering* (throwing trash on the ground).
- Pair students and have them answer the question.
- Go over the answers with the whole class.

B GROUPS. Discuss. Are the actions in the...

- Form groups. Try to mix students from different countries.
- Call on volunteers to answer the question.

2 LISTEN

A David is telling his cousin Solange...

- Have students look at the photo. Ask: *What is a curfew? Is there a curfew in the area where you live?*
- Play CD 2, Track 50.
- Have students discuss what happened.
- Answer the question with the whole class.

Answer: The police called David. His daughter was out after 10 P.M. There's a curfew for teenagers now in the city. After 10 P.M., no kids below the age of eighteen are allowed downtown.

Controlled Practice — 5 minutes

B Read the statements. Listen to the...

- Have students read the statements silently and predict if they are true or false.
- Play Track 50 again.
- Have students do the exercise and compare answers with a partner.
- Check answers. Have students read the items and say if they are true or false. If an item is false, ask the student to correct it.
- Copy the sentences with the words *ordinance* and *incidents* on the board. Elicit definitions (*ordinance: a city law; incidents: events—in this case, crimes*).
- Pair students and have them read the conversation.

MULTILEVEL INSTRUCTION for 2B

Cross-ability Have the above-level student read the role of David. Instruct students to use their real names in the conversation.

Communicative Practice — 10 minutes

C GROUPS. Discuss. Do you think that a...

- Put students in groups. Give a time limit for discussion. While students are talking, walk around and provide help as needed.
- Review the discussion with the whole class. On the board, draw a two-column chart with the headings *Pro* and *Con*. Ask students to state the advantages and disadvantages of a 10 P.M. curfew. Take notes on the board.

Expansion: Speaking Practice for 2C

- In the recording, Caroline was arrested and taken to the police station for being out past curfew. Put students in groups and have them discuss the following questions: *1. Did the police act appropriately when they picked up Caroline? 2. Should there be a punishment for teenagers who are out past curfew? If so, what should it be? 3. Is it OK to impose a curfew in one part of a city but not in another part? Why or why not?*

Lesson 1 Identify misdemeanors

Presentation   5 minutes

3 CONVERSATION

 David and Solange are talking...

- Define *customs* as *the place at an airport or border where travelers' bags are examined to find out if they are bringing in any illegal goods to the country.*
- Play CD 2, Track 51. Have students listen and read along silently.
- Check comprehension. Ask: *What did the customs officer find in Solange's bags? What did the officer do with the items she found? Why?*
- On the board, write the words *contaminating* and *food supply.* Elicit definitions.

Controlled Practice   5 minutes

4 PRACTICE

Ⓐ PAIRS. Practice the conversation.

- Form cross-ability pairs and have students practice reading the conversation.
- Ask volunteers to perform the conversation.

> **MULTILEVEL INSTRUCTION for 4A**
>
> **Cross-ability** Have the pre-level student read the role of David. The above-level student should help with vocabulary and pronunciation.

Communicative Practice   20 minutes

Ⓑ ROLE PLAY. PAIRS. Role-play this situation.

- Read the role descriptions. Clarify that Student A was waiting for a person who did not live in the apartment building.
- Model the role play with an above-level student. Play the role of the building owner. Decide if you will call the police.
- Pair students. Give them time to practice.
- Have volunteers perform their role plays for the class.
- Select a few key errors. Say the incorrect forms. Have the class respond with the correct ones.

Ⓒ STEP 1. PAIRS. Discuss. Which of the...

- Read the list of misdemeanors. For *improper disposal of trash*, ask: *Do you know a word that has this meaning?* (*litter* or *littering*).
- Ask students to give examples of disturbing the peace, for example, *playing loud music late at night* and damaging someone's property, for example, *grafitti* or *knocking down a fence.*
- Pair students. Give them a time limit for the discussion.
- Have students vote for the most serious misdemeanor. Ask why it is the most serious.
- With the whole class, discuss the need for misdemeanor laws.

STEP 2. GROUPS. Each of the actions above...

- Define *felony: a serious crime that is punished more severely than a misdemeanor, often by spending time in prison; burglary: illegally entering someone's home with the intention of stealing; murder: killing someone.*
- Form groups. Give a time limit for the discussion.
- To wrap up, discuss question 1 with the whole class. Then have one student from each country answer question 2.

> **Expansion: Speaking Practice**
>
> - Students have a debate. Divide the class into two groups. Designate each group as *pro* or *con.*
> - Say: *You will discuss reasons why jaywalking should or should not be a misdemeanor, punishable by a fine.*
> - Give a time limit for discussion.
> - Have each group select two speakers to present the group's side of the argument. Each group should have a note taker. The speakers may use the group's notes while speaking.
> - The pro side speaks first, then the con side. Next, audience members can ask either side questions. To conclude, the other speaker from each team gives a short rebuttal.
> - Audience members vote on who won the debate.

Extra Practice

Interactive Practice

3 CONVERSATION

CD2 T51

David and Solange are talking about a problem Solange had with customs. Listen and read.

David: How was your trip? Did you have fun?

Solange: We had a great time, but we did have a bit of a problem on the way back.

David: Really? What happened?

Solange: We were going through customs when an officer stopped us and searched our bags. She found the mangoes I wanted to bring home.

David: They're worried about contaminating the food supply. I don't think you can bring in meat or bread, either.

Solange: Well, the officer threw all the mangoes out.

David: That's too bad. But she was just doing her job.

4 PRACTICE

A PAIRS. Practice the conversation.

B ROLE PLAY. PAIRS. Role-play this situation.

Student A: You are sitting on the front door step of an apartment building, waiting for some friends to pick you up in their car. Someone comes out of the building and asks you to leave. You refuse because you aren't doing anything wrong, and there is nowhere else to sit.

Student B: You own the building where Student A is sitting. You explain to Student A that it is illegal to trespass or loiter on private property. You tell him or her to leave.

C STEP 1. PAIRS. Discuss. Which of the following misdemeanors do you think is most serious? Why do you think there are misdemeanor laws?

- Driving without a valid license or insurance
- Improper disposal of trash
- Disturbing the peace
- Deliberately damaging someone's property

STEP 2. GROUPS. Each of the actions above is not as serious as a felony, such as burglary or murder, but it is punishable by law. Discuss.

1. Why do you think that these actions are illegal in the U.S.?

2. Are they illegal in your home country? If not, should they be? Why?

Grammar

Past continuous for interrupted action

Main clause	Time clause
I **got** a call on my cell	**while** I **was watching** the news.
We **were going** through customs	**when** an officer **stopped** us.

Grammar Watch

- Use the past continuous with the simple past to talk about an action that was interrupted by another action.
- Use *while* to introduce a time clause with the past continuous.
- Use the past continuous for the action that was interrupted.
- Use *when* to introduce a time clause with the simple past.
- Use the simple past for the interrupting action.
- A time clause can start or end a sentence. Use a comma after a time clause when it starts a sentence: *While I was watching the news, I got a call on my cell.*

1 PRACTICE

Read the sentences. Then read the questions and circle the correct answers.

1. Felipe was loitering in the hallway of the apartment building when the landlord came out of his apartment and asked him to leave.
   Who was in the hallway first?
   (a.) Felipe   b. the landlord

2. While Isaac was listening to loud music, his neighbor became angry and reported him to the police.
   What happened first?
   (a.) Isaac was listening to loud music.   b. The neighbor reported him to the police.

3. The Chang family was walking through a private garden when an elderly man told them that it was private property and asked them to leave.
   When did the Chang family start walking out of the garden?
   (a.) before the man talked to them   b. after the man talked to them

4. A security guard told Huang to put out his cigarette while he was standing in the lobby of the building.
   What happened first?
   a. The security guard talked to Huang. (b.) Huang started smoking.

Getting Started   10 minutes

- Do a short pantomime: Sit at your desk and pretend to correct papers. After a minute or so, have a student (with whom you made arrangements ahead of time) knock on the door. Call out *Come in!*

- On the board, write the following (the times are examples): *1. 7:30 began correcting papers. 2. 7:45 [name] knocked on door; stopped correcting papers.*

- Say: *At 7:30 I began correcting papers. What was I doing at 7:35? (You were correcting papers.)* Then ask: *What happened at 7:45? ([name] knocked on the door.)*

- Write on the board: *I was correcting papers when [name] knocked on the door.* Point to the verb in the main clause, underline it, and say: *This verb form is called the* past continuous. Point to the verb in the dependent clause, underline it, and say: *This verb is in the past.* Circle *when* and draw an arrow to the verb *knocked*.

- Ask the class: *Do you know another way to say the same sentence?* As a hint, write *While* on the board and see if students can complete the sentence. If not, write *While I was correcting papers, [name] knocked on the door.* Again, underline the verbs. Circle *While* and draw an arrow to the past continuous verb.

Presentation   15 minutes

Past continuous for interrupted action

- Read the first Grammar Watch note. Use the sentences already on the board as examples. Point to *correcting papers* and say *This action was interrupted.* Point to *knocked* and say *This is the interrupting action.*

- Copy the sentences from the grammar chart onto the board. Have students identify the interrupting action and the action that interrupted.

- Read the second and third notes. Explain that *while* means *during that time.* It's usually used with the action that started first, which has a longer duration.

- Read the fourth note. Explain that *when* means *at that time.* People usually use *when* with the interrupting (short) action.

- Read the final note. Rewrite the example without a comma, switching the order of the clauses.

Language Note

For the sake of simplicity, students are usually taught to use *while* with the past continuous and *when* with the simple past. In fact, however, speakers of English frequently use *when* with both verb forms. Thus a sentence like the following is acceptable in spoken English: *My sister dropped by last night when we were eating dinner.*

Expansion: Grammar Practice

- Have students write the examples from the grammar chart in all possible ways. For example, *1. I got a call on my cell while I was watching the news. 2. While I was watching the news, I got a call on my cell. 3. I was watching the news when I got a call on my cell. 4. When I got a call on my cell, I was watching the news.*

- Walk around and check students' sentences while they are writing. Check for correct punctuation and verb forms.

Controlled Practice   20 minutes

1   PRACTICE

Read the sentences. Then read the questions...

- Do item 1 with the class. If necessary, remind students to use the past continuous for the action that began first, the action that was interrupted.

- Pair students and have them complete the exercise.

- Check answers.

2 PRACTICE

Ⓐ Complete the conversations. Use the simple...

- Read the example.
- Have students complete the exercise alone or in pairs. Give a time limit. Walk around and provide help as needed.
- Go over the answers and write them on the board. After each answer, ask the class: *Is this correct? Why?* Elicit the correct answers from students and write them on the board.

Expansion: Speaking Practice for 2A

- Form cross-ability pairs and have students practice the conversations.
- Call on pairs to perform the conversations for the class.

Ⓑ Complete the conversation. Circle the...

- Read the conversation.
- Have students do the exercise.
- Check answers.

Expansion: Speaking Practice for 2B

- Ask: *In your area, what do you think will happen in the following situations? 1. A driver is stopped by the police for speeding. The person does not have a valid driver's license. 2. A driver is stopped for speeding. The person has a valid driver's license, but he or she forgot it at home.*

Expansion: Vocabulary Practice for 2B

- Divide the class into two teams. On the board, write synonyms or definitions for some of the vocabulary in the exercise. Note: You can also say the synonyms instead of writing them. As soon as you write a synonym, students can call out the word or phrase it matches, and that team gets a point. Then write the next synonym.
- You can use the following synonyms and definitions: *1. a parking space (parking spot); 2. illegally park next to another parked car (double park); 3. leave (exit) a parking space (pull out); 4. doubt; think that someone is lying (suspicious); 5. planning to do something very soon (about to); and 6. happening (going on).*

Communicative Practice   15 minutes

Show what you know!

GROUPS. Discuss. Talk about a legal problem...

- Provide a model by telling the class about a legal problem you know about. Be sure to make the problem a simple one and use simple past and past continuous.
- Put students in groups. Have them choose a timekeeper.
- Give a time limit. While students are talking, walk around and provide help as needed.
- Ask one or two volunteers to repeat their story for the whole class. Based on the stories, have the class form sentences with the simple past and past continuous.

Progress Check

Can you . . . talk about legal problems?

Say: *We have practiced talking about legal problems. Now, look at the question at the bottom of the page. Can you talk about legal problems? Write a checkmark in the box.*

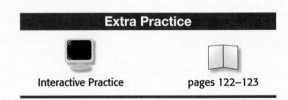

Extra Practice
Interactive Practice   pages 122–123

2 PRACTICE

A Complete the conversations. Use the simple past and the past continuous.

1. **A:** So why did Kyle and Lenny get arrested?

   B: They __were having__ an argument at a restaurant when Kyle got mad at Lenny

(have)
   and __knocked__ over a table. The table __fell__ against a mirror on the

(knock)   (fall)
   wall and __smashed__ it. While a waiter __was trying__ to clean up the mess,

(smash)   (try)
   the owner __called__ the police.

(call)

2. **A:** Did you know that you can get a ticket if you don't clean up after your dog in this

   city? While my friend __was walking__ his dog this morning, he __stopped__ to

(walk)   (stop)
   chat with a friend. While they __were talking__, the dog __did__ what dogs

(talk)   (do)
   do. When my friend started to walk again without cleaning up after the dog, a

   policeman gave him a ticket.

   B: I guess he'll remember to clean up after his dog next time.

B Complete the conversation. Circle the correct words.

Marco is the owner of a restaurant. One day he double-parked his minivan outside the
restaurant and told his busboy, Emilio, to keep an eye out for a parking spot. While Emilio
looked /(**was looking**)for a spot, a car(**pulled out**)/ **was pulling out** of a space nearby,
and Emilio(**called**)/ **was calling** Marco. Marco told Emilio to move the car for him. But
while Emilio **moved** /(**was moving**)the car, a policeman(**stopped**)/ **was stopping** him and
asked him for his driver's license. Emilio(**didn't have**)/ **wasn't having** his driver's license
with him while he **drove** /(**was driving**), which is illegal. The policeman(**got**)/ **was getting**
suspicious while Emilio **tried** /(**was trying**)to explain the situation. He thought Emilio was
trying to steal the car. The policeman was about to take Emilio down to the station, when
Marco(**arrived**)/ **was arriving** and explained what was going on. The policeman decided
not to give Emilio a ticket.

Show what you know! Talk about legal problems

GROUPS. Discuss. Talk about a legal problem you heard or read about. Describe
what happened. Use the simple past and the past continuous.

Can you...talk about legal problems? ☐

Life Skills

1 IDENTIFY PEOPLE IN A COURTROOM

GROUPS. Look at this picture. Read the definitions. Write the name of the person next to the correct definition.

___bailiff___	= the person who watches prisoners and keeps order in the courtroom
___court reporter___	= the person who records what people say at a trial
___defendant___	= the person who is accused of a crime
___defense attorney___	= the lawyer who tries to prove that the defendant is not guilty
___judge___	= the official who is in charge of a court and who decides how crimimals should be punished
___jury___	= a group of citizens who decide if the defendant is innocent or guilty
___prosecutor___	= the lawyer who tries to prove that the defendant is guilty
___witness___	= someone who describes what they know about a crime
___foreman___	= the leader of the jury

2 PRACTICE

PAIRS. Take turns. Read a definition. Have your partner name the person it describes.

Getting Started   5 minutes

Read the lesson title. Ask students to name the courtroom participants that they are already familiar with. Write the terms on the board.

Presentation   20 minutes

1   IDENTIFY PEOPLE IN A COURTROOM

GROUPS. Look at this picture. Read the...

- Have students study the picture for one or two minutes, taking in the people in the picture and the various labels.
- Say each vocabulary item. Have students repeat. Then read or have a student read each definition. Answer students' questions.
- Form groups and have students find the participants in the picture.

Culture Connection

- There are two common categories of law, *criminal* and *civil*. Criminal cases involve major crimes such as burglary, murder, rape, stealing, or driving under the influence of alcohol. If a person is convicted of these crimes, the punishment is usually imprisonment. Civil law addresses situations in which people have been harmed and a monetary compensation is requested. Examples of civil law cases include divorce and disputes involving property.
- In a criminal trial, the opposing attorneys are the *defense attorney* and the *prosecuting attorney*. The person accused of the crime is called the *defendant*. In civil cases, the accused person is also called the *defendant*, and the person who accuses the defendant is called the *plaintiff*. In civil cases there often is no jury; the decision is made by one or more judges.

 Expansion: Vocabulary Practice for 1

- Write the vocabulary items and definitions on index cards. Mix the cards and hand them out to students. Instruct students to mingle in order to match the vocabulary cards with their definitions. When students find their partners, have them sit together.
- Have each pair of students say their vocabulary item and read the definition.

Community Building

Arrange a field trip to a local court. If possible, arrange for students to view a trial in progress. Have them draw a sketch of the layout of the courtroom and label the participants.

Controlled Practice   10 minutes

2   PRACTICE

PAIRS. Take turns. Read a definition. Have...

- Pair students. Have them complete the task while covering the answers in Exercise 1 with a piece of paper. Have them check each answer one at a time.

3 PRACTICE

A Dan Jones is on trial for robbing a...

- Read item 1 with the class.
- Have students do the exercise. Have them compare answers with a partner.
- Call on students to read each quote and say who said it.

Communicative Practice   25 minutes

B CLASS. Discuss.

- Ask students about courtroom films or TV shows they have seen. Write the titles on the board.
- Have students say what they have learned from watching these programs.
- Be prepared to correct misconceptions or stereotypes that students may have. For example, students may get the impression from television that courtrooms are very dramatic, fast-paced places. In reality, most trials move very slowly and with little drama. A great deal of time is devoted to procedural matters that are quite uninteresting to spectators.

▬▬ Expansion: Speaking Practice for 3B

- If possible, record the opening scenes of a television courtroom show. It can be a courtroom drama or a reality program.
- View the recording with your students and have them identify the various participants in the courtroom.

Progress Check

Can you . . . identify people in a courtroom?

Say: *We have practiced identifying people in a courtroom. Now, look at the question at the bottom of the page. Can you identify people in a courtroom? Write a checkmark in the box.*

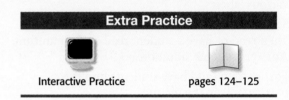

Extra Practice	
Interactive Practice	pages 124–125

A **Dan Jones is on trial for robbing a convenience store on March 8. Read each quote from his trial and write the name of the person who probably said it.**

> bailiff   defendant   foreman   prosecutor
> court reporter   defense attorney   judge   witness

1. "Do you solemnly swear to tell the truth, the whole truth, and nothing but the truth?" _the bailiff_

2. "Mr. Jones, the jury has found you guilty. I hereby sentence you to one year in prison." _the judge_

3. "I will show beyond a shadow of a doubt that Mr. Jones is guilty." _the prosecutor_

4. "We, the jury, find the defendant guilty." _the foreman_

5. "I saw Mr. Jones running out of the convenience store. He was wearing dark clothes and a baseball cap, but I saw his face under the streetlight." _the witness_

6. "The prosecutor said, 'Where were you at 7:45 P.M. on the night of March 8?' The defendant replied, 'I was in the convenience store on March 8. I did not rob the store. I ran out of the store because I was in a hurry to catch my bus.'" _the court reporter_

7. "I will show that Dan Jones, for reasons that will be made clear, could not have committed this robbery." _the defense attorney_

B **CLASS. Discuss.**

1. Do you ever watch reality TV programs about trials or films about courtroom dramas? Decribe one show or film you have seen.

2. What have you learned about the American legal system from watching these stories?

Can you...identify people in a courtroom? ☐

Listening and Speaking

1 BEFORE YOU LISTEN

GROUPS. Have you ever seen a TV courtroom show? Do you think these shows present courtrooms as they are in real life? Explain.

2 LISTEN

CD2 T52

A Lisa and Alex are watching TV. Listen to their conversation. How does Lisa feel about TV courtroom shows?   She doesn't like them.

CD2 T52

B Read the sentences. Then listen to the conversation again. Circle the phrase to complete each sentence.

1. Alex thinks courtroom TV shows are about (**real law and justice**) / **bad relationships**.

2. Lisa thinks courtroom TV shows are about **real cases** / (**made-up cases.**)

3. In the TV court case, the man borrowed money from his roommate to pay his **rent** / (**car payment.**)

4. The man refused to pay his roommate back because (**they had a fight**) / **he didn't have enough money**.

5. (**Alex owes Lisa**) / **Lisa owes Alex** fifty dollars.

C **GROUPS.** Discuss. If you had to go to court, would you want the case to be shown on TV? Why or why not?

Lesson 4 Describe what happens in a courtroom

Getting Started   10 minutes

1 BEFORE YOU LISTEN

GROUPS. Have you ever seen a TV courtroom...

- Ask students to raise their hands if they have seen a TV courtroom show. Make sure there is at least one such person in each group.
- Form groups and have them answer the questions. Encourage students to think of specific ways in which the TV shows are similar to and different from real-life trials.

Community Building

- Watch a courtroom drama with the class. TV shows include *Law and Order* or *Judge Judy*. Classic films include *12 Angry Men, To Kill a Mockingbird, Kramer vs. Kramer,* and *The Verdict*.

- Find a synopsis online and read it with the class before viewing. Note: For many movies you can also find the script online by searching with these prompts: [name of film] and script.

- Explain that many courtroom procedures are very old, and they preserve the language used at the time they were established. Students should not worry about understanding every word of the courtroom scenes.

- Prepare a list of questions for students to discuss after viewing. In particular, ask students if they agree with the verdict.

Presentation   5 minutes

2 LISTEN

Ⓐ 🎧 **Alex and Lisa are watching TV. Listen...**

- Have students look at the photo. Ask: *What is happening?*
- Tell students to listen specifically for the answer to the question. It is not necessary to understand every word.
- Play CD 2, Track 52.
- Call on a volunteer to answer the question. Ask: *How do you know? What did you hear?*

Controlled Practice   5 minutes

Ⓑ 🎧 **Read the sentences. Then listen...**

- Define *case* as *a legal action that is decided in a court of law*.
- Have students read the questions and predict the answers.
- Play Track 52 again.
- Check answers.
- If students have difficulty answering a question, replay the segment of the listening passage that answers it.

Communicative Practice   15 minutes

Ⓒ GROUPS. Discuss. If you had to go to court...

- If necessary, restate the situation without using the conditional. Say: *Imagine that you have to go to court. Do you want the case to be on TV?*
- Form groups. Give a time limit for discussion.
- Call on volunteers to answer the questions.

▬▬ **Expansion: Speaking Practice for 2C**

- Have the class watch a segment of a reality courtroom TV show, then discuss the following questions: *1. What is your opinion of the defendant and plaintiff in the show? 2. Why do you think people want to be on a show like this?*

Presentation   5 minutes

3 CONVERSATION

Pronunciation Watch

- Write sentences with *is, are, was,* and *were* on the board. For example: *The jury is discussing the case. Judges are elected by the people. The reality show was boring. The defendants were guilty.*
- Say each sentence. Be sure not to stress *is, are, was,* and *were.* Tell students to listen for the stressed words, then repeat them for you.
- Read the Pronunciation Watch note.

A 💿 **Listen to the sentences. Notice...**

- Play CD 2, Track 53. Have students listen.
- Play Track 53 again. Have students listen and repeat.
- Call on students to say the sentences.

Controlled Practice   10 minutes

B 💿 **Listen to the sentences. Circle...**

- Do item 1 with the class. Stop the recording and check answers.
- Play CD 2, Track 54. Have students do the exercise.
- Check answers.

C 💿 **Gina and Nick are talking about a...**

- Play CD 2, Track 55. Students listen and read silently.
- Check comprehension. Ask: *When did the incident happen? Where was Nick? What was he doing? What did he see? Why did he have to go to court?*

4 PRACTICE

A PAIRS. **Practice the conversation.**

- Form cross-ability pairs and have students read the conversation.
- Walk around and listen as students are practicing.
- Ask volunteers to perform the conversation.

■■ MULTILEVEL INSTRUCTION

Cross-ability Have pre-level students read the part of Gina. Instruct above-level students to quickly read their lines, then look up and say them without reading.

Teaching Tip

The look-up-and-speak technique can help students improve their ability to remember strings of words. In the technique, learners first read a phrase or sentence silently; then they look up and repeat it from memory. While reciting, students may change words as long as they retain the meaning and use correct grammar. Over time, students can practice with longer and longer strings of speech.

Communicative Practice   10 minutes

B MAKE IT PERSONAL. GROUPS. **Have...**

- If possible, tell about your own experience as a witness or having someone serve as a witness on your behalf. Encourage students to ask you questions about what happened.
- Have students raise their hands if they have ever been a witness. Distribute these students among different groups.
- Form groups and give a time limit for discussion.
- Call on volunteers to share their experience.

■■■ Expansion: Speaking Practice for 4B

- Have students do a role play in a courtroom. Assign two roles: a witness and the lawyer.
- The lawyer should ask questions such as *Where were you on [date and time]? What were you doing there? What did you see?*
- The witness should describe an accident like the one in Exercise 3C. Higher-level students can invent a different scenario. Students can also talk about the actual incident they described in Exercise 4B.

Extra Practice

Interactive Practice

Getting Started   10 minutes

- Introduce the passive using familiar situations. Use simple vocabulary so that students can focus on the grammar. For example, you can create a family chores chart like the following:

Benny	walk the dog
Mother	cook dinner
Cathy	wash the dinner dishes

- Put the chart on the board. Ask the class: *Who walks the dog every day? Who cooks dinner? Who washes the dinner dishes?* Write the answers in active voice. (*Benny walks the dog; Mother cooks dinner; Cathy washes the dinner dishes.*)
- Point to the sentences and explain: *If we want to emphasize the person who does each chore, we write the sentences this way. The word order is subject-verb-object. We call this the* active voice. Write *subject + verb + object* on the board.
- Continue the explanation as follows: *What if we want to emphasize the object instead of the subject? Then we can say the first sentence like this: The dog is walked by Benny every day. Dinner is cooked by Mother. The dinner dishes are washed by Cathy.* Write the sentences on the board.
- Point to the passive sentences and explain: *This kind of construction is called the* passive voice. *In a passive construction, the object of an active sentence becomes the object of a passive sentence.*
- Write the formula for the passive on the board: *subject + be + past participle + (optional)* by [someone or something].

Presentation   15 minutes

Passives: Present passive and simple past passive

- Copy the sentences from the grammar chart onto the board. It may be helpful to number them for ease of reference.
- Read the first Grammar Watch note and the example.
- Read the second note and the example. Then read the first sentence in the grammar chart. Ask the class: *In the first sentence, do we know who watches this show?* (no). Explain: *We don't know, and the speaker doesn't think it's important for us to know.*

- Read the third note and example. Then read sentences 2, 3, and 4 from the grammar chart. Explain: *These sentences have both a subject and an agent. The speaker decides whether to say the sentence in active or passive form, depending on what the speaker wants to emphasize.*
- Point out that subjects and verbs must agree in number in passive sentences.
- Read the last note and example.

 Expansion: Grammar Practice

- Erase the passive sentences about family chores on the board. Leave the active ones.
- Have students say the passive of each sentence, first with the agent and then without.
- Have students list at least three chores that are done by somebody in their household. Pair students and have them use the passive voice to tell their partner who does what. Tell them to include the agent in their sentences.

Controlled Practice   15 minutes

1 | **PRACTICE**

- Read the sentences. Is the sentence active or passive?
- Read the Vocabulary Note at the right. Then read the example with the class.
- Have students do the exercise, working alone or in pairs.
- Check answers.

 Expansion: Grammar Practice for 1

- Have students convert the sentences in Exercise 1 from active to passive and from passive to active, if possible. Remind students that a passive sentence can be changed to active only if it has an agent, in other words a *by* phrase.
- Explain that sentences with long objects, for example, *The defendant entered a plea of not guilty,* do not work well in the passive voice.

2 PRACTICE

Ⓐ Complete the sentences about criminal trials...

- Have students read the passage for meaning. Clarify vocabulary as needed, for example, *evidence: the objects or information used to show a defendant's guilt or innocence; outcome: a result.*
- Remind students that subjects and verbs must agree.
- Have students do the exercise and compare answers with a partner.
- Check answers. Call on students to give you their answers. Write them on the board and make corrections as needed.

Ⓑ Read part of Vincent's e-mail to a friend...

- As in the previous exercise, have students read the passage for meaning first. Read the definition of jury duty. Explain other vocabulary as needed, for example, *sue means to go to court to request money as compensation for damage that was done to a person or property; trip means to fall over something; the stand means the box in which witnesses sit while lawyers ask them questions in a courtroom.*
- Remind students that subjects and verbs must agree.
- Have students do the exercise. Have them compare answers with a partner.
- Check answers.

Communicative Practice 20 minutes

Show what you know!

GROUPS. Discuss a court case you read or...

- Explain or remind students that civil cases are often decided by a judge alone.
- Explain that *verdict* means *a jury or judge's decision at the end of a trial.*
- Model answers to the questions. You may wish to talk about a famous trial, such as the murder trial of O.J. Simpson.
- Form groups. Give a time limit for discussion. While students are talking, walk around and provide help as needed.
- To wrap up, have volunteers share their answers to the questions.

Progress Check

Can you ... describe what happens in a courtroom?

Say: *We have practiced talking about what happens in a courtroom. Now, look at the question at the bottom of the page. Can you describe what happens in a courtroom? Write a checkmark in the box.*

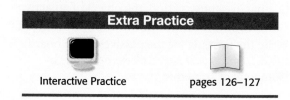

Extra Practice

Interactive Practice   pages 126–127

2 PRACTICE

A Complete the sentences about criminal trials with the simple present passive.

Criminal trials __are heard__ by a jury of twelve people. The defendant __is questioned__
       (heard)   (question)

by the prosecutor and the defense attorney. Then the witnesses __are questioned__. Evidence,
                                                   (question)

such as photos and documents, __are shown__ to the jury. The case __is discussed__ by the
                             (show)   (discuss)

jurors outside the courtroom. During the trial, jurors __are not allowed__ to read, watch, or listen
                                               (not/allow)

to stories about the trial. The outcome __is decided__ by the jury.
                                    (decide)

B Read part of Vincent's e-mail to a friend about his experience with jury duty. Complete the e-mail with the simple past passive.

> *Jury duty is a period of time when U.S. citizens must be ready to sit on, or be part of, a jury.*

Sorry I didn't call you yesterday. I __was called__ for jury duty. The case
                                   (call)

was unbelievable. A woman was suing the city because she broke her ankle when

she tripped over a bump in the sidewalk. She wanted the city to pay for her medical

expenses. But when she __was questioned__ in court, her story didn't make sense. When
                              (question)

she __was asked__ where she was when she tripped, she couldn't remember. Then
         (ask)

her doctor __was called__ to the stand. He said that she told him that she had fallen
             (call)

down the stairs in her house! The case __was dismissed__ soon after, and all the jurors
                              (dismiss)

__were sent__ home.
  (send)

Show what you know! Describe what happens in a courtroom

GROUPS. Discuss a court case you read or heard about. Use the active and passive voice. Answer the questions.

- Who was accused, and what was the person accused of?
- Was the case decided by a jury or a judge?
- What was the verdict? Was the defendant found guilty or not guilty?

Can you...describe what happens in a courtroom? ☐

Reading

1   BEFORE YOU READ

A GROUPS. Discuss. What kinds of evidence do police and lawyers use to prove that criminals are guilty of crimes?

B GROUPS. Read the definition for DNA. Discuss. What is DNA? How can it be used to find out whether someone committed a crime?

> DNA = deoxyribonucleic acid. DNA carries genetic information in a cell. Every person has different DNA.

2   READ

CD2 T56

Read and listen. Then review your answers to Exercise 1B. Was your background knowledge about DNA correct? Explain.

DNA and the Law

On May 7, 2008, three men robbed a bank in Waldorf, Maryland. They drove away in a van with a bag of money. They thought they had escaped. But the bank had put a pack of chemicals in the money bag, and the pack **exploded**. The robbers dropped the bag, got out of the van, and ran away. Soon afterward, the police arrested one of the robbers. How did the police find him so quickly? DNA from the robbers' blood was found on the bag of money.

DNA consists of genetic material that is found everywhere in our body, such as in our blood, skin, and saliva. DNA is our genetic fingerprint. All people have **similar** DNA, but no two people have the exact same DNA.

How is DNA used to identify a criminal when a crime has been

committed? The testing works like this: After a crime occurs, police collect **evidence** from a crime scene. Some of this evidence may be DNA **samples**, such as hairs or blood. The police then compare this DNA to DNA samples from an FBI **database**. The FBI database is computerized, and it has over 4 million DNA samples in it. These DNA fingerprints are taken from people all over the country who have been arrested or convicted of crimes. If the DNA in the evidence matches someone's DNA fingerprint, that person is probably guilty of the crime. But if the evidence does not match, the person is probably innocent.

DNA testing is not perfect. If DNA evidence is not collected or stored properly, for example, the tests may give wrong results. But it is still more **reliable** than other types of evidence. Witnesses may identify the wrong person. Lawyers, jurors, judges, and the police can make mistakes. DNA testing is usually accurate. It is the best way we have to prove that someone is guilty or innocent of a crime.

Before DNA testing, some innocent people went to prison for crimes they did not commit. The police are now using DNA testing to overturn wrongful convictions. As of 2008, DNA tests have been used to free more than 200 innocent people in the U.S.

Getting Started   10 minutes

1 BEFORE YOU READ

Ⓐ GROUPS. Discuss. What kinds of evidence...

- Remind students that the definition of *evidence* is *the objects or information used to show a defendant's guilt or innocence.* Elicit an example, such as a photo or a gun with fingerprints on it.
- Form cross-ability groups. Have them choose a note-taker and a reporter.
- Have the reporter share the group's list of kinds of evidence.

Ⓑ GROUPS. Read the definition for DNA...

- Keep students in the same groups as in Exercise A.
- Read the definition. Say *deoxyribonucleic acid* slowly and have students repeat, but point out that people seldom say the full name.
- Have students answer the questions to the best of their ability.
- Have students share their knowledge about DNA with the whole class. Provide additional explanation and clarification as needed. For example, you can explain that DNA determines every human characteristic, from physical characteristics such as eye color to mental abilities such as skill in mathematics.

Presentation   15 minutes

2 READ

Read and listen. Then review your answers...

- Have students read silently without using dictionaries.
- Give a time limit, but give students more time if necessary.
- Discuss the questions with the whole class.
- Play CD 2, Track 56 and have students listen to the passage and read.

▬▬▬ **Expansion: Grammar Practice for 2**

- Have students reread the article and underline all occurrences of the passive voice.
- Remind students of the structure of the passive: *be* + past participle.
- Instruct them to scan the article and raise their hand when they find the first occurrence (*was found* in the first paragraph). Then have them continue working on their own.
- Call on students to share answers.
- Point out that the passive is used very often in scientific writing.

Community Building

For a more comprehensive explanation of more information on how DNA evidence works, have students search online using terms such as *DNA evidence* or *how DNA evidence works.* Have students try to find the answers to the following questions: *1. How is DNA evidence used in a courtroom?* (to prove guilt or to clear an innocent person) *2. What are some ways that DNA evidence is used outside of a courtroom?* (paternity testing, identification, studying evolution and inherited diseases). Have students combine their answers into a class information sheet.

Controlled Practice   15 minutes

3 CHECK YOUR UNDERSTANDING

Reading Skill: **Understanding Longer Sentences**

- Read the Reading Skill. Say: *It can be useful to try to write long complex sentences as several shorter sentences.*
- Write the following long sentence on the board: *Even though DNA was first discovered in 1896, it wasn't commonly used in police work until forensic scientists developed DNA testing in the 1980s.*
- Break it down into shorter sentences as follows: *DNA was first discovered in 1896. At that time, it wasn't used in police work. Then scientists developed DNA testing in the 1980s.*

Ⓐ **Read the Reading Skill. Then draw lines...**

- Have students do the exercise.
- Check answers.
- Have students restate sentence 1 as two simple sentences.

Expansion: Reading Practice for 3A

- Have students look back at the reading and underline long sentences that are divided into "chunks."
- Have pre-level students find one sentence. Have above-level students find several.
- Call on several students to read out loud the sentences they underlined. Point out the different chunking devices that are found in the article (*commas and connecting words*).

Ⓑ **Read the sentences. Circle the correct word...**

- Do item 1 with the class. Have students scan the text to find the answer.
- Have students do the exercise. Then have them compare answers with a partner.
- Check answers.

4 WORD WORK

Find the boldfaced words in the article and...

- Remind students of the following tips for guessing from context: *1. Read each word in its sentence and determine the part of speech. 2. For verbs, determine if it is an action verb or not. For adjectives, determine if the meaning is positive or negative. For nouns, determine if the noun refers to a person or a thing. 3. Look at the sentences before and after the sentence in which the word appears to see if there is a synonym.*
- Form cross-ability pairs and have students do the exercise.

MULTILEVEL INSTRUCTION for 4

Cross-ability Have pre-level students find the words in the text and read out loud the sentences in which they appear. Have above-level students help with pronunciation. Next, have students discuss whatever clues are available to help guess. Have the pre-level student match the words with their definitions. Have the above-level student confirm the answers.

Expansion: Vocabulary Practice for 4

- Form pairs. Have them quiz each other on the words in Exercise 4. Instruct Student 1 to read a definition; have Student 2 respond with the word. Then tell them to switch roles.

Communicative Practice   20 minutes

Show what you know!

GROUPS. Discuss. Do you think that DNA...

- Form groups and have them choose a note-taker and a reporter.
- Have the reporter from each group share the group's opinion.

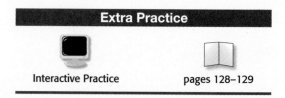

Extra Practice

Interactive Practice   pages 128–129

CHECK YOUR UNDERSTANDING

A Read the Reading Skill. Then draw lines to divide each sentence into "chunks."

Break long sentences into smaller "chunks" to make them easier to understand. One way to do this is to look for punctuation such as commas or connecting words such as *when*, *before*, *after*, *although*, and *if*.

1. Soon after the robbers dropped the bag and ran away, / the police arrested one of them.

2. If the DNA in the evidence matches someone's DNA profile, / that person is probably guilty of the crime.

B Read the sentences. Circle the correct word or phrase to complete each sentence.

1. The (bank) / police put a pack of chemicals in the money bag.
2. The bank robbers ran away from the van (with) / without the bag of money.
3. The police used DNA evidence to catch (one) / all of the bank robbers.
4. Two people (never) / almost never have the same DNA.
5. DNA databases contain DNA samples from people who **have never been in prison** / (**have been arrested.**)
6. It is **easier** / (**harder**) to make mistakes with DNA testing than with other types of evidence.

4 **WORD WORK**

Find the boldfaced words in the article and guess their meaning from the context. Then match the words with the definitions.

_f_ 1. explode
_a_ 2. similar
_e_ 3. commit
_g_ 4. evidence
_d_ 5. sample
_c_ 6. database
_b_ 7. reliable

a. almost the same
b. can be trusted or depended on
c. a large amount of data stored in a computer
d. a small amount of something
e. do something wrong or illegal
f. blow up
g. facts that prove that something is true

Show what you know! Talk about DNA evidence

GROUPS. Discuss. Do you think that DNA testing has improved the fairness of our legal system? Explain.

Listening and Speaking

1 BEFORE YOU LISTEN

A GROUPS. Make a list of all the traffic laws you can think of. What can happen if you break traffic laws?

B PAIR. Look at the words and their definitions. Which ones have you heard before?

contest (v) = to say formally that you do not think something is right or fair

fine (n) = money you have to pay as a punishment for breaking the law

be in the right = not to have broken the law or done something wrong

points on a license = penalties you receive for traffic violations. If you get too many points, you may lose your license.

run a stop sign = drive past a stop sign without stopping (a traffic violation)

ticket = a printed note saying that you must pay money because you have done something illegal while driving or parking your car

traffic school = a course in traffic safety and safe driving practices

2 LISTEN

CD2 T57

A Listen to a talk show about cars. What topic is Carl Mansfield answering questions about?

CD2 T57

B Read the statements. Then listen to the conversation again. Write *T* (true) or *F* (false). Correct the false statements.

__T__ 1. Caller 1 got a ticket because she didn't stop for a stop sign.

__T__ 2. A branch was covering the stop sign.

__T__ 3. Carl thinks that Caller 1 was in the right.

__F__ 4. Carl thinks that if Caller 1 shows a judge a picture of the sign, she ^probably won't have to pay the fine.

__T__ 5. Caller 2 wants to get the points on his license removed.

__T__ 6. Carl thinks that the police will clear Caller 2's driving record if he gets a traffic-school certificate.

C GROUPS. Discuss. Should people be required to go to traffic school if they have committed traffic violations? Why or why not?

Getting Started   5 minutes

- Read the lesson title.
- Ask the class: *Have you ever gotten a traffic ticket? What was it for? How much did you have to pay?* Have one or two volunteers share their experience.

1 BEFORE YOU LISTEN

Ⓐ GROUPS. Make a list of all the traffic laws...

- Form groups. Have them select a timekeeper, a note taker, and a reporter.
- Give a time limit. While students are talking, walk around and provide help as needed.
- Have reporters share the group's list. Write the items on the board. Define terms as needed.
- Call on a volunteer to answer the question.

Ⓑ Look at the words and their...

- Read the words. Have students repeat after you. Check that students are pronouncing the words correctly, for example, *conTEST* as opposed to *CONtest*.
- Read the definitions.
- Say each word in the context of a sentence, or ask students to do so.

Presentation   5 minutes

2 LISTEN

Ⓐ 💿 Listen to a talk show about cars. What...

- Play CD 2, Track 57. Have students listen for the answer to the question.
- Have students compare answers with a classmate.
- Call on students to share their answers.

Controlled Practice   5 minutes

Ⓑ 💿 Read the statements. Then listen...

- Have students read the questions before listening. Encourage them to predict the answers.
- Play Track 57 again. Have students listen and answer the questions.
- Have students compare answers with a partner.
- Check answers. Call on students to read each question and answer. Check to make sure that students understand *points* and *traffic school*.

Communicative Practice   15 minutes

Ⓒ GROUPS. Discuss. Should people...

- On the board, draw a two-column chart with the headings *Yes* and *No*.
- Form groups. Instruct students to think of reasons for and against requiring people to go to traffic school. Tell them to choose a note taker to take notes in the chart. They should also choose a reporter.
- Have reporters share their groups' ideas. List them in the chart on the board.

▬ Expansion: Speaking Practice for 2C

- Find out if anyone in the class has ever gone to traffic school. Ask: *Where and when did you go? How was the experience? Do you think it helped you to be a better driver?*

Presentation   10 minutes

 3   CONVERSATION

Pronunciation Watch

- Write this sentence on the board: *Go back to the stop sign and take a picture of it.*
- Say the sentence. Tell students to notice the stressed words. Underline them (*back, stop sign, take,* and *picture*).
- Say: *You've learned that content words, or words which carry meaning, like nouns, verbs, and adjectives, are usually stressed.*
- Read the Pronunciation Watch note.

Ⓐ Listen to the sentences. Notice the weak...

- Play CD 2, Track 58. Have students listen.
- Play Track 58 again. Have students listen and repeat.

Ⓑ Ana got a ticket. Listen and read.

- Play CD 2, Track 59. Have students listen and read along silently.
- Check comprehension. Ask: *Why did Ana get a ticket? What was her mistake? What could she have done to avoid getting the ticket?*

Controlled Practice   5 minutes

 4   PRACTICE

Ⓐ PAIRS. Practice the conversation.

- Form pairs and have students take turns reading each role.
- Have students switch partners and practice again.
- Go over the pronunciation errors.
- Ask volunteers to perform the conversation.

Communicative Practice   15 minutes

Ⓑ ROLE PLAY. PAIRS. Role-play this situation.

- Model the role play with an above-level student. Play the role of Student A. Tell Student B that you got a ticket. Student B should ask where you were

at the time. When you say you were near a school, Student B should explain the law to you.
- Form similar-ability pairs.
- Have volunteers role-play their conversation.

Culture Connection

In 2008, approximately 300 U.S. cities were using cameras at intersections to catch drivers running red lights.

▮ MULTILEVEL INSTRUCTION

Pre-level Have students write a script of their role play and practice reading it several times. Then tell them to practice without the script.

Above-level Have Student A express concern that his or her auto insurance rates will go up because he or she got a ticket. Have Student B advise Student A to go to traffic school.

Community Building

- Have students share their knowledge about the location of cameras at intersections in their city or town.
- Provide a model, for example, *There's a camera at the intersection of Olympic and Beverly.*
- If practical, bring in city maps and have students mark the location of the cameras.

Ⓒ MAKE IT PERSONAL. GROUPS. Discuss.

- Read the questions. If necessary, rephrase question 2 to avoid the unreal conditional. You can say: *Imagine that all these traffic laws don't exist. What will happen?*
- Form groups. Have them select a timekeeper, a note taker, and a reporter. The note taker should keep track of laws that the group feels should be changed.
- Give a time limit.
- Have reporters summarize their groups' discussion.

Extra Practice

Interactive Practice

3 CONVERSATION

CD2 T58

A 🔘 **Listen to the sentences. Notice the weak pronunciation of the words in blue. Then listen and repeat.**

Look at this.
Take a picture of the sign.
I got a ticket for running a stop sign.
How much is it for?

> ### Pronunciation Watch
>
> Words like *a, the, at, of,* and *for* are usually weak when another word comes after them. The vowel sound is quiet and short. Words like these have a stronger pronunciation at the end of a sentence.

CD2 T59

B 🔘 **Ana got a ticket. Listen and read.**

Ana: Look at this! I got a parking ticket!

Cho: Oh, no. How much is it for?

Ana: One hundred bucks! But why did they give me a ticket? I didn't get a ticket last night even though I parked in exactly the same spot!

Cho: Look! Your car is the only one on this side of the street.

Ana: You're right!

Cho: Let's see—look at this sign. It says that the city sweeps this side of the street every Tuesday morning. That's why everyone moved their cars to the other side of the street last night—except you!

Ana: That explains why I got the ticket! My car was blocking the street sweeping truck.

4 PRACTICE

A PAIRS. **Practice the conversation.**

B ROLE PLAY. PAIRS. **Role-play this situation.**

Student A: You received a speeding ticket in the mail. A camera took a picture of you while you were speeding by a school. You don't understand why you got the ticket, because you never drive above the regular speed limit.

Student B: Tell Student A that he or she was in a school zone and got a ticket for driving too fast past the school when children were in the area. Explain the posted speed limit shown at the right.

C MAKE IT PERSONAL. GROUPS. **Discuss.**

1. Why are there so many traffic laws?

2. What would happen if some of these laws didn't exist?

3. Are there any traffic laws that you think should be changed? If so, which ones? Why?

Grammar

Adverb clauses of condition and contrast

Adverb clause (condition/contrast)	Main clause (result)
As long as the traffic violations **aren't** too serious,	you **can go** to traffic school.
Even if you **are** mad at another driver,	you **shouldn't honk** your horn.
Even though I **parked** in the same spot,	I **got** a ticket.

Grammar Watch

- Use *as long as* to show the conditions needed for something to happen.
- Use *even if* to show that the condition in the adverb clause does not matter; the result does not change.
- Use *even though* when there is a surprising or unexpected contrast between the information in the two clauses.
- An adverb clause can start or end a sentence. Use a comma after an adverb clause when it starts a sentence.

1 PRACTICE

Read the first statement. Write *T* (true) or *F* (false) for each of the following statements.

1. Even if the road is empty, you aren't allowed to turn left at a red light.

    __F__ a. You can turn left at a red light if the road is empty.

    __T__ b. You can't turn left at a red light when the road is empty.

2. As long as you have a valid driver's license, you are allowed to drive anywhere in the country.

    __F__ a. You don't need a valid driver's license to drive anywhere in the country.

    __T__ b. You are allowed to drive anywhere in the country if you have a valid driver's license.

3. Even though she obeyed all the traffic laws, she had an accident.

    __T__ a. She obeyed all the traffic laws, but she had an accident anyway.

    __F__ b. She didn't obey all the traffic laws; that's why she had an accident.

4. Even if the speed limit is high, many drivers slow down in bad weather.

    __T__ a. Many drivers like to drive at a slower speed when the weather is bad.

    __F__ b. Many drivers like to drive at a higher speed when the weather is bad.

Lesson 8 Discuss traffic laws

Getting Started   10 minutes

- Remind students that they have already learned how to form sentences with adverb clauses of time (*before, after, since,* etc.), reason (*because, since*), and purpose (*so, so that*). Elicit examples of sentences with each subordinator. Write several sentences on the board and review their structure (dependent clause + independent clause with comma, or vice versa with no comma).

- Write the subordinators *as long as, even if,* and *even though* on the board. Say: *These phrases also introduce adverb clauses. Each one has a special meaning. We'll learn how to use them in this lesson.*

- On the board write an example sentence using each subordinator. Ask students if they can explain each sentence in different words. For example: *1. You can borrow my car as long as you don't stay out too late.* (You can borrow my car only if you don't stay out too late.); *2. Even if you're only going to the market, you have to wear a seatbelt.* (It doesn't matter if the market is very close, you have to wear a seatbelt in the car.); *3. Even though there's not much traffic, you have to obey the speed limit.* (There's not much traffic, but you still have to obey the speed limit.)

Presentation   15 minutes

Adverb clauses of condition and contrast

- Copy the sentences from the grammar chart onto the board.

- Read the first Grammar Watch note. Explain that *as long as* means *if,* but it has the added meaning of *only if* or *only under the special condition in the adverb clause.* Read the first example sentence and rephrase: *You can go to traffic school only if the traffic violation isn't serious. If it is serious, you can't go to traffic school.*

- Read the second Grammar Watch note and the second example. Explain that *even if* has the subtle meaning that it doesn't matter what the speaker thinks about the information in the clause (for example, whether the speaker likes or dislikes the information or agrees or disagrees with it); the result will not change. Say: *Thus, in the example, it doesn't matter whether you are mad at the other driver. It is still true that you shouldn't honk your horn.*

- Read the third note and the third example. To clarify, ask: *Normally, if you park somewhere and you don't get a ticket, do you expect to get a ticket if you park there again?* (no) Explain: *So in this sentence, if we read that the speaker got a ticket, that is surprising information. Even though is a signal to the listener that the speaker is going to say something surprising or unexpected.*

- Read the fourth note. Have three students rewrite the example sentences on the board switching the positions of the adverb clause and the main clause. Remind them not to use the comma.

Controlled Practice   15 minutes

| 1 | PRACTICE |

Read the first statement. Write *T* (true) or *F* (false)...

- Do item 1 with the class.
- Have students complete the exercise and compare answers with a partner.
- Check answers.
- Have students restate the meaning of each sentence. For item 1, for example, they can say: *It doesn't matter if the road is empty, you still aren't allowed to turn left at a red light.*

▬▬ **Expansion: Writing Practice for 1**

- Have students rewrite the four sentences in the exercise with the main clause first.
- Pair students and have them switch papers. Instruct them to check each other's sentences for correct capitalization and the use of the comma.

2 PRACTICE

A **Complete the sentences with the...**

- Read item 1 with the class.
- Have students continue working alone or in pairs.
- Check answers.

B **Complete the sentences with your own ideas.**

- Do item 1 with the class. Elicit several ways to complete the sentence.
- Have students complete the remaining items alone or in pairs.
- Have eight students write their sentences on the board (two students each for items 2 through 5).
- Call on other students to read the sentences and say if they are correct.

Communicative Practice 20 minutes

Show what you know!

GROUPS. Discuss.

- Form groups.
- Give a time limit for discussion. Walk around and provide help as needed.
- Call on volunteers to share their answers with the class.

Expansion: Speaking Practice for Show what you know!

- Have a series of debates on the questions. Divide the class into six teams, one pro group and one con group for each of the three questions.
- Give groups time to plan their arguments in support of the position they were assigned.
- Have each team select two speakers. Explain the structure of team debate: 1. The first pro speaker presents the pro position. 2. The first con speaker presents the con position. 3. Members of the audience can ask questions of either side. 4. The second speaker for the pro side sums up the pro position. 5. The second speaker for the con side sums up the con position. 6. The audience votes on the winning team. Instruct students not to vote for the position they agree with but rather for the side that presented more convincing arguments.

Progress Check

Can you . . . discuss traffic laws?

Say: *We have practiced discussing traffic laws. Now, look at the question at the bottom of the page. Can you discuss traffic laws? Write a checkmark in the box.*

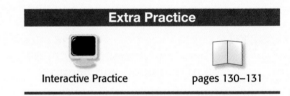

Extra Practice

Interactive Practice   pages 130–131

PRACTICE

A Complete the sentences with the conjunctions in the box. Use one conjuction more than once.

> even if   as long as   even though

1. _____As long as_____ you obey the traffic laws in your state, you won't get a traffic ticket.

2. _____Even though_____ her headlights didn't work, she drove her car at night. But then she got a ticket.

3. The police officer gave the Changs a ticket _____even though_____ they said that they would buy a car seat for their baby as soon as possible.

4. You shouldn't honk your horn in a traffic jam _____even if_____ you are really late for an appointment.

B Complete the sentences with your own ideas.

1. Even if everyone obeyed the traffic laws, _____.

2. Even if an intersection doesn't have a traffic light, _____.

3. As long as you drive carefully, _____.

4. As long as you wear your seat belt, _____.

5. Even though the light was red, _____.

Show what you know!   Discuss traffic laws

GROUPS. Discuss.

1. Should drivers be required to drive at lower speeds if the weather is bad?
2. Should people below the age of 16 be permitted to drive?
3. Should older people be allowed to drive as long as they pass vision and driving tests?

Can you... discuss traffic laws? ☐

Write about different legal systems

Writing

1 BEFORE YOU WRITE

A GROUPS. Read the rights of people who are arrested in the U.S. Discuss. What does each right mean? Do people have these rights in your home country?

- The right to remain silent while you are questioned by the police.
- The right to have a lawyer present while you are questioned.
- The right to a free lawyer if you cannot pay for one yourself.
- The right to a speedy, public, and fair trial.

B Read the writing model. What is the topic of the paragraph?

The Rights of the Accused in the U.S. and My Home Country

In the U.S., a person who is accused of a crime has the right to a speedy trial. In most states, the law says that a trial must take place within a certain number of months. But in my home country, people do not have the right to a speedy trial. They often have to wait in jail for many years before they go to trial. In the U.S., people have the right to a fair trial, with independent judges and competent lawyers. In contrast, when a person who is accused of a crime in my country finally does get a trial, the trial may not be fair. The judges are not always independent. Their decisions are often influenced by the wishes of politicians. Also, in my country, competent lawyers are very expensive, and many people cannot afford to hire one. Similarly, competent lawyers are expensive in the U.S. However, if a person cannot afford to hire a lawyer, the court will provide one. These are just some of the differences in the rights of accused people in the U.S. and my home country.

C PAIRS. Answer the questions.

1. What is the writer contrasting?
2. According to the writer, what are two differences between the rights of people accused of a crime in the U.S. and his home country?
3. What similarity exists between lawyers in the U.S. and lawyers in the writer's home country? What difference exists between the rights to a lawyer in the two places?

Writing Tip
Compare and Contrast

When comparing and contrasting two things, use words such as *similar, similarly,* and *like* to signal similarities and words such as *but, in contrast,* and *however* to signal differences.

Write about different legal systems

Getting Started
10 minutes

1 BEFORE YOU WRITE

A GROUPS. Read the rights of people who...

- Define *right* in the context of this exercise: *a freedom that people in a society have, such as the right to vote or the right to own a gun.*
- Discuss the first item. Explain that a person arrested in the U.S. cannot be forced to speak.
- Form groups.
- Discuss the answers with the class. Ask students about legal rights in different countries.

Culture Connection

In 1966, the U.S. Supreme Court ruled in *Miranda vs. Arizona* that a person arrested on suspicion of committing a crime has certain rights. The ruling states,

. . . The person in custody must, prior to interrogation, be clearly informed that he or she has the right to remain silent, and that anything the person says may be used against that person in court; the person must be clearly informed that he or she has the right to consult with an attorney and to have that attorney present during questioning, and that, if he or she is indigent, an attorney will be provided at no cost to represent him or her.

Presentation
15 minutes

B Read the writing model. What is the...

- Have students read the paragraph silently.

Writing Tip: Comparing and Contrasting

- Read the Writing Tip.
- Write a two-column chart on the board with the headings *Compare* and *Contrast*. Under each heading, elicit the words and phrases from the paragraph that express similarities and differences, respectively. For example, these terms signal differences: *different from, in contrast, another important difference,* and *but.* The word *both* signals similarity.

C PAIRS. Answer the questions.

- Form pairs.
- Check answers.

Possible answers:

1. The rights of the accused in the U.S. with the rights of the accused in the writer's home country.

2. In the U.S., the accused has the right to a speedy and fair trial. In the writer's home country, the accused often has to wait for years in jail while awaiting trial, and the trial may not be fair.

3. In both countries, competent lawyers are very expensive. But in the U.S., if a person can't afford a lawyer, the court will provide one. In the writer's home country, the court doesn't provide a lawyer.

▬ Expansion: Writing Practice for 1C

- Have students outline the writing model.
  - I. Differences in the rights of the accused
    - A. U.S.
      - _____
      - _____
    - B. Writer's home country
      - _____
      - _____
  - II. Legal representation _____
    - A. U.S.
      - _____
      - _____
    - B. Writer's home country
      - _____
      - _____

- Have students complete the outline.
- Discuss the outline with the class. First, point out that the outline does not have complete sentences; it contains main ideas only. Second, explain that the organization used in the model is called *point by point organization.* There are two points contrasted: the rights of the accused and legal representation. The points as well as the discussion of the two countries are separated by connectors.
- Have students circle the connecting words and phrases. Highlight the major transition between the two points. (*Another important difference*)

Lesson 9 · Write about different legal systems

Controlled Practice   15 minutes

2   THINKING ON PAPER

A BRAINSTORM. Think about your legal...

- If necessary, go over each item and review the rights that people have in the U.S.
- Have students discuss the rights with other people from their country of origin.

B Use your answers to the questions...

- Copy the chart onto the board. Model filling in one or two lines of the chart with information about the U.S. and another country you know about.
- Have students fill in their information. Encourage them to work together with other students from their native country.
- While students are working, walk around and provide help as needed.
- Have students share their charts with a partner from a different country of origin.
- Have two or three volunteers write their charts on the board. With the class, discuss how to organize a paragraph based on the information in the charts.

C Select two rights from your chart...

- Have students choose the topics they want to write about.

Communicative Practice   20 minutes

3   WRITE

Write a paragraph that explains similarities...

- Have the students outline their paragraph. If they did the Expansion activity outline from page T-222, they can use it as a model.
- Have students read the checklist items in Exercise 4 before writing. Tell them: *Keep these points in mind while you write.*
- Have students write in class. While they are writing, walk around and provide help as needed.

■ MULTILEVEL INSTRUCTION for 3

Pre-level Have students write about one difference between the legal rights of the accused in their country and the rights of the accused in the U.S. Have them use the introduction and organization from the model paragraph.

Above-level Have students write about several similarities and differences. Tell them to write the similarities and differences in two blocks, as in the model.

4   CHECK YOUR WRITING

- Have students read their paragraph and check the items in the checklist.
- If students are unable to check something off because they left it out, or if they want to rewrite part of their paragraph, encourage them to do so.

■ Expansion: Writing Practice

- Have students rewrite their paragraphs in class.
- Pair students and have them read their paragraphs to each other.

Teaching Tip

You may want to collect student papers and provide feedback. Use the scoring rubric for writing on page T-xiv to evaluate each student's vocabulary, grammar, mechanics, and how well he or she has completed the task. You may want to review the completed rubric with the students.

Extra Practice

Interactive Practice   page 132

2 THINKING ON PAPER

A BRAINSTORM. Think about your legal rights in two places: the U.S. and your home country. Compare or contrast how an accused person is treated.

Do you have the right to remain silent if you are questioned by the police?

Do you have the right to have a lawyer with you if you are questioned by the police?

Do you have the right to a free lawyer?

Do you have the right to a speedy and public trial?

Do you have the right to a fair trial?

Do you have the right to a jury trial?

B Use your answers to the questions in Exercise A to complete the chart.

Citizen's Rights in the U.S.	Citizen's Rights in the _____
1.	1.
2.	2.
3.	3.
4.	4.
5.	5.
6.	6.

C Select two rights from your chart in Exercise B to compare or contrast the U.S. and your home country.

3 WRITE

Write a paragraph that explains similarities or differences between the legal rights of accused people in two places: the U.S. and your home country. Focus on the two points that you selected from the chart.

4 CHECK YOUR WRITING

☐ Did you focus on two specific points about legal rights in the U.S. and your home country?

☐ Did you describe how those legal rights are alike and/or different in both places?

☐ Did you use words to signal similarities and differences?

☐ Did you use correct capitalization, punctuation, and spelling in your paragraph?

1 REVIEW   For your grammar review, go to page 255.

2 ACT IT OUT   What do you say?

STEP 1. CLASS. Review the conversations on page 207 and 219 (CD2, Tracks 51 and 59).

STEP 2. ROLE PLAY. PAIRS. Role-play this situation.

Student A: You are upset. You moved yesterday, and you needed to throw out your broken air conditioner. It was too big to put in the trashcan, so you carried it out into the street and left it there. A police officer saw you and gave you a ticket for dumping trash illegally.

Student B: Student A is your friend. You tell him that large items like air conditioners cannot be left in the street. Explain that the Sanitation Department has special days and times that they make pickups.

3 READ AND REACT   Problem-solving

STEP 1. GROUPS. Read about Polly's problem.

Polly was visiting a friend and parked her car in a parking lot close to her friend's house. She didn't realize that the parking lot was part of an apartment complex. There were no signs saying that the parking lot was private property. When she came back to pick up her car, she found out it had been towed away. She had to take the bus to pick up her car, and she had to pay a big fine to get her car back. Polly thinks it was unfair to tow away her car, because there was no way for her to know that it was illegal for her to park in the parking lot.

STEP 2. What is the problem? Discuss a solution. Describe what Polly should do.

4 CONNECT   For your Self-Evaluation Activity, go to page 262.
For your Team Project, go to page 273.

Which goals can you check off? Go back to page 205.

 Go to the CD-ROM for more practice.

Show what you know!

1 **REVIEW**

Turn to page 255 for the Grammar Review.

2 **ACT IT OUT**

STEP 1. Review the conversations...

- Play CD 2, Tracks 51 and 59. If necessary, direct students to the script for Track 51 on page 207 and for Track 59 on page 219. Tell them they will use this conversation as a model for the role play in STEP 2.

STEP 2 ROLE PLAY. PAIRS. Role-play this...

> **Teaching Tip**
>
> While pairs are performing role plays, use the scoring rubric for speaking on page T-xiii to evaluate each student's vocabulary, grammar, fluency, and how well he or she completes the task. You may want to review the completed rubric with the students.

- Have students look at the illustration. Ask: *What is happening in this picture? Is the man doing anything wrong?*
- Read the role descriptions. If necessary, explain that *dump* means *to get rid of something you don't want*, and that the *Sanitation Department* is *the city department that is responsible for collecting garbage.*
- Model the role play with an above-level student. Play the role of Student B. You can begin the conversation like this: Student B: *How was the move? What's the matter? You look upset.* Student A: *Well, the move went OK, but there was a problem.* Student B: *What happened?*
- Tell students to practice at least twice.
- Have volunteers perform their role play for the class.

3 **READ AND REACT**

STEP 1. GROUPS. Read about Polly's problem.

- Read the text out loud while students read silently. To check comprehension, ask: *What is Polly's problem?* (Her car had been towed away.)

STEP 2. What is the problem? Discuss a solution....

- Form groups and have students choose a timekeeper, a note taker, and a reporter. The note taker should write down the group's solutions.
- Give a time limit for discussion. While students are talking, walk around and provide help as needed.
- Have the reporter from each group share the group's solutions. Write them on the board.
- Have students look at the list of solutions and vote on the one they think is the best.

4 **CONNECT**

Turn to page 262 for the Self-Efficacy Activity, and page 274 for the Team Project. See page T-xi for classroom management tips for these activities.

Progress Check

Which goals can you check off? Go back to page 205.

Ask students to turn to page 205 and check off any remaining goals they have reached. Call on students to say which goals they will practice outside of class.

 Go to the CD-ROM for more practice.

If students need more practice with the vocabulary, grammar, and competencies in Unit 11, encourage them to review the activities on the CD-ROM.

12 Saving and Spending

Unit Overview

Goals

• See the list of goals on the facing page.

Grammar

• Articles: *a, an, the,* no article (∅)
• Future real conditionals
• Present unreal conditionals

Pronunciation

• Stress in compound words
• *Would you*

Reading

• Talk about starting a business
• Reading Skill: Summarizing

Writing

• Write about giving money to a charity

Life Skills

• Interpret and complete an income tax form

Preview

• Say the unit title. Ask: *What do you think this unit will be about?*
• Hold up your book or have students look at their books. Set the context by asking the preview questions. You can also ask: *Do banks look like this in your home country?*

Unit Goals

• Point to the Unit Goals. Have students read them silently.
• Tell students they will be studying these goals in Unit 12.
• Say each goal and explain unfamiliar vocabulary as needed, for example, *budget: a plan for spending money during a particular period of time; income tax: a portion of one's income that is paid to the government each year.*
• Tell students to circle one or more goals that are very important to them. Call on several volunteers to say the goals they circled.
• Write a checkmark (✓) on the board. Say: *We will come back to this page again. You will write a checkmark next to the goals you learned in this unit.*

Saving and Spending

Preview

Read the title. Where are the people? What are they doing?

UNIT GOALS

- ☐ Describe bank services

- ☐ Talk about starting a business

- ☐ Prepare a monthly budget

- ☐ Interpret and complete an income tax form

- ☐ Talk about dreams for the future

- ☐ Write about giving money to a charity

Listening and Speaking

1 BEFORE YOU LISTEN

A CLASS. Discuss. How often do you go to the bank? What kinds of bank services are important to you?

B GROUPS. Look at the online advertisement for a checking account. Talk about the services. What does each statement mean? Discuss any unfamiliar vocabulary.

interest rate = money that a bank pays you when you keep your money in an account

The Federal Deposit Insurance Corporation (FDIC) protects bank customers by guaranteeing deposits up to $250,000.

🌐 ⊖ ⊕ ◄ ► ↻   http://www.apollo.com

Special Online Offer

FREE CHECKING ACCOUNT!

- No monthly maintenance fee
- No minimum balance required
- Current interest rate: 1.5%
- Free online banking service
- Overdraft protection available

Apollo Bank, N.A. Member FDIC

2 LISTEN

A CD2 T60 — John Foster, a customer service officer at Apollo Bank, is talking to Ling Wu. What kind of account does Ling decide to open? Why?

B CD2 T60 — Read the statements. Then listen to the conversation again. Write *T* (true) or *F* (false). Correct the false statements.

__T__ 1. The MyMoney account has a good interest rate.

__F__ 2. A MyMoney account requires a minimum balance of ~~$1,000~~. $1,500

__T__ 3. Ling can get a free checking account, but it doesn't pay interest.

__F__ 4. The interest-free checking has ~~a maintenance~~ an overdraft protection fee of $30 per month.

__T__ 5. If Ling gets overdraft protection, she will have to pay a fee if she uses the service.

__F__ 6. Ling thinks she ~~will~~ won't make a lot of overdrafts.

C GROUPS. Would you open an account at Apollo Bank? Which kind of account would work best for you? Explain.

Getting Started — 10 minutes

1 BEFORE YOU LISTEN

A CLASS. Discuss. How often do you go to...

- Read the two questions. With the class, brainstorm services that are offered by banks and write them on the board. (*checking account, savings account, loans, ATM, overdraft protection,* etc.)
- Have students turn to a classmate and take turns answering in pairs.
- Go around the room and have students say which bank services are important to them. Define services not already listed on the board.

B GROUPS. Look at the online advertisement...

- Read the definitions of *interest rate* and *FDIC*.
- Ask the class: *Who has a checking account?*
- Form cross-ability groups. Try to put at least one student who has a checking account in each group.
- Have students read the advertisement line by line and discuss what each item means.
- Tell students to place a mark next to items that no one in the group can explain.
- With the whole class, explain the items that students marked.

MULTILEVEL INSTRUCTION for 1B

Cross-ability Have above-level students help pre-level students with pronunciation and vocabulary.

Presentation — 5 minutes

2 LISTEN

A John Foster, a customer service officer...

- Have students look at the photo. Ask: *Who are the speakers? Where are they?*
- Remind students to listen specifically for the answer to the question.
- Play CD 2, Track 60.
- Call on a volunteer to answer the question.

Controlled Practice — 5 minutes

B Read the statements. Then listen...

- Write the following terms on the board: *interest rate, minimum balance, maintenance fee, overdraft,* and *overdraft protection.* Have students speak with a neighbor and review the meaning of each term.
- Have students read the questions and predict the answers.
- Play Track 60 again.
- Call on students to read the questions and answers.
- If students have difficulty answering a question, play the corresponding part of the recording again.

Expansion: Speaking Practice for 2B

- Pair students and have them practice reading the Audio Script for Exercise 2B.
- Answer students' questions about the meaning of terms or bank procedures.

Communicative Practice — 10 minutes

C GROUPS. Would you open an account at...

- With the class, review the types of checking accounts offered at Apollo Bank and list them on the board (*MyMoney account,* and *interest-free checking*). Review the requirements and benefits of each account.
- Form groups. If students need to confirm or reinforce information about Apollo Bank, have them look at the Audio Script for Exercise 2B.
- Give a time limit for discussion. While students are talking, walk around the room and provide help as needed.
- To wrap up, go around the room and have students say the kind of checking account that would work best for them.

Presentation   5 minutes

3   CONVERSATION

Pronunciation Watch

- On the board, write: *password, online, overdraft,* and *website*. Ask: *What do you notice about the words?* (They are each made up of two words.)
- Say: *In each word, one syllable has the strongest stress. Listen.* Say each word.
- Instruct students to listen again and clap on the most heavily stressed syllable.
- Ask: *What do you notice about the stress?* (In each phrase, the first syllable is stressed most heavily.)
- Explain that each word has a unique meaning that is different from the meaning of the two words that make up the compound word. Two words that combine to make a unique word are called *compound* words. *Compound* means *composed of two or more.*
- Read the Pronunciation Watch note.

A **Listen to the compound words. Notice...**

- Play CD 2, Track 61. Have students listen.
- Play Track 61 again. Have students listen and repeat.
- Call on students to say each word. Correct as needed.

Controlled Practice   10 minutes

B **Underline the compound noun...**

- Have students underline the compounds and predict the stress. (All are stressed on the first word or syllable.)
- Play CD 2, Track 62. Have students listen and check their answers.
- Call on students to read each sentence. Correct errors in stress.

C **John and Ling are finishing their...**

- Play CD 2, Track 63. Have students listen and read.
- Check comprehension. Ask: *Which online services are offered? Is online banking safe? What is Ling going to do?*

4   PRACTICE

A PAIRS. **Practice the conversation.**

- Form pairs. Have students practice at least twice.
- Take notes on students' pronunciation of compound words. Correct errors on the spot.
- Ask volunteers to perform the conversation..

Communicative Practice   15 minutes

B ROLE PLAY. PAIRS. **Role-play this situation...**

- Read the role descriptions.
- Elicit from students the differences between checking and savings accounts.
- Form same-level pairs and have students plan their role play.
- Write the following conversation opener on the board: *B: Hello. Can I help you? A: Yes, I'd like to open a savings account. B: Well, we have two options. Our SaveMore account is . . .*
- Have volunteers perform their conversation.

▬▬ MULTILEVEL INSTRUCTION for 4B

Pre-level Have students write a script of a conversation about a specific savings account. Student A should ask about the interest rate, minimum balance, and maintenance fee. In the end, Student A should decide whether or not to open the account.

Above-level Instead of writing a script, have students make a chart with information about two kinds of checking accounts. Then have them practice using only their notes.

Extra Practice

Interactive Practice

---

3 CONVERSATION

When two words function together as one word, they form a compound word. You usually stress the first word in a compound word.

A CD2 T61

Listen to the compound nouns. Notice the stress. Then listen again and repeat.

pássword chécking account crédit card máintenance fee

B CD2 T62

Underline the compound noun in each sentence. Put a dot over the stressed syllable. Then listen and check your answers.

1. I'm thinking about opening a sávings account.
2. I looked at the wébsite for my bank.
3. One of their accounts has an ínterest rate of 3%.
4. You have to pay a sérvice fee if your balance is less than $1,000.

C CD2 T63

John and Ling are finishing their conversation. Listen and read.

John: OK, you're all set! Do you have any questions?

Ling: Actually, I do. Can I pay my bills online?

John: Definitely. You can even set up automatic payments for your bills. You can also check your account balance at any time.

Ling: Really? That sounds great. But is it safe?

John: Yes. Our website is secure, and you'll create your own password, so no one else can access your account.

Ling: Great. The online option really sounds like the best one for me.

4 PRACTICE

A PAIRS. Practice the conversation.

B ROLE PLAY. PAIRS. Role-play this situation. Use the conversation as a model.

Student A: You want to open a savings account. Ask the clerk about the options for savings accounts.

Student B: You are a customer service officer. A customer wants to open a savings account. Tell the customer about two different options. The SaveMore account has a 2.25% interest rate. There is a minimum balance requirement of $500. The regular savings account offers a 1.2% interest rate. You can open an account with as little as $25. There is no minimum balance requirement.

Grammar

Articles: *a*, *an*, *the*, no article (Ø)

Indefinite articles

Singular count nouns		
	Article	**Noun**
I'd like to open	**a**	**checking account.**
Please talk to	**an**	**assistant.**

Plural count nouns / Noncount nouns		
	Article	**Noun**
I won't have a problem with	**Ø**	**overdrafts.**
You don't earn	**Ø**	**interest.**

Definite articles

	Article	**Noun**
The bank replaced		**debit card** I lost.
The assistant told me about	**the**	**accounts** this bank offers.
The assistant gave us		**information** we wanted.

> **Grammar Watch**
>
> - Use the indefinite article with singular count nouns that are not specific.
> - Do not use an article (Ø) with plural count nouns or noncount nouns.
> - Use the definite article with a noun that is specific for you and your audience.
> - Use the definite article when you mention a person, place, or thing for the second time: *Please talk to an assistant. The assistant at that desk will help you.*
> - Do not use an article (Ø) with possessive adjectives: *Use your debit card for smaller purchases.*

---

1   PRACTICE

interest rate = the percentage you must pay to the credit card company that loans you money

Read the brochure about debit cards and credit cards. Circle the nouns without articles. Explain why there is no article.

What's the difference between debit cards and credit cards?

➤ When you use a debit card, you take out money from your bank account when you buy something. When you use a credit card, you borrow the money you spend from a credit card company or bank.

➤ Debit cards are easier to get than credit cards. Nowadays, when you open an account, the credit card company gives you a debit card.

➤ Most credit cards have very high interest rates. The credit card company charges you a monthly fee, or finance charge, for any unpaid balance.

Money Tip: Use a debit card for smaller purchases, like at the supermarket. Use a credit card for bigger purchases. But whichever card you use, make sure you don't spend too much!

Getting Started 5 minutes

- On the board, write *a, an,* and *the.* Tell the class: *These words are called articles. A and an are indefinite articles. The is a definite article. In this lesson, we'll learn when to use each kind of article. We'll also learn when to use no article.*

- Before class, collect a set of objects found in a bank or related to money. You'll need an array of items that allows you to demonstrate the various articles, for example, a checkbook, an ATM card, money, cash, a deposit slip, and a loan application.

- In class, elicit the articles and names of objects. Hold up an item and ask: *What's this?* Have the class respond with *It's a/an/[no article] _____.* List all items and articles on the board.

- To demonstrate *the,* name an article, then refer to it a second time. For example, ask a student: *Do you have an ATM card?* If the student says *yes,* follow up with *Where did you get the card?* Write both questions on the board. Underline the articles.

Presentation 15 minutes

Articles: *a, an, the, no article* (Ø)

- Read the first two Grammar Watch notes and the first two examples under *Indefinite Articles.* Explain the concept of *specific:* A noun is considered specific if the listener and speaker both know which noun is meant. In the first two examples, *checking account* and *assistant* are not considered specific because the speaker is not referring to one particular account or assistant.

- Note: Point out that Ø means *no article.*

- Read the example with the plural count noun. Explain, first, that *a* or *an* is never used with plural nouns. (*A* means *one.*) Give additional examples.

- Explain *noncount nouns.* Say: *A noun is* noncount *if you cannot put an indefinite article in front of it. For example, you cannot say* a water, a sand, a gasoline, *etc.* Money, cash, *and* interest *are noncount nouns.* Explain further: You cannot use *a* or *an* with noncount nouns, but it is possible to use *the* if the noun is specific according to the criteria explained above. For example, Teenager: *I'm broke. I need money.* Parent: *What happened to the money that I gave you last week?*

- Do not use an article with general statements. For example, *I trust banks* means *I trust banks in general.*

- Read the third note and the examples under *Definite Articles.* Explain that in each of these examples, the boldfaced noun is specific because it's modified by an adjective clause. Thus, both the speaker and the listener know which noun is meant.

- Read the fourth note. Explain that English speakers introduce a noun with *a* or *an.* After that, the noun is considered known, so if they mention it again, the article switches to *the.*

- Read the fifth grammar note and the example. Explain that possessives make a noun specific, so there's no need to use *the.*

Language Note

One way to think of specific nouns is that they are unique; that is, the speaker and listener both have enough information about the noun that they know which idea or thing is meant. Unique nouns—requiring the article *the*—include the following: 1. nouns modified by possessives, ordinal numbers, superlatives, adjectives, phrases, or adjective clauses; 2. nouns mentioned for the second time; 3. nouns of which there is only one in the world, for example, *the moon,* and *the Dead Sea;* 4. nouns which are known to the speaker and listener by virtue of prior knowledge, for example, *I'm going to the store.*

Controlled Practice 20 minutes

 PRACTICE

Read the brochure about debit cards and...

- Read the first sentence with the class.

- Explain such cases as *from a credit card company or bank.* Explain that *a* pertains to both *credit card company* and *bank.*

- Have students do the exercise in pairs.

Expansion: Grammar Practice

- Bring in an advertisement, brochure, or other type of reading passage. Have students circle the nouns and explain why they use *a, the,* or no article.

- Remind students that the rules in the Grammar Watch do not explain all uses of articles in English. Encourage students to explain as many as they can. Skip the others.

2 PRACTICE

Ⓐ Complete the advertisement. Circle...

- Go over the first answer with the class.
- Have students do the exercise.
- Have them compare answers with a partner.
- Call on students to say the answers. Correct as needed.

Ⓑ Complete the paragraph about home loans....

- Read the example with the class. Ask: *Why is no article needed?* (It is a general statement.)
- Have students complete the exercise alone or in pairs.
- Have students compare answers with a partner.
- Go over the answers with the class. Have students explain why they chose their answer. Correct as needed.

Expansion: Grammar Practice for 2B

- Copy the following conversation on the board. Say: *A customer is talking to a bank officer about getting a home loan.*
- Pair students. Have them find and correct seven errors.

Customer: Hi. I just bought a house, and I'd like an information about getting home improvement loan.

Bank Officer: Congratulations! We'd be happy to help you. Can you tell me what you plan to do with the loan?

Customer: Well, windows in house are very old. I'd like to replace them.

Officer: And how much a money do you want to borrow?

Customer: Four thousand dollars.

Officer: OK. To begin, you'll need to fill out application.

Customer: Can I take application home and fill it out there?

Officer: Of course. You can mail it back or return it in person.

Communicative Practice   20 minutes

Show what you know!

GROUPS. Discuss the bank services below....

- Form groups. Go over the list of services. Have students define or explain each one. Provide help as needed.
- When discussing business loans and mortgages, students may need the word *collateral*. Define it as *property or goods used as security against a loan; if the loan is not repaid, the borrower loses the property.* Walk around and provide help as needed.
- Give a time limit for discussion.
- Review the discussion with the whole class.
- *Optional:* Draw a continuum on the board. On the left, write *easy*. On the right, write *hard*. Have students organize the items from easiest to most difficult to obtain. (*savings account ➤ checking account and debit card ➤ mortgage and business loan*)

Expansion: Speaking Practice for Show what you know!

- Pair students. Have them discuss which of the services they have. Instruct them to say how easy or hard it was to obtain each item.
- Next, divide students into groups according to which services they have or have had. Have them discuss all of the steps involved in getting the service, explaining which steps were easy or difficult.
- Have each group choose one student to tell the whole class about the steps in the process.

Progress Check

Can you . . . describe bank services?

Say: *We have practiced describing bank services. Now, look at the question at the bottom of the page. Can you describe bank services? Write a checkmark in the box.*

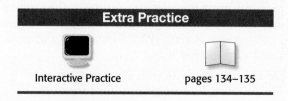

Extra Practice

Interactive Practice   pages 134–135

2 PRACTICE

A Complete the advertisement. Circle the correct answer. (Ø means no article is necessary.)

So you want to start **(a)**/ **the** business. Congratulations!
But where are you going to get **the** / **Ø** money you need?
At Monrovia Bank, we can help you.

- Do you want to buy **(a)**/ **the** car or truck for your business? Ask about our vehicle loans.

- Do you need **the** /**(Ø)** equipment, such as **the** /**(Ø)** appliances, tools, or computers? Our equipment loan may be **(the)**/ **Ø** loan for you.

- Do you need to buy **a** /**(Ø)** real estate? With our real estate loans, you can build **(a)**/ **the** new building or remodel **(an)**/ **the** old building.

Contact our loan officers at
www.monroviabank.com or
call 1-800-555-3000 today!

B Complete the paragraph about home loans. Use *a, an, the,* or Ø. More than one answer may be possible.

__Ø__ Houses are expensive. Most people have to borrow __Ø__ money if they want to buy __a__ house. But __Ø__ banks don't give __Ø__ home loans to everyone. To get approved for __a__ home loan, you need to show __the__ bank that you have __a__ job. You also need to have enough __Ø__ savings to pay for part of __the__ house. And you need __Ø__ good credit. To check people's credit, __Ø__ banks look at things like __Ø__ credit card payments and bill payments. If you have a lot of __Ø__ debt and your credit is bad, you should spend less and pay your bills on time. Try to make your credit good before you fill out __an__ application for __a__ loan.

Show what you know!   Describe bank services

GROUPS. Discuss the bank services below. Which services are easy to get? Which ones are more difficult to get? Why? Give reasons.

business loan   checking account   debit card   mortgage   savings account

Can you... describe bank services?   ☐

Reading

1 BEFORE YOU READ

CLASS. Discuss. If you were starting a business, what type of company or service would you choose? Where would you get the money to start your business? What else would you have to do?

2 READ

CD2 T64

Read and listen. What was Jose's dream? How did he try to achieve it?

A Dream Come True

An empty storefront **sat idle** with a FOR RENT sign. The storefront was inside a strip mall with a paint store, a pizza restaurant, and a barbershop. But to Jose Tenas, the storefront represented a dream.

Tenas, who came from Guatemala, had worked for years as a cook. He was an **aspiring** entrepreneur, and his dream had always been to own a restaurant. Prince William County, Virginia, has a large community of people from Central and South America, but there was not one Guatemalan restaurant. Jose called the landlord and took over the $2,400-a-month lease. He planned to open the restaurant right away.

But he had no idea how difficult it would be to open a restaurant. First, he needed start-up money for the business, which he borrowed from friends and relatives. He also took out a loan on his house. He needed to **pass** seven inspections and get seven **permits**. To prepare for the inspections, he hired contractors to help him fix up the restaurant.

Tenas passed the gas, plumbing, mechanical, fire, and electrical inspections. But the health inspection did not go well. As the health inspector walked around the restaurant, he made notes. When the inspector left, he gave Tenas a list of twenty health code violations. On the form was a stamp: NOT APPROVED. Tenas was upset, but he didn't give up. He cleaned up the restaurant and made the necessary improvements. Then he scheduled another appointment with the inspector. This time he passed.

Tenas had won his battle to open his business. Yet his success was still not a sure thing. One out of three restaurants fails. And Tenas owes $250,000 for fixing up the restaurant. But he is confident. "I know I will have the business," he says. "I have the **clientele**. The people who live here . . . they've been waiting for a Guatemalan restaurant." And indeed the restaurant fills up every day at lunchtime and hums with business all day long.

Getting Started 5 minutes

 1 BEFORE YOU READ

CLASS. Discuss. If you were starting...

- Read the questions. Go around the room and ask each student to answer (but limit the time allotted to each speaker). If your class is very large, call on selected pre-level, on-level, and above-level students to answer.

■■■ **MULTILEVEL INSTRUCTION for 1**

Pre-level Have students answer just the first question in Exercise 1. Let them use the future, for example, *I will start a donut shop.*

Above-level Have students answer all the questions. Encourage them to use the conditional, for example, *I would start a heating and air-conditioning service.*

Presentation 15 minutes

 2 READ

Read and listen. What was Jose's...

- Note: Do not pre-teach the boldfaced vocabulary. The items are practiced in Exercise 4.
- Read the title with the class. Ask: *Have you ever heard this phrase before? What does it mean?* (a dream that becomes a reality) Ask students to give an example of the appropriate use of the phrase. Then ask: *What do you think the* dream *might be?*
- Have students read silently without using dictionaries. Give a time limit, but allow more time to read if necessary.
- Ask: *Which paragraph answers the first question? (2) Which paragraph(s) answer the second question? (3 through 5)*
- Call on students to answer the questions.
- Play CD 2, Track 64. Have students listen and read.

Controlled Practice 20 minutes

3 CHECK YOUR UNDERSTANDING

Reading Skill: **Summarizing**

- Read the Reading Skill. Add the following information: *A summary is much shorter than the original article. Some summaries are only one sentence long. In addition, summaries are stated or written in the speaker's or writer's own words.*

- Explain that one way to summarize an article is to include the main idea (often the last sentence of the first paragraph) and the principal supporting details, that is, the main idea of each subsequent paragraph.

A Read the Reading Skill. Then check...

- Remind students that a good summary will include the main ideas from all the paragraphs.

- Working alone or in pairs, have students state the main idea of each paragraph.

- Have them do the exercise.

- Check answers.

▬▬▬ **Expansion: Speaking Practice for 3A**

- Ask: *Which summary did you choose? Why didn't you choose the other one? (It does not include the main ideas from all the paragraphs.)*

B Read the article again. Complete the...

- Have students read the article again and answer the questions.

- Have them compare answers with a partner.

- Check answers with the class. If necessary, have students read the section of the article that includes the answer to an item.

4 WORD WORK

Find the boldfaced words in the article...

- Do item 1 with the class. Remind students of the steps in the process of guessing; for example, students should read the word in its context and figure out the part of speech.

- Have students complete the remaining items and compare answers with a partner.

- Call on students to say the answers.

Communicative Practice 20 minutes

Show what you know!

GROUPS. Discuss. Do you think José started...

- Form groups. Try to put at least one student who owns his or her own business in each group.

- Give a time limit for discussion. While students are talking, walk around and provide help as needed.

- To wrap up, repeat the third question. Call on students who raise their hands.

Community Building

- Invite one or more small-business owners to come to the class and speak about starting a new business. Have students prepare a list of questions ahead of time.

- Inform students about the U.S. Small Business Administration (http://www.sba.gov/), which provides many services and tools to people wanting to start their own small businesses.

Extra Practice

Interactive Practice   pages 136–137

3

CHECK YOUR UNDERSTANDING

Reading Skill: Summarizing

Write a summary to show that you understand what you've read. Include the main idea and the most important information in the text.

A **Read the Reading Skill. Then check (✓) the better summary of the article.**

____✓____ Jose Tenas thought that there should be a Guatemalan restaurant in Prince William County. There were a lot of people from Central and South America in the area, but no Guatemalan restaurants. Jose started a restaurant in an empty storefront that he rented for $2,400 a month.

_____ Jose Tenas worked hard to reach his dream of owning a Guatemalan restaurant. He got loans from the bank as well as from his friends and family. It was not easy to pass the inspections and get the permits he needed, but eventually Jose succeeded.

B **Read the article again. Complete the statements.**

1. Jose Tenas dreamed of opening a ____restaurant____ in the strip mall.

2. Jose used to be a ____cook____.

3. Jose borrowed some of the money he needed to start his business from ____the bank____.

4. Jose failed the ____health____ inspection the first time.

5. In order to pass the inspection, Jose made a number of ____improvements____.

6. Jose believes his restaurant will be successful because there are many people from

____Central and South America____ in Prince William County, but only one Guatemalan restaurant.

WORD WORK

Find the boldfaced words in the article and guess their meaning from the context. Then match the words with their definitions.

1. __d__ sat idle   a. to be officially approved

2. __c__ aspiring   b. people who regularly go to a store, restaurant, etc.

3. __a__ pass   c. having a strong desire to achieve something

4. __e__ permits   d. was not being used for any purpose

5. __b__ clientele   e. official written statement giving you the right to do something

Show what you know!   Talk about starting a business

GROUPS. Discuss. Do you think Jose started his business in the right way? Did he make any mistakes? What would you do differently?

Listening and Speaking

1 BEFORE YOU LISTEN

A PAIRS. Are you good at managing money? Do you know how much money you earn and spend every month?

B GROUPS. Look at the budget worksheet. It shows Angela and Ricardo's income and their expenses. What is *income*? Which expenses are *fixed*? Which are *variable*? Explain how these two kinds of expenses are different.

INCOME		EXPENSES	
		FIXED EXPENSES	
Angela's job	$800/month	Rent	$600/month
		Bus fare	$120/month
Ricardo's job	$1600/month	VARIABLE EXPENSES	
		food	$400/month
		utilities	$200/month
		clothing	$60/month

C PAIRS. Think about your own expenses or spending habits. What *fixed* and *variable* expenses are in your budget? Make a list.

2 LISTEN

CD2 T65

A Patricia Wong, a financial expert, is giving advice to a caller on the radio show "MoneyWise." Listen to the conversation. What is the caller's problem? He has a lot of debt.

CD2 T65

B Read the statements. Then listen to the conversation again. Write *T* (true) or *F* (false). Correct the false statements.

___F___ 1. The caller wants ~~to take out a personal loan.~~ *advice on paying his bill*

___F___ 2. The caller owes a total of about ~~$20,000~~. *$25,000*

___F___ 3. The interest rate on the caller's credit cards varies from just under ~~9~~ *10* percent to 18 percent.

___T___ 4. Patricia tells the caller to ask the credit card company to reduce his interest rate.

___F___ 5. Patricia tells the caller to increase his monthly payment by ~~fifty~~ *twenty-five* dollars.

___F___ 6. Patricia tells the caller to ~~work overtime~~ *get a second job* in order to earn more money to pay off his debt.

Getting Started   5 minutes

Ask: *What is a budget* (a weekly or monthly plan for how someone will spend available money). Then ask: *Does your family have a budget? If so, who manages it?*

1   BEFORE YOU LISTEN

A PAIRS. Are you good at managing...

- Write *good at + present participle* on the board. Define: *When you're* good at doing *something, you are skilled or you have a talent.* Give examples, for example, *good at writing,* and *good at playing soccer.*
- Pair students and have them answer the questions.
- To conclude, ask the class: *Who is good at managing money?* Select a student who raises his or her hand and ask: *What do you do to manage your money?*

B GROUPS. Look at the budget worksheet. It...

- Have students look at the illustration. Ask: *How much money do Angela and Ricardo make each month?*
- Have students read the list of expenses. Based on the examples, ask them to define *fixed expenses (expenses that are the same every month)* and *variable expenses (expenses that change from month to month).*
- Form cross-ability groups. Give a time limit for discussing the questions.
- While students are talking, walk around and provide help as needed.
- Go over the answers.

C PAIRS. Think about your own expenses...

- Note: Students may be reluctant to discuss their personal finances. Tell those students to use their imaginations and pretend they are someone else, such as a pop star or the mayor of the city.
- Have students work alone to make their lists. Instruct them to include at least four fixed and four variable expenses.
- Form pairs and have them share their lists. Give a time limit for discussion.

Presentation   10 minutes

2   LISTEN

A Patricia Wong, a financial expert,...

- Remind students to listen specifically for the answer to the question. It is not necessary to understand every word.
- Play CD 2, Track 65.
- Call on a volunteer to answer the question.

Culture Connection

Fees and interest rates for credit cards can vary tremendously. Some cards do not charge a monthly fee; others do. However, all credit cards charge a very high interest rate on a cardholder's unpaid balance. The interest owed can accumulate dangerously in a very short time. Students should be warned to read the terms of their credit cards very carefully and, if possible, to pay off their cards each month.

Controlled Practice   20 minutes

B Read the statements. Then listen...

- Have students read the items and predict whether they are true or false.
- Play Track 65 again.
- Have students do the exercise.
- Check answers. If students have difficulty answering a question, play the corresponding part of the recording again.

Expansion: Speaking Practice for 2B

- Pair students and have them read the audioscript for Exercise 2A.
- Write the following questions on the board: *Why does Rafael have high interest on one of his credit cards? What advice does Patricia give him for reducing his credit card debt? What other suggestions would you give Rafael?* Have students discuss the questions in pairs.
- Ask the whole class: *Have you ever had a problem with credit card debt? What did you do about it?* Call on volunteers to answer.

Lesson 4 Prepare a monthly budget

3 CONVERSATION

 Pablo and his friend Luis are talking...

- Play CD 2, Track 66. Have students listen and read.
- Check comprehension. Ask: *Why doesn't Pablo want to go out? How does Pablo manage his money? What does Luis suggest?*

4 PRACTICE

A PAIRS. Practice the conversation.

- Form pairs and have students take turns reading each role.
- Have students switch partners and practice again.
- Walk around and listen as students are practicing.
- Ask volunteers to perform the conversation for the class.

Communicative Practice   25 minutes

B ROLE PLAY. PAIRS. Role-play this situation.

> ### Teaching Tip
> While pairs are performing role plays, use the scoring rubric for speaking on page T-xiii to evaluate each student's vocabulary, grammar, fluency, and how well he or she completes the task. You may want to review the completed rubric with the students.

- Read the role descriptions.
- Form cross-ability pairs.
- Model a role play with an above-level student. Play the role of Student B. Student A should start the conversation. For example, *I really need a new car, but I can never save any money. What can I do?*
- Call on pairs of students to perform their role play for the class.

▬▬ **MULTILEVEL INSTRUCTION for 4B**

Cross-ability Have the lower-level student play the role of Student A and ask for advice. Have the higher-level student play the role of Student B and explain how to make a budget.

C GROUPS. Look at the budget...

- Form groups. Have them select a timekeeper, a note taker, and a reporter. The note taker should write down the suggestions from the group.
- Give a time limit. While students are talking, walk around and provide help as needed.
- Have each group's reporter share the group's suggestions.

D MAKE IT PERSONAL. Look at the budget...

STEP 1. Create your own budget. Look at the...

- Have students copy the categories into their notebooks. Instruct them to write down their income first, then their fixed expenses, and finally their variable expenses.
- Tell students they can use imaginary information if they prefer.
- Pair students and have them describe their budgets to a partner.
- Have one or two volunteers write their budgets on the board. Have the class look at the budgets and recommend ways to cut expenses.

STEP 2. GROUPS. Discuss. Have you ever...

- Form groups.
- Give a time limit for discussion. While students are talking, walk around and provide help as needed.
- Discuss the last question with the whole class. Make a list on the board of things that are difficult to save money on. Elicit suggestions for saving money on those things.

Extra Practice

Interactive Practice

3 CONVERSATION

CD2 T66

Pablo and his friend Luis are talking about money. Listen and read.

Luis: Pablo, do you want to go out this weekend?

Pablo: I can't. I'm trying to cut expenses.

Luis: Seriously? But you have a good job.

Pablo: True, but I have to watch my money because I have many bills to pay.

Luis: Don't you keep a budget?

Pablo: No, not really. I just try to make sure I have enough to pay the bills.

Luis: Well, if you make a list of your regular expenses, you'll know exactly how much money you have for other things.

Pablo: That makes sense. And if I know exactly how much money I have, I won't worry so much all the time.

4 PRACTICE

A PAIRS. **Practice the conversation.**

B ROLE PLAY. PAIRS. **Role-play this situation.**

Student A: You want to buy a car, but you can't save up enough money to buy one. Talk to your friend about the situation.

Student B: You think your friend should make a budget. With a budget, he/she will find out what he/she is spending money on, and it will be easier to cut back and save.

C GROUPS. **Look at the budget worksheet in Exercise 1B. Imagine that Angela and Ricardo want to save money to buy a new car. How can they cut their expenses? What can they do to have more income? Make suggestions.**

D MAKE IT PERSONAL. **Look at the budget worksheet on page 276.**

STEP 1. **Create your own budget.**

STEP 2. GROUPS. **Discuss. Have you ever made a budget? Did it help you to save money? What are the most difficult things to save money on?**

Grammar

Future real conditionals

If clause	Result clause
If you **increase** your monthly payment,	you'**ll finish** paying off the loan sooner.
If you **don't cut** your expenses,	you **won't save** enough money.

⋮

Grammar Watch

- Use future real conditional sentences to talk about what will happen if something else happens.
- Use the simple present in the *if* clause. Use the future in the result clause.
- Use a comma after the *if* clause only if it starts the sentence: *You'll know exactly how much money you have if you keep a budget.*

1 PRACTICE

A Match the *if* clauses with the correct result clauses.

___c___ 1. If you figure out how much money you need to save every month,

___f___ 2. If you turn down the heat in your apartment,

___a___ 3. If you save your receipts,

___b___ 4. If you watch TV instead of going to the movies,

___d___ 5. If you don't smoke,

___e___ 6. If you can fix your own car,

a. you'll be able to keep track of your variable expenses.

b. you'll save money on entertainment.

c. it will be easier to meet your savings goals.

d. you'll be healthier and you'll save a lot of money.

e. you'll save money on repairs.

f. your utility bills will go down.

B Complete the conversations. Circle the correct words.

1. **A:** If I (don't) / won't go back to Colombia next summer, I / (I'll) miss my sister's wedding. But the airfare is so expensive.

   B: I know. But you can still go. If (you) / you'll save $100 every month, you / (you'll) have enough money to buy a ticket by next summer.

2. **A:** If (I) / I'll take some computer classes, I get / (I'll be able to get) a better job. But I don't have enough money to pay for the classes.

   B: Those classes are important. You should save up the money to pay for them. If (you) / you'll make a budget, you / (you'll) see how much you're spending and you can save more.

Getting Started   10 minutes

- Write several *if* clauses on the board. Make them relevant to the topic of money or events in the news. For example, *If I stop buying coffee at Starbucks every morning . . . ; If the United States doesn't reduce its dependence on oil . . . ; If I have any extra money next month . . .*
- Read each *if* clause. Go around the room and elicit different main clauses with *will*. Write some of them on the board.
- Explain: *It's possible that the situations in these sentences will happen in the future. That's why the form is called the* future real conditional.

Presentation   10 minutes

Future real conditionals

- Copy the examples onto the board and read them. Underline the verbs.
- Read the Grammar Watch notes. Emphasize the fact that the verb in the *if* clause is in the simple present.
- Review the contracted forms *I'll, you'll, he'll,* etc. Say each form and have the class repeat.
- Say the uncontracted forms. Have the class respond with the contracted ones. Then do the reverse.

Controlled Practice   20 minutes

1 PRACTICE

A Match the *if* clauses with the correct result clauses.

- Read item 1 with the class. Ask: *What does* figure out *mean? (determine)* Write the phrase on the board.
- Have students do the exercise. Then have them compare answers with a partner.
- Check answers.
- Write the following idioms on the board and elicit meanings: *turn down: reduce; keep track of: be aware; keep yourself informed about something.*

B Complete the conversations. Circle the...

- Do item 1 with the class. Remind students to use the present tense in the *if* clause and the future tense in the result.
- Have students complete the exercise and compare answers with a partner.
- Check answers.

Expansion: Grammar Practice for 1B

- Have each student write an *if* clause on a slip of paper. Remind students to use the present tense. Write one or two models on the board, for example, *If I get a raise . . . ; If my wife loses her job . . .*
- Collect the slips and put them in a box or hat.
- Call students to the front one by one. Have each one pull out a slip, read the *if* clause, and complete the sentence with a logical result clause.
- If your class is very large, do the activity as a mixer. Have students stand up and circulate. When they meet a classmate, they should read and complete each other's slips. They should then swap slips and move on to talk with other classmates.

Lesson 5 Prepare a monthly budget

2 PRACTICE

Complete Alicia and Oscar's conversation...

- Review the meaning of *don't mind*. (*If you don't mind doing something, it doesn't bother you; it is not a problem for you to do it.*)
- Have students do the exercise.
- Have them compare answers with a classmate.
- Call students up to the board to write the sentences with *if* clauses.
- Call on other students to read the sentences and correct as needed.

Communicative Practice 20 minutes

Show what you know!

Look at the budget you created on Page 276.

STEP 1. Think of how you can cut back...

- Have students write at least one sentence with *if*.

■ MULTILEVEL INSTRUCTION for STEP 1
Pre-level Have students write one sentence.
Above-level Have students write several sentences.

STEP 2. GROUPS. Discuss ways you can spend less...

- Form groups and have students share the sentences they wrote in Step 1.
- Instruct students to comment on one another's ideas. For example, they can say *That's a good idea. I'm going to try that.*

■ Expansion: Writing Practice for STEP 2

- Have students write sentences with *if* clauses about how their group members can reduce spending. For example, *If Alex takes the subway to work, he'll save $20 a week.* Remind students to add an *-s* ending to singular verbs.
- Collect the sentences and correct them. Before you return them, make a handout with errors from students' sentences. Write the sentences with errors on an overhead transparency or a handout.
- Have students work in pairs or groups to correct the errors.
- Return students' sentences.

Progress Check

Can you . . . prepare a monthly budget?
Say: *We have practiced preparing a monthly budget. Now, look at the question at the bottom of the page. Can you prepare a monthly budget? Write a checkmark in the box.*

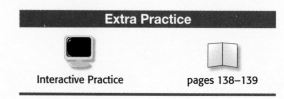

Extra Practice

Interactive Practice   pages 138–139

Complete Alicia and Oscar's conversation about their budget. Use the correct form of the verb in parentheses.

Alicia: I don't know what to do. My family in Mexico needs help, but with my salary, I don't think I can help.

Oscar: You know, I send money to my parents and sisters in Colombia. If I __don't help__ (not / help) them, my two sisters __won't be able to__ (not / be able to) go to school.

Alicia: Really? Can you show me how you do it? That is, if you __don't mind__ (not / mind).

Oscar: No, not at all. Budgeting is a lot of *ifs*. If you __don't do__ (not / do) this, then you __won't be able to__ (be able to) do that. For example, right now, you're renting a one-bedroom apartment. Here's one *if*. If you __don't mind__ (not / mind) living in a studio, then you __will save__ (save) a couple of hundred dollars in rent, maybe more. That's $200 that you can send to your family. Let's see you try another *if*.

Alicia: OK. I have a landline and a cell phone. If I __cut__ (cut) my landline, then I __will save__ (save) forty-nine dollars a month in phone bills!

Oscar: Yep. Let's see. How about commuting costs? Do you drive to work?

Alicia: Yeah. If I __take the bus__ (take the bus), . . .

Oscar: How much is bus fare? And how much do you spend on gas per week?

Alicia: Forty-two dollars a week in gas, and bus fare is $1.25 one way, that's $2.50 both ways. A savings of almost thirty dollars per week, for a total savings of $120 a month! Wow!

Oscar: See how your savings can mount up by cutting here and there?

Alicia: I sure do! Thanks, Oscar. I feel better now.

Show what you know!   Prepare a monthly budget

Look at the budget you created on page 276.

STEP 1. Think of how you can cut back on your monthly expenses. ("If I bring my lunch to work, I'll save seventy-five dollars a month.")

STEP 2. GROUPS. Discuss ways that you can spend less and save more.

Can you. . .prepare a monthly budget? ☐

Life Skills

1 LEARN ABOUT TAX FORMS

Read about how income tax is handled in the U.S.

When you work in the U.S., a portion of your salary is paid to the government for taxes. At the end of the year, your employer sends you a summary of your earnings and the amount of tax that you paid. This summary is called a wage and tax statement, or W-2 form. Taxpayers must use their W-2 forms to file income tax forms each year. The federal income tax form is called the 1040 ("ten forty"). The short version of the form is called the 1040EZ.

2 PRACTICE

Read the W-2 form below. How much money did Felipe Guzman earn in 2008? $35, 470.48

a Employee's social security number 354-00-7777	OMB No. 1545-0008	Safe, accurate, FAST! Use IRS e file	Visit the IRS website at www.irs.gov/efile.
b Employer identification number (EIN) 22-9006542	**1** Wages, tips, other compensation $35,470.38		**2** Federal income tax withheld $7,541.25
c Employer's name, address, and ZIP code Office World 10765 SW 6th Street Miami, FL 33174	**3** Social security wages $35,470.38		**4** Social security tax withheld $1,443.67
	5 Medicare wages and tips $35,470.38		**6** Medicare tax withheld $822.77
	7 Social security tips		**8** Allocated tips
d Control number	**9** Advance EIC payment		**10** Dependent care benefits
e Employee's first name and initial Last name Suff. Felipe J. Guzman	**11** Nonqualified plans		**12a** See instructions for box 12
	13 Statutory employee Retirement Plan Third-party sick pay		**12b**
f Employee's address, and ZIP code 32 NW 106th Ct. Miami, FL 33172	**14** Other		**12c**
			12d

15 State	Employer's state ID number 22-9006542	**16** State wages, tips, etc. $35,470.38	**17** State income tax $0	**18** Local wages, tips, etc.	**19** Local income tax	**20** Locality name

Form **W-2** Wage and Tax Statement   **2008**
Copy B—To Be Filed With Employee's FEDERAL Tax Return.
This information is being furnished to the Internal Revenue Service—Internal Revenue Service

Getting Started   5 minutes

- Ask: *What is a tax?* (money paid to the government) *What are some different kinds of taxes?* (gas, alcohol, sales, income, and property)
- Read the lesson title. Say: *In this lesson we'll read and talk about income taxes. An income tax is a tax on money that you earn from your job.*

Presentation   15 minutes

 LEARN ABOUT TAX FORMS

Read about how income tax is handled...

- If possible, bring real W-2 and 1040 forms to class.
- Read the information out loud while students read silently.
- Check comprehension. Ask: *What document do workers receive from their employers at the end of the year?* (a wage and tax statement) *What is this document called?* (W-2) *What is the name of the form that workers must fill out when they pay their income tax?* (Income tax return or 1040 forms)
- Show students the W-2 and 1040 forms.

▬ Expansion: Speaking Practice for 1

- Ask: *How many of you paid income taxes last year? Which form did you fill out—the 1040 or 1040EZ?*

Culture Connection

Income-tax forms can be obtained online at www.irs.gov. They are also available at Internal Revenue Service offices and at post offices.

Controlled Practice   20 minutes

2 PRACTICE

Read the W-2 form below. How much money...

- Tell students that they don't need to understand every word on the form. They should scan to find the answer to the question. Have them raise their hand when they have found it.
- Check the answer. Ask: *What are tips?* (gifts of money given to people who perform a service such as cutting hair or serving food) *What is other compensation?* (income that one receives from a source other than one's salary, such as rental income) If students do not know, provide the answers.

Culture Connection

There are three levels of taxes in the U.S.: federal, state, and local. Almost all workers must pay federal income taxes. Nearly all states have an income tax as well. (The exceptions are Alaska, Nevada, South Dakota, Washington, Texas, Wyoming, and Florida.) Cities do not usually have income taxes. Instead, they tax property (for example, to pay for schools) or impose a sales tax on top of the tax that the state may already impose.

Lesson 6 Interpret and complete an income tax form

3 PRACTICE

A Write the information using the W-2...

- Read item 1 with the class.
- Have students complete the exercise alone or with a partner.
- Go over the answers. Explain *Social Security tax: Social Security is the money people receive from the government each month when they retire, usually at age 65. The Social Security tax is money that workers pay into the fund that is used to pay the retirees.* Explain *Medicare tax: Medicare is the free health-care program available to people when they retire. Workers pay a portion of their income into the system each month.*

B Look at these sections of the 1040EZ form...

- Have students look at the 1040EZ form. For each item to be filled in, ask students to figure out where they need to look on the W-2 in order to get the information. For example, the answer to item 1 on the 1040 form can be found in box 1 of the W-2.
- Have students work alone or in pairs to fill in the information. As they are working, walk around and provide help as needed.
- Check answers. Explain as needed.

C CLASS. A *tax refund* is money that the...

- Provide more information about *tax refunds.*
- Help students figure out the answer if necessary. On the 1040 form, have them subtract the number in line 10 ($5,293.00) from the number in line 9 ($7,541.25). The difference ($2,248.25) is the amount of Felipe's refund.

Culture Connection

After taxpayers submit their 1040 forms (on or before April 15), the government recalculates their taxes. Sometimes it turns out that people haven't paid enough taxes, and they are required to send the government more money. Other times it happens that people have paid too much tax; in that event, they receive a tax refund.

Communicative Practice   20 minutes

D PAIRS. Turn to Page 277 and complete...

- Have students fill in an imaginary salary in line 1.
- Have them write *0* in lines 2, 3, and 8a.
- For line 7, tell people to choose a number that is roughly 25 percent of the number they wrote in line 1. This will be their imaginary tax payment.
- For line 10, they can choose the same number as line 7, a smaller number (in which case they will owe taxes) or a larger number (in which case they will get a tax refund).
- Pair students. Have them check each other's math.
- Have students share whether they will need to pay more tax or whether they will get a refund.

Community Building

- Have students write questions they have about filling out their W-2 forms and paying taxes.
- If possible, have an accountant come to class and answer students' questions.

Progress Check

Can you . . . interpret and complete an income tax form?

Say: *We have practiced interpreting and completing an income tax form. Now, look at the question at the bottom of the page. Can you interpret and complete an income tax form? Write a checkmark in the box.*

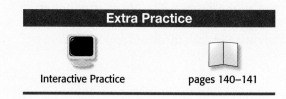

Extra Practice	
Interactive Practice	pages 140–141

3 PRACTICE

A Write the information using the W-2 form in Exercise 2.

1. Felipe Guzman's total compensation in 2008: ___$35,470.38___

2. Name of Felipe's employer: ___Office World___

3. Amount of federal income tax withheld from Felipe's pay: ___$7,541.25___

4. Amount of social security tax withheld from Felipe's pay: ___$1,443.67___

5. Amount of medicare tax withheld from Felipe's pay: ___$822.77___

6. Amount of state income tax withheld from Felipe's pay: ___$0___

B Look at these sections of the 1040EZ form. Use the information on Felipe's W-2 form to fill in lines 1, 4, 7, and 9. Line 10 is done for you.

Income **Attach** **Form)s W-2** **here.** Enclose, but do not attach, any payment.	1 Wages, salaries, and tips. This should be shown in box 1 of your Form(s) W-2. Attach your Form(s) W-2.	1 $35, 470.48
	2 Taxable interest. If the total is over $1,500, you cannot use Form 1040EZ.	2 0
	3 Unemployment compensation and Alaska Permanent Fund dividends (see page 10).	3 0
	4 Add lines 1, 2 and 3. This is your **adjusted gross income**.	4 $35, 470.48

Payments and tax	7 Federal income tax withheld from box 2 of your Form(s) W-2.	7 $7,541.25
	8a Earned income credit (EIC).	8a 0
	b Nontaxable combat pay election 8b	
	9 Add lines 7 and 8a. These are your **total payments**. ▶	9 $7,541.25
	10 **Tax.** Use the amount on **line 6 above** to find your tax in the tax table on pagaes 18–26 of the booklet. Then, enter the tax from the table on this line.	10 $5,293

C CLASS. A *tax refund* is money that the government gives back to you if you have paid too much in taxes. Look at the W-2 form and the 1040 EZ form. Will Felipe get a tax refund, or does he owe additional taxes? How much? Felipe will get a tax refund of $2,248.25

D PAIRS. Turn to page 277 and complete the 1040 EZ form. Make up the information about your compensation.

Can you...interpret and complete an income tax form? ☐

Listening and Speaking

1 BEFORE YOU LISTEN

CLASS. Discuss. Have you ever heard stories about people who suddenly come into a lot of money? What do they usually do with the money?

2 LISTEN

CD2 T67

A  **Chantal and Eduardo are friends. They're talking about what they would do if they suddenly got a lot of money. Listen to the conversation. What would Chantal do?** She'd go to medical school and then build a clinic.

CD2 T67

B **Read the questions. Listen to the conversation again. Circle the correct answers.**

1. How much money did the person who works in Eduardo's office get?
   a. $100,000
   b. $500,000
   c. $1,000,000

2. What is one thing the person did with the money?
   a. He bought a car.
   b. He bought a house.
   c. He went to medical school.

3. Why does Chantal want to go back to school?
   a. She doesn't like her current job.
   b. She's not good at her current job.
   c. She wants to become a doctor.

4. What would Chantal do after she was finished with school?
   a. set up a health clinic in the U.S.
   b. set up a health clinic in Haiti.
   c. give Americans free medical care

5. What would Eduardo do if he got a lot of money?
   a. move to Haiti
   b. stop working
   c. travel around the world

6. What would Eduardo buy if he got a lot of money?
   a. a new car
   b. a big house
   c. houses for all his friends and family

Getting Started   10 minutes

Read the lesson title. Ask students: *What are your dreams for the future?*

1   BEFORE YOU LISTEN

CLASS. Discuss. Have you ever heard stories...

- Define *came into (received) money*. Ask students: *How do people usually come into money?* They *inherit it* (receive it when someone dies and leaves it to them); *win it* (as in winning the lottery) or *perhaps receive it as a gift.*
- Read the questions. Tell students to think of books they've read, movies they've seen, or stories they've heard.
- Call on students who raise their hands to answer.

Presentation   5 minutes

2   LISTEN

A 🔊 **Chantal and Eduardo are friends...**

- Have students look at the photo. Ask: *How old are the people? What might they be talking about?*
- Remind students to listen for the answer to the question. They do not need to understand every word.
- Play CD 2, Track 67.
- Write on the board: *Chantal would . . .* Have students discuss the answer with a classmate.
- Check the answer with the whole class. Ask students what they heard that helped them find the answer.

Controlled Practice   10 minutes

B 🔊 **Read the questions. Listen...**

- Have students read the questions and predict the answers.
- Play Track 67 again.
- Call on students to answer the questions. If necessary, play the recording again.

▬▬▬ Expansion: Speaking Practice for 2B

- Pair students and have them practice reading the conversation from the Audio Script on Page 294.
- Have volunteers read the conversation for the class.
- Ask the class: *Which dream do you prefer, Chantal's or Eduardo's? Why?*

Presentation   10 minutes

3 CONVERSATION

Pronunciation Watch

- Speaking at normal speed and with natural pronunciation, ask: *Where would you like to go on your next vacation?* Call on students to answer (*I would like to go to . . .*)
- Say: *I'm going to repeat the question twice, once with slow pronunciation and once with fast, natural pronunciation.*
- Repeat the question, then ask: *What was the question?* Write it on the board. Underline *would you.*
- Read the Pronunciation Watch note. Explain: *When the two words are joined, the* d *and* y *combine to form a* j *sound.* You *is pronounced* ya. *Would you is therefore pronounced* wood-ja.

Ⓐ Listen to the pronunciation of *would*...

- Play CD 2, Track 68. Have students listen.
- Play Track 68 again. Have students listen and repeat.

Controlled Practice   10 minutes

Ⓑ Listen to the sentences. Circle the words...

- Do a quick minimal-pair drill. On the board, write *1—will you; 2—would you.* If you say *will you,* students should hold up one finger. If you say *would you,* they should hold up two.
- Play CD 2, Track 69.
- Check answers. Play the recording again if needed.

Ⓒ Omar and Linh are talking about what...

- Play CD 2, Track 70. Have students listen and read.
- *Optional:* You may want to have above-level students listen with their books closed.
- Check comprehension. Ask: *What would Linh do if she had a lot of money? What would Omar do?*

4 PRACTICE

Ⓐ PAIRS. Practice the conversation.

- Form pairs and have students take turns reading each role.
- Have students switch partners and practice again.
- Walk around and listen as students are practicing.
- Ask volunteers to perform their conversation.

Communicative Practice   15 minutes

Ⓑ MAKE IT PERSONAL. GROUPS. Discuss...

- On the board, write *If I had a lot of money, I would _____.*
- Model the answer with your own information.
- Form groups. Have each student complete the sentence.
- Have volunteers share their answer with the class.

▮▮ MULTILEVEL INSTRUCTION for MAKE IT PERSONAL.

Pre-level Restate the question using the simple future. Allow them to answer using the real conditional, for example, *If I get a lot of money, I will _____.*

Above-level Have students use the unreal conditional.

▮▮ Expansion: Speaking Practice for 4B

- Form pairs. Have them role-play the conversation in Exercise 3C, substituting their own dreams for the ones in the text.
- Have them practice several times.
- Have each pair of students perform their role play for another pair or for the whole class.

Extra Practice
Interactive Practice

Pronunciation Watch

In conversation, *would you* is often pronounced "wouldja." The words are joined together and pronounced as one word.

A CD2 T68 **Listen to the pronunciation of *would you*. Then listen again and repeat.**

What **would you** do if you had a lot of money?

Would you quit your job?

B CD2 T69 **Listen to the sentences. Circle the words you hear.**

1. (Will)/ Would you buy a house?
2. Will /(Would) you travel a lot?
3. Where **will** /(**would**) you go?
4. (Will)/ Would you go to South America?
5. What **will** /(**would**) you do there?

C CD2 T70 **Omar and Linh are talking about what they would do if they had a lot of money. Listen and read.**

Omar: What would you do if you had a lot of money?

Linh: I would quit my job at this convenience store and start my own business. I've always wanted to be my own boss.

Omar: That sounds like a good idea.

Linh: Why? What would *you* do if you had a lot of money?

Omar: I think I would travel for a year or two.

Linh: Where would you go?

Omar: Australia. And South America. I've always wanted to go to Argentina and Brazil.

Linh: Hmm…. Maybe I'd join you. My business can wait a year or two.

4 PRACTICE

A PAIRS. **Practice the conversation.**

B MAKE IT PERSONAL. GROUPS. **Discuss. What would you do if you had a lot of money?**

Talk about dreams for the future

Grammar

Present unreal conditionals

If clause	Result clause		
If you **had** a lot of money,	what **would** you **do**?		
If I **had** a lot of money,	I **would buy** a house. or: **I'd buy** a house.		
If that house **were** less expensive,	he	**could** **might**	**buy** it.

Grammar Watch

- Use present unreal conditional sentences to talk about things that are untrue, imagined, or impossible.
- Use the simple past in the *if* clause. Use *were* for all subjects when the verb in the *if* clause is a form of *be*.
- Use *would, could,* or *might* + the base form of the verb in the result clause. *Would* expresses desired results. *Could* and *might* express possible options.

1 PRACTICE

A Read the paragraph. Circle the *if* clauses and underline the result clauses.

> Let's face it, money is important. (If I had more money,) I would work less and I would have more time to do the things I want to do. (If I worked less,) I would spend more time with my family. And (if I had more time,) I might take college classes. I could get a better job (if I had a college degree.) There's no doubt that my life would be very different (if I had more money.)

B Complete the sentences. Circle the correct words. Then check the sentences that are true for you.

_____ 1. If someone **gives** / (**gave**) me a lot of money, I / (**I would**) start my own business.

_____ 2. If I **was** / (**were**) rich, **I'll** / (**I'd**) donate a lot of money to charity.

_____ 3. If I (**had**) / **would have** a lot of money, I **quit** / (**might quit**) my job.

_____ 4. If I **work** / (**worked**) part time, I / (**I would**) spend more time with my family.

_____ 5. If I **speak** / (**spoke**) better English, I **get** / (**could get**) a better job.

_____ 6. If I **have** / (**had**) health insurance, I **will** / (**would**) go to the doctor more often.

Getting Started

10 minutes

- To begin, ask the class: *Who has a lot of money? Nobody? OK, I want you to use your imagination and answer this question: If you had a lot of money, what would you do?* Say the sentence slowly, emphasizing *had* and *would*.
- On the board, write *If I had a lot of money . . .* Call on two above-level students to complete the sentence. Write their responses (*I would . . .*) on the board.
- Read the sentences. Point out the *if* clause and the result clause. Then point to the verbs in each phrase. Ask: *What's the form of the verb?* (if *clause: past; result clause:* would + *base form*) *What's the time?* (present) *Are we talking about a real or imaginary situation?* (imaginary)
- Say: *In English we change the form of the verb to show that we are talking about something imaginary.*

Presentation

10 minutes

Present unreal conditionals

- Copy the sentences from the grammar chart onto the board. Underline the verbs.
- Read the first Grammar Watch note. Then point to the *if* clause in each example and ask if it's true. For example, for the first example, ask: *Does the person in the* if *clause (you) have a lot of money?* (no) *In the third example, is the house less expensive?* (no)
- Read the second and third notes. Point again to the third example. Perhaps point out that *If that house were* sounds funny, but it is correct.
- Read the last note. Say: Would *expresses willingness or desire.* Might *means maybe; it's used to talk about possibility.* Could *means have the ability or possibility to do something.*
- Point out the contraction of the pronoun and *would*.

Language Note

Sometimes in conversation people will use *was* instead of *were* in *if* clauses with singular subjects, for example, *If that house was less expensive, I'd buy it.* In North America the use of *was* is so common that it probably does not need to be corrected in speaking. In writing, however, it is incorrect.

Controlled Practice

20 minutes

1 PRACTICE

Ⓐ Read the paragraph. Circle the *if* clauses...

- Read the paragraph out loud while students read silently.
- Ask: *What's the first* if *clause?* Have students circle it. Ask: *What's the first result clause?* Have students underline it.
- Have students complete the exercise alone or in pairs. Walk around and provide help as needed.
- Check answers.

Expansion: Speaking Practice for 1A

- Copy the following clauses based on Exercise 1A on the board: *If I had more money, If I worked less, If I had more time, I might take college classes if, I could get a better job if.*
- Put students in small groups. Instruct them to take turns completing each sentence. While students are talking, walk around and check verb forms. Make sure they are using the conditional.
- Call on volunteers to complete each clause with their ideas.

Ⓑ Complete the sentences. Circle the correct...

- Do item 1 with the class. Then say: *Raise your hand if this sentence is true for you.* Ask follow-up questions such as *What kind of business would you start?*
- Have students complete the exercise.
- Check the grammar. Have students read the sentences. Correct errors as needed.
- Pair students and have them share and discuss the statements they checked. Encourage them to ask follow-up questions, such as *What kind of business would you start? Where would you get the money? Who would your customers be? Where would you have your office? What kind of equipment would you need to buy? What kind of license would you need to get? How much would you charge?*

2 PRACTICE

Under what conditions, if any, would you...

- Explain that the items in the exercise express results. They belong in the result clause with *would, could* or *might*.
- Read item 1. Elicit several other *if* clauses that fit the sentences, for example, *If I lost my job, If I needed to buy a new car, If I had another baby.*
- Have students do the exercise in pairs. First, they should discuss the items, then write.
- Choose students to write their sentences on the board.
- Have other students read the sentences and correct errors as needed.

Communicative Practice   20 minutes

Show what you know!

STEP 1. Write sentences about different things...

- Have students work on their own. While they are writing, walk around and provide help as needed. Check students' sentences for correct use of the unreal conditional.
- If students are having difficulty, have them follow the model sentences in their book or on the board. Show them how to substitute different subjects and verbs but keep the same verb forms.

■■■ MULTILEVEL INSTRUCTION for STEP 1

Pre-level Have students write about the topics in the box, using the sentences from the lesson as models.

Above-level Have them write about what they would do if they had more money, time, or power. Encourage them to write original sentences.

STEP 2. GROUPS. Compare your answers.

- Form groups of similar ability. Instruct students to say their sentences to their group members. As you walk around, focus on the lower-level students and help them say their sentences correctly.
- As a second step, have students check and restate one another's sentences. Have students sit in a group and pass their papers to the person on their right. That person reads the sentences and checks the conditional forms and the comma. If they find an error, they should point it out to the writer.
- Next, students should restate one or more of the sentences, time permitting. For example, *If David had a lot of time, he'd volunteer more at his church.*
- Circulate and listen as students are talking. Check to make sure they are using the past in *if* clauses and pronouncing *would* or the *'d* contraction in the result clause.

STEP 3. CLASS. Present your ideas to the class...

- If possible, go around the room and have each student say one of his or her sentences. Take notes on students' ideas.
- Using your notes, conclude by telling the class which ideas seem to be most popular. Ask the class to suggest ways to make those dreams come true.

Progress Check

Can you . . . talk about dreams for the future?
Say: We have practiced talking about dreams for the future. Now, look at the question at the bottom of the page. Can you talk about dreams for the future? Write a checkmark in the box.

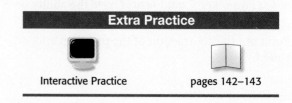

Extra Practice

Interactive Practice   pages 142–143

Under what conditions, if any, would you do these things? Write present unreal conditional sentences. Use *would*, *could*, or *might* in the result clause. Answers will vary.

1. cut back on your spending

   If I had a lot of expenses, I'd cut back on my spending.

2. loan money to a friend

   _____

3. ask a friend to loan you money

   _____

4. refuse to loan money to a family member

   _____

5. take out a loan for a large sum of money from a bank

   _____

6. quit your job

   _____

7. start your own business

   _____

Show what you know!   Talk about dreams for the future

STEP 1. Write sentences about the different things you would do if you had a lot of money/time/power. Use the topics in the box or your own ideas.

my family   my friends   my school   my community   my country

STEP 2. GROUPS. Compare your answers.

STEP 3. CLASS. Present your ideas to the class. Which ideas are the most popular? Can you think of any ways to make your "dreams" come true?

Can you...talk about dreams for the future? ☐

Writing

1 BEFORE YOU WRITE

A GROUPS. Read the facts about charitable giving in the U.S. Discuss. Why do people donate time or money to charitable causes?

- Americans give more money to charity than citizens of other developed countries.
- In 2006, Americans gave away almost $300 billion of their personal incomes to charity.
- On average, low-income working families give away 4.5 percent of their income compared to 2.5 percent among middle class families and 3 percent among high-income families.
- The average American household gives about $1,000 to charity a year.

B Read the writing model. What is the writer's main point?

Doctors Without Borders

If someone gave me $1,000 and told me to give the money away, <u>which organization would I choose?</u> Without a doubt, <u>it would be Doctors Without Borders</u>. This international organization believes that every person in the world has a right to medical care. Doctors Without Borders was started by a group of French doctors in 1971. Each year, the organization sends volunteer doctors, nurses, and administrators from different parts of the world to give medical care to people in more than seventy countries. The organization provides all kinds of medical care, from surgery and nutrition programs to mental health care and doctor training. In 1999, Doctors Without Borders received the Nobel Peace Prize for its good works. Doctors Without Borders helps victims of war, sickness, hunger, and natural disasters. I think this organization needs help more than any other organization in the world, so it is the one that would receive my financial support.

C PAIRS. Answer the questions.

1. What question does this paragraph ask and answer?
2. What facts and examples does the writer give to support her answer?
3. Why would the writer give her $1,000 to Doctors Without Borders?

D Reread the paragraph. Underline the writer's question and answer.

Writing Tip:

One way to focus a paragraph is to ask a question and answer it. You not only give an answer. You explain your answer by giving supporting details such as facts and examples.

Write about giving money to a charity

Getting Started — 10 minutes

- Discuss the word *charity* with the class. You could say, for example, *Charities are organizations that collect money and provide services to help people in need.* Give examples: The American Red Cross, United Way, local soup kitchens.
- Ask students to name charities they know about.
- On the board, write *charity = noun; charitable = adjective.*
- Ask: *Do you think Americans are charitable people?*

1 BEFORE YOU WRITE

Ⓐ GROUPS. Read the facts about charitable...

- Read the directions. Then read the facts.
- On the board, write the following additional discussion question: *Do any of the facts about charitable giving surprise you? If so, which one(s)? Why do they surprise you?*
- Form groups. Give a time limit for discussion.
- Go over the questions with the whole class. Repeat the question and call on volunteers to answer. List reasons for volunteering on the board.
- Repeat the question about surprising facts. Have a representative from each group share their answers.
- *Optional:* Follow up on the question of why people with lower incomes are more charitable than people with higher incomes. Why do students think this is the case?

Presentation — 15 minutes

Ⓑ Read the writing model. What is...

- Read the model out loud as students read silently.
- Have students read again silently. Tell them to underline the sentence or sentence parts that state the writer's main point. (Provide the following hint: *The main point can be stated in more than one sentence.*)
- With the class, discuss the main point. Encourage them to state it as an unreal conditional (*If someone gave me $1,000, I would choose to give it to Doctors Without Borders.*)

Ⓒ PAIRS. Answer the questions.

- Form pairs.
- While students are talking, walk around and provide help as needed.
- Go over the answers with the whole class. For question 2, have students read the sentences containing facts and examples.

Answers:

1. Which organization would I choose? It would be Doctor's Without Borders.

2. This organization believes every person in the world has a right to medical care. It provides all kinds of medical care, from surgery and nutrition programs to mental health care and doctor training. It helps victims of war, sickness, hunger, and natural disasters.

3. The writer feels this organization needs help more than any other organization in the world.

Writing Tip: **Asking and Answering Questions**

- Read the Writing Tip. Explain that it's common for writers to start paragraphs with questions, but it's important not to overdo this device. If one is writing a multiparagraph piece, for example, it would not be good writing to start each paragraph with a question.

Ⓓ Reread the paragraph. Underline the writer's...

- Have students work alone. Then have them compare answers with a classmate.

▆▆▆ Expansion: Writing Practice for 1D

- Have students focus on the organization of the paragraph. Point out that the questions in Exercise C provide an outline of the paragraph content.
- Say: *You are going to write a paragraph about a charity. What information will you include?*

Community Building

Go to the Doctors Without Borders website at http://www.doctorswithoutborders.org/. Under *Field News,* click on *Slideshows* or *Videos.* If possible, view these with your students.

Write about giving money to a charity

Controlled Practice   15 minutes

2   THINKING ON PAPER

A BRAINSTORM. Look at the list of...

- Write the categories in the students' book on the board. Elicit names and examples of each category and list those as well. (You might wish to add the category of animal welfare organizations such as the Humane Society.)

- Have each student say which charity he or she would like to write about. Find out if students have enough information about their charities or if they need to obtain more facts. In the case of large charities, direct students to the charity's website. For smaller, local charities, students might need to visit the charity and obtain a brochure on site.

B Complete the question-and-answer chart.

- Copy the graphic organizer on the board. Choose a charity with which you are familiar and demonstrate, using the organizer, to plan a paragraph about your charity.

- Base your question and answer on the model paragraph on page 242.

- Try to include at least five facts and examples. As needed, add more boxes for supporting details to your organizer.

- Try to select a mix of facts and examples for your supporting details.

- Have students plan their own paragraphs.

■ MULTILEVEL INSTRUCTION for 2B

Pre-level Plan the paragraph with the students. Select a well-known charity and bring in information about it. Read the information with them and have them underline details and examples they can use in their paragraphs. Have them fill in their organizers and show them to you before they begin writing.

Above-level Suggest that, at the end of their paragraphs, students include their personal experience with the charity they chose to write about. Do they perhaps volunteer there from time to time? Were they or members of their family ever the recipients of aid from the organization?

C Circle the most convincing facts, examples,...

- Explain to students that if they include many facts and examples in their graphic organizer, they need to select the most convincing ones to include in their paragraph.

- Demonstrate with your organizer from Exercise 2B. Pare the list of details down to three.

- Students who included only three facts or examples in their organizer can skip this step.

Communicative Practice   20 minutes

3   WRITE

Write a paragraph about a charity that you...

- Review paragraph format. Remind students to give their paragraph a title, indent the first line, begin each sentence with a capital letter, and double-space the lines.

- Have students read the questions in Exercise 4.

- Have students write in class.

4   CHECK YOUR WRITING

- Have students read their paragraphs and check the questions in the checklist. Have them revise according to the items in the checklist.

■ Expansion: Writing Practice for 3

- Have students rewrite their paragraphs.

- Pair students and have them read their paragraphs to each other.

- Have volunteers read their paragraphs to the class.

Community Building

Have the class select a charity and work together to contribute to it in some way. For example, they can volunteer to work at a local food bank or shelter or hold a carwash.

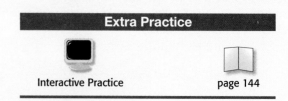

Extra Practice

Interactive Practice   page 144

THINKING ON PAPER

A BRAINSTORM. **Look at this list of charitable causes. Which one would you support? Why?**

- disaster relief organizations
- blood banks
- environmental organizations
- soup kitchens and homeless shelters
- child and family services
- religious organizations

B Complete a question-and-answer chart.

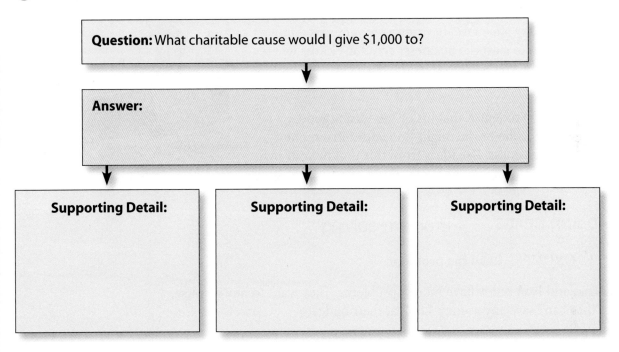

Question: What charitable cause would I give $1,000 to?

Answer:

Supporting Detail:

Supporting Detail:

Supporting Detail:

C Circle the most convincing facts, examples, and other supporting details on your chart.

3 **WRITE**

Write a paragraph about a charity that you would give $1,000 to. Use the information in your chart to organize the paragraph. Begin with your question. State your answer. Then explain your answer by giving facts, examples, and other supporting details.

4 **CHECK YOUR WRITING**

☐ Did you ask and answer a question?

☐ Did you explain the reasons for your answer by giving supporting details?

☐ Did you use correct capitalization, punctuation, and spelling?

1 **REVIEW**   For your grammar review, go to page 256.

2 **ACT IT OUT**   What do you say?

STEP 1. CLASS. Review the conversations on pages 232 and 233 (CD2, Tracks 65 and 66).

STEP 2. ROLE PLAY. PAIRS. Role-play this situation.

Student A: Talk to Student B about your dream of opening your own grocery store. You have some money saved up, but not enough to start the business. You don't know where to get the money you need to start the business.

Student B: Tell Student A that his or her idea is good. Suggest ways that he or she might find additional money for his or her business. Use ideas from this unit or your own ideas.

3 **READ AND REACT**   Problem-solving

STEP 1. GROUPS. Read the problem.

Oksana and Ivan Bulov have money problems. They want to buy a house, but they can't save any money. Look at their budget:

INCOME		EXPENSES	
		FIXED EXPENSES	
Oksana's job	$1,000/month	Rent	$1,000/month
		Train fare	$200/month
Ivan's job	$1,200/month	VARIABLE EXPENSES	
		food	$400/month
		utilities	$200/month
		clothing	$300/month

STEP 2. Discuss a solution. How can Oksana and Ivan save money to buy a house? Are there any expenses they can cut back on?

4 **CONNECT**   For your Self-Efficacy Activity, go to page 262.
For your Team Project, go to page 274.

Which goals can you check off? Go back to page 221.

 Go to the CD-ROM for more practice.

1 REVIEW

Turn to page 256 for the Grammar Review.

2 ACT IT OUT

STEP 1. Review the conversations...

- Play CD 2, Tracks 65 and 66. If necessary, direct students to the script for Track 65 on page 294 and for Track 66 on page 233.

STEP 2. ROLE PLAY. PAIRS. Role-play this...

> **Teaching Tip**
>
> While pairs are performing role plays, use the scoring rubric for speaking on page T-xiii to evaluate each student's vocabulary, grammar, fluency, and how well he or she completes the task. You may want to review the completed rubric with the students.

- Have students look at the illustration. Ask: *What is the woman thinking? What is her dream?*
- Read the role descriptions.
- With the class, review possible sources of money for a person wanting to start a new business.
- Model the role play with an above-level student. Play the role of Student B. *The conversation could start like this:* Student A: *If I had a lot of money, do you know what I would do?* Student B: *What?* Student A: *Start my own grocery store.* Student B: *Really? What's stopping you?* Student B: *I don't have enough money. . . .*
- Have volunteers perform their role-play.

▬▬ MULTILEVEL INSTRUCTION for 2

Pre-level Have students write out their dialogue. They can start with the suggested dialogue in Exercise 2, then continue with one or two suggestions for finding the money that Student A needs.

Above-level Have students practice without notes. Have Student B suggest at least three sources of money for starting a new business. Have Student A choose the idea he or she likes best and agree to try that one first.

3 READ AND REACT

STEP 1. GROUPS. Read the problem.

- Form groups. Have students study the budget together. Instruct students to figure out the couple's monthly income and their total expenses.

STEP 2. Discuss a solution. How can...

- Have groups select a note taker to write down the group's ideas for saving money. Have them write down the expenses to be cut and the amount that can be saved. Also ask groups to consider ways that Oksana and Ivan might increase their income.
- Have each group create a new budget for Oksana and Ivan.
- Have a representative from each group tell the class about their group's proposed new budget.

4 CONNECT

Turn to page 262 for the Self-Efficacy Activity and page 274 for the Team Project. See page T-xi for classroom management tips for these activities.

Progress Check

Which goals can you check off? Go back to Page 225.

Ask students to turn to Page 225 and check off any remaining goals they have reached. Call on students to say which goals they will practice outside of class.

 Go to the CD-ROM for more practice.

If students need more practice with the vocabulary, grammar, and competencies in Unit 12, encourage them to review the activities on the CD-ROM.

Grammar Review

UNIT 1

A Complete the conversation. Circle the simple present or the present continuous.

Patty: Hey, Chang. **(Are you working)**/ **Do you work** again today?

Chang: Yes. Marty usually **is working** / **(works)** on Fridays, but today **(I'm taking)**/ **I take** his shift.

Patty: Why? What **(is he doing)**/ **does he do**?

Chang: **I'm not knowing** /**(I don't know)** for sure. I think his family **(is visiting)**/ **visits**.

B Complete the conversation with the correct future form.

Alicia: Hey, Mom. I __'m leaving_____ in a few minutes.
_____(leave)

Mom: OK. What ____are you doing_____ tonight?
_____(you / do)

Alicia: Dania and I ____are going to see____ a movie.
_____(be going to / see)

Mom: What time ___are you going to be__ home?
_____(you / be going to / be)

Alicia: I'm not sure. But don't worry. I _____won't get_____ home too late.
_____(will not / get)

Mom: All right. Remember that you ___'re taking_____ me to work in the morning.
_____(take)

Alicia: Yep. I __'ll be_____ ready to leave at 7:00.
_____(will be)

C Complete the conversations. Use the simple past or the correct form of *used to*. Sometimes more than one answer is possible.

1. **A:** My husband and I _____moved_____ into a new apartment last weekend.
_____(move)
I'm glad, because our old apartment was far from my work.

   B: Really? Where __did you use to live__?
_____(you / live)

2. **A:** I saw you driving today. I _____didn't know_____ you had a car.
_____(not know)

   B: Well, I __didn't use to have__ one. I _____bought_____ that one about a month ago.
_____(not have)_____(buy)

3. **A:** How's your brother? He _____used to work_____ near me, but then he
_____(work)
_____got_____ a new job.
_____(get)

   B: He's doing well. He _____became_____ a manager a few months ago.
_____(become)

4. **A:** _____Did you learn_____ how to cook from your mother?
_____(you / learn)

   B: No. My grandmother _____taught_____ me to cook.
_____(teach)

UNIT 2

A Complete the conversation. Use gerunds or infinitives. If possible, write two answers.

A: Olivia doesn't like _working OR to work_ at the bank anymore. She wants
    (work)
_____to find_____ a new job. Actually, she's thinking about
    (find)
_____making_____ a career change. She's interested in
    (make)
_____becoming_____ a nurse.
    (become)

B: Really? Well, she'll probably need _____to get_____ a college degree
    (get)
before she can get a nursing job. Is she planning on _____going_____
    (go)
to school?

A: Actually, she started _____studying / to study_____ nursing at the community
    (study)
college a few years ago. Now she wants to continue _____working / to work_____
    (work)
towards her degree.

B: That's great. I think Olivia will be very good at _____taking_____ care
    (take)
of people. And I think she'll enjoy _____helping_____ others.
    (help)

B Complete the conversations. Circle the simple past or the present perfect.

1. A: How long (have you worked) / **did you work** at your current job?
   B: Well, I **have started** / (started) last June, so I (ve been) / **was** at this job for about six months.

2. A: I (ve learned) / **learned** so much in my business class already, and the semester is only half over.
   B: Yeah, I **have taken** / (took) a business class last year, and I really (learned) / **have learned** a lot, too.

3. A: Adela (has been) / **was** a manager at Data Tech, Inc. for twelve months now. She (has accomplished) / **accomplished** a lot in a very short time.
   B: She sure has. It's hard to believe that she **has taken** / (took) that job only a year ago.

4. A: Gabriel is a good employee. We **have hired** / (hired) him two years ago, and since then, he (has never missed) / **never missed** a day of work.
   B: Yeah, he **has had** / (had) a good reputation at his last job, too.

UNIT 3

A Complete the paragraph. Circle the correct participial adjective.

I used to be (worried)/ worrying about crime in our town, and I was (frustrated)/ frustrating by our litter problem. But things are changing. Community members are (interested)/ interesting in making a difference. It's **satisfied** /(satisfying) to see people working to improve the community, and it's **encouraged** /(encouraging) to see them working together. The community is making some **excited** /(exciting) changes, and I'm (amazed)/ amazing at our progress.

B Read the first sentence in each item. Then complete the second sentence to express a wish for the opposite.

1. There aren't a lot of restaurants in our neighborhood. We wish that
   _____*there were*_____ more restaurants in our neighborhood.

2. Richard doesn't have time to go to the movies very often. He wishes that _____*he had*_____
   time to go to the movies more often.

3. Mrs. Salas worries a lot. Her children wish that she _____*didn't worry*_____ so much.

4. The school can't get a computer for every student. Everyone wishes that _____*it could get*_____
   a computer for every student.

5. The bus is always late. I wish that _____*it weren't*_____ always late.

C Read the first sentence in each item. Then complete the second sentence. Include an object + infinitive.

1. The residents of our community don't participate in community events.
   We should encourage _____*them to participate*_____ in community events.

2. I parked in my neighbor's parking spot last night. She reminded _____*me not to park*_____ there.

3. Several people in our neighborhood were robbed last week because they opened the door
   for strangers. The police warned _____*them not to open*_____ the door for strangers.

4. We are all invited to attend meetings of the City Council. The City Council president urges
   _____*us to attend*_____ its meetings.

5. The streets in our neighborhood are dirty because people constantly litter. They just pay no
   attention to the signs that tell _____*them not to litter.*_____

A Complete the conversations. Put the words in parentheses in the correct order. If more than one answer is possible, write both answers.

1. Would you please _turn off the light OR turn the light off_ ?
   (turn / off / the light)

2. Can you look at this with me? I'm having a problem, and I can't quite
   figure it out .
   (figure / out / it)

3. If you ever need help, you know you can always _count on me_ .
   (count / on / me)

4. Do you have a moment? I'd like to _talk over these plans OR talk these plans over_ with you.
   (talk / over / these plans)

5. She was really hurt by her co-worker's remark. It won't be easy for her to
   get over it .
   (get / over / it)

B Read Person B's response. Then write a negative question that Person A could have asked.

1. **A:** _Shouldn't I take_ my break soon?

   B: Yes, you should. You should take it when Dina finishes her break.

2. **A:** _Didn't you hear_ about the schedule change?

   B: No, I didn't. I didn't hear anything about it.

3. **A:** _Haven't they cleaned_ the equipment yet?

   B: No, they haven't. They haven't cleaned it because they've been doing other work.

4. **A:** _Shouldn't she ask_ questions if she doesn't understand something?

   B: Yes, she should. She should ask questions any time she's not sure.

5. **A:** _Can't you finish_ the report tomorrow?

   B: No, we can't. We can't finish it tomorrow because Mr. Luna needs it today.

C Read the first statement in each item. Then complete the second sentence to make an indirect instruction or request with the same meaning.

1. My co-worker to me: "Wear comfortable shoes." My co-worker advised _me to wear_ comfortable shoes.

2. The supervisor to us: "Check the new schedule." The supervisor reminded _us to check_ the new schedule.

3. Anita to Sarah: "Don't be late for work." Anita warned _Sarah not to be OR her not to be_ late for work.

4. Shen to Franco: "Work carefully." Shen told _Franco to work OR him to work_ carefully.

UNIT 5

A Combine the two clauses to make a conditional sentence. Keep the clauses in the same order and add *if* to one clause. Include a comma if necessary.

1. a person is badly injured / don't move him or her

   If a person is badly injured, don't move him or her.

2. you don't have a smoke detector / you need to get one

   If you don't have a smoke detector, you need to get one.

3. get under a piece of furniture / there's an earthquake

   Get under a piece of furniture if there's an earthquake.

4. you are prepared for a fire / you have a better chance of surviving it

   If you are prepared for a fire, you have a better chance of surviving it.

5. call 911 / there's an emergency

   Call 911 if there's an emergency.

B Complete the sentences. Circle the correct adverb.

1. You should check the weather frequently **until /(when)** there's a severe weather watch.
2. **Until /(As soon as)** we felt the earth shake, we got under the table.
3. They didn't know about the hurricane **as soon as /(before)** they saw the weather report.
4. **(After)/ Before** the storm started, everyone stayed inside.
5. Stay on the phone with the 911 operator **(until)/ after** he tells you to hang up.

C Complete the sentences. Circle the correct answer.

1. I see smoke. There _____ be a fire somewhere.
   a. may   (b.) must   c. can't
2. In an emergency, some people _____ be very nervous.
   a. couldn't   (b.) might   c. must not
3. It _____ rain today. I didn't see the weather report, so I'm not sure.
   (a.) could   b. must   c. couldn't
4. Jane is allergic to milk, but she didn't have an allergic reaction after she ate that cookie. The cookie _____ have milk in it.
   a. may not   b. might not   (c.) must not
5. There's a hurricane watch for this area. The storm _____ affect us.
   (a.) may   b. must not   c. couldn't

UNIT 6

A Complete the sentences with the correct form of the verb. Make the sentence negative if necessary.

1. Tenants ___aren't allowed___ to have pets. It's against the rules.
   (allow)
2. Visitors ___aren't permitted___ to park in this lot. It's for tenants only.
   (permit)
3. Please don't throw away those soda cans. We ___'re supposed___ to recycle them.
   (suppose)
4. The landlord must put a smoke alarm in your apartment. He ___'s required___ to do it.
   (require)
5. The laundry room is open from 6:00 AM–9:00 PM. Tenants ___are allowed___ to use the
   (allow)
   laundry room during these hours only.

B Complete the sentences with tag questions.

1. You moved recently, ___didn't you?___

2. We don't have to pay the rent yet, ___do we?___

3. The tenants pay for electricity, ___don't they?___

4. The landlord didn't call back, ___did he? OR did she?___

5. The lock isn't broken, ___is it?___

6. The windows are closed, ___aren't they?___

C Read the first statement in each item. Then complete the second sentence with reported speech. Use formal English.

1. Tom told Beth: "I like my new neighbors."
   Tom told ___Beth (that) he liked his new neighbors.___

2. My landlord said, "Your dogs are too noisy."
   My landlord said ___(that) my dogs were too noisy.___

3. The tenant told his landlord, "I'll read the lease and return it to you on Friday."
   The tenant told ___his landlord (that) he'd read the lease and return it to him on Friday.___

4. Kim-Ly told the building manager, "Our lobby needs a new carpet."
   Kim-Ly told ___the building manager (that) their lobby needed a new carpet.___

5. Lucy told Mike, "My neighbor plays his TV really loudly."
   Lucy told ___Mike (that) her neighbor played his TV really loudly.___

UNIT 7

A Complete the conversations. Use the words in the box.

get	than	rather	would you rather
to	buying	prefer	would you prefer

1. **A:** Would you _____rather_____ take your car to a mechanic or do repairs yourself?

   B: I'd _____prefer_____ having a professional take care of any problems.

2. **A:** Would Theo prefer _____buying_____ a new car _____to_____ a used car?

   B: Well, he would rather _____get_____ a new car _____than_____ a used one.

   But he doesn't want to spend a lot either.

3. **A:** _____Would you prefer_____ a compact car or something larger?

   B: I'm not sure. What about you? _____Would you rather_____ drive a big car or a small one?

B Complete the conversations. Change the direct questions to embedded questions.

1. **A:** I wonder _if you can take a look at my car's tires._
   (Can you take a look at my car's tires?)

   B: Sure. Can you tell me _____what the problem is?_____
   (What is the problem?)

   A: Well, the treads are really worn. I wonder _____if / whether I need new tires._____
   (Do I need new tires?)

2. **A:** I just put new windshield wipers on my car, but they're not very good. I don't know

   _____why they don't work._____
   (Why don't they work?)

   B: Hmmm. I wonder _____if / whether you got the wrong size._____
   (Did you get the wrong size?)

   A: That might be it. I wasn't sure _____what size I should get._____
   (What size should I get?)

C Complete the conversations. Use the correct form of the past perfect.

1. **A:** My wife _____had wanted_____ a hybrid for a long time, so we finally bought one.
   (want)

   B: I think you'll be happy with it. We _____had decided_____ to get a more fuel-efficient car
   (decide)

   a long time ago. So when the hybrid cars came out, we bought one right away.

2. **A:** After she _____had saved_____ for about a year, Maritza got a new car.
   (save)

   B: Oh yeah? _____Had she looked_____ at a lot of cars before she made her choice?
   (she/look)

   A: Yes, she _____had_____. She _____had gone_____ to several dealers.
   (go)

UNIT 8

A Complete the conversation. Use the correct form of the present perfect continuous.

Dr. Pratt: Hello, Mrs. Lee. _____Have_____ you _____been waiting_____ long?
(wait)

Mrs. Lee: No, I haven't, thank you.

Dr. Pratt: Good. So, how _____have_____ you _____been feeling_____ since your last
(feel)
appointment?

Mrs. Lee: I _'ve been getting_ better every day. I _'ve been sleeping_ well at night, and I
(get)   (sleep)
haven't been taking naps during the day.
(not take)

Dr. Pratt: That's great. And _____have_____ you _____been taking_____ your medication?
(take)

Mrs. Lee: Yes, I have. My husband _has been reminding_ me every night.
(remind)

Dr. Pratt: Good. And _____have_____ you _____been exercising_____?
(exercise)

Mrs. Lee: Well, my daughter and I _have been walking_ together every day.
(walking)

Dr. Pratt: Very good. You _'ve been doing_ everything right!
(do)

B Complete the conversation. Circle the correct words.

Malena: Hey, you look great! What have you been doing?

Susana: Nothing special—just following my doctor's advice. She said I **better /(**'d better**)**
make some lifestyle changes to stay in good health.

Malena: Oh, yeah? What kinds of changes? Maybe I should make some changes, too.

Susana: Well, she said I **(ought to)**/ **ought** get more exercise. She thinks I **should to /(should)**
do some moderate exercise at least three times a week.

Malena: But I already have **(so many)**/ **so much** things to do. I'm **(so)**/ **such** busy that I don't
have time!

Susana: Well, you can start by doing small things like taking the stairs instead of the
elevator. It can make **so /(such)** a difference that you'll be amazed. Listen, we
had better /(ought to) take a walk a few days a week at lunchtime. Do you want to
go with me today?

Malena: Sure. Let's meet downstairs at 12:00, OK?

Susana: OK. And you **(had better)** / **have better** be there! Remember, your health is **such /(so)**
important that you must **making /(make)** time to take care of yourself!

UNIT 9

A Read the statements. Combine the sentences using either *because* or *since*. Don't change the order of the clauses.

1. <u>Since Lucia is having trouble with math, I want to talk to her teacher. OR:</u>

   <u>Because Lucia is having trouble with math, I want to talk to her teacher.</u>

2. Our son really likes to play sports. We encourage him to read books about them.

   Since our son really likes to play sports, . . . OR: Because our son really likes to play sports, . . .

3. Parents and teachers should communicate. It helps students do better in school.

   Parents and teachers should communicate since . . . OR: Parents and teachers should communicate because . . .

4. David's grades have improved. He started getting extra help after school.

   David's grades have improved since . . . OR: David's grades have improved because . . .

B Complete the conversations. Circle the correct words.

1. **Eliana:** I sent Manolo's teacher a note (**because**)/ **to** I want to set up a meeting with her. But she hasn't called or written me back.

   Victor: She (**might not have**)/ **must have** gotten the note. She doesn't seem like the kind of person **which** /(**who**) ignores messages. When did you send it?

   Eliana: Last week. I put it in Manolo's backpack (**so that**)/ **to** he could give it to her.

   Victor: You should check. Manolo (**could have**)/ **must not have** forgotten about it.

2. **Janet:** Did you go to the PTO meeting last night?

   Mi-Cha: No. I didn't go (**because**)/ **so that** I don't really know what the group does.

   Janet: Well, PTO stands for Parent Teacher Organization. It's a group **who** /(**that**) works to improve both the school and students' learning.

   Mi-Cha: It sounds like a good organization. I (**should have**)/ **must have** gone to the meeting.

   Janet: Don't worry. You can go to the next one (**to**)/ **so that** learn more about it.

3. **Farah:** Ugh—that test was so hard! Even Luisa said it was hard, and she's someone (**that**)/ **which** always gets good grades.

   Laila: I know. The people (**I talked to**)/ **which I talked to** all thought they got a bad grade. I **shouldn't have** /(**can't have**) done well on it.

   Farah: Me neither. I (**should have**)/ **may have** studied more.

4. **Mai:** Some schools are trying (**to**)/ **so that** help parents get involved. Many teachers meet with parents in the evenings. That's a big help for parents (**who work**)/ **work** during the day.

   Tien: Yeah, at my son's school there are translators (**that can**)/ **can** help parents (**who**)/ **which** are still learning English. A translator helped me last year, and she was great. Without her, I **may have been** /(**might not have been**) so involved in my son's education.

UNIT 10

A Complete the sentences. Use the words in the box.

| have | makes | lets | get | made | had |

1. They didn't want to work late, but the supervisor _____made_____ them stay until 9:00.
2. Please find Mr. Jones and _____have_____ him sign this. Then give it back to me.
3. The company _____lets_____ employees leave early the day before some holidays.
4. Can you _____get_____ someone to take your shift? Ask your co-workers.
5. The store was so busy yesterday! My boss _____had_____ me work on the cash register, and I usually don't do that.
6. Our company _____makes_____ us clock in and out for every shift.

B Complete the sentences with the correct reflexive pronouns.

1. Don't lift heavy objects by _____yourself_____. Get someone to help you.
2. I finished all the work _____myself_____. No one helped me.
3. Mrs. Yang burned _____herself_____ while cooking dinner.
4. Workers need to use caution with that machine. They could hurt _____themselves_____.
5. You and John can't do this project by _____yourselves_____. You'll need some help.
6. We're really proud of _____ourselves_____. We worked hard, and we got the job done.

C Complete the conversations. Use the words in the box.

Why don't you
Would you mind
Could I
Why don't I

1. **A:** _____Could I_____ borrow your pen for a minute?

   B: Sure. Here you go.
2. **A:** I can't go to lunch with you today because I forgot my wallet.

   B: _____Why don't I_____ lend you some money? You can pay me back tomorrow.
3. **A:** _____Would you mind_____ driving me home after work today?

   B: No, it's no problem at all.
4. **A:** _____Why don't you_____ talk to our supervisor about your problem?

   B: That's a good idea. I'll talk to her today after my shift ends.

UNIT 11

A Complete the sentences. Use the simple past or the past continuous.

1. While the defense attorney ___was preparing___ for the trial, the police
   (prepare)
   ___discovered___ new evidence.
   (discover)

2. I ___was waiting___ at a red light when an SUV ___hit___ my car.
   (wait)   (hit)

3. When his wife ___got___ home, Walter ___was watching___ courtroom TV.
   (get)   (watch)

4. The witness ___was talking___ when the attorney ___interrupted___ him.
   (talk)   (interrupt)

5. Paula ___saw___ a car accident while she ___was standing___ at the bus stop.
   (see)   (stand)

B Read the active sentences. Complete the passive sentences so they have the same meaning.

1. Attorneys on both sides of a case choose juries.

   Juries ___are chosen___ by attorneys on both sides of a case.

2. They sent the criminal to jail for 10 years.

   The criminal ___was sent___ to jail for 10 years.

3. The government calls most U.S. citizens to jury duty sometime in their lives.

   Most U.S. citizens ___are called___ to jury duty sometime in their lives.

4. Lawyers explained the details of the case to the jury.

   The details of the case ___were explained___ to the jury.

5. After hearing the facts, jurors discuss the case.

   After hearing the facts, the case ___is discussed___ by the jurors.

C Complete the sentences. Use the subordinating conjunctions in the box. You may use each conjunction more than once.

> even if
> as long as
> even though

1. Don't speed, ___even if___ you're in a hurry.

2. You won't get a ticket ___as long as___ you follow the traffic laws.

3. ___Even though___ I was really late for my appointment yesterday, I didn't speed.

4. ___Even if___ there aren't other cars around you, you should still use your turn

   signals. It's a good habit to get into.

5. ___As long as___ you study, you'll pass your driver's license test.

6. I always drive with my headlights on, ___even if___ it's not dark.

UNIT 12

A Complete the paragraph. Use *a, an, the,* or Ø.

With __a__ credit card, you can buy things now and pay for them later. This can be useful, but it can also be expensive. That's because __Ø__ credit card companies charge __Ø__ interest on the amount you owe them. __A__ debit card is different—it's linked to __a__ bank account. When you pay for something with __a__ debit card, the money comes out of __the__ account it's linked to.

If you have __a__ credit card, use it carefully. And make sure you always pay __the__ full amount of the bill as soon as you can. Try not to have __an__ unpaid balance so you don't have to pay __Ø__ interest charges.

B Complete the sentences so that they make future real conditional statements.

1. If I ___open___ a bank account, the bank ___will give___ me a debit card.
   (open)   (give)
2. We ___'ll be able to___ go on vacation, if we ___save___ our money.
      (be able to)   (save)
3. If she ___gets___ a loan, she ___'ll have to___ pay interest.
         (get)   (have to)
4. It ___will be___ easier to save money, if you ___make___ a budget.
      (be)   (make)

C Complete the sentences so that they make present unreal conditional statements.

1. They ___would start___ their own business if they ___had___ enough money.
         (start)   (have)
2. We ___would save___ money if we ___took___ the bus instead of driving.
        (save)   (take)
3. If I ___didn't eat___ out so much, I ___would spend___ a lot less on food.
        (not eat)   (spend)
4. If you ___opened___ a Mexican restaurant, people ___would come___.
          (open)   (come)

D Complete the sentences. Use the correct form of the verb.

1. If you suddenly ___got___ a lot of money, would you quit your job?
                   (get)
2. If she ___needs___ money, I'll lend it to her.
          (need)
3. I wouldn't do that if I ___were___ you.
                          (be)
4. If we stop buying coffee at the coffee shop, we ___will save___ about $20 a week.
                                                    (save)

Persistence Activities

Unit 1 Find Someone Who

A Write the names of classmates who can answer "yes" to these questions. Then ask the follow-up questions.

> Follow-up questions are questions that ask for more detail or additional information related to a previously asked question.

Find someone who . . .

1. has visited another city in
   the United States. _____
   Which city? _____

2. went to see a movie in the
   last month. _____
   Which movie? _____

3. knows how to play a musical
   instrument. _____
   What instrument? _____

4. did something fun or exciting
   last weekend. _____
   What did you do? _____

B PAIRS. Compare your answers. What did you learn that was interesting?

C After class, talk to a classmate who gave an answer you found interesting. Ask your own follow-up questions to get to know this classmate better.

Unit 2 Characteristics of a Good Learner

A Make a chart like the one below. Include ten rows.

B BRAINSTORM. GROUPS. What are the characteristics of a good learner? Record each idea in the first column.

Characteristic of a good learner	I do this.	I don't do this.	I want to work on this.
Plans a specific time to study	✓	✗	✓✓
Asks questions when he or she doesn't understand			

C Look at the learner characteristics in your chart. Put a check (✓) next to the ones you already do, an X next to the ones you don't do, and two checks (✓✓) next to the ones you want to work on.

D PAIRS. Share your charts. Look at the items with two checks (✓✓). Discuss ways you can help each other develop these learner characteristics.

Unit 3   Favorite Celebrations

A Think of your favorite holiday or celebration in your country or in the United States.

B Prepare to talk about this holiday or celebration with a partner. Use the following questions to help you remember and organize details.

> With whom do you spend the holiday or event?
>
> Where do you celebrate?
>
> What special things do you see?
>
> What sounds do you hear?
>
> What kinds of things do you smell?
>
> What foods do you eat?
>
> What special activities do you do?

C PAIRS. Tell your partner about your favorite holiday or celebration.

Unit 4   What Is Your Work Style?

A Look at the list of different work styles. Check (✓) the styles that are true for you. Put an X next to the styles that aren't true for you.

Work style preference	Yes	No
I like to work alone.		
I like to work in groups or teams.		
I like to have deadlines.*		
I like to get detailed instructions from my boss.		
I like to work with my hands.		
I like to solve problems.		
I like to work in an office.		
I like to create things.		
I like to do a lot of writing.		
I like to work with different people.		
I like to work within a definite schedule. No overtime!		

*Deadlines are specific times or dates when a task has to be completed.

B Look at the items you checked. Do your preferences match the job that you have now? How can knowing your work style preferences help you choose your job?

C PAIRS. Share your answers to Exercises A and B. Can you think of other jobs that might match your or your partner's preferences? Explain.

Unit 5 Snow Days

A Create a word web for the topic: "Reasons for school closings and class cancellations." Write those words in the center of a page. Draw a line out from the center and label it: "Weather-related reasons."

Reasons for school closings and class cancellations

Weather-related reasons

_____

_____

_____

B BRAINSTORM. Think about class cancellations.

1. What are the common weather-related reasons for school closings and class cancellations? List those specific examples below "Weather-related reasons."

2. What other reasons for class cancellations do you know? Add another line and label it. List specific examples for that reason.

C PAIRS. Discuss. How can you take advantage of school closings to learn English? Create a word web similar to the one in Exercise A to record your ideas.

Unit 6 How Far Have You Come?

A Think about what have learned in this English class. Leaf through your textbook, your workbook, and any written work.

B Make a chart like the one below. Include at least 10 rows. In the first column, list all the things that you have learned.

Things I have learned	Situations where I can apply what I have learned

C Look at the items you listed. How and where in your daily life can you apply each one? Write specific examples in the second column.

D PAIRS. Share your charts. Is there anything in your partner's list that is not in yours? Can it help you in your every day life? If so, add it to your chart.

Unit 7   Looking Forward

A What are you looking forward to studying in English class? Think about your goals and any daily activities or situations when you need to use English. Then look at the units in this book that you haven't studied yet. Identify at least five topics, grammar points, readings, vocabulary, or life skills that might help you in your daily life. Make a list.

1.
2.
3.
4.
5.

B GROUPS. Talk about each item on your list. Explain why it is important to you. Compare your lists. Talk about the similarities and differences. Agree on five things that are important to the whole group. Make a list.

C CLASS. Present your common list to the class.

Unit 8   Advertising English!

A PAIRS. Discuss. What is your favorite advertisement? Where are these advertisements—on billboards, television, radio, magazine, newspapers, brochures? What do you like about that advertisement? Does it have a slogan?

> Billboards are large outdoor signs for advertising.
> A slogan is a short, easily remembered phrase used in advertising, politics, etc.

B GROUPS. Describe your favorite advertisement. Talk about what makes an advertisement successful and memorable. Take notes.

C GROUPS. Discuss. Why is English important in your life? How can knowing how to speak, read, and write in English help you? What would happen if you didn't learn English? Take notes.

D GROUPS. Now create a poster advertising the importance of English in daily life. Think of a slogan for your advertisement. What colors will you use? Will you use pictures? How will you make your advertisement memorable?

E CLASS. Present your group's poster to the class. Display the posters in your classroom and, with your principal's permission, in your school to inspire others to learn English!

Unit 9   Then and Now

A   Think about how a pre-school child learns to speak a language, whether it is English or a native language. Then think of how you, as an adult, are learning English. Complete the chart below.

	Learning as a child	Learning as an adult
What strategies do children or adults use to learn a language? By imitating? By listening to an audio? By reading?		
Where do children or adults learn a language? At home? At school? In the playground?		
What do children or adults learn when learning a language? Vocabulary? Conversation? Grammar?		
From your observation, who is the faster learner, a child or an adult?		
In your opinion, what is the best way for children or adults to learn a language?		

B   PAIRS. Share your answers to Exercise A. How do you feel about learning English as an adult?

Unit 10   How Students Learn Best

A   Think of how you've been learning English. Check (✓) five types of activities you liked best.

- ☐ working alone
- ☐ working in pairs
- ☐ working in groups
- ☐ reading activities
- ☐ conversations
- ☐ grammar activities
- ☐ listening activities
- ☐ writing activities
- ☐ vocabulary activities
- ☐ using life skills materials (maps, graphs, forms, etc.)
- ☐ Other: _____

B   Look at the activities you checked. What did you like about them? How did they help you learn English?

C   PAIRS. Talk about other activities in the book. Which activities didn't you like? Why?

D   GROUPS. Compare your answers to Exercises A, B, and C. What are some similarities in the ways you prefer to learn English? Make a list of activities that help students learn effectively.

E   CLASS. Present your list to the class. Explain why these activities help students learn. Also discuss the activities that you didn't include. Why do you think those activities aren't as effective?

Unit 11 My Writing Checklist

A Look back at the checklists in Check Your Writing for each unit. Did those checklists help you write better paragraphs?

B Now look again at the paragraphs you wrote for this class. What common mistakes did you make? For example,

- Did you forget to use punctuation?
- Did you use capital letters correctly?
- Were there any misspellings?
- Did you make mistakes in subject-verb agreement?
- Did you forget to provide details to support a statement?

Create your own checklist for editing your writing. Include anything that will help you review, correct, and improve your writing.

C PAIRS. Compare your checklists. Explain why you included the items you did. Which items from your partner's checklist would you add to your checklist?

Unit 12 The Door of Opportunity

A Staple two pieces of paper together. On the first page, draw a picture of a door. You can make the door simple or elaborate. On the second page, make a chart like the one below.

What I will remember about English class	Where I will go from here

B Imagine yourself walking through a door and leaving your English class. What will you remember about the class? Who will you remember? What lessons and new knowledge will you take with you? Record these ideas in the first column.

C In the second column, write about where you want to go after this English class. Do you want to take more classes? Do you want to look for a new job? What are your plans now that English class is finished?

D CLASS. Share your door with the class. Describe one thing that you will remember about English class. Describe something that you will do now that you've finished class.

Team Projects

Unit 1 Routines <u>MAKE A POSTER</u>

TEAMS OF 2 Captain, Spokesperson

GET READY **Captain:** Ask your teammate about his or her current and past routines.
Find out how your routines are similar and different. Keep time.
You have ten minutes.
Assistant: Take notes in the chart.

Name	Current routines	Past routines

CREATE **Captain:** Get the materials. Then keep time. You have ten minutes.
Team: Create a poster about your routines. Use the information from your chart to make a Venn diagram. Label each of the circles with a team member's name. Write the routines that are the same for team members in the center. Write the routines that are different in the outer circles. If you can, take photos of the teammates and place them by the appropriate circles.

Maria

work in the evenings

used to go to the gym every day

TEAM

study English every day

used to speak my native language all the time

Antonio

listen to music every day

used to ride a bike

REPORT **Spokesperson:** Share your poster with the class. Describe your team's routines.

Unit 2   Job-Search Resources <u>MAKE A BOOKLET</u>

TEAMS OF 4 Captain, Co-captain, Assistant, Spokesperson

GET READY **Captain:** Ask your teammates about resources in your community where you can find information about job openings and careers. Ask what kind of information you can find from each resource.
Co-captain: Keep time. You have ten minutes.
Assistant: Take notes in the chart.

Materials
- 1 piece of white paper
- pens or markers
- stapler and staples

Resources	Services provided

CREATE **Co-captain:** Get the materials. Then keep time. You have fifteen minutes.
Team: Create a page for a booklet about career resources in your community. Use the information from your chart. Add art if you want.

REPORT **Spokesperson:** Share your page with the class. Describe the career resources in your area.

COLLECT **Captains:** Collect the page from each group. Staple the pages together to make a booklet about career resources in your community.

Unit 3 Community Services MAKE A POSTER

TEAMS OF 4 Captain, Co-captain, Assistant, Spokesperson

GET READY **Captain:** Ask your teammates about community services in your area. Ask them where the places are and how to get there.
Co-captain: Keep time. You have ten minutes.
Assistant: Take notes in the chart.

Place name	Location	How to get there

CREATE **Co-captain:** Get the materials. Then keep time. You have fifteen minutes.
Team: Choose one of the places you talked about. Use the information from your chart to create a poster about that place. Write directions to get there. Include a map if you want.

REPORT **Spokesperson:** Share your poster with the class. Describe the community service and how to get there.

Unit 4 Team Players MAKE AN OUTLINE

Materials
- 1 piece of white paper
- pens or markers
- stapler and staples

TEAMS OF 4 Captain, Co-captain, Assistant, Spokesperson

GET READY **Captain:** Ask your teammates how to be a successful team player. Ask what you should and shouldn't do at work to get along well with your co-workers.
Co-captain: Keep time. You have ten minutes.
Assistant: Take notes in the chart.

How to be a successful team player	
You should . . .	**You shouldn't . . .**

CREATE **Co-captain:** Get the materials. Then keep time. You have fifteen minutes.
Team: Imagine you will be giving a presentation to employees about how to be successful team players. Create an outline for your presentation. Include the information from your chart.

REPORT **Spokesperson:** Share your presentation outline with the class. Describe three ways to be a successful team player.

COLLECT **Captains:** Collect the outline from each group. Staple the pages together to make a booklet about how to be a team player.

Unit 5 Be Prepared MAKE A POSTER

TEAMS OF 4 Captain, Co-captain, Assistant, Spokesperson

GET READY **Captain:** Ask your teammates to name disasters that could happen where you live. Ask what supplies you need to prepare and what you need to do before a disaster strikes.
Co-captain: Keep time. You have ten minutes.
Assistant: Take notes in the chart.

Type of disaster: _____	
Supplies needed	**Things to do**

CREATE **Co-captain:** Get the materials. Then keep track of the time. You have fifteen minutes.
Team: Create a poster about how to prepare for a disaster. Use the information from your chart. Add art if you want.

REPORT **Spokesperson:** Share your poster with the class. Describe three ways to prepare for a disaster.

Unit 6   Website Design <u>MAKE A BOOKLET</u>

TEAMS OF 4 Captain, Co-captain, Assistant, Spokesperson

GET READY **Team:** Imagine you are on a website design team. The website is for newcomers to the United States. It is your job to design a page about renting an apartment. Suggest information for the website page.
Captain: Keep time. You have ten minutes.
Assistant: Take notes below.

_____

_____

_____

_____

_____

_____

CREATE **Co-captain:** Get the materials. Then keep time. You have fifteen minutes.
Team: Create a website page about renting an apartment. Use the information from your notes. Add art if you want.

REPORT **Spokesperson:** Share your website page with the class. Describe your website.

COLLECT **Captains:** Collect the website design from each group. Staple the pages together to make a booklet about renting an apartment.

Unit 7 Used Car for Sale DESIGN AN INTERNET AD

Materials
- large paper
- markers
- magazine or Internet car advertisements (optional)

TEAMS OF 4 Captain, Co-captain, Assistant, Spokesperson

GET READY **Team:** Imagine you have a used car that you want to sell.
Captain: Ask your teammates to describe the car you're selling.
Co-captain: Keep time. You have ten minutes.
Assistant: Take notes in the chart.

Make and model	
Year	
Mileage	
Options	
Other information	

CREATE **Co-captain:** Get the materials. Then keep time. You have fifteen minutes.
Team: Create an Internet ad for your car. Use the information from your chart. Add art if you want.

REPORT **Spokesperson:** Share your ad with the class. Describe the car you want to sell.

Unit 8   How to Reduce Stress <u>MAKE A BOOKLET</u>

Materials
- 1 piece of white paper
- pens or markers
- stapler and staples

TEAMS OF 4   Captain, Co-captain, Assistant, Spokesperson

GET READY   **Team:** Many people have a hard time staying relaxed with their busy and changing lives. This can cause stress. According to health experts, stress can affect our health in many ways. Discuss the health issues that can result from stress.
Captain: Ask your teammates to make suggestions for ways to reduce stress.
Co-captain: Keep time. You have ten minutes.
Assistant: Take notes below.

_____

_____

_____

_____

_____

_____

_____

CREATE   **Co-captain:** Get the materials. Then keep time. You have fifteen minutes.
Team: Create a page for a booklet about reducing stress. Use the information from your notes. Include a paragraph about ways to reduce stress.

REPORT   **Spokesperson:** Share your page with the class. Tell the class your suggestions.

COLLECT   **Captains:** Collect the page from each group. Staple the pages together to make a booklet of suggestions on reducing stress.

Unit 9 After-School Programs <u>MAKE A BOOKLET</u>

Materials
- 4 pieces of white paper
- pens or markers

TEAMS OF 4 Captain, Co-captain, Assistant, Spokesperson

GET READY **Team:** Imagine you are on a parent committee at your child's school. It is your job to design an after-school program for elementary students.
Captain: Ask your teammates to suggest eight after-school activities—for example, chess, sports, art, language.
Co-captain: Keep time. You have ten minutes.
Assistant: Take notes below.

_____

_____

_____

_____

_____

_____

CREATE **Captain:** Get the materials. Then keep time. You have fifteen minutes.
Team: Create a booklet about the after-school program. Include a sentence or two about each activity. Add art if you want. (Each student writes about two activities.)

REPORT **Spokesperson:** Share your booklet with the class. Describe your after-school program.

COLLECT **Captains:** Collect the booklet from each group. Staple the pages together to make a booklet of after-school programs.

Unit 10 Problem at Work WRITE AN ADVICE COLUMN

Materials
- 1 piece of white paper
- pens or markers
- stapler and staples

TEAMS OF 4 Captain, Co-captain, Assistant, Spokesperson

GET READY **Team:** Discuss issues you or someone you know has had at work. What was the problem? What happened? How was the problem solved?
Captain: Ask your teammates to choose one of the issues that you discussed.
Co-captain: Keep time. You have ten minutes.
Assistant: Take notes below.

_____

_____

_____

_____

_____

CREATE **Co-captain:** Get the materials. Then keep time. You have twenty minutes.
Team: Write a short letter to an advice columnist about the work issue you chose. (Each student writes for three minutes. Then check and correct your work.)

CREATE MORE **Team:** Exchange letters with another team. Imagine you are advice columnists. Write a short response to the other team's issue.

REPORT **Spokesperson:** Show the other team's letter and your response to the class. Describe the issue and your team's advice.

COLLECT **Captains:** Collect the letter and response from each group. Staple the letters together to make a booklet of advice on work problems.

Unit 11 Rights and Responsibilities <u>MAKE A POSTER</u>

TEAMS OF 4 Captain, Co-captain, Assistant, Spokesperson

Materials
- large paper
- markers

GET READY **Team:** In this unit, you learned about people's rights when they are arrested for a crime in the United States. Discuss. What other *rights* do people living in the U.S. have? What *responsibilities* do they have?

Captain: Ask your teammates to list both rights and responsibilities in the United States.

Co-captain: Keep time. You have ten minutes.

Assistant: Take notes in the chart.

Rights	Responsibilities

CREATE **Co-captain:** Get the materials. Then keep time. You have twenty minutes.

Team: Create a poster about rights and responsibilities in the United States. Use the information from your chart. Add art if you want.

REPORT **Spokesperson:** Share your poster with the class. Describe the rights and responsibilities you thought of.

Unit 12 A New Business MAKE A POSTER

Materials
• large paper
• markers

TEAMS OF 4 Captain, Co-captain, Assistant, Spokesperson

GET READY **Team:** Imagine you are going to start your own business.
What are some kinds of businesses you might start?
Captain: Ask your teammates to decide on the kind of business
you are going to start. Have the team choose a name for the business
and think of the products or services you will offer.
Co-captain: Keep time. You have ten minutes.
Assistant: Take notes below.

_____

_____

_____

_____

_____

_____

Co-captain: Get the materials. Then keep time. You have fifteen minutes.
Team: Create a poster about your business. Use the information from your
notes. Add art if you want.

REPORT **Spokesperson:** Share your poster with the class. Describe your team's
business. Be enthusiastic!

Employee's Report of Work-related Injury

To be completed immediately after the accident and submitted to your supervisor

Employee Name: _____ ID Number: _____

Male ☐ Female ☐ Date of Birth: _____ Marital Status: _____

Home Address: _____
        Street   City   ZIP Code

Home Phone No. _____ Cell Phone No. _____

Job Title: _____

Employment Start Date: _____

Date of Accident: _____

Location of Accident: _____

Describe in detail how the accident occurred:

[   ]

(describe the work you were engaged in, describe how the injury occurred, and explain the cause)

Part of body injured: _____
(be specific - example: right middle finger, left ankle, upper back)

Type of injury: _____
(example: sprain, burn and degree of burn, contusion, sutured)

Was medical treatment sought? If so: _____ _____
                             Name and address of medical provider   Phone Number

No. of days missed from work: _____

Return to work date (as stated by physician): _____

Type of leave used: _____

No. of days worked with restrictions: _____

Name of witness (es): _____ Phone No. _____

Was safety equipment provided? Yes ☐ No ☐

Was safety equipment used? Yes ☐ No ☐

Signature of employee: _____ Date: _____

Questions? Call 650-555-9827

MONTHLY BUDGET

INCOME	EXPENSES	MONTHLY AMOUNT
Wages or Salary:	**FIXED EXPENSES**	
Other:	Mortgage or Rent:	
	Car	
	Loan Payments:	
	Insurance:	
	Other Insurance:	
	Home:	
	Life:	
	VARIABLE EXPENSES	
	Utilities	
	Electric:	
	Gas:	
	Water:	
	Telephone:	
	Cable or Satellite TV:	
	Internet Access:	
	Car Expenses	
	Gasoline:	
	Maintenance:	
	Medical Expenses	
	Medical Bills	
	Prescription Drugs	
	Other Transportation:	
	Food & Groceries:	
	Toiletries	
	School Supplies:	
	Entertainment:	
	Meals Out	
	Newspapers, Magazines:	
	Gifts:	
	Charity:	
	Other:	
TOTAL INCOME:	**TOTAL EXPENSES:**	

Form
1040EZ

Department of the Treasury—Internal Revenue Service
**Income Tax Return for Single and
Joint Filers With No Dependents** **2010**

Label
Use the IRS label.
Otherwise please print or type.

L
A
B
E
L

H
E
R
E

Your first name and initial	Last name	Your social security number
If a joint return, spouse's first name and initial	Last name	Spouse's social security number
Home address (number and street).	Apt. no.	▲ You **must** enter your SSN(s) above.
City, town or post office, state, and ZIP code.		

Presidential Election Campaign ▶ Check here if you, or your spouse if a joint return, want $3 to go to this fund . . . . ▶ ☐ You   ☐ Spouse

Income
Attach Form(s) W-2 here.
Enclose, but do not attach, any payment.

1   Wages, salaries, and tips. This should be shown in box 1of your Form(s) W-2. Attach your Form(s) W-2. | 1

2   Taxable interest. If the total is over $1,500, you cannot use Form 1040EZ. | 2

3   Unemployment compensation and Alaska Permanent Fund dividends. | 3

4   Add lines 1, 2 and 3. This is your **adjusted gross income**. | 4

5   If someone can claim you (or your spouse if a joint return) as a dependent, check the applicable box(es) below and enter the amount from the worksheet on back.
   ☐ You   ☐ Spouse
   If no one can claim you (or your spouse if a joint return), enter $8,750 if **single**; $17,500 if **married filing jointly**. See back for explanation. | 5

6   Subtract line 5 from line 4. If line 5 is larger than line 4, enter -0-. This is your **taxable income**.   ▶ | 6

Payments and tax

7   Federal income tax withheld from box 2 of your Form(s) W-2. | 7

8a   **Earned income credit (EIC).** | 8a

b   Nontaxable combat pay election | 8b

9   Add lines 7 and 8a. These are your **total payments**.   ▶ | 9

10   **Tax.** Use the amount on **line 6 above** to find your tax in the tax table on pages 18–26 of the booklet. Then, enter the tax from the table on this line. | 10

Refund
Have it directly deposited!

11a   If line 9 is larger than line 10, subtract line 10 from line 9. This is your refund. | 11a
▶b   Routing number |⎵⎵⎵⎵⎵⎵⎵⎵| ▶ c Type: ☐ Checking   ☐ Savings
▶d   Account number |⎵⎵⎵⎵⎵⎵⎵⎵⎵⎵⎵⎵⎵⎵⎵|

Amount you owe

12   If line 10 is larger than line 9, subtract line 9 from line 10. This is the **amount you owe.**   ▶ | 12

Third party designee

Do you want to allow another person to discuss this return with the IRS? ☐ **Yes.** Complete the following.   ☐ **No.**
Designee's name ▶   Phone no. ▶ (   )   Personal identification number (PIN) ▶ |⎵⎵⎵⎵⎵|

Sign here
Keep a copy for your records.

Under penalties of perjury, I declare that I have examined this return, and to the best of my knowledge and belief, it is true, correct, and accurately lists all amounts and sources of income I received during the tax year. Declaration of preparer (other than the taxpayer) is based on all information of which the preparer has any knowledge.

| Your signature ▶ | Date | Your occupation | Daytime phone number (   ) |
| Spouse's signature. If a joint return, **both** must sign. ▶ | Date | Spouse's occupation | |

Paid preparer's use only

| Preparer's signature ▶ | Date | Check if self-employed ☐ | Preparer's SSN or PTIN |
| Firm's name (or yours if self-employed), address, and ZIP code ▶ | EIN | | Phone no. (   ) |

Form **1040EZ** (2010)

Grammar Reference

UNIT 1, Lesson 2, page 8

Stative (non-action) verbs

Emotions	Mental states	Wants and preferences	Appearance and value
admire	agree	hope	appear
adore	assume	need	be
appreciate	believe	prefer	cost
care	consider	want	equal
dislike	disagree	wish	look (seem)
doubt	expect		matter
fear	guess	**The senses**	represent
hate	hope	feel	resemble
like	imagine	hear	seem
love	know	notice	weigh
regret	mean	see	
respect	mind	smell	
trust	realize	sound	
	recognize	taste	
Possession and relationship	remember		
belong	see (understand)		
contain	suppose		
have	think (believe)		
own	understand		
possess	wonder		

Irregular verbs

Base form	Simple past	Past participle	Base form	Simple past	Past participle
awake	awoke	awoken	keep	kept	kept
be	was/were	been	know	knew	known
beat	beat	beaten	lead	led	led
become	became	become	leave	left	left
begin	began	begun	lend	lent	lent
bite	bit	bitten	let	let	let
blow	blew	blown	lose	lost	lost
break	broke	broken	make	made	made
build	built	built	mean	meant	meant
buy	bought	bought	meet	met	met
catch	caught	caught	pay	paid	paid
choose	chose	chosen	put	put	put
come	came	come	quit	quit	quit
cost	cost	cost	read	read	read
cut	cut	cut	ride	rode	ridden
dig	dug	dug	ring	rang	rung
do	did	done	run	ran	run
draw	drew	drawn	say	said	said
drink	drank	drunk	see	saw	seen
drive	drove	driven	sell	sold	sold
eat	ate	eaten	send	sent	sent
fall	fell	fallen	shake	shook	shaken
feed	fed	fed	sing	sang	sung
feel	felt	felt	sit	sat	sat
fight	fought	fought	sleep	slept	slept
find	found	found	speak	spoke	spoken
fly	flew	flown	spend	spent	spent
forget	forgot	forgotten	stand	stood	stood
forgive	forgave	forgiven	steal	stole	stolen
get	got	gotten	swim	wam	swum
give	gave	given	take	took	taken
go	went	gone	teach	taught	taught
grow	grew	grown	think	thought	thought
hang	hung	hung	throw	threw	thrown
have	had	had	understand	understood	understood
hear	heard	heard	upset	upset	upset
hide	hid	hidden	wake	woke	woken
hit	hit	hit	wear	wore	worn
hold	held	held	win	won	won
hur	hurt	hurt	write	wrote	written

UNIT 2, Lesson 2, page 28

Infinitives and Gerunds

Verbs followed by the infinitive (*to* + base form of verb)

agree	decide	mean	refuse
appear	deserve	need	request
arrange	expect	offer	seem
ask	fail	pay	volunteer
attempt	help	plan	wait
can('t) afford	hope	prepare	want
can('t) wait	learn	pretend	wish
choose	manage	promise	would like

Verbs followed by the gerund (base form of verb + *-ing*)

admit	escape	postpone
advise	explain	practice
appreciate	feel like	prohibit
avoid	finish	quit
can't help	forgive	recommend
consider	give up (stop)	regret
delay	imagine	report
deny	keep (continue)	risk
discuss	mention	suggest
dislike	mind	tolerate
enjoy	miss	understand

Verbs followed by the infinitive or the gerund

begin	hate	remember
can't stand	like	start
continue	love	stop
forget	prefer	try

UNIT 2, Lesson 5, page 34

Gerunds as Objects of Prepositions

Verb + Preposition			
admit to	complain about	insist on	rely on
advise against	count on	keep on	resort to
apologize for	deal with	look forward to	succeed in
approve of	dream about/of	object to	talk about
believe in	feel like/about	pay for	think about
choose between/among	go along with	plan on	wonder about

Adjective + Preposition			
afraid of	careful of	good at	satisfied with
amazed at/by	concerned about	happy about	shocked at/by
angry at	curious about	interested in	sick of
ashamed of	different from	nervous about	sorry for/about
aware of	excited about	opposed to	surprised at/about/by
awful at	famous for	ready for	terrible at
bad at	fed up with	responsible for	tired of
bored with/by	fond of	sad about	used to
capable of	glad about	safe from	worried about

UNIT 3, Lesson 2, page 48

Participial adjectives					
-ed	*-ing*	*-ed*	*-ing*	*-ed*	*-ing*
alarmed	alarming	embarrassed	embarrassing	overwhelmed	overwhelming
amazed	amazing	encouraged	encouraging	pleased	pleasing
amused	amusing	excited	exciting	relaxed	relaxing
annoyed	annoying	exhausted	exhausting	satisfied	satisfying
bored	boring	fascinated	fascinating	shocked	shocking
confused	confusing	frightened	frightening	surprised	surprising
depressed	depressing	horrified	horrifying	terrified	terrifying
disappointed	disappointing	humiliated	humiliating	thrilled	thrilling
disgusted	disgusting	interested	interesting	tired	tiring
disturbed	disturbing	irritated	irritating	touched	touching

-ed Adjective + Preposition			
alarmed at/by	disgusted with/by/at	frightened of/by	surprised at/about/by
amazed at/by	disturbed by	horrified at/by	terrified at/by
amused at/by	embarrassed by	interested in	thrilled at/with/by
bored with/by	encouraged by	irritated with/by	tired of
confused about/by	excited about	pleased with	touched at/by
depressed about	exhausted by	satisfied with	worried about
disappointed in/with	fascinated with/by	shocked at/by	

Phrasal verbs: Separable transitive

Phrasal verb	Meaning	Phrasal verb	Meaning
bring ... up	*raise (children)*	look ... up	*try to find (in a book, etc.)*
bring ... up	*call attention to*	make ... up	*invent*
call ... back	*return a phone call*	pass ... up	*decide not to use*
call ... off	*cancel*	pay ... back	*repay*
check ... out	*examine*	pick ... out	*choose*
cheer ... up	*cause to feel happier*	pick ... up	*lift; stop to get*
clean ... up	*clean completely*	point ... out	*indicate*
clear ... up	*explain*	put ... away	*put in an appropriate place*
close ... down	*close by force*	put ... back	*return to its original place*
cover ... up	*cover completely*	put ... off	*delay*
cross ... out	*draw a line through*	put ... together	*assemble*
cut ... up	*cut into small pieces*	set ... up	*prepare for use*
do ... over	*do again*	shut ... off	*stop (a machine, etc.)*
figure ... out	*understand*	sign ... up	*register*
fill ... in	*complete with information*	start ... over	*start again*
fill ... out	*complete (a form)*	take ... back	*return*
fill ... up	*fill completely*	talk ... into	*persuade*
find ... out	*learn information*	talk ... over	*discuss*
give ... back	*return*	tear ... down	*destroy*
give ... up	*quit, abandon*	think ... over	*consider*
hand ... in	*submit*	throw ... away	*put in the trash*
hand ... out	*distribute*	turn ... down	*lower the volume; reject*
help ... out	*assist*	turn ... off	*stop (a machine, etc.)*
leave ... out	*omit*	turn ... on	*start (a machine, etc.)*
let ... down	*disappoint*	turn ... up	*make louder*
look ... over	*examine*	write ... down	*write on a piece of paper*

Phrasal verbs: Inseparable transitive

Phrasal verb	Meaning	Phrasal verb	Meaning
count on	*depend on*	get over	*feel better after something bad*
fall for	*feel romantic love for*	look after	*take care of*
get off	*leave (a bus, train, etc.)*	look into	*investigate*
get on	*board (a bus, train, etc.)*	run into	*meet accidentally*
get through	*finish*	stick with	*not quit, not leave*

Phrasal verbs: Intransitive

Phrasal verb	Meaning	Phrasal verb	Meaning
act up	*cause problems*	go on	*continue*
break down	*stop working (a machine)*	go out	*leave*
catch on	*become popular*	grow up	*become an adult*
catch on	*learn, understand*	hang up	*end a phone call*
close down	*stop operating*	hold on	*wait*
come back	*return*	keep on	*continue*
come in	*enter*	keep up	*go as fast as*
dress up	*wear special clothes*	lie down	*recline*
drop in	*visit by surprise*	look out	*be careful*
drop out	*quit*	pay off	*be worthwhile*
eat out	*eat in a restaurant*	run out	*not have enough of*
end up	*reach a final place or condition*	show up	*appear*
find out	*learn information*	sign up	*register*
get ahead	*make progress, succeed*	sit down	*take a seat*
get along	*have a good relationship*	stand up	*rise*
get back	*return*	start over	*start again*
get off	*leave (a bus, train, etc.)*	stay up	*remain awake*
get on	*board (a bus, train, etc.)*	take off	*depart (a plane)*
get together	*meet*	turn out	*have a particular result*
get up	*rise from bed*	wake up	*stop sleeping*
give up	*quit*	watch out	*be careful*
go away	*leave a place or person*	work out	*be resolved*
go back	*return*	work out	*exercise*

UNIT 6, Lesson 8, p. 120

Reported speech: Changes to preserve meaning

Direct speech	Reported Speech
Lidia said, "**My** apartment **is** near the stairs."	Lidia said (that) **her** apartment **was** near the stairs.
The landlord told **us**, "**They didn't pay** last month's rent.	Tim's landlord told **us** (that) **they hadn't paid** last month's rent.
The building manager said, "**I've called** the plumber about the leak in **your** bathroom."	The building manager said (that) **he had called** the plumber about the leak in **my** bathroom.
The building manager told **me**, "The plumber **is fixing** the leak."	The building manager told me (that) the plumber **was fixing** the leak.
He explained, "**My** neighbor's dog **was barking** all night."	He explained (that) his neighbor's dog **had been barking** all night.
The tenants said, "**We've called** the landlord about that problem."	The tenants said (that) **they had called** the landlord about that problem.
The landlord replied, "**I'll call your** neighbor about the situation."	The landlord replied (that) **he would call our** neighbor about the situation.
My neighbor told **me**, "**You should send** a letter of complaint to the landlord!"	My neighbor told **me** (that) **I should send** a letter of complaint to the landlord.*

* Note: Do not change the modals *should, could, might,* and *ought to* when changing direct to reported speech.

UNIT 8, Lesson 5, page 154

Non-count nouns

Drinks	Food		Abstract ideas	School subjects	Other
coffee	beef	pasta	advice	art	furniture
juice	bread	pepper	beauty	ESL	homework
milk	broccoli	pie	fear	geography	information
soda	butter	rice	happiness	history	jewelry
tea	cereal	salad	help	language arts	mail
water	cheese	salt	love	math	medicine
	chicken	soup	luck	music	money
Community problems	chocolate	spinach	time	physical education	paper
	fish	sugar		science	
crime	fruit	yogurt		social studies	
garbage	ice cream			technology	
graffiti	jam/jelly			world languages	
noise	lettuce				
traffic	mayonnaise				
trash	meat				

UNIT 10, Lesson 5, page 194

Verbs and expressions used reflexively

allow oneself	be proud of oneself	help oneself	see oneself
amuse oneself	behave oneself	hurt oneself	take care of oneself
ask oneself	believe in oneself	introduce oneself	talk to oneself
be angry at oneself	cut oneself	keep oneself (busy)	teach oneself
be hard on oneself	dry oneself	look at oneself	tell oneself
be oneself	enjoy oneself	prepare oneself	treat oneself
be pleased with oneself	feel sorry for oneself	remind oneself	

Audio Script

UNIT 1

Page 6, Listen, Exercises A and C

Brenda: I need a burger, fries, and a garden salad.

Arturo: At 10:00 in the morning? I'm just making breakfast now. It's too early for lunch.

Brenda: Look, I agree, but that's what the customer wants. Can you do it?

Arturo: What the customer wants, the customer gets. Hey, I know you. You're Brenda. Brenda Kraig, right?

Brenda: Yes.

Arturo: I'm Arturo Pérez. My family lived next door to you on Juniper Street. Do you remember me?

Brenda: Arturo, hi. How are you? When did you start working at the Royale?

Arturo: About a year ago, but I usually work later. I'm a line cook six nights a week.

Brenda: So what are you doing here now? Where's Manny?

Arturo: Manny isn't working today. He's taking the day off to take care of some personal things.

Brenda: I hope nothing's wrong. But, hey, we can talk more during our break. Right now, my customer is waiting. I need the burger, fries, and salad.

Arturo: Coming right up.

Page 12, Listen, Exercises A and B

Brenda: Arturo, what are you reading?

Arturo: Some information I got from the Helman Culinary School. I'm starting cooking classes there next month.

Brenda: Why are you going to take cooking classes? You're already a cook.

Arturo: But I don't want to be a line cook forever. I want to become a sous-chef.

Brenda: A sous-chef? What's that?

Arturo: A sous-chef oversees just about everything that goes on in the kitchen and supervises the staff. That would be great preparation for what I'd really like to do.

Brenda: Which is what?

Arturo: Go out on my own! Ten years from now, I'd like to have my own restaurant.

Brenda: Wow! That's really ambitious. Are you going to quit your job at the Royale?

Arturo: No way! I have to keep my job.

Brenda: Hmmm … It won't be easy to work full time and go to school.

Arturo: I know, but I'll have bills to pay. Besides, I'll get a lot of great hands-on experience here.

Brenda: How long will it take to finish the culinary program?

Arturo: Two years. I'll take daytime classes and work in the evening.

Brenda: So you and I aren't going to have the same schedule anymore.

Arturo: Unfortunately, no. Manny will be back on his regular schedule next week, and I'll go back to my regular schedule after that.

Page 18, Listen, Exercises A and B

Hello, everyone. Welcome to "Real-Life Entrepreneurs." I'm your host, Holly Maxwell. This week, our show focuses on entrepreneurs in California.

Our guest today is Nadia Gorsky, founder of Grandma's Natural Frozen Soups. Nadia grew up in a three-generation household in northern California. When she was a child, her parents would go to work early in the morning, and Nadia's grandmother would watch her. Nadia used to help her grandmother around the house. In particular, Nadia used to help her grandmother make soup from her home country of Russia. One dish she often made was borscht, a beet soup usually served with sour cream.

Nadia's parents weren't able to finish high school, but they made sure that Nadia got a good education. They used to tell her that she could be anything she wanted to be. She received both a bachelor's and a master's degree in biology. Nadia's career goal was to be a nutritionist, and when she graduated, she got a job as a nutritionist at the local hospital planning healthy meals for the patients. But after a few years, Nadia realized that she wasn't satisfied. She began to dream about owning her own business.

In 2000, Nadia started Grandma's Natural Frozen Soups. The company makes and sells soups using all natural ingredients. Grandma's made almost a million dollars last year.

UNIT 2

Page 26, Listen, Exercises A and C

Catherine: Good afternoon. I'm Catherine Tote. I'm an employment specialist here at Sun County Career Center.

Nedim: Hello. I'm Nedim Buric. It's nice to meet you.

Catherine: People in Sun County come to our Career Center for many reasons—to learn English, to take training classes, to use our computer center. What brings you here today?

Nedim: I want to find a job as soon as possible.

Catherine: We can help you with that, Mr. Buric. But before we can start looking at available positions, there are several things we need to talk about.

Nedim: I'm sure you'd like to know about my work experience. I'm not employed at the moment. I came to the U.S. just last month. Before that, I was a university student in my home country, Bosnia.

Catherine: Do you have *any* job experience?

Nedim: Yes. My uncle is a lawyer. I worked in his office part time while I was in school.

Catherine: Do you have good computer skills?

Nedim: Yes. I've always been a fast learner when it comes to computers. I'm also a very organized person. I'm very careful with details, and I'm an excellent problem solver.

Catherine: I see. Did you finish school?

Nedim: Not yet. I studied for two years in Bosnia. But then I decided to come to the U.S. with my family. I expect to complete my degree in a year or so, in night school.

Page 32, Listen, Exercises A and B

Lisa: When I moved to the U.S. from Hong Kong twenty years ago, I didn't know anyone, and it was difficult for me to find a job. I tried looking in the newspaper, but there weren't a lot of things that I was capable of doing. I was really worried about not having enough money to live on when I finally saw a "Help Wanted" sign in the window of a flower shop. I went in and talked to the store manager, filled out an application, and started working the next day. I was lucky to get hired. It was difficult at that time to find out where the job openings were. Today, you have more ways to find a job. Just think about it ... You can go online to look for work, and there are several job placement agencies in our neighborhood. But in my opinion, networking is the best thing you can do. You have family, and we have friends and neighbors who might be able to help you. You should think about talking to everyone you know to get information about possible jobs.

Page 38, Listen, Exercises A and B

Mr. Lee: Tell me a little about yourself, Mr. Santos. How long have you been a driver?

Mr. Santos: Ten years. I've worked for Trends Supermarkets since 2006. Before that, I was with Grand Supermarkets.

Mr. Lee: OK. I see from your application that you have a commercial driver's license and you've driven a number of different kinds of trucks.

Mr. Santos: That's right. And I've never had an accident.

Mr. Lee: That's excellent. So, if you don't mind my asking, why are you thinking about leaving your current employer-- Trends?

Mr. Santos: A couple of reasons. First of all, I want to work days. Most of the driving I do now is at night. Also, I think there will be more opportunities for me in a company like yours. I'm interested in working as a dispatcher someday.

Mr. Lee: So, in other words, you'd like to work in the office some day?

Mr. Santos: Yes. I think it would present a new and different kind of challenge. I think I'd be good as a dispatcher because I've had so much experience as a driver and I would understand the big picture. Plus I'm good with technology and I like to problem-solve.

UNIT 3

Page 46, Listen, Exercises A and B

Mali: Hi, Eric. I'm going to the Thai Festival this weekend. Do you want to come? My friends and I go every year.

Eric: The Thai Festival? What's that, Mali?

Mali: It's a celebration of the Thai New Year. It's on the first Sunday in April. Come on. You'll have fun.

Eric: Do you think so?

Mali: Definitely. It's really fun. There's traditional dancing and music. They have kick boxing demonstrations. There are stands with traditional Thai crafts.

Eric: Well, it sounds interesting...

Mali: Oh, and the food! The food is amazing! All the restaurants are open, but there are also stands with food.

Eric: Hmm. I love Thai food. It's really hot!

Mali: Oh, one thing. Kids might throw water at you. Don't be surprised.

Eric: You're kidding, right?

Mali: No! It's part of the tradition. People have water guns or containers of water and throw it at each other.

Eric: Wow. OK. So what time do you want to go?

Page 50, Listen, Exercises A and B

Jenna: Hello, Mrs. Suarez. This is Jenna Smith from the Hanson Park Community Center. I'm returning your call about our after-school program.

Raquel: Oh, hello! Thank you for getting back to me.

Jenna: Your message said you were looking for art classes and tutoring in reading for your daughter who is in the 7th grade.

Raquel: Yes. My daughter loves art but could also use help with her reading.

Jenna: We actually have reading tutors at the center every day. Many children need extra help with reading.

Raquel: That's great. What about art classes?

Jenna: Unfortunately, we don't have art classes right now.

Raquel: Too bad. Do you have other kinds of classes?

Jenna: Yes, we have a lot of sports activities because we're located inside Hanson Park. We offer gymnastics, swimming lessons, basketball, and tennis.

Raquel: Those sound great!

Jenna: Do you think your daughter would like to be involved in sports?

Raquel: I think she'd like tennis, but I'll ask her.

Jenna: OK. Do you have any other questions?

Raquel: Yes. Um, what are your hours?

Jenna: We start classes right after school—at 3:00—and the last class ends at 7 P.M.

Raquel: So, my daughter could take classes from 3:00 to 7:00.

Jenna: Yes, that's right.

Raquel: What do I have to do to enroll her?

Jenna: You have to come to the center and fill out an application.

Raquel: Are there any fees?

Jenna: Our center is a partnership with the public school system, so no, there are no fees. All our classes are free.

Raquel: That's wonderful!

Page 51, Listen, Exercise B

Raquel: I'd like to come to the center after work today to fill out an application.

Jenna: Sure.

Raquel: Can you give me directions to the center?

Jenna: Yes. Where are you coming from?

Raquel: From work ... 82 Vine Street ... near the water.

Jenna: You're pretty close to us. First, you need to drive north on Vine Street.

Raquel: OK.

Jenna: Then you'll make a right on Route 10 and travel east.

Raquel: Uh-huh.

Jenna: Then you're going to make a left on Hanson Park Drive and travel two miles north. We're at 1200 Hanson Park Drive.

Raquel: What is your nearest cross-street?

Jenna: Our nearest cross-street is Memorial Boulevard.

Raquel: Great. Thank you. I'll see you around 6:30.

Jenna: I look forward to meeting you.

Page 52, Listen, Exercises A and B

Jamil: I wish the city would do something about cleaning up the park in our neighborhood. There's trash everywhere, and there's graffiti on all the benches.

Linlin: You know, when I go downtown, everything is nice and clean. I wish the Streets and Sanitation Department didn't spend all of their time downtown. I wish they would come to our neighborhood once in a while.

Jamil: They want things to look good downtown for the businesses and tourists, but you have a point. What about us? We pay taxes, too.

Linlin: And it's not just the streets and parks. I wish I had better garbage pick-up at my house. I'm never sure which day of the week the garbage truck is going to come, and last week they never came at all.

Jamil: Did you complain?

Linlin: I had no choice. But there was still no garbage pick-up until yesterday.

Jamil: We have the same problem. I keep calling to complain about it and about the vacant lot on the corner of Lawrence Avenue and River Street.

Linlin: The amount of trash in that vacant lot is horrible. It's a health hazard. Where does it all come from?

Jamil: Hmm, I think a lot of it is from the fast-food restaurants on Lawrence. The teenagers who go there eat their burgers and fries and throw the empty containers in the vacant lot.

Linlin: What are they doing hanging out by the vacant lot? They should be in school.

Jamil: And after school, they should be going to the community center. I just wish there were more after-school programs in the community.

Page 58, Listen, Exercises A and B

Clara Ramos: Thank you for coming here to meet with me this evening. As your City Council representative, it's my job to listen to the concerns of the community.

Hugo Lopez: Most of us in the neighborhood want to have better services. We don't want the city to take away services that we already have.

Clara Ramos: Exactly what services are you talking about, sir?

Hugo Lopez: The last time we met with you, we asked you to increase the number of police officers at the Southland District Police Station. Instead, the station is closing. Do you expect us to be happy with that decision?

Clara Ramos: Please, sir. I urge you not to believe everything you hear. The police station isn't closing. I spoke with the mayor and the chief of police. I couldn't convince them to provide more patrol officers, but don't worry. We have a plan.

Hugo Lopez: Let's hear it. We'd like you to explain how we can reduce the crime in this area.

Clara Ramos: The idea is to expand our community-policing program in the Southland District.

Hugo Lopez: Do you mean that we do the work instead of the police?

Clara Ramos: No, of course not. The program encourages neighborhood residents to work *with* the police to identify problems and find solutions. The police will still investigate specific incidents, but with community policing, they expect to see fewer crimes.

Hugo Lopez: I see. Because we can help the police identify problems before the crimes occur?

Clara Ramos: Exactly. The first meeting of the Southland Community Policing Program will take place next week. How many people in this room plan to attend?

UNIT 4

Page 66, Listen, Exercises A, B, and C

Robert: Welcome to People's Bank. I'm sure you'll like working here. Are you ready to get started?

Sandra: Yes. I'll just be observing you today, right?

Robert: That's right. For the first week, you'll be observing. By the end of the week, you should be ready to take over some duties and handle some customer needs on your own.

Sandra: Great. It'll be helpful to see the bank's procedures firsthand.

Robert: That's the idea. Let's start with deposits. This will be for a personal, not a business, account.

Sandra: Do many customers deposit cash?

Robert: No. Most deposits are checks, so let's talk about that. Make sure the customer endorses each check and fills out the deposit slip completely.

Sandra: With their name and address, right?

Robert: Yes, but pay special attention to the money amount on the deposit slip. It must be the same as the amount of the check. Then look for the customer's bank-account number and ask whether it's a savings or a checking account.

Sandra: And how do I print a receipt?

Robert: After you enter the amount of the deposit into the computer, put both the check and the deposit slip through this machine. It'll automatically print a receipt.

Sandra: Got it!

Robert: Well, it's almost one o'clock. We can pick up after lunch. How does this all seem to you so far?

Sandra: OK … I'm a little nervous, but I'll get over it.

Page 72, Listen, Exercises A, B, and C

Conversation 1

Doctor: So, how is Mr. Cordova doing today?

Resident: He's doing well. Let me take a look at his chart. Carolina, could you please give me Mr. Cordova's chart?

Carolina: Here it is.

Resident: Thank you. Hmm. I don't see any recent vital signs. Carolina, didn't someone take Mr. Cordova's vital signs this morning?

Carolina: Mercedes was the nursing assistant on duty this morning. I thought she did but you're right, they're not here. Maybe she forgot to record them. I'll take Mr. Cordova's vitals right now.

Resident: Thanks, Carolina.

Conversation 2

Doctor: How is Mrs. Worth doing?

Resident: She's coming along. Carolina, how many times has Mrs. Worth been out of bed since her gall bladder operation?

Carolina: She got up once and sat in the chair for an hour.

Resident: She had the procedure yesterday. She needs to start walking. Haven't any of the nurses tried to take her down the hall?

Carolina: There aren't a lot of nurses on the floor right now, but I'll walk with her down the hall as soon as I finish my rounds.

Resident: OK, good. Thank you.

Page 78, Listen, Exercises A and B

Dennis: Hi, Helena. How are you today?

Helena: Just fine, thanks. I'm a little nervous, though.

Dennis: Oh, you don't need to be nervous. The performance review is a conversation, really.

Helena: OK.

Dennis: First of all, I want you to know that we're happy in general with your work.

Helena: Oh, thank you!

Dennis: Yes, the quality of your work is very good. You're meeting your quotas, which is really important. I gave you a "3" in both categories.

Helena: Thank you. I understand how important it is to get all the packages out on time.

Dennis: Exactly. And you're good at following instructions. I gave you a "3" there, too.

Helena: Sometimes I have to ask for clarification…

Dennis: That's great. You should always ask if you're not sure. It's better to ask than to do the wrong thing.

Helena: OK. Good.

Dennis: I know you also have a positive attitude. That's really important.

Helena: Thanks. I agree. It makes things more pleasant when people are positive.

Dennis: I really appreciate that you work well with your co-workers. I've noticed that you often volunteer to help them if you finish your work early. You deserve the "4" I gave you for teamwork.

Helena: I enjoy working with everyone. I like being part of a team.

Dennis: Well, it shows. So I think the only thing that we need to talk about is the issue of clothing, well, jewelry and shoes, really. I had to give you a "2" in safety procedures. Employees are supposed to leave earrings and rings at home and not wear jewelry on the job. Yesterday you were wearing a long necklace that could have gotten caught in the machinery. And the other day, you were wearing sandals. You know that company policy requires all employees to wear shoes that will protect their feet and prevent them from slipping and falling if the floors are wet.

Helena: I'm so sorry. I stopped wearing my earrings and rings, but I didn't realize that I couldn't wear a necklace. It won't happen again. And I know about the shoes. I just forgot. I understand. Safety is very important.

UNIT 5

Page 86, Listen, Exercises A and B

Thank you all for being here this evening. I'm happy to see that so many people are concerned about fire safety. Tonight's class will focus on what you can do to prevent a fire in your home. Let's begin with a room that's very important in many homes—the kitchen.

Cooking is the number-one cause of house fires in the U.S. When you're in the kitchen, pay attention to what you're doing. Keep hair and clothing away from fire, and keep your cooking areas clean. If a pan of food catches fire, immediately put a lid over it and turn the stove off. Also remember to turn off the stove and oven when you finish preparing your food. And never leave the kitchen while food is still cooking on the stove. Remember that it takes only a few seconds for a fire to start.

If you have children, you should be extra careful. They're curious, so they'll want to know what's going on in the kitchen. Teach children not to touch anything on the stove.

Now, are there any questions before I go on?

Page 92, Listen, Exercises A, B, and C

Henry Ponce: Today we're discussing hurricanes with meteorologist Dr. Kay Wilkins. Dr. Wilkins, welcome.

Dr. Wilkins: Thank you, Henry. It's a pleasure to be here.

Henry Ponce: Let's begin with the basics. I know that hurricane season in the U.S. is during the summer months.

Dr. Wilkins: You're right, Henry, but not completely. Officially, hurricane season in the Atlantic Ocean is from June 1 through November 30. Most hurricanes will occur during these six months, but there have also been bad storms in May and December.

Henry Ponce: Tell me, Dr. Wilkins. What's the most important thing that everyone should know about hurricanes?

Dr. Wilkins: To take them seriously. Some people refuse to leave their homes during a hurricane. When the National Weather Service orders an evacuation, pay attention. Follow the evacuation order and go to a safe location.

Henry Ponce: Um hmm. There are very powerful winds and heavy rain during a hurricane. What are some of the other dangers?

Dr. Wilkins: Flooding is a major concern. In addition to the heavy rains, people who live along the coast should be prepared for high waves.

Henry Ponce: What about people who live inland? Do they have to worry about hurricanes?

Dr. Wilkins: Hurricanes get their power over water, so coastal areas are usually the hardest hit. After they hit land, hurricanes lose strength. But they can also cause damage in inland areas.

Henry Ponce: Can you explain the difference between a hurricane watch and a hurricane warning for our listeners?

Dr. Wilkins: I get that question a lot. The National Weather Service issues a hurricane watch when there is the possibility of a hurricane within the next 36 hours. The watch means that you should pay attention and begin to prepare for the severe weather.

Henry Ponce: Um hmm. I see. And a hurricane warning?

Dr. Wilkins: A hurricane warning means that you can expect a hurricane to arrive in your area within 24 hours. As soon as you hear the warning, make sure that your emergency preparations are complete.

Page 98, Listen, Exercises A and B

Hello. I'm emergency medical technician Iris Chen, and I want to remind you about Emergency Medical Services Week—EMS Week. During this week, please take time to honor 911 operators, EMTs, and other emergency personnel who provide our city with lifesaving services. Also use EMS Week as an opportunity to make sure that everyone in your family, including young children, knows how to make a 911 call.

In an emergency, some people may not think clearly, so be prepared. Put the 911 number and your own number next to every phone in your home. Then practice. With your phone turned off, show your family how to dial 911, and demonstrate what to do during the call. Stay calm and speak slowly. Explain what the emergency is in as few words as possible. Give information about whether there is anyone who is bleeding, unconscious, or not breathing. Give the location of the emergency. Listen carefully, and answer the operator's questions. Finally, don't hang up until the operator tells you to hang up.

Help us help you. A 911 call could save the life of someone you love.

UNIT 6

Page 106, Listen, Exercises A, B, C, and D

Mother: So, tell me about the apartment. It has three bedrooms?
Jessica: Yes. They're small, but that's OK.
Mother: You said the rent is $1200? Are utilities included?
Jessica: Water is included. So we just have to pay for gas and electricity.
Mother: How much was the security deposit?
Jessica: One month's rent--$1200. Between the three of us, we'll manage it. It'll be only $400 apiece.
Mother: All right. I might be able to help you a little with that.
Jessica: That'd be a big help, Mom.
Mother: So, remember, keep everything nice and clean. Be sure not to damage anything.
Jessica: Damage anything? Mom, don't worry. We won't damage anything.
Mother: Well, not on purpose you wouldn't. But you could by accident. And then, when you move out, the landlord will keep your security deposit.
Jessica: Oh Mom, stop worrying, we'll be careful.
Mother: I hope you have quiet neighbors.
Jessica: I know. Me, too. Well, at least there won't be any barking dogs. Tenants aren't allowed to have pets.
Mother: That's good. Now, what else can I worry about?

Page 112, Listen, Exercises A and B

Henry: Welcome to This Week. I'm your host Henry Sullivan. Our guest today is Manuel Rodriguez, a tenant rights lawyer. Today Manuel is going to answer questions on tenant law in Texas. Manuel, it's nice to have you back on our show.
Manuel: Thanks, Henry. Glad to be here.

Henry: Listeners, do you have problems with your landlord? If you do, give us a call. The number is 1-800-555-3333. …Ah, I see we have our first caller. Armando from Dallas, you're on the air.
Caller 1: Hi, Manuel. The smoke alarms in my apartment don't work anymore. I called the landlord several times but he never called me back. He has to replace the smoke detectors, doesn't he?
Manuel: Yes, in Texas, the landlord is required to put a working smoke detector outside each bedroom. But if the smoke detectors stop working, you have to notify the landlord in writing. Send your landlord a letter explaining the problem. Make sure to keep a copy of the letter.
Caller 1: I'll do that. Thank you, Manuel!

Page 112, Listen, Exercise C

Henry: Now for our next caller. Carla in San Antonio, you're on the air.
Caller 2: Hi, Manuel. My landlord is going to raise my rent to $700 a month. I can't afford to pay that much, and I'll have to move. Is he allowed to do that?
Manuel: How much time is left on your lease?
Caller 2: Six months. It's a one-year lease and it'll be up on September 1st.
Manuel: And have you ever paid your rent late or damaged the apartment?
Caller 2: No, I haven't. I'm a good tenant.
Manuel: It sounds like your lease is still in effect. That means the landlord is *not* allowed to raise your rent until after September 1st. But after that date, you'll have to sign a new lease, and he can raise the rent.
Caller 2: Oh well. At least I have six months to find a new apartment! Thanks, Manuel!

Page 118, Listen, Exercises A and B

Oscar: What's that noise? It's so loud.
Marta: The neighbors are watching TV.
Oscar: Which neighbors? The ones in 2A?
Marta: No, 2C.
Oscar: What's their name?
Marta: I don't remember. I've only seen them in the hallway.
Oscar: Well, I'm going over there and telling them they have to turn down the TV. We just got the baby to sleep.
Marta: I already went over there.
Oscar: You did?
Marta: Yes, I told them the baby was sleeping and I asked them if they could be quieter.
Oscar: What did they say?
Marta: They didn't say anything. They slammed the door in my face.
Oscar: What! I'm going over there right now!
Marta: Oscar, don't lose your temper. Yelling at them won't do any good. Let me call the building manager.
Oscar: What can he do?
Marta: He can call them and remind them about the building rules—no loud TV or music after 10 P.M. They might listen to him. He also said we could call the police if there's noise after 10 P.M.

Oscar: I'm not calling the police about noise. I'll go over there and settle it myself.

Marta: OK, fine, but let me call the building manager first. It's better if we let him handle it.

UNIT 7

Page 126, Listen, Exercises A and B

Eva: Mark, did you have a chance to look at the auto section this morning? Some of the ads looked interesting.

Mark: Yeah, … but some of the new cars are really expensive. I'm looking at these used-car ads from Tri-State Motors now.

Eva: Oh! I was looking at the used-car ads, too. There were some from dealers and others from private owners. Who would you rather buy from, a dealer or a private owner?

Mark: A dealer. We can get a warranty from a dealership but not from an individual seller.

Eva: You're right—good point. Does Tri-State have any of the models we're looking for—a compact that gets good gas mileage?

Mark: As a matter of fact they do. There are a few here with the features we want: four-doors with power steering, CD player, and air-conditioning. We can live without a sunroof, but air-conditioning is a must.

Eva: Don't forget about the safety features. We've got to have airbags.

Mark: Absolutely. With the newer cars, front airbags are standard, but we should look for a car that has side airbags—and antilock brakes, too.

Eva: I agree.

Mark: I just realized that we've never talked about color. Would you rather have a light color or a dark color—like black, maybe?

Eva: Hmm … Well, now that I think about it, I've always wanted to drive a *red* car.

Mark: Red, huh? I read somewhere that red cars get more speeding tickets.

Eva: Really? Hmm. How about this … Let's start looking and we'll see what's out there and what kind of deal we can get. Then we'll worry about the color.

Page 131, Practice, Exercise A

Amy: I'm thinking of buying a car.

Tom: Congratulations! Will it be your first car?

Amy: Yes, it will—well, at least in this country. I know you have to have insurance here when you own a car, but I really have no idea how to go about getting it. What did you do?

Tom: When I was shopping for my car, a friend of mine gave me the name and number of a good car insurance company. You can try them. I use All Country.

Amy: OK. I'll check them out. And I'm sure I can find information about other insurance companies on the Internet.

Tom: Good idea! You could also look through the yellow pages of the phone book.

Amy: Great. Thanks for the help.

Page 131, Practice, Exercises C and D

Amy: I'm ready to call and get a quote for car insurance.

Tom: Good. Are you ready for all the questions they'll ask?

Amy: I thought I would be asking most of the questions.

Tom: Actually, your premium will depend on how you answer some of their questions.

Amy: Really? What kinds of things will they ask?

Tom: They'll want to know what kind of car you drive. If you own a sports car, for example, the premium is usually higher.

Amy: OK. What else will they ask? How about safety features? A salesperson at the used-car lot told me that having lots of safety features would probably help keep my premium low.

Tom: Yes. That's true. And they'll want to know how many miles you expect to drive each year.

Amy: How can I predict how many miles I'll drive?

Tom: It's just a guess. Premiums are usually higher for people who drive a lot.

Amy: OK. Is there anything else I should know?

Tom: They'll probably ask you if you're single or married and also your age.

Amy: Why do my marital status and my age make a difference?

Tom: I think there are statistics that show that older, married people have fewer accidents.

Page 132, Listen, Exercises A and B

This is Jake Alexander, and you're listening to *All Things Auto*. It's time for our Car Care Question of the Week. I have an e-mail here from Nicole. Nicole writes, "Can you tell me what your number-one car-care tip is?" Well, listeners, when it comes to car maintenance, there's one thing you should always remember, and that is "Don't delay. Do it today." Of course, you should change the oil regularly. For most cars, that's every three months or every 3,000 miles. But there are other things that you should do regularly, too. Your car's tires are very important for your safety, so inspect them once a month. Check the tread, and check the air pressure. If you don't know how much air your tires should have, look in your owner's manual. Finally, check for leaks once a week. Look under the hood and under your car. And look for color. For example, transmission fluid is red. Engine coolant is bright green or yellow, and oil is light brown. If you see a problem, take your car to a good mechanic right away. Fix small problems before they become serious. It's impossible to say exactly how many years this will add to the life of your car, but you'll definitely save money and you'll have a vehicle that's safer and easier to drive. Remember, listeners—"Don't delay. Do it today!"

Page 138, Listen, Exercises A, B, and C

Nora: Are you OK? You aren't hurt, are you?

Frank: No, I'm fine. Are you all right?

Nora: Yes, but I can't say the same for my car. The right headlight is out, and there are huge dents in the hood and fender.

Frank: I don't know what happened. I'd already started moving into the right lane when I saw you. By that time, there was nothing I could do. I remember putting on my turn signal and looking for cars coming from the opposite direction, but I didn't see any cars.

Nora: I didn't see you either—until the very last minute. I had just slowed down because of the rain, but there still wasn't enough time for me to stop. You know, we should pull the cars to the side of the road. Now, where's my cell phone?

Frank: Are you going to call the police? I think we should do that.

Nora: Yes. We have to report the accident. It's the law. Besides, our insurance companies will definitely want a police report. You have insurance, don't you?

Frank: Of course. My insurance card and my driver's license and vehicle registration are in the car. I'll get them.

Nora: I'll get mine, too. Oh, by any chance, do you have a camera?

Frank: Why do we need a camera?

Nora: Well, my insurance agent told me to take pictures if I were ever involved in an accident.

Frank: That's a good idea. Actually, my cell phone has a camera. I'll get it.

UNIT 8

Page 146, Listen, Exercises A and C

Dr. Kim: Good morning, Mrs. Garcia. What brings you here today?

Irma Garcia: To tell you the truth, Doctor, I haven't been feeling well for the past couple of weeks.

Dr. Kim: What seems to be the problem?

Irma Garcia: For one thing, I can't sleep at night. I have a lot of congestion, so I can't breathe.

Dr. Kim: Anything else?

Irma Garcia: Yes. I feel achy. My whole body hurts! Oh, and I've been sneezing a lot lately.

Dr. Kim: Hmm … And you say this has been going on for about two weeks?

Irma Garcia: Right. At first, I thought I had a cold, but now I'm worried that it's something more serious.

Dr. Kim: I think you might have an allergy. The question is what's causing it. Is there anything different about where you live or work?

Irma Garcia: No, my husband and I live in the same house, and I still work in our family business.

Dr. Kim: OK. What about your diet? Have you been eating any new kinds of food?

Irma Garcia: Well, I eat the same food as always, but I've been cooking a lot more since my daughter came home from college a few weeks ago.

Dr. Kim: Aha! That could be the answer.

Irma Garcia: What? You think I'm allergic to my daughter?

Dr. Kim: No, Mrs. Garcia. Not your daughter, but maybe something your daughter brought into the house, such as perfume or a houseplant. We'll do a few tests to find out for sure.

Page 152, Listen, Exercises A and B

Operator: 911, what is your emergency?

Caller: I need an ambulance here.

Operator: OK. Where are you located?

Caller: 136 Elm Street.

Operator: OK. The paramedics are on their way. Can you tell me what's going on?

Caller: It's my husband and he's … I don't know, he's having chest pain. And he's sweating, really badly.

Operator: Is he conscious or unconscious?

Caller: He's conscious . . but he's having so much chest pain it's hard for him to breathe.

Operator: Try to stay calm. You need to help him until the paramedics get there. How old is your husband?

Caller: 58.

Operator: Does he have any ongoing medical problems?

Caller: Yes, he has diabetes.

Operator: Is he taking medication for that?

Caller: Yes.

Operator: Is he on any other medication?

Caller: No, I don't think so. Are the paramedics almost here?

Operator: Yes, help is on the way. You're doing great. Just continue to watch him. Call again if anything changes before the paramedics get there.

Page 158, Listen, Exercises A and B

The end of summer is almost here, and that means more than getting notebooks, pencils, and clothing for the new school year. School officials say that parents should not wait until the last minute to get their children the immunizations they'll need. State law requires specific vaccinations for all students entering school for the first time and for students in pre-school programs, kindergarten, grade 5, and grade 9. This is a reminder that student immunization records must be updated no later than September 15. Parents ought to have their children immunized now to avoid the early September rush. It's very important to make the September 15th deadline.

As part of a back-to-school effort, health clinics around the city will be offering free vaccination services. In addition, the annual Health for Life Fair will take place this weekend. Among the many activities at the health fair will be free medical check-ups for children ages 5 through 12 and free immunizations. All events and services will be in the Downtown Civic Center from 10:00 AM until 6:00 PM on Saturday and from noon until 6:00 PM on Sunday. For more information, look in the health news section of your local newspaper, or visit the Radio WDKM website at www.wdkm.com.

UNIT 9

Page 166, Listen, Exercises A and C

Mr. Bowman: Thanks for coming to my office today, Mrs. Adamski. I know you took time off from work to meet with me. I want to talk to you about your daughter.

Mrs. Adamski: Monika? Oh, Monika is a good student. My son has some problems with his grades, but not Monika.

Mr. Bowman: Oh, yes. Your daughter is an excellent student! And that's exactly why I want to talk with you. Since Monika will start high school next fall, it's time to start thinking about college.

Mrs. Adamski: College? Uh, Monika is only 13 years old. College is a long way off.

Mr. Bowman: Well, yes and no.

Mrs. Adamski: What do you mean, "Yes and no"?

Mr. Bowman: It's never too early to start thinking about college. I'd like Monika to have as many opportunities as possible, because she is one of our best students.

Mrs. Adamski: Thank you.

Mr. Bowman: But when I talk to Monika about college, she isn't interested, because she thinks she can't afford it.

Mrs. Adamski: Well, my husband and I can take care of our family, but we don't make a lot of money.

Mr. Bowman: Many schools offer scholarships and financial aid to help students pay for their education.

Mrs. Adamski: Oh, really? How can we make sure Monika gets a scholarship?

Mr. Bowman: Well, there are no guarantees. But the first thing to do is talk to Monika about classes that will prepare her for college.

Mrs. Adamski: OK, and I'd like to make another appointment with you. Next time I'll bring my husband so that we can both talk to you about scholarships and financial aid.

Page 172, Listen, Exercises A, B, and C

Secretary: Good morning. How can I help you?

Mr. Lopez: Hello. I'm Pablo Lopez, and this is my daughter, Marta. I need to enroll Marta in school. We just moved here.

Secretary: Oh, yes. You're the one I spoke with on the phone last week. Marta finished first grade at Newtown Elementary, right?

Mr. Lopez: Yes, that's right. She's ready for second grade.

Secretary: OK, I can help you get her enrolled. Do you have proof that you live in School District 15? For example, can you show me the lease for your new apartment?

Mr. Lopez: I don't have a lease, but I brought an electric bill that has my name and address on it.

Secretary: Perfect. Now, I'll need a few other things from you. Do you have Marta's school records from Newtown?

Mr. Lopez: Yes. I also brought her birth certificate and her medical and dental records.

Secretary: Excellent. I'll also need a phone number that we can call if there's an emergency. Here's a form you can fill out with that information.

Mr. Lopez: OK.

Secretary: And here's a list of school supplies—pencils, notebooks, and folders—which your daughter has to bring with her to class.

Mr. Lopez: Thank you.

Secretary: You're welcome. Let me know if you have any questions.

Page 178. Listen, Exercises A and B

I want to welcome you to the first meeting of this advisory committee. Before we do anything else, I'd like to explain the purpose of the committee.

Because he has talked about it so many times, you must have heard about the mayor's plan to improve school safety. He could not have come up with this plan without the support of parents' advisory committees all over the city. The plan requires all schools to identify five improvements to keep students safe and to create a better atmosphere for learning. I am asking you as advisory committee members to assist me in preparing a school safety plan for West Apollo Elementary School.

Every person in this room has something to contribute to our plan. Some of you are parents, and your children might have talked to you about problems at school. Some of you live near here, so you are familiar with problems in the neighborhood. The teachers in this group are familiar with how students behave in classrooms, in the cafeteria, and on the playground. Any one of you may have thought about changes that we should make in our procedures and school buildings. I hope all of you will contribute your ideas to our safety plan.

UNIT 10

Page 186, Listen, Exercises A and B

Sam: Oleg, have you finished the cabinets yet?

Oleg: I'm sorry, Sam. The supplier was out of the wood. It just came in yesterday.

Sam: Then we're a week behind schedule! Why didn't you tell me there was a problem with the supplier?

Oleg: I did. I called your office and left a message on your machine.

Sam: Why didn't you call the cell phone?

Oleg: I did. I called three times, but no one picked up. I even had Boris call you from the van.

Sam: Never mind . . . Now listen. You've got to finish the cabinets. How soon do you think you'll be done?

Oleg: Two weeks.

Sam: Come on. Can't you do it in a week and a half?

Oleg: Well, I need two weeks to make quality cabinets. You want me to do a good job, don't you?

Sam: OK, you're right. Two weeks. In the meantime, you need to let the counter guy measure space for the counter.

Oleg: Oh, sure. No problem.

Page 192, Listen, Exercises A, B, and C

Asad: Wait, Claudia! Don't turn on the press yet!

Claudia: What's the matter?

Asad: You can't wear a bracelet when you're operating the press. . . . See those moving rollers? Your bracelet could get caught in the roller. You could hurt yourself very badly.

Claudia: Oh. I'll take it off right now.

Asad: Didn't you go to the safety training?

Claudia: I did. But I thought they just said no loose clothing.

Asad: Or jewelry, like bracelets and necklaces. These machines are dangerous. Did you read the safety manual yet?

Claudia: Yes, of course, but I don't remember everything it said.

Asad: I see. OK. Let's do a safety check. I always do a safety check before I start. First, make sure the guards are all on the machine. Make sure you're not wearing long sleeves or jewelry. Keep your hands a safe distance from the rollers. OK, now it looks like you're ready to start. I'm going to watch you work for a while to make sure you're working safely.

Claudia: Thanks so much, Asad!

Asad: You're welcome.

Page 198, Listen, Exercises A and B

Don: Hi, Lisa. Could I talk to you for a minute?

Lisa: Oh, sure. Umm, is everything OK?

Don: Yes! Here, have a seat. I want to talk to you about your future with Parcel Movers.

Lisa: Oh, thanks! That's great.

Don: You've been doing an excellent job. Let's see. You started out with us six months ago as a sorter… You're very efficient. I can see you're moving 400 packages in an hour.

Lisa: Thank you.

Don: And you're accurate. I see you've made mistakes with only three packages in three months.

Lisa: I try my best.

Don: Also, when your co-workers need help, you try to help them.

Lisa: Well, thanks. I guess we're all part of a team.

Don: The other thing that's important is safety practices. You follow the safety practices you learned in the safety training course.

Lisa: Well, safety is important. I don't want to get hurt!

Don: Right, everyone wants to be safe. But you're especially conscientious. Vikram told me that you saw him lifting the wrong way and warned him . . .that's the kind of thing we like to see in a supervisor. So . . . I'm promoting you to the position of training supervisor.

Lisa: . . .Oh, wow! That's great . . .

Don: You'll be responsible for seven employees, starting on the 12th. Why don't you come to my office tomorrow morning—let's say at 10:15?—and I'll give you more details.

Lisa: Thank you, Don. I'm really excited to have this opportunity.

Don: You're welcome. You earned it.

UNIT 11

Page 206, Listen, Exercises A and B

Solange: David, what's the matter? You don't look so good.

David: I'm all right . . .but something happened last night that shook me up a little. While I was watching the 10 o'clock news, I got a call on my cell. When I picked up, I thought it would be Caroline telling me she was on her way home. But it was the police.

Solange: The police?

David: Yes, they had Caroline at the police station!

Solange: The police picked up *Caroline*?

David: It-it was OK. You know, when they first told me she was there I panicked—what was wrong—what might have happened—but she was fine, and she hadn't done anything wrong. —She'd just been out a little too late. There's a curfew for teenagers now in the city. After 10 PM, no kids below the age of 18 are allowed downtown. It was around 10:15 . . . Caroline and her friends had just been to the movies and were on their way home. An officer came by and picked them up for violating a city ordinance.

Solange: I didn't know there was a curfew.

David: Neither did I. But when I got to the station, the cops were very nice. While I was waiting, they explained the reasons for the ordinance.

Solange: Like what?

David: There have been some incidents downtown after dark. Someone got robbed. The curfew is meant to keep kids from being victims of crime.

Solange: I had no idea. I'd better tell Fabiola about the curfew. I don't want her getting into trouble or getting robbed.

David: Yeah. I told Caroline she has to be home by 10 PM in the future.

Page 212, Listen, Exercises A and B

Lisa: Alex! Don't tell me you're watching that program again.

Alex: What do you mean? What's wrong with this program?

Lisa: It's garbage.

Alex: How can you call it garbage? This program is watched by millions of people all over the country. It shows how the law works.

Lisa: Oh, do you really believe that? There's no real law on that show, just people complaining about their relationships.

Alex: Oh, come on, Lisa.

Lisa: Those aren't real cases at all—those stories are all made up. And they certainly aren't heard by real judges. They're all actors …

Alex: Ah ah ah not true—some of the shows are real cases. Or they're based on real ones.

Lisa: Oh, brother.

Alex: Listen to this case that was just on. It's really interesting. There were two roommates. One roommate was behind on his car payments, and the bank was going to repossess his car. So he got his roommate to lend him $2,000 for the car payment.

Lisa: Uh—not a good idea.

Alex: Uh, yeah! You're right about that! The roommates got into a big fight and moved out. And the guy with the car didn't pay back the $2,000 he owed his roommate. So they went to court, and the case was decided by a judge. He said to the guy who loaned his friend the money, "Well, your friend has to pay you the money back, but here's some advice. Never lend money to your friends."

Lisa: Hmm. That reminds me. . .

Alex: What?

Lisa: You owe me 50 bucks.

Page 218, Listen, Exercises A and B

Host: Welcome back to Car Chat! I'm your host Frank Evans, and I'm here with former traffic court judge Carl Mansfield. He's here to answer your questions about traffic violations. … Caller 1, you're on the air.

Caller 1: Hi, Carl. A police officer recently gave me a ticket for running a stop sign. But I couldn't see the sign because a tree branch was hanging over it. Do I really have to pay the fine?

Carl: It sounds like you're in the right. I advise you to ask for a trial to contest the ticket. But first go back to the stop sign and take a picture of it. Then you can show the picture to a judge in traffic court. He or she will probably dismiss the ticket.

Caller 1: Thanks, Carl.

Carl: You're welcome. Caller 2? How can I help you?

Caller 2: I've gotten a few traffic tickets, so I have some points on my license. I heard that if I go to traffic school, I can get the points on my license erased. Is that true?

Carl: Well, that depends on the state where you live. In this state, as long as your traffic violations aren't too serious, you can go to traffic school to get the points erased from your license. What kind of tickets are they?

Caller 2: Oh, they're mostly parking tickets. But I did get one ticket for speeding. How do I sign up for traffic school?

Carl: Well, it's easy. You can sign up online. After you complete the course, they'll give you a certificate. As soon as you show the certificate to the police, your driving record will be clean again.

Caller 2: Great! Thanks for the information!

UNIT 12

Page 226, Listen, Exercises A and B

John: Hello. What can I do for you?

Ling: Hi. I'd like to open a checking account.

John: OK. We have several options. Our MyMoney account is very popular. There's no monthly maintenance fee, and it has a pretty good interest rate.

Ling: That sounds good.

John: It requires a minimum balance of $1,500, though.

Ling: Uh … What happens if I go below fifteen hundred?

John: Well, you'll be charged a monthly maintenance fee.

Ling: I see. You know, a lot of banks offer free checking. Don't you have something like that?

John: Sure we do. You want an interest-free checking account then. There's no minimum balance requirement.

Ling: Yeah, interest-free checking—that's what I want. Are there any fees I should know about?

John: Well, the usual—you pay an overdraft fee if you write a check or make an automatic bill payment for more than the amount in your checking account. If you're interested, the bank offers overdraft protection for a monthly flat fee.

Ling: And how much is that?

John: $30.

Ling: No, thanks. I'll just have to keep an eye on my account balance.

John: OK … Interest-free checking then. Let me get your information …

Page 232, Listen, Exercises A and B

Host: Welcome back to MoneyWise. I'm Helen Duncan. We're here today with financial expert Patricia Wong. Patricia is taking questions from our listeners now. Here's our first caller.

Rafael: Hi, Patricia, I'm Rafael. Thanks for taking my call.

Patricia: No problem. I'm here to help you with your money questions. Go ahead.

Rafael: I have a lot of debt, and I'm having a hard time paying all my bills each month.

Patricia: What kind of debt, Rafael?

Rafael: Credit card and some personal loans.

Patricia: How much in personal loans and credit card debt are we talking about?

Rafael: Uh, I borrowed $5,000 from my credit union and I have about $20,000 in credit card debt.

Patricia: I see. That's $25,000 more or less. How old are you and what do you do?

Rafael: 27. I work in a hospital—I'm a technician.

Patricia: And what's the interest rate on your credit cards?

Rafael: They vary—from 9.99% to 18%.

Patricia: Whoa! What happened? Why 18%?

Rafael: Well, I missed a payment on one of my credit card bills.

Patricia: That's what usually happens. Well, your situation isn't hopeless, Rafael. The first thing that you should do is talk to the credit card companies. Try to get the rate lowered on the card with the 18% interest rate. If they lower the rate by just a point or two, it will make a big difference in your monthly payment.

Rafael: OK. I'll try.

Patricia: Next, if you can, pay off the cards with the highest interest rate by increasing your monthly payment. Let's say you're paying $50 a month now on a balance of $1000. If you increase your monthly payment to $75, you'll finish paying the loan seven months sooner.

Rafael: That sounds like something I can do. It's just $25 a month more than I'm paying now.

Patricia: Here's one more idea for you: try to get a second job and use your second income to pay off your debt. If you follow just one or two of those suggestions, you'll start reducing your debt in no time. Good luck.

Rafael: Thanks so much, Patricia. Those are all good suggestions.

Page 238. Listen, Exercises A and B

Eduardo: Hey, what would you do if you suddenly inherited a lot of money?

Chantal: I'd be quiet about it, and I'd keep working for a while. Why?

Eduardo: This guy in my office—turns out he had a rich uncle. Well, the uncle died and left him half a million!

Chantal: Really? What's he going to do with the money?

Eduardo: He already spent it! He bought a really expensive sports car and a motorcycle! Then he quit his job. And now he's traveling around the world.

Chantal: That's crazy. That money will disappear quickly. If I came into a lot of money, I would do something more useful with it.

Eduardo: Like what?

Chantal: I'd go to medical school. I've always dreamed of becoming a doctor.

Eduardo: You don't like being a nurse?

Chantal: I do, but I'd rather be a doctor.

Eduardo: Then you'd still work here?

Chantal: No, I'd go back home—to Haiti. I'd build a clinic in my village, and I'd give the people in my village free medical care.

Eduardo: You have such a good heart! As for me, if I found myself with a lot of money, I'd probably spend it on myself!

Chantal: What would you do?

Eduardo: I'd quit my job for sure. I don't like my job. Then I'd pay off all my debts. Finally, I'd buy a big house on the beach.

Chantal: But wouldn't you get lonely in that big house all by yourself?

Eduardo: Oh, no! I wouldn't live there by myself. I'd invite my parents, my brothers and sisters, cousins, even my closest friends to live with me.

Chantal: Whoa! That would be an entire village!

Eduardo: Exactly. Imagine what fun that would be. Of course, I'd invite you to come and visit me.

Chantal: It's a deal!

Index

Credits